INTRODUCTION TO Clinical Psychology

An Evidence-Based Approach

THIRD EDITION

INTRODUCTION TO

Clinical Psychology

An Evidence-Based Approach

THIRD EDITION

JOHN HUNSLEY | CATHERINE M. LEE

WILEY

Library and Archives Canada Cataloguing in Publication

Hunsley, John, 1959-
[Introduction to clinical psychology]
Clinical psychology : an evidence-based approach / John Hunsley, Catherine M. Lee. — Third edition.
Revision of: Introduction to clinical psychology : an evidence-based approach.
Includes bibliographical references and index.

ISBN 978-1-118-62461-6 (pbk.)

1. Clinical psychology—Textbooks. I. Lee, Catherine M. (Catherine Mary), 1955-, author
II. Title. III. Title: Introduction to clinical psychology.

RC467.2.H86 2014 616.89 C2013-906979-8

Production Credits
Acquisitions Editor: Rodney Burke
Vice President & Publisher: Veronica Visentin
Senior Marketing Manager: Patty Maher
Editorial Manager: Karen Staudinger
Editorial Assistant: Luisa Begani
Production Manager: Tegan Wallace
Production Editor: Yee Lyn Song
Media Editor: Channade Fenandoe
Typesetting: Thomson Digital
Cover Design and Interior Design: Joanna Vieira
Cover Image: Top row: Left, ©istockphoto.com/carterdayne; Middle, ©istockphoto.com/yellowcrestmedia; Right, ©istockphoto.com/Kangah
Bottom row: Left, ©istockphoto.com/RBFried; Middle, ©istockphoto.com/RushOnPhotography; Right, ©istockphoto.com/Plougmann
Printing & Binding: Sheridan

Printed and bound in the United States of America.

John Wiley & Sons Canada, Ltd.
5353 Dundas Street West, Suite 400
Etobicoke, ON M9B 6H8
Visit our website at: www.wiley.ca

To Rob and Nick

PREFACE

Between us, we have well over half a century of experience in clinical psychology. We share a passion for a profession that has the potential to make an important contribution to the understanding of human nature and to the alleviation of human suffering. We have written this book to introduce to students the theories and practices of clinical psychology and convey the important work done by clinical psychologists. The book is designed to be helpful not only to those who will go on to careers in clinical psychology, but also to those who will choose other career paths.

KEY FEATURES

Clinical psychology has evolved greatly in recent decades. In order to convey the nature of the contemporary practice of clinical psychology, we have incorporated three distinct features through all of the chapters.

Evidence-Based Approach

Concerns about health care costs, together with growing demands from well-informed health care consumers, have highlighted the need for clinical psychology to adopt evidence-based assessments and interventions. Unfortunately, many popular theories that have guided clinical practice for decades do not have supporting evidence. Throughout the text, we present theories and practices and examine the extent to which they are supported by research. If a technique or strategy is used frequently in practice but has not been supported empirically, we say so. We believe that our approach reflects the new realities in clinical psychology and the ongoing commitment of psychologists to deliver services that are the best science has to offer.

Diversity

Clinical psychology must address the needs of a diverse population. We highlight the need for sensitivity to gender, age, culture, ethnicity, sexual orientation, socioeconomic status, family type, and geographic location. Throughout the text, we include relevant assessment and treatment examples to illustrate the importance and the challenges of professional sensitivity to diversity issues in research and practice.

Lifespan Perspective

We have adopted a lifespan perspective throughout the text. We include examples illustrating issues with respect to children, adolescents, adults, and older adults. As many undergraduate students taking an introductory course in clinical psychology are unlikely to have decided on the age of clients with whom they eventually wish to work, it will be appealing to learn about clinical psychology across the lifespan. It is important for students to appreciate that assessment and treatment plans can vary depending on the age of the individual.

TEXT ORGANIZATION

The text can be divided into three sections. The first section provides an overview of issues that set the stage for the second section, which is on assessment; and that section, in turn, is the foundation for the third section on intervention in clinical psychology. In Chapter 1, we provide a definition of clinical psychology, describing its history and explaining similarities and differences between clinical psychology and other mental health professions. Chapter 2 addresses the diverse roles of clinical psychologists, all of which are based on the pillars of science and ethics. The importance of attention to ethical issues is highlighted not just in this chapter but throughout the text. The third chapter is an overview of issues related to classification and diagnosis. In this chapter, we introduce two individuals, an adult (Melissa) and an adolescent (Noah), whose psychological services we describe in subsequent chapters. Chapter 4 presents key issues on research methods, underlining the ways these methods are employed to address clinically meaningful questions.

In the second section, Chapters 5 to 9 address assessment issues in clinical psychology, highlighting ethical issues that must guide psychological practice. Chapter 5 provides an overview of the purposes of psychological assessment, a review of key concepts in psychological testing, and an examination of the distinction between testing and assessment. Chapter 6 presents information on clinical interviews and clinical observation, emphasizing developmental considerations relevant to these commonly used assessment methods. Intellectual and cognitive assessments are discussed in Chapter 7. Chapter 8 covers self-report and projective assessment, with in-depth examination of the usefulness of different assessment strategies. The challenges of integrating assessment data and making clinical decisions are illustrated in Chapter 9, with reference to services for Melissa (who was introduced in Chapter 3).

The third section, on intervention, covers both prevention and treatment. Chapter 10 highlights issues in prevention, describing programs designed for at-risk children and youth. In Chapter 11, we provide a brief overview of approaches to psychological intervention, describing the theoretical foundations of current evidence-based approaches and presenting data on the nature and course of psychotherapy. Chapters 12 and 13 present an overview of current evidence-based treatments for adults (Chapter 12) and for children and adolescents (Chapter 13). The case of Noah (who was introduced in Chapter 3) is used to illustrate issues in developing treatment plans. Chapter 14 provides information on evidence-based treatment elements derived from the therapy process and therapy process-outcome research. Finally, in Chapter 15, we examine issues in the practice of clinical psychology in the areas of health psychology, clinical neuropsychology, and forensic psychology.

Two appendices are included. The first lists journals in clinical psychology and should help students as they research topics in greater depth. The second appendix, entitled *Applications to Graduate School,* is designed to help students make decisions about graduate school applications as well as plan an application.

FEATURES OF INTEREST TO THE STUDENT

Within each chapter, many features have been incorporated to aid student learning. This text is designed to introduce clinical psychology in a reader-friendly and accessible manner, highlighting the varied and dynamic areas of the discipline.

Chapter Outline

Each chapter begins with an outline that prepares the student for the material to be covered.

Case Examples

In courses in clinical psychology, case examples are the tool through which abstract material is brought to life. In addition to the extended case presentations in Chapters 3, 9, and 13, case material is embedded throughout the text to illustrate issues in different developmental periods and with a diverse clientele. Reflecting the terminology in current practice, we alternate our use of the terms "patient" and "client." All the case examples we describe are based on our clinical experience. We have blended details about different people into composites to illustrate clinical issues. The case examples do not, therefore, represent specific individuals and all the names are fictitious.

Viewpoint Boxes

In each chapter, controversial issues and new directions in the field are highlighted in Viewpoint Boxes. Topics include:

- historically important themes, such as in *Distress in Clinical Psychologists and How They Deal with It* and *IQ and Its Correlates*
- new directions in clinical psychology, such as in *Psychological Resilience in the Face of Potential Trauma, Options for Increasing Psychotherapy Attendance,* and *Dissemination of Evidence-Based Treatments*
- controversies, such as in *What Do Psychologists Need to Know about Psychopharmacology?, The Trials and Tribulations of DSM-5,* and *How Reliable Are the Findings Reported in Research Studies?*
- issues with a lifespan perspective, such as in *Issues in Interviewing Older Adults* and *Treatment of Childhood Attention-Deficit/Hyperactivity Disorder*
- debates around evidence-based assessment, such as in *Child Custody Evaluations, Risk Assessment,* and *Why Do Questionable Psychological Tests Remain Popular with Some Clinical Psychologists?*
- expansion of the practice of clinical psychology to health, such as in *Health Promotion and Prevention Programs for Older Adults* and *Insomnia: No Need to Lose Sleep Over It!*
- current issues in treatment research, such as in *Multiple Perspectives on Treatment Goals* and *Sudden Gains in Therapy.*

Profile Boxes

To bring to life the reality of being a clinical psychologist, we have featured 24 individuals in Profile Boxes. We invited Canadian clinical psychologists at different stages of their careers to answer questions about being a clinical psychologist. In addition, to give students a sense of the varied activities in which psychologists engage, we asked three psychologists who work in different types of settings to describe a typical work week. We invited colleagues whom we consider fine examples of clinical psychologists, and we chose people whom we hope students will find inspiring. Students reading the Profile Boxes will better appreciate the wide range of activities in which clinical psychologists engage, the range of challenges they address in their work, and the creativity with which psychological principles are applied to reduce human suffering and improve psychosocial functioning.

We have also included a profile about a graduate student in clinical psychology, to give students a sense of the life of a clinical psychology graduate student.

Critical Thinking Questions

Key questions have been designed to promote discussion and debate on both traditional and emerging issues in clinical psychology. These questions appear in the margins marked with a head with a question mark icon.

Think About It!

Throughout each chapter, we have also included questions that encourage students to consider specific text material more deeply and more personally. These questions, which are marked with a thought bubble icon, usually ask the reader to consider the impact that a certain professional or empirical issue could have on someone's life. There are also questions that encourage students to consider how the manner in which clinical psychologists make decisions about professional services is similar to and different from the manner in which people make routine decisions.

Summary and Conclusions

At the end of each chapter, a section draws together the material discussed in the chapter.

Key Terms and Key Names

Throughout each chapter, important names and key terms are highlighted in bold. In addition, key term definitions are included in the margin. These are important study aids to highlight the most salient points of each chapter.

Additional Resources

For students who wish to explore an issue in greater depth, additional resources have been cited for various journals and books. The *Check It Out!* feature provides website links that allow readers to find out more about important issues raised in the chapter.

CHANGES IN THE THIRD EDITION

As clinical psychology is a rapidly evolving profession, in this third edition we have updated the scientific and professional literature we review to highlight recent changes in the field.

In Chapter 1, this involved providing new estimates about the economic costs of mental disorders and the numbers of mental health care specialists (including clinical psychologists). Chapter 2 has updated information about the professional activities and theoretical orientations of clinical psychologists, characteristics of training programs and their graduates, accreditation standards, and registration/licensure. A new profile on a "week in the life of a graduate student" has also been added. Information on both DSM-5 and ICD-10 diagnostic systems is included in Chapter 3, along with updated information on the epidemiology of mental disorders. To encourage the critical evaluation of scientific research, Chapter 4 has new Viewpoint Boxes addressing media reporting of research and the reliability of research results.

New assessment-related information has been included in Chapters 5 to 9. This includes a discussion of the continuing growth of evidence-based assessment, information on the updated Wechsler scales, and details of updated versions of frequently used self-report measures. Also, Chapter 6 has been reorganized to help readers be better prepared for learning about the challenges in assessing clients across the lifespan.

The chapters on prevention and treatment (Chapters 10 to 14) include new evidence of the impact of a number of prevention programs, information on the American Psychological Association resolution about the effectiveness of psychotherapy, an expanded listing of evidence-based treatments, details on a range of clinical practice guidelines, and results from a task force on evidence-based psychotherapy relationships.

Chapters 12 and 13 have been revised to provide updated information on evidence-based treatments and the results of treatment efficacy and effectiveness research for clients across the lifespan. In Chapter 15, we have expanded information on the management of both chronic pain and insomnia, added information on the use of neuropsychological assessment to evaluate the capacity of older adults to live independently and manage their lives, and updated details on forensic risk assessment tools and challenges in their interpretation.

Overall, 7 new Viewpoint Boxes and 20 new Profile Boxes have been added. We have also increased the use of clinical case material to illustrate important points discussed in the text, and focused increased attention on diversity issues. Furthermore, to improve the readability and comprehensibility of the material, we have enhanced the cross-referencing across chapters.

ACKNOWLEDGEMENTS

We have appreciated the support and guidance of many people during the preparation of the third edition of this book. Thanks are due to Rodney Burke, the acquisitions editor, who championed the importance of a written-in-Canada text on contemporary clinical psychology. We are grateful to Georgina Montgomery, our copy editor for this edition, and production editor Yee Lyn Song who coordinated the phases of production with efficiency. We are grateful for the helpful feedback provided by Robert Hunsley and Majeeda Khan and the capable research assistance provided by Robert Hunsley and Kathryn LaRoche. The book is enriched by the contributions of the psychologists who agreed to be profiled. We appreciate their cooperation and willingness to talk about their careers, and special thanks go to them. They are Drs. Melanie Barwick, Peter Bieling, Christopher Bowie, Clarissa Bush, Christine Chambers, David A. Clark, Karen Dyck, Jennifer Frain, Heather Hadjistavropoulos, David Hodgins, Charlotte Johnston, Martin Lalumière, Christopher Mushquash, Randy Paterson, Martin D. Provencher, Adam Radomsky, Graham Reid, Don Saklofske, Katreena Scott, Colette Smart, Michael Sullivan, Henny Westra, Jonathan Weiss, and Sheila Woody. We deeply appreciate the contribution of graduate student Emma MacDonald.

Last, but not least, we are grateful for the ongoing support of friends and family.

ABOUT THE AUTHORS

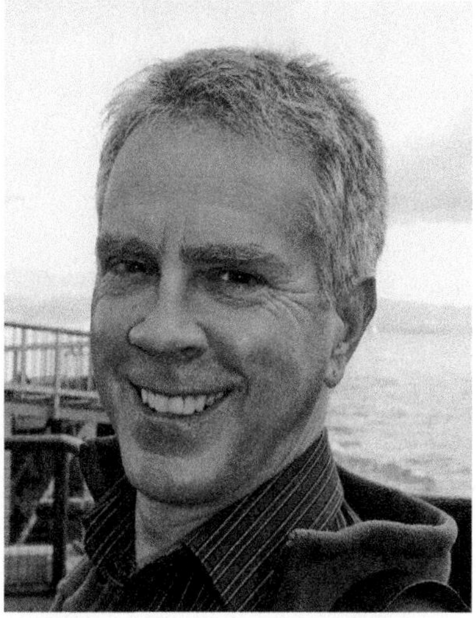

John Hunsley received a Ph.D. from the University of Waterloo in 1985. He is a full professor in the clinical psychology program at the University of Ottawa and is the director of the program. Dr. Hunsley teaches graduate courses in clinical research methods and psychological assessment. Dr. Hunsley's research interests focus on evidence-based psychological practice, the delivery of psychological services, and the scientific basis of psychological assessment. He has authored over 110 articles, chapters, and books on these topics. Dr. Hunsley is a Fellow of the Association of State and Provincial Psychology Boards, the Canadian Psychological Association (CPA), and the CPA Clinical Psychology Section. He has received the CPA Award for Distinguished Contributions to Education and Training in Psychology. From 2007 to 2011, he served as the editor of *Canadian Psychology*. He has also served on the editorial board of *Assessment, Journal of Personality Assessment, Professional Psychology: Research and Practice,* and *Scientific Review of Mental Health Practice.*

Catherine M. Lee earned a Ph.D. from the University of Western Ontario in 1988. She is a full professor of psychology at the University of Ottawa. Dr. Lee teaches graduate courses in evidence-based services for children and families and an undergraduate course on Clinical Psychology, as well as supervising practicum students and interns at the Centre for Psychological Services and Research. Her research interests focus on the provision of evidence-based services to promote positive parenting. She has authored over 70 articles, chapters, and books on this and related topics. Dr. Lee is a Fellow of the Canadian Psychological Association (CPA) and the CPA Clinical Psychology Section. She is an ad hoc reviewer for many granting agencies and scholarly journals and she serves on the editorial boards of *Clinical Child and Family Psychology Review* and *Cognitive and Behavioral Practice.* She is the former chair of the Clinical Psychology Section of the CPA and was President of the CPA in 2008–2009. She is a site visitor for the Canadian Psychological Association Accreditation Panel.

BRIEF TABLE OF CONTENTS

TABLE OF CONTENTS

THE EVOLUTION OF CLINICAL PSYCHOLOGY

1 CHAPTER

INTRODUCTION

> *Mental health is a state of well-being in which every individual realizes his or her own potential, can cope with the normal stresses of life, can work productively and fruitfully, and is able to make a contribution to his or her community.*
>
> World Health Organization (2007)

- More than 450 million people have mental disorders. Many more have mental health problems.
- About half of all mental disorders begin before people reach age 14.
- Worldwide, 877,000 people commit suicide every year.
- In emergencies, the number of people of mental disorders is estimated to increase by 6–11%.
- Mental disorders increase the risk for physical disorders.
- Many health conditions increase the risk of mental disorders.
- Stigma prevents many people from seeking mental health care.
- There are great inequities in the availability of mental health professionals around the world.

Adapted from World Health Organization (2007)

In the second decade of the 21st century, the potential for clinical psychology to make important contributions to the health of individuals, families, and society is abundantly clear. In this opening chapter, we introduce you to the profession of clinical psychology, its scope, and its remarkable history. Throughout this text, we will illustrate with compelling evidence that clinical psychologists have developed assessments that are helpful in understanding problems and interventions that are effective in preventing, treating, and even eliminating a broad range of health problems and disorders.

To fully appreciate the importance of such health services, it is necessary to understand the scope of the public health problem facing health care systems in North America and other parts of the world. A national survey of the mental health and well-being of Canadians aged 15 years and older found that as many people suffered from clinical depression as from common chronic health conditions such as heart disease and diabetes (Statistics Canada, 2003). Furthermore, 1 out of every 10 Canadian adolescents and adults reported symptoms consistent with a diagnosis of a mental disorder such as alcohol or illicit drug dependence, a mood disorder (i.e., major depressive disorder or bipolar disorder), or a serious anxiety disorder (i.e., social phobia, panic disorder, or panic disorder with agoraphobia). It is estimated that the cost of mental illness to Canadian society—including absenteeism, underemployment, unemployment, disability costs, health care services and supports, and premature death—may be as high as $63 billion annually (Wilkerson, 2012).

Perhaps due to the stressfulness of living and/or working conditions, the rate of mental health problems is even higher among certain groups than in the general population. For example, a health survey of members of active Canadian military personnel found that 15% reported a mental disorder in the previous year and 23% believed they required mental health services (Sareen et al., 2007). Being deployed to combat operations and witnessing atrocities were associated with increased risk of disorder and need for services. Participation in peacekeeping operations was not associated with increased risk, unless such assignments were associated with exposure to combat and witnessing atrocities. Similar results have been reported for American troops deployed to Iraq and Afghanistan (Smith et al., 2008).

In 1999, the Surgeon General of the United States released a report on the mental health of Americans (U.S. Department of Health and Human Services, 1999). Using data from national epidemiological studies, he estimated that, over a one-year period, 21% of Americans suffered from anxiety disorders, mood disorders, schizophrenia and other psychotic conditions, antisocial personality disorder, anorexia nervosa, or severe cognitive impairments. The estimate that one in five people suffers from a mental disorder applied to all age groups, including children, adolescents, adults, and older adults. The report also presented data showing that, in countries with established market economies (such as Canada, the United States, the United Kingdom, Australia, and New Zealand), the economic burden of mental disorders, mental illness, and suicide in terms of health care costs and lost productivity is second only to that of cardiovascular conditions.

The Depression Report, released in 2006 by the London School of Economics, translated epidemiological data into economic terms (London School of Economics Centre for Economic Performance, Mental Health Policy Group, 2006). Despite the estimate that one family in three is affected by depression or anxiety, only 2% of the expenditures of the National Health Service (NHS) in the United Kingdom (UK) are allocated to the treatment of these disorders. Lost output due to depression and anxiety is estimated to cost the UK economy £12 billion a year—representing 1% of the total national income. A million people in the UK receive disability benefits because of mental disorders, at a cost of £750 a month (about $1,500 Canadian) per person.

The UK National Institute for Health and Care Excellence (NICE) is an independent interdisciplinary organization with the mandate to provide national guidance on promoting good health and preventing and treating ill health. Systematic literature reviews by NICE concluded that evidence-based psychological therapies, which cost approximately £750 per person, are effective for at least half the people with anxiety and depression and are at least as effective as medication in tackling these mental health problems. The UK government therefore decided to improve access to psychological therapies by training mental health professionals, including, but not limited to, psychologists. Policy-makers predict that this investment will, in addition to offering enormous potential human benefits in reduced suffering and increased well-being, yield significant economic benefits in terms of both reduced claims for disability and increased productivity.

Data from the World Health Organization (presented in Exhibit 1.1) illustrate the scope of mental health problems in different countries. Worldwide, hundreds of millions of people suffer from mental disorders. However, most mental disorders are overlooked or misdiagnosed, and only a small percentage of those individuals who suffer from a mental disorder ever receive treatment. Even if they do receive treatment for other health concerns, in most cases—regardless of the wealth or level of development of the country in which these people live—mental health problems are neglected. This is particularly troubling because effective, relatively inexpensive treatments (psychological and/or pharmacological) exist for most of these conditions. Viewpoint Box 1.1 describes the initiatives undertaken by the Mental Health Commission of Canada to enhance the health and well-being of Canadians.

Are mental health problems as serious as physical health problems?

In addition to the pressing problems posed by mental disorders, there is mounting evidence that lifestyle and psychosocial factors are related to many of the causes of death in Western countries. As you will learn in Chapters 10 and 15, there is evidence that psychological services can dramatically reduce the negative health impact of these lifestyle and psychosocial risk factors. A large-scale study of the causes of mortality in the United States reached startling conclusions (Mokdad, Marks, Stroup, & Gerberding, 2004). Although dramatic causes such as motor vehicle accidents accounted for 2% of deaths, and shooting fatalities accounted for 1% of deaths, the leading causes of death were related to tobacco smoking (18.1%), poor diet and physical inactivity (16.6%), and alcohol consumption (3.5%). Adding the numbers together, these data demonstrate that at least 40% of fatalities were attributable to entirely preventable—or treatable—factors.

Exhibit 1.1 World Health Organization Mental Health: The Bare Facts

- At any given time, there are 450 million people worldwide suffering from mental, neurological, and behavioural problems.
- It is predicted that the number of people suffering from these problems will increase in the future.
- Mental health problems are found in all countries.
- Mental health problems cause suffering, social exclusion, disability, and poor quality of life.
- Mental health problems increase mortality.
- Mental health problems have staggering economic costs.
- One in every four people seeking other health services has a diagnosable mental, neurological, or behavioural problem that is unlikely to be diagnosed or treated.
- Mental health problems are associated with poor compliance with medical regimens for other disorders.
- Cost-effective treatments exist for most disorders and, if applied properly, could enable people to function better in their communities.
- There is greater stigma associated with mental health problems than with physical health problems.
- Most countries do not allocate sufficient funds to address mental, neurological, and behavioural problems.

Adapted from World Health Organization (2004b).

DEFINING THE NATURE AND SCOPE OF CLINICAL PSYCHOLOGY

As we consider the pain and suffering experienced by people with mental and physical health problems, the interpersonal effects of their distress on their family, friends, and co-workers, and the tragedy of untimely death, the need for effective services to identify and address these problems is evident. It is inevitable that, at many points in our lives, each of us will be affected, either directly or indirectly, by the emotional distress of psychological disorders. The first experience may be helping a friend through confusion and anger stemming from a loved one's suicide. As a university student, you may be faced with the challenges of helping a roommate with an eating disorder who binges and purges. Young parents may provide support to another young parent who is desperate to find appropriate services for a child with autistic disorder. In mid-life, you may be faced with the burden of caring for an elderly parent suffering from dementia, or you may be attempting to support a partner who is chronically anxious and avoids social gatherings. As you age, you may face the death of your partner and friends, and may have to cope with your own increasing infirmity and pain. Clinical psychology is the branch of psychology that focuses on developing assessment strategies and interventions to deal with these painful experiences that touch everyone's life.

VIEWPOINT BOX 1.1

MENTAL HEALTH COMMISSION OF CANADA

MHCC | CSMC

In Canada, although health services are provided by the provinces, federal initiatives have underlined the need for a national strategy with respect to mental health. *Out of the Shadows at Last*, published in 2006, reported on the Senate Commission on Mental Health, chaired by Senator Michael Kirby. Testimony from people with mental disorders, their families, service providers, and researchers drew attention to the urgent need for increased government investment to address the needs of the high numbers of Canadians suffering from a mental disorder. The incomplete and patchwork nature of mental health services available across the country was emphasized in the report. Following one of the key recommendations of the report, the federal government established the Mental Health Commission of Canada (MHCC).

The MHCC is a national non-profit organization designed to enhance the health and well-being of those living with a mental disorder by focusing national attention on mental health issues. The MHCC is designed to foster collaboration among different levels of government, service providers, researchers, people with mental disorders, and the families of those individuals. The MHCC has two clear messages about people living with a mental disorder:

- They have the right to receive the services and supports they need.
- They have the right to be treated with the same dignity and respect as those struggling to recover from any kind of illness.

The MHCC currently has six initiatives and projects:

1. *Opening Minds*: a campaign to reduce the stigma associated with mental disorders and to eradicate discrimination faced by those living with mental health problems
2. *Mental Health First Aid*: a program for training members of the public to assist a person developing a mental health problem or experiencing a mental health crisis
3. *Mental Health Strategy for Canada*: an initiative for developing a national mental health strategy (over two-thirds of countries already have one; Canada lags behind the rest of the world in this regard)
4. *Knowledge Exchange Centre*: an initiative designed to make evidence-based information about mental health widely available to both service providers and the public
5. *Housing First*: a program for providing people with housing and support services tailored to meet their needs
6. *Peer Project*: a project designed to enhance the use of peer support by creating and applying national guidelines of practice

Think about the challenges and stressors that you have faced and those faced by those you care about. Can you identify the things that made your distress worse? On the other hand, what helped you in dealing with difficulties?

Throughout the text, to give you a clear sense of who clinical psychologists are and the variety of things they do in their work, we introduce you to a number of Canadian clinical psychologists. In our first example in the text, Profile Box 1.1, you will meet psychologist Dr. Jennifer Frain, who is the executive director of a social service agency in Winnipeg, Manitoba.

PROFILE BOX 1.1

DR. JENNIFER FRAIN

Courtesy of Jennifer Frain

I did my undergraduate degree in psychology in my hometown at the University of Winnipeg. My master's degree in clinical psychology was completed at the University of Saskatchewan, followed by my Ph.D. in clinical psychology at Concordia University in Montreal. I completed my internship/residency at the Clarke Institute of Psychiatry in Toronto (which is now part of the Centre for Addictions and Mental Health). I returned to Winnipeg to begin my career and have now worked for over 15 years in social services. In 2006, I became the executive director of New Directions for Children, Youth, Adults and Families, Inc., the largest social service agency in Winnipeg, serving the Winnipeg community since 1885.

I joined the board of directors of the Manitoba Psychological Society (MPS) in 2000, as I wanted to connect with colleagues in the psychology community. I became president of MPS for the first time in 2002 and was re-elected in 2005. During my time on the MPS board of directors, I had the great fortune to work with other psychology advocates from across Canada, and in 2005 I became the chair of the Council of Professional Psychologists. It was in this role that I joined the board of directors of the Canadian Psychological Association (CPA). It was my privilege to serve as the president of the CPA in 2012–2013.

HOW DID YOU CHOOSE TO BECOME A CLINICAL PSYCHOLOGIST?

I was actually heading toward medical school (following a long tradition of MDs in my family) when, in my second year of undergraduate study, I took a Psychology of Sex Differences course with a well-known and brilliant psychologist. Although the course content was very interesting, I was most affected by the professor and the way she interacted with others, the way she approached questions, and the way she thought. She was a dynamic teacher and, for the first time in my life, I became totally fascinated with course material.

CONTINUED . . .

Other psychology courses followed and I veered away from a medical career and into graduate training in clinical psychology. I have never once regretted this decision.

WHAT IS THE MOST REWARDING PART OF YOUR JOB AS A CLINICAL PSYCHOLOGIST?

The breadth of skill development in clinical psychology training has been essential to my success in social services. I was trained to conduct interviews and perform assessments that require the distillation, analysis, and synthesis of diverse sources of information. Graduate training also helped me learn to use my reactions, empathic abilities, and problem-solving skills to provide therapeutic interventions to help an individual move forward positively in his or her life. In my work, I am required to supervise staff at all levels of my organization and to engage at a systems level with civil servants, elected officials, other organizations, and community and family stakeholders. It is incredibly rewarding and stimulating to be able to use my scientist and practitioner skills as a clinical psychologist working in a community setting.

WHAT IS THE GREATEST CHALLENGE YOU FACE AS A CLINICAL PSYCHOLOGIST?

The greatest challenge that I face as a clinical psychologist is my relative isolation in the area of social services. Although my training provided ideal preparation for what I do, few clinical psychologists consider a career in the social services. This is highly unfortunate, as many of the day-to-day issues dealt with are of serious consequence (e.g., the care and protection of children, the intervention with youth who are heavily involved in street culture, the provision of programs and services for persons with cognitive disabilities living in the community). The significance of the work, the high stakes, and the miserable outcomes for people when service is not available or not done right are huge, both for the individuals and for society at large.

WHAT DO YOU SEE AS THE MOST EXCITING CHANGES IN THE FIELD OF CLINICAL PSYCHOLOGY?

We are witnessing the participation of clinical psychologists throughout the health care system and I am very excited about that, as clinical psychologists can be providers of both health and mental care. It is encouraging to see a growing number of psychologists working in primary care clinics, oncology clinics, pain clinics, and cardiology units. The increased employment of psychologists in government is also terrific, as psychologists are being sought out to develop, identify, and institute policies that address population-level concerns, such as modifying poor behavioural choices and strategies to help people make better choices to ward off future problems (e.g., positive parenting strategies, healthy eating, active lifestyle adoption). So, for me, the most exciting changes I see are that psychologists are now working in diverse roles, which is enabling them to bring their breadth of knowledge and skills to bear on a wide range of challenges in society.

Let's consider some definitions of clinical psychology. Exhibit 1.2 provides examples of definitions and descriptions of clinical psychology from the United States, Britain, and New Zealand. Despite some differences in emphasis, a common theme running through these definitions is that clinical psychology is based firmly on scientifically supported psychological theories and principles. Clinical psychology is a science-based profession. Furthermore, the development of effective assessment, prevention, and intervention services relies on basic research into the nature of emotional distress and well-being. The practice of clinical psychology uses scientifically based methods to reliably and validly assess both normal and abnormal human functioning. Clinical psychology involves gathering evidence about optimal strategies for delivering health care services.

Exhibit 1.2 International Definitions of Clinical Psychology

AMERICAN PSYCHOLOGICAL ASSOCIATION, SOCIETY OF CLINICAL PSYCHOLOGY

The field of Clinical Psychology involves research, teaching and services relevant to the applications of principles, methods, and procedures for understanding, predicting, and alleviating intellectual, emotional, biological, psychological, social and behavioral maladjustment, disability and discomfort, applied to a wide range of client populations. In theory, training, and practice, Clinical Psychology strives to recognize the importance of diversity and strives to understand the roles of gender, culture, ethnicity, race, sexual orientation, and other dimensions of diversity.
(www.div12.org/about-us/)

BRITISH PSYCHOLOGICAL SOCIETY, DIVISION OF CLINICAL PSYCHOLOGY

Clinical psychology applies the scientific knowledge base of psychology to 'clinical' problems. After completing a psychology undergraduate degree, postgraduate training is undertaken in the application of psychology to a variety of human difficulties. Clinical psychologists aim to reduce psychological distress and to enhance and promote psychological well-being. A wide range of psychological difficulties may be dealt with, including anxiety, depression, relationship problems, learning disabilities, child and family problems and serious mental illness.
(dcp.bps.org.uk/dcp/clinical_psychology/role_home$.cfm)

NEW ZEALAND PSYCHOLOGSTS BOARD

Clinical Psychologists apply psychological knowledge and theory derived from research to the area of mental health and development, to assist children, young persons, adults and their families with emotional, mental, developmental or behavioural problems by using psychological assessment, formulation and diagnosis based on biological, social and psychological factors, and applying therapeutic interventions using a scientist-practitioner approach.
(www.psychologistsboard.org.nz/scopes-of-practice2)

Over the decades, the nature and definition of clinical psychology has shifted, expanded, and evolved. From an initial primary focus on assessment, evaluation, and diagnosis, the scope of clinical psychology has grown. Clinical psychology now also includes numerous approaches to intervention and prevention services that are provided to individuals, couples, and families. The practice of clinical psychology also covers indirect services that do not involve contact with those suffering from a mental disorder, such as consultation activities, research, program development, program evaluation, supervision of other mental health professionals, and administration of health care services. Given the ever-changing nature of the field, the only certainty about clinical psychology is that it will continue to evolve. Only time will tell whether this evolution ultimately leads to a decreasing focus on traditional activities of assessment and treatment (as predicted by some experts), to an increasing focus on the use of psychopharmacological agents to treat mental illness and mental health problems (as promoted by some psychologists and some psychological associations), or to the adoption of universal prevention programs designed to enhance our protection from risk. The changing nature of clinical psychology does, however, require that any definition of the field be treated as temporary, to be maintained only as long as it accurately reflects the field. The definition of clinical psychology must be altered and updated as innovations and new directions emerge.

The Canadian Psychological Association's Section on Clinical Psychology developed an excellent document that defines the current nature of clinical psychology, provides general principles intended to apply to future changes in the field, and firmly grounds the practice of clinical psychology in the context of professional ethics and responsibility. An excerpt of this definition is presented in Exhibit 1.3. In developing this

Exhibit 1.3 Canadian Definition of Clinical Psychology

APPROVED BY THE CLINICAL SECTION AND THE BOARD OF DIRECTORS OF THE CANADIAN PSYCHOLOGICAL ASSOCIATION, MAY 1993

Clinical psychology is a broad field of practice and research within the discipline of psychology, which applies psychological principles to the assessment, prevention, amelioration, and rehabilitation of psychological distress, disability, dysfunctional behaviour, and health-risk behaviour, and to the enhancement of psychological and physical well-being.

Clinical psychology includes both scientific research, focusing on the search for general principles, and clinical service, focusing on the study and care of clients, and information gathered from each of these activities influences practice and research.

Clinical psychology is a broad approach to human problems (both individual and interpersonal), consisting of assessment, diagnosis, consultation, treatment, program development, administration, and research with regard to numerous populations, including children, adolescents, adults, the elderly, families, groups, and disadvantaged persons. There is overlap between some areas of clinical psychology and other professional fields of psychology, such as counselling psychology and clinical neuropsychology, as well as some professional fields outside of psychology, such as psychiatry and social work.

Clinical psychology is devoted to the principles of human welfare and professional conduct as outlined in the Canadian Psychological Association's *Canadian Code of Ethics for Psychologists*. According to this code, the activities of clinical psychologists are directed toward: respect for the dignity of persons; responsible caring; integrity in relationships; and responsibility to society.

definition, the Section on Clinical Psychology sought input from numerous sources, including the members of the section, the executive committees of other sections within the Canadian Psychological Association, and the executive committees of several national organizations in Canada for which the definition might be relevant, such as the Canadian Council of Clinical Psychology Programs, the Council of Provincial Associations of Psychology, and the Canadian Register of Health Service Providers in Psychology (Vallis & Howes, 1996). Throughout this textbook you may notice other examples that illustrate the importance of conducting wide-ranging consultation in order to achieve consensus on important issues in the profession. Consultation is a hallmark of successful initiatives in clinical psychology.

EVIDENCE-BASED PRACTICE IN PSYCHOLOGY

Despite the apparent overlap in the various definitions of clinical psychology that we presented in Exhibit 1.2, there is still very active debate about the extent to which clinical psychology can or should be based solely on the science of psychology. Some psychologists doubt that clinical psychology can ever be effectively guided by scientific knowledge. Critics of a science-based approach to clinical psychology express the following concerns:

- Group-based data cannot be used in working with an individual—Critics argue that because a great deal of psychological research is based on research designs that involve the study of groups of individuals, it is difficult to determine the relevance of research results to any specific individual.
- Clients have problems now and we cannot afford to wait for the research—Critics argue that developing, conducting, and replicating research findings takes substantial time and thus the information provided by researchers inevitably lags behind the needs of clinicians to provide services to people in distress.
- Each individual's unique constellation of life experience, culture, and societal context makes it unlikely that general psychological principles can ever provide much useful guidance in alleviating emotional distress or interpersonal conflict.
- There is simply no research evidence on how to understand or treat many of the human problems confronted by clinical psychologists on a daily basis.

Although these kinds of concerns sound reasonable enough, they lead to the suggestion of basing clinical practice on the individual psychologist's gut feelings, intuition, or experience. The idea that clinical psychology is primarily a healing art rather than primarily a science-based practice is extremely problematic. As we discuss in subsequent chapters, there is ample evidence that people are prone to a host of decision-making errors and biases. Because clinicians are not immune from these errors and biases, they risk making serious mistakes in evaluating and treating clients. Thus, over-reliance on the clinician's professional experience and general orientation to understanding human functioning can be risky if it is not balanced with the application of scientifically based knowledge and with a scientific approach to developing and testing clinical hypotheses.

At the other end of the spectrum, there are clinical psychologists for whom the current definitions of clinical psychology do not go far enough in ensuring that science is at the heart of all clinical services offered to the public. A passionate proponent of this position is Richard McFall, who, in his 1991 presidential address to the Society for a Science of Clinical Psychology (a section of the American Psychological Association's Society of Clinical Psychology), challenged the field to provide only psychological services that research has shown to be effective and safe (McFall, 1991). The key elements of his *Manifesto for a Science of Clinical Psychology* are presented in Exhibit 1.4.

Exhibit 1.4 McFall's Manifesto for a Science of Clinical Psychology

CARDINAL PRINCIPLE

Scientific clinical psychology is the only legitimate and acceptable form of clinical psychology.

First Corollary

Psychological services should not be administered to the public (except under strict experimental conditions) until they have met the following four minimal criteria:

Criterion 1 The exact nature of the service must be described clearly.
Criterion 2 The claimed benefits of the service must be stated explicitly.
Criterion 3 These claimed benefits must be validated scientifically.
Criterion 4 Possible negative side effects that might outweigh any benefits must be ruled out empirically.

Second Corollary

The primary and overriding objective of doctoral programs in clinical psychology must be to produce the most competent clinical scientists possible.

Adapted from McFall (1991).

McFall's manifesto adopted a position on the role of science in clinical psychology that many clinical psychologists initially found too extreme. McFall's demand that only scientifically supported treatments should be offered to the public met with strong opposition from many clinical psychologists. The manifesto sparked a lively debate about the appropriateness and the ethics of routine psychological service (or any health service for that matter) that does not have documented, scientifically sound evidence demonstrating its effectiveness. There is no doubt that the vast majority of people who seek psychological services are in significant distress and hope to receive treatment that will reduce their distress and improve their overall functioning.

Do you think it is responsible to offer services that have no evidence of effectiveness? When effective treatments exist, is it reasonable to continue to offer services of undocumented effectiveness? If you were advising a friend to seek services, wouldn't you suggest looking for services that have been shown to be helpful for similar problems? If not, then why not?

In recent years, questions surrounding the appropriateness of adopting a science-based approach for the practice of clinical psychology have taken centre stage in discussions about the nature of clinical psychology. Originally developed within medicine, the **evidence-based practice** (EBP) model:

evidence-based practice: a practice model that involves the synthesis of information drawn from research and systematically collected data on the patient in question, the clinician's professional experience, and the patient's preferences when considering health care options.

a. requires the clinician to synthesize information drawn from research and systematically collected data on the patient in question, the clinician's professional experience, and the patient's preferences when considering health care options (Institute of Medicine, 2001; Sackett, Rosenberg, Gray, Haynes, & Richardson, 1996); and
b. emphasizes the importance of informing patients, based on the best available research evidence, about viable options for assessment, prevention, or intervention services.

The EBP model is now being integrated into many health and human service systems, including mental and behavioural health care, social work, education, and criminal justice (McHugh & Barlow, 2010; Mullen & Streiner, 2004). In order to practise in an evidence-based manner, a health care professional must be familiar with the current scientific literature and must use both the research evidence and scientifically informed decision-making skills to determine the ways in which research evidence can inform service planning for a patient.

As we describe in the next chapter, current training models in clinical psychology all emphasize the need for psychologists to be competent in the use and interpretation of scientific methods. Indeed, the EBP model has been endorsed by the both the Canadian Psychological Association (CPA Task Force on Evidence-Based Practice of Psychological Treatments, 2012) and the American Psychological Association as the basis for the professional practice of psychology (APA Presidential Task Force on Evidence-Based Practice, 2006).

It is fascinating to note that the movement for evidence-based practice in health care services places demands on all health services that are remarkably similar to those expressed by McFall's first corollary. Within two decades, a position that was originally considered extreme became mainstream in many health care systems and a goal espoused by several health care professions. Moreover, in a position paper on the implications of EBP for psychiatrists, the Canadian Psychiatric Association indicated that the single most compelling reason for practising in an evidence-based manner was an ethical one (Goldner, Abass, Leverette, & Haslam, 2001). In essence, because their code of ethics obliges psychiatrists to provide those receiving their services with the best available information about service options, these authors argued that psychiatrists must adopt the EBP model.

MENTAL HEALTH PROFESSIONS

The definitions of clinical psychology provide an important perspective on the nature and function of modern clinical psychology. However, it is useful to describe other health care professions whose services and client populations overlap those of clinical psychology. In the following pages, we describe several other professions, some of which also involve extensive training in psychology.

In what ways is clinical psychology similar to other mental health professions?

Within the field of psychology, what is unique about clinical psychology? The definitions we presented emphasized that clinical psychology is primarily concerned with the *application* of psychological knowledge in assessment, prevention, and/or intervention in problems in thoughts, behaviours, and feelings. Of course, in addition to providing psychological services, many clinical psychologists also conduct psychological research and contribute important information to the science of psychology. Nevertheless, the objective of research in clinical psychology is to produce knowledge that can be used to guide the development and *application* of psychological services.

Clinical psychology shares many of the research methods, approaches to statistical analysis, and measurement strategies found in other areas of psychology. Many areas of psychology, such as cognitive, developmental, learning, personality, physiological, and social, generate research that has direct or indirect applicability to clinical psychology activities. However, the key purpose of research in these other areas of psychology is to generate basic knowledge about human functioning and to enhance, in general terms, our understanding of people. The fact that some of this knowledge can be used to assess and treat dysfunction and thereby improve human functioning is of secondary importance.

Many psychologists apply their knowledge in diverse applied fields. In Chapter 15, you will learn about health psychologists, forensic psychologists, and neuropsychologists—typically these professionals are trained in clinical psychology and also have specialized training in their specific areas of research and practice. Two other areas of applied psychology, counselling psychology and school psychology, also provide important mental health services to the public. Although there is some similarity to clinical psychologists in their training and practices, these psychologists bring unique skills to the assessment, prevention, and treatment of mental health problems.

Counselling Psychology

It is important to distinguish between counselling psychology and counselling. Counselling is a generic term used to describe a range of mental health professions with various training and licensure requirements (Robiner, 2006). Estimates indicate that there are 49.4 counsellors per 100,000 people in the United States. The comparable figure for psychologists is 31.1 per 100,000 (Robiner, 2006). Turning specifically to counselling psychology, this profession has a great deal in common with clinical psychology. Historically, the distinction between clinical and counselling psychology was in terms of the severity of problems treated. Traditionally, the focus of clinical psychology was on the assessment and treatment of psychopathology—that is, manifestations of anxiety, depression, and other symptoms that were of sufficient severity to warrant a clinical diagnosis. On the other hand, counselling psychologists provided services to individuals who were dealing with normal challenges in life: predictable developmental transitions, such as leaving home to work or to attend university or college, dealing with changes in work or interpersonal roles, and handling the stress associated with academic or work demands. Simply put, counselling psychologists dealt with people who were, by and large, well adjusted, whereas clinical psychologists dealt with people who were experiencing significant problems in their lives and who were unable to manage the resulting emotional and behavioural symptoms.

Another distinction between the two professions was the type of setting in which the practitioners worked. Counselling psychologists were most commonly employed in educational settings (such as college or university counselling clinics) or general community clinics in which various social and psychological services are available. Clinical psychologists, in contrast, were most likely to be employed in hospital settings—both in general hospitals and in psychiatric facilities. These traditional distinctions between clinical and counselling psychologists are fading due to changes within both professions. Contemporary counselling psychologists provide services to individuals who are having difficulty functioning, providing, for example, treatment to university students suffering from disorders such as major depressive disorder, panic disorder, social phobia, or eating disorders (Benton, Robertson, Tseng, Newton, & Benton, 2003; Kettman et al., 2007). Both clinical and counselling psychologists are now employed in a wide range of work settings, including public institutions and private practices. In 2009, to aid in clearly defining and describing counselling psychology as a specialty within professional psychology, the Canadian Psychological Association adopted a definition of Canadian counselling psychology (Bedi et al., 2011).

©iStock.com/nullplus

Traditionally, counselling psychologists were most commonly found in educational settings, such as university clinics.

Over time, clinical psychologists have expanded their practice to address human problems outside the usual realm of mental health services by providing other services such as couples therapy, consultation, and treatment for people dealing with chronic illness and stress-related disorders. Thus, clinical psychologists developed services for individuals whose problem would not meet criteria for any psychopathological condition. Clinical psychologists have also begun to develop programs that are designed to prevent the development of problems. At one level, it is a rather tenuous decision to mark professional boundaries between counselling and clinical psychology on the basis of the possible differences between what constitutes "normal" range distress and abnormal levels of distress. Depending on the point in time in which someone seeks help, the same person might present with symptoms severe enough to meet diagnostic criteria for a mental disorder or with less severe, subclinical symptoms.

In many countries, there is no distinction between clinical and counselling psychology. In others, the distinction is becoming less and less meaningful for any practical purpose. In Canada, for example, the regulatory body for the profession of psychology in Ontario (the College of Psychologists of Ontario) requires that both counselling and clinical psychologists have the training and expertise to diagnose mental disorders. Just like clinical psychology, counselling psychology promotes the use of scientifically based interventions. This drive to provide evidence-based services is likely to have substantial implications for both training and practice in counselling psychology (Waehler, Kalodner,

Wampold, & Lichtenberg, 2000). The source of the distinction between the two psychology professions in some countries is that clinical and counselling psychologists are usually trained in different academic settings and in different academic traditions. Counselling psychology programs are found, for the most part, in faculties of education and/or departments of educational psychology. Clinical psychology programs, on the other hand, are based in psychology departments.

Data from surveys by Norcross and his colleagues indicate that clinical psychology programs attract far more applicants than do counselling psychology programs (Norcross, Kohout, & Wicherski, 2005; Norcross, Sayette, Mayne, Karg, & Turkson, 1998) and that counselling programs have a greater representation of ethnic minority students (Norcross et al., 1998). Research on clinical disorders is more commonly conducted in clinical psychology programs, and research on minority adjustment and academic/vocational issues is more frequently conducted in counselling psychology programs.

School Psychology

School psychologists have specialized training in both psychology and education. In the United States, school psychologists are employed in diverse organizations such as schools, clinics, and hospitals, and in private practice. In Canada, most school psychologists are employed by school boards. Given the focus on children's functioning, there is a natural overlap between school psychology and child clinical psychology. Historically, school psychology emphasized services related specifically to the learning of children and adolescents, including the assessment of intellectual functioning; the evaluation of learning difficulties; and consultation with teachers, students, and parents about strategies for optimizing students' learning potential. Clinical child psychology focused on the treatment of a diagnosable mental disorder.

Over time, the scope of school psychology has expanded in response to the demands of parents, school systems, and governments. Because of growing awareness of the deleterious effects on learning of child and adolescent psychopathology, parental psychopathology, and stressful family circumstances, the work of school psychologists now addresses students' mental health and life circumstances more broadly. The role of school psychologists now includes attention to social, emotional, and medical factors in a context of learning and development. These changes, combined with legal obligations that schools provide the most appropriate education for all children, have resulted in school psychologists diagnosing a range of disorders of childhood and adolescence, as well as developing school and/or family-based programs to assist students to learn to the best of their abilities. School psychologists have

School psychologists now take into account the social, emotional, and medical influences on students' learning and development.

also taken a leadership role in the development of school-based prevention programs designed to promote social skills, to reduce bullying, to facilitate conflict resolution, and to prevent violence (Kratochwill, 2007). These are described in detail in Chapter 10.

In the United States, there are estimated to be 11.4 school psychologists per 100,000 people (Robiner, 2006). Despite the increasingly close connections between school and child clinical psychology, it is likely that the two disciplines will remain distinct, at least in the near future. A survey of American school and child clinical psychologists clearly illustrates this point. Tryon (2000) found that, in a sample of school psychologists and clinical psychologists, the majority of school psychologists endorsed the position that training programs in school and clinical psychology should merge in order to provide improved services for school-based and school-linked mental health services, whereas fewer than half of the child clinical psychologists endorsed a merger. It therefore appears likely that distinctions in training will continue.

Psychiatry

Although we have focused on psychology-based professions thus far, it is important to note that primary care physicians provide more mental health services than any other health care profession (Robiner, 2006). As medical generalists, these physicians are usually the first health care professionals consulted for any health condition, be it physical or mental. Psychiatrists are physicians who specialize in the diagnosis, treatment, and prevention of mental illnesses. Like all physicians, in four years of medical school training they learn about the functioning of the human body and the health services that physicians provide. As with other medical specialties, training as a psychiatrist requires five years of residency training after successful completion of basic medical training. A range of residency options are possible, including both broad training in psychiatric services and specific training in subspecialties such as child psychiatry or geropsychiatry. Once they have completed specialization in psychiatry, psychiatrists rarely examine or treat the basic health problems that were covered in their medical training.

Psychiatric training differs in important ways from applied psychology training. First, psychiatric training deals extensively with physiological and biochemical systems and emphasizes biological functioning and abnormalities. Psychiatrists are well qualified to determine whether mental disorders are the result of medical problems and to unravel the possible interactions between physical illnesses and emotional disturbances. Psychiatric training provides the skills to evaluate the extent to which psychological symptoms result from or are exacerbated by medications used to treat physical ailments and

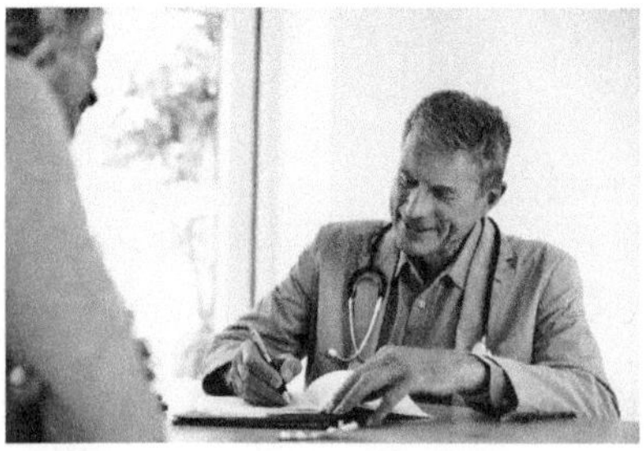

©iStock.com/Squaredpixels

Psychiatric services often emphasize both psychopharmacological and psychological treatments.

chronic illnesses. On the other hand, compared with psychologists, psychiatrists receive relatively little training in human psychological development, cognition, learning, or psychological functioning in general. Standard psychiatric training provides only limited training in research skills such as research design and statistical analysis. Many psychiatrists have become active researchers and have contributed in important ways to the knowledge base of the neurosciences and human sciences. Nevertheless, the average psychiatry resident receives far less training in research than does the average graduate student in clinical psychology. An expert panel in the United States warned that unless research training in psychiatric residency programs was dramatically strengthened, research by American psychiatrists risked dwindling to the point of "extinction" (McLellan, 2003).

Another fundamental difference between training in clinical psychology and psychiatry is that psychiatric training generally emphasizes psychopharmacological treatment over psychological treatment. Accordingly, compared with psychologists, psychiatrists tend to receive less training in the use of scientifically based psychological assessment and psychotherapy. Historically, psychiatrists were trained in forms of psychoanalytic and psychodynamic treatments such as those developed by Sigmund Freud, Carl Jung, and Alfred Adler. Due in part to the proliferation of effective psychopharmacological treatments in recent decades and the growing emphasis on evidence-based practice in psychiatry, there has been a waning of emphasis on training in psychoanalytic and long-term psychodynamic psychotherapy. There is growing attention paid to training psychiatrists in evidence-based treatments, which may include cognitive-behavioural and interpersonal therapies (cf. Hoge, Tondora, & Stuart, 2003; Martin, Saperson, & Maddigan, 2003). Despite the tendency for many psychiatrists to favour psychopharmacological approaches to treatment, psychiatrists were among the pioneers in the development of evidence-based psychological treatments: Aaron Beck was the primary developer of cognitive therapy for depression (and subsequently other disorders), Gerald Weissman was the primary developer of the interpersonal treatment of depression, and Isaac Marks has played a prominent role in the development of cognitive-behavioural treatments for anxiety disorders. Thus, although the relative emphasis of psychotherapy within the profession differs from that in clinical psychology, the provision of psychotherapeutic services remains, for many psychiatrists, a central aspect of psychiatric services. Attesting to this, the Canadian Psychiatric Association issued a position statement characterizing the provision of psychotherapy as an integral component of psychiatric care (Chaimowitz, 2004). Similarly, in 1998, the American Academy of Child and Adolescent Psychiatry took the position that psychotherapy must remain a core skill in the practice of child and adolescent psychiatry.

Until recently, an important distinction between clinical psychologists and psychiatrists was that only psychiatrists could prescribe medication. However, in some American jurisdictions, this is no longer the case. Programs through the federal Department of Defense and the Indian Health Service, as well as some state legislatures, have made provisions for psychologists to receive training to prescribe psychoactive medication. Canadian psychologists do not currently have prescription privileges. In Chapter 2, we will discuss this issue in greater detail.

There are currently approximately 4,100 psychiatrists in Canada (Canadian Psychiatric Association, 2013). In the United States, there are estimated to be 13.7 psychiatrists per 100,000 people (Robiner, 2006). The profession of psychiatry is facing a worldwide problem in recruiting new professionals. In many countries, even those as socially and economically different as Britain and India, the number of graduating medical students who wish to specialize in psychiatry has been insufficient to meet the demand for psychiatrists (Brockington & Mumford, 2002; Tharyan, John, Tharyan, & Braganza, 2001). In the United States, the number of medical students seeking psychiatric residencies has fallen by over 40% since the 1980s—only 3% of American medical students seek psychiatric training (Tamaskar & McGinnis, 2002). Several surveys of medical students have found that psychiatry is considered less professionally satisfying than other medical specialties. Feifel, Moutier, and Swerdlow (1999), for example, found that internal medicine, pediatrics, and surgery were all seen as more desirable career choices than psychiatry.

Clinical Social Work

Social workers focus on ways to improve the health and well-being of individuals, families, groups, and communities. Social work practice includes activities such as policy development, program planning, program management, research consultation, case management, discharge planning, counselling, therapy, and advocacy (Canadian Institute for Health Information [CIHI], 2011). Social workers are employed in diverse settings, including hospitals, community mental health centres, mental health clinics, schools, advocacy organizations, government departments, social service agencies, child welfare settings, family service agencies, correctional facilities, social housing organizations, family courts, employee assistance programs, school boards, and private counselling and consultation agencies (CIHI, 2011). The titles "social worker" and "registered social worker" are protected in legislation and can be used only by those who meet the regulations and standards of their provincial or territorial regulatory bodies. However, not all social workers are required to be registered with a regulatory authority (CIHI, 2011).

The number of registered social workers in Canada has been growing steadily, increasing by 114.2% over the 10-year period 1995–2004. This increase reflects not only the growing popularity of the profession, but also changes in legislation requiring the registration of social workers. (For comparison purposes, during the same period, there was a 33.1% increase in the number of registered psychologists). In 2009, there were almost 35,000 licensed social workers in Canada, 34.5% of whom were in Ontario and 21.8% in Quebec (CIHI, 2011).

Many social workers function as part of a mental health team in the role of case manager who, in collaboration with the patient, coordinates services with a range of social and community agencies, medical services, and other services (such as vocational or sheltered employment activities). In their role as case managers, social workers assist patients to navigate what is often experienced as a maze of service providers and a series of conflicting demands presented by various agencies. Case management is especially important in assisting people who suffer from severe and debilitating mental disorders such as schizophrenia and bipolar disorder.

Across jurisdictions, there is variability in the education required to practise social work. For example, the Alberta College of Social Workers requires a two-year diploma, whereas other Canadian provinces require an undergraduate or a master's degree in social work. Social work training programs emphasize the social determinants and consequences of mental health and illness. As is the case in applied psychology and psychiatry, clinical social work faces increasing demands to provide evidence-based services (e.g., Myers & Thyer, 1997). Given the move across so many mental health professions toward evidence-based services, evidence-based therapy, such as interpersonal therapy or cognitive therapy for the treatment of adult depression, could be provided by psychologists, psychiatrists, or clinical social workers.

Other Mental Health Professions

Psychiatric nurses are professionals who offer services to individuals whose primary care needs relate to mental and developmental health (Canadian Institute for Health Information [CIHI], 2011). Psychiatric nurses are responsible for managing administrative matters in inpatient settings, providing psychoeducation and counselling, and supervising ancillary services provided by others (such as nurses' aides and volunteers).

In the four western Canadian provinces, where registered psychiatric nurses are regulated as a distinct profession, there were 5,214 registered nurses in 2009 (CIHI, 2011). Psychiatric nurses are employed in diverse settings, including acute psychiatry, long-term geriatric care and home care, residential and community programs for the developmentally handicapped, forensic psychiatry, institutional and community-based corrections facilities, community mental health programs, special education programs for children, employee assistance programs, child guidance and family therapy clinics, chemical dependency programs, hospitals and special care homes, women's shelters and clinics, residential and community programs for adolescents, psychiatric nursing education, sheltered workshops, rehabilitation programs, vocational programs, self-help groups, and private practice (CIHI, 2011). In all these settings, psychiatric nurses are on the front lines, providing direct services, as well as training and consultation. Practitioners of this specialty typically receive their training as part of a two- or three-year diploma program or during a baccalaureate degree. In addition to the regular training in general nursing, psychiatric nurses receive training in the management and treatment of those with mental disorders warranting admission to a hospital or other similar institution.

In the residential care of children and adolescents with emotional and behavioural problems, front-line services may also be offered by child and youth care workers. Child and youth care workers usually have two-year college training in child development and behaviour management. In an attempt to meet the demand for mental health services while minimizing costs of services, outpatient services are often provided by mental health counsellors. In most cases, these counsellors have a college diploma or certificate based on a structured training program (often less than two years in duration) focused on the assessment and treatment of specific mental health problems such as addictions or trauma. There are also a growing number of counsellors trained in applied behavioural analysis, a systematic form of assessment and intervention that is the treatment of choice for pervasive developmental disorders such as autistic disorder. Of all the professionals presented in this chapter, child and youth care workers and counsellors have the least training and are the least likely to be members of a regulated profession.

As you can see, mental health services are offered by diverse professionals with varied backgrounds and training. There is a movement across all mental health professions to adopt evidence-based practice. This clearly requires an appreciation of the research foundations of our assessment tools and interventions. Psychologists are well placed to conduct and interpret the research foundations of effective practice. The composition of the mental health workforce is constantly shifting as professions seek more cost-effective strategies to ensure that their

Shutterstock/ Miriam Doerr

Psychiatric nurses often provide direct services, such as home care.

services can be accessed by a broad range of people who require care. As it becomes clear that evidence-based services can be provided effectively by trained professionals with different backgrounds, the roles of clinical psychologists will inevitably alter.

AVAILABILITY OF MENTAL HEALTH SERVICE PROVIDERS

There is wide variability in access to major mental health professions in different countries. Data from the World Health Organization indicate that the mental health needs of approximately half the world's nations are woefully underserved by trained professionals, with fewer than 1 psychologist, psychiatrist, or social worker for every 100,000 people (World Health Organization, 2004b). If we recall the data on the prevalence of mental health problems, even conservative estimates indicate that 1 in 10 people suffer from a mental disorder. Thus, in half the world, there is only 1 mental health professional for every 10,000 people who suffer from a mental disorder.

Canadian data indicate that, in 2009, there were 16,156 licensed psychologists practising in the country (Canadian Institute for Health Information, 2011). Table 1.1 provides details on the relative numbers of psychologists and psychiatrists in different countries. You may notice that some of the values presented for Canada and the United States differ slightly from those presented in the previous section. It is important to note that there is always some imprecision in calculating workforce estimates, as different organizations and researchers may refer to different sources and time periods to generate their estimates.

TABLE 1.1 ■ World Health Organization Data on Psychologists and Psychiatrists in Selected Countries

	Psychologists (per 100,000 people)	Psychiatrists (per 100,000 people)
Canada	35.0	12.0
United States	31.1	13.7
United Kingdom	9.0	11.0
Ireland	12.7	6.8
Australia	5.0	14.0
New Zealand	28.0	6.6
France	5.0	22.0
Germany	51.5	11.8

Adapted from World Health Organization (2005).

In Germany, Canada, the United States, New Zealand, and Ireland, there are substantially more psychologists providing mental health services than there are psychiatrists. By comparison, the United Kingdom has about the same proportion of psychologists as psychiatrists, whereas Australia and France have substantially more psychiatrists than psychologists.

Although the number of professionals providing mental health services in a country provides some indication of the adequacy of the health care system, it can mask regional disparities that affect the population. Key among such regional disparities is the difference between services available in urban and rural areas. By and large, those living in rural areas have fewer mental health professionals than do those living in urban areas. In Canada, for example, although the ratio of psychologists to psychiatrists is approximately 3 to 1 averaged for the whole country, in rural areas of Alberta, Newfoundland and Labrador, and Quebec, that ratio is an estimated 15 to 1 (Canadian Psychological Association, 1999). In Chapter 11, you will learn about an innovative training program to prepare psychologists for rural practice.

A BRIEF HISTORY OF CLINICAL PSYCHOLOGY

In considering the history of clinical psychology, it is useful to think in terms of interwoven threads that include the history of assessment and intervention within clinical psychology, the history of clinical psychology becoming a profession, the history of the treatment of mental illness, the history of prevention, and the history of psychology itself. In the remainder of the chapter, we will provide an overview of key aspects of clinical psychology's history.

Because clinical psychology has developed in differing ways and rates in various countries, we cannot do justice to the multitude of important events that have shaped, and continue to shape, the discipline worldwide. In this section, we highlight events that have contributed significantly to the current form of clinical psychology evident in most English-speaking countries. Due to space constraints, we have not included all critical occurrences that were instrumental in the development and application of clinical psychology in non-English-speaking countries. Nevertheless, in reading the following pages, you should get a general sense of the influences that contributed to the growth of clinical psychology in North America and elsewhere. Given the key role of American clinical psychology in shaping the face of clinical psychology worldwide, much of what follows highlights key events in the United States. You will notice that not all the key figures who were influential in the development of clinical psychology were psychologists.

Others include philosophers, psychiatrists, and members of related professions.

The Roots of Clinical Psychology

Numerous scholarly texts on the history of psychopathology and its treatment describe early proponents of the view that mental disturbances were caused by natural causes rather than by demonic possession. Among the early Greek scholars in the period of 500–300 B.C., Hippocrates (often called the father of medicine) emphasized what is now known as a **biopsychosocial approach** to understanding both physical and psychological disorders (i.e., that biological, psychological, and social influences on health and illness must be considered). In abnormal psychology and personality textbooks, you will have learned about Hippocrates' "bodily fluid" theory that imbalances in the levels of blood, black bile, yellow bile, and phlegm are responsible for emotional disturbance. The philosophers Plato and Aristotle are both credited with promoting some of Hippocrates' ideas, even though they did so in different ways. Plato emphasized the role of societal forces and psychological needs in the development and alleviation of mental disorders, whereas Aristotle emphasized the biological determinants of mental disorders.

biopsychosocial approach: a theoretical framework that takes into account biological, psychological, and social influences on health and illness.

In the late 1500s, St. Vincent de Paul proposed that mental and physical illnesses were caused by natural forces and that the extreme manifestations of mental disturbances such as psychotic behaviour were not caused by witchcraft or satanic possession. Unfortunately, the dominant approach to the treatment of mental illness in Europe and North America in the subsequent centuries was anything but humane. Those suffering from severe mental illness were isolated in asylums, most of which were far from conducive to the promotion of mental health. Numerous accounts of these institutions paint a picture of pain, despair, and desolation. Living conditions were often squalid and the more aggressive patients were chained to walls. Treatments included calming extreme behaviour using bleeding with knives or leeches (this was believed to reduce excitation due to an excess of blood) or immersion in frigid water.

During the period of the Enlightenment in Europe and North America that began in the latter half of the 1700s, a new world view emerged in which problems could be analyzed, understood, and solved and the methods of science could be applied to all natural phenomena, including the human experience. The impact of this philosophical movement on the treatment of the mentally ill was astounding. Reformer Philippe Pinel, the director of a major asylum in Paris in the late 1700s, ordered that the chains be removed from all mental patients and that patients be treated humanely. Around the same time in England, William Tuke advocated for the development of hospitals based on modern ideas of appropriate care and established a country retreat in which patients lived and worked. In the United States, Benjamin Rush promoted the use of moral therapy with the mentally ill (a treatment philosophy that encouraged the use of compassion and patience rather than physical punishment or restraints).

In what ways has scientific thinking shaped the evolution of clinical psychology?

About this time, within European medicine the specialty of neurology was growing rapidly. The increased attention to mental disorders led to the recognition that a number of conditions, such as hysteria (i.e., extreme, dramatic, and often odd behaviour, including limb paralysis), could not easily be accounted for with purely biological explanations. Jean-Martin Charcot, in France, is credited with being the primary developer of clinical neurology. As his fame grew, so did his emphasis on the role of psychological factors in hysteria. Charcot's use of suggestion and hypnosis to treat this condition initially attracted the attention of many physicians and medical students. Notable members of this group include Pierre Janet and Sigmund Freud, who initially embraced Charcot's theories and his use of hypnosis, but later went on to develop their own theories to account for hysteria.

The History of Assessment in Clinical Psychology

The early history of clinical psychology is largely the history of clinical assessment, as clinical psychology developed from psychology's focus on measuring, describing, and understanding human behaviour. Indeed, with some exceptions we discuss in the next section, clinical psychology was almost entirely an assessment-based discipline until the middle part of the 20th century. Milestones in the history of assessment in clinical psychology are noted in Exhibit 1.5.

By the latter part of the 1800s, the influence of the Enlightenment world view was also evident in the burgeoning application of scientific principles to understanding both normal and abnormal human behaviour. In England, Francis Galton studied individual differences among people, especially differences in motor skills and reaction times, which he believed were related to differences in intelligence. In Germany, Wilhelm Wundt, who studied sensation and perception, established the first psychology laboratory and was a central figure in advocating for psychology as the study of human experience. The American James McKeen Cattell, who at one time worked with Wundt, focused scientific attention on the connection between reaction time and intelligence. He is credited with coining the term *mental tests* to describe the battery of tests and tasks he developed to evaluate people's cognitive functioning.

Hulton Archive/Stringer/Getty Images

Wilhelm Wundt established the first psychology laboratory.

Exhibit 1.5 Timeline for the History of Assessment in Clinical Psychology

1879	Germany: *Measurement.* Wundt opens the first psychology laboratory measuring sensory processes.
1899	Germany: *Diagnosis.* Kraepelin develops the first diagnostic system.
1905	France: *Intelligence testing.* Binet and Simon develop a test to assess intellectual abilities in school children.
1917	U.S.: *Intelligence testing.* Army Alpha and Army Beta tests are developed to assess select soldiers.
1920s	Switzerland: *Projective testing of personality.* Rorschach publishes a book on the interpretation of inkblots.
1939	U.S.: *Intelligence testing.* Wechsler develops the Wechsler-Bellevue test of adult intelligence.
1940s	U.S.: *Projective testing of personality.* Murray and Morgan publish Thematic Apperception Test.
	Canada: *Intelligence testing.* Revised Examination M is used for selection and assignment in the military.
1943	U.S.: *Actuarial assessment of personality.* Hathaway publishes Minnesota Multiphasic Personality Inventory.
1952	U.S.: *Diagnosis.* The American Psychiatric Association publishes *Diagnostic and Statistical Manual of Mental Disorders.*
1954	U.S.: *Challenge to clinical decision-making.* Meehl distinguishes between statistical and clinical decision-making.
1968	U.S.: *Challenge to personality assessment.* Mischel proposes an alternative behavioural approach to assessment.
	U.S.: *Diagnosis.* The American Psychiatric Association publishes the second edition of *Diagnostic and Statistical Manual of Mental Disorders.*
1970s	U.S.: *Dimensional approach to child problems.* Quay, Achenbach, and Conners publish empirically based rating scales of child problems.
1980	U.S.: *Diagnosis.* The American Psychiatric Association publishes the third edition of *Diagnostic and Statistical Manual of Mental Disorders.*
1990s	Worldwide: *Increasing incorporation of behavioural assessment techniques into typical assessment practices.*
	Worldwide: *Widespread use of computers for scoring and interpreting psychological test results.*
1994	U.S.: *Diagnosis.* The American Psychiatric Association publishes the fourth edition of *Diagnostic and Statistical Manual of Mental Disorders.*
2000s	Worldwide: *Increased attention to the development of country-specific norms for commonly used measures of intelligence.*
	U.S. and Canada: *Increased attention to principles of evidence-based assessment in the selection and use of assessment instruments.*
2013	U.S.: *Diagnosis.* The American Psychiatric Association publishes the fifth edition of *Diagnostic and Statistical Manual of Mental Disorders.*

Without a doubt, the pre-eminent individuals who influenced the early work on assessment in clinical psychology are the German psychiatrist Emil Kraepelin and the French psychologist Alfred Binet.

Kraepelin was convinced that all mental disorders were due to biological factors and that these biological causes of the disorders could not be effectively treated by the rather primitive methods available in the late 1800s and early 1900s. Accordingly, he devoted his career to the study and classification of mental disorders in the hope that his work would result in a scientifically based classification system that would have treatment implications. Consistent with scientific approaches of the time, a key component of Kraepelin's approach to classification was to examine the way in which various symptoms covaried. Kraepelin assumed that by examining the symptomatic behaviour of a large number of patients, it would be possible to discern the kinds of disturbances of affect, thought, and behaviour that typically co-occurred. In Kraepelin's view, this would provide insights into the nature of mental disorders. Kraepelin called these groups of symptoms that frequently co-occurred **syndromes**, and his classification system was built around identifying the ways in which these syndromes related to and differed from each other. Thus, the presence of a single symptom was considered of little value in determining the nature of the disorder suffered by the patient. However, Kraepelin assumed that by considering the entire range of symptoms exhibited by the patient, it should be possible to identify the precise disorder from which he or she was suffering. As his study of symptoms and syndromes deepened, he realized that there were consistent differences between disorders in terms of when the symptoms first occurred (i.e., onset of the disorder) and the manner in which the disorder progressed subsequently (i.e., the course of the disorder). Kraepelin's classification system was unparalleled, and his classification of what is now known as schizophrenia was one of his major accomplishments. Even though some clinical psychologists have reservations about the value or validity of psychiatric diagnosis, Kraepelin's influence on modern psychiatry and clinical psychology is substantial. The nature and structure of current mental disorder classification systems, such as the American Psychiatric Association's *Diagnostic and Statistical Manual* and the World Health Organization's *International Classification of Diseases* (which are discussed in Chapter 3), have their origins in Kraepelin's work. Reference to these classification systems is an integral part of routine professional activities, ranging from conducting psychopathology research to billing for psychological services.

syndrome: group of symptoms that frequently co-occur.

Alfred Binet's contribution to clinical psychology is quite different, although no less substantial. In the early years of the 20th century, the French government wanted all children to receive schooling to maximize their potential to learn and develop. In particular there was concern to provide an education to those children with limited cognitive abilities who were unlikely to benefit from typical teaching methods. Before any special educational programs could be implemented, it was necessary to reliably identify children in need of such programs. Binet and his colleague Theodore Simon were invited to develop a strategy to measure mental skills that could yield information relevant to the identification of children with limited intelligence. By 1908, the two colleagues had developed the Binet-Simon scale of intelligence that consisted of more than 50 tests of mental skills that could be administered to children between the ages of 3 and 13 years. Binet and Simon gathered extensive data on a large number of children—that is, they established norms. As we describe in more detail in Chapter 5, norms allow for the comparison of test scores obtained by an individual to the range of scores within the general population or within specific subgroups of the general population. Thus, by comparing the intelligence test score obtained by a particular child with norms for children of the same age, the child's level of intelligence could be determined. In 1916, Lewis Terman published a modification of this scale for use in the United States, the Stanford-Binet Intelligence Test, which was the first widely available, scientifically based test of human intelligence. Binet's work established the importance of standardization in the development of psychological tests and the importance of references to normative data in interpreting test results.

Building on Binet's pioneering work and Terman's adaptation of the Binet-Simon test, the field of psychological assessment grew rapidly. With the entry of the United States into the First World War, the American government needed procedures to quickly determine the fitness of many thousands of recruits to serve in the military. Physicians were employed to evaluate the physical fitness of the recruits for various military activities. In addition, it was necessary to find a way to evaluate mental fitness and mental abilities. Therefore, a committee of the recently established American Psychological Association (APA, established in 1892) was struck to develop a system for classifying the men in terms of their mental functioning. This committee was chaired by Robert Yerkes, APA president. Within a short time, the committee developed a measure of verbal mental abilities, called the Army Alpha test, which could be administered in a group format (thus minimizing the cost and time of administration). They also developed a test of nonverbal mental abilities, the Army Beta test, for assessing recruits who were unable to read or who had limited English language skills. This involvement of psychologists in a key American government initiative set the stage for psychologists to be recognized in North America for their expertise in test construction and the measurement of individual differences. A second legacy of this process was the establishment of the first standards for the development of scientifically sound psychological tests. A third legacy was that, as a result of the value placed on these testing-related skills, the discipline of clinical psychology was officially recognized within the APA by the creation of the Section on Clinical Psychology in 1919.

During the next two decades, several approaches to clinical assessment flourished. Measurement of abilities continued to be a central focus for clinical psychologists. A milestone in the development of intelligence tests for adults was reached in 1939 with the release of the Wechsler-Bellevue test. Its developer, David Wechsler, subsequently developed intelligence tests for the entire age range (Wechsler Preschool and Primary Scale of Intelligence, Wechsler Intelligence Scale for Children, Wechsler Adult Intelligence Scale) and the most commonly used general measure of memory (Wechsler Memory Scale). Although other intelligence scales have since been developed for children and adults, the Wechsler scales are considered the *gold standard* in the assessment of intellectual abilities. The Wechsler scales will be discussed at length in Chapter 7. This period also saw the development of interest tests, with measures such as the Strong Vocational Interest Blank and the Kuder Preference Record, which were developed for training and personnel hiring purposes. Early self-report measures of temperament and personality became available with the release of Woodworth's Personal Data Sheet and the Allport-Vernon Study of Values.

Time & Life Pictures/Getty Images

Psychological testing in World War I.

The 1930s also witnessed the emergence of projective tests to evaluate personality and psychological functioning. Whereas intelligence tests measure performance on a task, and paper-and-pencil personality tests are based on self-description, projective tests are predicated on the notion that an individual's interpretation of a situation is determined by his or her personality characteristics. Thus, a person's response to an ambiguous stimulus is presumed to tell us something about the person's mental functioning. One of the most influential and widely used projective tests, the Rorschach Inkblot Test, was published by Swiss psychiatrist Hermann Rorschach in 1921. Although the test received a decidedly cool reception among psychiatric and psychological circles in Europe, it received a new lease on life when German psychologist Bruno Klopfer, who emigrated to the United States in 1934, began instructing psychology students at Columbia University on the use of the inkblots. The Rorschach Inkblot Test was also used in assessing children. Another projective technique that was considered suitable for both adults and children was the House-Tree-Person Test that involved interpretation of the psychological meaning of qualities of a person's drawing. Around the same time, American psychologists Henry Murray and Christina Morgan, working at the Harvard Psychological Clinic, published the Thematic Apperception Test (TAT), which comprised 20 pictures. Strongly opposed to the growing tendency to study psychological phenomena with experimental methods, Murray distanced himself from the mainstream of academic psychology, but he was greatly influenced in his thinking by the psychoanalytic writings of Sigmund Freud and Carl Jung. The development of projective tests proceeded without attention to the basic test construction objectives of standardization, reliability, validity, and norms, which has led to long-standing concerns about the quality and utility of many projective tests. These issues will be discussed at greater length in Chapter 8.

With the advent of the Second World War, psychologists once again became actively involved in the development and use of selection tests for the armed forces. In Canada, the Test Construction Committee of the Canadian Psychological Association was responsible for the development of the Revised Examination M that consisted of both verbal and non-verbal ability tests used in the selection and assignment of military personnel. However, the assessment milestone of the 1940s was unquestionably the publication of the Minnesota Multiphasic Personality Inventory (MMPI) by psychologist Starke Hathaway in 1943. The MMPI was, for many years to come, the epitome of the criterion-oriented approach to psychological test construction. The goal of the MMPI was to provide an easily administered test that could effectively screen for psychological disturbances among adults. To this end, Hathaway generated hundreds of test items that were administered to psychiatric patients. Items that were strongly associated with specific diagnoses were retained and then combined to make scales within the test. The ability of these scales to distinguish between people with and without psychiatric diagnoses was examined and modifications to the scales were made based on these data. Evidence for the final scales' reliability and validity was gathered and normative data (although rather poor) were obtained. Thus, in contrast to the projective tests, the development and interpretation MMPI relied extensively on attention to statistical procedures and test development criteria. Research on the MMPI is discussed in Chapter 8.

The fundamental differences between projective tests, which rely heavily on clinical judgment, and the MMPI, which relies on statistical analysis, set the stage for a critical evaluation of the value and accuracy of assessment in clinical psychology in the 1950s and 1960s. Paul Meehl's 1954 review of the relative strengths of clinically and statistically based assessment highlighted a number of problems that plagued the assessment enterprise in clinical psychology. In essence, Meehl's review of the literature found that a purely clinical approach to assessment was typically inferior to a more statistically oriented approach to accurately describing or diagnosing adults. By clinical, Meehl referred to the typical collection of interview and other information that was then used, sometimes with standardized test data, to generate descriptions and predictions of behaviour. The statistical approach, in contrast, involved the use of basic demographic information (such as age, gender, and health information) and data from standardized tests that were entered into statistical equations to yield descriptions and/or predictions. This latter approach was similar to risk estimates calculated by insurance companies to assign differential insurance policy costs based on estimated risk. A point often lost in the ensuing debate about the value of clinical judgment was that Meehl advocated strongly for the use of clinical experience in generating hypotheses about human functioning or about particular client characteristics. He maintained, however, that once these hypotheses were formulated, whether for research or clinical purposes, scientific methods (including, whenever possible, standardized psychological measures) must be used to test the viability of the hypotheses.

A little over a decade after Meehl's critique of clinical assessment practices, the publication in 1968 of Walter Mischel's compelling analysis of the shortcomings of personality traits for understanding human behaviour further eroded many clinical psychologists' confidence in the validity of their assessment work. Up to then, much of the research on personality had focused on the measurement and study of traits—that is, co-occurring characteristics that not only defined the personality of an individual but were also the primary influences in determining how an individual would react in a given situation. Mischel's work illustrated that these personality traits had more to do with how a person was viewed by others than with what a person actually did. Moreover, research on the predictive validity of personality traits typically yielded results of only moderate strength—in other words, knowing someone's personality traits provided very little useful information if you wished to know what someone would actually feel, think, or do in a particular situation. Much more accurate predictions of psychological experience could be obtained by considering both the person's past experiences in similar situations and the environmental influences on the person's behaviour in the situation.

Although many personality researchers and clinical psychologists believed that Mischel had underestimated the influence of personality factors and overestimated the power of social situations in determining behaviour, his analysis bolstered the rising influence of behavioural assessment approaches on clinical assessment. Initial behavioural approaches to assessment involved the identification of specific behaviours deemed to be central to the person's distress, by virtue either of being a key symptom that should be changed in therapy or being a central factor responsible for causing and/or maintaining the person's distress. Based on learning principles encompassed under operant, classical, and observational learning paradigms, behavioural assessment focused on easily defined and observable events, current behaviours, and situational/environmental determinants of behaviour. For much of the 1960s and 1970s, behavioural assessment largely involved obtaining frequency, rate, and duration measures describing the behaviours of interest. Compared with the self-report and projective personality assessment approaches, behavioural assessment was much more focused on gathering clinical data that had immediate and obvious value in the planning and evaluation of treatment strategies. As behavioural strategies often require observation by a third party, they were most commonly applied in treating problems of children and patients in hospitals or residential institutions. Observation strategies are described in Chapter 6.

Although sound tools for the assessment of children's intellectual functioning were developed early in the 20th century, empirically based assessment of children's emotional and behavioural problems did not begin in earnest until the 1970s with the publication of the first rating scales of children's behaviour. Different scales pioneered by Thomas Achenbach, Herbert Quay, and Keith Conners shared the same reliance on description of behaviours and on empirically derived scales to assess children's functioning. These scales required parents to rate the extent to which a particular behaviour was typical of their child. Like the MMPI, the items on these scales were subjected to factor analysis, so that scale scores were derived empirically. Such rating scales provide information on children's functioning on a number of dimensions rather than yielding a categorical diagnosis.

In the 1980s, the publication of the third edition of the American Psychiatric Association's *Diagnostic and Statistical Manual of Mental Disorders* (DSM) led to increased attention on the value of structured interview approaches to gathering diagnostic information. For many years, research had consistently demonstrated that clinicians (including clinical psychologists and psychiatrists) were very inconsistent in how they interviewed patients. Such inconsistencies were evident both from clinician to clinician and even by the same clinician over time. The result of these inconsistencies often led to the same individual being assigned very different diagnoses from clinicians. Such diagnostic inconsistency has the potential to dramatically affect the types of treatments recommended to the patient. The DSM-III was an explicit attempt to improve the reliability of psychiatric diagnoses by providing as clear guidance as possible on specific criteria that must be met to render a diagnosis. Based on the common measurement strategy in psychopathology research of using a standardized, structured interview to generate diagnostic information, clinicians were strongly encouraged either to use scientifically established structured interviews to diagnose DSM-III disorders or, at a minimum, to ensure that the necessary diagnostic criteria were met before a diagnosis was assigned. Particular attention has been paid to the development of structured diagnostic interviews for children, to ensure that questions are formulated in a manner that is developmentally appropriate. For example, it is not suitable to put complex questions about the duration of a problem to a child who has not yet developed a concept of time. Issues related to interviewing are addressed in Chapter 6.

Finally, there have been a number of striking changes in psychological assessment over the past three decades. One important change has been a rapprochement among different perspectives on how best to conduct psychological assessments. For most assessment purposes, it is generally accepted that assessment data should be obtained from (a) multiple methods, such as interviews, observations, and self-reports; and, increasingly, (b) multiple informants (i.e., not just from the client). A second important change has been the recognition that best practices in assessment should be based on assessment methods and measures that have solid scientific support. Issues of the psychometric properties of measures and the representativeness of norms used to interpret test scores are now commonly considered by psychologists. We will comment more on these issues in the chapters on assessment.

Another important change has been the increased attention to the relevance of assessment data for treatment planning and treatment evaluation. Decades of research amply demonstrate that psychologists can create assessment tools for myriad constructs. Many thousands of studies have been published on the reliability and validity of a huge range of psychological measures. However, it has become increasingly clear that, to justify the time and expense involved in clinical assessment, this vast knowledge must be applied in ways that are directly pertinent to improving the lives of people suffering psychological distress. Combined with concerns about costs and accountability of health care systems worldwide, this has highlighted two issues that clinical psychologists involved in assessment are beginning to address. The first issue is one of **clinical utility**: that is, does having assessment data on a patient actually provide information that leads to a clinical outcome that is better (or faster or less expensive) than would be the case if the psychologist did not have the assessment data? This issue reflects the problem that research on clinical psychology is often disconnected

clinical utility: usefulness of assessment data to provide information that leads to a clinical outcome that is better (or faster or less expensive) than would be the case if the psychologist did not have the assessment data.

service evaluation: activities designed to examine whether or not services work.

from research on interventions in clinical psychology and vice versa. As concerns about health care costs mount, clinical psychologists must justify to those who pay for their services the relevance of their assessment activities. The second, and related, current issue is one of **service evaluation**. Put bluntly, individual clinical psychologists are under increasing pressure to demonstrate that their services work. This has resulted in renewed attention to the role of clinical assessment in documenting progress and outcome in treatment. However, this need to demonstrate treatment effectiveness leads to a different type of clinical assessment than has often been used in the past. Whereas many clinical psychology measures were developed to give a broadly based psychological picture of the whole person, current assessment practices require that measures focus on specific problems (or strengths), be brief, and be amenable to repeated use. The measurement tools that are useful for generating an individual's psychological profile are not necessarily the ones that are relevant to the repeated assessment of someone receiving treatment. Accordingly, a minor revolution in the nature of clinical assessment is currently underway, with some traditional measures falling from favour, and some long-standing but underused assessment strategies coming to the fore. These issues are discussed in greater detail in Chapters 6, 7, and 8.

The History of Intervention in Clinical Psychology

Milestones in the evolution of intervention in clinical psychology are noted in Exhibit 1.6. The modern history of psychotherapy is typically seen as beginning with the work of Sigmund Freud and the development of psychoanalysis. As indicated earlier in this chapter, a number of European psychiatrists, such as Charcot and Janet, were actively involved in using verbal rather than physical approaches to the treatment of mental disorders in the late 1800s. Freud is credited with developing the first elaborated approach to the psychotherapeutic treatment of common psychological difficulties, even though subsequent historical analysis of his work suggests that it may not have been as original or revolutionary as he often suggested (Ellenberger, 1970). The 1900 publication of his book *The Interpretation of Dreams* marked an important milestone for the psychoanalytic movement and attracted both supporters and detractors. In subsequent years, psychiatrists such as Carl Jung and Alfred Adler joined Freud to develop and promote a psychoanalytic approach to the understanding and treatment of mental disorders. Ultimately, they and other followers split from Freud to develop their own theories and interventions.

Exhibit 1.6 Timeline for the History of Intervention in Clinical Psychology

1896	U.S.: Witmer opens the first psychology clinic.
1900–1930s	Europe, U.S., UK: Development of psychoanalytic approaches.
1920s	U.S.: First behavioural treatment of anxiety by Cover Jones.
1940s	U.S. and Europe: Increased demand for services to deal with war-related distress.
1942	U.S.: Rogers publishes *Counseling and Psychotherapy,* introducing a client-centred approach.
1952	UK: Eysenck publishes a review questioning the usefulness of psychotherapy with adults.
1957	U.S.: Levitt publishes a review questioning the usefulness of psychotherapy with children.
1958	South Africa: Wolpe publishes an article on the behavioural treatment of phobias.
1977	U.S. and Canada: Meichenbaum publishes *Cognitive-Behavior Modification: An Integrative Approach.*
1979	U.S.: Beck, Rush, Shaw, and Emery publish *Cognitive Therapy for Depression.*
1980	U.S.: Smith, Glass, and Miller publish *Effects of Psychotherapy*, providing results of a meta-analytic review of treatment for adults.
1987	U.S.: Weisz, Weiss, Alicke, and Klotz publish a meta-analytic review of treatment for children and adolescents.
1995	U.S.: The American Psychological Association's Division of Clinical Psychology defines criteria to evaluate the degree of empirical support for treatments.
1996	UK: Roth and Fonagy publish *What Works for Whom? A Critical Review of Psychotherapy Research.*
1998	U.S.: Nathan and Gorman publish *A Guide to Treatments That Work.*
2005	U.S.: The American Psychological Association adopts its policy on *Evidence-Based Practice in Psychology.*
2012	Canada: The Canadian Psychological Association adopts its policy on *Evidence-Based Practice of Psychological Treatments.*

The early decades of the 1900s were marked by the growth of numerous psychodynamic treatment approaches in Europe, which then spread to North America. These approaches differed widely in their core principles and techniques, but all were based on the assumption that most psychopathology stemmed from unconscious processes. For Freud, the unconscious was the source of all psychic energy as well as the repository of all our disappointments, hurts, and unfulfilled sexual and aggressive desires. He hypothesized that, to protect ourselves from the pain of continually re-experiencing these negative emotions and memories, we use a number of strategies called defence mechanisms such as denial, repression, and intellectualization. The goal of treatment is for the patient to gain insight into the origin of his or her problems (i.e., the painful contents of the unconscious) and the ways in which the defence mechanisms inadvertently block the person's full psychological development. Jung's model involved an aspect of the unconscious similar to Freud's (called the personal unconscious), but also included a much more positive form (called the collective unconscious) that could promote the individual's psychological growth. Jungian treatment emphasized, therefore, the importance of not only developing an awareness of the personal unconscious but also appreciating and harnessing the power of the collective unconscious.

Later psychodynamic models tended to de-emphasize the importance of unconscious determinants of behaviour. Alfred Adler's approach, for example, focused on the role of societal forces and socialization pressures in the development of personality and the treatment of disorders. His theory emphasized the impact of birth order on personality and the impact of social comparison processes in which we may underestimate or overestimate our personal strengths and weaknesses. Anna Freud, a daughter of Sigmund Freud, who had received analysis from her father when she was a child, developed ego psychology that encourages the person to develop skills that can help address current problems. Although her approach still considered the unconscious a force to be reckoned with, she highlighted the role of conscious efforts to adjust to past difficulties and current life obstacles. Anna Freud took a leading role in modifying psychoanalytic approaches in treatment with children.

Even though they were undoubtedly influential in the development of clinical psychology treatments, these psychodynamic approaches were not the only contributors to our current forms of psychotherapy. Two other distinct approaches to the treatment of psychological distress emerged during the first decades of the 20th century. Lightner Witmer, an American student of Wundt's credited with being the first to use the term *clinical psychology*, established a clinic offering psychological services in 1896 and university training in clinical psychology in 1904. Witmer was a university professor whose interests lay primarily in the application of research to learning and memory processes. He consulted with teachers and others in school settings to apply the new science of psychology to the assessment and remediation of learning difficulties, intellectual and developmental delays, and, to some extent, behaviour problems. In retrospect, it is ironic that the psychologist often described as the father of clinical psychology was really setting the stage for what would now be seen as school psychology.

A second example of the application of scientific psychology to the understanding and treatment of psychological disorders can be found in conditioning research in the 1920s. Through his famous experiment with little Albert and furry white animals and objects, John Watson demonstrated that it was possible to use conditioning principles to explain the development of phobias. The next step that had important implications for treatment purposes was when Mary Cover Jones showed that the principles of conditioning could be used to extinguish a phobic reaction in a child. This initial work, using animal and human learning concepts and procedures, set the stage for what would later become behaviour therapy.

In the 1940s and 1950s, the demand for psychotherapy grew dramatically, due largely to the need to provide mental health services both to members of the military and to members of the public who were affected by the horror and losses of the war. In the United States, for example, the need for mental health professionals to provide counselling and therapy to returning soldiers could not be met by the relatively small number of psychiatrists practising in the country. As a result, the Veterans Administration agency turned to the profession of clinical psychology, hiring many psychologists and providing a substantial infusion of funds to aid in the formation of new training programs in clinical psychology. This led to an enormous increase in the number of clinical psychologists in the United States and to the eventual establishment in later decades of clinical psychologists' reputation as being among the best trained practitioners of psychotherapy.

The 1940s and 1950s also saw a proliferation in the forms of psychotherapy available to the public. A major new movement in psychotherapy was initiated with the publication in 1942 of Carl Rogers' book *Counseling and Psychotherapy*. In contrast to the then dominant psychoanalytic approach, Rogers' approach was rooted in an assumption that people were inherently capable of developing in a positive, healthy manner. The primary goal of therapy, therefore, was to provide a supportive environment in which clients could reconnect with their emotions, their losses, and their aspirations and thereby discover their true potential for growth. Rogers' work was crucial in the development of humanistic approaches to the understanding and treatment of human problems, an approach that has been termed the third force in psychotherapy (with psychodynamic and behavioural approaches being the first two). Of equal, if not greater importance, Rogers was an early and firm advocate of the need to conduct systematic research on the process and outcome of psychotherapy. His position was markedly different from that typical of the time, as what frequently passed as psychotherapy research was little more than case studies. You will learn more about the limitations of the case study approach to the study of human functioning in Chapter 4.

Carl Rogers in 1979.

Changes were occurring in the psychodynamic approach to treatment as well, with Alexander and French publishing their book *Psychoanalytic Therapy* in 1946, in which they made a compelling case for briefer forms of psychoanalytic treatment. In the mid-1950s, Harry Stack Sullivan provided details on interpersonally focused strategies for intervening with patients. Outside the psychodynamic realm, new approaches within a humanistic/existential/experiential tradition were introduced, including Fritz Perls' concepts and procedures of gestalt therapy and Viktor Frankl's logotherapy. Finally, Joseph Wolpe published his work on systematic desensitization in 1958, thus setting the stage for the dramatic growth of the behavioural (and cognitive) therapies.

Hans Eysenck's (1952) critique of the effectiveness of psychotherapy was a turning point for psychotherapy research and training. Eysenck argued that the rates of improvement among clients receiving either psychodynamic or eclectic (i.e., an unspecified mix of theories and techniques) therapy were comparable to rates of remission of symptoms among clients receiving no therapy at all. He contended, therefore, that there was no evidence that the most commonly used forms of psychotherapy had any demonstrable effect. Although later proponents of these treatments pointed out substantial flaws in his arguments, Eysenck's review had two dramatic effects on the field. First, it crystallized dissatisfaction among many psychologists who did not agree with a psychodynamic approach to treatment, and led to efforts to establish treatments that were directly connected to psychology's empirically derived knowledge. Second, it resulted in a flurry of research activity in the following decades focused on evaluating both new and traditional forms of psychotherapy. As we will see throughout this book, advances in psychological services for children and families often follow the same trends as are seen in services for adults; however, there is usually a time lag of a few years. Reviews of the child psychotherapy research (Levitt, 1957) reached similar conclusions to Eysenck with respect to adult psychotherapy.

The 1960s and 1970s, consequently, were decades marked by an increase in both the numbers of psychotherapies available to the public and the amount of research devoted to understanding whether psychotherapy was effective (and, if it was, what made it effective). In the early 1960s, Albert Ellis developed Rational Emotive Therapy and Eric Berne introduced Transactional Analysis (an early forerunner of therapies aimed at enhancing personal growth and development as much as treating psychopathology). Using learning principles such as contingencies, shaping, and reinforcement, behaviour modification and behaviour therapy became widely adopted during this time to address problems as diverse as self-injurious behaviour, phobic avoidance, hyperactive behaviour, and sexual dysfunction. In tune with the growing attention to cognitive phenomena in psychology in general, behaviour therapy began to address cognitive elements in treatment. The publication in the late 1970s of two influential

Dr. Michael Fenichel
Aaron Beck and Albert Ellis.

books laid the foundation for what is now known as cognitive-behaviour therapy. These now classic texts were Don Meichenbaum's *Cognitive-Behavior Modification: An Integrative Approach,* which was published in 1977; and the first comprehensive treatment manual, *Cognitive Therapy of Depression: A Treatment Manual,* by Aaron Beck and his colleagues John Rush, Brian Shaw, and Gary Emery, which appeared in 1979. Cognitive-behavioural approaches are equally applicable to adults' and children's problems and gained popularity in the 1970s.

Another milestone was reached in 1980 when Smith, Glass, and Miller used a statistical technique called **meta-analysis** to review 475 controlled studies of psychotherapy. This technique (described in detail in Chapter 4) provides a means by which groups of studies can be statistically combined and compared. The authors' primary finding was that psychotherapy, in general, was clearly very effective, with the average person receiving therapy being better off after therapy than 80% of people with similar problems who did not receive therapy. The researchers also examined the efficacy of various types of treatment. Using different analytic techniques, they found that although there was general equivalence across divergent forms of psychotherapy, some therapies were superior to others for specific disorders and clinical problems. As we will see in Chapters 12 and 14, these results fuelled debates about the relative merits of psychotherapies that persist to the present.

meta-analysis: a review technique by which groups of studies can be statistically combined and compared.

Seven years later, a meta-analysis reported similar results for psychotherapy for children and adolescents, with 79% of treated children being better off after treatment than children and adolescents with similar problems who did not receive psychotherapy (Weisz, Weiss, Alicke, & Klotz, 1987). The impact of research such as this is addressed in Chapter 13.

The 1980s and 1990s saw several key developments in the history of psychotherapy. There was a dramatic increase in the amount of research on psychotherapy. Furthermore, there was a profound improvement in the methodological sophistication of those studies, with an increasing use of treatment manuals to guide interventions and standardized diagnostic criteria for assessing those receiving treatment. Numerous societal and health care pressures fuelled the demand for the development and dissemination of effective short-term treatments (i.e., treatments involving fewer than 20–25 sessions). This demand for short-term treatments was welcomed by proponents of disorder-specific cognitive-behavioural treatments. In addition, psychodynamic and humanistic/existential/experiential approaches were adapted to provide services over a shorter period of time. Numerous forms of interpersonally focused psychodynamic treatments emerged in Britain, Canada, and the United States, including Time-Limited Dynamic Psychotherapy developed by Hans Strupp and his colleagues. Within the experiential orientation, the emphasis was on more structured and directive interventions that melded traditional principles and values with contemporary knowledge of emotional functioning. Key among the proponents of this process-experiential treatment approach were Les Greenberg in Canada and Robert Elliott in the United States.

It should be clear from this overview that the practice of clinical psychology has been influenced by research on the impact of psychotherapy. Another landmark event occurred in 1995 with the release of the report by the American Psychological Association Division of Clinical Psychology's *Task Force on Promotion and Dissemination of Psychological Procedures.* The impetus for this task force came from increasing pressure in the United States for health care practices to be demonstrably effective as well as cost-effective. Legislation and state case law were being used to shape the nature of federal and state health care policy, and there appeared to be a very real danger that access to mental health and behavioural health care services might be diminished because of perceptions that such services were both expensive and relatively ineffective. Clearly a response from organized psychology was needed to underscore the efficacy of psychological interventions for certain disorders and conditions. The task force developed empirical criteria to aid in the determination of whether an intervention was efficacious in the treatment of a given disorder or clinical problem. Using these criteria, the task force then produced an initial list of efficacious treatments. The term **efficacy** is used to denote evidence that a treatment was shown to work under research conditions that emphasized internal validity, with the term **effectiveness** being reserved to describe evidence that the treatment was shown to work in real-world conditions. Predictably, this initiative was embraced by some clinical psychologists and treated with scorn by others.

efficacy: evidence that a treatment has been shown to work under research conditions that emphasized internal validity.

effectiveness: evidence that a treatment has been shown to work in real-world conditions.

Regardless of the strengths or limitations of this and related initiatives (which we discuss in Chapters 12 and 13), it has forever changed how clinical psychologists view the connection between empirical evidence and their therapeutic services. In the 1990s, the first editions of several books were published that reviewed the research base of psychological treatments for a range of disorders. Key among the books was *What Works for Whom? A Critical Review of Psychotherapy Research* by Roth and Fonagy (1996) and *A Guide to Treatments That Work* by Nathan and Gorman (1998). These influential texts have been updated to include recent research findings, and we will discuss them more in the chapters on psychological treatments.

The emphasis on grounding psychological services firmly in science culminated in the adoption of policies on evidence-based practice by both the American and Canadian psychological associations, which we described earlier in this chapter. Although the policies touch on all aspects of psychological services, it is likely that they will have the most impact on the treatment services provided by psychologists both within and outside these countries.

The History of Prevention in Clinical Psychology

Unfortunately, the history of prevention efforts in clinical psychology is much shorter than the history of assessment or intervention. This is because, as outlined above, the profession of clinical psychology started with an assessment focus and then added the dimension of intervention. As clinical psychologists were incorporated into national health care systems in both public and private sectors, they adopted the priorities of these systems, which, until very recently, did not include much in the way of prevention efforts. Due to growing concerns about the dire health consequences of smoking and the need to promote safer sex practices to reduce the incidence of AIDS and sexually transmitted diseases, clinical psychologists now frequently play an important role in public health initiatives to change lifestyle-related illnesses. Concerns about the apparent increase in depression in the United States have led a number of clinical psychologists to develop prevention programs aimed at educating adolescents and young adults about depression and the types of psychological coping skills that can be used to maintain good mental health. Another societal problem, violence in intimate relationships, is also the focus of preventive efforts headed by clinical psychologists. In Chapter 10, we describe the current status of prevention programs in clinical psychology.

THE FUTURE

Predicting future events is always an uncertain business. Nevertheless, some brave psychologists have ventured to give their prognostications for future developments in clinical psychology. A 2009 survey of clinical child and adolescent psychologists asked respondents to predict major directions in clinical practice, research, and training for the coming decade (James & Roberts, 2009). In all three domains, evidence-based practice was predicted to have the greatest influence on the specialty area of clinical child and adolescent psychology. Groth-Marnat (2000), an authority on psychological assessment issues, offered some predictions about what is likely to transpire in the realm of clinical assessment in the next 50 years. Some of his predictions are almost sure bets, such as revisions to the DSM, the Wechsler intelligence tests, and the MMPI.

For others, he went out on a limb, predicting that advances in virtual reality technology will, by 2020, allow ability testing based on the simulation of life and work situations. His most dramatic prediction was that by 2035 measures based on the results of human genome research will be incorporated into clinical assessments.

Of course only time will tell which, if any, of these predictions will come to pass. Given the history of clinical psychology, perhaps the only certainty for the future is that exciting changes are in store for the profession and for those who practise it. That being said, trends starting in the past decade or two can give us some idea of the ways in which clinical psychology will develop and grow. Accordingly, it is almost certain that clinical psychology will be influenced by, among other factors, increasing need to: provide psychological services for an array of health problems, not just mental health problems; develop services that respond to the health care needs of an aging population; ensure that psychological assessments, prevention programs, and treatments are both evidence-based and appropriate for the diverse range of people who receive these services; and enhance the impact of concurrent use of psychological and pharmacological interventions.

SUMMARY AND CONCLUSIONS

Worldwide, mental health problems have staggering emotional and financial costs. Compared with physical health problems, mental health problems are woefully underserved. There is a trend across all mental health professions to develop and disseminate evidence-based services so that these serious problems can be effectively and economically addressed.

Clinical psychology shares with other mental health professions a focus on assessment and intervention in the prevention and treatment of emotional, behavioural, and neurological problems. In contrast to psychiatry and psychiatric nursing, which have their roots in the treatment of pathology, psychology is grounded in the science of human behaviour. Among the mental health professions, psychology is unique in its long-standing research tradition. From the beginning of their academic training, students in psychology learn to understand, interpret, and conduct methodologically sound research.

In tracing the history of psychological assessment, intervention, and prevention, it is clear that systematic observation and evaluation are hallmarks of clinical psychology. Drawing on a wealth of knowledge about human functioning and development, clinical psychologists have earned recognition for their expertise in assessment, treatment, and prevention of serious problems. The field of clinical psychology is in a process of constant evolution.

KEY TERMS

biopsychosocial approach: a theoretical framework that takes into account biological, psychological, and social influences on health and illness.

clinical utility: usefulness of assessment data to provide information that leads to a clinical outcome that is better (or faster or less expensive) than would be the case if the psychologist did not have the assessment data.

effectiveness: evidence that a treatment has been shown to work in real-world conditions.

efficacy: evidence that a treatment has been shown to work under research conditions that emphasized internal validity.

evidence-based practice: a practice model that involves the synthesis of information drawn from research and systematically collected data on the patient in question, the clinician's professional experience, and the patient's preferences when considering health care options.

meta-analysis: a review technique by which groups of studies can be statistically combined and compared.

service evaluation: activities designed to examine whether or not services work.

syndrome: group of symptoms that frequently co-occur.

KEY NAMES

Alfred Binet

Hans Eysenck

Emil Kraepelin

Richard McFall

Paul Meehl

Carl Rogers

ADDITIONAL RESOURCES

Journals

Clinical Psychological Science

Clinical Psychology: Science and Practice

Clinical Psychology Review

Professional Psychology: Research and Practice

Books

Barlow, D. H. (Ed.). (2011). *Oxford handbook of clinical psychology.* New York: Oxford University Press.

Dobson, K., & Dobson, D. (Eds.). (1993). *Professional psychology in Canada*. Toronto, ON: Hogrefe & Huber Publishers.

Routh, D. K. (1994). *Clinical psychology since 1917: Science, practice, and organization*. New York: Plenum Press.

Check It Out!

The website of the Canadian Psychological Association provides information on the diverse sections of psychology, accreditation, and licensure: www.cpa.ca

The website of the American Psychological Association includes information related to the sciences and practice of psychology: www.apa.org

Psychologist Kenneth Pope's website provides resources on ethics, intervention, and critical thinking: www.kspope.com

The website for the National Institute of Mental Health provides information on diagnosis and treatment of mental disorders: www.nimh.nih.gov

The website of the UK National Institute for Health and Clinical Excellence provides clinical guidance on health issues: www.nice.org.uk

CONTEMPORARY CLINICAL PSYCHOLOGY

2 CHAPTER

INTRODUCTION

Clinical psychology is a fascinating profession. Few university graduate programs prepare students for such varied and challenging careers. Depending on personal preferences and job requirements, a clinical psychologist may devote professional time to (a) providing psychological services, (b) conducting research and providing clinical training, (c) consulting with other professionals and agencies, or (d) all of the above. Moreover, it is common for the relative balance of activities to shift over the span of a career, so that a clinical psychologist may have periods when she or he devotes most time to research and in other periods devotes most time to administration or teaching. In this way, the psychologist has a multitude of different interests within a single career in psychology. Clinical psychologists work with individuals (at any stage in life), couples, families, groups, and organizations. Many clinical psychologists work in the domain of mental health (e.g., treating anxiety disorders, disruptive behaviour disorders, mood disorders, schizophrenia, or substance abuse disorders). A large number of clinical psychologists conduct research and provide health services outside the traditional practice domain (e.g., dealing with stress, coping with pain, or promoting adherence to medical treatment regimens) and/or provide services related to relationship functioning (e.g., couples therapy, parent training, or family therapy).

In 2011, the Canadian Psychological Association commissioned Ekos Research to conduct a survey of attitudes toward psychologists and accessing psychological services. Participants in the survey ($N = 2{,}832$) were asked to identify the mental health professionals best able to help them with various mental health problems. Psychologists were among the top three professionals considered able to care for people living with depression and anxiety disorders, and also among the top three best able to care for people coping with the stress of diagnosis with a disease like cancer. It is heartening to know that the public views psychologists as helpful mental health care providers. However, there are enormous international disparities in the extent to which people have access to mental health services from psychologists. The Scandinavian countries, along with New Zealand, Canada, and the United States are, relatively speaking, well served by psychologists. Unfortunately, the same cannot be said of many other countries, especially those in Africa and Asia.

In this chapter, we will describe the range of activities in which clinical psychologists engage and some of the settings in which they work. To bring these activities to life, we have asked three Canadian clinical psychologists who work in different settings to describe their usual professional activities over the course of a week. In reading these descriptions of professional activities in the three profile boxes, you will probably be struck by the busy and varied nature of their professional time. As it will be many years until you could be a licensed clinical psychologist, you may also be interested to learn about the activities of a graduate student in clinical psychology. You can imagine yourself just a few years from now engaging in the activities she describes as part of a typical week.

You may recall that in Chapter 1 we talked about what we consider a touchstone of clinical psychology: science-based practice. In this chapter, we introduce a second touchstone of clinical psychology: professional ethics. Because clinical psychologists, as health care providers, must meet training and licensing requirements in order to practise, we provide a perspective on licensing requirements. In the final sections of the chapter, we will present the nature of clinical psychology and the nature of training in clinical psychology in Canada.

ACTIVITIES OF CLINICAL PSYCHOLOGISTS

Over the years, a number of surveys have documented the nature of the activities undertaken by clinical psychologists. Some activities, such as assessment and research, have stayed relatively constant in terms of the numbers of psychologists who frequently engage in them. As we explained in Chapter 1, following the Second World War, there was a steady rise in the number of clinical psychologists providing psychotherapy. Table 2.1 shows data from a survey of U.S. psychologists (Norcross & Karpiak, 2012) that indicate the percentage of clinical psychologists who engage in different professional activities. Table 2.2 shows data from a survey of Canadian psychologists (Hunsley, Ronson, & Cohen, 2013) that

TABLE 2.1 ■ Professional Activities of Clinical Psychologists in the United States

Activity	Percentage of Psychologists Who Engage in Each Activity
Assessment and Diagnosis	58
Psychotherapy	76
Consultation	38
Research	47
Teaching	49
Supervision	47
Administration	46

Adapted from Norcross & Karpiak (2012).

indicate the proportion of time that clinical psychologists in this country spend, in general, on their main professional activities.

As you can see, the majority of psychologists engage in many different professional activities. In interpreting these data, it must be remembered that survey information can provide a useful overview of general trends among clinical psychologists, but does not indicate the variability in professional activities among individual clinical psychologists.

Profile Boxes 2.1 to 2.4 introduce three Canadian clinical psychologists and one graduate student in clinical psychology. Dr. Clarissa Bush is employed in a children's hospital in Ontario (Profile Box 2.1); Dr. Sheila Woody is the director of the clinical psychology program at the University of British Columbia (Profile Box 2.2); Dr. Randy Paterson is a psychologist in private practice in British Columbia (Profile Box 2.3); and Emma MacDonald is a graduate student in the clinical psychology program at Ryerson University in Ontario (Profile Box 2.4). You will notice that from graduate school onward, these psychologists have full and varied schedules.

TABLE 2.2 ■ Professional Activities of Clinical Psychologists in Canada

Activity	Percentage of Time Spent by Psychologists in Each Activity
Assessment	28.5
Intervention	41.3
Consultation	13.3
Research	5.5
Teaching	5.9
Other	5.6

Adapted from Hunsley, Ronson, & Cohen (2013).

Assessment and Diagnosis

It is virtually impossible to be a clinical psychologist and not do some form of psychological assessment. You may recall from Table 2.1 that Norcross and Karpiak (2012) found that more than half of the respondents to their survey engaged in assessment and diagnosis, and Hunsley et al. (2013) found that the psychologists who responded to their survey spent almost a third of their professional time in assessment activities (Table 2.2). As you can see in the profile boxes, all three psychologists spend part of their time conducting psychological assessments and diagnoses.

PROFILE BOX 2.1

DR. CLARISSA BUSH

After finding that a secretarial career was not for me, I enrolled at Queen's University. Once I discovered the course description for Psychology 100, I never looked back, moving to McGill University to finish my honours degree and then a Ph.D. in clinical psychology in 1984. After graduation, my first job was at Ottawa's St. Vincent Hospital stroke program and eventually I worked in most of the other programs there as well. Moving to Elizabeth Bruyère (later called Sisters of Charity Ottawa Health Services, or SCOHS), I worked for many years in the Memory Disorder Clinic. The diagnostic assessment of dementia remains one of the most rewarding of my clinical activities. In 1995, I trained as a designated capacity assessor, and capacity assessment remains part of my private practice work. In 2005, I obtained additional training and extended my neuropsychology practice to include children and adolescents. I currently work part-time in the oncology program at the Children's Hospital of Eastern Ontario (CHEO) and I maintain a part-time private practice with clients across the lifespan.

I served on the Council of the College of Psychologists from 2002 to 2008 in various roles, including president and chair of the Registration Committee. I am currently on the Discipline Committee of the College.

Clinical teaching has always been a part of my professional life, and my workload usually includes the supervision of a practicum student or intern. Together with a colleague, I developed an internship program at the SCOHS and am now the director of training in psychology at CHEO. More recently, I have taught courses in clinical neuropsychology and in professional ethics in the graduate program at the University of Ottawa, where I am a clinical professor.

A TYPICAL WEEK

I work at CHEO on Mondays, Tuesdays, and Thursdays. Although in theory Thursday is reserved for training program activities, in practice these activities can need attention at any point in the week. The flexibility of a third day available for clinical care is helpful in scheduling young patients who are on chemotherapy and may not be feeling up to neuropsychological testing some of the time.

I began Monday morning by replying to emails dealing with training issues. After that, most of my day was spent with a practicum student who is working under my supervision to assess a 9-year-old boy who has recently finished treatment for leukemia. After a brief planning meeting, I conducted an interview with his parents, accompanied by the practicum student. During the rest of the morning, I observed parts of the assessment she was conducting. In the afternoon, I reviewed a draft report the practicum student had written on another patient, and wrote a report on a patient

CONTINUED . . .

I recently assessed. I also met with the psychometrist to plan Tuesday's assessment activities.

On Tuesday I had an assessment with an 18-year-old woman who had been treated for a brain tumour when she was very young. After a brief meeting with her and her mother to explain the assessment, review limits of confidentiality, and obtain consent, the psychometrist working under my supervision began testing with the client while I interviewed her mother. I learned that the patient was hoping to attend a college-level nursing program, but was struggling in school and might not be able to achieve this. Later in the day I completed an interview with the client and suggested a referral to our academic/vocational counsellor, who would be able to work with her to obtain accommodations at college or suggest other career options for her.

Wednesday was a day at my private practice. After attending to various administrative details (going through the mail, entering payments into my accounting system, paying bills, and returning phone calls about possible referrals), I met with the psychometrist I supervise to review the plan we had made for the client I had interviewed the previous week and who would be completing neuropsychological testing that day. Later in the morning I conducted an intake interview with a man who had developed memory problems. With his consent, I interviewed his wife separately, as she felt better able to tell me about some of the personality changes she had observed when he was not present. I worked on a report for the balance of the day, with a lunchtime meeting with the psychometrist to discuss the progress of testing and plan for next week's assessment.

On Thursday I completed paperwork at the hospital before chairing a meeting of the Internship Training Committee. We reviewed the plan for upcoming internship interviews and the requirements of the Association of Psychology Professional Postdoctoral and Internship Centers for communicating with internship candidates. Later I had my monthly meeting with the current interns and we discussed some aspects of our evaluation system and reviewed some of their clinical work. During the remainder of the day, I reviewed a draft report written by a practicum student and met with her to discuss it. I suggested some readings on research relevant to the particular cognitive problems experienced by the client she had assessed.

Friday morning I spent at my practice, where I had planned to meet with a mother and her adopted 17-year-old son for a feedback interview. Her son had been exposed to alcohol and drugs in utero and had been making poor and risky choices in the past few months. As it turned out, the young man chose not to attend the feedback interview, but as I had his consent, I met with his mother alone. I then spent the afternoon teaching the graduate ethics seminar at the university, which included a planned debate on the use of social media by psychologists.

Most commonly, assessment activities involve evaluating the psychological functioning of an individual or a relationship (such as a couple, a parent–child relationship, or a family). Some assessments focus on the way a social unit functions (such as interactions within and between departments of an agency, or between an agency and the recipients of the agency's services). The precise nature of the assessment activities depends, to a large part, on the purpose of the assessment. Let's take an example of a psychologist who wants to be able to judge with confidence whether 7-year-old Ethan has behaviour problems that are serious enough to justify placement in a special service. The psychologist may focus on whether Ethan's behaviour meets criteria for a diagnosis of oppositional defiant disorder. If, however, the psychologist is conducting an assessment prior to beginning parent training, the focus of the assessment will be to gain a precise understanding of the behaviours that the parents wish to change (such as the intensity, frequency, and duration of defiant behaviour) and contextual variables that affect Ethan's behaviour (such as parental consistency, marital conflict, or the presence of a replacement teacher in the classroom). Thus, if the goal of the assessment is to determine eligibility for a service, assessment may be the sole function of the psychologist's service. On the other hand, even when the primary service is psychotherapy, assessment plays an important role in the planning, monitoring, and evaluation of the intervention.

In the later chapters on assessment, you will see the ingenuity with which psychologists have developed scientifically sound assessment tools to assess a host of psychological phenomena in infants, children, adults, and older adults. Generally speaking, these tools fall into one of several categories that will be discussed in Chapters 6 (interviews and observational systems), 7 (intellectual and cognitive measures), and 8 (self-report measures and projective measures). Moreover, as you will learn in Chapter 9, in reaching a clinical formulation, most clinical psychologists combine data obtained from a number of assessment methods, such as interviews, self-report measures, observations, performance (or skill) tasks, and reports from informants other than the patient.

As you will see in Chapter 5, regardless of the precise form and purpose of the assessment activity, all clinical assessments share a primary goal of aiding the understanding of the person's current level of psychosocial functioning. Without a sense of how the person is doing now, in terms of such important human variables as emotions, behaviours, symptoms, and relationships, it is simply not possible to provide meaningful psychological services. However, as you will learn in Chapter 9, psychological assessment is much more than just testing: it involves the collection of multiple types of data that are then integrated into a coherent formulation of the problem experienced by the person or groups being assessed.

In many instances, formulating a diagnosis is part of the assessment process. As we describe in more detail in Chapter 3, diagnoses provide a concise statement about the nature of a person's disorder or dysfunction. Having established a diagnosis, the psychologist can efficiently search the scientific literature to update his or her knowledge of the disorder's etiology, course, prognosis, and beneficial treatments. In Canada and the United States, the dominant diagnostic system used by clinical psychologists is the *Diagnostic and Statistical Manual of Mental*

Disorders (DSM) published by the American Psychiatric Association, now in its fifth edition (DSM-5). Other countries have adopted the World Health Organization's *International Classification of Diseases* (ICD), now in its 10th edition (ICD-10).

To what extent do you think you would welcome the challenge of conducting psychological assessments? What would you find most interesting about assessment activities? Are you the kind of person who enjoys addressing questions by gathering and integrating diverse data?

PROFILE BOX 2.2

DR. SHEILA WOODY

Courtesy of Laura Leyshon

I read Freud's *Interpretation of Dreams* for an independent study project in high school. I'm not sure why I picked that particular book, but it ignited my interest in a career involving psychology. After learning more about the different types of mental health professionals, I decided (at age 14!) to become a clinical psychologist. I am still glad I did. My Ph.D. in clinical psychology is from the American University in Washington, D.C. Although I had begun graduate school intent on a clinical career, I soon began to prepare for an academic career because I loved doing research and wanted the freedom and variety of academia. Working as a professor gives me opportunities to conduct research, write, mentor individual students, teach larger groups of students, and serve the profession as a leader—in addition to seeing clients and supervising graduate students who are learning to offer psychological services. After my internship, I completed a two-year clinical research postdoctoral fellowship in the Department of Psychiatry at the University of British Columbia (UBC).

My first faculty job was as an assistant professor at Yale University, so I was first licensed as a psychologist in the state of Connecticut. In 2000, I returned to beautiful British Columbia. I am still at UBC; as a full professor, I do research, teach, mentor students, and co-direct our graduate program. My research examines different aspects of anxiety disorders, including treatment outcome studies and psychopathology research. I am registered as a psychologist in British Columbia. In addition to supervising students in our clinical training program, I have a small private practice where I see adults with anxiety disorders.

A TYPICAL WEEK

On Monday morning, I had a meeting with some City of Vancouver employees. We are working together to estimate the prevalence of hoarding in poor neighbourhoods of the city. We are educating each other as we go, finding ways to use their real-life experiences in ways that meet the demands of research, with a goal toward expanding knowledge about hoarding. After this meeting, I went to campus, where I had a couple of meetings with undergraduate students. I advised one student on his applications to graduate school and then met with an honours student to discuss his progress on research we are conducting together. After that

CONTINUED . . .

meeting, I had about 30 minutes to prepare for teaching. I refreshed my memory about my lecture, checked the online discussion board for student questions, and packed up my laptop to walk across campus to teach 150 undergraduate students about behavioural disorders. When I finished teaching, I prepared minutes from my earlier meeting with the City of Vancouver workers and emailed the minutes to them.

Tuesday morning I worked at home for a few hours. I edited a graduate student's proposal for ethical review of her master's thesis research, planned lectures for next week, and resubmitted a manuscript that my students and I had revised following peer review. When I went to campus, I met with other graduate program administrators to discuss the recent round of fellowship applications. Later, I consulted with a counsellor who treats compulsive hoarding to discuss some of her difficult cases. I then attended a talk in my department on information security, where I learned more about how to protect clients' and students' private information online. The end of my workday involved observing the practicum students I supervise as they conducted group cognitive-behavioural therapy for compulsive hoarding. I sat behind an observation window and took notes on the session.

Wednesday morning I met with one of my doctoral students about the design of her dissertation research. I spent a bit more time preparing for teaching, and then I consulted with a younger colleague about how she can help one of her students who is not succeeding academically. Afterward, I met with my practicum students for 90 minutes of clinical supervision. We discussed things that had gone well in yesterday's group session and engaged in role plays to help them build skills related to things that had not gone so well in the session. Then we planned next week's session. When supervision was finished, I went to teach my undergraduate class on behavioural disorders before returning to my office to see a client who is experiencing social anxiety in her work environment.

Thursday and Friday began much like Tuesday, with my working at home on research and teaching preparation. On Thursday afternoon, I accompanied a practicum student to do an assessment at the home of one of our clients who has problems with hoarding. Friday I once again taught my large class and finished the week with an afternoon lab meeting with my graduate and undergraduate students.

Intervention

As noted in Tables 2.1 and 2.2 earlier, survey data reported by Norcross and Karpiak (2012) indicate that the majority of clinical psychologists offer psychotherapy, and data collected by Hunsley et al. (2013) showed that psychologists devoted over 40% of their professional time to providing psychological interventions. Canadian clinical psychologists in that survey most frequently provided individual therapy (with 85% of psychologists offering this service). Marital/couples therapy and family therapy were also provided by 27% of Canadian psychologists, whereas group therapy was offered less frequently (20%).

As we describe in Chapters 12 and 13, there is a wealth of evidence to suggest that psychological treatments can be effective in treating a wide range of health problems. In Chapter 14, we provide information about a range of client and clinician factors, including the quality of the therapeutic alliance that influences the outcome of treatment.

As illustrated in the profile boxes, the proportion of time devoted to psychotherapy varies across the different employment settings. However, as we discussed in Chapter 1, psychologists are not the only health care professionals who offer psychotherapeutic services. Survey data from Ontario indicated that, of those people aged 15 to 64 years who sought health care services for mental health reasons, only 10% were seen by psychologists (Lin, Goering, Offord, Campbell, & Boyle, 1996). Many of the services provided by medical practitioners involved the provision of psychoactive medications, a form of treatment that cannot be provided by psychologists in most jurisdictions (see Viewpoint Box 2.1 for more details).

What are the advantages and disadvantages of psychologists having the privilege of prescribing psychoactive medication?

VIEWPOINT BOX 2.1

WHAT DO PSYCHOLOGISTS NEED TO KNOW ABOUT PSYCHOPHARMACOLOGY?

Given the soaring rates of prescription for medications designed to treat mental disorders, it is not surprising that many of the people who receive psychological services are also receiving pharmacotherapy to address their problems. What roles can or should psychologists play with respect to the treatment of mental disorders with medication? There is a middle ground between the two extremes of suggesting that (a) psychologists focus exclusively on psychological approaches and ignore medication or (b) psychologists should become able to prescribe medication: specifically there is considerable need for psychologists to serve in the role of consultant about medication for mental health problems.

In the United States, the issue of prescriptive authority for psychologists has been a hot-button issue since the 1990s. Although the states of Louisiana and New Mexico, and the military, allow psychologists to be trained to prescribe psychoactive medication, to date fewer than 100 psychologists have received the necessary postdoctoral qualification to prescribe medication. Advocates of prescription privileges for psychologists argue that psychologists can be at least as competent as other health care professionals in prescribing medication for psychological disorders. They suggest that underserved segments of the population, such as those in rural areas and older adults, could benefit from the extension of prescription privileges to psychologists. Within psychology, critics argue that psychologists' distinctive expertise is in the development and application of evidence-based assessment and psychological interventions. They express concern that the inclusion of adequate training in psychopharmacology would inevitably come at the expense of training in psychological issues (e.g., Stuart & Heiby, 2007).

Within Canada, the strongest support for prescription privileges comes from the Canadian Psychological Association Section on Psychopharmacology. Canadian critics of prescription privileges for psychologists have highlighted that the Canadian Code of Ethics encourages psychologists to work in a collaborative fashion with other health care professionals rather than attempting to duplicate their services (Dobson & Dozois, 2001). Fundamental differences between the American and Canadian health care systems also play a role in the debate. Under Canada's publicly funded health care system, it is likely that the federal government would have concerns that additional numbers of practitioners eligible to prescribe expensive psychopharmacological treatments would contribute to mushrooming health care costs

CONTINUED . . .

(Romanow & Marchildon, 2003; Westra, Eastwood, Bouffard, & Gerritsen, 2006). Given the importance of these issues for both health care services and the training of clinical psychologists, the Canadian Psychological Association formed a task force to examine the issue in a Canadian context. The task force report, published in 2010, recommended that psychologists focus their attention on becoming knowledgeable about best practices in psychopharmacology in their area of practice so that they can serve as competent consultants with respect to medication, without seeking the authority to prescribe medication themselves.

In popular movies or television series, psychotherapy is often presented as a lifelong commitment to frequent treatment sessions with a psychologist or psychiatrist. In reality, the majority of people who receive psychotherapy attend fewer than 10 sessions. Approximately a third of clients attend only one or two sessions, and fewer than 1 in 10 clients attend more than 20 sessions of therapy (Olfson & Marcus, 2010).

As the expression "talk therapy" implies, psychotherapy uses verbal means for the therapist to promote change. But what actually happens in psychotherapy? An innovative survey examined this question. In a Web-based questionnaire, the Practice Directorate of the American Psychological Association (APA, 2003b) asked 241 clinical psychologists questions right after they completed a psychotherapy session. Across theoretical orientations, virtually all psychologists reported discussing current stressors related to the client's problems and interpersonal relationships or relationship patterns. The most commonly reported techniques (reported by more than 75% of respondents) were to identify or challenge thoughts, relate thoughts to feelings, focus on affect by validating or labelling emotions, gather information, and guide or direct the client.

As we indicated in Chapter 1, different theoretical approaches to psychotherapy emphasize different aspects of human experience in understanding and treating psychological distress and disorder. The dominant approaches include psychodynamic, cognitive-behavioural, experiential, and interpersonal (which, in some forms, is closely related to psychodynamic). Additionally, a number of clinicians describe their orientation as eclectic or integrative, meaning they blend concepts and strategies from two or more approaches.

Table 2.3 presents data from surveys on the theoretical orientation of clinical psychologists and graduate students in clinical psychology in Canada and the United States. The general picture suggests that, in North America, a cognitive-behavioural approach is the most popular single orientation among clinical psychologists. This is likely to continue given that graduate students also endorse this orientation more commonly than any other. Although cognitive-behavioural approaches are popular, substantial numbers of clinical psychologists describe

TABLE 2.3 ■ Theoretical Orientations of Clinical Psychologists and Clinical Psychology Graduate Students

	Canadian Psychologists[1]	Canadian Students[2]	U.S. Psychologists[3]	U.S. Students[4]
Cognitive-behavioural	80%	70%	46%	68.9%
Psychodynamic	26%	21%	18%	27.4%
Experiential	31%	41%	4%	27.1%
Interpersonal	23%	35%	4%	27.1%
Eclectic	–	28%	22%	34.3%

Note: In some cases, the total reported exceeds 100% because respondents were permitted to indicate more than one orientation in the survey.

[1]Hunsley et al. (2013).

[2]Singer, Cassin, & Dobson (2005).

[3]Norcross & Karpiak (2012).

[4]Cassin, Singer, Dobson, & Altmaier (2007).

their practice as eclectic. A similar conclusion was reached based on the results of a survey of psychological treatment services offered in hospitals in Canada (Humbke et al., 2004). Respondents to the survey were asked to rank order the theoretical orientations of psychologists working in hospital settings. Across the country, cognitive-behavioural treatments were the most popular, with 46% of hospitals offering such therapies as the main therapeutic approach. A significant minority of hospitals (16%) offered treatment described as eclectic. Relatively few hospitals reported that the treatment approach was predominantly psychodynamic (6.5%) or experiential (6.5%).

Do you find the idea of offering psychological interventions appealing? Are you surprised to learn that most clients attend very few sessions? Does the idea of helping clients to learn ways to change the ways they think, feel, and behave interest you?

Does the theoretical orientation actually make a difference in what therapists do in sessions? Although the evidence from the APA (2003b) online survey revealed a number of commonalities in therapy sessions across clinical psychologists, clear orientation-related differences were also apparent. For example, compared with psychodynamic clinicians, cognitive-behavioural clinicians were significantly more likely to spend time providing psychoeducation by informing the client about the nature of the presenting problem. They were also more likely to encourage the client to ask questions, to collaboratively set an agenda for the session with the client, to encourage the client to engage in specific activities (including homework assignments to be done between therapy sessions), and to teach coping skills. In contrast, those espousing a psychodynamic approach were significantly more likely to explore the client's childhood experiences, to relate the client's reactions to the therapist to patterns in the client's family of origin, and to explore dysfunctional patterns of behaviour and relationship expectations.

PROFILE BOX 2.3

DR. RANDY PATERSON

Courtesy of Fabrice Grover

I received a Ph.D. at the University of Western Ontario in 1990 and, after working in academic and clinical settings in London, Ontario, moved to Vancouver, B.C., in 1993. There I became the coordinator of the Changeways Program at the University of British Columbia Hospital. A cognitive-behavioural group program for depression, Changeways was designed to reduce the rate of hospital readmission among clients treated locally for depression. A successful program evaluation led to the dissemination of the group protocol to hospital and mental health centres throughout British Columbia and, later, across Canada. Subsequent developments include the development of stress management and assertiveness training programs, public education initiatives, and participation on the B.C. Depression Strategy, which resulted in the *Self-Care Depression Program* (co-authored with project leader Dr. Dan Bilsker).

In 2002, I established Changeways Clinic, a private clinic in central Vancouver. We currently have seven psychologists on staff, and we employ two assistants. The clinic provides one-to-one therapy for depression, anxiety disorders, and related difficulties. Changeways also offers training programs for professionals on evidence-based practice (across Canada and internationally), and offers materials based on its clinical and training programs for sale via the clinic website (www.changeways.com). In addition, I consult to government and private organizations on the enhancement of evidence-based service provision. A member of the gay community, I also provide clinical services on gay issues and training programs on sexual orientation for health care providers. I have published three books through New Harbinger Publications: *The Assertiveness Workbook, Private Practice Made Simple,* and *Your Depression Map.*

A TYPICAL WEEK

There really are no typical weeks at Changeways Clinic, due to the combination of activities and services provided. One week may involve more consulting work, another more clinic administration. Here, however, is a composite.

Mondays, Tuesdays, and Wednesdays are generally clinical days for me. I usually arrive around 8:30 a.m. and spend time checking email and voicemail messages. Many clients who work regular hours like to have early or late appointments, so my 9 a.m. and

CONTINUED . . .

4:30 p.m. time slots are almost always booked, with my other meetings scattered through the day. I complete notes before heading home, so the day typically ends about 6 p.m.

I aim for four to five client appointments per day. This is a relatively light clinical load. The rest of my office time is split among a variety of tasks. Administering the clinic takes perhaps five hours a week, including filing taxes, dealing with equipment issues, consulting with the clinic assistants, reviewing our finances, and working on the clinic website. I also write a weekly blog (www.psychologysalon.com). The content of the posts varies: some are written with the general public in mind, while others are designed more for therapists. The blog helps keep the clinic in the public eye, and it serves as a way of announcing new workshops and products.

Workshop planning and preparation take a fair chunk of my time. I have tried to offer a standard set of workshops that I can simply dust off and present, but in practice every program is revised on a regular basis and most are tailored to the expected audience. Some programs are purchased and hosted by outside agencies. Workshops in Vancouver are organized by our clinic, which entails much more work: event promotion, booking space and catering, registering participants, and so on. As the date for a program nears, the materials we will give each participant are created, boxed, and, if necessary, shipped.

Our clinic has also begun hosting occasional talks for the general public on psychological issues. Topics have included the nature of depression, the disadvantages of optimism, the effect of exercise on mood, and the nature of cognitive therapy. Currently, this program—called Psychology Salon (like the blog)—is co-hosted by the Vancouver Public Library, who provides the presentation space and handles all of the promotion.

Recently I have become interested in the prospect of offering continuing education workshops and programs for the public online. I have been writing and filming programs to be hosted by an online education service. This may enable people to see some of the programs that they wouldn't otherwise attend, and may provide the clinic with a source of revenue that will compensate for the time spent in program development . . . or not.

Thursdays and Fridays I set aside as non-clinical days. This is when most of the continuing education programs are booked. Workshop days begin early, with my arrival at the hotel or convention space an hour and a half before the scheduled start time to finalize set-up and ensure that all electronics are working, before greeting attendees and helping them sign in. The workshop might be on treating depression, conducting exposure therapy, enhancing assertiveness skills, becoming aware of sexual orientation issues, managing a private practice, or conducting cognitive therapy. At the end of the day supplies and leftovers are packed up and returned to the clinic for the assistant to sort through. If I have had to travel to offer the program, I usually fly home the evening it ends, which makes for a long day.

I usually plan to offer only one or two workshops per month, and so most weeks I have Thursday and Friday free to work on other projects. Lately I have spent these days on the video programs, but I have also used them for other longer-term projects such as writing or revising manuals, creating new workshops, and developing conference presentations.

In addition to my practice, I have a small orchard outside the city. From April to October, I spend most weekends at the farm, and I try to leave town Thursdays whenever possible. The practical nature of the farm work, with its directly observable effects (a repaired fence, an irrigation system that finally pumps water, a mowed lawn), provides an excellent counterpoint to the often uncertain and intangible effects associated with psychological practice. I often alternate between work-related writing projects and farm chores over the weekend.

Prevention

You may remember from Chapter 1 that prevention activities are a relatively new addition to the skill set of clinical psychologists. Accordingly, only a small percentage of clinical psychologists devote professional time to this activity. Prevention services are categorized according to the stage in the course of a disorder at which they are introduced. Primary prevention involves the prevention of a disease or disorder before it actually occurs. Secondary prevention is designed to reduce the recurrence of a disease or disorder that has already developed and been diagnosed. Tertiary prevention refers to efforts to reduce the overall disability that results from the disease or disorder.

You will learn more about prevention in Chapter 10. Generally speaking, prevention activities tend to focus on either reducing risk factors or enhancing protective factors. Risk factors are characteristics of an individual or of an individual's life circumstances that increase the likelihood of the development of a disorder. You are probably quite familiar with physical factors such as smoking, being overweight, having high cholesterol levels, and having a family history of heart disease that are all risk factors for the development of heart disease. Protective factors, on the other hand, are individual or environmental characteristics that lessen the likelihood of eventually developing a disease or disorder. Regular exercise and a diet low in saturated fats are considered protective factors that reduce the risk of developing heart disease. As we describe in more detail in Chapter 10, risk factors for the development of many psychological disorders in children and adolescents include inconsistent discipline, conflict in the family, and parental psychopathology.

Prevention efforts are usually based in community settings, as opposed to institutional settings such as hospitals or private clinical psychology practices. Prevention programs can be offered to large groups of people at a time, such as educating children about ways to resist pressures to abuse alcohol or educating parents about issues around bullying in the schoolyard. Alternatively, prevention programs may be offered in a one-on-one format, as is often done in teaching life skills to individuals already diagnosed with severe mental illness. Most commonly, the role of the clinical psychologist is to develop, implement, and evaluate the prevention programs. The prevention program is often delivered by mental health professionals such as nurses, counsellors, or social workers.

Can you recall any prevention programs that were offered when you were in school? What features of the prevention programs did you like and what features do you think might make the programs effective?

Consultation

Clinical psychologists often act in the role of consultant, as Dr. Woody described in her profile (Profile Box 2.2). Providing information, advice, and recommendations about how best to assess, understand, or treat a client is called **clinical consultation**. When the focus of the consultation is related to developing a prevention or intervention program, evaluating how well an organization is providing a health care or related service, or providing an opinion on policies on health care services set by an organization, the terms **organizational consultation** or "community consultation" are typically used. Dr. Paterson (Profile Box 2.3) spends a lot of time in organizational consultation with government and private agencies on the delivery of evidence-based services.

clinical consultation: the provision of information, advice, and recommendations about how best to assess, understand, or treat a client.

organizational consultation: services to an organization focused on developing a prevention or intervention program, evaluating how well an organization is doing in providing a health care or related service, or providing an opinion on policies on health care services set by an organization.

Throughout the history of the profession, clinical psychologists have offered clinical consultation. As a member of a multidisciplinary team, a clinical psychologist receives requests to provide guidance about a patient who is under the care of another professional. For example, one of us was asked to suggest how hospital staff could best handle a demented older adult's confusion and growing anger over his inability to understand what was being served to him in his meals. Another request came from a child daycare centre that wanted help in dealing with a disruptive 2-year-old. It is a common (and highly ethical) practice for clinical psychologists to request an opinion from a fellow clinical psychologist on how to handle a particularly difficult or challenging assessment or treatment issue that has arisen.

Consultation to agencies often falls into one of several categories: needs assessment, program development, program evaluation, and policy consultation. Needs assessments are required to determine the extent of an unmet health care need in an identified population. A clinical psychologist might be asked, for example, to conduct a needs assessment to determine whether there are mechanisms to ensure that new immigrants are aware of health care services available in their community. Once a needs assessment has established the scope of the need, a psychologist might be hired to develop a program to educate the target population about the available services. The final step involves determining whether or not the program was successful in achieving its goal, by conducting a program evaluation. The program evaluation assesses the extent to which the program was carried out as intended and the extent to which the program objectives were met. Another type of consultation, policy consultation, focuses on determining whether an agency's policy is congruent with its mission or is consistent with professional standards or scientific evidence. For example, a clinical psychologist might be engaged to provide an opinion on the suitability of a health care company's policy regarding reimbursement of psychotherapy services to health care providers.

How interested are you in consultation services? In what way do you think consultation skills may be similar to, and different from, the skills required in providing direct services like psychotherapy?

PROFILE BOX 2.4

EMMA MACDONALD

Courtesy of Emma MacDonald

I completed a B.Sc. (Honours) in psychology at St. Francis Xavier University in Antigonish, Nova Scotia, in 2009. My undergraduate research focused on sex differences in pain responding. During my undergraduate education, I was a research assistant to Dr. Margo Watt, who later became my honours thesis supervisor. My experiences in Dr. Watt's lab inspired me to pursue a career in clinical psychology. I am continuing my training at Ryerson University in Toronto under the supervision of Dr. Naomi Koerner. When I started, the graduate psychology program at Ryerson was newly formed and I was part of the third class to be enrolled. We were very pleased when the clinical psychology program received accreditation from the Canadian Psychological Association in 2012. My master's thesis investigated the use of a computerized training program to change the way people think about their anxiety symptoms. I am in the process of preparing this manuscript for publication. I completed the M.A. program in 2011.

I am currently enrolled as a Ph.D. student and, in addition to other research projects, am planning my dissertation research, which will focus on obsessive-compulsive disorder (OCD). In addition to my studies at Ryerson, I am involved in several professional psychology associations. I currently hold the position of student representative on the Executive Committee of the Clinical Section of the Canadian Psychological Association. My goal for the future is to have a career that includes both research and delivery of psychological services.

A TYPICAL WEEK

A typical week in the life of a graduate student in clinical psychology varies greatly based on classes, clinical placements, and research commitments. During my first year in graduate school, I spent most of my time in classes. Now that I am more advanced in the program, I have one class in a given semester and much more time for research and clinical work, which is a great balance. The best part of this is the diversity in my daily activities, so I rarely get bored with anything!

I spend Mondays in a practicum placement at the St. Michael's Hospital Family Practice Clinic and Ryerson's Clinical Psychology Training Clinic. In the morning, I prepare for the clients I will see during the day. One client has a major depressive disorder and the other has a social anxiety disorder. After completing progress notes following each session, I prepare for the afternoon when I co-lead group therapy for panic disorder with another clinical psychology practicum student. The day ends with group supervision, in which all students at the clinic discuss their clients with the supervising psychologist and with each other.

Tuesday is dedicated to research. This can include testing participants for studies, preparing manuscripts to submit for publication, or conducting ad hoc manuscript review for journals with my research supervisor. This week I focused on my dissertation research by working on a literature review and reading articles related to OCD.

CONTINUED . . .

Wednesday is also a clinical day. In the morning I complete an assessment on a new client, which includes administering a structured interview. This takes about two hours to complete, after which I write the assessment report. In the afternoon I have a client who is struggling with depression. I also have individual supervision with my clinical supervisor where I can discuss my clients, their progress, and the plan for treatment.

Thursday is my catch-up and meeting day. Sometimes I meet with the undergraduate student whose thesis I am co-supervising with Dr. Koerner. This week I met with my research supervisor to discuss my research projects and dissertation. I also do the readings for my class the following day. If I have any free time, I also use Thursdays for research.

Fridays are busy, starting with class in the morning. This semester I am taking a graduate seminar on eating disorders. Friday afternoons are reserved for clinical student meetings. Some weeks we attend clinical rounds, which are brief clinical skills workshops conducted by psychologists. This week we met with Ryerson's director of clinical training to discuss clinical requirements of the program. At the end of the day, I have a lab meeting with my research supervisor and the other students in my lab.

Graduate school is a marathon, not a sprint. For this reason, it is important to have a good work/life balance. One of the best parts of graduate school is that I have the flexibility to make sure I achieve that balance. Although some weeks I have to work long hours or throughout the weekend, I make sure to take some time off the next week. Taking care of yourself is one of the keys to succeeding in graduate school.

Research

All clinical psychologists are trained to conduct and evaluate research. University coursework provides initial training in research methods, which is put into practice by conducting a doctoral dissertation. The profession's ethical codes require clinical psychologists to continue to attend to practice-relevant research throughout their professional careers. Even though all clinical psychologists should be informed research consumers, only a minority of clinical psychologists regularly engage in producing research. Both Dr. Paterson and Dr. Bush both devote time to keeping up with the latest research and disseminating this knowledge to other professionals and to the public.

In the past, much of the research in clinical psychology came from university settings and was conducted or supervised by clinical psychology faculty members in departments of psychology or in medical schools. Faculty members in university are typically expected to devote their professional time to research and teaching. In their review of the research productivity of professors in Canadian clinical psychology programs, Carleton, Parkerson, and Horswill (2012) found that most professors publish between one and three articles each year. With the growing recognition of the need for science-based health care in many parts of the world, it is now increasingly common for clinical psychologists in publicly funded institutions such as hospitals to devote part of their workload to research. Because of psychologists' extensive training in research methodology and statistics, some hospital-based clinical psychologists are employed primarily as researchers, with psychological service delivery as a secondary component of their work. Such psychologists may actually have a greater proportion of their workload devoted to research than most academics do. A survey of clinical psychology faculty members in American universities (Himelein & Putnam, 2001) found that conducting and supervising research accounted for only 17% of professors' work time. Because of the central role that empirical evidence plays in guiding the provision of psychological services, some private practitioners have also made it a priority to be regularly involved in research activities.

Clinical psychologists conduct research on an impressive range of topics, including normal human functioning, psychopathology, assessment, intervention, and/or prevention. Let's consider examples of the types of research conducted by clinical psychologists. In studying normal human functioning, clinical psychologists conduct research on personality, memory processes, intimate relationships, parenting, child development, and aging. Clinical psychologists carry out research aimed at improving our understanding of the nature and causes of conditions as varied as sexual pain disorders, depression in older adults, disruptive behaviour disorders, pathological gambling, and insomnia. Measures of perfectionism, anxiety sensitivity, infant pain, trauma, and scores of other phenomena have been developed in recent years. With respect to prevention and intervention, clinical psychologists study resilience in the face of adversity, treatments for marital conflict, early intervention strategies for childhood anxiety disorders, factors that predict premature termination from therapy, and patterns of mental health service use in various countries. To help you locate clinical psychology research, Appendix 1 provides an overview of the major journals in the field.

Think of your research experiences thus far in your psychology training. Which parts of the research process were most challenging? Which were most rewarding? Are you a person who enjoys formulating testable questions and gathering the data to answer them?

Teaching and Supervision

Full-time professors in clinical psychology engage in different types of teaching activities. They typically teach both undergraduate and graduate courses in psychology and, in some programs, they also supervise graduate students in the provision of psychological services.

Himelein and Putnam (2001) found that these different teaching activities accounted for 26%, 11%, and 4% of the average American clinical psychology professor's work time.

Courses

The type of courses taught depends on the professor's areas of specialization and expertise. Undergraduate courses commonly taught by clinical psychology professors include psychopathology, personality theories, human adjustment, interpersonal processes, psychology of women, family psychology, geropsychology as well as introduction to clinical psychology. In addition, these professors teach advanced courses to small groups of graduate students on topics such as professional ethics and issues, psychological assessment, psychotherapy, multicultural counselling, psychopathology, clinical research methods, program evaluation, and health psychology.

University courses are taught by both full-time and part-time professors. In most universities, some clinical psychologists who work in the community are employed as part-time instructors and teach one or two undergraduate courses each year. Clinical psychology programs also hire these professionals to teach specialized graduate courses in areas not covered by full-time faculty (e.g., neuropsychology or rehabilitation psychology). Psychologists employed in hospital settings often contribute to the training of both psychology and medical students by offering seminars or workshops on select aspects of clinical psychology. Dr. Bush (Profile Box 2.1) is a great example of a community-based psychologist who makes a substantial contribution by teaching graduate courses in clinical neuropsychology and professional ethics.

What are the qualities that make an excellent teacher? What do you think would be the rewards of teaching others about clinical psychology?

Clinical Supervision

A central part of the training of clinical psychologists involves conducting psychological assessment and intervention. After taking advanced courses in these topics, graduate students provide services to the public under the close supervision of licensed clinical psychologists. Clinical supervision is offered in either a group or individual format. This first clinical experience under the supervision of a licensed psychologist is called a **practicum**. Some clinical psychology programs operate an

practicum: the initial supervised training in the provision of psychological services that is a requirement of the doctoral degree; usually part-time.

in-house psychology training clinic in which faculty members supervise students in the provision of services such as intellectual assessment, diagnostic evaluation, individual therapy, group therapy, and family therapy. All training programs, including those that offer in-house training, rely on the active participation of clinical psychologists in the community in providing training opportunities for graduate students. Within the clinical psychology community, there are strong links between university-based training programs and community-based training in diverse settings. Dr. Woody's duties include establishing these links so that students can benefit from the wealth of training opportunities in the community. Thus, clinical psychologists in general medical hospitals, residential treatment settings for adolescents, rehabilitation centres, and psychiatric hospitals may all contribute to the supervision and training of future clinical psychologists. For example, both Dr. Bush and Dr. Paterson are actively engaged in the supervision of practicum students and interns.

In most Canadian clinical psychology programs, graduate students obtain between 1,000 and 2,000 hours of practicum experience during their graduate training (see www.cpa.ca/docs/File/Accreditation/Tables-Doctoral_Programme_ARs-2011-12.pdf). Following the completion of all other aspects of their training (with the possible exception of the defence of a doctoral thesis), students then complete a full-time, year-long **internship** or **residency** in which they are supervised in the provision of psychological services in settings such as hospitals, workers' compensation boards, or community agencies. In their survey of clinical supervision in Canadian academic and community service settings (mainly hospitals), Johnston and Stewart (2000) found that practicum students were supervised primarily by academic clinical psychologists, whereas interns were more likely to be supervised by clinical psychologists in service settings.

internship: the period of supervised training in the provision of psychological services that is a requirement of the doctoral degree; sometimes referred to as residency; usually a one-year, full-time period.

Research Supervision

The guidance provided by the research supervisor (who may be a psychologist working outside the university) is evident at many stages of the student's program. Initially supervision involves assisting graduate students in understanding the research literature in a chosen area and then conceptualizing the research that the student will conduct as part of his or her degree. Before the research is conducted, the supervisor ensures that it will be done in an ethical manner and is approved by an institutional research ethics board. The supervisor typically provides input on study design, sampling considerations, measurement selection, statistical analysis, and, finally, the interpretation and presentation of the research. Dr. Woody devotes many hours a week to research supervision, and graduate student Emma MacDonald spends many hours receiving research supervision.

> In considering professors who may supervise your honours thesis in psychology, have you thought of asking their current students to describe the professors' research supervision skills?

Administration

Out of necessity, most clinical psychologists are involved in administrative activities. In a private practice, this includes the activities necessary to maintain an efficient and professional business, such as bookkeeping and supervision of personnel. Dr. Paterson notes that many hours are devoted to these responsibilities. In institutional settings such as hospitals and universities, psychologists are expected to contribute to the overall running of the institution by serving on committees and assuming management positions. For example, clinical psychologists often serve on the research ethics boards of institutions. In hospital settings, they may sit on committees dealing with research, quality assurance, and community relations. Dr. Bush is engaged in various multidisciplinary committees within the hospital and at a regional level. Within universities, clinical psychologists often serve on committees that may include those involved in the hiring of new professors, running of the undergraduate psychology program, and selecting of new graduate students. Management positions in universities are likely to include director of the clinical psychology program, director of the training clinic, chair of the psychology department, and possibly dean of the faculty. Clinical psychologists in hospital or related medical settings may be found in a range of management positions, including discipline leader within a mental health team, chief psychologist in a department of psychology, or director of an entire service (e.g., rehabilitation services or child mental health services). The opportunity to assume administrative responsibilities begins in graduate school. Emma MacDonald has already served in administrative capacities, both in her program and in the national organization for psychologists.

EMPLOYMENT SETTINGS

So far, we have mentioned a range of work settings in which clinical psychologists might be employed. Surveys examining the employment settings of clinical psychologists indicate that the number of clinical psychologists like Dr. Paterson working in independent practice has grown considerably over the past three decades (Hunsley et al., 2013; Norcross

& Karpiak, 2012). Moreover, even those psychologists employed in an institutional setting, like Dr. Bush, frequently have part-time private practices. Hunsley et al. found that in addition to the 27.5% of Canadian clinical psychologists who reported that they worked exclusively within a private practice, another 50% reported private practice as a secondary work setting.

In Canada, a large number of clinical psychologists are employed in hospitals or outpatient clinics. Historically these settings were linked to departments of psychiatry, rehabilitation services for war veterans, or pediatric services (Hearn & Evans, 1993). Currently within hospitals, traditional organizational structures based on departments have been replaced by program models in which health professionals, including psychologists, are appointed to a specific program or service, and by matrix models in which psychologists have responsibility to both a specific program and to general psychological services. A survey by Humbke and colleagues (2004) found that only a fifth of Canadian hospitals had an identified department of psychology. These researchers also found that, although the ratio of full-time psychologists to hospital beds had improved from 1:131 in 1992 to 1:53 in 1999, one-third of hospitals did not employ a full-time clinical psychologist.

The survey data we have presented do not include information on a number of alternative employment opportunities for clinical psychologists. For example, clinical psychologists are often employed in residential treatment clinics, correctional and forensic settings, government agencies focused on personnel selection and training, and private research and consulting firms. Some clinical psychologists with expertise in public policy are employed in government ministries and departments, public health organizations, or research granting agencies.

THE TWO PILLARS OF CLINICAL PSYCHOLOGY: SCIENCE AND ETHICS

How do theories inform the practice of clinical psychology?

As we emphasized in Chapter 1, the profession of clinical psychology is founded on the application of the results of empirical research to address emotional, behavioural, and neurological problems. In all their activities, whether providing psychological services to the public, planning new research endeavours, teaching undergraduate courses, or providing input on health care policy matters, it is crucial that clinical psychologists maintain their knowledge of research relevant to their activities. This is not simply a reflection of the model in which they are trained. As you will learn in this section, ethical codes of conduct require that clinical psychologists maintain their knowledge of the scientific foundation of their professional activities. All three psychologists profiled in this chapter devote regular time to keeping up to date with research in their field.

Ethical principles set out fundamental guidelines for the way that psychologists work professionally. These principles include respect for people, the responsible provision of services, the maintenance of integrity in professional relationships, and professional responsibilities to society. In all their professional activities, clinical psychologists must remain aware of the importance of questioning one's services. Clinical psychologists must always keep in mind questions such as "What is the evidence for what I am planning to do?" and "What are the relative risks and benefits to my patients (or students or research participants) of the course of action I am considering?"

Most clinical psychologists agree that professional services should be informed by research evidence. Disagreement starts to creep in when the discussion turns to just *how* the research should inform (or determine) practice and just *what* constitutes research evidence. You may recall that in Chapter 1 we described McFall's manifesto for a science of clinical psychology, which urged that no service should be provided unless there is empirical evidence that it is valid and effective. At the other extreme, some psychologists take a position that they should simply be mindful of general, basic research findings on human functioning. Answers to the *what* issue range from the position that all personal and clinical experience should be considered research evidence, to the position that only the results of experimental studies should constitute the knowledge base of clinical psychology.

Of course, very few psychologists hold opinions represented by these extremes. Nevertheless, there is considerable variability in how the role of science is interpreted. For example, Peterson (2004) suggested that we should accept that some of the problems facing clinicians cannot be studied by scientific methods. Accordingly, he argued that we must rely on intuition and experience in such cases. In response to this, Nathan (2004) suggested that one must be aware of the potential harm that may occur to patients when there is no science to guide practice. Rather than relying on intuition, he countered that the best practice would be to offer no service in such situations rather than risk providing the wrong or harmful treatment.

What role should intuition play in the practice of clinical psychology?

Despite the large body of evidence available to clinical psychologists, science cannot provide a research-based solution for each situation confronted by a clinician. From our perspective, an evidence-based approach to clinical services involves the use of the research evidence whenever it is available. However, when no research evidence is available to guide services, the clinical psychologist can optimize services by maintaining a scientific frame of mind. This involves taking a systematic, questioning, and self-critical approach to determining the relevance of a service and then monitoring its effects to determine whether the outcome is primarily beneficial or harmful. Lilienfeld, Lynn, and Lohr (2003) suggested this requires the clinician to strike a balance between excessive open-mindedness (i.e., "anything goes") and excessive scepticism (i.e., "only proven services are acceptable"). Science is an evolving compilation of ideas, theories, and facts. Science is also a method of formulating and testing hypotheses. As you will find in Chapter 4, the same type of scientific thinking that influences methodological designs behind multi-million-dollar treatment studies can also be employed by each individual clinical psychologist to ensure that clients receive the most effective services.

So what, exactly, is the problem with the call from Peterson (and many other clinical psychologists) for clinicians to use their intuition and experience to guide their work? Intuition is often described as a felt-sense about something that cannot be entirely described, put into words, or accounted for. From a scientific perspective, the problem with using intuition to guide service delivery is that, by definition, a systematic, questioning, and self-critical approach is the polar opposite of intuition. From a health care system perspective, there is another issue: how would you feel about a dentist, surgeon, or gynaecologist using intuition in providing services to you or to someone you care about? Imagine your reaction to a dentist who told you that she *felt* that fluoride treatments were not useful, a surgeon who said he had a *sense* of the tissue that needed to be removed and so did not rely on laboratory analysis, or a gynaecologist who said she knew that some women find PAP tests difficult and *guessed* you looked healthy enough so would not bother with the test? Similarly, how would you feel on learning that a psychologist failed to provide a treatment that was known to be effective for a problem such as agoraphobia, explaining that he had a strong intuition that you would be better served by another approach?

What about relying on clinical experience? After all, it only seems reasonable to assume that experienced clinicians are better than novice clinicians, doesn't it? Unfortunately, this assumption is contradicted by most research on clinical psychologists and other health service providers. Numerous studies have shown that when given identical information, experienced clinicians are no better than clinicians in training at making accurate, valid decisions (Garb, 1998). The main reason that experience does not necessarily guarantee the highest quality service is that it is exceedingly difficult to learn from clinical experience. Clinical psychologists must frequently deal with complex and ambiguous situations in which they must make decisions and, in almost all instances, they receive no feedback about the accuracy of these decisions (Garb & Boyle, 2003). Without corrective feedback, it is extremely unlikely poor practices can be detected and stopped or that good practices can be identified and enhanced. Therefore, a scientifically oriented clinical psychologist must be constantly aware of the need to check his or her assumptions and activities.

We often rely on the basic assumptions of a theoretical orientation to guide our clinical practice. That is, of course, the whole point of a theoretical orientation: it directs the clinician's attention to phenomena and to possible explanations that are deemed most relevant, and it diverts attention from aspects of the client's experience that are deemed irrelevant. It must be remembered, however, that theories of human functioning are essentially maps and that, to truly know if the map is accurate, it must be put to the test. Sometimes, theories are wrong, and the failure to test a theory can have serious consequences. You may recall from previous psychology courses how Freud became puzzled at the number of young female patients who reported sexual abuse. It seemed inconceivable to him that so many women had been abused as children, so he developed an alternative explanation or theory that these women were expressing sexual fantasies. Freud's theories carried great conviction and were accepted as correct without scientific testing. Surveys conducted many years later revealed that alarming numbers of children of both genders are, indeed, sexually abused. It is deeply troubling to think of the very serious consequences suffered by many people because of reliance on the credibility and authority of the proponent of a theory, rather than on data stemming from appropriate tests of the theory.

Fortunately, most theorists have permitted their theories to be scientifically tested. The best illustration of this is the work of Carl Rogers. As you learned in Chapter 1, Carl Rogers proposed that therapy must provide a supportive environment in which clients reconnect with aspects of themselves and thereby discover their potential for growth. Rogers balanced his own strong convictions with powerful advocacy of the need for research into psychotherapy. He masked the identity of his clients, then provided researchers with transcripts of his therapy sessions. Truax (1966) analyzed sessions of a successful long-term therapy case to determine whether client-centred therapy's key therapeutic condition of *unconditional positive regard* occurred and, if it did, whether it was linked to positive client outcomes. Contradicting Rogers' own model, Truax found that Rogers did not provide positive regard *unconditionally*. Instead (consciously or unconsciously), he employed empathy, acceptance, and directiveness as reinforcers of selective client behaviour. In other words, consistent with basic learning models, Rogers *shaped* client behaviour over the course of the therapy and used the reinforcers of empathy and acceptance to bring about client change.

So, for example, he paid more attention when the client talked about emotions than he did when the client talked about other issues. This is, of course, important information about how a therapist can help a client change, but it also illustrates that the client-centred condition of *unconditional* positive regard is not likely to be a key aspect of successful treatment. We owe a debt of gratitude to Carl Rogers for being more concerned with learning about the process of change than he was about promoting his own views. Adopting a scientific position involves putting our ideas to the test and risking the discovery that some ideas that make a lot of sense to us may, in fact, be wrong. The best scientists are driven by curiosity that is twinned with openness to input and a willingness to be proved wrong.

How willing are you to put your cherished beliefs to the test? What do you think it requires to submit for evaluation an intervention that you have spent years developing? As a psychologist, would you be willing to gather the data that may show that you were wrong? As a consumer of psychological services, would you prefer to see a psychologist who was 100% convinced that his or her approach is the best, or a psychologist who was willing to examine the evidence?

informed consent: an ethical principle to ensure that the person who is offered services or who participates in research understands what is being done and agrees to participate.

Popperfoto/Getty Images

Dr. Karl Brandt, Hitler's personal physician and head of the Nazi euthanasia program, on trial at Nuremberg. Horror at the atrocities committed under the name of science led to the development of ethical codes.

Basing clinical psychology services on research is crucially important, but so is the need to provide services ethically. The modern interest in developing ethical codes for research and professional services can be traced to the Nuremberg war crime trials that occurred after the Second World War (Sinclair, 1993). After the horrific discovery of atrocities conducted by the Nazis under the guise of medical science, a code of ethics in medical research was developed. This code was the first to incorporate the idea that the person who is being experimented on must understand what is being done and must agree to participate. This concept of **informed consent** is applied both to patients and to research participants and is the cornerstone of professional and research ethical codes. The American Psychological Association (APA) developed a code of ethics for psychologists shortly after the Second World War and has revised it several times, most recently in 2010 with amendments that underline that ethical principles must always respect basic principles of human rights. Within Canada, there was agreement to adopt the early versions of the APA code of ethics and it was not until the 1980s that a uniquely Canadian code of ethics for psychologists was developed. The Canadian code was designed to reflect Canadian legal traditions, apply to all areas of psychology, and serve as a teaching tool.

The *Canadian Code of Ethics for Psychologists* published by the Canadian Psychological Association (2000) is now in its third edition and is intended to provide guidance to all members of the CPA in all the capacities in which a psychologist might function, including research, clinical service, teaching, consultation, administration, and social policy activities. The same ethical standards are expected of psychologists in all their roles.

There are four ethical principles in the Code: respect for the dignity of persons, responsible caring, integrity in relationships, and responsibility to society. A definition is provided for each principle and a list of specific ethical standards illustrates the application of the principle. These standards include minimal expectations about the attitudes and behaviours of Canadian psychologists performing their work as psychologists. Two examples illustrate the nature of these standards. Under the principle of respect for the dignity of persons, there is a standard regarding non-discrimination. According to this standard, psychologists should not practise, condone, facilitate, or collaborate with any form of unjust discrimination. Under the principle of responsible caring, there is a standard regarding the maximizing of benefits: psychologists should select interventions that are relevant to the needs and characteristics of the client and that are likely to be effective based on established theory or empirical evidence. Psychologists also have an ethical obligation to ensure that their services are not affected by their own distress, an issue discussed in Viewpoint Box 2.2.

VIEWPOINT BOX 2.2

DISTRESS IN CLINICAL PSYCHOLOGISTS AND HOW THEY DEAL WITH IT

Ethical codes require psychologists to be self-aware and not to offer psychological services when their own functioning is impaired. Just as any health care professional should not offer services when suffering from incapacitating allergies or a vicious flu virus, psychologists should not offer psychological services when their own emotional health gets in the way of them doing their job effectively.

Are psychologists psychologically healthy?

Psychologists are not immune from the life events that affect everyone. Like everyone else, psychologists experience painful events such as the death of a loved one, serious illness, or accidents. Psychologists are human: they sometimes doubt their professional competence, they have children who get into trouble, they argue with their partners, worry about their elderly parents, and feel lonely when they are away from their friends and loved ones for an extended time. Not surprisingly, in a survey of 522 practising psychologists, Sherman and Thelen (1998) found that the more life events psychologists experienced, the more impairment in professional roles they reported.

What kinds of work stress do psychologists face?

Like many health care professionals, psychologists face challenges in effectively managing their time, making sure that they find a balance between offering services, writing notes and reports, answering phone

CONTINUED . . .

calls, supervising training activities, providing service to the profession, and engaging in continuing education to keep up to date with research advances in the field. Furthermore, the nature of their work may expose psychologists to particular stressors. People often wonder how psychologists cope with a professional life spent working with troubled clients who have experienced trauma or abuse or who are angry, sad, afraid, confused, or difficult to get along with. Sherman and Thelen reported that almost three-quarters of the psychologists who responded to their survey worked with clients who had serious emotional problems or who were suicidal. A meta-analysis of studies of psychotherapists' work lives found that those who reported working long hours and who felt as though they made greater effort than their clients did reported greater emotional exhaustion. Those who felt that they received constructive feedback at work reported a higher sense of personal accomplishment (Lee, Lim, Yang, & Lee, 2011).

Are psychologists traumatized by their work?

Concern has been expressed that working with people who have experienced trauma can cause psychologists to experience symptoms such as intrusive thoughts, extreme distress, and changes in beliefs and attitudes. This phenomenon has been referred to as vicarious traumatization, burnout, compassion fatigue, and secondary traumatic stress. Although there has been a great deal of clinical attention to this phenomenon, there has been relatively little systematic research on the topic. Reviews (e.g., Elwood, Mott, Lohr, & Galovski, 2011; Sabin-Farrell & Turpin, 2003) found evidence that mental health professionals have emotional responses to hearing traumatic material, but noted that these responses are a natural and short-term reaction. Some studies have found more intense psychological distress to be associated with the percentage of trauma survivors in the caseload and to being newer to that type of work. Research has not demonstrated evidence that working with trauma survivors is associated with changes in beliefs and attitudes.

Regular exercise promotes good health and can aid in dealing with work stress.

How do psychologists cope?

Research has found that psychologists engage in a number of health-promoting activities. Work-related strategies include taking breaks during the workday, consulting with colleagues on difficult issues, practising good time management such as scheduling time for paperwork and phone calls, and limiting the caseload in terms of both volume and the types of clients seen. Other health-promoting activities include devoting time to hobbies, taking vacations, engaging in regular exercise, and taking part in church and spiritual activities. A survey of 595 psychologists conducted by Rupert and Kent (2007) underlined the importance of having a sense of humour, maintaining a balance between work and personal life, and spending time with friends and family. In dealing with personal and professional challenges, psychologists engage in constructive problem-solving. Psychologists also seek psychological services to address serious difficulties. So, just as a dentist needs to practise oral hygiene and have regular checkups, psychologists need to adopt healthy lifestyles and seek professional help when they encounter difficulties.

Strength through adversity

A small but growing literature identifies ways that psychologists show resilience in their work with traumatized individuals. They report enhanced compassion, re-evaluation of the significance of their own problems, as well as a sense of satisfaction from being able to help others and an appreciation of the human capacity to heal and to recover from exposure to unimaginable horrors (Horrell, Holohan, Didion, & Vance, 2011).

How easy is it for you to maintain a healthy balance in your life? Which coping strategies do you find helpful in dealing with stress? Are there other coping strategies that you would need to develop if you were to become a clinical psychologist?

Several features of the Canadian Code set it apart from other codes of ethics for psychologists (Hadjistavropoulos, 2011; Sinclair, 1998). First, all versions of the Code were developed from an analysis of the international and interdisciplinary literature on codes of ethics. Second, empirical methods were used to incorporate the knowledge of Canadian psychologists into the Code. Third, an explicit model of ethical decision-making is embedded in the Code, in contrast to other codes that rely primarily on absolute and prescriptive standards. So, instead of listing what psychologists should and should not do, the decision-making model promotes a way of thinking and a way to resolve apparent dilemmas or situations in which two principles seem to conflict. There is evidence that the model works well, as both psychologists and non-psychologists are able to use the principles to achieve acceptable solutions to ethical dilemmas (Seitz & O'Neill, 1996). Fourth, the Code uses differential weighting of the four ethical principles so that it is clear that respect for the dignity of persons should usually be given greater weight in decision-making than the principle of responsibility to society. Overall, there is evidence that, compared with other codes, the Code meets the goal of enhanced educational value and provides a clear rationale for decision-making (Malloy, Hadjistavropoulos, Douaud, & Smythe, 2002; Hadjistavropoulos, 2011).

TRAINING IN CLINICAL PSYCHOLOGY

Psychology programs are extremely popular in all universities and colleges. Data from the Canadian Association of University Teachers (CAUT) convincingly demonstrate that psychology is very attractive to students (CAUT, 2012). With 429 doctorates awarded in psychology in 2009/2010, psychology was surpassed only by engineering (1,050 doctorates) and by biological and biomedical sciences (843 doctorates) and in terms of the number of doctorates awarded within a discipline (CAUT, 2012). The majority of students enrolled in psychology doctoral programs were women (74.8%).

For many years, clinical psychology has been the most popular field within graduate programs in psychology. Clinical psychology programs attract far more applications than do other graduate programs in psychology and they also graduate more students. The 2011 data

How does training in the different models of clinical psychology (scientist-practitioner, clinical scientist, and practitioner-scholar) prepare students for different types of positions in clinical psychology?

for American universities show that 34% of doctorates in psychology were in clinical psychology. In comparison, 12% of Ph.D awarded that year were in counselling psychology and 3% were in school psychology (National Opinion Research Center, 2012).

Models of Training in Clinical Psychology

Three models guide the training of clinical psychologists: the scientist-practitioner model, the clinical scientist model, and the practitioner-scholar model (McFall, 2006). Most doctoral programs awarding the Ph.D. in clinical psychology endorse the scientist-practitioner model. This training model was first endorsed by the American Psychological Association at a training conference held in Boulder, Colorado (Raimy, 1950), and is known as the *Boulder model.*

scientist-practitioner model: a training model that emphasizes competencies in research and psychological service provision.

In the **scientist-practitioner model**, graduate students must develop and demonstrate competencies in research and psychological service provision. As in any other Ph.D. program, students demonstrate competency in research by undertaking original research, which they write up in a dissertation and successfully defend in an oral examination. Clinical skills, such as interviewing, test administration, assessment report writing, psychotherapy, and clinical consultation are learned in practicum training throughout the program. These skills are enhanced and refined during the internship year, a period in which the student is employed full-time to deliver psychological services under the supervision of licensed psychologists in an organized health care setting.

The guiding philosophy underlying the scientist-practitioner model is that clinical psychologists should be capable of producing research and using empirical evidence to guide their clinical services. There is substantial variability among scientist-practitioner oriented programs regarding the relative balance of science and practice in training and, more importantly, regarding the manner in which students are trained in the integration of science and practice (Sayette, Norcross, & Dimoff, 2011). Some programs that strongly promote the development of research skills now identify themselves as espousing a **clinical scientist model**, a model in which the primary goal is to have graduates who are equipped to contribute to the knowledge base of psychology and related disciplines.

clinical scientist model: a training model that strongly promotes the development of research skills.

In the 1950s and 1960s, most graduates from Boulder model programs were employed in practice settings with primary responsibility for clinical service. These psychologists very rarely conducted any research after completing the doctoral dissertation. At a training conference in Vail, Colorado, participants expressed their dissatisfaction with the manner in which the scientist-practitioner model was applied in many training programs and developed a new model, the **practitioner-scholar model**, which was refined at subsequent conferences (Peterson et al., 1991).

practitioner-scholar model: a training model that emphasizes clinical skills and competencies as a research consumer.

The practitioner-scholar model emphasizes training in the clinical skills that most clinical psychologists need in a service setting and places less emphasis on research skills taught in Ph.D. programs. Programs training students in the practitioner-scholar model offer a different degree, the Psy.D. Many Psy.D. programs have developed research requirements that include considerable research training and the completion of a research project. Compared with Ph.D. programs, Psy.D. programs place less emphasis on experimental designs and large sample analyses and greater emphasis on naturalistic designs and the evaluation of individual cases or service-oriented programs. In general, Psy.D. programs are designed to train research consumers who are informed by science in their service activities, but who do not need the skills to conduct research.

In both the United States and Canada, all Ph.D. programs in professional psychology are offered by universities. In the United States, Psy.D. programs are found both at universities and in free-standing professional schools. Many in the profession have expressed concerns about the proliferation of the free-standing schools. Critics note factors that negatively affect the quality of students' training, including larger class sizes, lower financial support, and an overreliance on part-time instructors with little experience in research or teaching (McFall, 2006). In Canada, because of the concerns about the quality of training offered in some free-standing professional schools, Psy.D. programs can be offered only in universities.

The main distinction between Ph.D. and Psy.D. models of training is the weight given to science and practice. Using survey data from APA-accredited scientist-practitioner and practitioner-scholar programs, Cherry, Messenger, and Jacoby (2000) found distinct profiles consistent with the nature of each model. Students in each type of program had comparable amounts of clinical service delivery during their training, but students in scientist-practitioner programs were more involved in research than were students in practitioner-scholar programs. Similarly, graduates of both programs spent the majority of their professional time providing clinical services (around 60%), whereas graduates from scientist-practitioner programs spent more time in research activities than did graduates from practitioner-scholar programs (10% versus 2%).

There are other important factors to consider, however, in selecting a training program. Norcross, Ellis, and Sayette (2010) compared the characteristics of APA-accredited clinical psychology programs across five types of programs on the practice-research continuum, ranging from free-standing Psy.D. programs and university professional school Psy.D. programs to practice-oriented Ph.D. programs, equal-emphasis Ph.D. programs, and research-oriented Ph.D. programs. The overall acceptance rate into clinical programs was 17%, but it ranged from a high of 50% in free-standing Psy.D. programs, declining across the practice research continuum to a low of only 7% acceptance in research-oriented Ph.D. programs.

If you are considering applying to graduate school in clinical psychology you will want to learn not only about acceptance rates, but also about the financial support typically offered in different types of programs (unless you are very wealthy or have recently won the lottery). Financial assistance can be in the form of a fee waiver, some kind of fellowship or assistantship, or a combination of fee waiver and assistantship or fellowship. Norcross and his colleagues found that the likelihood of funding was lowest in free-standing Psy.D. programs, in which only 1% of incoming students could expect a waiver and assistantship or fellowship. Funding increased in a linear fashion across the continuum, so that the highest support was offered in research-oriented Ph.D. programs, in which 89% of incoming students received both a fee waiver and assistantship or fellowship. Across all clinical psychology programs, students took about 6 years to complete the program, including the internship. Length of time in the program also increased linearly, with students graduating with a Psy.D. from a free-standing school in a mean of 5 years and students in Ph.D. programs in a mean of 6.3 years.

In terms of theoretical orientation, there are some clear differences in programs as well. Although behavioural and cognitive-behavioural orientations are the dominant orientation in all clinical psychology programs, the highest number of faculty endorsing cognitive-behavioural orientations is in research-oriented Ph.D. programs (74% versus 28% in free-standing Psy.D. programs). Humanistic/phenomenological approaches are more commonly endorsed by faculty in free-standing professional schools (18%) than they are by faculty research-oriented Ph.D. programs (6%).

Which training model appeals most to you? How do you weigh the benefits of higher acceptance rates against the disadvantages of lower funding in free-standing professional programs? If you were seeking services, would it matter to you whether the psychologist was trained in a university-based program or in a free-standing professional school?

accreditation: a process designed to ensure that training programs maintain standards that meet the profession's expectations for the education of clinical psychologists.

Accreditation of Clinical Psychology Programs

The American Psychological Association (APA) was the first to develop an **accreditation** process designed to ensure that training programs maintain standards that meet the profession's expectations for the education of clinical psychologists. In 1969, the Ontario Psychological Association (OPA) developed accreditation guidelines for university programs and hospital internships in the province. By 1980, there were four Canadian university training programs accredited by APA and six Ontario university training programs accredited by the OPA (Doyle, Edwards, & Robinson, 1993). In response to the growth of clinical psychology training throughout Canada, accreditation standards and processes were established by the CPA in 1984. A few years later, in recognition of CPA accreditation, the OPA ceased its accreditation activities. In 2008, the APA discontinued the accreditation of programs outside the United States, such that after 2015, no Canadian programs will be accredited by the APA. However, the Academy of Psychological Clinical Science (acadpsychclinicalscience.org) will soon begin accrediting university training programs and internship programs that emphasize training in a clinical scientist model. It is possible that some Canadian institutions will apply to be accredited by this organization.

Until 1998, the CPA had consistently reaffirmed the scientist-practitioner model of training as the only acceptable form of training in accredited clinical psychology programs. A change of policy occurred in 1998 with the CPA's approval of the accreditation of Canadian Psy.D. programs. The CPA accreditation requirements for such programs are very similar to those used for accrediting Ph.D. programs and stipulate that, to be eligible for accreditation, a Psy.D. program must be university based. Thus, both the APA and CPA have accreditation criteria for evaluating the quality of clinical psychology training in the two clinical training models. A program that receives accreditation from one or both associations has therefore met the high standards of training set by the profession, and graduates from the program are likely to receive some of the best training available in clinical psychology. Students are therefore strongly advised to seek training in an accredited clinical psychology program. Table 2.4 lists the professional psychology programs in Canada that are accredited by the CPA. All of the English-speaking programs are Ph.D. programs. In Quebec, two universities offer both the Ph.D. and the Psy.D. (referred to as D.Psy.).

How can a psychologist prepare for all the diversity he or she will encounter in a professional career?

A major challenge facing all training programs is to ensure that students are prepared to provide psychological services to an increasingly diverse population. The 2006 census revealed that, with growth in immigration, one in six Canadians belongs to a visible minority (Statistics Canada, 2008a). There has also been growth in Canada's Aboriginal population, which passed the one-million mark in 2008 (Statistics Canada, 2008b). Because the issue of diversity is influenced by geographical, historical, and sociological factors, there is no single way for clinical psychology training to address diversity training. For example, think of the

TABLE 2.4 ■ Professional Programs Accredited by the Canadian Psychological Association

	Clinical	Counselling	Neuropsychology	School
Alberta				
University of Alberta		Ph.D.		
University of Calgary	Ph.D.	Ph.D.		
British Columbia				
Simon Fraser University	Ph.D.			
University of British Columbia	Ph.D.	Ph.D.		
University of Victoria	Ph.D.			
Manitoba				
University of Manitoba	Ph.D.			
New Brunswick				
University of New Brunswick	Ph.D.			
Nova Scotia				
Dalhousie University	Ph.D.			
Ontario				
Lakehead University	Ph.D.			
Queen's University	Ph.D.			
Ryerson University	Ph.D.			
University of Guelph	Ph.D.			
University of Ottawa	Ph.D.			
University of Toronto, OISE	Ph.D.	Ph.D.		Ph.D.
University of Waterloo	Ph.D.			
University of Windsor	Ph.D.			
Western University	Ph.D.			
York University	Ph.D.*			
Quebec				
Concordia University	Ph.D.			
Laval University	Ph.D., D.Psy.			
McGill University	Ph.D.	Ph.D.		
Université de Montréal	Ph.D., D.Psy.		Ph.D.	
Saskatchewan				
University of Regina	Ph.D.			
University of Saskatchewan	Ph.D.			

*There are two accredited programs, one in clinical developmental psychology and one in adult clinical psychology.

challenges for a training program in developing a curriculum and a set of training experiences to educate students in working with indigenous peoples. Such programs in Canada, the United States, and New Zealand would look very different for several reasons. One reason for these differences would be the degree of cultural heterogeneity within the indigenous population (greater in North America than in New Zealand). Another reason for the differences would stem from the history of relations of the indigenous communities with the dominant culture in each country. The history of open conflict and of treaty agreements is starkly different when comparing the First Nations and Inuit in Canada, the Native Americans in the United States, and the Maori in New Zealand.

Even neighbouring countries such as Canada and the United States differ dramatically with respect to population characteristics such as age and income. Bowman (2000) noted major differences in the cultural composition of the two countries. She also noted that visible minorities constitute a smaller proportion of the Canadian than the U.S. population. The most common cultural origins of Canadian visible minorities are (in descending order of frequency) Asian, First Nations, and African. For the American population, the most common origins of visible minorities are (again in descending order of frequency) African, Latin American, Asian, and Native American. Differences in linguistic diversity are also important to consider. A larger proportion of Americans than Canadians speak English at home. Furthermore, Canada has twice as many new immigrants per capita as does the United States.

Clinical psychologists must be aware that in addition to culture and language, diversity encompasses age, income, sexual orientation, disability, family structure, and geographical location. Those wishing to provide services in a rural setting, for example, need to be aware of the distinct nature of stressors people face in rural areas (e.g., higher levels of unemployment and accidents) and of the fact that rural areas tend to have higher levels of indigenous people and people with a lower overall level of education compared with urban settings (Barbopoulos & Clark, 2003; Helbok, Marinelli, & Walls, 2006). In Chapter 11, we describe an innovative program to offer services to people living in remote areas, as well as a program to train psychologists for rural practice (McIlwraith, Dyck, Holms, Carlson, & Prober, 2005).

Because of the myriad ways in which diversity is expressed in a country, it is highly unlikely that all clinical psychologists could develop special knowledge of all the types of diversity they may encounter. What is more important (and more respectful of the ways in which diversity might be expressed among a psychologist's clients), therefore, is for a psychologist to (a) be aware of diversity issues, (b) be open to discussing these issues with clients (when appropriate), (c) have the interpersonal skills to effectively communicate about these issues, and (d) have the research skills to interpret and design research that is sensitive to diversity factors (cf. Hertzsprung & Dobson, 2000; Whaley & Davis, 2007). Attention to diversity issues requires a balancing act in which universal human norms, specific group norms, and individual characteristics are considered in tandem with the continuum of normal-abnormal behaviour.

LICENSURE IN CLINICAL PSYCHOLOGY

Health care professionals are licensed to provide their services in the jurisdiction in which they practise. Licensed health care professionals, such as clinical psychologists, must meet minimal requirements for their academic and clinical training and are required by law to provide ethical and competent services. They are also regulated by a professional organization (e.g., a College of Psychologists) that holds them accountable for their professional activities. Without some form of licensing, there is no regulatory body to ensure that the public is protected when receiving health care services.

licensure: regulation to ensure minimal requirements for academic and clinical training are met and that practitioners provide ethical and competent services; regulation of the profession helps to ensure the public is protected when receiving services.

Licensure requirements in clinical psychology vary from country to country. In some countries, such as the United States, to become a clinical psychologist requires training at the doctoral level. In most European countries, a master's degree is required, whereas elsewhere, such as in Canada, Australia, and the UK, doctoral level training is preferred, although it may be possible for someone with master's level training to become licensed as a clinical psychologist.

Table 2.5 provides information on the level of graduate training required for licensure in Canada. In some jurisdictions, those with a master's degree can be registered as psychologists; in others, the title "psychologist" is reserved for those with doctorates, and the title "psychological associate" is used for those with a master's degree. As we mentioned in Chapter 1, in 2009, there were over 16,000 licensed psychologists and psychological associates in Canada (Canadian Institute for Health Information, 2011). In British Columbia and Ontario, the scope of practice of the two titles is identical (i.e., those holding either title can provide all forms of psychological service), whereas in Manitoba, a psychological associate can practise only under the auspices of a supervising psychologist. In all jurisdictions except British Columbia and Quebec, the registration process involves a period of supervision by licensed psychologists (or psychological associates) before a person is able to practise autonomously. In most provinces, the length of this supervised period is longer for those with a master's degree, in recognition that doctoral

TABLE 2.5 ■ Licensure Requirements for Psychologists in Canada

Province/Territory	Degree	Supervision	Examinations
Alberta	Master's	1 year post-master's	EPPP* Oral
British Columbia	Doctorate (Psychologist)	1 year predoctoral	EPPP Jurisprudence
	Master's (P. Associate)	4 years' post-master's	Oral
Manitoba	Doctorate (Psychologist)	1 year predoctoral and 1 year postdoctoral	EPPP Jurisprudence
	Master's (P. Associate)	2 years' post-master's	Oral
New Brunswick	Doctorate	1 year predoctoral and 1 year postdoctoral	EPPP
	Master's	3 years' post-master's	Oral
Newfoundland & Labrador	Doctorate	1 year predoctoral and 1 year postdoctoral	EPPP
	Master's	2 years' post-master's	
Northwest Territories	Master's	1 year post-master's	Exam may be required
Nova Scotia	Doctorate	1 year predoctoral and 1 year postdoctoral	EPPP
	Master's	4 years' post-master's	Oral
Nunavut	Master's	1 year on registry	Exam may be required
Ontario	Doctorate (Psychologist)	1 year predoctoral and 1 year postdoctoral	EPPP Jurisprudence
	Master's (P. Associate)	4 years' post-master's and 1 year on registry	Oral
Prince Edward Island	Doctorate	1 year predoctoral and 1 year postdoctoral	EPPP
	Master's	2 years' post-master's	Oral
Quebec	Doctorate	2,300 hours supervised predoctoral	None
Saskatchewan	Master's	1 year post-master's	EPPP Oral
Yukon	No legislation governing licensure of psychologists		

*Note: P. Associate = Psychological Associate; EPPP = *Examination for Professional Practice in Psychology.*

applicants receive far more supervised training during their graduate degree.

The final requirement for registration in most jurisdictions involves examinations of knowledge of psychological and professional issues. Typically this includes a written examination of knowledge of basic and applied psychology (the *Examination for Professional Practice in Psychology* [EPPP] is a standard exam used across North America, set by the Association of State and Provincial Psychology Boards) and an oral examination that assesses knowledge of professional practice, professional ethics, and jurisprudence relevant to the practice of psychology. British Columbia and Ontario also require that psychological associates and psychologists pass a written examination that covers jurisprudence and ethical issues. As is readily evident from Table 2.5, even after a person completes a graduate degree in psychology, it takes at least another year before he or she has the right to use the title "psychologist" and to autonomously offer psychological services to the public.

As Table 2.5 demonstrates, there is considerable variability in licensure requirements across Canada, including variability in educational requirements, supervision requirements, and examination requirements. To ensure that psychologists licensed in different provinces have comparable levels of competence in providing services to the public, representatives of the regulatory bodies responsible for the licensing of psychologists and psychological associates in Canada signed a *Mutual Recognition Agreement* (MRA) in 2001. The MRA specifies that, to be licensed as a psychologist or psychological associate in Canada, an individual must have been evaluated as possessing core competencies in interpersonal relationships, assessment and evaluation, intervention and consultation, research, and ethics and standards. Before the agreement was fully implemented, provincial legislation that governs the practice of psychology had to be changed.

A fundamental goal of the MRA was to establish the conditions under which a licensed psychologist could have his or her qualifications recognized in another Canadian jurisdiction. The MRA should also prove to be a significant benefit for the public. Currently, it is possible to become registered as a psychologist without having completed a training program in clinical psychology (accredited or unaccredited). In Canada, all that is required in any jurisdiction is a graduate degree in psychology. This made sense at a time when there were few accredited clinical psychology programs. We recognize that many competent clinical psychologists who have made important contributions to the field obtained their training outside of accredited programs. In our opinion, however, the profession of clinical psychology has developed to the point where the completion of a clinical training program (preferably one that is accredited) should be the academic requirement for licensing and the ability to autonomously provide clinical services to the public. In some American states, training in an accredited program (or training comparable to that received in an accredited program) is required for licensure. Despite the fact that the number of accredited clinical training programs in Canada has grown in recent years, the MRA does not require that someone applying for licensure be a graduate of a clinical program. The MRA does provide a set of very clear training requirements that must be met by all people applying for licensure. Therefore, individuals with graduate degrees in experimental psychology who wish to become licensed will require additional training in professional service provision to be eligible for licensure. Although this falls short of the ideal of requiring accredited clinical training for licensing, we see this as a significant step forward in the profession of clinical psychology.

To assist students who may be considering a career in clinical psychology, Appendix 2 describes procedures for applying to graduate school in clinical psychology. The appendix begins with the important question of how to decide whether pursuing training in clinical psychology is the right choice for you. Subsequent sections address whether you would be eligible for admission to a doctoral program in clinical psychology, the application process itself, and, finally, strategies to strengthen your application.

SUMMARY AND CONCLUSIONS

Clinical psychologists engage in diverse activities and are employed in many different settings. Graduate training in clinical psychology involves coursework, supervised practicum training, a doctoral dissertation, and a full-time internship. There is debate within the field about the relative weight that should be given to research in both training and the practice of clinical psychology. In North America, there is an increasing number of accredited programs with well-developed training models that vary in research emphasis. Both science and ethics are important in the practice of psychology, and Canada has been a world leader in the development of a code of ethics to guide decision-making that is respectful of individuals and that promotes well-being.

Both across and within countries, there are different requirements to become licensed as a clinical psychologist. Anyone considering a career in clinical psychology should carefully consider these licensing requirements before undertaking a course of graduate study in psychology.

KEY TERMS

accreditation: a process designed to ensure that training programs maintain standards that meet the profession's expectations for the education of clinical psychologists.

clinical consultation: the provision of information, advice, and recommendations about how best to assess, understand, or treat a client.

clinical scientist model: a training model that strongly promotes the development of research skills.

informed consent: an ethical principle to ensure that the person who is offered services or who participates in research understands what is being done and agrees to participate.

internship: the period of supervised training in the provision of psychological services that is a requirement of the doctoral degree; sometimes referred to as residency; usually a one-year, full-time period.

licensure: regulation to ensure minimal requirements for academic and clinical training are met and that practitioners provide ethical and competent services; regulation of the profession helps to ensure the public is protected when receiving services.

organizational consultation: services to an organization focused on developing a prevention or intervention program, evaluating how well an organization is doing in providing a health care or related service, or providing an opinion on policies on health care services set by an organization.

practicum: the initial supervised training in the provision of psychological services that is a requirement of the doctoral degree; usually part-time.

practitioner-scholar model: a training model that emphasizes clinical skills and competencies as a research consumer.

scientist-practitioner model: a training model that emphasizes competencies in research and psychological service provision.

ADDITIONAL RESOURCES

Books

Evans, D. R. (Ed.). (2011). *The law, standards, and ethics in the practice of psychology* (3rd ed.). Toronto, ON: Carswell Publications.

Sturmey, P., & Hersen, M. (Eds.). (2012). *Handbook of evidence-based practice in clinical psychology. Volume 1: Child and adolescent disorders.* New York: John Wiley and Sons, Inc.

Sturmey, P., & Hersen, M. (Eds.). (2012). *Handbook of evidence-base practice in clinical psychology. Volume 2, Adult disorders.* New York: John Wiley and Sons, Inc.

Truscott, D., & Crook, K. H. (2004). *Ethics and the practice of psychology in Canada.* Edmonton, AB: University of Alberta Press.

Check It Out!

The American Psychological Association provides information on accreditation as well as a listing of accredited programs. It provides links to licensing organizations in the United States: www.apa.org

The Association of State and Provincial Psychology Boards is the association of Canadian and U.S. licensing boards in psychology: www.asppb.org

The Australian Psychological Society provides information on licensure in Australia, including an assessment of psychology qualifications for candidates from overseas who wish to be registered as a psychologist in Australia: www.psychology.org.au/

The British Psychological Society includes an excellent publication, *So you want to be a psychologist,* which is packed with information about training and careers in psychology in the United Kingdom: www.bps.org.uk

The Canadian Psychological Association provides information on accreditation, as well as a listing of accredited programs. It provides links to licensing organizations in Canada: www.cpa.ca

The New Zealand Psychological Society provides links to the regulatory body, the New Zealand Psychologists Board: www.psychology.org.nz

CLASSIFICATION AND DIAGNOSIS

3 CHAPTER

INTRODUCTION

Every person is unique. Each has his or her own aspirations, goals, challenges, vulnerabilities, and problems. Everyone is influenced by genetics, physiology, life experiences, and current life circumstances. Yet, as we all know from daily experience, in order to describe, understand, and predict the responses of others, we must search for common elements of human behaviour in this ocean of uniqueness. To manage the complexities of life, we tend to categorize, classify, and search for patterns. Without a way to conceptualize and categorize the reactions of friends, family members, and co-workers, it would be impossible for us to navigate through life.

Classification is also a central element of all branches of science and social science. A classification system allows scientists to organize, describe, and relate the subject matter of their discipline, whether it is subatomic particles, microscopic forms of life, social systems, or celestial bodies. A range of features can be used to classify objects or concepts, including form, function, and purpose. Moreover, any object can be classified in a number of ways: a stone can be classified based on its composition, its shape, its value, its site of origin, or the geological period in which it was formed. As we will see in this chapter, two key aspects of the adequacy of classification systems are validity and utility (Kendell & Jablensky, 2003). **Validity** refers to the extent to which the principles used in classifying an entity are effective in capturing the nature of the entity. **Utility** refers to the usefulness of the resulting classification scheme.

We begin our discussion of classification by considering the underlying structure of classification systems. As you will see in this chapter, this issue is critically important in the diagnosis of mental disorders. Classification can be based on a **categorical approach** in which an

classification validity: the extent to which the principles used in classifying an entity are effective in capturing the nature of the entity.

classification utility: the usefulness of a classification scheme.

categorical approach to classification: an entity is determined to be either a member of a category or not.

What are the benefits of classification?

dimensional approach to classification: classified entities differ in the extent to which they possess certain characteristics or properties.

entity is determined to be either a member of a category or not. The assumption underlying categorical classification is that there is an important qualitative difference between entities that are members of a category and those that are not. An extreme example of a categorical approach is to classify entities as living or non-living. A categorical approach to psychopathology involves assigning a diagnosis such as major depressive disorder: the person is judged to have the disorder or not to have the disorder. In a categorical classification system, categories may or may not be overlapping, but those assigned to a category should be very similar to one another.

In contrast to the categorical approach, a **dimensional approach** to classification is based on the assumption that entities differ in the extent to which they possess certain characteristics or properties. This approach focuses on quantitative differences among entities and reflects the assumption that all entities can be arranged on a continuum to indicate the degree of membership in a category. Weight and height are prime examples of ways that dimensional approaches are used to classify people. Within a dimensional classification system, the different dimensions may or may not be related, but it is essential that the dimensions reflect significant higher order constructs rather than simple descriptive features (e.g., a construct such as neuroticism, rather than specific psychological phenomena such as sadness, nervousness, loneliness, poor self-esteem, or poor self-confidence).

Take a moment and think about how you classify people, including your friends, family members, classmates, and even strangers you see on a bus or in a coffee shop. What qualities do you tend to use in classifying them? Physical characteristics? Style of dress? Interpersonal style? Do you tend to think in terms of categories (e.g., friendly or not friendly) or dimensions (e.g., friendliness) when you compare people you know?

Child psychopathology researcher **Thomas Achenbach** gathered information about children's difficulties from multiple informants and then used factor analysis to identify the symptoms that tend to co-occur (e.g., Achenbach, 2010; Ivanova et al., 2007). Achenbach's work yielded two broad dimensions of problems: externalizing problems and internalizing problems. Externalizing problems are acting-out behaviours such as yelling, destroying things, stealing, and showing aggression. Internalizing problems refer to feelings of sadness, worry, and withdrawn behaviour. Using a dimensional approach, a child's functioning can be described according to the intensity of externalizing and internalizing problems. Later in the chapter, we will examine ways in which these two dimensions may underlie psychopathology across all age ranges. Achenbach's work also resulted in the development of the *Achenbach System of Empirically Based Assessment* (ASEBA; Achenbach, 2002). The ASEBA is a family of empirically derived assessment tools to measure competence and problems (internalizing and externalizing) across the lifespan. We describe this set of instruments in greater detail in Chapter 8.

©iStock.com/skynesher

How do you categorize people?

Whether based on a categorical or a dimensional approach, a **diagnostic system** is a classification based on rules used to organize and understand diseases and disorders. When these decision-making rules are applied to the symptoms of a specific individual, the classification system yields a **diagnosis** that concisely describes the symptoms that comprise the person's condition. Exhibit 3.1 lists some of the purposes of diagnostic systems used by psychologists and psychiatrists. Most health care practitioners find diagnostic systems useful, for all the reasons listed in the exhibit. Despite the advantages of diagnosis, there are also possible drawbacks, such as stigmatization of the person receiving the diagnosis and the potential for an inaccurate diagnosis to result in harmful or inappropriate treatment. Most clinical psychologists (whether practising in an institutional setting such as a hospital or in a private practice setting) are required to diagnose a patient to determine if the patient is eligible for certain services (e.g., extra academic support for students with learning disabilities). Furthermore, many insurance companies require a diagnosis before authorizing reimbursement of the charges for psychological services.

diagnostic system: a classification based on rules used to organize and understand diseases and disorders.

diagnosis: the result of applying the decision-making rules of a diagnostic system to the symptoms of a specific individual.

Exhibit 3.1 The Purposes of a Diagnostic System for Mental Disorders

- Provide a concise description of essential aspects of the patient's condition
- Reflect best current scientific knowledge of psychopathology
- Provide a common language for clinicians, researchers, and, increasingly, patients to use in discussing mental health conditions
- Indicate possible causes of the current condition (i.e., etiology)
- Indicate possible future developments in the condition (i.e., prognosis)
- Provide guidance on possible co-existing problems or conditions that should be evaluated
- Provide guidance on treatment options to be considered
- Provide a key term that can be used by clinicians to search the scientific literature for the most current information on the condition
- Provide a framework for determining reimbursement of health services and eligibility for special programs or services

As you learned in Chapter 1, modern attempts to classify and diagnose abnormal human behaviour began with the work of Emil Kraepelin, whose initial examination of dementia praecox (now called schizophrenia) and manic-depressive insanity (now called bipolar mood disorder) laid the foundation for current psychiatric diagnostic systems. The so-called neo-Kraepelinian approach to classification has several characteristics. These include viewing each diagnosis as a medical illness using specific criteria to define a category, and emphasizing the importance of diagnostic reliability (Blashfield, 1991).

prototype model: members of a diagnostic category may differ in the degree to which they represent the concepts underlying the category.

In the past few decades, this approach to psychiatric classification has been augmented with elements of a prototype model. The defining feature of the prototype model approach is that members of a diagnostic category may differ in the degree to which they represent the concepts underlying the category. As an example, if you think of all the features pertinent to the category "mammals," dogs are more prototypic of the category than are platypuses. Applying the prototype model to psychiatric diagnosis implies that not all people receiving the same diagnosis have exactly the same set of symptoms. Accordingly, in contrast to strict neo-Kraepelinian assumptions, two people with the same diagnosis may not have exactly the same disorder (i.e., the same set of symptoms) and therefore may require somewhat different treatment.

In this chapter, we will present the classification and diagnostic systems most commonly used by clinical psychologists. The examples we will examine are the *Diagnostic and Statistical Manual of Mental Disorders* (DSM) of the American Psychiatric Association and the *International Statistical Classification of Diseases and Related Health Problems* (ICD) of the World Health Organization. We will concentrate much of our discussion on determining the validity and utility of a diagnostic system. We begin by examining what constitutes abnormal human behaviour and how researchers try to understand the ways such behaviours develop into full-blown clinical disorders.

DEFINING ABNORMAL BEHAVIOUR AND MENTAL DISORDERS

Why should we care about whether a behaviour is abnormal or not?

As we discussed in Chapter 1, clinical psychologists now provide a range of psychological services to people with and without diagnosable conditions. Therefore, you may wonder, who cares about determining what constitutes abnormal behaviour? The quick answer is that most of us care about whether our experiences and behaviours are normal or abnormal. Many people consult psychologists to find out whether the problems and symptoms they (or their loved ones) are experiencing are normal or abnormal. For example, Ryan may be very concerned that he and his wife are having occasional disagreements and do not have sexual intercourse as often as they used to when they were first married; Rebecca may be concerned that she sometimes feels sad about the recent death of her father; Crystal may be worried about her son Matt who counts backward from 100 and says a prayer every time he begins to feel nervous; and Courtenay may be worried by the frequent thoughts of hurting herself that seem to be put into her mind by other people. In all likelihood, Ryan and Rebecca are experiencing normal, predictable events that occur to almost everyone in a similar situation. A responsible psychologist should convey this information to them and determine whether any treatment is truly warranted. In some cases, brief psychoeducation may provide sufficient reassurance. In contrast, Crystal's son Matt may be developing a clinical disorder (depending on how much the activities interfere with his daily functioning), and Courtenay is clearly having an experience that is abnormal. The psychologist is likely to recommend further assessment and treatment for Matt and Courtenay.

©iStock.com/Linda Yolanda

Individuals may seek psychological services to find out if their difficulties are normal.

How does culture influence definitions of normality and abnormality?

Abnormal behaviour is not just rare, unusual, or bizarre behaviour. Determination of whether a behaviour is abnormal requires knowledge of the context in which the behaviour occurs. Consider the following behaviours: Lizzie throws herself on the floor when asked to do anything such as take a bath, tidy up her things, or stop an enjoyable activity; Paul cannot be left alone with the family pets as he treats them roughly; Jonathon says he and his stuffed turtle are going on a magic adventure; Heather often rubs her genital area in public; and Danielle cries uncontrollably for extended periods and is disinterested in food. Are these behaviours abnormal? Without more information, we cannot say. One important issue is the person's age. We will interpret Lizzie's temper tantrums and oppositional behaviour differently according to whether she is 2, 22, or 82. If she is 2 years old, there is likely no cause for alarm. Although the behaviour would be grossly abnormal for both a 22-year-old and an 82-year-old, it is likely that the underlying cause would be different at different ages. Similarly, rough treatment of animals is not unusual in a preschool-age child, but is often associated with serious psychopathology when it occurs in older children. We cannot judge the behaviour of Jonathon or Heather without knowing their ages: what would be age-appropriate in a very young child would be very troublesome in an adolescent or adult. Danielle's sad behaviour cannot be understood without knowing the context. If she has just learned of the death of a loved one, her behaviour is likely part of a normal reaction to grief. Her cultural heritage will also contribute to the way in which her grief is expressed: in some cultures a grieving person is expected to appear outwardly unmoved by a loss, whereas in other

PhotoDisc/Getty Images

Without knowing the context of a person's behaviour, we cannot say whether that person's behaviour is normal.

cultures it may be common for the person to wail and rip her clothing. Diagnostic criteria for many childhood disorders specify that the symptom must be developmentally inappropriate. Therefore, the psychologist must have a good sense of the range of normal behaviour in a particular developmental period to be able to judge what is abnormal.

Developmental Psychopathology

developmental psychopathology: a framework for understanding problem behaviour in relation to the milestones that are specific to each stage of a person's development.

A **developmental psychopathology** approach examines problem behaviour in relation to the milestones that are specific to each stage of development. This approach underlines that biological and psychological systems are constantly changing. It also emphasizes the importance of major developmental transitions (such as starting daycare, learning to speak, going to high school, or moving into a long-term care facility) as well as disruptions to normal patterns of development (such as loss of a loved one, the effects of poverty, or exposure to trauma). Central to this approach is a reliance on empirical knowledge of normal development. So, for example, in understanding problems in very young children, it is essential to be informed by research on a wide range of issues, including interpersonal attachment, cognitive development, and sleep patterns. Understanding difficulties that are evident in preschool-age children requires, in particular, knowledge of language development and of ways that adults promote children's self-esteem and self-control. Problems in school-age children can be considered in the context of what we know about academic functioning, peer relationships, and harmonious families.

The developmental psychopathology approach has been particularly useful in understanding problems of infancy and childhood, but it can also be applied to help us understand the challenges of later phases in development such as retirement. A developmental psychopathology approach involves not only a snapshot of the client's current difficulties, but also consideration of the course of the problem if left untreated. The adoption of this approach has allowed clinical psychologists to draw on a vast literature about parenting, child neglect and abuse, the effects of conflict on family members, cognitive changes over the life course, and changing societal values when considering diagnostic issues.

Diagnosis

No diagnosis is based on a single symptom. Diagnostic criteria always include a cluster of symptoms that co-occur. Medical students often report that, in learning about different disorders, they recognize symptoms that they have experienced and worry that they may suffer from the serious disorder they are studying. Parents, too, hear about symptoms that are associated with childhood disorders and may be tempted to speculate on a diagnosis of attention-deficit/hyperactivity disorder to the child at the next table in a restaurant who is whooping with delight and flicking food at a friend.

The diagnosis of mental disorders involves challenges that are less common in the diagnosis of physical conditions (Hyman, 2010). Most medical diagnostic systems focus not only on symptoms but also on the etiology of the condition and the ways in which external agents or external causes (such as bacteria, infectious agents, or malnutrition) gave rise to symptoms. Data from laboratory tests such as X-rays, ultrasound scans, and blood tests provide markers for many physical disorders and diseases. To date, there are virtually no comparable lab tests available for mental disorders. As a result, classification systems for mental disorders rely almost entirely on the observation of symptoms. This means that, in practice, most diagnostic decisions are derived largely from client self-report data. (We discuss the use and value of data from multiple informants in several subsequent chapters.)

©iStock.com/tbel

©iStock.com/ArtisticCaptures

Children and adults express happiness in different ways.

Personal, cultural, or professional values influence the determination of what is abnormal or disordered. In defining abnormality, it is extremely important to rely on scientific evidence, not just value judgments. For example, beliefs based on theoretical models of human functioning may, at times, interfere with an ability to see forms of psychological distress and suffering. One of the clearest examples is the diagnosis of depression in youth. Although the problem of depression in adults has been recognized for centuries, until the 1980s mental health professionals did not evaluate or treat childhood depression. The major reason for this apparent negligence is that, based on tenets of the dominant theoretical models, childhood depression could not occur. According to psychoanalytic models, depression is a disorder of the superego. It is therefore impossible to develop depression until the stage of development at which the superego emerges. Prior to this stage, a child's psyche is not sufficiently developed to use the types of defences that result in the experience of depression. Application of behavioural models developed on adults also made it impossible to detect depression in children. A primary symptom of adult depression is sadness. However, children express both happiness and sadness in different ways from adults. A very young child may laugh out loud, expressing spontaneous pleasure, or may sing, or skip exuberantly. Such overt expressions of pleasure are unusual in adults. Adults may express sadness verbally, whereas children are more likely to express disinterest or boredom.

Defining Disorder

The *Diagnostic and Statistical Manual of Mental Disorders,* fifth edition (DSM-5; American Psychiatric Association, 2013) defines a mental disorder in the following manner:

> *A mental disorder is a syndrome characterized by clinically significant disturbance in an individual's cognition, emotion regulation, or behavior that reflects a dysfunction in the psychological, biological, or developmental processes underlying mental functioning. Mental disorders are usually associated with significant distress or disability in social, occupational, or other important activities. An expectable or culturally approved response to a common stressor or loss, such as the death of a loved one, is not a mental disorder. Socially deviant behavior (e.g., political, religious, or sexual) and conflicts that are primarily between the individual and society are not mental disorders unless the deviance or conflict results from a dysfunction in the individual, as described above.*
>
> *American Psychiatric Association (2013, p. 20)*

This definition covers both what is and is not a mental disorder. It is intended to underlie any diagnosis formulated and/or communicated by a mental health professional using the DSM-5 classification system.

Thus, the diagnosis of a disorder does not just require the co-occurrence of a set of statistically rare symptoms or behaviours; it also requires that there is something wrong or dysfunctional and that this dysfunction causes harm to the individual or to those around him or her, a concept that was originally referred to as **harmful dysfunction** (Wakefield, 1992). In other words, some form of pathology is evident and this pathology causes impairment. The requirement that both conditions be satisfied is critical, as it is relatively common to have some form of pathology without it necessarily resulting in impairment. For example, a fear of heights that does not restrict a person's usual daily activities would not constitute a harmful dysfunction.

harmful dysfunction: the behaviours associated with a mental disorder are dysfunctional and the dysfunction causes harm to the individual or to those around him or her.

Terms such as *dysfunctional* and *harmful* are, of course, value-laden, but as we presented in the section on developmental psychopathology, research evidence can be used, at least partially, to operationalize these concepts. Widiger (Widiger, 2004; Widiger & Sankis, 2000) has suggested that the concept of **dyscontrol** should be part of the definition of mental disorder. That is, the resulting impairment must be involuntary or, at least, not readily controlled. This addition is important, especially in legal contexts, because it means that someone who intentionally and willfully engages in unacceptable behaviour such as sexually abusing a

dyscontrol: the impairment resulting from a disorder must be involuntary or not readily controlled.

child or shooting participants at a summer camp would not be considered to have a mental disorder. Dyscontrol, however, is also a value-laden term that is difficult to operationalize. After all, how can you accurately determine whether another person is unable to control a behaviour or is simply choosing not to control the behaviour? To give you a sense of the work of clinical psychologists that contributes to the understanding and treatment of people with schizophrenia, Profile Box 3.1 introduces you to Dr. Christopher Bowie.

PROFILE BOX 3.1

DR. CHRISTOPHER BOWIE

Courtesy of Christopher Bowie

I received my graduate training in clinical psychology and neuropsychology at Hofstra University and Mount Sinai School of Medicine. My mentors, Drs. Mark Serper and Philip Harvey, specialize in the assessment and treatment of schizophrenia, arguably the most severe mental illness. I followed this education with a postdoctoral fellowship at Hillside Hospital with Dr. Barbara Cornblatt, who leads one of the most successful centres for the study of the risk for schizophrenia. My education and training occurred simultaneously at a university psychology department and hospital psychiatry department. This allowed me access to some of the most clinically interesting experiences I could imagine. I am currently an associate professor at Queen's University, where I direct a laboratory studying schizophrenia. I am also the head consulting psychologist for an early-intervention-for-psychosis program.

HOW DID YOU CHOOSE TO BECOME A CLINICAL PSYCHOLOGIST?

After two years studying business and finance as an undergraduate, I switched my major to psychology following two seemingly different classes: abnormal psychology and perception. My professors shared a passion for the science of psychology. Perhaps more importantly, they opened the window for me into what the life of a psychologist is like in an academic and hospital setting. I was drawn to the concept of academic freedom, the scientific search for answers to complicated questions about disabling illnesses, and the ability to redefine each workday.

WHAT IS THE GREATEST CHALLENGE YOU FACE AS A CLINICAL PSYCHOLOGIST?

Traditionally, we think of clinical psychologists having a role in treating a wide range of mental disorders, but the reality is that many of the more severely ill individuals, perhaps those who stand to benefit the most from our services, are often considered to be "psychiatric" patients. This distinction is important, because for several decades it has guided the way treatments have been offered and has meant that patients were offered psychopharmacological rather than psychotherapeutic interventions. The hallucinations and delusions that those with schizophrenia often experience are the most striking symptoms, and these respond well to medications. However, these symptoms alone actually explain very little of the breadth and depth of problems functioning in everyday life. As a clinical psychologist, I have been able to use the tools of our profession to more

CONTINUED . . .

carefully examine the core of the illness and develop treatments aimed at these symptoms. Thus, the goal of my work is balanced more on the improvement of functioning than on the reduction of symptoms.

TELL US ABOUT YOUR RESEARCH ON SEVERE MENTAL ILLNESS

My research program at Queen's University investigates neurocognitive abilities and their relationship to everyday functional outcomes in people with schizophrenia. Many individuals with schizophrenia have a favourable clinical response when taking medications, but they continue to struggle with living skills like going to work, socializing, and living independently. Neurocognitive impairments are present well before the person who would later be diagnosed with schizophrenia even experiences psychosis. Their early and lifelong presence make it difficult for those with schizophrenia to attend to, learn, remember, sequence, and generalize the wide range of skills that are typically acquired during adolescence and early adulthood. Schizophrenia-associated neurocognitive impairments interrupt the acquisition of these critical developmental skills early in life and continuously throughout adulthood. This makes living independently, working, and socializing a challenge for many people with schizophrenia. My work has identified neurocognitive impairments as a key reason why many people with schizophrenia experience difficulties in these many domains of functioning. Building on my correlational research, I have more recently examined the effects of a psychological treatment called cognitive remediation. Thus, unlike brain injury, where we are hoping to *rehabilitate* skills that were lost, in schizophrenia we have to consider more of a *habilitative* approach, to help people acquire the skills that they never fully developed. My recent data suggest that cognitive remediation works very well in promoting gains in everyday living skills and behaviours, but these results are more likely to be meaningful and durable if cognitive remediation is paired with an explicit component that teaches these skills. Interestingly, teaching these skills is much less effective without also offering cognitive remediation.

HOW DO YOU INTEGRATE SCIENCE AND PRACTICE IN YOUR WORK?

Without carefully studying the etiological factors and functional relationships of neurocognition, staging effective clinical treatments is impossible. Our years of examining the core features of cognitive impairment, and how these deficits relate to different areas of functioning, has led to the development of new treatments. In my clinical work with those who have early psychosis, we continuously monitor treatment outcomes and collect a wide range of baseline and treatment engagement variables to determine who is recovering, at what pace, on which abilities.

WHAT DO YOU SEE AS THE MOST EXCITING CHANGES IN THE FIELD OF CLINICAL PSYCHOLOGY?

It is by treating the hyphen in the scientist-practitioner link as a unifying rather than dividing symbol that we can make substantial contributions to the quality of life for those with mental disorders. To me, the re-emergence of psychology in the study and treatment of schizophrenia and related conditions is a very exciting phenomenon. Clinical psychology's historical contributions when many of those with the condition were living in institutional settings were important, but now that those with schizophrenia are living in the community, our field has more opportunities to help understand and treat the condition using more of our clinical tools than ever. A major challenge going forward is convincing policy-makers that there is value in short-term clinical care cost in the long-term plan to reduce disability.

Prevalence of Mental Disorders

So, just how common are mental disorders? You may recall learning in Chapter 1 of the Statistics Canada survey (2003) of the mental health and well-being of Canadians aged 15 years and older which found that 1 out of every 10 Canadian adolescents and adults reported symptoms consistent with a diagnosis of a mental disorder such as alcohol or illicit drug dependence, a mood disorder (major depressive disorder or bipolar disorder), or a serious anxiety disorder (social phobia, panic disorder, or panic disorder with agoraphobia).

What is the role of basic research in psychology in informing the diagnosis of mental disorders? How can we make sense out of differing prevalence rates of mental disorders among countries?

How does that rate compare with the rates in other countries? Using diagnostic criteria from DSM-IV (the predecessor to DSM-5) for anxiety disorders, mood disorders, impulse control disorders (such as bulimia and attention-deficit/hyperactivity disorder) and substance abuse disorders, the World Health Organization (WHO) Mental Health Survey Consortium (2004) surveyed people 18 years of age and older in 14 countries: Colombia, Mexico, and the United States (the Americas); Belgium, France, Germany, Italy, the Netherlands, Spain, and Ukraine (Europe); Lebanon (the Middle East); Nigeria (Africa); and Japan and China (Asia). All survey interviews were conducted in person by trained interviewers. To ensure the comparability of data obtained from all countries, the WHO Consortium used standardized interviewer training procedures, WHO translation protocols, and numerous quality control procedures. Sample sizes ranged from approximately 1,700 participants in Japan to almost 9,300 participants in the United States. Twelve-month prevalence data (i.e., the percentage of people in a year who met diagnostic criteria) from this massive survey are presented in Table 3.1.

You will notice that the Statistics Canada survey had a broader age range (15 and older, versus 18 and older), whereas the World Health Organization data used broader definitions of disorder. As you can see in the table, overall prevalence rates varied greatly from country to country, ranging from 4.3% in Shanghai to 26.4% in the United States. In all but one country (Ukraine), anxiety disorders were the most common mental disorder, with mood disorders being the next most common set of mental disorders. It is interesting to note that the six countries included in the surveys that are classified by the World Bank as having lower per capita income (China, Colombia, Lebanon, Mexico, Nigeria, and Ukraine) had some of the lowest and highest total prevalence rates. The authors of the report recognized that the failure to include schizophrenia in the surveys was problematic. They argued, however, that previous research has shown that many people diagnosed with schizophrenia would also receive a diagnosis that was included in the surveys. Therefore, the authors believed that the overall picture

TABLE 3.1 ■ Prevalence of Selected Mental Disorders

Country	Anxiety	Mood	Impulse-Control	Substance Abuse	Any Disorder
Colombia	10.0%	6.8%	3.9%	2.8%	17.8%
Mexico	6.8%	4.8%	1.3%	2.5%	12.2%
United States	18.2%	9.6%	6.8%	3.8%	26.4%
Belgium	6.9%	6.2%	1.0%	1.2%	12.0%
France	12.0%	8.5%	1.4%	0.7%	18.4%
Germany	6.2%	3.6%	0.3%	1.1%	9.1%
Italy	5.8%	3.8%	0.3%	0.1%	8.2%
Netherlands	8.8%	6.9%	1.3%	3.0%	14.9%
Spain	5.9%	4.9%	0.5%	0.3%	9.2%
Ukraine	7.1%	9.1%	3.2%	6.4%	20.5%
Lebanon	11.2%	0.8%	1.7%	1.3%	16.9%
Nigeria	3.3%	0.8%	—	0.8%	4.7%
Japan	5.3%	3.1%	1.0%	1.7%	8.8%
China-Beijing	3.2%	2.5%	2.6%	2.6%	9.1%
China-Shanghai	2.4%	1.7%	0.7%	0.5%	4.3%

Adapted from the World Health Organization Mental Health Survey Consortium (2004).

of the worldwide prevalence of people meeting criteria for at least one mental disorder is accurate.

Other studies have presented even higher estimates for the prevalence of mental disorders. Wittchen et al. (2011) reviewed the literature on mental disorder prevalence in the member states of the European Union (plus Switzerland, Norway, and Iceland) and re-analyzed existing data sets based on population samples from these countries. Unlike the previous studies we described, Wittchen et al.'s research included data on all mental disorders, including neurological disorders, and on all age groups. As a result, they estimated that each year approximately 38% of the European Union population suffers from a mental disorder and/or neurological disorder. The most frequently occurring mental disorders were anxiety disorders, insomnia, depression, somatoform disorders, and alcohol and drug dependence. Based on disability data, the most disabling disorders were depression, dementias, alcohol use disorders, and stroke.

In addition to collecting prevalence data, the WHO Mental Health survey also collected data on the disability and treatment of mental and physical disorders (Ormel et al., 2008). The results from the survey may surprise you. Across countries, mental disorders were viewed as being more disabling than physical disorders such as chronic pain, heart disease, cancer, and diabetes. The disabilities associated with mental disorders were seen as especially elevated in the spheres of social and personal relationships. At the time of the interview, survey participants with mental disorders were much less likely to be receiving treatment for their disorders than were those with physical disorders, and this was especially true for lower-income countries. Specifically, in higher-income countries, 65% of all physical disorders were treated, compared with 24% of mental disorders. For lower income countries, treatment rates were 53% for all physical disorders and 8% for mental disorders.

Knowing that millions of people worldwide suffer from mental disorders and that these disorders cause substantial disability is important, but it is also necessary to be able to imagine what life is like for an individual who suffers from a mental disorder. To provide you with a greater appreciation of what mental disorders are like, we have included cases describing two people—Noah, an adolescent, and Melissa, an adult—who were referred to us for the treatment of anxiety symptoms. The cases we present in the book are based on our clinical practice. Whenever we present an example of a person suffering from a mental disorder, we have taken care to conceal the person's identity by changing their names and some parts of the background information. You will learn more about the services Noah and Melissa received in later chapters, when we focus on assessment and intervention.

case example **NOAH**

Noah is a 13-year-old boy whose family left his country of origin when he was 10. He was referred for psychological services to address symptoms of anxiety, hypervigilance, and sleep disturbance. According to his mother, Noah was a normal child whose birth and early childhood were unremarkable. However, when Noah was 3 years old, his country suffered extreme strife and conflict that culminated in ethnic cleansing. Noah, his mother, and twin sister were separated from his father and learned only months later that the father had been brutally killed. Following the loss of his father, repeated exposure to mob violence, and months of sheltering from continued threat of death, Noah displayed behaviour that is found in some very young children's response to trauma—he withdrew from the world and became mute. Although he has made remarkable progress and in many ways has a normal life, to this day Noah continues to re-experience images of the scene in which the family was fleeing for their lives, the small children clinging to their parents. In addition, he re-experiences images of corpses, blood, and body parts, drawn not only from direct experience, but also from personal accounts he has heard and media images he has seen.

As his mother attempted to rebuild the family life following such horrific loss and exposure to violence, Noah sought reassurance by clinging to two attachment figures: his mother and his twin sister. The availability of these two people to provide comfort and reassurance enabled him to gradually venture into the world by attending school. During this time, as safety was slowly re-established, Noah was surrounded by evidence of the genocide. All the adults in his life had experienced terror and loss. The fragile equilibrium that had been achieved by the time he was 9 years old was shattered when the family was exposed to renewed threats of death unless they dropped charges against those accused of killing Noah's father.

In contrast to the experience at the age of 3, when he was too young to cognitively understand what was happening and could respond only on an emotional level, at the age of 9 Noah was intellectually mature enough to understand that his family could be harmed. He was terrified at the possibility of unprovoked attacks and at the risk of dying or losing yet another family member.

Since leaving his country of origin, Noah has begun the process of rebuilding his life. He attends school and has friends with whom he enjoys spending time. He is a keen soccer player. Although he and his twin no longer cling to one another, they are very important to one another. Nevertheless, Noah continues to be haunted by his experiences. Images of the violence disturb his sleep. He is fearful at night, unwilling to sleep alone, and troubled that noises are of intruders coming to murder the family. Battle scenes in movies evoke memories and a panic response. Noah is troubled by talk about the genocide experiences, covering his ears and yelling at his mother to stop talking about it. Noah experiences somatic symptoms of anxiety including pounding heart and dizziness. This symptom profile is consistent with a diagnosis of post-traumatic stress disorder. In addition to experiencing unusual symptoms, Noah shows clear evidence of harmful dysfunction: the symptoms get in the way of him enjoying all the regular experiences of a teenager, they interfere with his sleep, and they are distressing to him. Despite his best efforts and that of his family, Noah is unable to control these symptoms.

Noah's current adjustment is a testament to his mother's resolute determination to create security for her children. He has benefited from the secure life he experienced prior to the genocide, by his mother's steadfast efforts to create a normal life, and by the availability of a twin sister. However, he was exposed not to a single life-threatening experience, but to sustained life-threatening experiences over a prolonged period. Nothing will erase the memories and psychological scars of his early childhood trauma. Toward the end of the book, we will discuss evidence-based psychological services that could reduce symptom severity, so that Noah will be able to function without daily, debilitating anxiety.

case example **MELISSA**

Melissa is a married 27-year-old mother with a 6-month-old baby, Evan. Melissa was referred for psychological services by her family physician due to intrusive worries and repeated checking behaviours. Melissa had a regular childhood in a loving family. She describes herself as always having been a worried person, but as never previously having sought psychological services. Her husband, Erik, is a successful executive in an information technology company. The couple lives in a pleasant suburb and enjoys an above-average income. They attend social activities associated with Erik's work. In addition, Melissa attends a mother and baby group with other young mothers whom she met in prenatal classes. Melissa reports that in recent years she has been increasingly preoccupied with worries about making mistakes that might harm other people. She first became aware of these worries in her role as a nurse. Having been proud of her profession for several years, Melissa became preoccupied with worries that she might make an error in dispensing medication and that one of the people in her care would be harmed by her actions. As her worries increased, she became progressively more distressed at the potential harm she might cause, and devoted more and more time to checking that she was not making errors. She finally dealt with her stress by quitting her job when she became pregnant with her first child.

Even though Melissa eliminated her work stress, she continued to feel worried. She is particularly troubled by fears when driving that she has inadvertently knocked over a pedestrian or a cyclist. These thoughts are triggered whenever she hits a bump in the road or if she has momentarily lost concentration during her driving. When Melissa has such thoughts, she imagines the victim lying injured in the road, so she circles back looking for him or her. She has a tendency to stop the car and examine the pavement for signs of blood. She may ask passersby if they witnessed an accident or if they have seen an injured person limping away. Only when she has circled the area many times without discovering evidence of an accident is she able to continue. Episodes of checking delay most journeys, including grocery shopping, trips out with the baby, and picking Erik up from work. Even after she has searched for evidence, Melissa is vigilant in listening to the radio and watching television to check for reports of a hit-and-run accident. She also quizzes people she knows about whether they have heard about an accident.

As well, Melissa worries that she may accidentally harm her baby. Cleaning the house poses a special challenge, as she becomes distressed at thoughts she may have spilled a household cleaning product near the baby. She responds to these worries by changing the baby's clothes and washing the area in which the baby is located. The cleaning routines required to reassure her that the baby has not been contaminated with a toxic product can take several hours.

Melissa recognizes that these worries are unusual. She believes her thoughts are excessive and that her checking is out of proportion to the likelihood she has actually caused any harm. She is embarrassed by her symptoms and worries that other people will think she is crazy. She is grateful to Erik for tolerating her extreme thoughts and behaviours. Melissa's symptom profile is consistent with a diagnosis of obsessive compulsive disorder.

Even though Melissa recognizes that these thoughts and behaviours are out of proportion to the likelihood that she has harmed anyone, she is unable to control them. Her husband's attempts at reassurance and reasoning have also met with failure. Despite his desire to be loyal and supportive, Erik is frustrated at Melissa's odd behaviours. Her need for reassurance is emotionally draining and he is embarrassed to think his wife may be crazy. In the assessment chapters, we will present tools that can be used to assess the extent of Melissa's problems and describe the process of assessing her difficulties.

Understanding the Development of Mental Disorders

Modern theories of the etiology of mental disorders are all based on a biopsychosocial model. Although theories vary in the emphasis they give to different factors within the general biopsychosocial model (e.g., some biological theories emphasize genetic elements, whereas most psychological theories tend to emphasize cognitive, developmental, and interpersonal elements), there is a consensus among psychopathology researchers that the presence of a mental disorder is determined by a blend of biological, psychological, and social factors (e.g., Kendler, 2008). Of course, the precise contribution of each of the three factors is likely to vary from disorder to disorder. The contribution of these factors may also change over the course of life: for example, in a longitudinal study of common fears, the impact of genetic factors that influenced fear intensity during childhood tended to diminish over time, whereas the impact of life experiences increased over time (Kendler et al., 2008).

What are the advantages and disadvantages for a young person such as Noah of receiving a diagnosis of a mental disorder?

In keeping with our emphasis on the need for empirical evidence in evaluating theories and services, we move now to consider some of the research on the development of abnormal behaviour. We have space to highlight only a few of the most important issues in the emergence of psychological disorders from the huge scientific literature on this subject.

Research by Turner and Lloyd (2004) illustrates how the build-up of life stress places people at risk for developing a disorder. In interviews with more than 1,800 young American adults (aged 18–23 years), the researchers asked about a wide range of major stressful experiences, such as parental unemployment, being abandoned by one or both parents, life-threatening illness, forced sexual intercourse, being shot at with a gun, witnessing someone being seriously injured or killed, being in a serious car crash, and experiencing physical abuse from a dating partner. Some, but not all, of the experiences they asked about are potentially traumatic. In addition, they asked questions about both current psychological symptoms and lifetime experience of diagnosable disorder. The researchers' goal was to examine the links between stress and first episodes (i.e., the first occurrence of a diagnosable condition) of anxiety and depressive disorders. Of the 33 stressors they examined, 26 were associated with significantly increased risk of subsequently developing an anxiety or mood disorder. Across gender and ethnicity (Hispanic American, African American, and non-Hispanic white American), the odds of developing a disorder increased with the number of stressors experienced.

A second example, using an interpersonal stress model, comes from a study by Hammen, Shih, and Brennan (2004) that examined the complex intergenerational transmission of depression among approximately 800 Australian adolescents and their mothers. The researchers found that depression in maternal grandmothers predicted maternal depression and interpersonal stress. The maternal depression, in turn, influenced the mothers' interpersonal stress and the development of their children's social competence. The interpersonal stress experienced by the mothers also contributed to the children's interpersonal stress and to their children's depression. The final piece of the stress/disorder chain was that the poor social competence and high interpersonal stress in the children predicted their own development of depressive symptoms.

©iStock.com/Marina_Ph

Natural disasters are associated with increases in anxiety disorders and in posttraumatic stress disorder (PTSD).

Although life stress is clearly implicated in the development of many disorders, not all people exposed to major stressors develop a disorder and, if disorders do develop, they do not do so at the same time or rate for all people. As you will see in Viewpoint Box 3.1, the majority of tsunami and hurricane victims do not meet criteria for diagnosis of a mental disorder despite having experienced tremendous loss and devastation. It is relatively easy to understand how a natural disaster can provoke debilitating psychological symptoms—most of us can imagine that we would feel distraught if we were to witness the sudden death of many loved ones and the loss of our homes. It is equally important to try to understand the variables that enable some people to survive trauma without developing a psychological disorder.

VIEWPOINT BOX 3.1

PSYCHOLOGICAL RESPONSES TO NATURAL DISASTERS

Natural disasters such as tornados, floods, hurricanes, and earthquakes strike with little warning and can result in enormous devastation and loss of life. Each year, many thousands of people experience such disasters and, in this Viewpoint Box, we examine the psychological effects that can accompany these tragic events. Whether they occur in less developed countries or in highly developed countries, disasters have the potential to adversely affect the well-being of numerous individuals, often for many months and years after the disaster. Long after homes have been rebuilt and life has returned to some semblance of normality, the psychological scars will remain for some people.

In December 2004, a massive tsunami devastated parts of East Africa and South Asia. The island country of Sri Lanka was particularly affected, with over 31,000 deaths, over 23,000 people injured, and over half a million people displaced by the devastation. The scope of the disaster in southern Sri Lanka was almost unimaginable: people lost family members and friends; whole villages and towns were destroyed; many people's livelihoods were swept away by the disaster; and much of the infrastructure supporting daily life activities, including transportation and communication systems, were wiped out in the region. Initial studies of the disaster's psychological impact indicated that approximately 40% of youth and 20% of their parents experienced post-traumatic stress disorder (PTSD) four months after the tsunami (Wickrama & Kaspar, 2007). Studies from other countries in the affected regions also found high rates of PTSD as a result of the disaster.

A little over a year and a half after the tsunami, researchers conducted a thorough survey of one severely affected region in Sri Lanka to determine the prevalence of psychological symptoms and disorders. Using questionnaires adapted for use in the region, Hollifield et al. (2008) interviewed 89 adults by approaching one-third of the 223 inhabited homes in one town. Among their sample, 51% lost family members in the tsunami, 80% lost friends, and 75% had extensive damage to their property and belongings. One-quarter of respondents had moderate to severe PTSD symptoms, 16% had clinically elevated depression symptoms, and 30% had clinically elevated anxiety symptoms. Taken together, the researchers estimated that 40% of those interviewed were experiencing mental disorders many months after the tsunami.

In August 2005, Hurricane Katrina formed in the Atlantic Ocean. After striking the Bahamas and Florida, it crossed over the Gulf of Mexico, gaining strength as it progressed. The Category 5 hurricane ripped into several states, with its strongest effects felt in Alabama, Louisiana, and Mississippi. As a result of the hurricane and the associated storm surge, over 1,800 people died, more than half a million people were displaced, and over $100 billion in damages occurred. It was the worst natural disaster in the United States for many decades. Galea et al. (2007) surveyed over 1,000 adults

CONTINUED . . .

living in the affected areas in Alabama, Louisiana, and Mississippi. Several months after the hurricane passed, over a quarter of these people met criteria for an anxiety or mood disorder and 12.5% met criteria for PTSD. Among the residents of New Orleans, a city devastated by the hurricane and the breaching of levees, the rate of mental disorders was much higher. Almost 50% met criteria for an anxiety or mood disorder and 30% met criteria for PTSD. The researchers speculated that the slow government response to the disaster served to exacerbate the stress experienced by respondents, and thus negatively affected the mental health of the people who lived through Hurricane Katrina. Researchers also found that people with pre-existing mental disorders were particularly vulnerable to the negative mental health effects of the disaster. In their sample of 499 veterans, Sullivan et al. (2013) reported that the likelihood of meeting diagnostic criteria for any new mental disorder on a screening instrument was 6.8 times greater for those with a pre-existing mental disorder compared with those without a pre-existing disorder. The odds of screening positive for a new mental disorder were particularly elevated for individuals with pre-existing PTSD.

Another survey of adults who survived Katrina adds an important element to our understanding of the effects of natural disasters. Wang et al. (2008) interviewed over 1,000 adults about mental health needs and mental health treatments in the aftermath of Katrina. Because of disruptions caused by the hurricane, almost one-quarter of individuals who had been receiving mental health services prior to Katrina experienced a reduction in, or termination of, services following Katrina. Among adults who developed a mental disorder as a result of the disaster, fewer than 20% received any type of mental health treatment and, of those who did receive treatment, almost two-thirds received medication without any form of psychological treatment. As a result of their findings, the researchers recommended that disaster management plans should be designed to address both the widespread failure to initiate needed mental health treatment and the disruptions that occur to existing mental health services.

Etiological research also explores individual differences in the emergence of psychological disorders. This requires the longitudinal study of large numbers of people and the use of sophisticated statistical analyses. A fascinating example of such research is a study by Cole et al. (2002) in which 12 waves of data were collected (Grades 4 to 11) from 1,570 American children/adolescents and their parents. The study was designed to investigate normative developmental shifts in the rate at which depressive symptoms emerge. The researchers found that the rate at which depressive symptoms occurred in children and adolescents was not consistent over the course of their development. Data from both parents and children indicated that there was a significant increase in the rate of depressive symptoms between Grades 6 and 7. The average rate of change before this period and after this period was relatively stable, suggesting that there are destabilizing factors influencing child development and the subsequent experience of depressive symptoms in late childhood/early adolescence. Also worth noting was that the symptoms of depression increased much more rapidly for girls than for boys, starting at the period between

Grades 5 and 7. Based on these data, researchers interested in examining the initial development and maintenance of depression can now focus on the critical time period identified by Cole and colleagues to more closely investigate factors implicated in the emergence (and non-emergence) of depression.

Using data from the Baltimore Longitudinal Study of Aging which began in 1958, Sutin et al. (in press) used data from over 2,300 participants to estimate the trajectory of depressive symptoms across the adult lifespan. They found that depressive symptoms were highest in young adulthood, decreased during middle adulthood, and then increased in older adulthood. Longitudinal studies can also inform us about what happens to people following the development of a depressive episode. Eaton et al. (2008) collected data on almost 3,500 American adults in 1981 and then obtained follow-up data 23 years later. Of most interest were the 92 people who had their first episode of diagnosable depression during the course of the follow-up. Fully 15% of these 92 adults did not have a single year free of depressive episodes following their initial episode. In contrast, approximately 50% of people who experienced a first episode of depression recovered and had no subsequent episodes of depression. These findings are like the proverbial glass of water that is half full: the good news is that half of people who experience depression are unlikely to have a recurrence. The bad news is that half of people who experience depression will have recurrent depression, with some of these individuals experiencing depression that is virtually unremitting. The challenge for researchers, of course, is to try to determine the factors that discriminate between the individuals who comprise the "good news" and "bad news" groups.

A final line of etiological research we'd like to illustrate deals with the importance of having solid normative data on what constitutes typical distress and problem behaviours. All children, adolescents, and adults have occasional psychological challenges and difficulties, but just how many of these problems is it normal to have? Bongers, Koot, van der Ende, and Verhulst (2003) examined this question using parent-reported data from the Child Behavior Checklist for a representative sample of more than 2,000 Dutch children. The sample was recruited through municipal registers and data were collected over a 10-year period at 2-year intervals. The researchers examined normal levels of such problems as anxiety, somatic complaints, aggressive behaviour, attention problems, and social problems. Results from this study provide psychologists with valuable normative data for each year between the ages of 4 and 18 (for girls and boys separately). For example, a clinical psychologist providing services to a family can

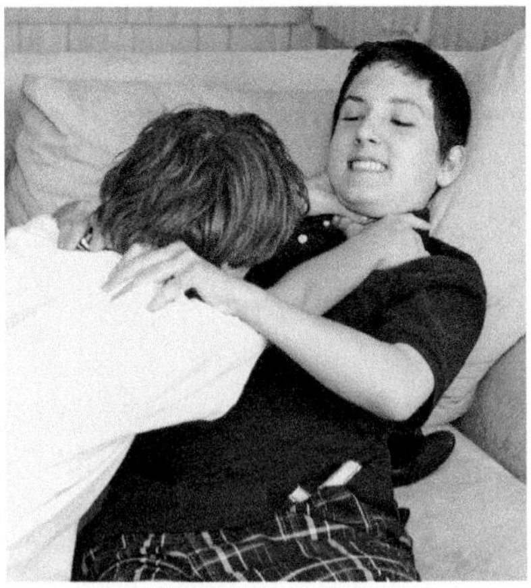

Shutterstock/Lisa F. Young

Normative data help us to determine the need for services.

determine whether the level of a child's aggressive behaviour reported by a parent is comparable to, or much greater than, what is normally expected for a child of that age and gender. This information, in turn, is likely to influence the nature of the information and services offered to the family.

THE *DIAGNOSTIC AND STATISTICAL MANUAL OF MENTAL DISORDERS* (DSM) SYSTEM

In the following sections, we describe the DSM system, the diagnostic system that has long been used by many North American mental health professionals, including clinical psychologists. We begin by considering the historical context for the development of the current diagnostic system DSM-5 and then describe the main features of the DSM-5. Following this, we move on to consider the *International Statistical Classification of Diseases and Related Health Problems* (ICD) system, which is the internationally used diagnostic system for mental disorders and the main alternative to the DSM.

The Evolution of the DSM

Each edition of the DSM reflects the status of diagnosis at the time of its publication. The first edition of the DSM published by the American Psychiatric Association in 1952 heavily emphasized psychodynamic etiological factors for the majority of the disorders and provided only vague diagnostic descriptions. The shortcomings of the original DSM did not have a significant impact on services, as only one form of treatment—psychoanalysis—was available (Shea, 1991). By the time of the publication of the second edition in 1968, new treatment options were becoming available (including drug treatments), and psychiatric researchers were increasingly examining biological and neurological aspects of mental disorders. As a result, in the second edition, the psychodynamic orientation was less prominent and there was greater precision in terminology (Shea, 1991).

The third edition of the DSM, published in 1980, marked a dramatic departure from the first two editions. Under the guidance of the task force chair, Robert Spitzer, enormous effort was devoted to improving the organization and classification of mental disorders. This was evident in many different ways. First, the manual was explicitly atheoretical, which allowed for the possibility of greater acceptance within the mental health field and for the introduction of concrete behavioural descriptions of most disorders. Second, the diagnostic criteria were much more explicit than they were previously, with lists of symptoms provided for each diagnosis. Third, as a significant part of the effort to improve upon the reliability of psychiatric diagnoses, thousands of patients and hundreds of clinicians were involved in field trials of the diagnostic system. These ambitious changes demonstrated greater attention to the scientific literature and to scientific classification principles. Advances in the burgeoning psychopathology literature were reflected in an update of the DSM-III published in 1987.

Given the widespread acceptance of DSM-III and its revision, DSM-III-R, great efforts were made in the preparation of the DSM-IV, which was published in 1994. Work groups composed of research experts and clinicians in the field were established for each major class of mental disorders. Exhaustive literature reviews were conducted and proposals were developed for diagnostic criteria. Liaisons were established with scores of mental health and professional organizations, both within the United States and internationally. The resulting manual was developed in a far more collaborative and scientifically informed manner than were any of the preceding editions of the DSM. The DSM-IV-Text Revision, published in 2000, corrected errors identified in the DSM-IV text, updated the scientific information about disorders, and enhanced its educational value. The text revision did not, however, include changes in the criteria used to diagnose a disorder or changes in the listing of disorders.

Beginning in 1999, the groundwork for DSM-5 began at a planning conference that established research priorities for developing the new diagnostic manual. In subsequent years, research plans were formalized, position papers on issues related to psychiatric classification were commissioned, international consultations were undertaken with the World Health Organization and the World Psychiatric Association, and a number of conferences were held that focused on specific diagnostic categories or issues. By 2008, the membership of the working groups for each diagnostic category within the overall DSM-5 task force was set. Subsequently, these working groups finalized the information and criteria for each diagnostic category, reviewed data on the field testing of the diagnostic criteria, and solicited feedback from multiple stakeholders. The American Psychiatric Association released the DSM-5 at its annual convention in 2013. Although most new DSM editions have sparked controversy in the mental health field, there was unparalleled criticism levelled at the DSM-5 and the process underlying its development. We describe some of these issues in Viewpoint Box 3.2.

VIEWPOINT BOX 3.2

THE TRIALS AND TRIBULATIONS OF DSM-5

Long before the release of DSM-5, a host of criticism was directed at both the process of developing the classification system and at some of the new content. The revision of a classification system is an enormous task requiring extraordinary efforts from numerous knowledgeable and committed experts. Nevertheless, it is an enterprise fraught with potential problems, for well-intentioned plans can easily go awry during committee deliberations on how to interpret scientific evidence and translate that evidence into meaningful diagnostic criteria and disorder classification. Since the work on DSM-III, each DSM edition has faced considerable public and professional scrutiny, with many concerns raised about the validity of mental health diagnoses and the impact of these diagnoses on the lives of millions of people. Nevertheless, the level of discontent, disappointment, and outrage provoked by the DSM-5 development process is unprecedented.

Early in the development of DSM-5, Dr. Robert Spitzer, the psychiatrist who chaired the DSM-III task force, raised a number of concerns. In a series of commentaries, open letters, and emails to professional association listservs, he expressed grave reservations about the lack of transparency in the development process. Examples he provided included the inability of professionals to obtain minutes of DSM-5 task force meetings and the requirement that members of the DSM-5 task force sign confidentiality agreements forbidding them from releasing information about any materials or discussions that were part of the development process. Subsequently, Dr. Allen Frances, the psychiatrist who chaired the DSM-IV task force, joined with Spitzer in expressing concerns about the apparent "growth" in new disorders planned for inclusion in the DSM-5. In numerous articles, editorials, commentaries, and blogs, Frances highlighted flaws in the rationales used to support the expansion of what constitutes a mental disorder and argued against applying psychiatric labels to everyday problems and challenges in life. In books intended for professional (Frances, 2013a) and public (Frances, 2013b) audiences, he set out his views about problems with the DSM-5 and how "diagnostic inflation" might affect many individuals seeking professional help with normal reactions to common events and stressors.

Adding to criticism from those responsible for the previous two major editions of the DSM, many other individuals and associations voiced reservations about the planned DSM. Some of these objections were based on opposition to the principle of mental health diagnosis. Many were reactions to the content of documents in which the task force sought feedback on their plans for various aspects of the new DSM. Concern was also expressed about the over-representation of medical/biological views on mental disorders and their treatment, with 70% of the members of the DSM task force having a financial association with pharmaceutical companies (Collier, 2010). Taken together, these concerns led to the publication of an open letter about proposals for the DSM-5 (www.ipetitions.com/petition/dsm5). Signatories to this letter included several divisions of the American Psychological Association (including the Division of Clinical Psychology), the British Psychological Society, the American Family Therapy Association, and the Society for Personality Assessment. Subsequently, some members of the personality disorders work group resigned because they considered that proposals for altering the diagnosis of personality disorders were inconsistent with the scientific evidence (Gornall, 2013). Criticism mounted when Regier et al. (2013) reported initial results of field trials of the new diagnostic system: very poor results were found for the reliability of diagnoses for such common disorders as depression and generalized anxiety disorder, and the reliability among clinicians of diagnosing mixed anxiety-depressive disorder had essentially a no-better-than-chance level of agreement.

CONTINUED . . .

Outcry from public and professional bodies may be ignored. However, two decisions taken by major bodies in the United States have had considerable practical impact on the use of the DSM. The first decision relates to the use of the DSM system for billing purposes. Health care providers covered by the Health Insurance Portability and Accountability Act (HIPAA) are required to use the *International Statistical Classification of Diseases and Related Health Problems* (ICD) system for billing purposes. This means that although DSM-5 provides numerical codes for diagnoses in the ICD system, it is not the system used for diagnosis of patients receiving care under Medicaid and Medicare. The ripple effects from this are likely to mean a reduction in the use of the DSM system for many other patients receiving mental health services. The second decision relates to the use of the DSM in research. In 2013, the director of the National Institute of Mental Health (NIMH), Dr. Thomas Insel, announced that, due to lack of validity data on the DSM system, the NIMH would be encouraging efforts to develop a new diagnostic system for mental disorders based on biological markers for these disorders (Gornall, 2013).

The DSM-5

The DSM-5 is based on a categorical approach to classification. As you learned earlier in the chapter, this means that mental disorders are classified on the basis of specific defining criteria. However, because some disorders may be better represented by dimensional categorization, the classes of disorders were clustered with similar disorders. Using the concepts of internalizing and externalizing disorders that you learned about earlier in the chapter, disorders with anxiety, depressive, and somatic symptoms were grouped together (i.e., internalizing features), as were disorders with impulsive, disruptive conduct, and substance use symptoms (i.e., externalizing features). In addition, the DSM-5 adopts a lifespan approach, listing disorders more frequently diagnosed in childhood at the beginning of the manual, and disorders more frequently diagnosed among older adults at the end of the manual. The DSM-5 task force did not consider the research base adequate to develop dimensional approaches to define classes of disorders.

One of the guiding principles was to maintain continuity with previous editions. Nevertheless, a number of controversial changes in diagnoses and diagnostic criteria were introduced in DSM-5 (including allowing a diagnosis of depression to be made when an individual is bereaved). Other key principles included the need for revisions to the previous edition to be based on scientific evidence and for the manual to be feasible for use by clinicians working in a variety of settings. As you learned in Viewpoint Box 3.2, not everyone agrees that these principles have been met in the DSM-5.

The DSM-5 is more than just a list of classes of disorders and diagnostic criteria. For each mental disorder listed in the manual, there is a wealth of information on diagnostic features; subtypes (if applicable);

associated features and disorders; prevalence; course; familial pattern; differential diagnosis; and specific culture, age, and gender features. These details facilitate a fuller appreciation of what is known about the mental disorder and alert the clinician to important aspects that should be considered during the evaluation of the person. Although it is desirable to have this information, the multi-year cycle between editions cannot keep pace with the emergence of research and, thus, information presented may quickly become outdated or obsolete. Exhibit 3.2 provides a listing of all DSM-5 diagnostic classes.

Exhibit 3.2 DSM-5 Diagnostic Classes

Neurodevelopmental Disorders
Examples: Intellectual Disabilities, Autism Spectrum Disorders, Attention-Deficit/Hyperactivity Disorder
Schizophrenia Spectrum and Other Psychotic Disorders
Examples: Schizophrenia, Delusional Disorder, Schizoaffective Disorder
Bipolar and Related Disorders
Examples: Bipolar I Disorder, Bipolar II Disorder, Cyclothymic Disorder
Depressive Disorders
Examples: Major Depressive Disorder, Dysthymia, Premenstrual Dysphoric Disorder
Anxiety Disorders
Examples: Separation Anxiety Disorder, Panic Disorder, Generalized Anxiety Disorder
Obsessive-Compulsive and Related Disorders
Examples: Obsessive-Compulsive Disorder, Body Dysmorphic Disorder, Hoarding Disorder
Trauma- and Stress-Related Disorders
Examples: Posttraumatic Stress Disorder, Acute Stress Disorder, Adjustment Disorders
Dissociative Disorders
Examples: Dissociative Identity Disorder, Dissociative Amnesia, Depersonalizaton/Derealization Disorder
Somatic Symptom and Related Disorders
Examples: Somatic Symptom Disorder, Illness Anxiety Disorder, Conversion Disorder
Feeding and Eating Disorders
Examples: Pica, Anorexia Nervosa, Bulimia Nervosa
Elimination Disorders
Examples: Enuresis, Encopresis, Other Specified Elimination Disorder
Sleep-Wake Disorders
Examples: Insomnia Disorder, Central Sleep Apnea, Restless Legs Syndrome
Sexual Dysfunctions
Examples: Erectile Disorder, Female Orgasmic Disorder, Male Hypoactive Sexual Desire Disorder
Gender Dysphoria
Examples: Gender Dysphoria in Children, Gender Dysphoria in Adolescents and Adults, Other Specified Gender Dysphoria

CONTINUED . . .

Disruptive, Impulse-Control, and Conduct Disorders
Examples: Conduct Disorder, Antisocial Personality Disorder, Kleptomania
Substance-Related and Addictive Disorders
Examples: Alcohol-Related Disorders, Inhalant-Related Disorders, Tobacco-Related Disorders
Neurocognitive Disorders
Examples: Major and Mild Neurocognitive Disorder Due to Alzheimer's Disease, Major and Mild Neurocognitive Disorder Due to Traumatic Brain Injury, Major and Mild Neurocognitive Disorder Due to Huntington's Disease
Personality Disorders
Examples: Paranoid Personality Disorder, Borderline Personality Disorder, Avoidant Personality Disorder
Paraphilic Disorders
Examples: Exhibitionistic Disorder, Pedophilic Disorder, Transvestic Disorder
Other Mental Disorders
Examples: Other Specified Mental Disorder Due to Another Medical Condition, Other Specified Mental Disorder, Unspecified Mental Disorder
Medication-Induced Movement Disorders and Other Adverse Effects of Medication
Examples: Neuroleptic-Induced Parkinsonism, Medication-Induced Acute Dystonia, Tardive Dyskinesia
Other Conditions That May Be a Focus of Clinical Attention
Examples: Relational Problems, Abuse and Neglect, Education and Occupational Problems

Adapted from *Diagnostic and Statistical Manual of Mental Disorders* (5th ed.) (2013). American Psychiatric Association.

Based on information we presented about Noah, look over Exhibit 3.2 and think about what diagnostic class or classes might contain diagnoses consistent with his symptoms.

In the development of the DSM-5, considerable attention was focused on ethnic and cultural considerations. This is extremely important for the system to be relevant and valid for international use and use in culturally diverse populations within a country. The DSM-5 includes several types of information that enhance the cultural relevance of the diagnostic system. First, when the scientific evidence exists for cultural/ethnic variations in the clinical presentations of a mental disorder, this information is provided in the text accompanying the diagnostic criteria. Second, a limited number of cultural syndromes (often called culture-bound syndromes) are described in an appendix. Examples include *Dhat syndrome* (a syndrome observed in South Asia in which young men attribute their psychological symptoms to semen loss), *malady moun* (a cultural explanation in Haitian communities involving interpersonal conflict viewed as responsible for multiple mental and physical disorders), and *nervios* (a description of distress among Latinos/Latinas in North America that includes a broad range of symptoms including headaches, nervousness, and sleep disturbances). Finally, a section on cultural formulation provides information to assist the clinician in making a culturally sensitive and appropriate diagnosis and overall clinical formulation. This information includes directing attention to the cultural identity of the person being evaluated, cultural explanations for the individual's disorder, cultural factors related to the psychosocial environment and the person's functioning, and cultural aspects of the relationship between the person and the clinician.

THE *INTERNATIONAL STATISTICAL CLASSIFICATION OF DISEASES AND RELATED HEALTH PROBLEMS* (ICD) SYSTEM

The *International Statistical Classification of Diseases and Related Health Problems* (ICD) is the statistical classification of *all* health conditions developed and adopted by the World Health Organization and is now in its 10th edition (ICD-10; WHO, 1992a). A section of the ICD covers mental and behavioural disorders. The ICD is available in 42 languages. The international development and field testing of the classification system ensured relevance across countries and cultural populations. ICD is available online, permitting the system to be updated annually to reflect changes in scientific evidence. There is no cost for access to the ICD.

The way in which the ICD is used varies from country to country. The first use is to provide population level data on different illnesses and causes of death. Many countries modify ICD for use in their health care systems so that it can inform service provision to individual patients. In the United States and some other countries, a clinical modification of the ICD (ICD-CM) provides greater precision about each diagnosis and the person's condition, going beyond the information required for statistical purposes. As of October 2014, the United States Department of Health and Human Services requires the use of the ICD-10-CM version for all billing and reporting purposes.

In broad terms, ICD-10-CM is compatible with DSM-5 and, for each disorder described in DSM-5, ICD-10-CM numerical codes are provided. As Exhibit 3.3 shows, there are some differences in diagnostic classes and specific diagnoses. Differences are also apparent in the way in which some diagnoses are described and conceptualized. For example, the ICD acute stress reaction is defined differently than is the DSM-5 acute stress disorder. In ICD-10 an acute stress reaction is not seen as a potential precursor to PTSD (as it is in DSM-5); a broader, more diffuse set of anxiety and depressive symptoms is presented than in DSM-5, and symptoms resolve within three days—a much shorter course than described in DSM-5. Although ICD-11 (planned for release in 2015) will follow the organizational structure of diagnostic classes used in DSM-5, there will likely continue to be differences between the two systems with respect to the precise diagnostic criteria used for many disorders.

Exhibit 3.3 ICD-10 Diagnostic Classes

Organic, Including Symptomatic, Mental Disorders
Examples: Dementia in Alzheimer's Disease, Dementia in Huntington's Disease, Delirium Not Induced by Alcohol or Other Psychoactive Substances
Mental and Behavioural Disorders Due to Psychoactive Substance Use
Examples: Mental and Behavioural Disorders Due to Use of Alcohol, Mental and Behavioural Disorders Due to Use of Cocaine, Mental and Behavioural Disorders Due to Use of Tobacco
Schizophrenia, Schizotypal, and Delusional Disorders
Examples: Schizophrenia, Schizotypal Disorder, Persistent Delusional Disorders
Mood (Affective) Disorders
Examples: Bipolar Affective Disorder, Depressive Episode, Persistent Mood (Affective) Disorders
Neurotic, Stress-Related, and Somatoform Disorders
Examples: Obsessive-Compulsive Disorder, Post-Traumatic Stress Disorder, Somatoform Disorders
Behavioural Syndromes Associated with Physiological Disturbances and Physical Factors
Examples: Eating Disorders, Nonorganic Sleep Disorders, Sexual Dysfunction Not Caused by Organic Disorder or Disease
Disorders of Adult Personality and Behaviour
Examples: Histrionic Personality Disorder, Pathological Gambling, Gender Identity Disorders
Mental Retardation
Examples: Mild Mental Retardation, Moderate Mental Retardation, Profound Mental Retardation
Disorders of Psychological Development
Examples: Expressive Language Disorder, Specific Reading Disorder, Childhood Autism
Behavioural and Emotional Disorders, with Onset Usually Occurring in Childhood and Adolescence
Examples: Hyperkinetic Disorders, Conduct Disorders, Separation Anxiety Disorder of Childhood

Adapted from the ICD-10 *Classification of Mental and Behavioural Disorders* (1992b). World Health Organization.

The World Health Organization has also developed a companion classification system for the ICD called the *International Classification of Functioning, Disability and Health* (ICF). Moving beyond the classification of disease and illnesses, the ICF provides a system for describing health and health-related conditions. With respect to functioning and disability (i.e., impairments in functioning, activity limitations, or participation restrictions), information is coded for both the person's body (functions of body systems and body structures) and the person's societal involvement (activities and participation). It is also possible to use the ICF to code environmental factors that affect a person's health functioning. The focus on overall functioning and disability, as opposed to just a clinical diagnosis, is particularly important for psychologists working in rehabilitation and pain management services.

LIMITATIONS OF DIAGNOSTIC SYSTEMS

The current process of requiring systematic research reviews, international collaborations, and expert working groups has done much to reduce concerns that science is taking a backseat to professional considerations in the development of diagnostic systems. However, both the DSM-5 and ICD-10 are not without problems. In this section, we will highlight questions that have been raised about the systems in the following realms: the definition of abnormality; diagnostic reliability; the heterogeneity of symptom profiles within a disorder; the validity of diagnoses; and the continuing use of a categorical approach to classification.

Defining Abnormality (Revisited)

Top left: © Laureen March/CORBIS; Top right: ©iStock.com/mammamaart; Bottom: © Zave Smith/Corbis

What is a normal response to common life events?

One of the concerns that have been raised repeatedly since the 1980s is that, in an effort to ensure coverage of all forms of clinical distress, diagnostic systems may over-diagnose mental disorders. The statistic cited earlier in the chapter—that approximately one-quarter of all American adults have a mental disorder—is not an isolated finding, with other estimates suggesting that at least 30% of American adults meet diagnostic criteria for a mental disorder (e.g., Regier et al., 1998). Findings such as these are what led Frances (2013b) to raise concerns about what he has termed the "medicalization of ordinary life."

Such epidemiological data have led to calls for more stringent definitions of mental disorder, as many experts doubt that the prevalence of mental disorders can be this high. A number of researchers have responded to these concerns. For example, Kessler et al. (2003) used epidemiological data to examine the extent to which diagnostic data predicted psychosocial functioning a decade later. They began by categorizing the diagnostic data based on the severity of the condition: 3.2% of survey respondents met criteria for severe disorders, 8.7% were classified as having a moderate severity disorder, and 16.0% were classified as mild cases of disorders. Next, they related this classification information to data gathered for the decade following the diagnosis. These included data on hospitalization for mental health problems, work disability due to a mental disorder, suicide attempts, and whether the survey participants met the criteria for serious (or severe) mental disorder. Kessler and colleagues found a linear relation between disorder severity and subsequent problems in psychosocial functioning. The elevated risk for subsequent psychosocial problems was evident even among those classified as having mild disorders. In fact, compared with people with no diagnosable condition, those suffering from a mild disorder were 2.4 times more likely to develop significant psychosocial problems. Accordingly, the researchers argued that although mental disorders, like physical disorders, vary in severity, even mild mental disorders are associated with substantial subsequent risk for impaired functioning and should therefore be represented within a diagnostic system. Importantly, comparable findings were reported by Rai, Skapinakis, Wiles, Lewis, and Araya (2010). Using ICD-10 diagnostic criteria and UK epidemiological data, they found that over half of the functional disability occurring during mental disorders was accounted for by symptoms that were below the diagnostic threshold.

Diagnostic Reliability

Since the 1980s, there has been substantial focus on ways to enhance the reliability of clinical judgments about the presence or absence of a specific mental disorder. Each new version of the DSM and ICD systems has undergone field testing to determine the extent to which the goal of improved reliability has been attained. Without question, in comparison to early diagnostic systems, there have been substantial improvements in diagnostic reliability. However, evidence from these field trials and other research indicates that the level of inter-rater reliability on the assigning of diagnoses falls below acceptable levels.

Kirk (2004) summarized reliability data for several child and adolescent disorders. In evaluating diagnostic reliability, it is important to consider two types of reliability. First, reliability studies have examined the ability of independent evaluators to provide diagnoses that fall within the same general category (e.g., within the category of attention-deficit and disruptive behaviour disorders). Most studies examining this form of reliability have found that reliability values can sometimes, but not always, attain a good level (i.e., a value of at least .70 on a measure of inter-rater reliability known as the kappa statistic). Second, reliability studies have also examined the extent to which independent evaluators agree on the same specific diagnosis (e.g., separation anxiety disorder, conduct disorder). Kirk reported that, in such studies, reliability levels often fail to attain an acceptable level. He also noted that there is often extreme variability in reliability values noted from different sites in DSM field trials, with reliability (kappa) values ranging from extremely low (e.g., .18) to extremely high (e.g., 1.0). Because the presence or absence of a diagnosis often determines whether a child is eligible for special health and/or educational services, much more needs to be done to improve the reliability of the DSM system.

There have been calls for mental health researchers and clinicians to be less stringent in their expectations for inter-rater reliability. Kraemer, Kupfer, Clarke, Narrow, and Regier (2012), all of whom were involved with the DSM-5 task force, suggested that kappa values for as low as .2 are acceptable when considering diagnostic agreement. Concretely, this would mean that, for many conditions, it would be acceptable to find a level of agreement between raters that is only somewhat better than chance agreement. In response, Spitzer, Williams, and Endicott (2012), all of whom led the development of DSM-III, argued that any inter-rater reliability value below .6 is a cause for concern in how clinicians diagnose mental disorders. A value of .6 is also the lower limit proposed by Hunsley and Mash (2008) to describe an acceptable level of inter-rater reliability for interview or observational coding instruments.

Part of the problem with the inter-rater reliability of any diagnostic system is the challenge of accurately identifying uncommon conditions. In general, the less frequently a disorder occurs, the more likely clinicians will disagree about its presence during a diagnostic interview. The rarer the mental disorder, the lower the odds of adequate inter-rater reliability. As we describe a bit later, another part of the problem may be the continuing reliance on a diagnostic system that is based on categories rather than dimensions. Simply put, the coding of a symptom as a dichotomous variable (i.e., present or absent) can negatively affect the reliability of symptom coding compared with rating the same symptom as a continuous variable.

Heterogeneity of Symptom Profiles

Another aspect of the DSM and ICD systems that could contribute to problems with reliability is the polythetic nature of most of the disorders (i.e., the same diagnosis can be applied to individuals with a range of identical and different symptoms). Although it would be unrealistic to have a rigid set of criteria that must be met by everyone who has the same disorder, the fact that such extensive symptom variability is permitted in both systems negatively affects inter-rater reliability. There may also be another critical drawback to the polythetic approach to diagnosis. Variability in response to treatment, whether psychological or pharmacological, could be related to variability in symptom profiles among treated patients. Yet, because the level of analysis is typically on the relation between diagnosis and outcome, the connection between different symptom profiles and treatment responsiveness could be overlooked. For example, simply knowing that the symptoms of 55% of depressed patients improve when using a certain medication tells us nothing about why the medication helps many, but not all, patients. On the other hand, knowing that 85% of those with elevated physical symptoms of depression responded well to the medication in contrast to only 25% of those with elevated cognitive symptoms yields important information for subsequent research and has implications for prescription practices.

Limitations of a polythetic approach have been recognized for decades, and attempts to address these limitations have often focused on establishing clinically relevant subtypes within a diagnosis. As Clark et al. (1995) noted, few of these efforts have been successful and many of the subtypes described in the two diagnostic systems have only limited empirical support. As Clark and colleagues also pointed out, an incredible range of specifiers is available for the DSM category of major depressive disorder, including severity, chronicity, and the nature of some symptoms (e.g., catatonic or melancholic features). The resulting range of symptoms and features covered under this diagnosis is so diverse that it seems verging on impossible—or meaningless—for a single diagnosis to be applied to all the possible patient profiles.

Diagnostic Validity

As we discussed earlier in the chapter, validity is a central criterion that must be considered in evaluating a classification system. Kendell and Jablensky (2003) viewed diagnostic validity as an indication that a disorder is a discrete entity that has clear boundaries with other disorders. Kendell and Jablensky suggested that very few mental disorders have demonstrated diagnostic validity. It is noteworthy that all the examples of valid diagnoses that they listed were conditions with clear biological causes, including Down's syndrome and Huntington's disease.

How does low inter-rater reliability for the presence of a diagnosis affect the validity of a diagnosis?

A prime example of a diagnosis with questionable validity is the DSM acute stress disorder (ASD). This diagnosis involves the development of anxiety, dissociative features, and other symptoms within a month following exposure to a traumatic stressor. As Harvey and Bryant (2002) noted, ASD was introduced into DSM-IV to fill a vacuum that existed around the diagnosis of PTSD. A DSM diagnosis of PTSD cannot be applied to such symptoms if they occur within a month of the traumatic event. ASD was defined, therefore, as a disorder in which PTSD-like disorders occurred shortly after the trauma. If symptoms of ASD persist for more than a month after the event, then a

©iStock.com/Johncairns

Is acute stress disorder a valid diagnosis?

diagnosis of PTSD may be appropriate and the ASD diagnosis would be superseded. This opens the possibility that researchers might be able to establish the nature of connections between initial distress following trauma (i.e., ASD) and more chronic distress (i.e., PTSD).

There have been a number of criticisms raised about ASD, all of which raise major questions about its diagnostic validity. The initial criticisms, as summarized by Harvey and Bryant (2002), included the following: the requirement for dissociative symptoms is not consistent with research on trauma reactions; it was inappropriate to introduce a diagnosis into DSM-IV in order to predict another diagnosis; it was inappropriate to introduce a diagnosis that has almost no supporting empirical evidence; it is not justifiable to distinguish between two diagnoses with comparable symptoms simply on the basis of symptom duration; and there is a great likelihood that the diagnosis could pathologize transient stress reactions that do not require the attention of mental health professionals. Importantly, many studies have found that there is only a weak association between meeting DSM criteria for ASD and, after more time has passed, meeting DSM criteria for PTSD (e.g., Creamer, O'Donnell, & Pattison, 2004; Kangas, Henry, & Bryant, 2005). On the other hand, the introduction of the ASD diagnosis has served to promote research into acute stress reactions. In reviewing this research, Cardeña and Carlson (2011) suggested that there is now considerable evidence that acute reactions to trauma do predict later distress and adjustment problems. There is an emerging consensus that dissociation experienced around the time of trauma, not ASD per se, is one of the strongest predictors of subsequent PTSD. Viewpoint Box 3.3 presents some of the evidence that many people are resilient when faced with potentially traumatic events in their lives.

Comorbidity

comorbidity: when a person receives diagnoses for two or more disorders at the same point in time.

Comorbidity occurs when a person meets criteria for two or more disorders at a specific point in time. The extent of comorbidity in clinical populations is substantial. Brown, Campbell, Lehman, Grisham, and Mancill (2001) assessed the comorbidity of current and lifetime DSM-IV anxiety and mood disorders in more than 1,100 American adults seeking services for stress and anxiety disorders. Among individuals currently meeting diagnostic criteria for an anxiety or mood disorder, 57% also met criteria for another disorder. For example, among those diagnosed with panic disorder, 36% met criteria for another anxiety disorder and 17% met criteria for a mood disorder. Among those diagnosed with major depressive disorder, 64% met criteria for an anxiety disorder. Comorbidity is also evident in youth. In the National Comorbidity

VIEWPOINT BOX 3.3

PSYCHOLOGICAL RESILIENCE IN THE FACE OF POTENTIAL TRAUMA

When reading the case of Noah, and the extent to which natural disasters can cause extreme psychological distress (Viewpoint Box 3.1), you might have the impression that psychological disorders such as depression and PTSD are the inevitable result of experiencing life-threatening situations. Actually, the contrary is more accurate: people are amazingly resilient and most are able to recover their psychological equilibrium after experiencing potentially traumatic events. For example, in population surveys, researchers have found that, although two-thirds of children report experiencing at least one traumatic event by the age of 16 years, less than 15% develop post-traumatic stress symptoms and less than 1% will meet criteria for PTSD (Copeland, Keeler, Angold, & Costello, 2007).

©iStock.com/Aldo Murillo

The presence of supportive relationships enhances resilience in the face of trauma.

In a series of studies and reviews, Bonanno (e.g., Bonanno, 2004; Bonanno, 2005; Mancini & Bonnano, 2006; Bonanno, Westphal, & Mancini, 2011) has underscored the fact that most people are surprisingly resilient when faced with extreme circumstances. One of the most important findings in Bonanno's research is that, regardless of the nature of the potentially traumatic events that people must confront, approximately one-third to one-half demonstrate psychological resilience. In other words, such individuals experience only a passing period of mild distress and/or disruption in daily activities. After the normal initial distress that almost everyone feels when dealing with life-threatening situations or the death of loved one, resilient individuals quickly regain their previous level of well-being and mental health, often within days or weeks. Recovery, defined as (a) the experience of moderate to severe distress in the face of trauma and (b) a gradual return to normal functioning, is a second common response to potential trauma. Across all types of trauma, Bonnano and colleagues have estimated that 15–35% would be classified as recovered within two years of the trauma.

What are the factors that characterize resilient individuals? They include the presence of supportive relationships and the ability to flexibly adapt to change when required. You will learn more on this in Chapter 10, when we describe how educational and treatment programs build on these "protective factors" in an effort to prevent the development of clinically significant distress. Bonnano and colleagues have also found that expressing more positive emotions than negative emotions is characteristic of many resilient people. Moreover, they also reported, consistent with a great deal of research on the mental health benefits of overly positive views of oneself (e.g., Taylor & Brown, 1988), that the tendency to overestimate one's own abilities and positive qualities is frequently associated with resilience. Given the fact that loss and trauma are invariably part of the human condition, research on resilience holds great promise for helping countless individuals better cope with both predictable and unpredictable severe stressors.

Survey–Adolescent Supplement (NCS-AS), which surveyed 10,123 youth aged 3–18, 40% of young people who met criteria for one disorder also met criteria for another lifetime disorder (Merikangas et al., 2010).

Overall, whether based on clinical samples (i.e., those seeking services) or on community samples, most epidemiological surveys find, in country after country, comorbidity rates that exceed 40% (Clark et al., 1995). When individuals with a single disorder are compared with those with comorbid disorders, a very clear pattern emerges: those with comorbid conditions are more severely impaired in daily life functioning, are more likely to have a chronic history of mental health problems, have more physical health problems, and use more health care services (Newman, Moffitt, Caspi, & Silva, 1998). These characteristics have clear consequences for both research and clinical services. On the research side, accurately representing the extent of comorbidity in research samples is necessary to accurately estimate the relation between a disorder and its correlates. On the clinical service side, people with comorbid disorders are likely to present with psychosocial characteristics that make the planning and delivery of services more complex (Newman et al., 1998). Moreover, if these services are based on treatment research that used patients without comorbid disorders, or if these services are focused on only one of the disorders, the services may be suboptimal and may underestimate the scope or duration of treatment necessary for satisfactory outcomes. Because of these concerns, as we will see in the chapters on psychological treatment, researchers are increasingly attuned to the importance of not excluding individuals with co-existing disorders from their studies.

Categorical versus Dimensional Classification

As the above studies demonstrate, comorbidity is a clinical fact. Presence of comorbidity contradicts the assumption that diagnostic categories are discrete and non-overlapping. The DSM-5 explicitly acknowledges that each category of mental disorder need not be a discrete entity—yet doing so opens up the possibility that a dimensional system may better represent the nature of mental disorders. As noted in the DSM-5, there are no commonly agreed-upon dimensional systems that could replace the prevailing categorical approach. However, that may be changing, as numerous steps have been taken to conceptualize many disorders within dimensional models (e.g., Krueger, Watson, & Barlow, 2005; Widiger & Trull, 2007).

The question of dimensionality can be considered within a specific disorder. There has been a great deal of controversy in the area of depression research about whether depression is a discrete diagnostic category or should be viewed as existing on a continuum that includes both clinical symptoms and subclinical distress. The most sophisticated research now suggests that depression may encompass both a specific condition and a continuum. Santor and Coyne (2001), for example, obtained clinician ratings of symptoms on samples of clinically depressed adults and non-clinically depressed—but distressed—adults. When depressed and non-depressed individuals with comparable levels of clinician-rated depressive symptoms were compared, group differences on specific symptoms were apparent. Depressed mood, anhedonia (lack of pleasure), and suicidality were more likely to be evident in the depressed group, whereas hypochondriasis and insomnia were more evident in the non-depressed group. Thus, although the severity of depressive symptoms can be expressed on a continuum, Santor and Coyne argued that the use of a continuum (or dimensional) model might mask important and diagnostically relevant group differences. Using self-report measures of depressive symptoms, research on both clinical samples (Ruscio & Ruscio, 2000) and non-clinical samples (Beach & Amir, 2006; Hankin, Fraley, Lahey, & Waldman, 2005) have found evidence for both categorical and dimensional features. Generally speaking, analyses of self-report items expressing distress (e.g., discouragement, loss of interest in others) appear to yield a dimensional perspective on the continuum of subclinical to clinical depression. In contrast, analyses of self-report items of somatic symptoms (e.g., sleep disturbance, weight loss) appear to provide strong evidence that some depressive symptoms are best understood as constituting a discrete disorder.

In conducting research on the underlying dimensions of mental disorders, we can also step back from examining a specific disorder and explore patterns that may exist across disorders. Based on epidemiological data, it is increasingly clear that comorbidity cannot be explained as being simply due to either symptom overlap among diagnostic categories or methodological problems in research. Instead it seems that there are a number of core pathological processes that underlie the overt expression of a seemingly diverse range of symptoms (Krueger & Markon, 2006). For example, the internalizing and externalizing dimensions that were first identified with respect to American children's problems have been found to be applicable across countries as diverse as Ethiopia, Iceland, Korea, Israel, and Jamaica (Ivanova et al., 2007). These dimensions are also helpful in understanding adult problems. A major cross-cultural study examining the structure of psychiatric comorbidity in 14 countries (Netherlands, Germany, United Kingdom, France, Italy, Greece, Turkey, Japan, China, India, Nigeria, Brazil, Chile, and the United States) tested for the presence of these factors. Krueger et al. (2003) found that depression, somatic disorders, and anxiety consistently formed a single factor, whereas symptoms of alcohol abuse consistently formed a second factor. The inclusion of data from a variety of Western and non-Western countries strengthens the conclusion that there may be internalizing and externalizing psychopathological characteristics that underlie many mental disorders. Subsequent research by Wright et al. (2013) replicated these findings using epidemiological data from over 8,800 adult Australians. The dimensions of internalizing and externalizing disorders—with the addition of a dimension representing psychotic experiences—appeared to underlie the range of psychological symptoms reported in the survey. In sum, dimensions rather than categories consistently appear to be a better way to describe and understand mental disorders.

SUMMARY AND CONCLUSIONS

Classification is a fundamental human activity. The classification of mental disorders draws on both a neo-Kraepelinian tradition as well as on a more recent developmental psychopathology approach that takes into account contextual variables such as developmental stage. The definition of a mental disorder requires not only that behaviours are abnormal, but also that they cause harm to the individual and are outside the individual's control. In North America, the most commonly used system has been the *Diagnostic and Statistical Manual of Mental Disorders*. Increasingly, however, the *International Statistical Classification of Diseases and Related Health Problems* is used for the diagnosis of mental disorders. Over time, both of these diagnostic systems have moved toward placing a greater reliance on evidence-based diagnosis. In turn, the development of clear decision-making rules has enabled advances to be made in the study of psychopathology. Cross-cultural studies using these systems have revealed great variability across countries in the incidence of disorders. The most common types of disorders found in all countries are anxiety disorders and mood disorders. An alternative approach to the categorical diagnosis used in these two diagnostic systems is to assess individuals on important dimensions of functioning. In particular, the dimensions of internalizing and externalizing problems that were originally identified from studies of child psychopathology are proving to be useful in understanding psychopathology and mental disorders across the lifespan.

KEY TERMS

categorical approach to classification: an entity is determined to be either a member of a category or not.

classification utility: the usefulness of a classification scheme.

classification validity: the extent to which the principles used in classifying an entity are effective in capturing the nature of the entity.

comorbidity: when a person receives diagnoses for two or more disorders at the same point in time.

developmental psychopathology: a framework for understanding problem behaviour in relation to the milestones that are specific to each stage of a person's development.

diagnosis: the result of applying the decision-making rules of a diagnostic system to the symptoms of a specific individual.

diagnostic system: a classification based on rules used to organize and understand diseases and disorders.

dimensional approach to classification: classified entities differ in the extent to which they possess certain characteristics or properties.

dyscontrol: the impairment resulting from a disorder must be involuntary or not readily controlled.

harmful dysfunction: the behaviours associated with a mental disorder are dysfunctional and the dysfunction causes harm to the individual or to those around him or her.

prototype model: members of a diagnostic category may differ in the degree to which they represent the concepts underlying the category.

KEY NAMES

Thomas Achenbach　Emil Kraepelin　Robert Spitzer

ADDITIONAL RESOURCES

Books

American Psychiatric Association. (2013). *Diagnostic and statistical manual of mental disorders* (5th ed.). Washington, DC: American Psychiatric Publishing.

Frances, A. (2013b). *Saving normal.* New York: William Morrow.

Journals

American Journal of Psychiatry

Archives of General Psychiatry

Canadian Journal of Psychiatry

Journal of Abnormal Child Psychology

Journal of Abnormal Psychology

Check It Out!

Information on the DSM system, including its history and use, can be found on this American Psychiatric Association site: www.psychiatry.org/practice/dsm

Information on the World Health Organization's International Classification of Diseases (links to a copy of the ICD-10 Classification of Mental and Behavioural Disorders can be found at the bottom of the webpage): www.who.int/classifications/icd/en

The Canadian Mental Health Association is a great resource for information on mental health and mental disorders: www.cmha.ca/mental-health/understanding-mental-illness

The National Institute of Mental Health provides a wealth of data on mental disorders and their treatment: www.nimh.nih.gov/health/index.shtml

RESEARCH METHODS IN CLINICAL PSYCHOLOGY

4 CHAPTER

INTRODUCTION

Will this therapy help me be less anxious in social situations?

My father has bipolar disorder, so how likely is it that I will have it too?

Is there anything that can be done to help my son who has autism?

How much time is my mother likely to have before her dementia makes it impossible for her to safely live on her own?

What effect will my divorce have on my young daughter? Would it help if we stayed together until she leaves home?

Psychologists who provide services to the public face questions like these on a daily basis. To properly answer these questions, clinical psychologists need solid research data. The people asking these and myriad similar questions deserve far more than a response based simply on a hunch—they deserve the best information that science can provide them. That is why a review of clinical research methods is essential in understanding clinical psychology. You may recall learning in Chapter 1 that, among the health professions, clinical psychology provides the strongest research training. In this chapter, you will learn about the ways that research methods can inform and guide the delivery of psychological services.

This chapter provides a brief introduction to the kinds of issues that must be considered in designing and interpreting research in clinical psychology. The majority of issues that we touch on apply to research in other areas of psychology, but we will highlight their relevance to the practice of clinical psychology and discuss some challenges that only clinical researchers face in testing their research hypotheses. Our intent is to provide an overview of the issues and methods that are central to conducting research in clinical psychology. Although they are important for clinical practice, we will not touch on various applied research/evaluation strategies, such as program evaluation. Likewise, we will not address qualitative research approaches (such as focus groups, participant observations, and document analysis) used in some areas of clinical psychology research. The quantitative research designs we discuss in this chapter focus on testing hypotheses generated by the researcher, whereas, in general, qualitative research tends to be more exploratory in nature. (Interested readers can learn more about qualitative research methods in psychology from helpful publications such as Creswell [2012] and Silverman [2011]).

To give you a sense of the whole research endeavour, we begin by discussing why we need research, and the ways that research hypotheses can be generated. Then we emphasize ethical issues in planning, conducting, and reporting research. Next, we describe a number of clinically relevant research designs and highlight aspects of sampling, measurement, and statistical analyses. We conclude this chapter by attending to factors that influence the reporting and utilization of research results. You may be surprised to learn that the type of disciplined thinking required to design a good study is also necessary to design and evaluate psychological services. A scientist-practitioner is well trained to develop testable clinical hypotheses, gather the data necessary to test those hypotheses, weigh the evidence, and reach sound conclusions.

According to our professional standards and our ethical codes, people have a right to expect psychological services that are firmly based on psychological science. As described in Chapter 1, this is known as evidence-based practice, which means basing clinical services and health care policy, whenever feasible, on replicated evidence gathered from scientific studies (Institute of Medicine, 2002; Sackett, Rosenberg, Gray, Haynes, & Richardson, 1996). Evidence-based practice requires psychologists to be not only sensitive and empathic, but also well informed about current research relevant to the services they provide. The effective scientist-practitioner thinks in a scientific manner and applies knowledge derived from research with care and compassion.

What are the differences between evidence-based practice and eminence-based practice?

The antithesis of evidence-based practice is practice based on tradition and authority, what some have facetiously called *eminence-based practice*, in which recommendations are accepted because the person delivering them is seen as an expert. The public should be sceptical about accepting opinions simply because they come from a supposed expert on a television talk show. As Mullen and Streiner

(2004) rightly stated, the opinions of even recognized experts are just that—opinions—unless their views are supported by the best available empirical evidence. Moreover, as illustrated in Exhibit 4.1,

Exhibit 4.1 Common Errors in Thinking

Faulty Reasoning: A form of argument that is inaccurate or misleading in some way.
Example: "Psychologists have provided effective services for decades without having research available on what makes treatment effective. Therefore, there is no reason for me to bother reading this research in order to be effective." One of the ways in which this is inaccurate is that the argument does not provide any proof that the services of these unspecified psychologists were effective.

False Dilemma: This fallacy takes the form of reducing the range of options available to just two (usually extreme) options.
Example: "Either I accept the treatment that the psychologist is suggesting or I just give up trying to change." Clearly other options are available, including asking the psychologist what treatment options might be available or consulting another psychologist (or other health care provider) to obtain a second opinion.

Golden Mean Fallacy: This logical error involves assuming that the most valid conclusion to reach is a compromise of two competing positions.
Example: "I have heard that both cognitive and psychodynamic treatments can be helpful for the type of problems I have, so I really should look for a treatment that combines both cognitive and psychodynamic elements." Assuming that the original statement about effective treatments is correct, there is no reason to assume that a synthesis of the two treatments would be more effective than either treatment on its own.

The Straw Person Argument: This involves mischaracterizing a position in order to make it look absurd or unpalatable.
Example: "Anyone who would prescribe a drug to treat my son's symptoms just wants to turn active kids into zombies." It is highly unlikely that the health care professional recommending medication has this goal in mind, but it provides a simplistic rationale for rejecting the possibility of taking the medication.

Affirming the Consequent: This logical error takes the following form: first, assume that *x* is a cause of *y*. Then, when *y* is observed, conclude that *x* must have caused it.
Example: "People who have schizophrenia always act in a bizarre manner. This person is acting bizarrely. So, obviously, this person has schizophrenia." There are problems with this, including the fact that people with schizophrenia do not always act in a bizarre manner and that there can be many explanations for bizarre behaviour other than the presence of a psychotic disorder.

Appeal to Ignorance: This mistake takes the form of arguing that, because there is no evidence to prove a position is wrong, the position must be correct.
Example: "There is no scientific evidence that having my patients sing and dance while they remember the trauma that they experienced harms them or is ineffective. So, of course, this new form of therapy has to be helpful." The lack of evidence to demonstrate harm or ineffectiveness is not, of course, equivalent to the presence of evidence for the beneficial effects of the treatment.

Adapted from Pope (2003).

we cannot simply rely on common sense as a guide to appropriate decision-making, as there are often logical inconsistencies in the way that people process information and make decisions. Although such inconsistencies may be of little consequence in a decision about what brand of breakfast cereal to buy, they can have enormous effects in a decision related to seeking and following through on health care services.

How can science help if the treatment is unhelpful?

The evolution of the treatment of obsessive-compulsive disorder (OCD) is a good example of the way that research can inform practice (Thomas & Rosqvist, 2011). You may recall that in Chapter 3 we described Melissa, who suffered from OCD. Literature dating back centuries describes people who suffered from what we now call obsessions and compulsions. The clinical focus on OCD started in the 1800s, when these obsessions and compulsions were seen as a mental problem. Until the 1960s, OCD was considered an untreatable disorder, so someone like Melissa might have received a diagnosis but no services that were likely to help. However, the prognosis for individuals with OCD changed dramatically with the development of behavioural treatments that included the key treatment components of exposure and response prevention. Exposure involves generating anxiety for the individual by deliberate exposure to the anxiety-provoking thoughts or external stimuli. Response prevention involves stopping the person from engaging in the rituals that are typically used to inappropriately manage the anxiety. Research has shown that when this form of treatment is used, most people with OCD experience substantial improvements in functioning (Rosa-Alcázar, Sánchez-Meca, Gómez-Conesa, & Marín-Martínez, 2008).

However, the road to the development of effective behavioural therapy for OCD was not a direct one, and there were many dead ends and wrong turns along the way. For example, it was common in the 1970s and 1980s for a thought-stopping component to be included in OCD treatments. This required the person to yell "Stop" or to make a loud noise whenever unwanted, intrusive thoughts occurred. Although this strategy fit with a behavioural theory about obsessions and compulsions, it was not very practical. Even more problematic were the findings of later research, which showed that trying not to think about something often has a paradoxical effect: it results in the increased persistence of intrusive thoughts! This is a good example of how clinical psychology practice must change when evidence shows that a theoretically sound intervention does not work. Profile Box 4.1 introduces Dr. Adam Radomsky whose research examines the nature and treatment of OCD.

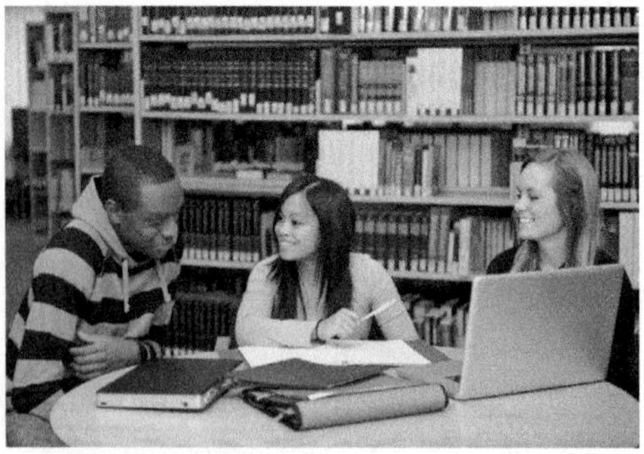

©iStock.com/CEFutcher

Imagine the response from these students if you were working at the next table and all of a sudden yelled "Stop" as part of your thought-stopping treatment.

If we ask you not to think about taking a break from studying and having a delicious snack, you may notice that images of appetizing snacks keep popping into your head. If you kept this up for a period of time, repeatedly trying not to think about snacks, you would find that you were spending more and more time thinking about snacks.

PROFILE BOX 4.1

DR. ADAM RADOMSKY

Courtesy of Adam Radomsky

I received a Ph.D. in clinical psychology at the University of British Columbia and completed a fellowship at Harvard Medical School/Massachusetts General Hospital. Currently, I am a full professor of psychology at Concordia University, where I direct the Anxiety and Obsessive-Compulsive Disorders Laboratory. My research investigates cognitive therapy for OCD and anxiety disorders, as well as cognitive, behavioural, and emotional aspects of these disorders. I have received several national and international awards, including the Canadian Psychological Association's President's New Researcher Award (2007), being named a Beck Institute Scholar (2005–06), and a Canadian Institutes of Health Research (CIHR) New Investigator Award (2004–09). I have published a number of peer-reviewed articles and book chapters related to cognition, behaviour, OCD, and the anxiety disorders and am frequently invited to speak at national and international conferences. My research is funded by the Canadian Institutes of Health Research. I am a member of l'Ordre des psychologues du Québec and am board certified in cognitive therapy by the Academy of Cognitive Therapy and by the Canadian Association of Cognitive and Behavioural Therapies. In my clinical practice, I specialize in cognitive-behavioural therapy (CBT) for adult OCD and anxiety disorders.

HOW DID YOU CHOOSE TO BECOME A CLINICAL PSYCHOLOGIST?

As an undergraduate student, I was fascinated by abnormal behaviour. I spent some time as a volunteer at a large mental health hospital and concluded that the psychologists there served a role that was appealing to me. An outstanding lecture on classical conditioning (in which the professor conditioned an entire class to startle whenever he said "CS," for conditioned stimulus) sealed the deal.

WHAT IS THE MOST REWARDING PART OF YOUR JOB AS A CLINICAL PSYCHOLOGIST?

There are two extremely rewarding parts of my job. I feel lucky to be able to see first-hand the progress of those struggling to overcome often crippling levels of anxiety, most often with remarkable success. I also really enjoy the creativity associated with research, from designing interesting and novel experiments to learning—even discovering—new scientific information about OCD, anxiety disorders, and their treatment.

WHAT IS THE GREATEST CHALLENGE YOU FACE AS A CLINICAL PSYCHOLOGIST?

It can be quite complicated to try to replicate the everyday experience of OCD within a laboratory context. People diagnosed with OCD often feel excessively responsible for protecting themselves and

CONTINUED . . .

others from harm, but this responsibility is often confined to their home and/or belongings. A great deal of creativity is required to design a study through which we can investigate this in the lab. Occasionally, much time and expense is devoted to a study that "doesn't work." This can happen when an experimental manipulation of perceived responsibility, for example, doesn't actually produce differing levels of perceived responsibility in our participants (measured through a manipulation check), or when we design a study that participants describe as "interesting, but not relevant to me or my problems." Of course, these are simply opportunities to go back to the drawing board and try again.

TELL US ABOUT YOUR RESEARCH ON OBSESSIVE-COMPULSIVE DISORDER.

I am very fortunate to have a laboratory that includes a fully functioning kitchen for the study of OCD through ecologically valid methodologies. It allows me to examine cleaning and checking behaviour in real time of real objects (appliances, switches, door knobs, etc.). I've been very interested in memory as it applies to OCD; when research participants are asked to repeatedly check our laboratory stove, for example, their confidence in their memory declines dramatically. This phenomenon occurs both for student participants and for participants who have clinically significant problems. Interestingly, this and other work I've done in this area shows that memory accuracy in OCD is excellent—often better than in those without the disorder. These findings indicate that previous research suggesting the presence of memory deficits in OCD may have failed to take into account the differences between memory for varying types of words and memory for real, threatening situations and stimuli.

HOW DO YOU INTEGRATE SCIENCE AND PRACTICE IN YOUR WORK?

The integration of science and practice is not only key to my work, it's integral to my identity as a clinical psychologist. The clients I see in my practice are the inspiration for much of my research. That is, many of my laboratory studies are based on observations, questions, and/or obstacles raised by those with whom I'm working clinically. In turn, my research has a strong influence on how I help people, with results of specific experiments or studies being directly relevant to the problems faced by my clients. For me, these two elements of my work are completely interwoven. I simply couldn't be a good researcher without my practice and couldn't be a good clinician without my research.

WHAT DO YOU SEE AS THE MOST EXCITING CHANGES IN THE FIELD OF CLINICAL PSYCHOLOGY?

In countries like Australia and the United Kingdom, governments are recognizing that there is a great need for clinical psychology. Importantly, they've reached the conclusion that evidence-based psychological treatments should be funded through their national health care systems. This is a huge step forward; it recognizes the fact that psychologists need to do what works, not just what is pleasant, historical, or requested by others. This is the most exciting advance in clinical psychology and promises to change the lives of thousands of people in need. It will also help to advance treatment research and the profession of clinical psychology.

How do theories affect the research process?

GENERATING RESEARCH HYPOTHESES

How does a researcher decide what to study? Exhibit 4.2 shows some of the many possible sources of research ideas, including personal experience, professional experience, and knowledge of the scientific literature. As Dr. Radomsky noted, clinical work is often a rich source of research hypotheses. You will see that many of the psychologists profiled in this book also emphasize that they generate many of their hypotheses from observations they make in the delivery of psychological services, then they test these hypotheses in their research.

Dr. Adam Radomsky

This research laboratory, designed like a kitchen, makes it possible to observe obsessive-compulsive behaviours in a context that is similar to everyday life.

Whatever the source or inspiration for our research ideas, our thinking is always influenced by the type of theory we hold about human behaviour. In some instances, the researcher uses a formal theory to generate a research idea. This is known as following a deductive process. In other instances, the researcher follows an inductive process; for example, deriving an idea from repeated observations of everyday events. Even though the inductive process is not explicitly guided by theory, it is influenced by the researcher's informal theories, including his or her theoretical orientation and general world view. So with a strong cognitive-behavioural background, Dr. Radomsky is likely to pay attention to aspects of learning and thinking that may explain obsessive-compulsive behaviour. Not only do theories influence the types of research ideas

Exhibit 4.2 Possible Sources of Research Ideas

Everyday Experience and Observation

Example: Noticing that your children's friends are troubled by their parents' divorce.

Professional Experience and Observation

Example: Noticing a pattern among one's patients that suggests a connection between feelings of social rejection and specific early childhood experiences.

Addressing Applied Problems and Needs

Example: Testing whether a successful psychoeducational treatment package for helping police officers better manage work stress can be adapted to alleviate the distress of victims of serious motor vehicle accidents.

Previous Research

Example: Attempting to reconcile contradictory findings in previous research by comparing the phenomenon in clinic and community samples, as variations in sampling may be responsible for these inconsistent findings.

Theory

Example: Directly comparing the ability of two different theories of motivation to predict which distressed couples will stay in couples therapy and which couples will terminate services prematurely.

the researcher generates, they also influence the way the researcher interprets the data he or she obtains from the completed research study. In other words, researchers are not immune from the potential biasing effects of their own beliefs and values. Despite the potential for theories to mislead researchers in their interpretation of research data, science could not progress without theories, for theories serve to organize and give meaning to the results of research endeavours and to generate new ideas to be tested in future research. Theories are not a problem, unless the researcher forgets that they are only one way to look at phenomena and slips into treating them as facts. As long as the researcher is willing to formulate and test hypotheses, theories are extremely useful.

How is the science of clinical psychology different from the science of other types of psychology? What ethical issues are particularly important in the science of clinical psychology?

After developing a general research idea, scientists follow a number of steps to ensure that the hypothesis is properly formulated and tested. First, the researcher conducts a systematic search of the published research on the phenomenon of interest. Second, assuming that there is no research that has directly tested the idea, the researcher begins to formalize ideas so that they can be tested in a scientific manner. This requires translating abstract ideas into something that can be measured. For example, a researcher interested in violence may decide to measure the frequency and intensity of violent acts in the previous year. Part of this task of operationalizing an abstract concept requires that the researcher consider the precise nature of the relations among the concepts that form the research idea (see Exhibit 4.3). A major challenge in operationalizing an idea is ensuring that the resulting operational definition fully captures the key aspects of the original idea. In the third step, the researcher must carefully consider the extent to which the research idea may be based on cultural assumptions that may limit the applicability or relevance of the planned research (American Psychological Association, 2003a). The value of the research is enhanced by ensuring the cultural relevance of the planned research and the use of appropriate samples of participants. Fourth, the researcher must consider ethical issues in testing of the idea. For example, ethical considerations might make some research designs unsuitable, such as using random assignment in an experiment to determine the effects of violence. Finally, the researcher must draw together all the results of the previous steps to sketch out the study procedures. Along the way, some aspects of the planned study may need to be dropped or modified due to practical constraints (e.g., insufficient funds or a lack of appropriate measures).

How are different research designs suitable at different stages of the development of knowledge in a field?

Choices about the ethical conduct, type of research design, sample of participants, and measures used all influence the research hypothesis that will be tested. For example, a simple statement, such as "Increased anxiety is associated with more errors in social interactions," could be translated into a number of very different research hypotheses, each dependent on choices made about methodological features of the study. To determine whether increased anxiety was associated with more errors in social interaction across people with different levels of trait anxiety, the design would include research participants who have varying anxiety levels. If the researcher wished to determine whether the statement was true within individuals as they became more or less anxious, then the design would require that participants be tested repeatedly as they experienced different levels of anxiety. This might also involve the researcher attempting to manipulate the participants' anxiety levels, in which case the hypothesis would be recast as "An increase in anxiety causes more errors in social interactions." If the researcher wished to determine if the statement was true for all ages, this would require participants of different ages. The bottom line is that researchers must ensure that the research methods match the hypothesis to be tested.

Exhibit 4.3 Conceptualizing the Relations Among Concepts/Variables

1. **What are the relations among the variables of interest?**
   Correlation: The variables are associated with each other.
   Example: Mothers' ratings of children's behaviour problems are correlated with fathers' ratings of children's behaviour problems.
   Cause: One variable directly or indirectly influences the level of a second variable.
   Example: A child's hyperactive symptoms result in parental stress.
2. **What are the factors that influence the relations among variables?**
   Moderation: One variable influences the direction or size of the relation between two other variables.
   Example: The negative effects of marital conflict on children are lower in families with a strong parental alliance than they are in families with a poor parental alliance.
3. **How does one variable influence a second variable?**
   Mediation: The influence of one variable on a second variable is due, in whole or in part, to the influence of a third variable.
   Example: The link between maternal HIV status and children's depressive symptoms is partially explained by maternal depressive symptoms.
4. **Is it possible to alter an outcome of interest?**
   Prevention: An attempt to decrease the likelihood that an undesirable outcome occurs.
   Example: School-based programs to decrease bullying.
   Intervention: An attempt to decrease or eliminate an undesirable outcome that has already occurred.
   Example: Treatment to reduce bingeing and purging.

Adapted from Kazdin (1999).

If you wanted to test a hypothesis that mental disorders are associated with experiencing stigma, what kind of hypotheses might you generate?

ETHICS IN RESEARCH

We cannot overemphasize the importance of paying close attention to ethical factors in the design, conduct, and reporting of research. This is true for all science, but is especially important in clinical psychology research in which research participants may be vulnerable due to their psychological distress and/or may be receiving psychological services as part of the research. The quest for knowledge must never compromise the welfare of research participants. In the *Canadian Code of Ethics for Psychologists* (Canadian Psychological Association, 2000), described in Chapter 2, psychologists are required to apply the same type of ethical decision-making in both research and the provision of psychological services. Psychologists are expected to apply the general principles (respect for the dignity of persons, responsible caring, integrity in relationships, and responsibility to society) in a research context just as they would in other parts of their professional role. Other psychological organizations, such as the American Psychological Association (APA), the Australian Psychological Society, and the British Psychological Society, include in their ethical codes sections that specifically address the application of ethical principles in a research context (Rae & Sullivan, 2003).

Illustrating the range of ethical issues that must be considered throughout the research process, Exhibit 4.4 provides a summary of research-relevant ethical principles found in the APA Ethical Principles of Psychologists and Code of Conduct (2010a). These principles underline that attention to the welfare of research participants (and animal subjects) and to honesty in the presentation of research findings are overarching themes to which psychologists must attend.

As indicated in Exhibit 4.4, researchers have an ethical obligation to those involved in their studies. The issue of informed consent from research participants is particularly important, as this provides an assurance that a research participant is fully aware of the possible benefits and risks of research involvement. An example of a consent form for a clinical psychology research study is presented in Exhibit 4.5.

Once researchers have published the results of their studies, they also have an ethical obligation to share their data with other

Exhibit 4.4 American Psychological Association Ethical Principles for Research and Publication

1. **Institutional Approval**
   When required, institutional approval for research must be obtained and the research must be conducted in accordance with the approved research protocol. If a study is conducted through multiple institutions, multiple approvals may be required.
2. **Informed Consent for Research**
   When obtaining informed consent, potential participants must be informed of the purpose of the research, their rights to decline or withdraw participation, the possible consequences of declining or withdrawing, the possible consequences of being involved in the research, any benefits stemming from research involvement, limits of confidentiality, incentives for research participation, and whom to contact with questions about the research and participants' rights.
3. **Informed Consent for Recording**
   Informed consent for recording voices or images must be obtained prior to the recording unless the research consists solely of observations in public places or the research design involves some form of deception that requires that informed consent be sought after the recording has been completed.
4. **Client/Patient, Student, and Subordinate Research Participants**
   When research is conducted with clients/patients, students, or subordinates, steps must be taken to protect the potential participants from the adverse consequences of declining or withdrawing participation.
5. **Dispensing with Informed Consent**
   It may be possible to dispense with informed consent only where the research would not be expected to cause harm or distress or where permitted by law or government regulation.
6. **Offering Inducements for Research Participation**
   Excessive or inappropriate monetary or other inducements for research are to be avoided if such inducements are likely to coerce participation in the research.
7. **Deception in Research**
   Deception is not used in research unless it is justified by the study's likely value and the use of non-deceptive procedures is not feasible. Deception cannot be used if the research is likely to cause physical pain or severe emotional distress. When deception is used, participants must be informed about the nature of deception as early as is feasible.
8. **Debriefing**
   Participants must have an opportunity to promptly obtain information about the nature, results, and conclusions of the research and steps must be taken to attempt to correct any misconceptions about the research.
9. **Humane Care and Use of Animals in Research**
   Animals used in research must be acquired, cared for, used, and disposed of in compliance with laws, government regulations, and professional standards. All those involved in the use of animals in research must be instructed in the care, maintenance, and handling of the animals. Reasonable efforts are made to minimize the discomfort and pain of animal subjects and, if an animal's life is to be terminated, the act must proceed rapidly and with an effort to minimize pain.
10. **Reporting Research Results**
    Data must not be fabricated, and reasonable steps must be taken to correct any significant errors found in published research reports.

CONTINUED . . .

11. **Plagiarism**
    The work or data of others must not be presented by a researcher as his or her own.
12. **Publication Credit**
    Authorship of a publication must accurately reflect the contributions of the author(s); minor contributions to the research or the writing of the publication do not merit authorship.
13. **Duplicate Publication of Data**
    Data that have been previously published must not be published subsequently as original data.
14. **Sharing Research Data for Verification**
    After results are published, researchers must ensure that their data are available for verification or re-analysis by other competent professionals.
15. **Reviewers**
    Those who review material submitted for publication or for grant support must respect the confidentiality of the material.

Adapted from APA (2010a).

Exhibit 4.5 Sample Consent Form

Dr. Chris Brown
Department of Psychology
University of Canada
Telephone number: (123) 456-7890
Email address: chrisbrown@ucanada.ca

We are conducting a study to better understand the factors that are involved in decisions to seek and receive psychological services. This study is being conducted by Dr. Chris Brown, a professor in the Department of Psychology at the University of Canada. We would like to interview you about the factors that played a role in your decision to request psychological services at the Department of Psychology's Psychological Service Centre and about the expectations you have for therapy or counselling. The interview will take place either prior to or following an appointment you have at the Psychological Service Centre. Participation in the interview will take approximately 30 minutes. You will receive an honorarium of $15 for your participation in this study. This will be given to you following the interview. If you choose to end the interview, you will still receive $15.

I consent to participate in this study. I understand that I am agreeing to be interviewed and that the interview will involve approximately 30 minutes of my time. I understand that as the questions deal with personal decisions about seeking psychological treatment, I may experience some slight distress in answering the questions. I have received assurances from the researcher that every effort will be made to minimize the likelihood of any distress. I understand that if I am uncomfortable with any question I do not have to answer it. I also understand that I am free to withdraw from this study at any time. Any decision to withdraw from the study will not affect the status of the services I am receiving at the Psychological Service Centre.

I understand that all my answers will be kept strictly confidential; not even my therapist will have access to any information related to this study. My information will be kept in a locked filing cabinet, and only members of the research team will have access to the information.

CONTINUED . . .

I understand that my anonymity will be assured by never using my name or identifying information in the analysis and reporting of this study. Only a code number will be used to identify my information and all reports of this study will involve combined information from all participants.

I understand that, if I have any questions or concerns about the study, I can contact Dr. Brown at (123) 456-7890 or at chrisbrown@ucanada.ca. If I wish, I can also contact the university protocol officer for ethics in research, at (123) 456-0000 or at protocolethics@ucanada.ca, to obtain information or to make a complaint about the ethical conduct of this study.

Finally, I understand that I can receive a summary of findings at the completion of the study.

There are two copies of this consent form, one of which I may keep.

Participant's Signature: ______________________________

Date: ______________________________

Researcher's Signature: ______________________________

Date: ______________________________

I wish to receive a summary of the findings of this study upon its completion.

YES ❑ NO ❑

researchers (see Exhibit 4.4). This ensures that other qualified scientists can access the data and verify the results of the research. However, such sharing may occur much less frequently than is desirable. For example, after many months and repeated efforts to obtain data from the authors of studies published in some of the best journals in psychology, Wicherts, Borsboom, Kats, and Molenaar (2006) reported that almost three-quarters of the authors refused to provide their data for re-analysis.

Prior to data collection, the researcher must obtain approval for conducting the research from the institution in which he or she works. In Canadian institutions, research ethics boards (REBs) ensure that the proposed research conforms to the Tri-Council Policy statement *Ethical Conduct for Research Involving Humans,* formulated by a joint body representing the Canadian Institutes of Health Research, the Natural Sciences and Engineering Research Council of Canada, and the Social Sciences and Humanities Research Council of Canada. The researcher must provide extensive details about the proposed study to the institution's REB. This involves providing both general information about the nature of the study and the procedures involved, as well as information specific to ethical considerations in the recruitment and research involvement of participants. Exhibit 4.6 lists the types of information that a researcher must provide when seeking REB approval to conduct a study.

Exhibit 4.6 Sample Form for Requesting Ethics Evaluation of a Research Project

This application form must be completed and submitted by all researchers planning to use human participants in their research study. All questions must be answered fully.

1. **Type of Research**
   Example: Honours student thesis project, doctoral dissertation, professor's research.
2. **Researchers**
   Please provide names, addresses, phone numbers, email addresses, and institutional affiliations.
3. **Research Project**
   Please provide title, anticipated starting and completion dates, and funding source. Please provide a summary (i.e., no more than six pages) of the proposed research that includes full details of the proposed methodology.
4. **Research Participants**
   Please provide details about the number of participants required and their ages and any special characteristics they must possess.
5. **Participant Recruitment**
   Please provide details on how and where participants will be recruited. If an organization has consented to provide support for participant recruitment, please provide evidence of this consent. Who will be responsible for contacting potential participants? Please provide copies of all forms or scripts used to recruit participants. If children are to be recruited, what steps have been taken to ensure that they and their legal guardians are provided with developmentally appropriate descriptions of the research and the nature of participation in the research?
6. **Screening of Participants**
   Will any steps be taken to select or exclude individuals from research participation? If yes, please include copies of the materials used for this screening.
7. **Research Participation**
   What, exactly, are the participants asked to do in the research? Please provide copies of all measures or interviews that will be completed and a full description of all tasks that participants will be asked to complete.
8. **Informed Consent**
   Please provide a copy of the consent to research form. What steps have been taken to ensure that there is no coercion to participate in the research? What steps have been taken to ensure that all requests for participants and descriptions of the research are done in a respectful and culturally appropriate manner?
9. **Potential Risks and Benefits**
   Please describe the potential risk to research participants, including physical harm, psychological harm, legal harms or inconveniences, or economic inconveniences. What steps are to be taken to minimize these risks? Please describe the potential benefits of the research and why the potential benefits of the study outweigh its potential risks.
10. **Anonymity**
    What steps will be taken to ensure the anonymity of participants during the research and in any presentation of the research results?
11. **Confidentiality**
    Please describe who will collect the data, who will have access to the data, and how the data will be stored. How long will the data be maintained?

RESEARCH DESIGNS

Are the findings of experimental studies more convincing than the results of other types of research designs?

As we describe in the following sections, numerous research designs are used in clinical psychology research. These designs vary in the degree of experimental manipulation (from naturalistic observation of behaviour to true experimental designs) and in the number of participants involved (from single participant designs to epidemiological designs using tens of thousands of participants). Although it is tempting to view certain designs as better or stronger than others, this is an oversimplification of research in a given domain. All designs have advantages and disadvantages. As we describe below, some designs are better than others in their capacity to control certain threats to research validity. We cannot determine the value of a design without knowing the state of knowledge in a research domain. For example, once a research area is well developed, correlational designs are unlikely to add anything new to the scientific literature. On the other hand, in a relatively new research area, even a relatively simple case study may make a meaningful contribution to the literature.

No single study can answer all of the important questions in a research area. Often a good study generates far more questions than answers. Research must be seen as cumulative, with each study contributing to the knowledge base of an area. Clinical psychology, as broadly defined in Chapter 1, involves the application of scientific knowledge to the understanding, assessment, prevention, and treatment of psychological disorders and distress. Many different research areas are relevant to the practice of clinical psychology. It is obvious that clinical practice should be informed by research on assessment, prevention, and intervention. In addition, clinical practice can be enriched by knowledge of research on psychopathology, stress and coping, normal development, normal family processes, and many other areas.

Some psychology students may find the rationale behind a number of research design features obscure or hard to comprehend. It is useful to think of these design features as strategies that address potential shortcomings of psychological research. For example some studies use control (or comparison) groups to examine similarities and differences between groups. This is done to address the criticism that a pattern seen in the research group of interest—such as the tendency for depressed adolescents to report conflictual relationships with their parents—may also be true for other groups (i.e., adolescents who are not depressed).

In experimental designs, participants are randomly assigned to the experimental groups. This strategy increases the likelihood that all groups are comparable prior to the experimental manipulation (such as receiving treatment or being on a waiting list prior to receiving treatment). After all, if groups are not equivalent before the manipulation, it is much more difficult to argue that any group difference evident after the manipulation is indeed due to the manipulation. So, for example, in examining the efficacy of a computer-based treatment for depressed adolescents, it would be necessary to ensure that adolescents were randomly assigned to treatment or waiting-list groups. Otherwise, positive changes in the computer-based treatment group might be attributed to pre-existing differences between the groups, such as their level of education, rather than to the effects of the specific treatment.

Although initial results are very exciting and rewarding, researchers should remain cautious about study results until the study is replicated, preferably by a different group of researchers. No matter how important the results of a study appear to be, they are of limited value unless similar results are independently obtained by others working in the field. Imagine that a car manufacturer advertises a new car with incredible fuel efficiency. These claims are not very convincing unless they are obtained by others who, independently of the manufacturer, evaluate the same model of car and obtain comparable results. Bearing this in mind, Viewpoint Box 4.1 raises some questions about the way in which the media often report on research findings.

VIEWPOINT BOX 4.1

IF IT IS REPORTED IN THE MEDIA, IT MUST BE TRUE—RIGHT?

You have seen or heard these types of headlines many times: fantastic claims are made about advances in our ability to cure life-threatening illnesses, change human behaviour, unlock hidden potentials of the human mind, or "turn back the clock" on the aging process. It is not just advertisements, tabloid newspapers, or websites of questionable accuracy that report such claims. Major news agencies and television networks also report claims like these every day of the week. "Science writers" trawl the scientific journals to locate articles that will be of interest to the general public. Most of these advances are presented as coming from legitimate researchers working in universities, government institutions, or multinational corporation laboratories. It all sounds so tempting to believe any great news that offers hope of relief from suffering—but should you? Clearly it would be impossible to evaluate all of these claims, but researchers have begun to examine the accuracy of the information presented in media reports.

The American Association for the Advancement of Science (AAAS) operates an online, global news service through which research institutions can release their research results to the public. EurekAlert! (www.eurekalert.org/index.php) provides coverage of press releases in all areas of science. Yavchitz and colleagues (2012) were interested in the extent to which a positive "spin" (i.e., over-emphasizing the possible beneficial effects of an experimental treatment) was evident in the results of randomized controlled trials

CONTINUED . . .

of health care interventions reported in EurekAlert! They searched for all press releases on the site, dated between December 2009 and March 2010, about research that compared an experimental treatment to a control condition or comparison treatment. For the 70 studies they found, they then obtained (a) the published article on which the press release was based and (b) copies of news items based on the press releases. The researchers found an inappropriate or unwarranted emphasis on the benefits of the experimental treatment (such as focusing only on findings showing an effect for the experimental treatment) in 40% of the journal abstracts, 47% of the press releases, and 51% of the news items based on the press releases. In most instances the spin found in the press releases and media reports originated in the journal abstract. This suggests that researchers themselves are likely responsible for at least some of the "overselling" of research findings.

©iStock.com/101cats

News stories often exaggerate the effects of new findings.

There are indications, though, that media outlets also bear some responsibility, as they do not provide appropriate coverage in cases in which exciting or promising initial research results are not replicated in subsequent research. Gonon, Konsman, Cohen, and Boraud (2012) examined the reporting in English-language newspapers of influential research studies on attention deficit/hyperactivity disorder (ADHD). As most psychology students know, replication is essential in the scientific process, and these researchers were interested in determining whether media outlets displayed an awareness of the importance of replication. They searched the *Dow Jones Factiva* database to locate scientific publications on ADHD reported in newspapers in the 1990s and identified the 10 most frequently mentioned studies. Then they searched the *PubMed* database until the end of 2011 for all research studies that were on the same topic as these 10 most mentioned studies. Of key interest to the researchers was the extent to which (a) the results of subsequent research were consistent with the findings of the most mentioned studies and (b) there was newspaper coverage provided to these later research publications. According to Gonon and colleagues, most findings reported in the newspapers during the 1990s were not replicated in subsequent research, with only 2 of the 10 most cited studies having results that were supported by later research investigations. In addition, they found only one newspaper article that reported on the fact that the research findings stemming from one of most commonly mentioned studies were not supported by subsequent research.

So, the bottom line appears to be that, to really understand what was found in a research study, it is essential to locate and read the research study, and related research studies, rather than simply relying on media reports of the findings. Media reports tend to focus on the most sensational aspects of study findings and rarely fully explain the state of scientific knowledge on a topic. It is far more appealing to state that a study holds the key to resolving Alzheimer's disease than it is to explain how a study adds a tiny piece to our understanding of a very complex issue.

Syracuse University (Archives)

Dr. Donald Campbell encouraged researchers to pay more attention to potential design problems that can undermine a study's validity.

You've probably noticed that published research studies include extensive detail about how the study was conducted, what statistical analyses were used, and what the results were. You may find these details boring and tend to skip over them. Now imagine that you are reading a study in order to attempt to replicate it for your honours thesis. In this case, you will be eager to know the precise details so that you can conduct your study in the same way.

internal validity: the extent to which the interpretations drawn from the results of a study can be justified and alternative interpretations can be reasonably ruled out.

external validity: the extent to which the interpretations drawn from the results of a study can be generalized beyond the narrow boundaries of the specific study.

statistical conclusion validity: the extent to which the results of a study are accurate and valid based on the type of statistical procedures used in the research.

Over the years, psychologists have identified a relatively large number of design problems that can undermine the validity of a research study. Of course, if steps are taken to overcome these problems prior to conducting a study, the validity of a study is protected or strengthened. Therefore researchers have gone to great lengths to develop and promote the use of a classification system that covers the majority of potential problems. As originally conceptualized by **Donald Campbell** (e.g., Cook & Campbell, 1979), these potential design problems are classified as representing threats to the **internal validity**, **external validity**, or **statistical conclusion validity** of a study. We will deal with the first two categories of threats to validity now and discuss threats to statistical conclusion validity later in the chapter.

Internal validity refers to the extent to which the interpretations drawn from the results of a study can be justified and alternative interpretations can be reasonably ruled out. Exhibit 4.7 describes the types of threats to internal validity that psychologists must attend to in designing their research. **External validity** refers to the extent to which the interpretations drawn from the results of a study can be generalized beyond the narrow boundaries of the specific study in question. Exhibit 4.8 describes the types of threats to external validity that psychologists must attend to in designing their research.

Exhibit 4.7 Threats to the Internal Validity of a Study

History: This threat involves the influence of events that occur outside the context of the study that influence or account for the results of the study.

Maturation: Changes in the participants due to their psychological or physical development that cannot be disentangled from the experimental manipulation can pose a threat to internal validity.

Testing: Repeated testing may influence the results of a study due to the participants' familiarity with a test and memory of how they responded previously on a test or measure.

CONTINUED . . .

Instrumentation: In longitudinal studies, changes in the definition of constructs and in their measurement can make the interpretation of changes in participants' responses much more difficult, if not impossible.
Statistical Regression: Extreme scores on measures, both high and low, tend to be less extreme upon retesting. This may mean that changes in scores in a study may be due to regression rather than to an experimental manipulation.
Selection Biases: This threat involves the effect that systematic differences in recruiting participants or assigning participants to experimental conditions may have on the outcome of the study.
Attrition: The loss of participants in a study over time may bias the results if there are systematic differences between those who remain in the study and those who withdraw.

Adapted from Cook and Campbell (1979).

Exhibit 4.8 Threats to the External Validity of a Study

Sample Characteristics: External validity can be limited because of the degree to which the characteristics of the research participants, such as their sociodemographic and psychological characteristics, map onto other samples and populations of interest.
Stimulus Characteristics and Settings: Aside from the participants, features of the study such as the institutional setting and the characteristics of those involved in the conduct of the study (e.g., therapists in a treatment study) may constrain the generalizability of obtained results.
Reactivity of Research Arrangements: By virtue of being in a study, participants may respond differently than they would in other contexts. This can severely limit the extent to which the results of the study provide information about how people behave outside of the research context.
Reactivity of Assessment: Participants' awareness that their behaviours, moods, attitudes, etc. are being monitored may influence how they respond in the study and these alterations in response may not be consistent with their responses once the study is completed.
Timing of Measurement: The decision about when to measure variables may result in conclusions that are not true for all time points (e.g., observed effects that appear stable over time may in fact not be stable between measurement periods).

Adapted from Cook and Campbell (1979).

A close reading of these two exhibits shows that there is no perfect study and researchers must balance internal and external validity. Generally speaking, the more a researcher attempts to deal with threats to internal validity, the more he or she opens up the study to threats to external validity, and vice versa. By reducing threats to internal validity, the researcher opts to have as "clean" a study as possible. Typically, scientists initially give priority to concerns about internal validity, as this allows a relatively straightforward interpretation of the study's findings. Once again, though, the need to give priority to addressing internal or external validity threats depends on the state of the research field.

How does a psychologist decide whether to maximize internal validity or external validity?

Take, for example, the field of psychotherapy research. Research from the 1970s to the 1990s emphasized the need to control threats to internal validity. Treatment manuals were used to operationalize the nature of treatments, and numerous methodological and statistical strategies were developed to minimize effects due to selection biases and to attrition. Careful attention to threats to internal validity enabled scientists to gather relatively unambiguous evidence of the clinical efficacy of many treatments.

As you learned in Chapter 1, "efficacy" is the term used to describe treatment effects in tightly controlled experimental designs. Once psychotherapy researchers know these treatments are helpful under tightly controlled conditions, they can loosen some experimental controls on internal validity in order to enhance the external validity of subsequent treatment studies. Thus, in the next stage of treatment research, participation selection criteria may be relaxed, monitoring of therapist interventions may be through limited supervision or quality assurance practices rather than through intense supervision, and timelines for the delivery of services may be made more flexible, permitting an assessment of clinical effectiveness. In Chapter 1, you learned that effectiveness refers to treatment effects in "real world" treatment settings and contexts, with typical patients and typical therapists.

In the following sections, we describe a variety of research designs, starting first with those that offer only limited protection against threats to validity. Designs such as these are often used in early research on a particular topic. As the knowledge on a topic evolves, there is a tendency for the research designs to become progressively more rigorous. Accordingly, we also describe designs that offer considerable protection against threats to validity, especially threats to internal validity.

Case Studies

Like in medicine, case studies have a long and important history in clinical psychology. Descriptions of unusual presenting problems or of novel treatments have enriched the professional literature. A typical case study involves a detailed presentation of an individual patient, couple, or family illustrating some new or rare observation or treatment innovation. Case studies are a valuable format for making preliminary connections between events, behaviours, and symptoms that have not been addressed in extant research. Case studies can be a rich source of research hypotheses regarding the etiology or maintenance of disorders. They can also be the initial testing ground for innovative assessment or intervention strategies. Case studies have heuristic value—that is, they draw the attention of other professionals to a phenomenon.

The scientific value of case studies is in their potential to generate hypotheses, but they do not allow for the rigorous testing of hypotheses. The major weakness of the case study method is that most threats to internal validity cannot be adequately addressed (Kazdin, 1981). Take, for example, a case study on the treatment of Zach's temper tantrums around homework. Usually, the author of a case study reports the client's symptoms or presenting problems prior to and following treatment (such as the number of tantrums and their intensity). Although the author would probably like to claim that any improvement was due to treatment effects, alternative explanations cannot be ruled out in this simple research design. The observed changes could be due to a number of other factors unrelated to therapy, including normal developmental changes (i.e., maturation—the simple effects of Zach growing older or having no homework during the holidays), the abating of symptoms that typically occurs over time (i.e., regression to the mean), or life events outside of therapy (i.e., history effects, such as getting a new teacher).

Changes in Zach's difficulties around homework might occur for many different reasons.

Single Case Designs

The limitations of the case study can be at least partially addressed in a number of ways, even when the focus of the study remains on an individual patient (or couple or family) or on a very small number of patients (Hayes, Barlow, & Nelson-Gray, 1999; Morgan & Morgan, 2001). Threats such as maturation and regression to the mean can be easily handled by the simple strategy of extending the period of time that the person is assessed and the frequency with which the assessments occur. To address the threat of changing criteria or definitions of the problems/symptoms (i.e., instrumentation), the same measures can be used at each assessment point rather than, for example, relying on one parent's ratings for pre-test and the other parent's ratings for post-test. Also, the measures should be standardized and, if at all possible, well established rather than being potentially unstable and biased clinician observations.

The possibility that observed changes are due to extra-treatment events can be partially addressed by clearly defining the nature of the therapeutic intervention and precisely noting when it occurred. Thus, *if* the problems were relatively consistent and stable prior to the target intervention *and* the change occurs very shortly after the intervention, *then* a case can be made for the change being due to the intervention. Figure 4.1 illustrates a number of these features in what is commonly known as an A-B single case design, with the A period representing the level of symptoms prior to the intervention (also known as the baseline) and the B period representing the level of symptoms following the intervention. Although intervention effects are typically determined by

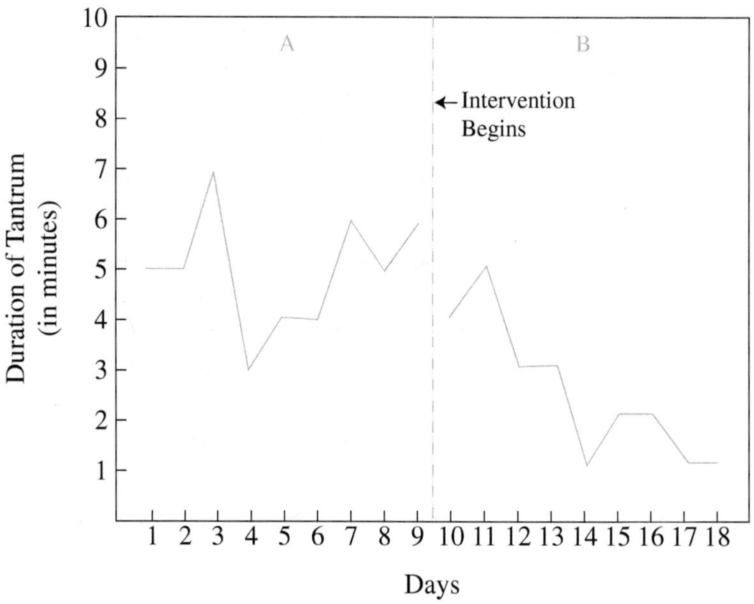

Figure 4.1 A-B design

visual inspection of graphed data (such as represented in Figure 4.1), a number of statistical tests can be used to determine if statistically significant changes occurred (e.g., Morley & Adams, 1989). Such tests can be especially valuable if the baseline assessment of symptoms shows a very variable pattern.

Two design strategies improve on the straightforward A-B design by ruling out the threat of history to the validity of the study. The first option is to conduct a small series of A-B designs using the same intervention with a number of individuals who present with similar problems. If the data for three or four cases are collected sequentially (i.e., the people receiving the intervention do not all receive the intervention at the same time) and the symptom levels consistently appear to change following the intervention, then support for the contention that the intervention was responsible for the change is very strong. A second option is to use what is known as an A-B-A single case design. This is similar to the A-B design except that the treatment is withdrawn after a few weeks and data continue to be collected for a second A period (i.e., a period in which no treatment occurs). For example, after the psychologist collaborates with Zach's parents to precisely define what constitutes a tantrum, they could be asked to ignore tantrums and reward homework completion during period B, and to return to their regular reaction of reminders and threats during the second A period. If Zach's tantrums return to pre-treatment levels, then a strong case can be made for the effectiveness of the intervention. The major drawbacks to this design are that (a) it may not be possible to have the person refrain from using the treatment strategies during the second A period, especially if the strategies have been effective in reducing symptom levels for a few weeks, and (b) ethical considerations may make clinicians unwilling to remove, however briefly, a treatment strategy that appears to be working well.

Correlational Designs

Correlational designs are probably the most commonly used research designs in clinical psychology. The focus of these designs, no matter how complex they are, is on the examination of association among variables. Perhaps the most common error is to make causal statements about associations in the data, but this is inappropriate, as correlational designs can never determine causality. Even when one variable temporally precedes another variable, a causal connection cannot be established, as the apparent effect of the first variable on the second could be due to the influence of an unmeasured third variable. The hallmarks of the scientific study of causality in human functioning are the use of experimental manipulation and random assignment to conditions. Both of these design features are absent in correlational designs.

It is a mistake to equate correlational *analyses* with correlational *designs*. Correlational designs can be analyzed with all types of statistics, including correlations, partial correlations, multiple regression, *t*-tests, or analysis of variance (ANOVA). For example, many studies compare the performance on a laboratory task (e.g., a simulated social interaction) of people diagnosed with a DSM disorder with that of people with no diagnosis. Even though there are discrete groups and an ANOVA is conducted to analyze group performance on the lab task, the design of the study is correlational in nature. This is because no manipulation occurs (i.e., all participants experience the same conditions in the study) and participants are not randomly assigned to conditions.

Sometimes researchers using a correlational design decide to artificially create groups from the data they collected by using median splits or some type of cut-off score to categorize participants as high or low on a dimension. Again, the use of group comparisons in the data analysis should not be confused with an experimental design. It is also worth noting that the common strategy of dichotomizing continuous variables is rarely appropriate and can frequently yield misleading results (MacCallum, Zhang, Preacher, & Rucker, 2002; Streiner, 2002). One of the main drawbacks of this strategy is that median splits are often used to form the two groups (i.e., half of the participants are assigned to each group), and whether a participant is assigned to the "high" group or the "low" group on the basis of his or her score depends on the median score for the set of participants. Therefore, as median scores are likely to differ across studies, the same participant score may be assigned to the high group in one study and the low group in another. This makes it extremely difficult to summarize findings across studies, as the precise nature of a "high score" varies from study to study.

Correlational designs come in many forms. Some are purely descriptive, such as the bulk of epidemiological research on the study of the incidence (the rate of new cases of a disorder in a specific time period), prevalence (the overall rate of cases of a disorder in a specific time period), and distribution (rates of disorders across geographic areas and/or sociodemographic characteristics) of disorders in a population. A good example of this type of study is the one by the WHO World Mental Health Survey Consortium (2004) of the prevalence of mental disorders, that you learned about in Chapter 3.

factor analysis: a statistical procedure used to determine the conceptual dimensions or factors that underlie a set of variables, test items, or tests.

Correlational designs can be used to examine the underlying structure of a measure or a set of measures. This is known as **factor analysis**. Factor analysis is often used in the development of a measure to determine which items contribute meaningfully to the test. Despite the test developer's best efforts, some items may simply not work as well as others in assessing the construct the test was designed to evaluate. Factor analysis can reveal which items "work" and which don't. Factor analysis can also be used to determine the conceptual dimensions that underlie a set of tests. For example, a researcher may have data from participants who completed measures on a range of variables such as anger, anxiety, loneliness, shyness, and dysphoria. Through the use of factor analytic techniques, the researcher can determine whether these measures all assess distinct constructs or whether they are better understood as tapping into a single, broad construct often labelled *general distress or negative affectivity*. Figure 4.2 illustrates the way test items form different factors.

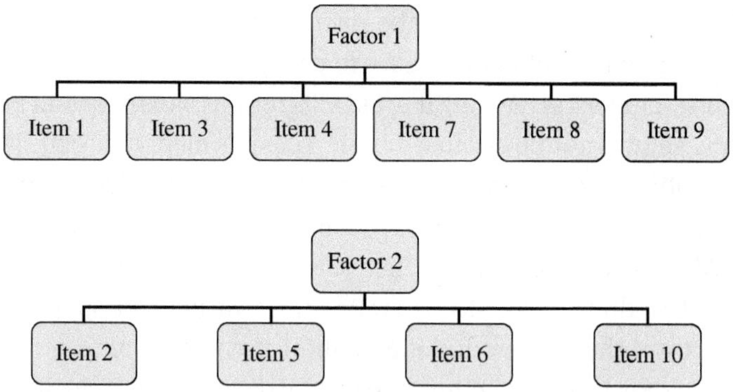

Figure 4.2 An illustration of how items in a test form different factors

Although factor analysis comprises a large range of statistical techniques, there are two basic forms. Exploratory factor analysis is used when the researcher has no prior hypotheses about the structure of the data. In this situation, the pattern of correlations among variables or test items provides the evidence for the underlying factor structure in the data. In contrast, a more demanding form of factor analysis, known as confirmatory factor analysis, is used to test a specific hypothesis regarding the nature of the factor structure. With confirmatory factor analysis, the researcher specifies, a priori, what the factor structure should be and how each variable or test item contributes to this structure. The statistical analysis then provides information on how well the structure observed in the data fits with the hypothesized factor structure.

Most frequently, correlational designs are employed to examine the relations among discrete variables in an effort to develop or test a conceptual model. One such design involves the testing of a **moderator** variable (see Exhibit 4.3). A moderator variable is one that influences the strength of the relation between a predictor variable and a criterion variable (Holmbeck, 1997). For example, the relation between the experience of stressful life events and psychological distress may be moderated by the type of coping strategies used. Given comparable levels of life stress, the greater use of coping strategies designed to actively engage and resolve problems may result in lower levels of distress. In general, moderator analyses are used to enhance the researcher's ability to predict as much variance as possible in a criterion variable by exploring the ways in which other variables can be combined to predict the criterion.

moderator: a variable that influences the strength of the relation between a predictor variable and a criterion variable.

Another common design involves the testing of **mediator** variables. A mediator variable explains the mechanism by which a predictor variable influences a criterion variable (Holmbeck, 1997). For example, the relation between parental psychopathology and child adjustment may be due, partially or entirely, to the quality of the relationship between parent and child. In general, mediator analyses are used to explicate the conceptual link among variables. As an aside, moderator and mediator analyses can be used with both correlational and experimental designs (Kraemer, Wilson, Fairburn, & Agras, 2002).

mediator: a variable that explains the mechanism by which a predictor variable influences a criterion variable.

A final correlational design that is increasingly used in clinical psychology research is known as **structural equation modelling** (SEM; e.g., Ullman, 2006). SEM is a comprehensive approach to testing an entire theoretical model. This design combines elements of confirmatory factor analysis and mediator analyses. First, the researcher lays out a structural model that shows how all the variables in the model are related to each other. This is akin to mediator analyses. For example, the model may be one in which both client beliefs about the benefits of treatment and the severity of client problems are hypothesized to

structural equation modelling: a comprehensive statistical procedure that involves testing all components of a theoretical model.

predict the extent to which treatment is successful. The effect of beliefs about treatment on treatment outcome is hypothesized to be mediated by motivation to engage in the various aspects of treatment, whereas the effect of problem severity on treatment outcome is hypothesized to be direct, with no mediating variables. In SEM, the ability of the whole model to predict treatment outcome is assessed.

In a second step, the researcher considers how best to measure each variable in the model (in our example, this includes treatment expectations, problem severity, treatment motivation, and treatment outcome) and selects multiple measures for each variable. The specification and testing of this measurement model is akin to confirmatory factor analysis. There are several strengths to this design. The analysis of the measurement model allows the researcher to obtain relatively pure measures of a construct that are derived from multiple measures used for each variable. These measures are then used to test a comprehensive structural model rather than isolated aspects of the model one at a time, as is typically done in mediator analyses. However, despite the complexity and strength of this design, SEM can determine only the extent to which a hypothesized causal model fits the study's data—it cannot unequivocally demonstrate that the hypothesized causal model is true. Nevertheless, it is possible to apply SEM to data gathered from experimental designs to make stronger statements about causal relations among some variables (MacCallum & Austin, 2000). One challenge in conducting SEM is that it requires a relatively large sample (i.e., more than 200 participants). For research on relatively infrequent conditions, such as aphasia or clinically significant hoarding, it may be difficult to recruit sufficient numbers of participants so that SEM procedures can be used.

Quasi-Experimental Designs

Quasi-experimental designs involve some form of manipulation by the researcher, such as variations in the nature of the information provided prior to undertaking some task, exposure to different levels of noise while completing a task, or different types of treatment conditions. Quasi-experimental designs do not, however, involve random assignment to experimental conditions. A weakness of this design is that, because participants are not randomly assigned to the different conditions or levels of the independent variable, the effect of the independent variable on the dependent variable may be confounded with extraneous influences.

Of course, this raises the question of why anyone would choose not to use an experimental design. The answer is simple: in many situations it is simply not ethical or feasible to randomly assign participants to conditions. A study of health care systems by Bickman (1996) illustrates the usefulness of quasi-experimental designs when experimental designs are not suitable. The study was designed to determine whether the provision of enhanced mental health care services, in addition to usual care, resulted in improvements in participants' psychological and social functioning. The enhanced care condition was extensive, with cost and training considerations limiting the availability of the condition to a single American site. Because all participants in the area knew that the enhanced care was available, it would have been impossible to randomly assign participants to enhanced and usual care conditions. Instead, the researchers selected a site elsewhere in the United States that was comparable in terms of the population of potential participants and in terms of the usual mental health services available. Data were collected from participants at both sites to determine the effect of the enhanced care intervention.

The most frequently used quasi-experimental designs involve the comparison of two previously established groups of participants. In the simplest design, one group receives the intervention, the other doesn't. Data are collected after the intervention and then analyzed. This design is cost-effective and relatively straightforward because only one wave of data collection is required. However, this must be balanced against the obvious weakness of this design: that the two groups may differ substantially before the intervention, thereby confounding the results. Data collection prior to the intervention strengthens the design, as pre-intervention differences can be controlled for statistically.

Experimental Designs

Experimental designs involve both random assignment to condition and experimental manipulation. These features allow the researcher to draw relatively unambiguous conclusions about the effects of the independent variable on the dependent variable. We say "relatively" unambiguous because results may be confounded by unplanned variability in the manner in which the manipulation occurred (e.g., therapists who are supposed to be providing the same treatment may differ in how closely they follow the treatment protocol) or by the random assignment of participants failing to yield groups equivalent on all dimensions prior to the intervention (this is often due to using too small a sample).

Compared with all other research designs, experimental designs provide the best protection against threats to internal validity. As with quasi-experimental designs, the strongest design is one in which both pre-intervention and post-intervention data are collected. Sometimes, however, concerns about reactivity to testing may lead a researcher to dispense with obtaining pre-intervention data, which weakens the ability to determine the initial equivalence of groups. By skimming the pages of scientific journals in clinical psychology, you will find many examples of experimental designs, often called true experiments. In the realm of psychotherapy research, these types of designs are typically known as **randomized controlled trials**. Randomized controlled trials involve the random assignment of participants into one of two or more treatment conditions. In many instances, a no-treatment condition (often called a wait-list condition) is included, in which research participants do not immediately receive any form of intervention. Then, in order to meet ethical standards, once a period that is comparable to the duration of the treatment or treatments being investigated has passed, those in the no-treatment condition are offered treatment.

randomized controlled trial: an experiment in which research participants are randomly assigned to one of two or more treatment conditions.

PROFILE BOX 4.2

DR. DAVID HODGINS

Courtesy of David Hodgins

I am a full professor in the program in clinical psychology in the Department of Psychology, University of Calgary. I am also the head, Department of Psychology and a coordinator with the Alberta Gaming Research Institute. I received my B.A. (Honours) (1981) in psychology from Carleton University, and my M.A. (1983) and Ph.D. (1987) in clinical psychology from Queen's University. I am registered as a clinical psychologist in Alberta. My research interests focus on various aspects of addictive behaviours, including relapse and recovery from substance abuse and gambling disorders. I have published over 100 peer-reviewed articles in top journals on these topics. I have conducted a number of randomized clinical trials of both brief and more traditional addiction treatment models. My self-directed treatment model for gambling problems is recognized as an evidence-based treatment by the United States Substance Abuse and Mental Health Administration. In 2010, I received the Scientific Achievement Award from the U.S. National Center for Responsible Gaming. I maintain a private practice in Calgary in addition to providing consultation to a number of organizations internationally.

HOW DID YOU CHOOSE TO BECOME A CLINICAL PSYCHOLOGIST?

I attended a small rural high school and remember clearly in my final year selecting pamphlets labelled Psychologist, Psychiatrist, and Social Worker from the career information display outside the guidance counsellor's office. Even though I did not really know the difference between them, I was more drawn by the description of psychology than the alternatives. I don't think I locked into a career path at that point. Instead, I took a variety of introductory courses in my first year of university and psychology ended up being the most stimulating. I particularly liked the abnormal module and I remember special lectures by a graduate student on the topic of death and dying. Although I don't remember what I learned from the pamphlet in high school, I do know that my undergraduate courses at Carleton University helped me appreciate psychology's scientific approach to understanding behaviour. By the end of my B.A., I knew that I wanted to attend

CONTINUED . . .

graduate school in clinical psychology. At that point, I was interested in developmental psychology and envisioned myself being a scientist-practitioner working with children and families. However, I didn't appreciate yet the role serendipity plays in determining the path that one ultimately takes!

WHAT IS THE MOST REWARDING PART OF YOUR JOB AS A CLINICAL PSYCHOLOGIST?

I particularly enjoy the diversity that psychology has offered me. Before moving to academia, I held a number of clinically focused positions. After graduate school, I worked as a psychologist in Cape Breton, half-time in a mental health service and half-time on a long-stay inpatient unit. These positions taught me a lot about the diversity of clients in terms of severity and types of disorders and how to work with other disciplines to ensure optimal care. My second position was an addiction position in Calgary, which had ultimately been my area of focus in graduate school. The Calgary position was diverse, busy, and challenging, although in different ways than in Cape Breton. The position was in a major teaching hospital that had both education and research mandates in addition to the clinical mandate. Supervision of psychology students and trainees in other disciplines was expected. Research and evaluation was possible. My research involvement and more serendipity allowed me to move to a full-time academic position in 2001.

WHAT IS THE GREATEST CHALLENGE YOU FACE AS A CLINICAL PSYCHOLOGIST?

Like a lot of psychologists, I find that information overload is a constant challenge. From my desktop, laptop, or iPad, I can now access almost any type of psychological knowledge and there is simply too much to process, even within my specific area of focus (and without considering all the other areas for which I'd like to know the latest developments). Add to that burden, the daily onslaught of emails, listservs, and texts and it is simply overwhelming to know how to filter everything to a manageable level. At least my phone does not ring as often as it used to.

TELL US ABOUT YOUR RESEARCH ON ADDICTIVE BEHAVIOURS

My most recent area of focus has been on helping individuals recover from gambling problems "by themselves." This is not the oxymoron that it appears to be. People who recover without using formal treatment programs use the same recovery strategies that are taught in treatment. We are investigating various methods of promoting this self-recovery process. Our latest project is testing the efficacy of an online Web-based self-recovery toolkit.

HOW DO YOU INTEGRATE SCIENCE AND PRACTICE IN YOUR WORK?

For me, the integration of science and practice is so essential to clinical psychology that I can't imagine how I could separate them. I need to have a theoretical model to direct what I do clinically and I feel compelled to track the empirical foundation of the model as it unfolds in the research literature. At the same time, my clients have taught me a lot and it is clear that my years as a front-line clinician have informed the types of research questions that I ask.

WHAT DO YOU SEE AS THE MOST EXCITING CHANGES IN THE FIELD OF CLINICAL PSYCHOLOGY?

Basing policy and clinical practice on research evidence is a strong trend in health care and other government systems. As a science-based discipline, psychology has been ahead of the pack and it is good to see us provide some leadership in this area. It is also good to see psychology responding to the increased consumer perspective in mental health, helping to design accessible and effective treatments.

Meta-Analysis

Until the 1980s, reviews summarizing research findings in a specific research realm were based on qualitative (that is, non-numerical) methods. Somewhat like a sophisticated term paper, reviews provided a narrative account of the various studies, their strengths, weaknesses, and findings, and then drew conclusions about the state of knowledge in the research area. This traditional form of review is still used for summarizing conceptual and methodological approaches used in researching a topic. However, a quantitative form of research review known as **meta-analysis** is now the standard for making a general statement about the findings in a research field (Harris, 2003).

meta-analysis: a set of statistical procedures for quantitatively summarizing the results of a research domain.

Meta-analysis brings scientific rigour to the process of reviewing the results of research, allowing investigators to use explicit decision rules and computations in reporting findings. Consequently, meta-analytic studies are more frequently cited in the work of researchers than are studies using the other research designs we have described (Patsopoulos, Analatos, & Ioannidis, 2005). Meta-analysis involves a complex set of statistical procedures to quantitatively review research in an area. An analogy to a typical research study may be helpful to explain what meta-analysis is. A typical research study involves the collection of data from multiple research participants. The data are then summed up and overall trends in the group of participants are examined using statistical procedures. The same general process occurs in meta-analysis, but the "participants" in a meta-analysis are research studies rather than individuals.

In a single research study, similar data are collected from all participants. Obviously this is not possible in a meta-analysis, for the original research studies are likely to have employed different measures for assessing outcome. Meta-analysis combines the results of prior research using a common metric called an **effect size** (Rosenthal & DiMatteo, 2001). Effect sizes can be calculated for almost all types of research designs and statistical analyses. For correlational analyses, the correlation coefficient is typically used as the effect size. For analyses involving differences among groups, the effect size is obtained by calculating the difference between the means of two groups (e.g., the treatment and no-treatment groups) and then dividing by the standard deviation of either one of the groups or the pooled sample of both groups. Although it may seem that these are relatively simple calculations, researchers have found that great care must be taken in quantitatively summarizing a research area, as it is very easy for errors to creep into the calculations of effect sizes (Gøtzsche, Hróbjartsson, Marić, & Tendal, 2007).

effect size: a standardized metric, typically expressed in standard deviation units or correlations, that allows the results of research studies to be combined and analyzed.

Meta-analysis offers numerous advantages over traditional research reviews or single empirical studies. For example, statistical analyses, rather than the author's impressions, guide the conclusions drawn about a research topic. Moreover, by including data from many studies, the number of research participants on whom conclusions are based is dramatically increased. This greatly enhances the researcher's power to detect an effect and improves the generalizability of the conclusions drawn on the basis of the literature. Given its methodological and statistical strengths, meta-analysis is increasingly used to determine the current state of knowledge about many areas of research and to assist in the development of health care policies regarding the provision of medical and psychological services. In Chapters 12 and 13, we describe several meta-analyses that have been influential in shaping views of the efficacy of psychological treatments for patients of all ages.

SELECTING RESEARCH PARTICIPANTS AND MEASURES

We cannot emphasize enough that no single study can answer all the questions in a research field. At best, a study adds a small amount of knowledge to a field. To be certain that this knowledge is meaningful, researchers must be aware of the strengths and limitations of their studies and must strive to reduce threats to the validity of the research. As we described in Exhibits 4.7 and 4.8, many of the threats to the internal and external validity of a study can be addressed by considering a number of participant sample and measurement parameters. In the following sections, we highlight some issues that researchers must consider in order to maximize the validity of a study.

Selecting the Sample

Biases in sample characteristics and selection can have an enormous impact on the researcher's ability to accurately interpret study results. For example, a study based on data obtained from White male university students registered in an introductory psychology course is likely to have rather limited generalizability, and the researcher must ensure that his or her conclusions accurately reflect the fact that the findings may not apply across age, gender, ethnicity, educational level, and socioeconomic status. Likewise, a study of parenting values based on data from two biological-parent Chinese Canadian families residing in the same home may provide very valuable information, but the results may not generalize to other ethnic groups or to other family constellations, such as step-families, single-parent families, or families with

Researchers need to be aware of how differences in the sociodemographic characteristics of research participants may affect the generalizability of their research results.

same-sex parents. As a starting point, therefore, the researcher needs to consider how best to optimize the fit between (a) the characteristics of the population to which the results will be generalized and (b) the type of sample that should be recruited for the study. It is also important that the researcher fully describe the characteristics of the participants involved in the research and the manner in which participants were recruited for the study. Surprisingly, this is not always done in published research (Lee et al., 2007). Without such information, it is not possible to determine whether the results may be biased by the sample composition.

Selecting the Sampling Strategy

It is rarely possible to obtain data from all members of a population, regardless of whether the population is defined as all citizens of a country, all those who experienced a specific stressor (such as surviving a hurricane), or all people with a specific mental disorder (such as schizophrenia). Accordingly, researchers must make decisions about how to obtain data from a subset of the population of interest. This subset is known as the research sample. Decisions about the strategies used to recruit participants can affect the validity and generalizability of a study.

If a psychologist wants to study people diagnosed with a specific disorder, why does it matter how they are recruited into the study?

Two examples illustrate the potential research limitations of sampling strategies. A number of studies have examined the extent to which victims of childhood sexual abuse exhibit psychological symptoms and disorders as adults. Contradictory findings have been reported with respect to dissociative symptoms, with some studies finding little evidence of dissociative symptoms and others finding substantial evidence of the link between childhood victimization and later dissociative symptoms. Much of the apparent discrepancy between such findings appears to be due to variations in sampling strategies. The studies finding little or no connection tend to use community samples, whereas studies reporting strong connections tend to use samples from psychological or psychiatric clinics. Thus, evidence for dissociative symptoms depends on the extent to which participants are experiencing clinical distress and/or seeking services for their distress (Rumstein-McKean & Hunsley, 2001). A second example comes from research on marital functioning. Karney and colleagues (1995) conducted two studies: in the first, couples were recruited through newspaper advertisements and, in the second, research participants were solicited from public records of marriage licences. The two samples of participants differed on many sociodemographic, psychological, personality, and marital quality variables. Because of these differences, many of the significant associations found among these variables in one study were not found in the second. These two examples demonstrate the need for researchers to attend to sampling strategies, both in the design of a study and in interpretation of findings.

There are two basic forms of sampling: probability sampling and non-probability sampling (Henry, 1990). Probability sampling focuses on the use of numerous strategies to ensure that the research sample is representative of the population (e.g., obtaining data from every 10th household in a neighbourhood; using census information to determine how many participants with different levels of income need to be recruited in a study; contacting a randomly selected 20% of all psychologists licensed in a jurisdiction and requesting their involvement in a study). The term *probability sampling* comes from the fact that, with these types of sampling strategies, the researcher knows the probability of selecting participants from the population of interest. This is the type of sampling used in surveys that are frequently reported in the media on topics such as preferences for political parties or candidates, views on government priorities, and attitudes on issues such as immigration, health care, and the environment. Probability samples are required when the researcher is interested in obtaining an accurate and precise estimate of the strength, level, or frequency of some construct in the population. For this reason, probability sampling is typically used in epidemiological studies of the prevalence of mental disorders or the utilization of mental health services.

Although some psychological research uses probability sampling strategies, psychologists more commonly rely on non-probability sampling approaches. These sampling strategies may include advertising for research participants in a newspaper, on a website, or in a mental health treatment setting. As you probably know from experience, many psychological studies rely on university students as research participants. Because the researcher does not know how many people saw a recruitment poster or opened a recruitment email for participation in the study, it is not possible to determine the probability of obtaining participants from the pool of potential participants. Furthermore, because the researcher is not specifically recruiting in order to ensure the representativeness of the sample, data from non-probability samples are unlikely to be as generalizable as data obtained from probability samples. However, in much psychological research, this is assumed not to be a major problem.

Setting the Sample Size

The final consideration is the number of participants required for the study. Without a sufficient number of participants, a study will not have the statistical power needed to detect the very effect it was designed to examine. Psychotherapy outcome research illustrates this challenge. Most experimental studies in which a treatment condition is compared with a no-treatment control condition have sufficient sample sizes and power to detect an effect due to treatment. However, an early and influential review of experiments in which two treatments were compared with each other found that only half of published studies had sufficient sample sizes and power to detect a difference between treatments (Kazdin & Bass, 1989). Although the conclusions of this review have been available for many years, there are still frequent problems with studies having low power to detect treatment effects. As we will discuss in Chapter 14, this means that a common interpretation that all psychotherapies have comparable effects may be based, at least partially, on research design weaknesses. Many tools, developed using the statistical work of Jacob Cohen, are available to assist researchers in determining the optimal number of participants to recruit for a study based on the phenomenon under investigation, the research design, and the type of planned data analysis (e.g., Cohen, 1992).

Measurement Options and the Importance of Psychometric Properties

A multitude of measurement options are available to clinical psychologists conducting research. No option is necessarily the best for all types of studies. Instead, as we have repeatedly emphasized, the strengths and limitations of a measurement option (or a research design or a sampling strategy) must be carefully considered, along with the degree to which the measurement option fits the research hypothesis and other aspects of the planned study. Exhibit 4.9 provides a summary of the range of general measurement modalities that may be appropriate for a study. In many studies, multiple measures of each variable are selected. This enhances the likelihood that the variable of interest has been fully or adequately measured in the study. However, as the time required for study participation increases, this may have an effect on the study by selectively influencing the type of person who is able and willing to take part, thereby affecting the study's external validity.

The psychometric properties of a measurement strategy have a dramatic effect on the outcome of a study. Reliability—the degree of consistency in the measurement—and validity—the degree to which the construct of interest is accurately measured—both affect the quality of a study and the likelihood that a hypothesis is tested appropriately. Exhibit 4.10 provides a summary of the psychometric properties that a researcher should consider in selecting a measurement tool. Although there are literally thousands of established measures and assessment procedures available, in some instances researchers may choose to develop a measurement tool specifically for the study. In such cases, researchers must ensure they use a measure that is both reliable and valid.

Exhibit 4.9 Measurement Options

Self-Report Measures: The research participant completes a questionnaire describing some aspect of himself or herself. This may range from global self-ratings, such as overall happiness or psychological adjustment, to very specific self-ratings, such as anxiety while completing a research task.

Informant-Report Measures: Information about a target research participant is gathered from other individuals. In clinical psychology research, this is typically someone who is well acquainted with the participant, such as a partner, a parent, or a teacher. Data may also be obtained for individuals with only limited experience with the participants. In studies of social interaction, for example, informant-report measures may be gathered from all the participants who interacted with a given participant.

Rater Evaluations: Data may be obtained from someone knowledgeable about a participant's involvement in a study, such as a rater who viewed videotapes of the participant performing a task or a therapist who provided treatment to the participant. Such ratings can range from evaluations of very specific to very global features.

Performance Measures: Participants may be asked to complete tasks in a study, such as a visuomotor task, a response time task, an identification task, or a task related to specific intellectual or social skills. The quality of the participant's performance on the task is used as data in the study.

Projective Measures: A technique, such as a storytelling task, may be used to assess the underlying needs or motives of a research participant. The assumption in using such measures is that they provide data that are different from those obtained through self-report.

Observation of Behaviour: Coding systems or general ratings may be used to summarize elements of a participant's actual behaviour. This may occur in either naturalistic settings such as the family home or in laboratory settings.

Psychophysiological Measures: A range of measurement options is available to evaluate a participant's biological characteristics. These include measures of autonomic arousal, cardiovascular activity, and neurological functioning.

Archival Data: Research data are often obtained from information sources that exist apart from the actual research study. This may include such sources as police records, health care utilization records, and academic records.

Exhibit 4.10 Psychometric Properties of Measures

Reliability

Internal Consistency: The degree to which elements of the measure (such as items on a test) are homogeneous.

Test-Retest Reliability: The stability over time of scores on a measure.

Inter-Rater Reliability: The consistency of scores on a measure across different raters or observers.

Validity

Content Validity: The extent to which the measure fully and accurately represents all elements of the domain of the construct being assessed.

Face Validity: The extent to which the measure overtly appears to be measuring the construct of interest.

Criterion Validity: The association of a measure with some criterion of central relevance to the construct, such as differentiating between groups of research participants.

Concurrent Validity: The association of a measure with other relevant data measured at the same point in time.

CONTINUED . . .

Predictive Validity: The association of a measure with other relevant data measured at some future point in time.
Convergent Validity: The association between a measure and other measures of either the same construct or conceptually related constructs.
Discriminant Validity: The association between measures that, conceptually, should not be related.
Incremental Validity: The extent to which a measure adds to the prediction of a criterion beyond what can be predicted with other measurement data.

ANALYZING THE DATA

Once data are collected, the researcher must conduct data analyses to determine the extent to which his or her research hypotheses have been supported. Appropriate data analysis is an integral part of a valid study, so researchers must carefully choose from a multitude of options for data analysis when designing the study. Guidelines on statistical methods and how to report research findings are available to assist a researcher in making these important decisions (e.g., APA Publications and Communications Board Working Group on Journal Article Reporting Standards, 2008; Wilkinson & the Task Force on Statistical Inference, 1999). Just as there are a number of threats to the internal and external validity of a study, so too are there many threats to the statistical conclusion validity of a study. Statistical conclusion validity refers to aspects of the data analysis that influence the validity of the conclusions drawn about the results of the research study. Common threats to statistical conclusion validity are outlined in Exhibit 4.11. As with other threats to validity, careful attention to these threats during the design of a study can increase the likelihood of accurately detecting an effect in the study. Viewpoint Box 4.2 provides a perspective on how ignoring these threats may dramatically influence the conclusions drawn about research findings.

Exhibit 4.11 Common Threats to the Statistical Conclusion Validity of a Study

Low Statistical Power: Statistical power refers to the ability to detect group differences when such differences truly exist. If a study has low statistical power, often caused by the use of samples that are too small, the researcher may not be able to accurately conclude that group differences were found in the study.
Multiple Comparisons and Their Effects on Error Rates: Most studies involve the testing of multiple research hypotheses, with multiple measures used to operationalize key constructs. The researcher needs to consider how many analyses to conduct and the error rate to use for analyses in order to have a reasonable balance between the desire to avoid Type I errors (i.e., concluding there is an effect when no true effect exists) and Type II errors (i.e., concluding there is no effect when a true effect exists).

CONTINUED . . .

Procedural Variability: Even with clear instructions and procedures to follow, those conducting the research (such as interviewers, observational raters, and therapists) may differ in how they interpret or use the instructions and procedures. Increases in variability in a study decrease the ability to detect a phenomenon or experimental effect.
Participant Heterogeneity: Variability in participant characteristics may result in differential results within the sample. Again, by increasing variability within a study, it is more difficult to detect a true effect.
Measurement Unreliability: The less reliable a measure, the more that measurement error influences the data obtained from participants. This increases within-study variability and negatively affects the ability to detect an effect.

VIEWPOINT BOX 4.2

HOW RELIABLE ARE THE FINDINGS REPORTED IN RESEARCH STUDIES?

As we described in Viewpoint Box 4.1, the findings of an initial study in a research domain are not always replicated in subsequent research. But just how widespread is this pattern? There is growing evidence that it is common and that it occurs in a broad range of research areas. Here are some examples:

- Many research studies have reported that, compared to what is observed in non-distressed adults, adults experiencing various mental health conditions show brain volume abnormalities in diverse parts of the brain. Ioanndis (2011) reviewed this literature, using the effect sizes typically found in this research area to calculate the power of each study to detect statistically significant results. He was surprised to find that, across 461 data sets, there were at least twice as many significant results reported as there should have been based on each study's statistical power.
- Reboxetine, a selective noradrenalin reuptake inhibitor, has been approved for the treatment of depression in many countries. Using data from published studies and unpublished data from the drug manufacturer, Eyding and colleagues (2010) conducted a meta-analysis of the use of reboxetine for treating major depression in adults. Overall, when all published and unpublished data were used, they found no evidence that the drug had effects superior to those obtained with placebo medication. Moreover, compared to the unpublished data, data from published studies greatly overestimated the benefits of reboxetine and underestimated the extent of adverse drug effects.
- Research on the interaction of genes and environmental conditions has grown rapidly. In examining the first decade of such research (i.e., during the period 2000–2009), Duncan and Keller (2011) focused on published replications of initial gene-by-environment interaction studies. Across 103 published studies, they found that 96% of hypothesized effects in the initial studies were statistically significant, but only 27% of attempts to replicate these novel findings were statistically significant.

So what is going on here? Underlying the problem is the fact that journals are more likely to accept studies with statistically significant findings. So, the most likely explanations involve the selective use of statistical analyses and the selective reporting of outcomes in a study (Munafò & Flint, 2010). That is, researchers are likely conducting multiple statistical tests on their data without correcting the significance level for the fact that multiple tests were conducted. For example, they may report a difference as significant at $p < .05$ when they ought to have been using a more stringent

CONTINUED . . .

criterion because of the number of analyses conducted. This is considered to be "cherry picking" the significant results in order to increase the likelihood that their research will be published. The result is that research in many areas may include substantial numbers of false positive findings, giving the impression of stronger research support for some hypotheses than is actually warranted. The solution to this problem is ensuring that (a) research studies have sufficient statistical power, (b) adjustments are made for conducting multiple statistical analyses, and (c) researchers accurately report and represent major analyses of their data.

©iStock.com/RapidEye

Beware of the possibility of false positive findings in published research.

Statistical and Clinical Significance

Researchers in psychology commonly rely on statistical tests to determine the outcome of a study and the degree to which a research hypothesis was supported. However, it is important to remember that, for many psychological measures, there is no direct correspondence between the scores on a measure and a person's experience in the world. For example, what does it mean to receive a score of 11 on a measure of anxiety: how is a score of 11 manifested in the person's day-to-day life? Because many psychological measures have an arbitrary metric with limited or no real-world correspondence, it is important that researchers learn more about what the score on a measure actually means in the life of a person and just how meaningful, in real-life terms, differences in scores really are (Blanton & Jaccard, 2006; Kazdin, 2006). Knowing that two groups differ in a statistically significant manner on their scores on a particular measure is important, but it does not provide information about whether the difference is a meaningful one. Therefore, in many types of clinical psychology research, statistical significance is necessary but not sufficient to fully evaluate the results of a study.

Because the field of clinical psychology focuses on the application of psychological knowledge to improve human functioning, researchers must also address whether the results have any practical significance. In treatment research, this is known as **clinical significance**. Clinical significance has been defined in a number of ways, but all definitions share an emphasis on evaluating the degree to which the intervention has had a meaningful impact on the functioning of the treated participants.

clinical significance: in addition to the results of a study attaining statistical significance, the results are of a magnitude that there are changes in some aspects of participants' daily functioning.

Just as there are different definitions, so too are there several distinct methods for calculating clinical significance, some of which use group data and others that focus on the data from individual participants in a treatment study (Kraemer et al., 2003; Wise, 2004). One commonly used approach is to evaluate, for each participant, whether the participant could be said to be in the normal range of functioning. This may involve the use of norms, cut-off scores on scales, or pre-determined criteria (such as being employed or being able to function without assistance when performing self-care tasks) to operationalize normal range functioning. A second commonly used method, developed by Neil Jacobson and colleagues, called the *reliable change index*, determines whether a participant's pre-treatment to post-treatment change on a scale is statistically greater than what would be expected due to measurement error. If it is, and if the score on the scale has moved to within two standard deviations of the mean score for a non-disordered sample, then a clinically significant change is said to have occurred (Jacobson & Truax, 1991). It is important to note that different methods for calculating clinical significance may yield different conclusions (Bauer, Lambert, & Nielsen, 2004), so, as with traditional data analyses, the researcher must make sure that appropriate clinical significance methods are used in a study.

SUMMARY AND CONCLUSIONS

Throughout this book, we emphasize the importance of a solid research foundation for the practice of clinical psychology. In this chapter, we have given a brief overview of the research process, highlighting the decisions that the researcher must make at all stages of the process in order to conduct ethical research and to balance the needs of internal and external validity. Perhaps the most important message is that there is no perfect study and that the different methodological features all have advantages and disadvantages. Just as the researcher must weigh different choices carefully, so too must the informed research consumer be aware of the effects of different methodological features in interpreting results in a reasonable manner.

Exhibit 4.12 summarizes a number of issues that, as novice research consumers, you should consider when reading the clinical psychology research literature.

Exhibit 4.12 How to Critically Evaluate a Research Study

The fact that a study is published does not mean that it is perfect. In fact, there is no such thing as a perfect study. Instead, studies vary in the degree to which the researchers have successfully addressed important issues and have successfully dealt with threats to internal, external, and statistical conclusion validity. To help you develop a critical eye for research, here are some questions you should ask yourself when reading a published study:

Title: Does the title accurately reflect the content of the article?

Introduction: Is the background information on the research area presented clearly and logically? Is there unnecessary detail that is confusing or misleading? Is there a clear statement of the purpose of the study and/or of the research hypotheses?

CONTINUED . . .

Participants: Are the chosen participants appropriate for the study topic? To what extent can results be generalized from the study's sample to other populations of interest? Are recruitment methods described? Were any analyses conducted to determine if there were effects due to differing methods? Was there attrition in the study and, if so, how was it handled statistically and interpretatively? If control/comparison groups were used, were they appropriate for the hypotheses being tested? In an experiment, was assignment to condition truly random?

Measures: Are the psychometric properties (i.e., reliability and validity) found in previous research reported and are they adequate? Likewise, is the reliability for the current sample reported, and is it adequate? If interviewers or coders were used, are inter-rater reliability values reported? Are the chosen measures developmentally and culturally appropriate for the participants? How well do the measures evaluate the variables included in the research hypotheses?

Procedures: In general, are the procedures appropriate for testing the research hypotheses? For example, was the training of raters/interviewers/therapists reported and does it seem adequate? Overall, are the procedures described in sufficient detail that the study could be replicated?

Results: Are the statistical analyses appropriate for the research hypotheses and the research design? Are the assumptions for the analyses met or were they violated? Was there any attention to whether the sample size was sufficient to detect a true effect in the study? Was there an appropriate balance between avoiding Type I and Type II errors? Do the tables provide enough detail (or too much) to aid in understanding the obtained results? Were post hoc analyses conducted and, if they were, did the researchers exercise caution in interpreting the findings? If the study was a randomized clinical trial, were clinical significance methods used?

Discussion: Are the results fully discussed? Are there clear statements about the extent to which the research hypotheses were supported? Does the researcher inappropriately interpret non-significant results? Is there a reasonable discussion of the limitations of the study? How well does the researcher integrate his or her findings with previous work in the area? Are viable alternative explanations of the obtained results considered in a meaningful manner?

KEY TERMS

clinical significance: in addition to the results of a study attaining statistical significance, the results are of a magnitude that there are changes in some aspects of participants' daily functioning.

effect size: a standardized metric, typically expressed in standard deviation units or correlations, that allows the results of research studies to be combined and analyzed.

external validity: the extent to which the interpretations drawn from the results of a study can be generalized beyond the narrow boundaries of the specific study.

factor analysis: a statistical procedure used to determine the conceptual dimensions or factors that underlie a set of variables, test items, or tests.

internal validity: the extent to which the interpretations drawn from the results of a study can be justified and alternative interpretations can be reasonably ruled out.

mediator: a variable that explains the mechanism by which a predictor variable influences a criterion variable.

meta-analysis: a set of statistical procedures for quantitatively summarizing the results of a research domain.

moderator: a variable that influences the strength of the relation between a predictor variable and a criterion variable.

randomized controlled trial: an experiment in which research participants are randomly assigned to one of two or more treatment conditions.

statistical conclusion validity: the extent to which the results of a study are accurate and valid based on the type of statistical procedures used in the research.

structural equation modelling: a comprehensive statistical procedure that involves testing all components of a theoretical model.

KEY NAMES

Donald Campbell   Jacob Cohen   Neil Jacobson

ADDITIONAL RESOURCES

Books

Hayes, S. C., Barlow, D. H., & Nelson-Gray, R. O. (1999). *The scientist practitioner: Research and accountability in the age of managed care* (2nd ed.). Needham Heights, MA: Allyn & Bacon.

Kazdin, A. E. (2003). *Research design in clinical psychology* (4th ed.). Needham Heights, MA: Allyn & Bacon.

Kazdin, A. E. (Ed.). (2003). *Methodological issues and strategies in clinical research* (3rd ed.). Washington, DC: American Psychological Association.

Roberts, M. C., & Ilardi, S. S. (2003). *Handbook of research methods in clinical psychology*. Oxford: Blackwell Publishing Ltd.

Thomas, J. C., & Hersen, M. (Eds.). (2011). *Understanding research in clinical and counseling psychology* (2nd ed.). New York: Routledge.

Check It Out!

The American Psychological Association has a number of sources of information and links to resources for conducting research: www.apa.org/research/tools/index.aspx

Although the focus of the Social Psychology Network is on social psychology, this is a wonderful website that contains numerous links to resources on research methodology, research ethics, and statistics: www.socialpsychology.org/methods.htm

The VassarStats website has extensive resources for understanding statistical procedures commonly used in psychology, along with online calculators that provide you with the option of conducting statistical analyses: vassarstats.net

The *British Medical Journal* provides a collection of short, easy-to-read articles on statistics: www.bmj.com/about-bmj/resources-readers/publications/statistics-square-one

If you are interested in learning more about meta-analysis, free meta-analysis software is available at several sites: ericae.net/meta/metastat.htm

www.lyonsmorris.com/ma1/index.cfm

You can access the Tri-Council policy on ethical conduct of research involving humans at the following website: www.pre.ethics.gc.ca/eng/policy-politique/initiatives/tcps2-eptc2/Default/

5 CHAPTER

ASSESSMENT: OVERVIEW

INTRODUCTION

Aden is having difficulty concentrating in school. He is having a hard time learning to read. Is he entitled to receive special education services?

Kayla has been cranky and unwilling to do her homework. She seems to get upset at the slightest provocation. Is this just regular teenager moodiness or does she have a serious problem?

Since he received a potentially lethal electric shock at work, Boris has had difficulty managing his temper. He is moody and unpredictable. What are the prospects for him returning to work?

As we outlined in Chapter 3, the classification of phenomena is a central feature of all sciences and social sciences. Classification requires the collection of data in a process known as assessment. People are routinely assessed and classified for a variety of purposes. In the educational system, students are assessed virtually every day from the time they begin school at the age of 4 or 5 until they complete their education some 12 to 25 years later. Assessments of knowledge and skill through examinations, projects, homework assignments, and class presentations are used to assign grades and to determine whether the person has met criteria to graduate. On the basis of these grades and other assessment data (such as personal interviews and entrance examinations), decisions will be made about students' applications to private

Is Kayla a regular teen or does she have a serious disorder?

schools, universities, or graduate programs. In the work realm, most people undergo some form of assessment to determine whether they should be offered a job. In many cases, such assessments are highly subjective and are thus potentially biased and unfair. Once hired, employees undergo constant informal assessment of their job performance by their supervisors. Increasingly, salary increases or advancement in the organization are related to results of performance evaluations. Even when you apply for a credit card, loan, or mortgage, you (or more precisely your credit history and credit risk) are assessed.

Psychological assessment strategies and tools are used increasingly for a number of educational and employment purposes. In this chapter and in the following four chapters, you will learn about the use of psychological assessment for clinical purposes. Along the way, we introduce you to the domains and methods of assessment most commonly found in clinical psychology. In these chapters, we will show you the potential value of clinical assessment and make you aware of the challenges that clinical psychologists face in gathering and integrating assessment information.

PSYCHOLOGICAL ASSESSMENT

As we just highlighted, we are all assessed on a regular basis. Moreover, as human beings, we all constantly engage in informal assessment activities related to our day-to-day lives. We use information (i.e., assessment data) to help us make both small decisions (such as whether to ask a professor to explain a concept that is unclear or whether to accept an invitation to have a meal with a friend) and more important decisions (such as whether to accept an offer for graduate school or to move in with an intimate partner). Data such as facial expressions, tone of voice, previous experiences with a person, and our own emotional reactions all influence our decisions. In most cases, these assessment processes occur automatically. As you will learn in Chapter 9, automatic decision-making can be vulnerable to many types of errors.

How is psychological assessment different from other types of assessment?

What makes psychological assessment, or more specifically clinical assessment, different from other types of assessment? Psychological assessment is an iterative decision-making process in which data are systematically collected on the person (or persons); the person's history; and the person's physical, social, and cultural environments. Based on an initial understanding of the problem to be assessed, preliminary information is gathered that, in most cases, leads to a refinement of the understanding of the problem and to an alteration in assessment activities. This cycle then repeats itself until the psychologist decides enough information has been collected to adequately respond to the assessment question. Psychological assessment involves the gathering and integration of multiple types of data from multiple sources and perspectives. At a minimum, this involves information provided by the client and information based on the psychologist's observation of the client during a clinical interview.

All psychological assessments are undertaken to address specific goals, such as (a) evaluating a child's cognitive abilities to determine whether the child is eligible for remedial services; (b) identifying the characteristics and behaviours associated with an adolescent's repeated social rejection, so that a treatment plan can be devised to help improve the youth's social functioning; or (c) determining the extent of emotional impairment experienced by an adult who was in a car accident.

Guided by assessment goals, the psychologist clearly and precisely formulates the questions to be addressed during the assessment. In turn, these questions inform the selection of the most appropriate assessment methods and instruments. Throughout the process of data collection, the psychologist generates hypotheses about the client and, therefore, may alter or refine the initial assessment questions in order to examine these hypotheses. This typically leads to the use of additional assessment procedures and the review of other data. Once all the assessment data have been collected, the psychologist must then make sense of the information and meaningfully address the inevitable inconsistencies and contradictions that occur in all assessment situations.

As part of this integration and interpretation process, the psychologist generates more hypotheses and strives to evaluate the strength of the evidence for and against these hypotheses. In most instances, prior to generating a final set of conclusions designed to answer the questions that originally led to initiating the psychological assessment, the psychologist consults with the client (and possibly others) about the accuracy of these conclusions. Of course, as with all psychological services, psychological assessment must be conducted in a manner that is informed by an awareness of human diversity and is sensitive to client characteristics, including, but not limited to, age, gender, ethnicity, culture, sexual orientation, and religious beliefs.

All clinical psychologists should be competent in conducting assessments. The 1999 presidential task force of the American Psychological Association's Division 12 (Clinical Psychology) established a model training curriculum in clinical assessment. You can see in Exhibit 5.1 the knowledge and skills that graduate students in clinical psychology must master in order to be competent in conducting psychological assessment. You will notice that the applied skills build on the foundational knowledge of psychometric theory that is covered in undergraduate programs. Information provided in this chapter and in the next four chapters will help you become better acquainted with these topics.

Exhibit 5.1 A Model Curriculum for Clinical Psychology Assessment: Recommendations from the American Psychological Association, Division 12 Presidential Task Force (1999)

Conceptual Areas

Normality, norms, and standardization
Reliability
Validity
Threats to validity (bias, deception, malingering)
Clinical decision-making (sources of error, optimal strategies)

Applied Topics

Intellectual assessment
Self-report personality assessment
Neuropsychological assessment
Diagnostic assessment (meaning of diagnoses, reliability, sources of data)
Structured interviews and behavioural observation with children and adolescents
Parent rating scales for child/adolescent assessment
Specific skills relevant to the focus of the graduate program (e.g., test construction, assessment of individuals with disabilities, risk assessments)
Assessment data integration and report writing
Ethics and legal issues in assessment

As part of a major conference on defining and evaluating competencies in professional psychology, in 2002 a psychological assessment working group identified core competencies for professional psychologists. As you can see in Exhibit 5.2, achieving and maintaining competence in psychological assessment is no easy feat. Consistent with the recommendations for training in Exhibit 5.1, competence in assessment requires both conceptual knowledge and practical assessment skills. Although not explicitly recognized in the competency listings, another significant challenge is for clinical psychologists to ensure their knowledge and skills are up to date. As we will see in Chapters 7 and 8, new measures continue to be developed and many of the major psychological tests are regularly updated every few years. So, even though students may learn about the most recent advancements during their graduate training, the process of staying up to date requires a commitment to career-long learning.

Exhibit 5.2 Core Competencies in Psychological Assessment

- Knowledge of:
  - psychometric theory
  - the scientific, theoretical, empirical, and contextual bases of psychological assessment
- Knowledge, skills, and techniques to assess cognitive, affective, behavioural, and personality dimensions of human experience
- Ability to:
  - assess intervention outcomes
  - evaluate critically the multiple roles, contexts, and relationships in which clients and psychologists function and the reciprocal impact of these on the assessment activity
  - establish, maintain, and understand the collaborative professional relationship involved in the assessment activity
- Understanding of the relation between assessment and intervention, assessment as an intervention, and intervention planning
- Technical assessment skills, including problem/goal identification and case conceptualization; understanding and selection of appropriate assessment methods; effective use of the assessment methods; systematic data gathering; integration and analysis of information; understandable, useful, and responsive communication of findings; and development of recommendations

Adapted from Krishnamurthy et al. (2004).

The Purposes of Psychological Assessment

As you may remember learning in Chapters 1 and 2, psychological assessment has always been an important professional activity for clinical psychologists. Even though the roles of clinical psychologists have expanded over the decades, assessment activities remain a central part of the profession. Psychological assessments are conducted for myriad reasons. The first important distinction is between situations in which psychological assessment is the primary clinical service provided and situations in which the psychological assessment is just one element of the clinical service.

©iStock.com/Maica

Psychological assessments may be initiated to diagnose learning disorders.

Assessment-Focused Services versus Intervention-Focused Services

Some psychological assessments are stand-alone services. Examples include child custody evaluations to determine the best parenting arrangements for children whose parents are separating or divorcing, psychoeducational assessments to diagnose learning disorders and to identify cognitive strengths and weaknesses, neuropsychological assessments to evaluate the extent of cognitive and memory impairment following a severe concussion, and psychosocial functioning/diagnostic assessment to evaluate the psychological aftermath of a motor vehicle accident. In these cases, an assessment is initiated to answer basic questions about the person's current functioning or suitability for services and to provide recommendations for remediation of problems, whether by a psychologist or by another health care or education specialist. In some instances, the clinical psychologist may also be asked to provide an opinion on whether the person's current level of functioning is substantially different from a prior level of functioning (e.g., before a car accident or a work-related injury).

assessment-focused services: services conducted primarily to provide information on a person's psychosocial functioning.

These **assessment-focused services** are conducted primarily to provide information that can be used to address a person's current or anticipated psychosocial deficits. Thus, the conclusions and recommendations provided by the psychologist may have an enormous impact on the person's life circumstances, such as whether a child will have primary residence with one parent or whether an injured worker will receive a disability pension. Given the importance of the decisions that are based on assessment results, psychologists must use evidence-based assessment tools and must follow all ethical standards in providing these services (a point we address more fully later in the chapter).

An individual may make a request for a psychological assessment. At other times, the request for an assessment is made by another person or an organization (e.g., a court-mandated child custody evaluation—see Viewpoint Box 5.1 for a discussion of issues around child custody evaluations). In conducting the assessment, the psychologist must be cognizant of these referral factors, for they may influence the extent to which the person wishes to cooperate with the assessment, as well as motivation to emphasize psychological strengths or psychological impairments (see Exhibit 5.2 regarding the importance of awareness of the context of assessment). It is also important that psychologists have thorough knowledge of the legal context in which their assessments will be used. It is possible, for example, that their assessments may be challenged by the person being assessed or by an institution or agency that initially requested the assessment (e.g., an insurance company).

Parents seeking a child custody evaluation should consult professional guidelines, which are easily accessed on websites, so that they can ensure that the professional who is offering to conduct a child custody evaluation will complete a comprehensive and valid assessment that will yield helpful recommendations.

VIEWPOINT BOX 5.1

CHILD CUSTODY EVALUATIONS

The majority of divorcing parents reach an agreement about the arrangements for parenting their children on their own or with the help of legal and mental health professionals. Although it is preferable for parents to reach their own agreement on post-divorce parenting arrangements, this is not always possible. A small minority of parents who are unable to reach an agreement turn to the legal system to determine parenting arrangements after divorce. Judges in turn seek advice from mental health professionals by ordering a child custody evaluation by a mental health professional.

With training in child development and expertise in psychological assessment, clinical psychologists should be well placed to offer informed opinions about optimal parenting plans for these high-conflict families. However, the provision of child custody evaluations is a professional minefield, yielding large numbers of complaints about professional misconduct. In response to these problems, guidelines have been drawn up by various organizations, including the American Psychological Association (APA, 2010b) and the Association of Family and Conciliation Courts (AFCC, 2006). One of the most comprehensive sets of guidelines was prepared by the College of Psychologists of Alberta (2002). The guidelines lay out in detail the many types of assessment data that must be gathered to perform an adequate assessment.

It is easy to see how the process of conducting interviews with parents, children, and new partners; carrying out observations of various family members; administering psychological tests to adults and children; and synthesizing reports from collateral sources such as teachers and therapists is likely to be a lengthy and costly procedure. A survey of American psychologists indicated that the evaluation process took on average 21.1 hours (Ackerman & Ackerman, 1997). Given the hourly rates charged by psychologists, it is clear that the cost of the average child custody evaluation runs into thousands of dollars.

Ackerman and Ackerman also presented some very troubling data on the tests most commonly used by psychologists in child custody evaluation. In assessing children, psychologists reported commonly using a range of projective tests such as the Children's Apperception Test, the Sentence Completion Test, the Rorschach Test, and projective drawings. These projective tests for children fall far short of the scientific standards of demonstrating reliability and validity, and having norms (Hunsley, Lee, Wood, & Taylor, in press). In assessing adults, the most commonly used test was the MMPI-2, followed by the Rorschach. No validity studies have supported the usefulness of these tests in predicting the best parenting arrangement for divorced families. Of particular concern are several websites describing the subscales of the MMPI-2 and advising parents on the most appropriate responses to provide in order to appear well functioning.

To more directly assess what evaluators do, Horvath, Logan, and Walker (2002) conducted content analyses of 135 reports included in official court documents. In contrast to the self-report methodology used by Ackerman and Ackerman (1997), this strategy allowed the investigators to directly examine what evaluators did rather than what they said they do. Horvath and colleagues found great variability in the extent to which APA guidelines were followed. Interviews sometimes failed to address critical issues such as domestic violence and child abuse. Results of this study underline the need for practitioners to use multiple methods to evaluate family functioning, and to rely only on evidence-based assessment strategies in making recommendations that are of such importance to children and their families.

©iStock.com/TatyanaGl

Psychological assessment may be used to make recommendations about parenting after divorce.

intervention-focused assessment services: assessments conducted in the context of intervention services.

As clinical psychologists have become more involved in providing intervention services, there has also been a shift in the type of assessments they conduct. Psychological assessments are most commonly conducted in the context of intervention services. In these **intervention-focused assessment services**, the psychological assessment is not a stand-alone service, but is conducted as a first step in providing an effective intervention. All intervention should involve some assessment. For example, an initial evaluation of the person's life circumstances and psychosocial functioning is necessary to determine whether psychological treatment is warranted or whether some other form of intervention should be recommended. Pre-treatment assessment findings are used to determine appropriate psychological interventions. These data also provide a useful point of comparison for interpreting subsequent assessment findings obtained during or after treatment.

Thus far we have categorized assessment activities as roughly falling into one of two domains: stand-alone assessment in which the main intent is to present conclusions and recommendations about the person's functioning; and assessment in which the main intent is to intervene to improve the person's functioning, with the assessment data being used in support of this service. Although this dichotomy is useful in thinking about psychological assessment, it is rather simplistic and does not fairly represent the variety of purposes for which assessment is conducted. Therefore, to deepen your knowledge of why psychologists conduct assessments, we will focus on the following range of interrelated assessment purposes: screening, diagnosis/case formulation, prognosis, treatment design and planning, treatment monitoring, and treatment evaluation. We will return to several of these topics in Chapter 9 when we examine the decision-making processes associated with the clinical use of assessment data.

Screening

screening: a procedure to identify individuals who may have problems of a clinical magnitude or who may be at risk for developing such problems.

Given their expertise in measurement and psychometrics, psychologists are often called on to assist in the development or implementation of **screening** measures. Depending on the nature of the screening and the screening site, psychologists may or may not be directly involved in conducting screening assessments. The purpose of screening for a disorder, condition, or characteristic is to identify, as accurately as possible, individuals who may have problems of a clinical magnitude or who may be at risk for developing such problems. Individuals who are screened may not have sought out assessment services; rather, they are receiving the assessment as part of the routine operations of a clinic, school, hospital, or employment setting. For example, there are now a number of instruments that are routinely used in schools to identify youth with mental health problems. Psychological services are then offered to those who have been identified as having problems (Levitt, Saka, Romanelli, & Hoagwood, 2007).

People may also actively seek out a screening assessment. In the United States, there are national screening days for a number of psychological disorders, including the National Alcohol Screening Day and the National Depression Screening Day. These screening days have many sponsors, including the American Psychological Association. The screening can be done online or in person at many community-based health care settings such as general hospitals, mental health clinics, and specialty health care providers' offices. Hundreds of thousands of Americans each year are screened for mental health problems in this manner. Information on the websites for these screening services is included at the end of this chapter.

Although screening is useful in identifying those at risk, it is important to remember that screening tools are not the same as tools used in diagnosis. So, for example, if you score high on a depression-screening instrument, it does not mean that you would necessarily meet diagnostic criteria for depression.

Diagnosis/Case Formulation

As you learned in Chapter 3, assessment data are used to formulate a clinical diagnosis such as those listed in the DSM-5. Interview data, psychological test data, and reports from significant others provide information on the symptoms the person is experiencing. Information on symptoms is compared with diagnostic criteria to determine whether the symptom profile matches criteria for DSM diagnoses. As we described in Chapter 3, knowing the diagnosis for a person helps clinicians communicate with other health professionals and search the scientific literature for information on associated features such as etiology and prognosis. Diagnostic information can also provide key information on the types of treatment options that have been found to be effective in clinical trials (Nelson-Gray, 2003). Thus, diagnosis can provide an initial framework for a treatment plan that can be modified to fully address the client's concerns and life circumstances.

Historically, the term *diagnosis* was used to describe the entire process of conducting a psychological assessment and formulating a clinical picture of the client. The term originated when diagnostic criteria for psychological and psychiatric disorders were ambiguous and relatively uninformative for clinical purposes (i.e., during the era of DSM-I and DSM-II). Thus, in the past, *diagnosis* or *psychodiagnosis* referred to the process in which the psychologist used interview and testing data to render a comprehensive representation of the patient's psychological makeup (cf. Rapaport, Gill, & Schafer, 1968). Although the term psychodiagnosis is still used by some clinicians (primarily those with a psychodynamic orientation), the term **case formulation** is now more commonly used to describe the use of assessment data to develop a comprehensive and clinically relevant conceptualization of a patient's psychological functioning. Typically a case formulation provides information on the patient's life situation, current problems, and a set of hypotheses linking psychosocial factors with the patient's clinical condition.

case formulation: a description of the patient that provides information on his or her life situation, current problems, and a set of hypotheses linking psychosocial factors with the patient's clinical condition.

Prognosis/Prediction

Whether or not it is stated explicitly, psychological assessment always implies some form of prediction about the patient's future. For example, recommendations that the person seek psychotherapy to address bulimic symptoms or that special academic tutoring is needed to compensate for a learning disability imply that, without some form of intervention, the present problems will either continue or worsen. A dentist would not recommend implants to deal with a lack of teeth in a patient aged six months—it would be assumed that, in time, the teeth would grow. Similarly, if the psychologist believed that bingeing was simply related to an adolescent growth spurt, or that a child's reading difficulties were an inevitable part of the learning process, then it would be unnecessary to recommend intervention—the passage of time would be sufficient to correct the problem.

prognosis: predictions made about the future course of a patient's psychological functioning, based on the use of assessment data in combination with relevant empirical literature.

Prognosis refers to the use of assessment data, in combination with relevant empirical literature, to make predictions about the future course of a patient's psychological functioning. Although the psychopathology literature provides information for this task, it must always be remembered that these studies deal with future outcomes at the group level. The clinician's task is to use this probabilistic information (e.g., "60% of patients with this diagnosis experience a recurrence of their symptoms within two years") in a manner that takes into account the unique circumstances of the patient being assessed.

One of the biggest challenges for clinicians is to predict possible client outcomes as accurately as possible. In considering ways to enhance the accuracy of predictions, the psychologist must weigh a number of variables such as time and cost, the consequences of inaccurate decisions, and the base rate of the predicted outcome. Although it is always possible to collect more and more assessment data, this is not always desirable. Time spent on assessment may mean less time is available to provide an intervention for the patient. The cost of an assessment should not be underestimated: more time spent on assessment means that someone (e.g., the client) or some organization (e.g., the client's health insurance plan) must cover these costs. The clinician must therefore strike a balance between the desire to obtain more information and the need to be conscious of the very real constraints that influence the scope of the assessment.

Prediction errors are inevitable—no one can predict with 100% accuracy. However, not all errors have the same psychological or financial cost. Psychologists should be aware of these issues, and their selection of assessment strategies and instruments should be based on conscious choices about the types of errors they wish to minimize. A failure to detect attention-deficit/hyperactivity disorder (ADHD) may result in several years of frustration and academic and social failures for a child and his or her family, whereas a failure to detect a mild specific phobia is unlikely to have the same generalized impact. In older adults, symptoms of impaired memory, difficulties in thinking, and problems in concentration may occur as features of both major depressive disorder and dementia. A misdiagnosis has the potential not only to result in ineffective treatment, but also to add to the burden experienced by the individual. Errors can also occur in which a person is diagnosed when, in fact, no diagnosis is warranted. For example, if a person showing signs of social awkwardness was mistakenly diagnosed with Asperger's syndrome or autism spectrum disorder, it could lead to both unnecessary treatment and stigmatization.

All of these types of errors are influenced by the **base rate** of a problem or diagnosis: that is, the frequency with which the problem/diagnosis occurs in the population. In a nutshell, the less frequently a problem occurs, the more likely a prediction error will occur. As many of the predictions that clinical psychologists make are about rare conditions or *low base rate events*—such as the presence of an eating disorder, the likelihood that the person will be violent in the future, or the likelihood of a future suicide attempt—the consequences of error must be seriously considered.

base rate: the frequency with which a problem or diagnosis occurs in the population.

Errors in clinical prediction can occur in many assessment activities, including screening, diagnosis, and case formulation. To better understand how clinical psychologists attempt to address the issue of error, it is necessary to understand some of the basic concepts of decision theory. To begin, there is, of course, the situation in which the prediction is accurate. As presented in Exhibit 5.3, this can mean either that the prediction that an event will occur was accurate (*true positive*) or that the prediction of a non-event was accurate (e.g., that no diagnosis was warranted or that a specific event such as a suicide attempt would not occur—*true negative*). However, just as a prediction can be correct in two distinct ways, there are two types of incorrect predictions. A *false positive* occurs when the psychologist predicts that an event will occur but, in fact, it does not occur (e.g., the psychologist diagnoses ADHD in a child who does not have the disorder). Conversely, a *false negative* occurs when an event occurs that was not predicted by the psychologist (e.g., the psychologist fails to diagnose someone who has a personality disorder).

Exhibit 5.3 Accuracy and Errors in Clinical Prediction

Prediction	True Event	True Non-Event
Event	True Positives (A)	False Positives (B)
Non-Event	False Negatives (C)	True Negatives (D)

Sensitivity: A / (A + C)

Specificity: D / (D + B)

sensitivity: proportion of true positives identified by the assessment.

specificity: proportion of true negatives identified by the assessment.

In referring to accuracy in clinical predictions, psychologists employ two additional concepts: sensitivity and specificity. **Sensitivity** refers to the number of times an event is predicted, across cases, compared with the total number of times that the event actually occurs. More simply, sensitivity (or selectivity; Hogan, 2007) is the proportion of true positives identified by the assessment (Haynes, Smith, & Hunsley, 2011). Sensitivity is determined arithmetically by dividing the number of true positives by the sum of true positives and false negatives. In contrast, **specificity** deals with the prediction of non-events. It refers to the number of times a non-event is predicted across cases compared with the total number of times that no event occurred; alternatively, it can be considered as the relative proportion of true negatives (Haynes et al., 2011). Arithmetically, it is determined by dividing the number of true negatives by the sum of true negatives and the false positives.

Let's assume that a psychologist conducted assessments on hospital inpatients in a patient care unit in order to predict who was at risk for future suicide attempts. In our example, sensitivity provides information on how well the assessment procedures were able to detect future suicide attempts, and specificity provides information on how well the assessment procedures were able to identify individuals who would not attempt suicide. There are serious consequences associated with failing to detect a person who went on to make a suicide attempt, but there are also costs and consequences for each non-suicidal person who is erroneously categorized as potentially suicidal—the person's freedom and privacy will have been restricted and considerable personnel resources will have been directed toward monitoring the person. Of course, it would be ideal if an assessment had both high sensitivity and high specificity but, in reality, this is rarely the case. Therefore, a decision about which assessment procedures to select should be informed by a thorough consideration of the procedure's sensitivity and specificity and the psychological and financial costs stemming from inaccurate clinical predictions.

Treatment Planning

As we discussed earlier in the chapter, a great deal of psychological assessment is designed to inform treatment-related decisions. Once the psychologist and client have reached a decision that some treatment is required, the next step is to determine what exactly the treatment should be. Treatment planning is the process by which information about the client's context (including sociodemographic and psychological characteristics, diagnoses, and life circumstances) is used in combination with the scientific literature on psychotherapy to develop a proposed course of action that addresses the client's needs and circumstances. Treatment planning provides a clear focus for treatment and gives the client realistic expectations about the process and likely outcome of treatment. The plan also establishes a standard against which treatment progress can be measured.

Within the context of health service provision, a treatment plan is a valuable tool that facilitates communication among professionals working with the client, provides a clear statement about the nature of the planned services to agencies that may need to authorize and/or pay for the services, and provides a document that can be reviewed as part of an agency's quality assurance activities to ensure that appropriate services are being provided. The collaborative effort between psychologist and client to develop and implement a treatment plan should also establish a good foundation that will help in navigating the subsequent challenges of psychotherapy. Rather than simply agreeing to a vague statement about therapy, a

It is always necessary to tailor the treatment to suit the client's unique circumstances.

formal treatment plan ensures that a client can provide truly informed consent for the procedures he or she is about to undertake.

The first step in developing a treatment plan is to determine whether there are treatment options with established effectiveness for the types of problems the client presents. The psychologist must consider the extent to which the characteristics of the client match those of research participants in relevant clinical trials. The better the fit, the greater the psychologist's confidence in choosing one form of treatment. However, even if the fit is relatively poor—as may be the case in dealing with clients with a minority ethnic/cultural background—treatment outcome studies can still provide a useful starting point for developing a treatment plan. Regardless of the fit, it is always necessary to tailor the treatment to the client's unique circumstances.

A useful treatment plan must cover three general areas: problem identification, treatment goals, and treatment strategies and tactics (Mariush, 2002). A clear statement of the problems to be addressed provides the necessary starting point for understanding the proposed treatment and for, eventually, determining the treatment's success. For treatment to be efficient and focused, goals must be specified. Goals can include both ultimate goals for treatment and intermediate goals that must be attained in order to reach the ultimate treatment goals. For example, in helping Carolina overcome bulimic symptoms, the ultimate treatment goal may be the development of appropriate body image and of effective emotion regulation skills. The short-term goal, on the other hand, may be the reduction of bingeing behaviour by establishing a routine of eating three healthy meals a day. For Hannah, who has been cutting her arms, the short-term goal may be a reduction in self-harming behaviour, with a longer-term goal of establishing good study habits, enlarging her social network, and dealing with conflict in her family. In Chapter 6 you will learn about interviewing strategies that are useful in helping clients to define their problems and goals.

Finally, a description of treatment strategies provides information on the general approach to addressing the clinical problems, whereas a description of treatment tactics provides details of specific tasks, procedures, or techniques that will be used in treatment. To address Justin's symptoms of depression and relationship conflict, for example, the treatment strategy may be to use individual interpersonal therapy or to use emotionally focused couples therapy (EFT) with both Justin and his partner Pat. The treatment tactics, however, would deal with the specific elements of treatment, such as, within EFT, having the couple work on emotionally reconnecting with each other and developing renewed trust in each other's emotional availability.

Only with a thorough and accurate assessment is it possible to specify the type of strategies and tactics that are best suited to deal with a client's presenting problems.

Treatment Monitoring

Once a clear treatment plan is in place, the psychologist closely monitors the impact of treatment. Treatment monitoring is a crucial element of effective treatment as it enables the psychologist to change the treatment plan based upon the patient's response to treatment. If a patient is progressing extremely well, it may be possible to shorten treatment or to focus subsequent phases of treatment on other issues of concern to the patient. Alternatively, if the treatment is less than optimally effective, close monitoring of treatment progress provides an opportunity to alter the treatment. Figure 5.1 shows an example of treatment monitoring data for Hannah, who received services to deal with self-harming behaviour. All clinicians have an implicit sense of how the patient is progressing, but treatment monitoring refers to explicitly tracking progress through the use of specific questions or psychological measures. By providing data on problems in the process of treatment (such as difficulties in the therapeutic relationship) and obstacles the patient is encountering in following through on therapeutic activities (such as not doing assigned tasks outside the therapy session), treatment monitoring can provide an opportunity to reorient treatment efforts to avoid potential treatment failure (Mash & Hunsley, 1993).

To repeatedly evaluate elements of the treatment process (such as the therapeutic relationship and compliance with tasks) and alterations in psychological functioning (including changes in symptom frequency,

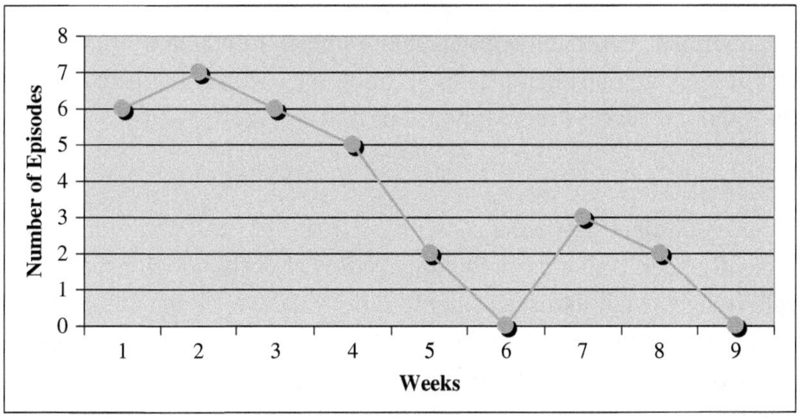

Figure 5.1. Frequency of Hannah's self-harm episodes during each week of treatment

intensity, and duration), psychologists use interviews, brief psychological tests, and/or tests specifically tailored to the client's problems and goals (Kazdin, 1993). Research by psychologist Michael Lambert, a major contributor to the research on assessing changes due to treatment, demonstrated that routine treatment monitoring can substantially affect treatment outcome. In a meta-analysis of three large-scale studies, Lambert et al. (2003) found that by using monitoring data to alert clinicians to treatment progress (or lack of progress), the likelihood of client deterioration was reduced and the positive effects of psychotherapy were enhanced. In these studies, treatment monitoring data were routinely collected on more than 2,500 patients in a range of treatment settings such as university counselling centres and outpatient treatment clinics. Services were provided by qualified professionals who espoused the full range of theoretical orientations typically found in practice settings. The same very simple experimental manipulation was used in all studies: patient and clinician dyads were randomly assigned to a "no feedback condition" in which the treatment monitoring data were not provided to the clinician or to a "feedback condition" in which the clinician was given the data. Across the studies, in the no feedback condition, Lambert and colleagues found that 21% of patients deteriorated and 21% experienced clinically important improvements in functioning. However, in the feedback condition, the number of clients who experienced deterioration was reduced by a third (to 13%) and the proportion of successful treatment cases increased by two-thirds (to 35%). Similar results have been reported in subsequent large-scale studies of individual psychotherapy outcome (Shimokawa, Lambert, & Smart, 2010). Moreover, there is growing research demonstrating that monitoring progress in couples therapy also has an extremely positive effect on treatment outcome (Anker, Duncan, & Sparks, 2009; Reese, Toland, Slone, & Norsworthy, 2010). These results present a convincing argument that clinical psychologists have an ethical responsibility to routinely gather treatment monitoring data in order to enhance the likelihood of successful treatment outcome.

Treatment Evaluation

In most clinical psychology settings, treatment outcome data have typically been collected to document the extent to which psychological services such as psychotherapy are effective in achieving stated goals. A comparison of outcome data with intake data provides an indication of how much change, if any, has occurred during treatment of a particular individual. You might wonder why such data are necessary—surely health care providers know how much their patients have improved. Research evidence indicates that this is not usually the case. For example, in a study of services provided by a group of 23 mental health professionals (including psychologists) who routinely provided therapy to children, no significant correlations were found between the professionals' perceptions of client improvement and data from self-report measures completed by both parents and children (Love, Koob, & Hill, 2007).

Outcome data can also be used as indicators of how well an entire system of care is functioning. Data gathered for treatment monitoring can affect treatment services provided to an individual client, but data gathered for treatment outcome purposes can yield information relevant to an entire psychological practice or service (Whipple & Lambert, 2011). At the level of individual psychologists working in an agency, aggregating data across patients can provide useful information about a psychologist's success in working with patients. When compared with data obtained from other psychologists in the agency, these data also have the potential to yield information about psychologists who are performing at above- or below-average levels. Those psychologists whose treatment services are less successful could receive feedback and be given additional supervision or training to rectify the situation. On the other hand, a practice analysis of the relatively successful clinicians' activities could provide indications of certain clinical skills or knowledge that set these individuals apart from their colleagues. Training sessions for all clinicians could then focus on the dissemination of these identified areas of strength in order to improve the overall effectiveness of those working in the service setting. Of course, whether providing feedback to an individual psychologist or making group comparisons among practitioners, it is essential to take into account the service context. For example, if one psychologist in an agency provides services to clients with chronic mental health problems and a history of unsuccessful treatment, it would be unfair to compare outcome data with those obtained by psychologists working with less distressed clients.

Treatment outcome data can also be used to document the typical range of outcomes clients experience and the nature and duration of treatment required to obtain successful outcomes. With these data in hand, clinicians can then provide accurate estimates to clients and any third-party payers about the likely benefits, duration, and costs of treatment. Comparing these data across agencies providing similar services may reveal particular strengths and weaknesses in an agency. Consultation with other agencies could then yield avenues for improved outcomes through changes in administrative and/or clinical procedures (e.g., adopting more effective treatment strategies for dealing with clients diagnosed with cocaine dependence and cocaine abuse). Based on data available from published clinical trials of psychotherapy or from treatment centres acknowledged to be leaders in the field, individual practitioners and agencies can set benchmarks against which their own treatment outcome data can be compared. Such comparisons can lead to quality assurance strategies for improvements in areas of suboptimal service delivery.

Data on typical treatment responses can be used to enhance the outcome of a course of treatment for a client. Several groups of psychotherapy researchers have used large data sets based on repeated measures of client progress to establish profiles of symptom reduction and improvements in functioning over the course of treatment. When this information is used by clinicians in the context of treatment monitoring, it becomes possible to identify when the client's progress is less than what is typically found for those with similar problems. Whipple and Lambert (2011) described a data monitoring system in which a graph depicting typical client progress is used as a comparison against which the progress of a specific client can be charted. On a session-by-session basis, if the client's assessment score is significantly less than that obtained by the typical client, the clinician is alerted to the suboptimal progress and the possibility of eventual treatment failure. With this knowledge, the psychologist can then engage the client in discussions about problems in the process of treatment, thus potentially resulting in changes in the treatment plan.

PSYCHOLOGICAL TESTING

You will have learned in many of your psychology courses that psychologists have expertise in the development and use of tests in the study and treatment of human functioning. Although you may find websites and magazines filled with quick tests of various concepts, developing a scientifically sound psychological test requires more than simply writing a few questions and finding a good name for the test. The *Standards for Educational and Psychological Testing* (American Educational Research Association, American Psychological Association, & National Council on Measurement in Education, 1999) set out principles that psychologists must follow in developing and using tests and assessment procedures. As you will see in the following sections, a number of criteria must be met if a psychological test is to have any value in research or clinical practice.

But first, let's consider what exactly a psychological test is. Although it might seem to be a relatively simple task to define a test, it is in fact a rather difficult thing to do. In the *Standards* (AERA et al., 1999), a test is defined in the following manner: "An evaluative device or procedure in which a sample of an examinee's behavior in a specified domain is obtained and subsequently evaluated and scored using a standardized process" (p. 183). This definition, although general enough to encompass various methods of testing (including interviewing, observation, and self-report), is rather awkward and may not be immediately understood by non-psychologists. Hunsley et al. (in press) defined a test according to its intended use. *If* (a) the clinician's intent is to collect a sample of behaviour that will be used to generate statements about a person, a person's experiences, or a person's psychological functioning *and* (b) a claim is made or implied by the clinician that the accuracy or validity of these statements comes from the way in which the sample of behaviour was collected and interpreted and not just from the clinician's expertise, authority, or special qualifications, *then* the process used to collect and interpret the behavioural sample is a psychological test and must meet the standards established for psychological tests. So, for example, although you may be able to quickly develop a questionnaire designed to measure some aspect of human functioning, it is not a test until it has been demonstrated to have met the standards of reliability, validity, and norms.

Why does it matter how a psychological test is defined? Although there are numerous technical reasons why it is important, there is a practical reason that has very important real-world consequences. Psychological tests are frequently used in legal and quasi-legal contexts, such as when a judge must decide on child custody or when a tribunal rules on whether to award a disability pension to an injured worker. Without safeguards to ensure that psychological tests meet scientific standards, it would be possible for any set of questions to be called a test and its results to be assumed to provide scientifically accurate and valid information. Viewpoint Box 5.2 presents further issues to consider with respect to psychological testing on the Internet.

If you are considering psychological testing on the Internet, you need to be just as careful as if you were seeking psychological testing in a traditional format. Consider the credentials of the organization that is offering services and the scientific basis of the tools. No score should ever be interpreted in isolation. To be useful, it must be considered part of the information gathered in the process of psychological assessment.

VIEWPOINT BOX 5.2

PSYCHOLOGICAL TESTING ON THE INTERNET

According to Statistics Canada data, the majority of Canadian households have at least one regular Internet user (Statistics Canada, 2011). Although children in single-parent families and those living in rural areas are less likely to have Internet access at home, the widespread availability of computers in school increases access for all young people. With the exponential growth in access to the Internet and its increasing use in diverse activities, it is inevitable that mounting numbers of people may use the Internet to find information about health issues. A U.S. survey found that 59% of American adults have searched online about health information and that 35% conducted Internet searches specifically to try to diagnose a condition they might have (Pew Internet, 2013).

As you surf the Internet, you have probably come across sites that offer psychological testing. Some of these sites are offered as a public service by health organizations. Others are more like commercials for pharmaceutical companies—once you have agreed that you suffer from a number of symptoms of a disorder, you may receive a recommendation to talk to your physician about the usefulness of a particular medication in treating those symptoms. Some sites offer psychological testing as a form of "infotainment" and others are commercial enterprises requiring you to pay for psychological testing. It is important to know that these online services are psychological *testing* rather than psychological *assessment*. Online testing is not the same as having a psychological assessment. Online testing may be part of a psychological assessment, but it can never be considered a substitute (Buchanan, 2002).

Many paper-and-pencil psychological tests in questionnaire format can easily be adapted for online administration. Currently, many well-respected psychological tests may be completed online through secure sites. Online completion of tests allows for accurate scoring and rapid feedback. Tests can be updated quickly and new versions introduced at very low cost. Test administration can be adapted to clients with special needs, and versions can be made available in many different languages. The potential to offer psychological testing services cheaply to large numbers of people, some of whom may live in remote areas and who may have only limited access to face-to-face services with a mental health professional, is very appealing.

Research shows that Internet samples are diverse and that results found through Internet responses are similar to those obtained by traditional methods (Gosling, Vazire, Srivastava, & John, 2004). For example, there is growing evidence that online versions of tests demonstrate the same pattern of responses and psychometric properties that are found when paper versions of the tests are completed at home or in a research setting (Weigold, Weigold, & Russell, 2013). This suggests that the use of the Internet for psychological research and testing can be done appropriately and, therefore, will likely increase in the coming years.

However, before we unconditionally accept the potential benefits of psychological testing via the Internet, we must consider psychometric, ethical, legal, and practical issues (Naglieri et al., 2004). The use of psychological tests on the Internet should be guided by the same principles that guide the use of any psychological tests. However, as you are aware, the Internet is unregulated. Ethical practices dictate that the test developer must demonstrate that the test has been found to be reliable and valid when used for specific purposes with specified populations. In most instances, it is also critical that the test developer provide appropriate norms for the test. The issue of the availability of appropriate norms is particularly important as Internet access may make a test that was normed on a homogenous sample available to a much broader sample of the population. One of the most important professional issues is whether Internet testing is conducted as part of a psychological assessment

CONTINUED . . .

in which the psychologist also gathers other data about the client and in which the client is provided face-to-face feedback about the assessment results. Smith et al. (2011) provided a fine example of how Internet testing can be conducted in a fully ethical manner. Their clinic has a range of instruments available for clients to complete online, including measures of anxiety, depression, problem gambling, conduct disorder, and relationship difficulties. As part of the assessment services provided to clients, these measures can be completed prior to and during treatment services. Additionally, a range of presenting problems can be tracked by clients using online self-monitoring diaries (an approach we describe in detail in Chapter 6). All assessment data gathered via the Internet are reviewed with clients at treatment sessions and collaborative decisions are made about which measures to use for the next phase of services.

Assessment versus Testing

Not all information gathered by a psychologist involves psychological testing. This underscores a more general point that psychological assessment and psychological testing are not synonymous. Consistent with the definitions of psychological tests, testing occurs when a particular device is used to gather a sample of behaviour from a client, a score is assigned to the resulting sample, and comparisons with the scores of other people are made in order to interpret the client's score. Assessment is more complex and multifaceted than testing and may or may not involve the use of psychological tests. Assessment requires the integration of life history information and clinical observation of the client with, in most cases, the results obtained from psychological tests and information provided on the client by significant others in the client's life (Groth-Marnat, 2009). The result from a test is a score that can be interpreted based on comparisons with the scores of others; the result from an assessment is a coherent, unified description of the client or selected aspects of the client's experience.

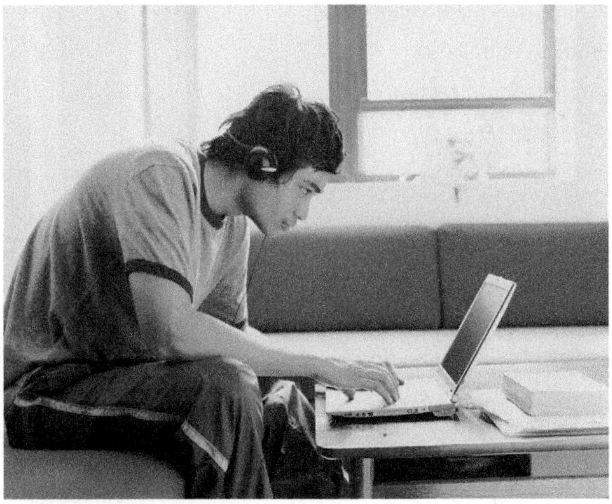

Digital Vision/Getty Images

Many Internet sites offer psychological testing.

All mental health professionals conduct assessments, but, compared with other mental health professionals, psychologists receive far more training in issues related to testing and are far more likely to use tests. The data in Table 5.1 illustrate this point. Palmiter (2004) surveyed a sample of professionals providing mental health services to children and adolescents in the United States. As shown in the table, according to the survey, all mental health professionals are likely to interview the child/adolescent and the family. However, compared with other mental health professionals, psychologists are much more likely to use tests to obtain information about their young clients. These

TABLE 5.1 ■ Assessing Children and Adolescents: What Do Mental Health Professionals Do?

Assessment Method	% Clinicians[1]	% Psychologists[2]
Family interview	89.1	90.9
Individual child/adolescent interview	83.0	83.3
Review previous treatment records	70.7	63.6
Review previous educational testing	50.9	62.1
Naturalistic observation	44.3	33.3
Review recent report cards	37.4	54.5*
Parent behaviour rating scales	34.8	60.6*
Teacher behaviour rating scales	33.5	50.0*
Child/adolescent self-report rating scales	25.7	40.9*
Intelligence testing	26.1	40.9*
Achievement testing	17.8	33.3*
Personality testing	16.5	33.3*

[1]Data are from a sample of 230 American clinicians (psychiatric social workers, psychiatric nurses, counsellors) who work with children and adolescents (Palmiter, 2004).

[2]Data are from a sample of 66 American doctoral-level psychologists who work with children and adolescents (Palmiter, 2004).

*Percentages using this method are significantly different at $p < .05$.

differences were evident for all forms of tests, including measures completed by parents and teachers, measures completed by the child/adolescent, and measures of intelligence and academic achievement. The accurate psychological assessment of children and youth poses a considerable challenge. Compared to adults, children and adolescents are in a process of rapid cognitive, physical, and emotional development. Furthermore, children and adolescents rarely refer themselves for psychological services—they are referred by adults such as parents and teachers. The lives of children and adolescents are best understood with reference to the contexts in which they are embedded—in families, schools, and peer groups. Therefore, assessment of children and adolescents requires that a much larger number and variety of tests and measures be used than is typically the case for adults (Mash & Hunsley, 2007). Adding to this challenge is the fact that child and adolescent assessment, by its very nature, involves the integration of information obtained from multiple methods (e.g., interviews, ratings, direct observations), informants (e.g., child, parent, teacher), and settings (e.g., home, classroom).

The collection of diverse forms of information and the subsequent integration of this information are defining aspects of psychological assessment. As previously outlined in Exhibit 5.2, there are many distinct competencies that are required for psychologists to conduct meaningful assessments. Gary Groth-Marnat (2009), who has authored some of the most commonly used resources for teaching psychological assessment, nicely captured what is required of a clinical psychologist when conducting an assessment:

> *The central role of the clinician performing psychological assessment is that of an expert in human behavior who must deal with complex processes and understand test scores in the context of a person's life. The clinician must have knowledge concerning problem areas and, on the basis of this knowledge, form a general idea regarding behaviors to observe and areas in which to collect relevant data. Doing this involves an awareness and appreciation of multiple causation, interactional influences, and multiple relationships (p. 4).*

PROFILE BOX 5.1

DR. MICHAEL SULLIVAN

Courtesy of Michael Sullivan

I completed my undergraduate training at McGill University and my M.A. and Ph.D. in clinical psychology at Concordia University in Montreal. I am currently a full professor of psychology, medicine and neurology at McGill University. I also hold a cross-appointment with the School of Physical and Occupational Therapy and am scientific director of the University Centre for Research on Pain and Disability. I have lectured nationally and internationally on the social and behavioural determinants of pain-related disability. My research focuses on the relation between catastrophic thinking and pain experience, and the development of community-based approaches to the management of pain-related disability. I am licensed as a clinical psychologist in Quebec. I currently hold a Canada Research Chair in Behavioural Health. In 2011, I received the Canadian Psychological Association Award for Distinguished Contributions to Psychology as a Profession.

HOW DID YOU CHOOSE TO BECOME A CLINICAL PSYCHOLOGIST?

The road to becoming a clinical psychologist was actually a bit convoluted. I had almost finished my undergraduate degree in psychology and was still unclear about what my next step should be. I took a year off school, worked as a research assistant in the daytime, and played guitar in Irish pubs at night. Through that year, I became more and more fascinated with health psychology and became more and more convinced that trying to make a living playing guitar in Irish pubs would be challenging. I went back to school and completed my graduate degrees at Concordia. During that time, I saw clients through the university clinic and at a chronic care psychiatric facility. These experiences exposed me to a wide range of clinical conditions, from the mildly distressed student to the severely thought-disordered inpatient. Increasingly, I became intrigued by the forces

CONTINUED . . .

that impact on mental health and the nature of the tools required to ameliorate mental health conditions. I slowly became convinced that understanding the human psyche and effectively treating mental health problems represented two of the greatest challenges facing humankind.

TELL US ABOUT YOUR RESEARCH ON THE ASSESSMENT OF PAIN.

In 1995, my colleagues and I developed the Pain Catastrophizing Scale (PCS). This instrument was designed to assess the degree to which individuals engaged in "catastrophic interpretations" of their pain experience. Our research suggested that individuals who had a tendency to catastrophize about their pain, compared to others with pain, experienced more intense pain, more emotional distress, and were more disabled. Over the past 25 years, catastrophic thinking has emerged as one of the best psychological predictors of pain severity, pain duration, and pain-related disability. The PCS has now been translated into 20 languages and incorporated in the standard assessment protocols of pain clinics around the world. Although research has been consistent in showing that catastrophic thinking can augment the physical and emotional distress associated with painful health conditions, little is known about the processes by which this occurs. Understanding the processes by which catastrophic thinking impacts on pain experience is one of the big challenges of future research.

HOW DO YOU INTEGRATE SCIENCE AND PRACTICE IN YOUR WORK?

A major focus of much of the research that has been conducted in my laboratory has been the quest for a better understanding of psychological influences on pain experiences. I believe that this work has contributed in important ways to the development of useful theoretical models of the psychology of pain. Theory is a crucial element of our efforts to understand the world around us, but theory by itself does not change clinical problems. On the heels of our theoretically based research, we have also been involved in the development of intervention programs designed to target psychological risk factors (such as catastrophic thinking) for problematic health and mental health outcomes associated with pain. In this manner, our research findings become the fuel for the development of interventions aimed at improving the physical health and mental health of individuals who suffer from painful conditions.

WHAT DO YOU SEE AS THE MOST EXCITING CHANGES IN THE FIELD OF CLINICAL PSYCHOLOGY?

One of the most exciting changes in the field of clinical psychology has been the re-emergence of "behaviour" as a primary target of intervention, at least in the domain of pain management. Although the widespread adoption of cognitive-behavioural interventions in the early 1980s was a positive step forward in clinical practice, somehow the "behavioural" element of treatment was eventually discarded. In essence, clinical psychologists began to focus all their attention on changing cognition and neglected the behavioural side of physical health and mental health problems. Consequently, for the problem of pain-related disability, clinical psychology lost considerable credibility. Psychologists were seen as useful interventionists for changing how people feel, but not so useful in changing what people do. This was problematic because reducing disability is really about changing what people do. In recent years, we have seen a reconsideration of the importance of behaviour as a central and distinct target of intervention in the treatment for individuals with pain-related conditions. This I see as a very exciting change in the field of clinical psychology.

Psychometric Considerations

What are the essential ingredients of a useful psychological test?

The entire range of issues involved in test construction and validation are covered in courses on test construction and psychometric theory. As many of you have probably already completed such a course, we restrict our discussion here to reviewing the basic requirements for a test to be both scientifically sound and clinically useful. These psychometric elements, which hold for all types of psychological tests, are standardization (of stimuli, administration, and scoring), reliability, validity, and norms.

Most students find that psychometric considerations are not as interesting as case material. However, before you skip over them, it may be useful to imagine that you are in the emergency room, having broken your hand in a fall on the ice. Would you wish to have your X-ray read by a person who has aced the anatomy course, or by someone who had skipped the anatomy class that covered the bones in the hand because it was simply too boring? To conduct competent, evidence-based assessments, psychologists must have a sound understanding of psychometrics.

Standardization

standardization: consistency across clinicians and testing occasions in the procedure used to administer and score a test.

Standardization is an essential aspect of a psychological test, and it implies consistency across clinicians and testing occasions in the procedure used to administer and score the test (Anastasi & Urbina, 1997). Without standardization, it is virtually impossible for the psychologist to replicate the information gathered in an assessment or for any other psychologist to do so. Furthermore, without standardization, test results are likely to be highly specific to the unique aspects of the testing situation and are unlikely to provide data that can be generalized to testing by another psychologist, let alone to other situations in the person's life.

To reduce variability in the testing situation, test developers provide detailed instructions regarding the nature of the stimuli, administrative procedures, time limits, and the types of verbal probes and permissible responses to the client's questions. Instructions are provided for scoring the test. For many tests, only simple addition of responses is required; however, for many other tests, there are complex scoring rules that may require extensive training to achieve proficiency. It is essential that psychologists are trained in scoring the test and that they adhere to established scoring criteria. Unfortunately, it is relatively common for some psychologists to disregard the use of such scoring criteria in favour of non-standardized, personally developed approaches to scoring. For example, as you will see later in this chapter, the Thematic Apperception Test (a storytelling test in which respondents provide stories to pictures presented by the clinician) is frequently used by some psychologists. However, despite this test being clinically available for many decades, there is no consensus among clinicians on how to score and interpret client responses to pictures (Teglasi, 2010).

What problems might there be with basing decisions on unstandardized tests?

How would you feel if a psychologist made decisions about your psychological adjustment based on an untested and unstandardized scoring system?

Reliability

We briefly touched on the psychometric properties of reliability and validity in Chapter 4 (see Exhibit 4.10). You may remember that reliability refers to the consistency of the test, including whether all aspects of the test contribute in a meaningful way to the data obtained (**internal consistency**), whether similar results would be obtained if the person was retested at some point after the initial test (**test-retest reliability**), and whether similar results would be obtained if the test was conducted and/or scored by another evaluator (**inter-rater** or **inter-scorer reliability**). Reliable results are necessary if we wish to generalize the test results and their psychological implications beyond the immediate assessment situation. Standardization of stimuli, administration, and scoring are preconditions for good reliability, but do not ensure adequate test reliability. A test may consist of too many components that are influenced by irrelevant client characteristics, the testing situation (such as the demand characteristics associated with the purpose of the testing), or the behaviour of the assessing psychologist. It is also possible that the scoring criteria for the test may be too complicated or lacking in detail to permit reliable scoring.

internal consistency: the extent to which all aspects of a test contribute in a similar way to the overall score.

test-retest reliability: the extent to which similar results would be obtained if the person was retested at some point after the initial test.

inter-rater reliability/inter-scorer reliability: the extent to which similar results would be obtained if the test was conducted by another evaluator.

A question that typically arises in both clinical and research situations is just how reliable a test must be. As with many questions in psychology, the answer to this is not entirely straightforward. First, strictly speaking, the test itself does not have reliability—reliability must be considered in a broader context that takes into account both the purpose for which the test is being used and the population it is being used with. So, simply because high levels of reliability have been found for an instrument when used with young adults, it should not be assumed that comparable levels of reliability will be found when used with older adults. Second, there are numerous psychological tests for which one would not expect internal consistency or test-retest reliability to be very high (Streiner, 2003). Take the example of a measure of stressful life events. You have probably seen such tests in other psychology courses, on websites, or in popular magazines. They involve the listing of various possible life events that an individual may experience (e.g., death of a significant other, loss of employment, marriage, birth of a child) and usually ask the respondent to indicate which events occurred in the last year. Internal consistency of such tests is irrelevant, as the items are not necessarily related to each other. Likewise, if such a test was taken at the age of 18 and then again at the age of 25, one would not necessarily expect high test-retest reliability—such a test is not intended to measure a characteristic that is stable over time.

Why is it important for clinical psychologists to understand psychometric considerations?

Let's return to the question of how much reliability is necessary. As Hogan (2007) suggested, this is a similar question to how high a ladder should be—the answer in both cases is that it depends on the purpose you have in mind. Nevertheless, there is a clear consensus that the level of acceptable reliability for tests used for clinical purposes must be greater than it is for tests used for research purposes. In considering internal consistency reliability, a number of authors have suggested that a value of .90 is the minimum required for a clinical test (e.g., Nunnally & Bernstein, 1994). For research purposes, values greater than .70 are typically seen as sufficient, with lower values being unacceptable (e.g., Hunsley & Mash, 2008; Kaplan & Saccuzzo, 2001). The main reason that high reliability is so important for clinical purposes is that reliability influences how much error there is in a test score. This can be extremely important in clinical work where precise test cut-off scores are used, such as in determining whether a child's measured intelligence is high enough to warrant access to a gifted school program.

Validity

When we consider test validity we are evaluating the degree to which the test truly measures what it purports to measure. A standardized test that produces reliable data does not necessarily yield valid data, because a test purporting to measure one construct may in fact be measuring a different construct. Test validity is a matter of ensuring that the test includes items that are representative of all aspects of the underlying psychological construct the test is designed to measure

content validity: the extent to which the test samples the type of behaviour that is relevant to the underlying psychological construct.

concurrent validity: the extent to which scores on the test are correlated with scores on measures of similar constructs.

predictive validity: the extent to which the test predicts a relevant outcome.

discriminant validity: the extent to which the test provides a pure measure of the construct that is minimally contaminated by other psychological constructs.

incremental validity: the extent to which a measure adds to the prediction of a criterion above what can be predicted by other sources of data.

(**content validity**), that it provides data consistent with theoretical postulates associated with the phenomenon being assessed (**concurrent validity** and **predictive validity**), and that it provides a relatively pure measure of the construct that is minimally contaminated by other psychological constructs (**discriminant validity**).

In applied contexts, such as in clinical assessment, an additional form of validity should be considered, namely **incremental validity**: the extent to which a measure adds to the prediction of a criterion above what can be predicted by other sources of data (Hunsley & Meyer, 2003; Sechrest, 1963). It is not necessarily a case of "the more data the better" in clinical assessment. As described previously, there are costs associated with the collection of assessment data. The collection of excessive amounts of data can lead to both unnecessary costs and the introduction of unnecessary error creeping into the assessment. Despite the clear importance of incremental validity in conducting clinical assessments, there is currently very little research available to guide clinical psychologists in their selection and use of tests.

Although it is common to talk about a test being either valid or invalid, validity is not a dichotomous variable. Many psychological tests consist of subscales designed to measure specific aspects of a more general construct. For such tests, it is inappropriate to refer to the validity of the test *per se,* because the validity of each subscale must be established. Moreover, validity is always conditional and must be established within certain parameters. Simply because a test is valid for specific purposes within specific groups of people, it does not follow that it is valid for other purposes or groups (Haynes et al., 2011). For example, knowing that an intelligence test is a valid predictor of academic functioning does not also automatically support its use as a test for determining child custody arrangements.

We should not automatically assume that a test that has been shown to be valid for members of one ethnic group will be valid for members of a different ethnic group. When deciding if it is appropriate to use a test with a client, the psychologist should determine whether there is validity evidence based on research with members of the same ethnic group as the client. Fernandez, Boccaccini, and Noland (2007) outlined a four-step process psychologists can use in identifying and selecting translated tests for Spanish-speaking clients (and which is applicable to translated tests in other languages). First, the range of translated tests should be identified by reviewing the catalogues and websites of test publishing companies. Next, research evidence for each relevant translated test, not just the original English-language versions, must be examined. Third, the nature of the Spanish-speaking samples used in the studies should be examined to determine if the results are likely to be relevant to the client (e.g., research conducted in Spain may not be generalizable to a client who recently emigrated from Ecuador). Finally, the strength of the validity evidence must be weighed in determining whether the test is likely to be appropriate and useful in assessing the client.

Norms

To meaningfully interpret the results obtained from a client, it is essential to use either norms or specific criterion-related cut-off scores (AERA et al., 1999). Without such reference information, it is impossible to determine the precise meaning of any test results. So, if you were told you had a score of 44 on a test of emotional maturity, it would provide no meaningful information unless you knew the range of possible scores and how most other people score. In psychological assessment, comparisons must be made to either criteria that have been set for the test (e.g., a certain degree of accuracy, as demonstrated in the test, is necessary for the satisfactory performance of a job) or to some form of norms.

For most purposes in clinical psychology, test developers establish norms. Most importantly, decisions must be made about the populations to which the test is to be applied. It is possible to establish norms for comparing a specific score to those that might be obtained within the general population or within specific subgroups of the general population (e.g., gender-specific norms). So, if your score of 44 for emotional maturity turned out to be significantly higher than the average in the general population, you might be very pleased. It is also possible to establish norms for determining the likelihood of membership in specific theoretical or concrete categories (e.g., non-distressed versus psychologically disordered groups). As with validity considerations, it may be necessary to develop multiple norms for a test based on the group being assessed and the testing purpose (i.e., norms relevant for different ages and ethnic groups).

A critical aspect of test norms is the quality of the normative sample. It is very common to find tests that have norms based on samples of convenience—in other words, data were obtained from a group of research participants in a specific location and may not be representative of scores that would be obtained by others. Common convenience samples include undergraduate students, hospital inpatients, or patients in a single psychology clinic. Such norms should be treated very sceptically, as no effort was made to ensure that the members of the normative group were comparable in age, gender, ethnicity, or educational level (for example) to those who are likely to take the test as part of a clinical assessment. There are some commonly used psychological tests, such as the Wechsler intelligence scales (see Chapter 7), that have nationally representative norms. With these types of norms, great care has been taken to ensure that test scores were obtained from a group of research participants selected to be representative of the national population for whom the test will be used. Accordingly, one can have much more confidence in the value and relevance of such norms.

As you may remember if you have taken a course in psychometrics and test construction, there are three main categories of test norms: percentile ranks, standard scores, and developmental norms (Hogan, 2007). A percentile rank indicates the percentage of those in the normative group whose scores fell below a given test score. If a test score of 25 is associated with a percentile rank of 81, this indicates that 81% of those in the normative group scored at or below a test score of 25. As you may have seen in Appendix 2, most students applying to graduate programs in clinical psychology are required to take the Graduate Record Examination (GRE). Typically, the results from this test are reported as percentile ranks. The use of standard scores is very common with psychological tests. To develop a standard score, a *z*-score is calculated. This involves subtracting the mean of the test scores from a specific test score and dividing the resulting number by the standard deviation of the test scores. Many psychological tests, such as the Minnesota Multiphasic Personality Inventory-2 (MMPI-2; described in detail in Chapter 8), convert a calculated *z*-score to a distribution in which the mean score is 50 and the standard deviation is 10 (i.e., a *T*-score). The GRE uses a different distribution in which the mean score is set at 500 and the standard deviation is 100.

Figure 5.2 presents the distribution of scores under a normal curve and allows you to interpret the normative meaning of a percentile rank or a standard score. Using this figure, you can see that a *T*-score of 71 on the MMPI-2 means that the score is greater than that obtained by more than 98% of the normative sample.

Finally, developmental norms are used when the psychological construct being assessed develops systematically over time. The intelligence test developed by Alfred Binet used mental age equivalents to quantify the intellectual status of children (i.e., a child's score was comparable to the average child of a given age). The Woodcock-Johnson III Test of Cognitive Abilities uses both age equivalents (i.e., the age level in the normative sample at which the mean score is the same as the test score under consideration) and grade equivalents (i.e., the grade level in the normative sample at which the mean score is the same as the test score under consideration) to quantify achievement performance.

Testing Practices in Clinical Psychology

In Chapter 2, we described testing and assessment as central activities for most clinical psychologists. In Chapters 7 and 8, we describe in detail a number of commonly used psychological tests, with a particular

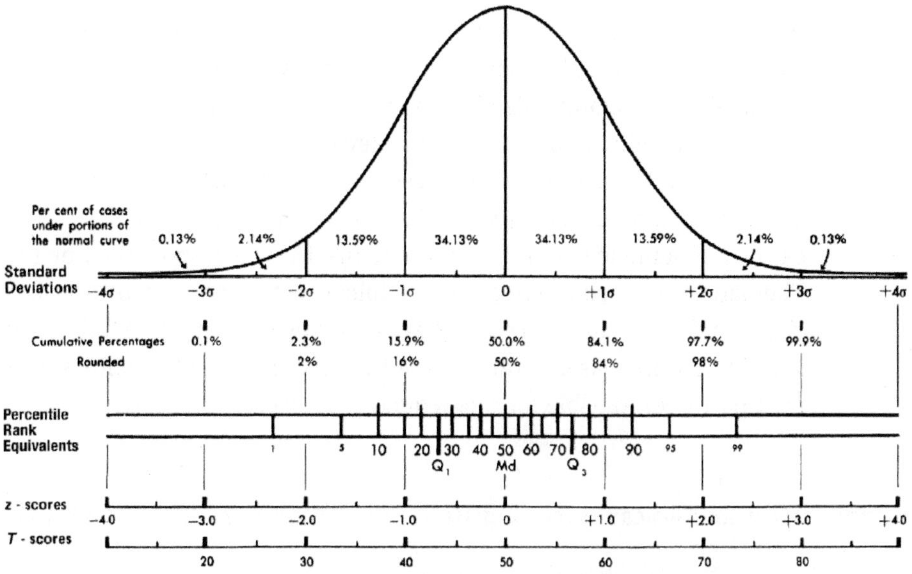

Figure 5.2 Equivalence of several types of norms in the normal curve

Test Service Notebook 148: Methods of Expressing Test Scores. Courtesy of NCS Pearson, Inc., Educational Assessment, San Antonio, TX.

emphasis on those that have substantial evidence of reliability and validity. Our intent in this section is to briefly present to you the tests that clinical psychologists typically use. As you read the following paragraphs, we'd like you to keep in mind the unfortunate fact that, as Groth-Marnat (2009) noted, many clinical psychologists fail to take into account the psychometric properties of tests or the strength of the research regarding the tests. In other words, although some commonly used tests have outstanding psychometric properties, others fall woefully short of professional standards. We will have much more to say about this lamentable state of affairs in subsequent chapters.

There is a long history of surveys of clinical psychologists' practice activities and use of different types of tests. Exhibit 5.4 presents information from surveys of American clinical psychologists. Data from Cashel's (2002) survey of 162 clinical psychologists working with children and adolescents suggested that intelligence tests, behaviour rating scales completed by parents and teachers (and, in some cases, the youth themselves), and brief projective tests are commonly used. In their survey of 137 clinical psychologists, Piotrowski, Belter, and Keller (1998) asked respondents about the most important tests used in clinical practice. Although the specific tests differed from those reported in the Cashel (2002) study, a similar pattern emerged, with intelligence, self-report personality inventories, and projective measures seen as most important. Of concern in both these surveys is the frequent reliance on projective tests. Compared with intelligence tests, personality inventories, and behaviour rating scales, projective tests are far less likely to be standardized, to have norms, or to possess acceptable levels of reliability and validity (Hunsley et al., in press). For example, although the Rorschach Inkblot Test can be administered, scored, and interpreted in a standardized manner, this is not the case for the clinical use of sentence completion tasks, the Draw-A-Person Test, or the Thematic Apperception Test. The clinical use of projective tests has declined dramatically in recent years (Norcross & Karpiak, 2012) and it is likely that increased awareness of these scientific shortcomings is at least partly responsible for this reduction in use.

Exhibit 5.4 Test Usage Among American Clinical Psychologists

Five Tests Most Commonly Used in Child and Adolescent Assessment[1]

Wechsler Intelligence Scale for Children
Achenbach System of Empirically Based Assessment
Sentence Completion Tests
Conners' Parent and Teacher Rating Scales
Draw-A-Person Test

Five Tests Rated As Most Important in Assessment Practices[2]

Minnesota Multiphasic Personality Inventory (both adult and adolescent versions)
Wechsler intelligence scales (both adult and child versions)
Rorschach Inkblot Test
Millon inventories
Thematic Apperception Test

[1]From Cashel (2002).
[2]From Piotrowski, Belter, and Keller (1998).

Why do psychologists collect multiple types of information in their assessments?

Both country of practice and nature of doctoral assessment training appear to influence psychologists' test usage. Bekhit, Thomas, Lalonde, and Jolley (2002) found that British psychologists were much less likely than American psychologists to use psychological tests. In a survey of 158 British clinical psychologists, the tests seen as most important for clinical practice were the Wechsler intelligence scales (adult and child versions), the Wechsler Memory Scale, the Beck Depression Inventory, the National Adult Reading Test, and the Millon Personality Inventories. Extremely few respondents rated the Thematic Apperception Test and the Rorschach as important for clinical use. Childs and Eyde (2002) surveyed approximately half the APA-accredited clinical psychology programs in Canada and the United States. They found that more than two-thirds of surveyed programs taught doctoral students to use the Wechsler intelligence scales, the MMPI scales, the Rorschach Inkblot Test, and the Thematic Apperception Test. This definitely helps explain the Piotrowski et al. (1998) data: psychologists are simply using the tests that they were trained to use. If we consider the model curriculum recommendations found in Exhibit 5.1 and the competency requirements found in Exhibit 5.2, the Childs and Eyde (2002) data suggest that there are some very significant weaknesses in the way in which most programs approach assessment training. For example, although almost every surveyed program provided training in the interpretation and reporting of test results, less than two-thirds provided instruction on the topics of reliability and validity, and only 20% had a course that covered issues related to norms.

EVIDENCE-BASED ASSESSMENT

In recent years, we have witnessed a renewed emphasis on the scientific evidence underlying psychological tests and assessment. This is attributable to the increased focus on the use of scientific evidence to guide the provision of health care services, as well as greater awareness of shortcomings in the ways in which some clinical psychologists assess their clients. **Evidence-based assessment** (EBA) is an approach to psychological evaluation that uses research and theory to guide (a) the variables assessed, (b) the methods and measures used, and (c) the manner in which the assessment process unfolds. It involves the recognition that the assessment process is a decision-making task in which the clinician must repeatedly formulate and test hypotheses by integrating data obtained throughout the assessment (Hunsley & Mash, 2007).

evidence-based assessment: the use of research and theory to guide (a) the variable assessed, (b) the methods and measures, and (c) the manner in which the assessment process unfolds.

The first step in the development of EBA has been the identification of psychological instruments (including interviews, self-report measures, observational coding systems, and self-monitoring measures) that have been demonstrated to possess solid psychometric properties. Hunsley and Mash (2008) developed a rating system for instruments used for specific assessment purposes (e.g., diagnosis, treatment monitoring, treatment evaluation) within specific conditions (e.g., depression, self-injurious behaviours, couple conflict). The rating system requires the attainment of predetermined psychometric levels in the areas of reliability, validity, and norms across published studies (e.g., repeated evidence of internal consistency values of .90 and above is designated as "excellent"). The next step is using statistical procedures to integrate assessment data for individual clients and to develop scientifically sound procedures for client data to directly inform important clinical decisions (e.g., De Los Reyes, Thomas, Goodman, & Kundey, 2013; Youngstrom, 2013).

ETHICAL CONSIDERATIONS

As we described in Chapter 2, the profession of clinical psychology is founded on two main pillars: science and ethics. Thus far in the chapter, we have focused almost exclusively on the scientific side of psychological assessment. It is now time to consider the main ethical issues psychologists encounter in conducting assessments.

In Chapter 2, we described the ethical principles, such as responsible caring, that are represented in the *Canadian Code of Ethics* (CPA, 2000). Obviously, all those principles apply when assessments are conducted by Canadian psychologists. Both the American Psychological Association (APA, 2010a) and the Association of State and Provincial Psychology Boards (ASPPB, 2005) have codes of conduct that contain elements specific to assessment activities. In order to avoid differences in codes and legal requirements across jurisdictions, we focus our presentation of ethical issues on generic issues in assessment rather than on a specific code of conduct.

People considering a psychological assessment should ensure that they receive sufficient details about the assessment to be able to make an informed decision about participation. They require information about the nature and purpose of the assessment, the fees, the involvement of other parties in the assessment, and any limits to confidentiality.

When considering ethical issues in assessment, the first and foremost issue is that of informed consent. In some instances, it may not be possible to obtain freely given informed consent because the person is, in some fashion, being compelled to undergo the assessment. Common examples include situations in which a court has mandated an assessment or an assessment is being undertaken to determine an individual's competence or capacity to make decisions. For example, Toni, a seriously depressed mother who is engaged in a battle for the custody of her child with her formerly abusive partner, may feel that she has little choice about whether to participate in a child custody evaluation if she wishes to retain her parenting arrangement with her child. Similarly, Trent, who was charged with manslaughter following a motor vehicle accident, may feel he has little choice about participating in a psychological assessment that will address whether symptoms of attention-deficit/hyperactivity disorder contributed to the accident. In these situations, psychologists should still strive to provide as much information about the assessment as is appropriate in these cases. Most codes of conduct indicate that psychologists have a responsibility to adequately communicate the results of the assessment to the client. Not only must the psychologist provide the information, but he or she must take reasonable steps to ensure that the client understands the results.

All information collected as part of a psychological assessment must be treated as confidential. This means that no information gathered in the assessment can be released to others without the client's consent. Although this seems rather straightforward, there are exceptions to this. For example, if the psychologist learns that the client is intent on committing suicide, has a clear plan for this, and has the means to carry out the plan, the psychologist has an obligation to break confidentiality in order to secure the client's safety. When a child volunteers in the course of intelligence testing that he or she is upset because a parent punished him or her with a belt, then the psychologist has a legal obligation to inform the child protection authorities. Limits to confidentiality must thus be explained to the client as part of the informed consent procedures.

In most jurisdictions, legislation allows people to access their health records. In other words, whatever is in a client file, with very few exceptions, can be seen by the client, and clients can authorize the release of file information to others such as teachers, lawyers, or other health care providers. This poses a potential challenge for psychologists, as they are also required to protect the security and copyright of test materials. As a result, it is becoming standard practice among psychologists to distinguish between test data and test material per se. Test data, like other parts of a client file, may be released to others upon the request of the client (or the client's guardian or legal representative). Test material, including actual test questions and manuals, are not part of the file and must not be released. The distinction between test data and test material has caused publishers of psychological tests to alter the format of some tests. It was common practice for self-report measures, for example, to have both the test questions and a space for scoring the test on the same sheet. This made it impossible to physically separate the test data (i.e., the client's score or circled responses to questions) from the test itself. Accordingly, the format of many of these tests has been altered to provide a separate sheet on which the client provides a response and the test is scored.

In conducting assessments, psychologists have an ethical responsibility to be knowledgeable about test properties such as standardization, reliability, validity, and norms. They must also be familiar with the proper use and interpretation of the tests they use. It is particularly important that psychologists be aware of the tests' strengths and limitations with respect to psychological characteristics such as age, gender, ethnicity, and cultural background. When providing feedback about the assessment to the client or to others designated by the client, psychologists have a responsibility to clearly indicate the limits to the certainty of their findings. This pertains to all aspects of assessment results, including diagnoses, clinical judgments, and clinical predictions. They also have an obligation to indicate the basis for their results and must clearly indicate the sources of data used in an assessment. It is becoming increasingly common for psychologists to use computer-generated interpretive reports when using personality, intelligence, or achievement tests. Psychologists who use the interpretive statements contained in the computer-generated report should acknowledge the sources of the statements in the assessment report. This ensures that the basis for the conclusions obtained from the interpretive report is clearly presented.

SUMMARY AND CONCLUSIONS

In this chapter, we have reviewed some of the many purposes of psychological assessment. We have highlighted that, in addition to stand-alone assessment services, psychological assessment can be used in screening, diagnosis and case formulation, prediction, treatment planning, and monitoring the effectiveness of interventions. An important distinction was drawn between psychological assessment, which refers to an entire process of inquiry, and psychological testing, which may be used as part of that process. We have argued that psychologists have special expertise in the use of tests, and that for a tool to be considered a psychological test it must meet strict criteria in terms of standardization, reliability, validity, and norms. The development of principles for evidence-based assessment holds the promise of enhancing the scientific quality of instruments used by clinical psychologists. Finally, we reviewed ethical issues related to consent to assessment services.

KEY TERMS

assessment-focused services: services conducted primarily to provide information on a person's psychosocial functioning.

base rate: the frequency with which a problem or diagnosis occurs in the population.

case formulation: a description of the patient that provides information on his or her life situation, current problems, and a set of hypotheses linking psychosocial factors with the patient's clinical condition.

concurrent validity: the extent to which scores on the test are correlated with scores on measures of similar constructs.

content validity: the extent to which the test samples the type of behaviour that is relevant to the underlying psychological construct.

discriminant validity: the extent to which the test provides a pure measure of the construct that is minimally contaminated by other psychological constructs.

evidence-based assessment: the use of research and theory to guide (a) the variables assessed, (b) the methods and measures used, and (c) the manner in which the assessment process unfolds.

incremental validity: the extent to which a measure adds to the prediction of a criterion above what can be predicted by other sources of data.

internal consistency: the extent to which all aspects of a test contribute in a similar way to the overall score.

inter-rater reliability/inter-scorer reliability: the extent to which similar results would be obtained if the test was conducted by another evaluator.

intervention-focused assessment services: assessments conducted in the context of intervention services.

predictive validity: the extent to which the test predicts a relevant outcome.

prognosis: predictions made about the future course of a patient's psychological functioning, based on the use of assessment data in combination with relevant empirical literature.

screening: a procedure to identify individuals who may have problems of a clinical magnitude or who may be at risk for developing such problems.

sensitivity: proportion of true positives identified by the assessment.

specificity: proportion of true negatives identified by the assessment.

standardization: consistency across clinicians and testing occasions in the procedure used to administer and score a test.

test-retest reliability: the extent to which similar results would be obtained if the person was retested at some point after the initial test.

KEY NAMES

Gary Groth-Marnat

Michael Lambert

ADDITIONAL RESOURCES

Books

Groth-Marnat, G. (2009). *Handbook of psychological assessment* (4th ed.). Hoboken, NJ: John Wiley & Sons Inc.

Haynes, S. N., Smith, G., & Hunsley, J. (2011). *Scientific foundations of clinical assessment.* New York: Taylor & Francis.

Hogan, T. P. (2007). *Psychological testing: A practical introduction* (2nd ed.). Hoboken, NJ: John Wiley & Sons Inc.

Hunsley, J., & Mash, E. J. (Eds.). (2008). *A guide to assessments that work.* New York: Oxford University Press.

Check It Out!

The Buros Center for Testing provides listings of tests and test reviews: www.unl.edu/buros

The American Psychological Association has a research database, PsycTESTS, that covers many types of psychological tests: www.apa.org/pubs/databases/psyctests/index.aspx

There are several websites with information on screening for psychological problems.

National Alcohol Screening Day: www.mentalhealthscreening.org/programs/colleges/nasd

National Depression Screening Day: www.mentalhealthscreening.org/events/national-depression-screening-day.aspx

Self-screening for anxiety and depression, offered by Freedom From Fear: www.freedomfromfear.org/screenrm.asp

ASSESSMENT: INTERVIEWING AND OBSERVATION

6 CHAPTER

INTRODUCTION

Among the myriad strategies used in clinical assessments, interviews and observations are the most commonly used by psychologists. Across diverse theoretical orientations, clinical psychologists gather assessment data by talking to clients and by observing them. Interviews are used in overlapping ways for both clinical assessment and psychotherapy (see Figure 6.1). Interviews play a vitally important role in the development of a collaborative relationship between a psychologist and client. They are an integral component of both stand-alone assessments and assessments that are part of the delivery of psychological services. Interviews are the most common strategy to gather information necessary to make a diagnosis and serve many additional purposes. They are also used to obtain information for case formulation, problem definition, and goal-setting. Interview data include material that cannot be easily assessed in psychometric tests and that is important in generating hypotheses and elaborating on themes that have been identified in other assessment strategies.

In this chapter, we will explain some of the differences between clinical assessment interviews and regular conversations. Psychologists are trained how to ask questions and how to listen. The way that questions are formulated can encourage clients to give a "yes-no" type answer, or to elaborate and explain in greater detail. Listening skills include verbal strategies to convey understanding and to clarify what the client has said, as well as non-verbal behaviours that convey that the psychologist is attentively tracking the conversation. In this chapter, we will describe confidentiality issues that must be addressed prior to

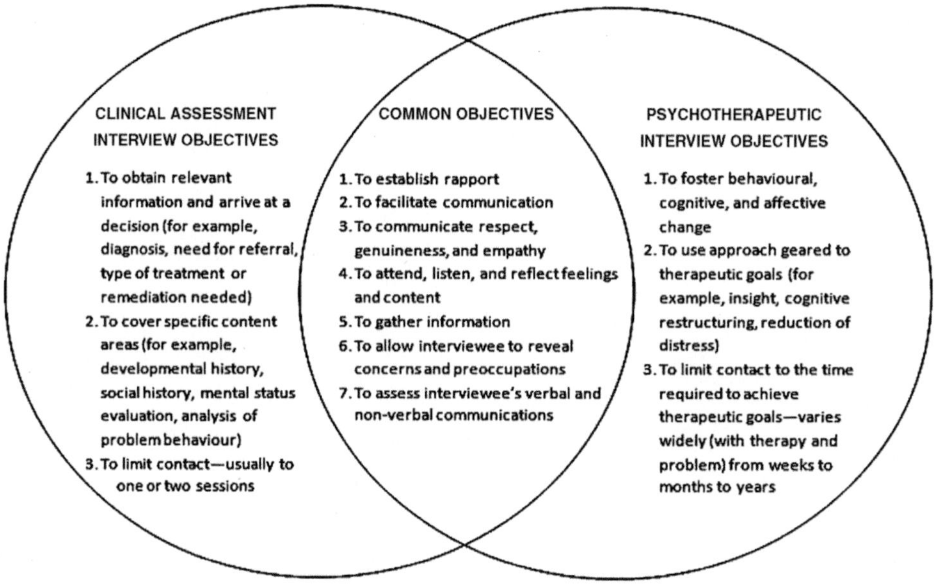

CLINICAL ASSESSMENT INTERVIEW OBJECTIVES
1. To obtain relevant information and arrive at a decision (for example, diagnosis, need for referral, type of treatment or remediation needed)
2. To cover specific content areas (for example, developmental history, social history, mental status evaluation, analysis of problem behaviour)
3. To limit contact—usually to one or two sessions
COMMON OBJECTIVES
1. To establish rapport
2. To facilitate communication
3. To communicate respect, genuineness, and empathy
4. To attend, listen, and reflect feelings and content
5. To gather information
6. To allow interviewee to reveal concerns and preoccupations
7. To assess interviewee's verbal and non-verbal communications
PSYCHOTHERAPEUTIC INTERVIEW OBJECTIVES
1. To foster behavioural, cognitive, and affective change
2. To use approach geared to therapeutic goals (for example, insight, cognitive restructuring, reduction of distress)
3. To limit contact to the time required to achieve therapeutic goals—varies widely (with therapy and problem) from weeks to months to years

Figure 6.1 Differences and similarities between clinical assessment interviews and psychotherapeutic interviews

Reproduced with permission from Mash & Sattler (1998).

beginning any interview. We will outline strategies used in interviews to define the client's problems, formulate client goals, and obtain an accurate description of ways the client has attempted to solve similar problems in the past. We will also present ways that the skills required in interviewing an individual must be adapted when the psychologist is interviewing a couple or a family. For example, you can imagine that a clinical psychologist interviewing 13-year-old Michael and his mother would quickly lose rapport with the teenager if all the focus of the interview was on his mother. So, in working with more than one client, the psychologist must be adept at ensuring each person has an opportunity to talk.

©iStock.com/Maica

The psychologist must maintain rapport with the teenager and the parent.

Different purposes require different types of interviews that vary in their degree of structure. In unstructured interviews, the psychologist decides what questions to ask and to follow up on as the interview unfolds. Semi-structured interviews allow the psychologist some flexibility in questioning and the order of questions. Highly structured interviews specify the precise ways that questions should be posed and queries made, as well as define the types of responses necessary to score a particular symptom as present. You may recall that, in Chapter 4, we discussed the need to balance threats to internal validity and external validity. Similarly, in considering interview formats, the psychologist must weigh the advantages of structure against the advantages of flexibility. In practice, most clinical assessment interviews are unstructured and follow the format preferred by the individual psychologist. Even though unstructured clinical assessment interviews do not follow a set script, they are distinct from regular conversation in important ways we describe later.

For many decades, children were considered to be unreliable informants, so all pertinent clinical information was gathered from the significant adults in their lives. Psychologists now know that children can provide important information about their experiences, thoughts, and feelings. However, it is not sufficient to simply scale down an adult interview for use with children. Although face-to-face interviews are a common way to gather information from adults, this strategy poses special challenges with children. We will describe some of the developmental issues that must be taken into account when interviewing children, including their level of cognitive development, their emotional expression, and their suggestibility. Given the limitations of child interviews, diagnostic information is also obtained from adults who know the child well, such as parents, teachers, and caregivers.

Interviews offer rich opportunities for the psychologist to observe the client. The psychologist is attentive to the client's appearance, behaviour, affect, and responses to questions. Couple, parent-child, and family interviews also provide the opportunity to observe the ways that family members interact including the way they take turns or how they handle disagreement. Psychologists also find it useful to observe children and families in more naturalistic environments, such as in a playroom, at home, or at school. We will discuss the types of information that can be gathered from such observations. In the final section of the chapter, we will discuss the usefulness of self-monitoring as a clinical assessment strategy, in which the client keeps track of and records the details of relevant thoughts, behaviours, or feelings.

What are some of the major goals of assessment interviews?

ETHICAL ISSUES: LIMITS OF CONFIDENTIALITY

Ethical codes dictate that psychologists must provide confidential services. This means that the psychologist is required to maintain secrecy with respect to the material that is revealed in the course of providing psychological services. The psychologist is bound to respect the client's privacy and must not discuss details with other people without the client's permission. Even though privacy legislation in all jurisdictions in Canada limits the use and release of private information, there are limits to the confidentiality of information provided to a psychologist. As we discussed in Chapter 5, in some cases, a third party such as a school board, an insurance company, or a family court judge has requested the assessment. In those circumstances, the client must give permission for the results of the assessment to be sent to the third party. There are also legal obligations to break confidentiality when a person's safety is at risk. Canadian provinces all have child protection laws that require professionals to inform the local child protection agency if there is a suspicion that a child may be in need of protection. Psychologists are required to take steps to ensure that clients are protected from self-harm and that others are protected if a client plans to harm someone else. Psychological reports and records can be subpoenaed by the court, and the psychologist can be required to testify with respect to the psychological services provided to the client.

Psychologists must ensure that the client understands the limits of confidentiality before he or she enters into an agreement to receive psychological services (which is why we are discussing ethical issues so early in this chapter!). The client has a right to know what will be kept confidential and under what circumstances confidentiality may be broken. The limits of confidentiality can vary considerably from province to province, so the psychologist must be fully aware of these limits, too. Exhibit 6.1 provides an example of the way that a psychologist might introduce the **limits of confidentiality** at the beginning of a first appointment. Although it is highly unusual to begin a first conversation with a statement that sets out all kinds of unpleasant scenarios, such as child abuse, suicide, homicide, and court cases, an explanation of the limits of confidentiality gives a very clear signal that the conversation that will follow is a professional one. By calmly explaining the limits of confidentiality, the psychologist demonstrates that, in the context of psychological services, the client's rights are protected and the person's safety is considered paramount, and that it is possible to talk about very difficult issues. As you can imagine, students in training sometimes wonder whether a client who has been told the limits of confidentiality will be afraid to say anything to a psychologist; however, this is not the case. Knowing that the psychologist will need to take action, clients still disclose painful experiences such as being the victim of abuse or having thoughts of suicide.

limits of confidentiality: situations in which the psychologist is legally obliged to break confidentiality by disclosing information provided by the patient to another person or agency.

Exhibit 6.1 Limits of Confidentiality: A Heavy Way to Start a Conversation, but a Professional Way to Start an Assessment Interview

Everything that is said here is private. I will not tell other people what's talked about. However, there are some important exceptions to that rule. First, if you told me that a child was being harmed in some way, then by law I have to do something to protect the child; that is, I'd have to report the information to the child protection services. Second, if I heard that you were finding things so tough that you felt life just wasn't worth living anymore, then I'd have to take steps to protect you. Basically, if I hear anyone is in danger of being hurt by someone else or by himself or herself, then I can't keep things private, but must do something to protect the person. Third, if there was ever some kind of a court case, then a judge could ask me to give testimony, could ask me about these sessions, or ask to see my notes.

Do you understand the limits to confidentiality that I just described? Do you have any questions? I know this is a heavy way to get started, but I believe it is important to describe this to all clients, just so you know where you stand.

What is your reaction to the information provided in Exhibit 6.1? How would this affect your views of psychological services? What kind of skills does it require to begin a conversation this way?

UNSTRUCTURED ASSESSMENT INTERVIEWS

In conducting clinical interviews, psychologists strive to create a safe environment designed to make the client more at ease to talk about the issues that are troubling to him or her. The assessment interview is conducted free from disruptions; the psychologist does not answer the phone, read text messages, or respond to email during interviews. Ideally, offices are soundproofed to limit distracting background noises. The psychologist adopts a calm and relaxed stance designed to put clients at ease. However, the clinical interview is not a social visit. It differs in important ways from the conversations a client may have with friends, with the hairdresser, or with a stranger on a long train journey. Allowing a person to simply tell his or her story is not the same as conducting a clinical assessment interview. Empathic listening may be sufficient to provide temporary relief to a distressed friend, but it is not sufficient to enable the psychologist to formulate a diagnosis or to begin treatment planning. Exhibit 6.2 lists some of the ways that clinical interviews differ from regular conversations. Because an assessment interview is not a regular conversation, the client may feel more at ease in discussing painful or embarrassing issues than he or she would be willing to discuss in chats with friends.

What are the major differences between assessment interviews and conversations with friends?

Exhibit 6.2 Differences between Clinical Interviews and Social Conversations

Social Conversation	Clinical Interview
Can take place anywhere	Usually in an office
May be overheard by others	Private
Variable duration	Usually 50 minutes to an hour
Details may be repeated in other conversations	Confidential, except to protect safety or with client's written permission
Purpose is relationship maintenance	Purpose is both information gathering and establishing a collaborative relationship
Free-flowing according to each person's interest	Goal-directed, keeps to an agenda, clear sequence, keeps to relevant themes
Reciprocal: *Something similar happened to me . . . That reminds me of the time when I . . .*	Focused on the client
Each person waits for an opening to make a comment: *Now that you mention worries . . .*	Clinician interrupts and redirects conversation: *Do you ever worry . . .*
Maintenance of relationship usually takes precedence	May require persistent questioning over gathering information
Commonly avoids painful topics	Clinician raises painful topics such as abuse, violence, suicide
Participants rarely take notes	Psychologist may take notes
Not documented	Notes of session are kept by the psychologist
Not recorded	With client's permission may be audio or video recorded

If you choose a career in clinical psychology because you always liked talking to people and are considered by your friends to be a good listener, you may be surprised to discover that you will need to learn to interact in a very different way in your future role as a psychologist.

The psychologist is responsible for structuring the session to ensure that relevant topics are covered during assessment interviews. The psychologist's theoretical orientation and training determine the extent to which he or she explicitly directs the session, the manner in which the questions are asked, and the topics that are covered. In general, though, psychologists are trained to formulate questions in a manner that facilitates the client's engagement in the interview.

open questions: questions that allow elaborate responses and cannot be answered with a simple *yes* or *no*.

closed questions: questions that can be answered with a single word.

One important distinction is between **open questions** and **closed questions**. Open questions allow the client to provide elaborate responses and cannot be answered with a simple *yes* or *no*. Closed questions, on the other hand, can be answered with a single word. Each has advantages and disadvantages. Open questions allow the client to give a more complex answer and do not suggest a particular response is required. However, open questions may invite the client to begin a long, tangential story that may be of limited relevance, in which case the psychologist must direct the client back to the topic at hand. Closed questions, on the other hand, yield brief, less ambiguous answers, allowing the rapid coverage of many topics. Exhibit 6.3 gives examples of open and closed questions. Many psychologists find it useful to begin discussion of a topic with an open-ended question and to follow up with closed questions that clarify details of the response.

Exhibit 6.3 Open and Closed Questions

Open	Closed
Who lives in your house?	*Does your dad live with you?*
What was your reaction when you found out you were pregnant?	*Were you pleased when you found out you were pregnant?*
How do you show affection?	*Do you kiss your partner?*
What do your parents do when you break curfew?	*Do you get grounded when you break curfew?*
What happens when you argue?	*Do you hit her when you argue?*
Tell me about the kinds of things that make you feel anxious.	*Were you anxious when you gave a presentation to the class?*
How did your reactions compare to what you usually feel?	*Did you feel better after taking a deep breath?*
How would your life be different if you make the changes you want in therapy?	*Do you think you will be able to work again when you no longer feel depressed?*

Pay attention to your usual style of questioning in your conversations with friends. Do you notice any difference in the impact on the conversation when you use open and closed questions? If you have a favourite interviewer or talk show host, notice the type of questions that person uses and the way the questions alter the conversation.

Although some people worry that asking questions about difficult issues such as suicide will increase the likelihood of suicidal behaviour, this is not the case. Because the phrasing of the question can influence the type of answer, psychologists are careful not to ask leading questions or to put words in the client's mouth. The client's initial response to a question may be non-committal or vague, requiring the psychologist to encourage the client to elaborate or to explain: *Tell me what you mean . . .; Tell me more about that.* Contrary to the conventions of regular conversation, the psychologist gently persists with a line of questioning until the question has been answered. So, for example, after Jessica changed the topic or made a joke when asked about her new relationship, a friend might conclude that she did not wish to discuss it, and move on to other topics, whereas a psychologist might ask her if she noticed that she seemed to be having difficulty talking about the relationship. As clinical assessment interviews are not the same as regular conversation, the psychologist may ask questions that people may find difficult to answer (e.g., *What was it like for you when you had the miscarriage? What went through your mind as you were forcing yourself to vomit? How do people respond to you when you tell them that you have schizophrenia?*). Sometimes clients are at a loss how to answer and must reflect before answering. Psychologists use silence to allow the client time to reflect and, therefore, do not feel obliged to fill in the gaps in conversation as they might in a social context.

STRUCTURED DIAGNOSTIC INTERVIEWS

What are the advantages and disadvantages of structured diagnostic interviews?

In Chapter 3, we described the evolution of diagnostic systems used to categorize different types of psychopathology. You may remember that each version of the *Diagnostic and Statistical Manual of Mental Disorders* (DSM) provided more precise decision rules for the diagnosis of disorders. Researchers noted that although most mental health professionals agreed on the general features of a disorder, there was poor inter-rater reliability in assigning diagnoses; that is, there was low agreement between two interviewers about the precise diagnostic category. To address this problem, a number of **structured interviews** were developed. These interviews vary in their coverage of symptoms and life context. They have a specific format for asking questions and a specific sequence in which questions are asked. Based on initial client responses, the interviewer is then directed to use follow-up questions that help confirm or rule out possible diagnoses. Although structured interviews can be designed to address almost any clinical issue, the majority are designed to provide diagnostic information. As you will see, most of the structured interviews we present were developed for use with the DSM-IV. With the release of DSM-5, these interviews will require updating and validation.

structured interviews: interviews with a specific format for asking questions and a specific sequence in which questions are asked.

The most widely used clinical interview in North America, the Structured Clinical Interview for Axis I Disorders (SCID; First, Spitzer, Gibbon, & Williams, 1997), permits diagnosis of a broad spectrum of disorders. Two versions have been developed. The SCID-I is an interview designed for research that includes almost the entire spectrum of DSM disorders, whereas the shorter SCID-CV covers only the most common disorders. The SCID begins with an open-ended interview on demographic information, work history, chief complaint, history of present and past psychopathology, treatment history, and assessment of current functioning. This less structured format is designed to develop rapport with the client prior to beginning the structured symptom-focused questions that are designed to yield diagnostic information. It is clear, therefore, that the SCID is not a completely standardized instrument. The structured portion includes required probe questions as well as recommended follow-up questions. Each probe corresponds to a specific DSM criterion. For some types of disorder, such as bipolar disorder, good inter-rater reliability values have been reported, whereas for others, such as agoraphobia, the findings are mixed (Keller & Craske, 2008). Given the increasing use of information technology to deliver health care services, it is important to note that the SCID is as reliable when administered via videoconferencing as it is when administered in person (Shore, Savin, Orton, Beals, & Manson, 2007). The developers assumed that, as the SCID criteria parallel DSM criteria, this provided sufficient evidence of its validity. So, in a sense, the validity of the SCID is tied to the validity of the DSM itself. The strength of the SCID lies in the breadth of the disorders it covers. The weakness, which may be related to the breadth of coverage, is the variable reliabilities that are obtained for different disorders and the lack of strong validity data. Because the SCID covers all Axis I diagnoses, it also can be very time-consuming to administer—an important consideration in clinical use.

In contrast to the broad coverage of the SCID, the Anxiety Disorders Interview Schedule for DSM-IV (ADIS IV; Brown, Di Nardo, & Barlow, 1994) is a semi-structured diagnostic interview that focuses on anxiety disorders and disorders that are commonly comorbid with anxiety disorders (mood disorders, substance-related disorders, and somatoform disorders). There are two versions for adults (one that addresses current diagnosis only and a longer version that assesses both current symptomatology and lifetime history of problems) and parallel child and parent versions for assessing anxiety disorders in youth. Like the SCID, the ADIS includes general background information as well as questions that relate directly to DSM-IV criteria. There is considerable evidence of the reliability and validity of the ADIS. Its main advantage over more general diagnostic interviews lies in the depth of coverage of the disorders that are assessed (Summerfeldt & Antony, 2002).

A brief measure, the Primary Care Evaluation of Mental Disorders (PRIME-MD), was developed for use in primary health care settings (Spitzer et al., 1995). The main advantage of the PRIME-MD is as a rapid screening device (Summerfeldt & Antony, 2002). Although it cannot be considered a substitute for a full diagnostic interview, its brevity makes it very appealing for use in medical clinics. There is growing evidence of the reliability of the PRIME-MD, as well as support for its validity (e.g., Jackson, Passamonti, & Kroenke, 2007). As a result, it has been translated into many languages and research evidence supports its use in primary care settings in a wide range of countries, such as France (Norton et al., 2007), Hungary (Voros et al., 2006) and Iraq (Hussein & Sa'Adoon, 2006).

Exhibit 6.4 presents information on the diagnostic interviews we have discussed. As you can see, the comprehensive interviews take at least an hour to administer, whereas the screening measures are completed more quickly. Most of these interviews can be administered by

Exhibit 6.4 Comparison of Features of Diagnostic Interviews

Name	Age Range	Training Required	Breadth of Coverage	Time to Administer	Correspondence to DSM-IV
Structured Clinical Interview for Axis I Disorders (SCID)	Adult	Trained mental health professional	Broad	60 minutes	Yes
Anxiety Disorders Interview Schedule (ADIS) IV	Adult	Trained mental health professional	Medium	45–60 minutes	Yes
Anxiety Disorders Interview Schedule (ADIS) IV Child-Parent Version	Child	Trained mental health professional	Medium	45–60 minutes parent; 45–60 minutes child	Yes
Primary Care Evaluation of Professional Mental Disorders (PRIME-MD)	Adult	Trained health professional	Narrow	10–20 minutes	Somewhat
Dominic Interactive	6–11 years	Trained mental health professional	Broad	10–15 minutes	For screening only; no frequency and duration data

mental health professionals who have received additional specialized training.

Some of the structured diagnostic interviews that were originally developed for adults have been modified for use with children. For example, in adapting the ADIS for use with youth (ADIS Child and Parent Versions, Albano & Silverman, 1996), visual cues such as the Feelings Thermometer were introduced. On a Feelings Thermometer respondents are asked to indicate on a picture of a thermometer how they are feeling. Zero might represent totally calm and 100 might represent very afraid. The Feelings Thermometer is designed to enable children to better communicate different gradations of feelings when their vocabulary for expressing these distinctions is limited. So, whereas a child might be able to verbalize only crude distinctions like *kind of scared* and *really scared*, he or she may be able to convey that in some situations the level of fear is a 20, whereas on others it is a 60 or 80. Nevertheless, some features of diagnostic interviews are particularly problematic with children. These include the length of the interview, which often exceeds children's attention capacity, as well as questions requiring a more precise response than children are capable of providing. Diagnostic interviews for children and adolescents usually have parallel versions that are completed by parents. This of course raises the challenging issue of how to make sense of disagreements between different informants (Silverman & Ollendick, 2008).

To address some of the challenges of assessing very young children, some creative interview formats have been developed. Ablow and colleagues have used puppets in the assessment of children aged 4 to 8 years (Ablow et al., 1999; Measelle, Ablow, Cowan, & Cowan, 1998; Measelle, John, Ablow, Cowan & Cowan, 2005). Children are presented with two identical puppets, Iggy and Ziggy, who describe themselves in different ways. So, for example, Iggy says, *I am not shy when I meet new people*, and Ziggy says, *I am shy when I meet new people*. Children are then asked to indicate which puppet they are similar to. Ablow and colleagues have reported encouraging test-retest reliability and discriminant validity for the interview. Children appear to be able to reliably report on their personality traits (Measelle et al., 2005) and on basic symptoms of anxiety and depression (Luby, Belden, Sullivan, & Spitznagel, 2007).

A group of Canadian researchers have developed a diagnostic interview for children aged 6 to 11 years, Dominic Interactive, which uses cartoon drawings as cues (Valla, Bergeron, & Smolla, 2000). Children are shown a series of drawings and asked whether or not they would behave like the target child. The stimuli are available in different formats that vary in gender, age, ethnic background, and language. Given

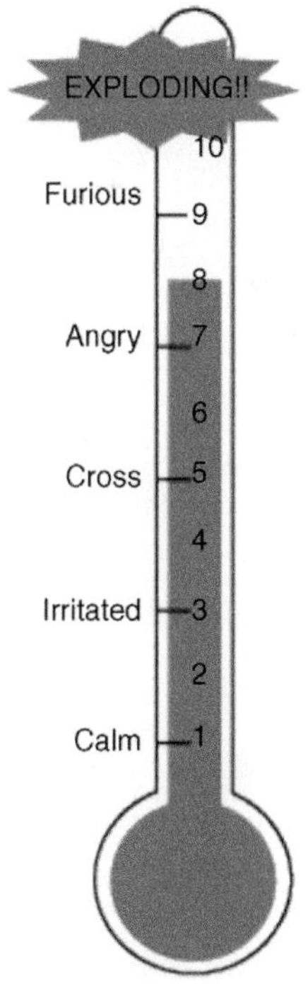

Courtesy of the Mental Health Foundation of Australia

An anger thermometer allows the child to identify different intensities of anger that he or she is feeling.

www.dominicinteractive.com

Illustration from the Dominic Interactive interview.

children's difficulties with the concept of time, there is no attempt to determine the frequency of behaviours, so the interview cannot yield full information required for diagnosis, nor does the information yield contextual data. Valla and colleagues (2000) have reported adequate test-retest reliability and criterion validity to support the use of the Dominic Interactive as an effective, brief screening instrument for mental disorders. An interactive version in which the stimuli are presented via computer and the child responds by clicking the appropriate box has also been found to be a simple and effective way for children to present an overview of their symptoms (Shojaei et al., 2009). Dominic Interactive is a good example of the use of computers to administer interviews to clients, a trend that is becoming increasingly popular and holds the promise of improving the quality of data collected as part of psychological assessments (cf. Garb, 2007).

Do you respond differently to an interview administered by a person versus one administered by a computer? Why?

GENERAL ISSUES IN INTERVIEWING

Attending Skills

Clinical assessment requires skills not only in asking questions, but also in listening. Exhibit 6.5 lists a number of listening skills that are crucial for a psychologist to develop. In an assessment interview, the psychologist attends carefully to what is being said as well as observes non-verbal behaviour. There may be important discrepancies between what a person is saying and how he or she is behaving (e.g., Nathan agitatedly rubs his hands together while simultaneously reporting that everything is fine in his relationship). The psychologist also uses non-verbal behaviour such as nods, eye contact, and vocalizations such as *Mmm . . .* and *Uh-huh* to communicate that he or she is tracking the conversation without interrupting the flow of what is being said. Periodically, the psychologist summarizes and paraphrases the client's statement as a way of clarifying that he or she understands what is being said. Emotional reflections are statements related to the client's non-verbal behaviour and the content of the responses that focus attention on the client's affect: *It sounds as though that was very painful for you*, or *You seem very angry about that.*

Exhibit 6.5 Listening Skills

Non-Directive Listening Response	Description	Primary Intent/Effect
Attending behavior	Eye contact, leaning forward, head nods, facial expressions, etc.	Facilitates or inhibits spontaneous client talk.
Silence	Absence of verbal activity.	Places pressure on clients to talk. Allows "cooling off" time. Allows interviewer to consider next response.
Clarification	Attempted restating of a client's message, preceded or followed by a closed question (e.g., *Do I have that right*?).	Clarifies unclear client statements and verifies the accuracy of what the interviewer heard.
Paraphrase	Rephrasing of the content of what the client said.	Assures clients that you hear them accurately and allows them to hear what they said.
Sensory-based paraphrase	Paraphrase that uses the client's clearly expressed sensory modalities.	Enhances rapport and empathy.
Non-directive reflection of feeling	Restatement or rephrasing of clearly stated emotion.	Enhances clients' experience of empathy and encourages their further emotional expression.
Summarization	Brief review of several topics covered during a session.	Enhances recall of session content and ties together or integrates themes covered in a session.

From Sommers-Flanagan & Sommers-Flanagan (2012). *Clinical Interviewing* (4th ed.), Table 3.1, p. 62. Reprinted with permission from John Wiley & Sons, Ltd.

A key difference between clinical assessment interviews and regular conversations is that they focus exclusively on the client. The psychologist does not take turns in describing similar experiences that he or she has had. In Chapter 14, you will learn that therapist self-disclosure can facilitate a positive therapeutic alliance; however, therapeutic self-disclosure is not the same as the reciprocal sharing of personal information that takes place in social relationships. In deciding whether or not to self-disclose, the therapist is guided by the client's interests, rather than by a personal need to vent or to gain approval from the client.

How do you think it would feel to have a conversation focus entirely on you for almost an hour? Would you feel comfortable, or awkward, or maybe intimidated? If you were in training as a psychologist, how easy would it be for you to modify your natural conversation style?

It is essential that the psychologist ask questions and listen to the client's answers in a manner that is respectful and non-judgmental. During the course of an assessment interview, clients reveal, often for the first time, painful, embarrassing, or frightening experiences they have had. They may be concerned about how they will be judged by others and how the psychologist will react to the disclosure of this sensitive information. Whether the client is someone coming to terms with his sexual identity, seeking to reconcile mixed feelings toward a parent who abandoned her as a child, or hoping that fears about going crazy are unfounded, the client requires support from the psychologist when providing details about concerns. In situations in which the client describes a behaviour that the psychologist cannot condone or finds abhorrent, the psychologist must still maintain a non-blaming stance and seek to understand the client's perspective. The psychologist's goal is to gather information and convey understanding of what the client is communicating, even if the psychologist does not approve of the behaviour. Exhibit 6.6 gives an example of the ways a psychologist might use questions and listening skills in interviewing a man who has been referred for an assessment to determine his suitability for an anger management program.

Exhibit 6.6 Sample Interview Illustrating Questions and Listening Skills

Psychologist:	*What happens when you argue*? (open question)
Client:	*Well, it sometimes gets out of hand.*
Psychologist:	*Tell me what you mean by that.* (clarification)
Client:	*Well, I never mean to hurt her.*
Psychologist:	*What is it that you do*? (open question)
Client:	*I am not proud of this, I am not a bully.*
Psychologist:	*Sounds like you are ashamed of what happens.* (emotional reflection)
Client:	*Yeah, it just gets out of hand sometimes. I don't think I am a wife-beater.*
Psychologist:	*When the two of you argue, you do things that you are not comfortable about, that you don't like.* (summarization)
Client:	*Mmm, hmm*
Psychologist:	*Tell me about the last time you argued and things got out of hand—what happened?* (open question)
Client:	*She was on my case, and I said let's just leave it, I didn't want a fight, but she kept on, then when I started to walk out, she stood in my way, so I pushed her out of the way.*
Psychologist:	*When you pushed her, was she hurt*? (closed question)
Client:	*Yeah, she kind of stumbled against the fridge, I didn't mean to hurt her, I just wanted to get out.*
Psychologist:	*How often do your arguments end up in pushing and shoving?* (open question)
Client:	*Not too often.*
Psychologist:	*Every day? Every week? Every month or so*? (closed question)
Client:	*Probably most weeks, I guess.*

Contextual Information

The assessment interview is often used to gather contextual information. This may include demographic information about the client's current context (such as age, living arrangement, family composition, school, or employment), developmental history, previous psychological services, medical history, educational background, and exposure to stressful or traumatic life events. Viewpoint Box 6.1 describes the importance of assessing the possibility that a client has been exposed to violence. The type of background information considered essential to an assessment depends on the theoretical orientation of the psychologist as well as on the type of services offered. For example, psychodynamically oriented psychologists typically devote more time to discussing childhood events and concerns than do psychologists with a cognitive-behavioural orientation. Regardless of orientation, many hours could be devoted to gathering information about a person's life—the challenge for clinical psychologists is to selectively focus on aspects that are most relevant for understanding the client's problems and the personal resources that could be brought to bear on the problems.

VIEWPOINT BOX 6.1

SCREENING FOR EXPOSURE TO VIOLENCE

Noah, aged 12, presented at a local mental health centre with symptoms of fearfulness, physiological arousal, and difficulties sleeping. He was diagnosed with generalized anxiety disorder.

Ashley, aged 14, was assessed prior to sentencing for assault charges and diagnosed with conduct disorder.

Sheila, aged 35, presented to her family physician with loss of pleasure in usual activities, weight loss, and difficulties concentrating. She was diagnosed with major depressive disorder.

Noah (who was introduced in Chapter 3) was not asked and did not volunteer information about the bloody scenes he had witnessed as his father was murdered in a war-torn country. As a result, the post-traumatic stress disorder (PTSD) diagnosis was overlooked and his anxiety symptoms were misinterpreted as generalized anxiety. Ashley was not asked and did not describe witnessing her father beating her mother. Similarly, she remained quiet about the violence in her current dating relationship. Sheila was not asked and was too ashamed to tell about the repeated violence she suffered from her partner.

Violence affected these three people profoundly. It caused pain, shame, self-doubt, fearfulness, and anger. It altered the way they thought about relationships, the way they thought about themselves, and their views of the world. Exposure to violence can result in feelings of numbing and avoidance. The person who has been a victim or witness to violence may avoid thinking about it; he or she may respond in a dull way that masks the intensity of her feelings. Repeated exposure to violence can also lead to desensitization and minimization so that the person feels that abusive treatment is to be expected and should not be complained about. The victim or witness of violence may be afraid of the repercussions of talking about the violence—fear of retribution by the perpetrator, and fear of blame by others for remaining in the relationship or for having provoked the abuse in the first place.

CONTINUED . . .

Psychologists and other mental health professionals are very concerned about the effects of violence. It is upsetting to discover that innocent people are harmed by strangers and also by those who are close to them. It is particularly troubling to know that nobody is immune from the threat of violence. Psychological assessment must include routine screening to determine whether the person has been a witness to and/or a victim of violence. Questions must be phrased in a sensitive and open way that allows the client to acknowledge what he or she has experienced. A client who is asked directly if she has been abused may reply that she has not, if she considers that she deserved to be slapped and pushed around for having left the house in a mess. Sensitive questioning offers a number of possible responses. The psychologist may note the following:

> *Sometimes when couples argue, one person leaves the room; in other couples, one person may give the silent treatment; sometimes one person may say very hurtful things; in some couples, one person may treat the other like a punching bag. What kinds of things does your partner do when he is angry?*

In addition to the types of questions that are asked, it is important to consider the context in which such screening is conducted. Asking a woman about partner abuse in the presence of her partner is likely to yield denial. She may simply not be safe to disclose what she has suffered. Research conducted in emergency departments, family medicine practices, and women's health clinics in Ontario found that although women preferred to answer questions about intimate partner violence on self-report measures, such measures may be less accurate than information collected via interviews (MacMillan et al., 2006).

Learning about Noah's witnessing of his father's murder leads the psychologist to understand his difficulties in a different way. If Noah is suffering from posttraumatic stress disorder, he may benefit from exposure-based treatment. Finding out that Ashley was a child witness to violence and is now the victim of partner abuse helps us understand her aggressive behaviour and underlines the necessity for her to learn ways to protect herself and ways to assert herself appropriately in relationships. Sheila's depression may be understood differently in the context of the abuse she has suffered. Issues around her current and future safety must take priority in treatment.

Culturally Sensitive Interviewing

Canada is increasingly a multicultural society. As the population becomes more ethnically diverse, greater attention is paid to the subtle and dramatic ways that different racial, ethnic, and linguistic groups think, act, and behave. Both the Canadian Psychological Association and the American Psychological Association have developed guidelines for ethical practice with diverse populations (American Psychological Association, 2002; Canadian Psychological Association, 2001). In interviewing clients, the psychologist must be sensitive to ethnic, socioeconomic, regional, and spiritual variables that affect the client's experience and behaviour with the psychologist (Sue & Sue, 2008; Takushi & Uomoto, 2001). For example, orthodox Jews observing *shomer negiyah* are not permitted to touch a member of the opposite sex, so may refuse to shake hands with the psychologist. The psychologist must therefore be careful not to interpret as social withdrawal, lack of engagement, or surliness what is actually observance of a religious edict. Importantly, there is growing research demonstrating that small slights, misunderstandings, and unwarranted assumptions based on stereotypes on the part of the psychologist (collectively called *microaggressions*) can have a substantial negative impact on the alliance with clients and on the clients' overall therapy experience (e.g., Constantine, 2007).

©iStock.com/aimintang

Psychologists must be sensitive to the fact that communication styles may differ across ethnic groups.

How can psychologists conduct culturally sensitive interviews?

As no psychologist can expect to be familiar with all of the cultural diversity he or she will encounter in his or her professional life, it is necessary to be aware of any cultural blind spots. This means that the psychologist must not assume that communication patterns and styles are universal. The same behaviour may have different significance in a different group. Eye contact is a good example. In the 1970s and 1980s, most clinical psychology training programs taught students to maintain eye contact with clients. Now, there is greater sensitivity that, in some cultures, too much eye contact may be perceived as intimidating. Similarly, it would be an error to interpret an averted gaze as evidence of avoidance, as it may simply represent a respectful stance toward an authority figure.

Cultures vary in the degree of importance that is paid to punctuality—arriving late to an interview may be a sign of disorganization and lack of motivation within some groups, but may simply reflect a more casual attitude toward time in others. A psychologist assessing a child who had recently arrived in Canada from Africa found that attendance at assessment appointments was sporadic, with the client and her mother often arriving late. On one occasion, when the client and her mother did not show up for an appointment, the psychologist called the family to reschedule and was surprised to hear that the outgoing message on the family's answering machine was for her, announcing that, as it was a beautiful day, the family had decided to go to the beach instead of coming to the psychologist's office. The psychologist also noted that during the assessment the child performed poorly on timed tasks. In understanding the challenges the child faced in adjusting to the Canadian school system, it was very helpful to appreciate culturally based differences in the importance of time.

There is great diversity across individuals with respect to their comfort with open-ended questions. A client who expected to be asked highly structured questions might appear disorganized and confused when faced with a less structured interview. Psychologists must be aware of potential differences such as these and must be willing to ask clients to explain the ways that things work in their cultural group. As psychologists expand their services to a diverse clientele, they may face challenges in assessing clients who do not speak English or French.

To address this, interpreters may be used. This presents new challenges in terms of confidentiality as well as in ensuring that the interpreter is competent in conveying the subtleties of what is said by both the psychologist and client.

There is emerging evidence that interpreter-mediated services can be successful. For example, d'Ardenne, Ruaro, Cestari, Fakhoury, and Priebe (2007) examined the effects of treatment for posttraumatic stress disorder among refugees in England: one group of patients received treatment in English; a second group (who required interpreters) received the same treatment but with the involvement of trained interpreters in the treatment sessions. Refugees in both conditions obtained comparable treatment results. The use of interpreters has also been found to have no effect on the sensitivity and specificity of an interview designed to assess depression and PTSD in refugees (Eytan, Durieux-Paillard, Whitaker-Clinch, Loutan, & Bovier, 2007). However, the pitfalls of poor translation are numerous. One early version of the Wechsler Intelligence Scale for Children asked children, *What is the thing to do if you cut your finger?* A poor French-Canadian translation that was in circulation in parts of Canada asked the child, *What is the thing to do if you cut your finger off?* It is clear that a small error made a big difference in the type of question being asked. Children asked the poor translation were more likely to provide an answer such as *I would cry*, for which they gained no points.

Defining Problems and Goals

Clients often arrive in psychologists' offices with vaguely defined complaints about themselves or other people. They make general statements about themselves such as *I can't get along with people* or describe their loved ones in unclear ways such as *he's irresponsible*. The challenge with these labels is that they could mean anything, as we all have somewhat different standards for judging behaviours and reactions. Does the person who cannot get along with others have violent outbursts or simply wish he or she had a more active social life? Many words that are diagnostic labels are also used regularly in everyday conversation. You may hear a parent describe a child as hyperactive or anxious, a co-worker describe a person as paranoid, or a television news announcer wonder if someone is schizophrenic.

In assessment interviews, the psychologist helps the client elaborate on the problem. Cognitive-behavioural psychologists, in particular, ask clients many questions designed to translate the complaint into a behavioural description of the problem. These details are essential for the psychologist to have a clear sense of the patterns within the problem area, as this information will form the basis of a treatment plan.

Exhibit 6.7 shows questions that might be asked to help the client move from a vague description to one that clearly describes the problem as well as its frequency, intensity, and duration. For many clients, this is not an easy task and requires gentle persistence on the part of the clinical psychologist to obtain a clear definition of the problem rather than a general and vague complaint.

Once the problem has been defined in specific, concrete terms, it is easier to determine whether the client meets criteria for diagnosis of a particular problem. In making these decisions, the psychologist must

Exhibit 6.7 Problem Definition Questions

Clients come to psychologists with vague complaints about themselves or other people:

- *I'm a loser.*
- *I'm depressed.*
- *I can't get along with people.*
- *I can't seem to get started.*
- *S/he never listens; s/he's defiant.*
- *S/he won't do anything; s/he's irresponsible/lazy.*
- *S/he hurts people; s/he's aggressive.*
- *S/he never thinks; s/he's impulsive.*
- *S/he's so clingy; s/he's dependent.*
- *S/he has trouble at school; s/he's dumb.*
- *S/he has fits/tantrums.*

To translate the complaint into a behavioural description of the problem, psychologists ask the following:

Tell me what you mean by "depressed."

"Trouble" means different things to different people. What does it mean to you?

When you say s/he is aggressive, what is it that s/he does?

Give me an example of what you mean by "clingy."

I'm trying to get a picture in my head of what you mean by "defiant." Help me imagine what s/he is doing when s/he is defiant.

Questions about the frequency of the problem:

How often does s/he . . .?

Does it happen every day? Many times a day . . .?

Questions about the duration of the problem:

When did this start?

Can you remember a time when this didn't happen? Are there times when s/he does not . . .?

How long has s/he been . . .?

Questions about the intensity of the problem:

How long does it last?

What does s/he break? How hard does s/he hit?

have a good understanding of normative behaviour. For example, in assessing a child who may suffer from attention-deficit/hyperactivity disorder, the psychologist must decide whether the child's activity level, impulsivity, and attention span are within normal limits for a child that age, or whether they are unusual.

After clarifying the definition of the problem, a cognitive-behavioural psychologist then seeks a clear definition of the client's goals. Like problems, goals are often defined in vague terms: *I'd like to feel better*; *I wish my child would be more respectful*; *I wish my partner and I could get along better*. Unless goals are formulated in more concrete terms, it is impossible to determine whether there is progress toward reaching them. So, the formulation of concrete goals is an essential step in determining whether psychological services may be helpful. Exhibit 6.8 gives examples of the types of questions psychologists ask to help clients more clearly identify their goals for treatment.

Exhibit 6.8 Goal Definition Questions

- Goal must be important to the client
- Goal must be expressed in terms of the ways people behave
- Goal must be small, simple, and achievable
- Goal must be in positive terms

Sample goal definition questions:

At the end of our sessions, what would lead you to decide that it had been worthwhile? How would you know you had not wasted your time?

If services here were to be helpful, what would be different?

If you and Chris were to get along better, what would you be doing that you are not doing now?

How would Marcel show he was happier?

If there was a change in the right direction, what would it be?

Yes, it would be great to win the lottery, but let's suppose that doesn't happen—what would have to happen for your financial worries to decrease a bit?

I understand that what you most want is to finish high school. If we were to break that down into steps, what would be the first step?

So, if François was not so inattentive, what is it he would be doing? How would you know he was more attentive?

Assessing Suicide Risk

As we have mentioned several times, assessment interviews are not like regular conversations. In assessment interviews, psychologists must be alert to client difficulties. Given the special risk for suicide among those suffering from a depressive disorder, in assessing a depressed client it is customary to ask questions to determine the risk that the client will make a suicide attempt. It is essential that those questions be based on what is known about the factors that increase the risk of suicidal behaviour. Psychologists ask direct questions about suicidal thoughts, plans and their lethality, and access to the means to attempt suicide. Given the strong links between a history of suicidal behaviour and risk for future suicidal behaviour, questions must also focus on a history of suicide attempts. As some suicidal clients may make only a general statement about their level of unhappiness or hopelessness, it is the psychologist's responsibility to follow up such comments with questions assessing the current risk. Exhibit 6.9 gives examples of the kinds of questions psychologists ask in assessing suicide risk. If the psychologist determines that a patient is at low risk for committing suicide, it would be appropriate to ensure that the person has emergency numbers for a suicide helpline and a local hospital. If the person appears to be at an elevated risk, the psychologist may need to accompany the patient to the emergency unit of the nearest hospital (Cuckrowicz, Wingate, Driscoll, & Joiner, 2004).

Exhibit 6.9 Empirically Supported Suicide Risk Assessment

Questions Used as Part of a Suicide Risk Assessment

Have you had any thoughts of suicide recently?
When you think about suicide, what exactly do you think about?
Have you ever attempted suicide?
Have you made any plans for taking your life, such as obtaining the means to commit suicide?
Do you think that you could follow through on a suicide attempt?
Have you ever hurt yourself intentionally, such as by cutting or burning yourself?
What are the reasons that you would consider suicide as an option?
Tell me about your family and friends. Do you feel supported and are you able to talk to them about your problems?
Do you think that anything can be done about your problems?

Adapted from Cukrowicz, Wingate, Driscoll, & Joiner (2004).

Interviewing Couples

So far, we have described interviews with an individual. In some circumstances, psychologists may interview a couple. Couple interviews may be conducted to focus on the partner's impressions of the client's problems, on couple problems, or on the problems that the couple's child is

©iStock.com/CEFutcher

Interviews allow the psychologist to observe how a couple interacts.

experiencing. Interviewing a couple requires the psychologist to simultaneously engage with two people. As the two partners may differ in style, opinions, and willingness to attend the interview, the psychologist requires flexibility and interpersonal skills to ensure that each person has an opportunity to talk without the conversation becoming out of hand. After all, it is quite likely that each person has a different view of the situation and that the views may not be at all compatible. The couple interview allows the psychologist to ask about and observe the way the couple interacts, their warmth toward one another, the way they handle differences, and the way they communicate in general (Snyder, Heyman, & Haynes, 2008).

The ability to direct and structure an interview is very important when there is a clear power differential in the couple, which may be evident from what is said by each partner or from one partner's reluctance to engage in the discussion. However, not all couple issues are best addressed in couple sessions and, for this reason, most couples therapists routinely have at least one individual session with each partner. For example, it is impossible to screen for partner abuse in the presence of the partner. One person may be too intimidated by an abusive partner to respond honestly to questions about violence in the relationship. Screening for partner abuse must be conducted individually.

Interviewing Families

Just as couple interviews can be more challenging to conduct than individual interviews, family interviews can be even more taxing for the psychologist. The psychologist has the daunting task of establishing rapport with several people who have different styles and different agendas for the assessment. A psychologist who devoted undivided attention to Tyler, who wanted greater freedom from his parents, would quickly lose rapport with Tyler's parents, Ethan and Lindy, who wanted to explain their worries that their son was failing in school and interacting with delinquent peers. Similarly, if the psychologist devoted undivided attention to the parents, Tyler would easily become disengaged. In assessing families, the psychologist ensures that, over the course of the interview, attention is devoted to each person. At the beginning of the interview, the psychologist tells family members explicitly that he or she would like to hear from each person. However, to put that into practice, the psychologist often must diplomatically cut off one family member to ensure each has a turn: *I would like to hear more from you, but am conscious of time and would also like to hear ideas from others in the family*. The psychologist also conveys that it is normal for each person to have a different perspective. Although each person is invited to speak, each also has the right to be silent. It may be necessary to remind parents of this. Family members are invited to comment from their own perspective.

VIEWPOINT BOX 6.2

ISSUES IN INTERVIEWING OLDER ADULTS

With an aging population, it is inevitable that there will be an increasing need for psychological services for older adults. Demographic forecasts predict that older adults will comprise a large percentage of the population in the coming decades. There is considerable overlap between the needs of older adults and the needs of adults in mid-life, so both geropsychologists and generalist clinical psychologists may be able to offer effective psychological services to older adults. Like younger adults, older adults seek psychological services to deal with a range of emotional, behavioural, and cognitive issues. However, as we have emphasized in other chapters, the provision of effective psychological services requires sensitivity to developmental issues that influence clients' seeking services, as well as the nature of assessment and intervention services that are appropriate. Guidelines for psychological practice with older adults have been developed by the American Psychological Association (2004) and by the Australian Psychological Society (Pachana, Helmes, & Koder, 2006). Guidelines for health care professionals addressing a range of mental health issues have also been developed by the Canadian Coalition for Seniors' Mental Health and can be downloaded at www.ccsmh.ca/en/natlGuidelines/initiative.cfm.

The American and Australian guidelines encourage psychologists to become knowledgeable about adult development and aging. Psychologists should be aware of the problems in daily living that are commonly faced by older adults; and, in addition to having general knowledge of psychopathology, they should know about patterns of psychopathology that are evident in older adults. In assessing older adults, psychologists must tailor their strategies to the specific needs of that population. This means that assessment strategies should take into account the older person's health status and cognitive and emotional functioning.

Compared with the general population, older adults are more likely to face issues around declining health, loss of autonomy, relationships with caregivers, bereavement, and mortality. Older adults are usually referred to psychological services by a primary health care provider. Given their declining health, older adults have more frequent contact with primary health care providers than do younger adults (La Rue & Watson, 1998). They may be referred to what seems to them a confusing array of health professionals. It is the psychologist's responsibility to ensure that the older adult is aware of the purpose of the psychological services and provides fully informed consent to any assessment procedure. If the older person is judged not capable of providing consent due to cognitive impairment, then consent is required from the person having legal authority for the older person, and the older person would be asked to provide a verbal assent to procedures.

Although the majority of older adults enjoy sound cognitive functioning, a significant number suffer some degree of cognitive impairment. The APA recommends that psychologists become skilled at recognizing cognitive changes in older clients. The extent of cognitive impairment varies from one person to another, with many people remaining capable of reaching decisions and acting autonomously despite some cognitive changes. The psychologist should ensure that the client understands the reason for referral, the nature of services offered, and the likely outcome of services. In offering services

CONTINUED . . .

jean gill/Getty Images

Psychologists must tailor interviews to meet the needs of older clients.

to older adults with serious cognitive impairment, the psychologist must pay particular attention to whether the person is capable of consent to services.

In interviewing older adults, the psychologist must be sensitive to the possible presence of cognitive impairment and to possible cohort effects. For example, the current population of older adults in the time of the economic depression of the 1930s, the Second World War, or the post-war recovery period. One developmental task of later life is to reminisce about one's formative years, so the sociopolitical influences these older adults experienced may figure prominently in their discussions of their lives. The interviewer must also be sensitive to the impact such events may have had on the interviewee.

The psychological assessment of older adults requires knowledge of the physical challenges that may affect the person. Issues around chronic illness and disability may be the reason that psychological services are required, but they may also introduce special challenges in conducting the assessment. Psychologists must be well informed about the possible effects of medication on client functioning. Skills in health psychology may be particularly important in working with older adults.

With declining health, some older adults may need to rely increasingly on both paid and unpaid caregivers. The cooperation of these caregivers may be essential in having the older adult attend an interview. The client may be unable to attend unless a caregiver agrees to provide transportation. Furthermore, when the older person suffers confusion or memory problems, it may be necessary to also gather important information from others. Like the challenges faced in integrating data from parents and children, the psychologist may face challenges in reconciling discrepant accounts from older adults and their caregivers. Unfortunately, some older adults are vulnerable to abuse by caregivers. Sensitive psychological services should include screening for maltreatment by family members or paid caregivers. The need for effective psychological services is bound to increase in the coming years. The provision of services will rely on the psychologist's sensitivity to the myriad health, cognitive, and social factors that affect the older adult.

Interviewing Children and Adolescents

In contrast to early approaches to the psychological assessment of children that relied primarily on adult accounts of child behaviour or on interpretations of children's play, current child assessment strategies often include the child as an important source of information about his or her thoughts and feelings. It is now recognized that children can provide unique information about aspects of their experience that are not fully tapped by measures completed by adult informants such as parents, teachers, or caregivers (Mash & Hunsley, 2007).

Interviews with children are designed to explore the child's perspective. They also allow the psychologist to assess the way the child interacts with an unfamiliar adult. The psychologist conducts the interview in a way that makes it seem like a conversation to the child, but that ensures the relevant topics are covered. Like adults, children are entitled to know about confidentiality and its limits. The psychologist must explain the purpose of the interview. As children may associate interviews with adults as evaluative in nature, it is important to reassure the child that there are no right or wrong answers to the questions, and that everyone has a different opinion. To engage the child in conversation, the psychologist maintains a varied voice tone and relaxed posture.

Interviewing techniques must be adapted when psychologists are interviewing children. Developmental considerations affect cognitive functioning and the young client's understanding of what is being asked. Young children differ from adults in terms of their attention span and capacity to stay focused on the interview. Furthermore, children differ from adults in their style of interaction.

How have psychologists adapted interview techniques to take into account developmental issues?

Think about a visit to the home of an adult friend and the way that you and your friend might talk together, perhaps seated at the kitchen table or on the sofa. As adults, you may sustain conversation over a lengthy period of time, maintaining eye contact, asking questions, and clarifying your understanding of what was said. Now think about a conversation you might have if a child was present (perhaps your friend's younger sibling, or your friend's child). In what ways would your conversation be different with the child? What if you and the child are not members of the same ethnic or cultural group—how might this make a difference? It is quite likely that the range of topics you would talk about with a child would be substantially different. In addition, you'd probably change the way you asked questions. You would be surprised if 6-year-old Emma joined in the conversation for a lengthy period—most likely she would chat for a while, then leave to do something she found more interesting. The type of conversation you have would also depend on the child's age: in talking to a preschool-age child, you'd probably talk about the immediate environment, such as the TV show the child had just watched, a toy the child was holding, the logo on a T-shirt, or the sport that the child was about to do. With an elementary school age child, you would be able to ask questions about the child's life—school, friends, activities, sports, or holidays. In other words, you would be able to talk about topics that were not in the child's immediate environment or planned activities. In general, with older children, it becomes increasingly possible to have them reflect on patterns in their experiences and to discuss how other

©iStock.com/pkruger

As children do not have the same sense of time as adults do, it is helpful to anchor interview questions for children to special events in their lives.

people might be feeling. Conversations with adolescents can cover a range of remote and abstract topics that younger children would be unable to discuss.

In interviewing children, psychologists must be careful not to use a sophisticated vocabulary that is incomprehensible to them. Although some children may announce they do not understand and ask for clarification, others may simply lose interest and become quiet. It is the psychologist's responsibility to ensure that a child client understands the questions that are being asked. A child who fails to understand a question may stare blankly, say *I don't know*, or give an answer based on erroneous understanding of what was being asked. Children find questions that relate to time particularly difficult. For example, a young child may be at a loss to say how many times over the last six months he or she has felt a certain way if the child has no concept of how long six months is. Generally, it is helpful to use special events or occasions that are personally relevant to them, such as the beginning of school, Halloween, or a birthday. However, some strategies that are effective in helping children give more detailed responses, such as using dolls, may also increase the number of errors in children's statements (Salmon, 2001). Careful attention must be paid to ensure that the interviewer does not inadvertently influence the child to give a particular response (Bruck & Ceci, 2004). Sometimes children may mistake a word for another that sounds similar. An 8-year-old girl who was asked if she ever thought about death replied that she did, almost every day. When asked to tell more about this, she explained, *There's a girl in my class called Kirsten who is death and she has to sit at the front and wear a special hearing aid so she knows what the teacher says*. Without this type of clarification, the psychologist might have wrongly assumed that this child felt suicidal, rather than recognizing that the child did not differentiate between the words *death* and *deaf*.

Although face-to-face contact and eye contact may be important ingredients of assessment interviews with most adults, we know that children and adolescents engage in some of their best conversations when they are not in eye contact. Teenagers who remain silent at the meal table may be much more talkative in the car on the way to an activity. Similarly, psychologists may invite child clients to play or draw while they are chatting. It is important to note, however, that using drawings and toys as aids to facilitate rapport is not the same as making interpretations about the child's drawings or play. In the first case, dolls and drawings are used to put the child at ease, whereas in the second they are used as projective material intended to reveal aspects of psychological functioning. We discuss issues around projective tests in Chapter 8.

Psychologists may also have challenges in understanding what the child is talking about. Children's fashions change quickly, so the psychologist may be uncertain whether Sensei Wu is the child's soccer coach, new friend, a character in a TV show, or a new vaccination. No psychologist can expect to remain constantly up to date with the changing trends in children's expressions, activities, games, or movies, just as no psychologist can expect to be equally knowledgeable about the mores and customs of all cultures. Instead, a psychologist must develop skills in listening to the child and in sensitively clarifying that he or she has properly understood what the child was saying. Rapport with children may be enhanced if the psychologist asks the child to explain details, whereas it may be impaired if the psychologist tries to give the impression of being familiar with all the details of the child's life. Children are different from adults, but they also differ from one another at different ages and developmental stages. Strategies that may be effective in engaging a young school-age child, such as bright decor, cheerful posters and soft toys on the bookshelf, may alienate the adolescent client.

Psychologists must also alter their style when interviewing adolescents. If they treat the adolescent as an adult, there may be concepts and terms that the client doesn't understand (and may not admit to not understanding). However, adolescents may also be sensitive to what they perceive as simplistic baby talk, such as *When I use the word depression, I mean when someone feels sad or kind of down*, or a kindergarten teacher style of questioning, such as *Do you know what I mean when I say "bulimia"?*

OBSERVATIONS

During the assessment interview, the psychologist is a keen observer of the client. In addition to the answers to questions, important data can be gathered by observing the client. Although clinical assessments used to routinely include comments on the client's appearance and grooming, it is only necessary to report noteworthy features that are relevant to the assessment. Comments on clients' attractiveness are often not salient to the referral question and are considered offensive by some people. The psychologist notices the client's activity level, attention span, and impulsivity. Careful attention is paid to the client's speech, noting any difficulties or abnormalities. The psychologist observes the physical movements and behaviours of clients as well as the ease of interacting with them. Profile Box 6.1 introduces Dr. Charlotte Johnston whose research involves analyses of direct observations of parents and children.

©iStock.com/michaeljung

Using drawings as aids to facilitate rapport between a psychologist and child is not the same as making interpretations about the child's drawing.

PROFILE BOX 6.1

DR. CHARLOTTE JOHNSTON

Courtesy of Charlotte Johnston

After completing my B.A. and M.Sc. degrees in psychology at the University of Calgary, I moved to the United States to complete my Ph.D. in clinical psychology at Florida State University, then returned to Canada for a psychology internship at the Child and Family Centre at McMaster University. I am currently a full professor in the clinical psychology program in the Department of Psychology at the University of British Columbia and a registered psychologist in British Columbia. I teach courses on clinical psychology at the undergraduate level and clinical child psychology at the graduate level. My clinical activities and research focus primarily on families of children with disruptive disorders and attention-deficit/hyperactivity disorder (ADHD). My research has investigated parent and child characteristics that are associated with parent-child conflict, and how parents' explanations of child behaviour are related to their responses to psychological and pharmacological treatments for child disorders. I also conduct workshops and public lectures on child disruptive disorders and ADHD for professionals and families. I live in Vancouver with my husband, an emergency physician, and our two cats.

HOW DID YOU CHOOSE TO BECOME A CLINICAL PSYCHOLOGIST?

When I first went to university, I knew I liked working with children. Psychology seemed to offer a chance to learn about a broad range of ways in which children develop and function, including how children fit within families. In psychology courses, I got hooked on research and its application in understanding and improving the problems of childhood. In graduate school, I wanted to be involved in both research and its application in the area of child disorders. Clinical psychology, with its focus on the integration of science and practice, was a perfect match for these interests and I haven't regretted the choice for a moment.

WHAT IS THE MOST REWARDING PART OF YOUR JOB AS A CLINICAL PSYCHOLOGIST?

The most rewarding aspect of this profession is the diversity of activities in which I participate. On any given day, I'm likely to do any or all of clinical practice, research, and teaching.

WHAT IS THE GREATEST CHALLENGE FACING YOU AS A CLINICAL PSYCHOLOGIST?

Integrating science and practice. This integration is essential and is what makes clinical psychology strong. However, it also makes our job difficult. I work to apply research findings to my clinical work and to ask research questions that have real clinical relevance. We are constantly challenged with educating others, including consumers of psychological services and policy-makers, about this integration and about the importance of clinical psychology being evidence based.

TELL US ABOUT THE CHALLENGES OF CONDUCTING STANDARDIZED INTERVIEWS AND OBSERVATIONS.

I recognize that young children with problems like oppositional behaviour or ADHD have limited ability to reliably recall and report their experiences. I typically don't use structured interviews with the child, but instead I rely on structured interviews with parents and sometimes the child's teacher to provide information about the child's

CONTINUED . . .

behaviour. Parents and teachers are able to provide more reliable and valid reports about the child's behaviour, particularly behaviours such as being argumentative or inattentive, than are children themselves. However, it is important to remember that reports by parents and teachers reflect not only the child's behaviour, but also the adults' expectations about child behaviour or potential biases. Thus, it is important to supplement parent and teacher reports with observations of the child's behaviour in the clinic or in a more naturalistic context such as home or school. I might observe the child during classroom activities, or in a one-to-one situation playing with the parent. These observations are more objective measures of the child's behaviour than parent or teacher reports, but they are not without problems. Practical constraints mean that observations are usually brief and children generally react and act differently because they are being observed. So, the behaviour I observe may not be representative of how the child usually behaves. In sum, the challenge is to use multiple assessment tools, like interviews and observations, and then to meaningfully integrate the information so as to capitalize on the strengths of each tool and minimize the effects of each method's weaknesses.

HOW DO YOU INTEGRATE SCIENCE AND PRACTICE IN YOUR WORK?

My clinical work and research are related, so each helps me to understand the other. For example, when I work with a family, this offers insight that I can use to design research studies to test the effectiveness of different parenting strategies, or how we can assess the barriers that prevent families from implementing these strategies. In my clinical work, I choose evidence-based assessments and interventions as much as possible. However, I also need to consider how applicable the research evidence is to the particular child and family that I am seeing. If the evidence is based on families or circumstances that are quite different from those of my client (e.g., the studies were conducted with two-parent, middle-class families and my client is being raised by a single grandmother living in poverty), I may need to modify the treatment. However, I will do this knowing that I am venturing into relatively uncharted territory and that I must evaluate the effects of the modified treatment on an ongoing basis (e.g., using brief measures to track progress on a session-by-session basis).

WHAT DO YOU SEE AS THE MOST EXCITING CHANGES IN THE PROFESSION OF CLINICAL PSYCHOLOGY?

Dissemination of our services. We need to invest greater efforts in communicating that psychological treatments exist that have proven useful for many people and many types of psychological problems. And these treatments are often more cost-effective than no treatment or than other forms of treatment.

Once we have evidence that an assessment or intervention is useful, we must consider the level of training that is needed for its implementation. Should these assessments or treatments be restricted to clinical psychologists? Alternatively, could individuals with less training deliver these services more efficiently and just as effectively? Although it is tempting to "protect the turf" of clinical psychology, these questions need empirical answers and it should be the evidence rather than professional protectionism that guides health service policies.

Client behaviour in the psychologist's office may not always be representative of the way the person behaves. For example, children with ADHD often respond well in novel situations with the undivided attention of an unfamiliar adult. Therefore, a psychologist could underestimate the extent of the child's problems by assuming that the child's behaviour during an intake interview was representative of how the child generally behaves. The purpose of naturalistic observations is to gather information that could not easily be obtained in the office. It allows observation of behaviours that clients may not describe in interviews or questionnaires because they are either unaware of them or uncomfortable about them. Home observations provide information about the ways the child and parents behave in a familiar setting. School observations provide information about the school context, teaching style, and the child's behaviour in a school context. Permission must be obtained to conduct observations outside the clinic. The parent (and the child if she or he is judged capable to consent) must give permission for the child to be observed. School personnel must also consent to observations at school. Naturalistic observations are scheduled at a time when the problem behaviour is most likely to occur. In many families with young children, the hours around supper, homework, and preparation for bed are times of conflict and difficulty. Depending on the particular assessment question, school observations may be scheduled to see the child in both preferred and non-preferred activities, with different teachers, in quiet study periods, and on the playground.

The observer's goal is to be like the proverbial fly on the wall, noticing everything but not being noticed. Observers dress in a professional, but unobtrusive style. After brief introductions, the observer invites everyone to behave as they normally do. A clipboard and pen are reminders to both adults and children that this is not like a regular social visit. Even though adults may initially try hard to make a good impression and behave at their best, children are extraordinarily effective in leading adults to behave authentically. Children comment on unusual behaviours that the adults may engage in to impress the observer, for example: *We're having dessert tonight? Why do you want us to eat at the table today? I really like the new toy you gave me.* At the end of the observation period, the observer takes a few minutes to ask how typical this day was of their usual routine, for example: *I know it is strange having someone watching, so can you tell me how typical today was? Was Jordan's behaviour the same as usual, worse than usual, or better than usual? In what way? What about your behaviour?*

Imagine having a psychologist observe your interactions while you are having a meal at home. How might you behave differently? Even if you were initially self-conscious about what you were doing and saying, how long do you think this would affect you?

Data from direct observations are used to generate hypotheses about the child's functioning that can be examined in light of other assessment data. It would obviously be inappropriate to draw diagnostic decisions solely based on observations, or to conclude that because a child appeared fine during the observation period that there were no difficulties. At most, these observations provide a limited window on how the child behaves with significant others at home and at school. But when combined with information from interviews, testing, and other people's reports, observational data can provide data that confirm or attenuate the evolving picture of the child's strengths and weaknesses.

A large body of psychological research demonstrates that people are influenced by appearances (Garb, 1998). A well-known example is the assumption that people who wear glasses are more intelligent than those who do not wear glasses. Other biases relate to hairstyle, grooming, posture, hand gestures, and tone of voice. Psychologists are not immune from these biases that may affect their decision-making. We are particularly prone to errors when interacting with an unfamiliar group. In some parts of Canada, a greeting may entail a barely perceptible nod of the head, whereas elsewhere it may involve a handshake, kisses on both cheeks, or touching of noses. Ethical guidelines require psychologists to become aware of the ways that their background influences their interactions with others and their interpretations of the behaviours of others.

Given the valuable insights that we have gained into parent-child and marital relationships based on research using systematic observation of interactions, you might expect that psychologists would have borrowed these systematic observation systems for use in the clinic. This is not the case at all. Although clinicians use observation as an essential tool in assessment, they rarely use observational coding systems that have been standardized or that have established reliability and validity (Mash & Foster, 2001). Although structured diagnostic interviews that were originally developed in a research context have been modified for use in clinical practice, the same transfer from research to clinical practice has not occurred in terms of observations. One major obstacle is expense. Some of the most useful research coding schemes require as much as 20 hours of coding to analyze 1 hour of interaction. In a cost-conscious health care system, these costs would be extremely difficult to justify.

SELF-MONITORING

In terms of data gathering, it would be ideal if a psychologist could observe a patient for many hours each day to see the precise nature of the symptoms or problems that are the focus of treatment. As this is not feasible, psychologists rely on patients' retrospective reports of events to get a sense of how frequently a problem occurs and exactly how the problem is handled. As we all know, however, memories for events become clouded over time and, despite the patient's best efforts, he or she might not remember the important details of an event that occurred six days prior to an appointment with the psychologist. To obtain accurate information as economically as possible, psychologists have developed a number of strategies for patients to observe themselves that collectively are known as **self-monitoring** strategies.

self-monitoring: strategies to monitor one's own behaviour, emotions, and/or thoughts.

Self-monitoring can take many forms. The client may be asked to simply record the occurrence of an event, such as when a cigarette was smoked, a meal was consumed, or a headache occurred. This kind of self-monitoring data can provide the type of information needed to establish baseline conditions for a behaviour or problem that will be the focus of treatment (such as using relaxation techniques to reduce the severity and frequency of headaches). With precise information about the frequency of these problems before and during treatment, it becomes possible to ascertain the degree to which treatment is effective or needs to be altered.

Self-monitoring can also involve the client keeping daily records of thoughts or feelings. This is particularly useful information for the psychologist as it provides access to variables that are not amenable to direct observation. A client may be asked, for example, to record pertinent details each time he or she has thoughts of being a failure. For cognitive-behavioural psychologists, obtaining information about the context in which these thoughts occur can provide useful information about factors that may provoke or maintain dysfunctional or non-productive behaviours.

How can self-monitoring strategies add useful data to an assessment?

In developing intervention strategies for working with a client, self-monitoring involves recording occurrences of symptoms and also the efforts made to manage or curtail the symptoms. Compared with a simple series of interview questions in the psychologist's office requiring retrospective recall, this is likely to provide a fuller picture of the client's usual strategies, both successful and unsuccessful, for dealing with the symptoms. Figures 6.2 and 6.3 provide examples of self-monitoring forms that might be used in the treatment of an eating disorder and an anxiety disorder, respectively.

Psychologists may choose to provide a client with a standard self-monitoring form that is appropriate for the symptom/behaviour to be reported. Alternatively, the psychologist may decide to construct a form with the client that has the potential of ensuring that the client better understands the nature of the reporting task. Many technological aids can be used in self-monitoring. Smartphones and tablets can prompt clients

FOOD INTAKE RECORD

NAME: ______________________________

DATE: ______________________________

TIME	PLACE	FOOD CONSUMED	MEAL OCCASION	SITUATION
7:15 am	home	1 cup coffee, black 1 bran muffin	breakfast	For a change I actually got up in time to have breakfast.
1:30 pm	university cafeteria	Small salad, no dressing Diet coke	lunch	I tried putting off eating as late as possible
3:15 pm	class	Bag of peanuts	snack	I was so hungry in class that I had to eat something from my backpack
6:30 pm	home	2 cheese sandwiches, (light cheese slices) 1 apple, 1 bran muffin	dinner	I tried to have a nutritious meal
11:30 pm	home	1 litre chocolate ice cream, 3 glasses skim milk Bag of cookies	snack	I couldn't sleep and I ended up bingeing

Figure 6.2 Self-monitoring of food consumption.

to keep track of changes over the course of treatment and graph treatment progress (Maheu, Pulier, McMenamin, & Posen, 2012). Moving beyond the recording of thoughts, emotions, and behaviours, some self-monitoring devices, known as ambulatory biosensors, are designed to measure physiological variables. These devices require virtually no effort on the part of the client, as data are recorded automatically, with no disruption in the daily activities of the person. A wide array of such devices is available, including those designed to assess cardiovascular activity, physical activity, and cortisol levels (Haynes & Yoshioka, 2007).

Despite the obvious strengths of the self-monitoring method, there are some challenges in implementation. Self-monitoring data are not always accurate, as the client may fail to record information at the appropriate time, may not have fully grasped the nature of the task given by the psychologist, or may be reluctant to report some undesirable

©iStock.com/MorePixels

Technology can be used as an aid in self-monitoring.

MY WORRY RECORD

DATE: ____________________

Please record every significant worry that you have during the day. As we discussed in our sessions, this would include anything that you find upsetting, that is difficult to stop thinking about, or that interferes with the things you are trying to do. Please be as specific as possible about each worry.

TIME	SITUATION	WORRY	ANXIETY LEVEL 0=calm 10=panicky	DURATION (minutes)
3:30 pm	at work	I will never get this done. I'm a failure. I won't be able to keep fooling them at work. I'm going to lose this job	8	45 minutes
7:40 pm	home, trying to relax	I know I can do it, but why do I have such a hard time with work deadlines? I spend so much time worrying and trying to understand my reaction. Why don't I just get things done? What is wrong with me?	6	30 minutes

Figure 6.3 Self-monitoring worry.

thoughts or behaviours (Korotitsch & Nelson-Gray, 1999). The psychologist must take the time to ensure that the client understands both the importance of obtaining self-monitoring data and how to accurately record the necessary information. As with interviews, there may need to be procedural alterations in using self-monitoring with children (Shapiro & Cole, 1999). To ensure that children are clear on the behaviours to be recorded, the self-monitoring form may include reminders in the form of words, pictures, or stick figures. Training to do the self-monitoring properly also requires that the purpose of the task and the instructions be presented in an age-appropriate manner. The issue of **reactivity** occurs in self-monitoring regardless of the client's age. Reactivity refers to a change in the phenomenon being monitored that is due specifically to the process of the self-monitoring. This has been found for a surprisingly wide array of symptoms and problems, including hallucinations, substance abuse, worry, and insomnia (Korotitsch &

reactivity: a change in the phenomenon being monitored that is due specifically to the process of monitoring the phenomenon.

Nelson-Gray, 1999). In almost all cases, such changes result in a decrease in the problem behaviour in question. Although this provides a therapeutic "bonus," it does undermine efforts to obtain the most accurate data possible. Viewpoint Box 6.3 describes strategies for obtaining repeated measures, in real time, of what a client is experiencing.

VIEWPOINT BOX 6.3

ECOLOGICAL MOMENTARY ASSESSMENT

In both clinical work and research, psychologists often use self-report measures to evaluate a person's behaviours, thoughts, and emotions (we describe such measures more fully in Chapter 8). However, measures that ask "how you usually feel" or "which statement best describes you" may not fully capture the complexities of daily life. For example, Verkuil, Brosschot, and Thayer (2007) asked university students to complete several commonly used self-report measures of worry and anxiety, and then to keep a self-monitoring diary of the frequency and duration of any worry they experienced over the next six days. Much to the researchers' surprise, there was only moderate correlation between the two types of measures, and self-report measures predicted less than half of the variance in students' experience of daily worry.

Many psychological interventions focus on altering clients' emotional distress and maladaptive behaviours as they occur in day-to-day life. Accordingly, it is important that the research used to guide such interventions can provide complete and accurate information about individual patterns of psychological experience as they occur across hours, days, and weeks. *Ecological momentary assessment* is the term used for a set of strategies that allow research participants (and patients) to report repeatedly on what is occurring to them in real time (Shiffman, Stone, & Hufford, 2008). Using either electronic recording strategies or pencil-and-paper diaries, participants provide information on their experiences in event-based designs (e.g., describing their thoughts, behaviours, emotions, and interpersonal interactions around the time when they experienced a specific problematic event, such as a panic attack) and/or time-based designs (e.g., recording their mood and physical activity levels every hour in order to obtain an accurate sense of how fluctuations in mood and activity affect each other). The results of ecological momentary assessment research allow psychologists to examine patterns in clinically relevant processes, such as efforts to quit cigarette smoking. Based on such research, we know that most smokers experience very little craving when they quit, although there may be some brief periods of intense craving; cravings experienced early in the morning are most likely to put people at risk for smoking a cigarette; and experiences of acute distress (e.g., getting angry) also lead to temptations to smoke (Shiffman et al., 2008). Bearing these findings in mind, psychologists can then help their clients be better prepared to manage the challenges of quitting smoking.

SUMMARY AND CONCLUSIONS

Interviews and observations are used by all clinical psychologists in their assessment activities. Clinical interviews are different from other types of verbal interactions, as they are directed by one person with a specific set of goals in mind. In interviewing and observing, psychologists must be sensitive to diversity issues, including cultural, regional, and generational norms. Cognizant of these issues, psychologists must also find ways to obtain the type of information they need, even when asking about sensitive or painful topics. Because a number of factors affect the quality of an interview, structured interviews have been developed for a range of tasks, most notably for diagnostic purposes. Although these interviews provide a reliable approach to diagnosis, they can be very time-consuming and limited in scope. A final assessment method used by many psychologists is self-monitoring. Instead of relying on retrospective accounts of important events or behaviours, the patient is provided with a structured format to record events shortly after they occur. This information, when combined with that available from interviews and observations, helps fill out the emerging clinical picture of the client and his or her experiences.

KEY TERMS

closed questions: questions that can be answered with a single word.

limits of confidentiality: situations in which the psychologist is legally obliged to break confidentiality by disclosing information provided by the patient to another person or agency.

open questions: questions that allow elaborate responses and cannot be answered with a simple *yes* or *no*.

reactivity: a change in the phenomenon being monitored that is due specifically to the process of monitoring the phenomenon.

self-monitoring: strategies to monitor one's own behaviour, emotions, and/or thoughts.

structured interviews: interviews with a specific format for asking questions and a specific sequence in which questions are asked.

ADDITIONAL RESOURCES

Books

McLeod, B. D., Jensen-Doss, A., & Ollendick, T. H. (Eds.) (2013). *Handbook of child and adolescent diagnostic and behavioral assessment.* New York: Guilford.

Segal, D. L. & Hersen, M. (Eds). (2003). *Diagnostic interviewing* (4th ed.). New York: Springer.

Sommers-Flanagan, J., & Sommers-Flanagan, R. (2012). *Clinical interviewing* (4th ed). New York: John Wiley & Sons, Inc.

Sue, D. W., & Sue, D. (2008). *Counseling the culturally diverse: Theory and practice* (5th ed.). New York: John Wiley & Sons, Inc.

Check It Out!

You can find information about the Structured Clinical Interview for DSM Disorders (SCID) here: www.scid4.org

You can find information about the Dominic Interactive here: www.dominicinteractive.com

For information on risks for suicide and understanding more about suicide prevention:

www.livingworks.net

www.canadiancrc.com/Youth_Suicide_in_Canada.aspx

Numerous websites provide examples of self-monitoring forms and procedures for personal concerns such as mood and weight loss. Here are just a few examples:

www.cognitivebehaviourtherapy.org.uk/guides/depression/monitoring/

web4health.info/en/answers/bipolar-self-monitor.htm

health-infocenter.org/reach-your-goal/self-monitoring—the-importance-of-a-food-and-activity-diary.html

ASSESSMENT: INTELLECTUAL AND COGNITIVE MEASURES

7 CHAPTER

INTRODUCTION

In 1946, an organization called Mensa was founded in England. Since its inception, membership has been restricted to people with an intelligence test score (usually referred to as an intelligence quotient or IQ) that is in the top 2% of the population. Today, more than 100,000 people worldwide are members of this organization, with members in more than 100 countries. For many years, people have been interested in knowing their IQ, which has led to the proliferation of many books and online tests purporting to provide valid IQ tests. One of the earliest of these products, Hans Eysenck's best-selling book *Know Your Own I.Q.*, originally published in 1962, has gone into multiple editions and can still be purchased today.

Western society has tended to place great value on intelligence, but also places a great emphasis on the idea of equality. As a result, there have frequently been intense public debates around the use of intelligence tests to make decisions about people's educational and occupational choices. For example, the publication of *The Bell Curve* (Herrnstein & Murray, 1994), a review of the history of research on intelligence, ignited a lengthy debate in the media about the meaning of intelligence and the advantages and disadvantages of using intelligence tests. Although many of the research-based conclusions presented in the book were not particularly original or controversial, the authors' attempts to link the results of research on intelligence to public policy initiatives (such as rescinding American affirmative action policies in education and hiring) drew the ire of many critics.

As you learned in Chapter 1, the history of assessment in clinical psychology and the history of intellectual assessment are closely connected, as both were greatly influenced by Binet and Simon's development of the first standardized test of intelligence. Many of the criteria that are now used to evaluate the qualities of any psychological test date back to efforts to develop the first intelligence tests in the early part of the 20th century. At that time, special education services were being designed and it was necessary to develop scientific instruments to identify those in need of such services. The vital importance of accurately identifying individuals who were unlikely to benefit from regular education led to the promotion of concepts such as standardization, reliability, validity, and norm-referenced interpretations. Another by-product of these initial assessment efforts is that both our concepts of intelligence and our intelligence assessment instruments have heavily emphasized aspects of intelligence that are directly relevant to educational and instructional initiatives. As you will see later, some of the more recent models of intelligence have tried to balance this focus with greater attention to non-academic skills that reflect intelligent behaviour.

In the testing of intelligence and cognitive capacities, there is a great deal at stake. Because of the important implications of the results of intellectual and cognitive assessment, in the latter half of the 20th century, test developers made great efforts to reduce test bias and measurement error. As a result, tests of intelligence and related cognitive abilities are among the psychometrically strongest tests that psychologists have developed.

We begin this chapter by outlining theories of intelligence and some of the research relevant to understanding the influences on intelligence and intelligence tests. Psychologists working in many different settings are often asked to assess an individual's intellectual and cognitive abilities. After describing some of the more common situations in which such evaluations are required, we move to describe the most commonly used intelligence tests and other tests of cognitive functioning.

A number of websites purport to provide online evaluations of intelligence. Do you know the Latin phrase caveat emptor? It means "buyer beware" and is as relevant for anyone taking self-administered intelligence tests as it is for purchasing yoga clothing, diet products, used cars, or anything that sounds like a deal that is just too good to pass up.

DEFINING INTELLIGENCE

We all have an intuitive idea of what intelligence is. We can point to individuals we consider highly intelligent; likewise, we can probably identify examples of intelligent behaviour (and probably some examples of not so intelligent behaviour). How can we define intelligence in a manner that is appropriate across skill sets, areas of performance, and cultural contexts? One option is to simply avoid the use of the term intelligence, and to use other concepts such as ability or, more accurately, general mental ability. Although a number of theorists and test developers have taken this approach, it doesn't really get us any further in trying to tease out the meaning of intelligence, as it just substitutes one word or phrase for another.

What are the problems in defining intelligence in terms of academic performance?

Throughout the years, psychologists have made many attempts to define intelligence. These include both broad definitions, such as the ability to learn or to adapt to the environment, and narrow definitions, such as the ability to engage in abstract thinking (cf. Aiken, 2003). Because Binet was working on the development of a tool to predict school performance, his definition focused on ability related to scholastic/academic tasks. You will probably agree that this yields a limited definition. Subsequent definitions of intelligence have focused on the context of life more generally. An influential definition was presented by Wechsler (1939), who defined intelligence as a person's global capacity to act purposefully, to think in a rational manner, and to deal effectively with his or her environment. Wechsler devoted his career to the development of scales to assess a range of problem-solving skills. He assumed that these abilities were acquired through education and life experiences. Wechsler's definition has had a profound influence on the way clinical psychologists evaluate intelligence. As we will see in the next section, current theories of intelligence explicitly acknowledge that intelligence is a combination of abilities in multiple areas of life. Gottfredson's (1997, p.13) definition nicely captures this in everyday language: "[Intelligence] . . . involves the ability to reason, plan, solve problems, think abstractly, comprehend complex ideas, learn quickly and learn from experience. It is not merely book learning, a narrow academic skill, or test-taking smarts. Rather it reflects a broader and deeper capability for comprehending our surroundings—'catching on,' 'making sense' of things, or 'figuring out' what to do."

THEORIES OF INTELLIGENCE

To provide a brief overview of the many theories of intelligence, we will categorize the dominant models into one of three domains: *factor models, hierarchical models,* and *information processing models.* Factor models involve two or more factors that are postulated to be at more or less the same structural level. In contrast, hierarchical models are based on the assumption that there are different levels of factors, with the higher-order or primary factors composed of lower-order or secondary factors. Information processing theories focus less on the organization of types of intelligence and more on the identification of the processes and operations that reflect how information is handled by the brain.

The earliest and probably most influential factor model of intelligence was developed by Charles Spearman (1927). Based on the intercorrelations among tests of sensory abilities (sensory discriminations, reaction time, etc.), Spearman proposed that all intellectual activities share a single common core, known as the *general factor* or g. The more highly correlated two tests of mental abilities are, the more they share a substantial loading on the *g* factor. However, because measures of intellectual abilities are not perfectly correlated, Spearman postulated that there are a number of *specific factors,* or *s,* that are responsible for unique aspects in the performance of any given task. The more a test is influenced by *s,* the less it represents the influence of *g.* Spearman's focus on *g* and *s* was known as the *two-factor model.*

***g*:** the general factor shared by all intellectual activities.

Although the idea of *g* is retained in most theories of intelligence, other factor models have been proposed. All of them suggest that there are related but distinct factors that comprise intelligence. Thurstone (1938) proposed one of the first alternatives to Spearman's model. Based on his research into the relatively low intercorrelations among many ability measures, Thurstone proposed a group of factors known as *primary mental abilities,* including spatial, perceptual, numerical, memory, verbal, word, reasoning, deduction, and induction abilities. These abilities, although relatively distinct, overlap to a very small extent and it was this small overlap that Thurstone suggested was Spearman's *g.* In contrast to the majority of researchers who developed a model of intelligence, Thurstone also developed a measure of intelligence based on his model.

The number of factors included in models of intelligence ranges from as few as 2 to well over 100 (Guilford, 1956). In an attempt to reconcile these different models, hierarchical model theoriests have proposed that there are a small number of main factors that are comprised of subfactors. One of the first and most influential of these models was proposed by Raymond Cattell (1963, Horn & Cattell, 1966). Cattell believed that existing intelligence tests were too focused on verbal, school-based tasks. In developing a test that assessed more perceptual aspects of intelligence, he proposed two general factors in intelligence: fluid intelligence (*g(F)*) and crystallized intelligence (*g(C)*). Fluid intelligence is the ability to solve problems without drawing on prior

fluid intelligence: the ability to solve novel problems; innate intellectual potential.

crystallized intelligence: what we have learned in life, both from formal education and general life experiences.

experiences or formal learning, and is therefore best understood as representing one's innate intellectual potential. Crystallized intelligence is what we have learned in life, both from formal education and general life experiences. Other hierarchical models represented attempts to reconcile many of the differences among the previous theories of intelligence, often with Spearman's *g* as the highest order factor (e.g., Carroll, 1993). Since the late 1990s, Cattell and Horn's theoretical work and Carroll's factor analytic work have been combined into a unified theory known as the Cattell-Horn-Carroll theory of intelligence. Many intelligence tests, including the Wechsler scales, now explicitly incorporate aspects of this theory.

In the 1980s, developments in cognitive psychology laid the groundwork for two influential information processing models of intelligence. Instead of examining intercorrelations among ability test scores (typically with some form of factor analysis), these models were based on research focused on explicating the manner in which people process information and solve problems. Unlike earlier models in which some form of *g* was seen as the dominant element of intelligence, Sternberg's (1985) *triarchic theory* involves three interrelated elements: componential, experiential, and contextual. The componential element deals with (a) the mental processes of planning, monitoring, and evaluating (referred to as executive functions); (b) performance, or the solving of a problem; and (c) knowledge acquisition, including encoding, combining, and comparing information. The experiential element addresses the influence of task novelty or unfamiliarity on the process of problem-solving. The third element, context, involves three different ways of interacting with the environment: adaptation, alteration of the environment, and selection of a different environment. Sternberg's model suggests that consideration of all these elements is necessary to understand intelligence. The explicit inclusion of the experiential and contextual elements sets it apart from other models as these elements underscore the need to incorporate learning history and environment in understanding intelligent behaviour.

©iStock.com/jcarillet

Do theories of intelligence capture the abilities required to live alone in the wilderness for a week without shelter, tools, or supplies?

A second information processing theory, Gardner's (1983, 1999) *theory of multiple intelligences* also assigns less importance to *g*. According to Gardner, there are multiple forms of intelligence, including linguistic, musical, logical-mathematical, spatial, bodily-kinesthetic, intrapersonal, interpersonal, naturalist, spiritual, existential, and moral. Not surprisingly, given the early connection of intelligence tests to academic performance, these different types of intelligence are inadequately assessed by traditional intelligence tests. Gardner argued that a culturally unbiased assessment requires recognition of the full range of different types of intelligence. His theory has been embraced by many

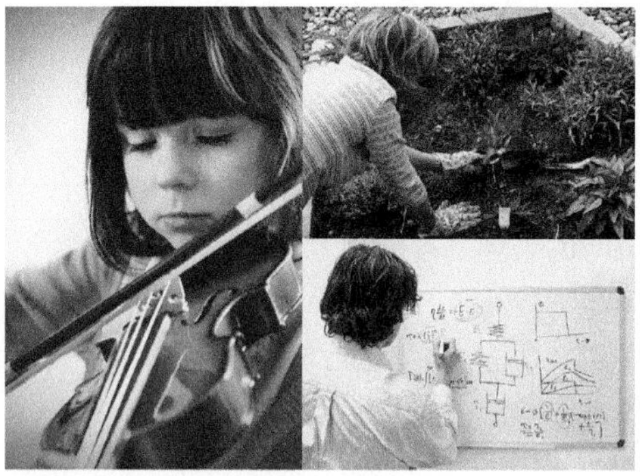

Left: ©iStock.com/Dori OConnell;
Top right: ©iStock.com/kmaassrock;
Bottom right: ©iStock.com/36clicks

Gardner identified multiple forms of intelligence.

educators and has led to the development of school curricula designed to maximize every student's potential to learn (Hogan, 2007). According to Gardner's model, instead of asking, "How intelligent are you?" a better question is "How are you intelligent?"

In summary, over the past century, a range of theories of intelligence has been proposed, with earlier theories focusing on the role of *g* and later theories placing much more of an emphasis on information processing skills. Because clinical psychology is usually described as a science-based discipline, it would be reasonable to assume a strong connection between theories and measures of intelligence. However, this has not consistently been true in the realm of intellectual assessment. As you will see later in the chapter, the most commonly used measures of intelligence are only partially based on current models of intelligence. Indeed, as we highlighted in Chapter 5, and as you will see again in many other chapters, a continuing challenge in clinical psychology is ensuring that psychological services are based on the best available research evidence.

Consider for a moment the following set of people: an Olympic athlete, an expert interpreter, a talented musician, a skilled carpenter, a popular comedian, and a successful fishing guide. To what extent are their different abilities reflective of intelligence, effort and practice, and/or biological predispositions? How broadly should we define intelligence and intelligent behaviour?

ASSESSING INTELLIGENCE: THE CLINICAL CONTEXT

What types of questions can assessment of intelligence and cognitive functioning address?

The assessment of intelligence is often an integral component of a psychological assessment. The following brief case examples provide an illustration of the range of situations in which an evaluation of intellectual functioning is required.

Nicole is a 63-year-old woman who has requested an evaluation of her cognitive functioning due to concerns about what she perceives to be recent memory problems. She is a senior manager in a successful marketing company and has always derived great satisfaction from her work. In the past year, Nicole has noticed that she often forgets her appointments and fails to complete her administrative duties on time because of a lack of attention to deadlines. She has purchased various aids to help her keep track of her work activities (including apps on her smartphone), but she fails to use them consistently. Although they occur less frequently in her home life, she does notice similar memory lapses, especially with social appointments and activities with her husband. Nicole is concerned that the memory lapses are becoming more frequent and that they may be the initial stages of a more serious memory or cognitive disorder.

David is a 47-year-old man who suffered a workplace accident two months ago. He is a bricklayer who was working on a job site repairing damage to the brickwork of a shopping mall when a car hit the scaffolding on which he was standing. The scaffolding collapsed and David fell from a height of two storeys onto a pile of bricks on the ground, injuring his back and breaking his wrist. He was also struck on the head by a falling brick. Although he did not lose consciousness at the time, he felt a bit dizzy for a couple of days after his fall. Initially, he was primarily concerned about the potential effect of his back and wrist injury on his return to work. In the past month, though, David has noticed that he often forgets where he is going and that he has a "fuzzy" feeling in his head that makes it difficult for him to concentrate. He was referred for an evaluation by the Workers' Compensation Board to determine if he is fit to return to work or if there are grounds for considering some form of disability pension stemming from his head injury.

Olivia is an 8-year-old girl whose parents requested an assessment as part of their efforts to have her enrolled in a gifted program. Her parents report that she began reading words at the age of 2 and that by the age of 5 she was reading books intended for those in Grade 2. Olivia is currently in Grade 3 and is often given additional work by her teacher because she rapidly completes the usual work assigned to the class. Despite being generally successful in school, Olivia is described by her parents as being rather fearful of new situations and has a tendency to focus on her school work rather than play with friends or get involved in games or athletic activities.

Joaquin is a 19-year-old university student who was referred for assessment because of academic problems. Although he reports always having had difficulty getting organized and completing his work on time, he found the first year of university extremely stressful because he consistently had to work through the night to complete assignments. In class, Joaquin refrains from asking any questions and borrows other people's notes because his own are poor and incomplete. Joaquin is an avid reader who frequently forgets about his other commitments when he is in the middle of reading a novel. He reports that his friends describe him as a daydreamer. Joaquin wonders if he has some type of learning problem that is interfering with meeting his academic goals.

In the preceding case examples, both Nicole and David are experiencing changes in their usual level of cognitive functioning. In one instance, there is a concern that this may be due to an underlying neurological condition, and in the other, there is a question about whether the changes are due to an injury. A common question addressed by psychologists in such cases is whether the current level of functioning represents a change from a previous level. Although it would be easy for a dentist to compare a person's dental status before and after an accident, people do not routinely have assessments of their intellectual functioning unless there is a problem. There can be conceptual and measurement problems associated with efforts to estimate what is known as a **premorbid IQ** (i.e., intellectual functioning prior to an accident or the onset of a neurological decline). However, psychologists have developed relatively effective strategies for making these estimates by consulting the client's achievement records, testing with measures of ability that are relatively insensitive to decline, and paying close attention to the intelligence scale subtests that are least affected by neurological impairment (Groth-Marnat, 2009). Progress has also been made in using demographic variables and scores for subtests of intelligence scales to predict premorbid IQ (Schoenberg, Lange, & Saklofske, 2007).

premorbid IQ: intellectual functioning prior to an accident or the onset of a neurological decline.

The cases of Nicole and David also present a challenge for the assessor because the extent and severity of the possible changes in psychosocial functioning must be determined. In both cases, the assessment will not be limited to the use of an intelligence scale as, at a minimum, self-monitoring data and interviews with relevant others will be necessary to document any decrements in functioning. The use of multiple sources of data, including intellectual test results, is relatively standard for assessment questions that involve possible alterations in cognitive functioning, whether due to an accident, disease, or dementia.

The cases of Olivia and Joaquin present another common set of assessment questions that hinge on the use of intelligence tests. Questions related to giftedness, intellectual disabilities, or learning disabilities rely heavily on the results of intelligence tests. Giftedness is defined, in most jurisdictions, as an intelligence test score in the top 2% of the population (IQ $\geq$ 130). A diagnosis of mental retardation requires that a person obtain an IQ score in the lowest 2% of the population (IQ $\leq$ 70) as well as have impairments in functioning in areas such as self-care, social skills, home living, and work. In most jurisdictions in Canada, to diagnose a learning disability (or a specific learning disorder in DSM-5 terminology), there must be a substantial discrepancy between scores on a standardized achievement test and the person's age and level of intelligence (Kozey & Siegel, 2008).

In all cases, though, psychologists are careful to differentiate between intelligence test scores and intelligence per se. For reasons described in the following section, commonly used intelligence tests do not tap the full range of abilities that are included in modern theories of intelligence. Instead, they tend to focus on those abilities that are related to academic performance and are not designed to measure social, emotional, and other domains. Because our intelligence tests have only limited content validity for the broader construct of intelligence (as currently understood), any result on an intelligence test does not fully represent a person's total intelligence.

As you learned in Chapter 5, surveys of American clinical psychologists identified the Wechsler scales as among the top five most commonly used tests in child and adolescent assessment (Cashel, 2002) and among the five tests rated as most important in assessment practice (Piotrowski et al., 1998). We turn now to an examination of these scales.

THE WECHSLER INTELLIGENCE SCALES

There are three main Wechsler intelligence scales: the Wechsler Adult Intelligence Scale–Fourth Edition (WAIS-IV), which is designed to assess individuals in the age range of 16 to 90 years; the Wechsler Intelligence Scale for Children–Fourth Edition (WISC-IV), which is designed to assess children and adolescents in the 6 to 16 age range; and the Wechsler Preschool and Primary Scale of Intelligence–Fourth Edition (WPPSI-IV), designed to assess children in the age range from 2 years 6 months to 7 years 7 months. An extended version of the WISC-IV, the WISC-IV Integrated, is available for situations in which more fine-grained testing of intellectual abilities is required. A brief test, the Wechsler Abbreviated Scale of Intelligence–Second Edition (WASI-II), is also available for testing people between 6 and 89 years of age.

In the rest of the chapter, we focus primarily on the Wechsler intelligence scales and associated cognitive tests for four main reasons. First, the Wechsler intelligence scales are the most commonly used individually administered measures of intelligence. Second, use of these scales allows for testing of people across almost the entire age range (i.e., 2.5 to 90 years). Third, there are current versions of the three main scales that have been developed for use in Canada. Fourth, and most importantly, for the past few decades these scales have been developed in ways that have enhanced the quality of the scales' psychometric properties and norms. In the following sections, we discuss a range of issues that are relevant to all of the Wechsler intelligence tests, such as factor structure, normative sample, administration, and interpretation. We then move on to provide some specific information about each of the three main tests.

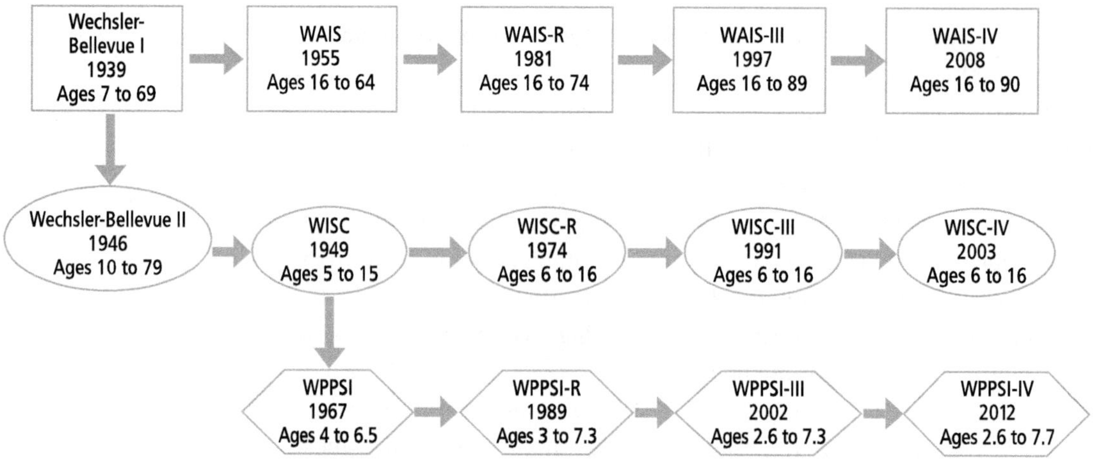

Note: WPPSI = Wechsler Preschool and Primary Scale of Intelligence; WISC = Wechsler Intelligence Scale for Children.
This material was modified and used by permission of John Wiley & Sons, Inc.

Figure 7.1 History of the Wechsler intelligence scales

Background Issues

Figure 7.1 shows the history of the three tests that are all derived from the original Wechsler-Bellevue Intelligence Scale. As the three tests share common origins, there is overlap in the concepts assessed and in the types of items. However, as we will see in the descriptions of each test, there are also important differences between tests that reflect not only evolving notions about how best to conceptualize intelligence, but also the necessity of assessing intelligence in a developmentally sensitive manner.

For psychologists, the name of David Wechsler, developer of the Wechsler intelligence scales, is synonymous with intelligence testing. Wechsler had extensive experience with the early intelligence tests, as he studied under Spearman and was an intelligence examiner in the First World War. You may remember learning in Chapter 1 that mental abilities were tested by administering the Army Alpha test in a group format. The Army Beta test was also administered in a group format and was used to assess recruits who were unable to read or who had limited knowledge of English. In the 1930s, Wechsler became chief psychologist at the Bellevue Hospital in New York, and it was in this context that he developed the Wechsler-Bellevue Intelligence Scale (1939), the first individually administered intelligence test intended for use in a general child and adult population. In constructing this intelligence scale, Wechsler's goal was to create a test that borrowed from and improved on other tests of intelligence, such as the Stanford-Binet and the Army Alpha and Beta tests (Kaufman & Lichtenberger, 1999). He did not set out to develop a test that reflected a particular theory of intelligence, but was motivated by the quest for an instrument that had substantial clinical utility. In his scale, similar to the Alpha and Beta tests, equal weight was accorded to verbal intelligence subtests (i.e., those requiring verbal responses) and performance intelligence subtests (i.e., those relying on non-verbal responses that are often timed).

An important innovation, introduced by Wechsler, was the use of deviation scores to measure intelligence. The Stanford-Binet test (briefly discussed in Chapter 1 and also later in this chapter) relied on comparisons between the chronological age (CA) and the person's mental age (MA—defined as the average age in the normative sample of those who achieved the same test score as the person). The formula for the intelligence quotient (IQ) obtained from the scale is then IQ = (MA/CA) × 100. Thus, if Krista's CA is 20 and her MA is 20 (i.e., the average age of those receiving the same test score as she did is 20 years), she will have an IQ of 100. If her father, Greg, has a CA of 50 and he has an MA of 50, he will also have an IQ of 100. Although this is simple enough, there is a problem with this IQ ratio approach if the standard deviation of the IQ distribution differs with age. Let's assume, for a moment, that the standard deviation is 15 IQ points for 20-year-olds and 10 points for 50-year-olds. So, if Krista and Greg both scored one standard deviation above the age mean, this would result in an IQ of 115 for Krista and an IQ of 110 for Greg. Suddenly the meaning of a ratio IQ is not quite so clear-cut. To remedy this problem, Wechsler translated raw scores into *standard scores* based on a normal distribution with a mean of 100 and a standard deviation of 15, thus ensuring comparability in the meaning of IQ scores across ages. In other words, going back to our example, if both 20-year-old Krista and 50-year-old Greg score one standard deviation above the mean, they will both obtain an IQ score of 115. Viewpoint Box 7.1 addresses the controversial issues surrounding IQ and its correlates.

Unlike the earliest IQ tests that were group administered (as we saw in Chapter 1), the most commonly used contemporary tests are individual.

VIEWPOINT BOX 7.1

IQ AND ITS CORRELATES

There is probably no more controversial area of psychological research than that of intelligence and its correlates. This is partially due to a misunderstanding about psychological research. There is, for example, a common confusion about correlation and causation. The fact that a variable is correlated with an IQ score does not mean it has a causal connection with intelligence.

A second source of error leading to controversy is the erroneous belief that intelligence (or any other psychological characteristic) must be due to *either* heredity *or* the environment. The results of decades of psychological research leave no question on this point: both heredity and environment interact in complex ways to influence intelligence.

CONTINUED . . .

Controversy and misunderstanding may also occur because of confusing an IQ score with the concept of intelligence. Remember that the content validity of most intelligence tests is related to performance in logical, educationally influenced tasks. Results of a study by Sternberg and colleagues (2001), who examined academic intelligence and practical intelligence in Kenyan children, nicely illustrate this point. These researchers used standard measures of fluid and crystallized intelligence (see the section on Theories of Intelligence) along with a measure assessing practical intelligence for adaptation to the environment (primarily knowledge of natural herbal medicines). The correlation between the measure of practical intelligence and crystallized intelligence (i.e., academic intelligence) was −.31. This inverse relation means that children with higher scores in terms of academic intelligence had lower scores in terms of their knowledge of natural herbal medicine. The researchers speculated that this might reflect that the more time children devoted to school and school work, the less time they were able to devote to developing tacit knowledge about aspects of the indigenous environment.

So, with these points in mind, what do we know about the correlates of intelligence? The following conclusions are based on summaries of the research literature presented by Nisbett et al. (2012):

- Approximately 40–80% of the variance in a population's IQ scores is attributable to heritability (i.e., genetic factors). This, however, does not indicate the genetic component of specific individual's intelligence, nor does it indicate how intelligent any individual is likely to be.
- The heritability of IQ can be strongly influenced by environmental factors. For example, in the United States, environmental factors account for most of the variance in IQ found in samples of low socioeconomic status (SES) children and adolescents. The most likely explanation for this is that youth living in poverty are unlikely to develop to their full genetic potential.
- Researchers have identified over 280 different genes responsible for specific forms of intellectual disability. In contrast, very little progress has been made in identifying the genes responsible for normal variation in IQ.
- There is some evidence that breastfeeding increases IQ for both normal weight infants and infants born prematurely.
- Socioeconomic class has a large effect on IQ. For example, children from lower SES backgrounds who are adopted by upper middle class parents will, in time, have an average increase of 12 IQ points.
- Good quality education, and in particular early schooling, affects intelligence. Children who are deprived of schooling for an extended period show substantial IQ deficits.
- For older adults, aerobic exercise can protect against declines in IQ.
- There are no overall sex differences for intelligence. That being said, there is consistent evidence of slight advantages for females on measures of verbal abilities and for males on measures of visuospatial abilities.
- There tend to be small ethnic differences in IQ. There is no evidence to indicate that genetic factors are responsible for any of these differences. The largest of these differences have been found between Black and White Americans. The Black–White difference has declined by a third since the 1970s, which clearly can only be due to environmental (e.g., education, social opportunities), not genetic, factors.
- The priming of psychological reactions to negative stereotypes (known as stereotype threat) can affect scores on a range of mental ability tests. For example, making women aware of the (inaccurate) stereotype that "girls aren't good at math" has been found to suppress their scores on math tests by an average of one-fifth of a standard deviation.

The early versions of the WAIS, WISC, and WPPSI provided three main summary scores: Verbal IQ (VIQ), Performance (non-verbal) IQ (PIQ), and **Full Scale IQ** (FSIQ; the sum of Verbal and Performance scales). The FSIQ is the total score for an intelligence scale and is the value that is usually referred to simply as the IQ. Over the years, numerous factor analytic studies of the Wechsler scales have found moderate intercorrelations among the various subscales in the three scales, suggesting they tap a *g* factor (e.g., Caruso & Cliff, 1999). This suggests it is reasonable to use a total score that combines verbal and non-verbal scores in order to assess general intelligence. However, very few factor analytic studies have found unqualified support for two separate verbal and performance factors, so the research evidence does not support the use of VIQ and PIQ scores on their own.

Full Scale IQ: the total score for an intelligence scale obtained by summing scores on verbal and non-verbal scales; usually referred to simply as the IQ.

Although there is some slight variability across the three main Wechsler scales, a four-component factor structure seems to best represent the underlying nature of the scales. Accordingly, the most recent versions of the scales emphasize these factors (usually referred to as indexes or composite scores) rather than the VIQ and PIQ. For example, the four index scores for the adult test, the WAIS-IV, are Verbal Comprehension (the ability to comprehend and use verbal material), Perceptual Reasoning (the ability to use visually presented material), Working Memory (the ability to do timed tasks that require the use of information in short-term memory), and Processing Speed (the ability to quickly process and use new information). Implicitly, the Wechsler scales reflect a hierarchical model, with the FSIQ as a measure of *g* and the separate abilities represented by the four index scores.

What is the significance of having an appropriate normative group for a psychological measure?

The Wechsler-Bellevue was greatly criticized for its very limited set of norms. Since that early test, Wechsler and his collaborators have devoted enormous efforts to establishing a solid normative base for the Wechsler intelligence scales. The most recent versions of the three scales have all used normative samples of at least 1,700 participants. For all scales, great care was taken to ensure that the demographic characteristics of the normative samples matched the most up-to-date American census data. Although this ensures the **representativeness** of the normative sample for testing in the United States, it does not guarantee that the norms are appropriate for testing in other countries. A norm-referenced test is useful to the extent that it provides accurate information about a normative group that is relevant to the tested individual. The most salient characteristics that must be considered in making these normative comparisons are age, grade, sex, geographic region, ethnicity, and socioeconomic status (Sattler, 2001). Interpreting the test result from any individual who differs from the normative

representativeness: extent to which a sample reflects the characteristics of the population from which it is drawn.

group on these characteristics may be problematic. Even though there is evidence that the Wechsler *scales* measure the same core set of cognitive abilities when used in countries other than the United States (e.g., Bowden, Lissner, McCarthy, Weiss, & Holdnack, 2007), there is evidence that the Wechsler *norms* are not always appropriate for use outside the United States. For example, Kamieniecki and Lynd-Stevenson (2002) found that Australian children under the age of 15 obtained slightly higher IQ scores than did American children of a similar age. If the American norms were used to classify giftedness or retardation among Australian children, for example, classification errors would occur.

There is, of course, another problem that may occur when testing someone who differs from the normative sample: the test itself may not be fair. For example, questions that are specific to an American context (e.g., "How many states were there when the United States was established?") may not be appropriate for assessing the general knowledge of a non-American test-taker.

Why have psychologists developed Canadian versions of tests of intelligence and achievement?

To address these issues, starting with the work on the WISC-III, revisions to all Wechsler scales include a Canadian standardization component. This involves ensuring that test items are appropriate to the Canadian context (and altering the items when necessary) and then establishing Canadian norms using a large sample of participants whose demographic characteristics are representative of Canadian national census data. As a result, psychologists in Canada can now use the Wechsler intelligence scales with great confidence. Similar efforts have been undertaken in other countries, including Australia and the UK. Building on this foundation, efforts are currently underway to ensure that all subsequent editions of the Wechsler Intelligence Scales have fair items and appropriate norms for testing French-speaking Canadians.

A final general point should be kept in mind with respect to the Wechsler intelligence scales. Wechsler modelled the original Wechsler-Bellevue scale on tests evaluating an examinee's abilities in academically related areas. This means that the tests are oriented to analytical forms of intelligence and do not measure abilities in the artistic, social, or emotional domains, among others. It also means that the focus of the Wechsler tests is on the examinee's current ability or some of the *products* of intelligence, with little or no attention directed to the *processes* that underlie intelligence. A person's performance on the Wechsler scales indicates a great deal about how well he or she can solve problems in a few important areas, but very little about exactly how he or she solves diverse problems (Groth-Marnat, 2009). Viewpoint Box 7.2 addresses the construct and measurement of emotional intelligence.

What are some of the limitations of the Wechsler scales?

VIEWPOINT BOX 7.2

EMOTIONAL INTELLIGENCE AND ITS CORRELATES

Among the multiple intelligences defined by Gardner (1983) are the abilities to understand oneself and others, labelled intrapersonal and interpersonal intelligence. In contrast to the wealth of literature on intelligence related to academic and occupational performance, emotional intelligence received relatively little attention until the 1990s. Adopting an approach similar to that used for other types of intelligence, Salovey and Mayer (1990) proposed that emotional intelligence (EI) is composed of related abilities that enable the person to perceive, understand, and regulate emotions. As the painstaking and scholarly work of developing sound measures progressed, the publication of the popular book *Emotional Intelligence: Why It Can Matter More Than IQ* (Goleman, 1995) catapulted the concept of EI to the attention of the general public.

The idea of EI has a great deal of intuitive appeal. The search to understand the qualities that enable people to be informed by emotions and to regulate their emotions in order to be well adjusted and to get along with others is clearly an important endeavour. Not surprisingly, the concept of EI has fuelled a thriving industry. A Google search will reveal many ways to assess EI, to enhance EI, and to become certified in helping others to do so. Improving EI is presented as an important goal in both education and the workplace. Many of the websites claim that their materials are scientifically validated and supported by many years of research. As you may be aware, marketing often progresses at a faster pace than science does, so some of the claims are not yet backed up by replicated scientific evidence.

It should not surprise you to learn that there are a variety of ways of defining EI, each leading to the development of different measures. For example, the Emotional Quotient Inventory and its short form, EQ-i-Short (Bar-On, 2002), are based on a definition of EI as a disposition made up of cognitive, personality, and motivational and affective factors (Parker, Saklofske, Wood, Eastabrook, & Taylor, 2005). This measure requires participants to rate themselves on intrapersonal, interpersonal, stress management, and adaptability scales, and yields a total EI score. Data suggesting that high scores on the scale can be easily faked raise concerns about its validity and practical usefulness (Grubb & McDaniel, 2007). The Mayer-Salovey-Caruso Emotional Intelligence Test (MSCEIT; Mayer, Salovey, Caruso, & Sitarenios, 2003) is an ability-based measure and contains questions that are akin to those found in intelligence tests. The model on which it is based hypothesizes that EI encompasses abilities in four areas: (a) perception of emotion, which refers to the ability to detect emotions in oneself and in others—this work developed from research on recognition of non-verbal cues; (b) use of emotional information in thinking—this refers to the ways that emotions influence our thinking and is grounded in cognitive psychology; (c) understanding emotions; and (d) managing emotions.

A comprehensive review of the research using ability-based measures (Mayer, Roberts, & Barsade, 2008) summarized findings indicating that EI is associated with the following:

- Better social relations for children (as reported by children, their family members, and their teachers)
- Better social relations for adults (according to self-report)
- Better family and intimate relations (reported by self and others)
- More positive perceptions by others—high EI individuals are considered more pleasant to be around and more empathetic
- Better academic achievement (reported by teachers)
- Better social relations during work performance
- Better psychological well-being (according to self-report)

CONTINUED . . .

There is also evidence from ability-based measures that EI is associated with positive adjustment, as rated by the individual and by others. Overall, though, comparisons of findings across studies in the EI literature are greatly complicated by the use of different models and different measures (Mayer, Salovey, & Caruso, 2008). Undoubtedly, the burgeoning field of EI research will continue to grow in the coming years, and many of the scientific gaps and challenges in the literature will be addressed by researchers committed to enhancing our knowledge of this fascinating psychological construct.

Administration, Scoring, and Interpretation Issues

Doctoral students in clinical psychology often spend an entire graduate course learning how to administer, score, and interpret the Wechsler scales. Standardized administration requires familiarity with all the subtests, ease in handling materials, and detailed knowledge of permitted prompts when an item is partially or incorrectly answered.

Administration of the Wechsler scales should be conducted in a comfortable but relatively nondescript room (i.e., with no distractions that influence the person's concentration). Typically, the psychologist sits opposite the test-taker or at a 90-degree angle to him or her—an important point if assessing an energetic child who is eagerly trying to peek at what the psychologist is getting ready to do next! The test-taker should be given information about the nature of the test (in an age appropriate manner) and should be allowed to ask questions. Testing with the scales can be time-consuming: Ryan, Glass, and Brown (2007) reported that about one-third of administrations of the WISC-IV took more than 80 minutes, and that child age, school grade, and FSIQ all correlated positively with administration time. That is, the older you are, the further along in school you are, and the higher your intelligence, the more items are administered and the longer the testing session. Unlike a coach or teacher, the assessor is not permitted to give the test-taker any feedback on performance or whether answers are correct or incorrect, so encouragement takes the form of noticing effort, concentration, and persistence rather than suggesting that the person is doing well. In some cases, such as with children, older adults, or individuals with brain damage, it is necessary to take breaks between subtests, otherwise the person's fatigue may interfere with the concentration necessary for the testing.

Extensive details about the administration, scoring, and interpretation of the Wechsler intelligence scales are provided in the manuals that accompany the measures. There are also many other sources available to aid psychologists in their use of these scales (e.g., Flanagan & Kaufman, 2009). Having mastered administration of the scales as part of their graduate training, clinical psychologists usually attend training sessions when a revised scale is published, so that they learn about and practise new procedures introduced in a revised edition. For the test scores to be meaningful, clinicians must follow administration guidelines scrupulously; otherwise, it is not possible to accurately use the normative data to interpret a person's test scores.

Administering and scoring these tests are not easy tasks. Numerous studies have found evidence of substantial errors in the administration and scoring of all three Wechsler scales (e.g., Hopwood & Richard, 2005; Loe, Kadlubek, & Marks, 2007; Ryan & Schnakenberg-Ott, 2003). Unfortunately, the consequences of administration and scoring errors can be serious. In addition to errors related to carelessness, errors also reflect how complex it is to accurately use the Wechsler scales. To give you a sense of this, consider the following example, which is similar to an item on the WAIS-IV. The test-taker is asked to indicate "In what way are a swimming pool and a baseball field alike?" The assessor must determine whether the person's response "You can have fun in both" is worth 2 points, 1 point, or 0 points. In the manual, information such as the following is provided: 2 points are awarded for answers that involve a recognition that both are used for sporting or athletic activities, 1 point is awarded for answers that indicate they are found in recreational areas or that both require maintenance, and 0 points are awarded for answers such as "You get wet in both" or "Both can be outside, but only a pool can be inside." Although the Wechsler manuals have been extensively tested and the most common responses (both good and poor) are listed, the assessor must know when to ask for more information in response to an answer that does not appear in the manual. If the examiner fails to ask for more information when such a prompt is required, the score may be underestimated; if however, the examiner prompts unnecessarily, it may incorrectly inflate the person's score. For testing to proceed at a reasonable rate, the psychologist must be familiar with all the scoring rules to make rapid scoring decisions. Lengthy delays while the examiner consults the manual may prolong the testing session, leading to boredom, frustration, and sub-optimal performance.

The general interpretive strategy, recommended by almost every source on the Wechsler tests, is to move from the general to the specific. Groth-Marnat (2009), for example, suggested that the FSIQ should always be interpreted first, followed by the factor scores (such as verbal comprehension and working memory). These steps allow the psychologist to understand the broad pattern of the examinee's IQ and his or her general strengths and weaknesses. FSIQ information, including the percentile rank, provides an overall indication of the person's mental abilities in comparison with the normative group. Interpretations of the factor scores allow for a more comprehensive picture of the examinee's cognitive abilities, including whether there are noteworthy aspects such as much superior functioning in verbal comprehension compared with perceptual reasoning. A difference such as this can be due to a host of factors, including educational background and brain damage. Careful consideration of these scores in the context of other assessment information can provide valuable information for determining the person's overall cognitive functioning and possible options for vocational or educational remediation.

The next step in the interpretation of a Wechsler scale is to examine additional factorial groupings of subtests that have been identified in the research literature. A common strategy is to use the distinction made in the Cattell-Horn-Carroll theory between crystallized and fluid intelligence. As we indicated earlier in the chapter, crystallized intelligence is defined as education-based knowledge and abilities, whereas fluid intelligence is the ability to solve novel problems. As we describe a bit later in the chapter, the WAIS-IV now incorporates measures of fluid intelligence and the WPPSI-IV has index scores similar to key aspects of the Cattell-Horn-Carroll theory. Most authorities then recommend that the psychologist interpret variability between and within the subtests of the scale. To this end, sources such as Flanagan and Kaufman (2009) provide detailed descriptions of the clinical considerations associated with each subtest and the factors that may influence each subtest. Although widely endorsed and practised, the analysis of subtest scatter is problematic because the internal consistency reliability of each subtest is typically much lower than that associated with the summary scores (i.e., the FSIQ score and factor scores). This translates into reduced assessment precision, which in turn means an increased likelihood of false positive and false negative statements about the person's ability as measured on each subtest. Decades of research have found that information contained in subtest profiles adds little to the prediction of academic achievement or of learning behaviours (Watkins, 2003).

Canadian Normative Data

Canadian standardization projects for the Wechsler intelligence scales began with the WISC-III (Wechsler, 1996). Since that time, Canadian norms have been developed for editions of the WPPSI, WISC, and WAIS. The general strategy for constructing Canadian norms involves using recent Canadian census data to establish the sampling frame for the project and then developing a stratified random sampling plan to ensure that the resulting sample is representative of English-speaking Canadians. This means that age, sex, ethnicity, educational level, and geographical representation are all taken into account. (As you will see later in the chapter, there are translated versions of these scales used for assessing French-speaking Canadians. These versions currently use Canadian norms or French-Canadian norms derived from samples in Quebec.)

Using data from Canadian normative groups, the test developers then derive scaled scores (i.e., standardized scores) from the raw scores. As a first step, the Canadian data are compared with the data from the American normative groups and the distribution of the scores for each age group is examined. Although there are some national differences in the mean raw scores in the normative groups, overall the distributions are similar. This similarity allows the developers to apply the same statistical procedures employed with the American data to derive estimates of population values for the Canadian data. As a final step, these estimates are transformed into standard scores so that each subtest has a mean of 10 and a standard deviation of 3.

Top row: Left, ©iStock.com/Art-Y; Middle, ©iStock.com/Johnny Greig; Right, ©iStock.com/szeyuen
Bottom row: Left, ©iStock.com/MBMdesigns; Middle (top), ©iStock.com/ProArtWork; Middle (bottom), ©iStock.com/francesco_de_napoli; Right, ©iStock.com/nycshooter

The WAIS-IV can be used to assess people from a broad age range.

Children, adolescents, and adults taking the Wechsler scales in Canada are now evaluated on the basis of how Canadians usually perform on the scales, which has very important implications in clinical settings. For example, Canadian norms yield an accurate estimation of the cognitive impairment experienced by Canadian patients with substantial neuropsychological problems, whereas use of American norms leads to an underestimate of cognitive impairment (Iverson, Lange, & Viljoen, 2006). The general pattern of intercorrelations among WAIS-IV subtest scores is very similar for the American and Canadian normative samples. However, the mean factor scores are higher in the Canadian samples than in the American samples (Bowden, Saklofske, & Weiss, 2011). Just as you learned earlier about an Australian study, this means that many errors would be made in identifying both high and low scores among Canadians if American norms were used. Profile Box 7.1 introduces Dr. Don Saklofske whose research focuses on the measurement of intelligence.

PROFILE BOX 7.1

DR. DON SAKLOFSKE

Courtesy of Don Saklofske

I earned my Ph.D. from the University of Calgary and am a full professor in the Department of Psychology, University of Western Ontario. Previous academic appointments (now adjunct professorships) were held at the Universities of Calgary and Saskatchewan. I am a visiting professor at Beijing Normal University (Psychology Department) and the Zhuhai campus, China. Past clinical practice settings include hospital, mental health clinics, schools, and private practice. I am a retired registered psychologist in Alberta and was previously registered in Saskatchewan.

CONTINUED . . .

My work currently focuses on teaching and training psychologists, carrying out professional association activities, and conducting research. My research focus on personality, intelligence, and psychological assessment is both theoretical and applied, and correlational and experimental. I have written or edited over 140 journal articles, 74 book chapters, and 29 books, and delivered several hundred conference presentations.

Motivating my study of emotions and social cognition is my current emphasis on prevention, resiliency, and psychological health. I serve on the advisory panel for the development of the Wechsler intelligence tests and am editor of two journals, associate editor for another, and editor of books for the Springer Series on Human Exceptionality. I have held positions in professional psychology associations at the provincial level (e.g., Psychologists' Association of Alberta) and national level (e.g., Canadian Psychological Association). Currently, I am president of the International Society for the Study of Individual Differences. It is an honour to have been elected a Fellow of both the Canadian Psychological Association and the Association for Psychological Science.

WHAT MADE YOU CHOOSE TO BECOME A CLINICAL PSYCHOLOGIST?

As an undergraduate, I was drawn to the scientist-practitioner perspective in clinically oriented courses and found the links between theory, research, and practice most compelling. As a graduate student, I was fortunate to have been academically supported by a number of talented and brilliant faculty members at the University of Calgary who encouraged my interests. My fascination with human behaviour and individual differences makes psychology the perfect fit for me.

WHAT IS THE MOST REWARDING PART OF YOUR JOB AS A CLINICAL PSYCHOLOGIST?

Being a psychologist is itself most exciting and rewarding. I am involved daily in the study of the very factors that describe human behaviour ... what makes us like all others, some others, and no others! The university setting provides a rich context to engage in both discovery and the application of knowledge. Applying psychology in direct clinical service and in the training of both graduate and undergraduate students has always been a very rewarding side of my work; it gives meaning to psychology as a scientific discipline and profession. The opportunity to make a real difference is a very big reward!

WHAT IS THE GREATEST CHALLENGE FACING YOU AS A CLINICAL PSYCHOLOGIST?

One challenge, given the many unknowns in present-day psychological science, is that our clinical efforts are not always successful. Also, there is the ongoing concern that our resources as a helping profession are limited and we constantly try to do too much with too little. Future challenges include finding ways to provide psychological services outside of large cities and to Canada's changing population demographics. And we must become even more active in promoting psychological wellness and resiliency and developing prevention services to complement our capacity to apply evidence-based therapies and interventions.

TELL US ABOUT THE IMPORTANCE OF CANADIAN NORMS FOR TESTS SUCH AS THE WECHSLER SCALES.

One of psychology's key contributions is defining and measuring human characteristics. Psychologists have developed measures to assess numerous constructs, including intelligence, personality variables such as extraversion, psychological conditions such as anxiety and depression, and various other factors ranging from self-concept to motivation. Standardized, norm-referenced tests allow us to compare the scores of one person to a relevant group. Some years ago, Canadian psychologists raised questions about differences in

CONTINUED . . .

scores between Canadians and Americans on intelligence tests such as the Wechsler scales. Two important questions were "Does this test, developed in the United States, work the same way in Canada?" and "Do Canadians score the same as Americans?" Although the factors that describe intelligence appear to be similar in both countries and in fact across many countries, the score distributions from one country do not always replicate in another country. The earlier Wechsler scales developed in the United States included questions with American content. Nevertheless, we initially found that when the WISC-III and WAIS-III were administered to Canadian children and adults, they scored higher than did their counterparts in the United States. These data provided a sound basis for developing Canadian norms. Our goal is to make these psychological tests as reliable and valid as possible for use in Canada, and this extends to developing Canadian norms if needed. More recent tests, such as the WISC-IV and the WAIS-IV, include subtests that are less influenced by culture and specific educational experiences, and are related to what psychologists call fluid intelligence.

HOW DO YOU INTEGRATE SCIENCE AND PRACTICE IN YOUR WORK?

The scientist-practitioner perspective is the foundation of my work and that of my colleagues. Although we remain open to ideas from other fields, disciplines, and cultures, the strength of psychology comes from being grounded in science. We must therefore search for evidence to determine whether our claims and clinical practices are supported or not, whether it be diagnosis, treatment, or the effectiveness of an intervention or prevention program.

WHAT DO YOU SEE AS THE MOST EXCITING CHANGES IN THE PROFESSION OF CLINICAL PSYCHOLOGY?

Everything! This is such an exciting time as advances in psychology are progressing at a very fast pace. The rapid growth of psychological knowledge and collaboration with other fields such as the neurosciences and behaviour genetics, and with professions such as medicine, kinesiology, and education, hold great promise for humankind. Although psychologists will continue to be confronted by many emerging and yet-to-be-answered questions, our potential to provide evidence-based assessment, intervention, and prevention at the primary, secondary, and tertiary levels has never been greater.

Wechsler Adult Intelligence Scale—Fourth Edition (WAIS-IV)

The WAIS-IV American and Canadian editions were released in 2008 (Wechsler, 2008). The WAIS-IV includes extensive changes from previous versions: some new subtests were added and some long-standing subtests were eliminated, changes were made to the items in many of the subtests that were retained, the age range was enlarged to include 16- to 90-year-olds, and, for the first time, the use of index scores replaced the use of verbal and performance intelligence quotients. These changes were designed to address several goals, including making the structure of the test consistent with results of factor analytic research on previous versions of the WAIS, improving the reliability and validity of the subtests, and reducing the overall administration time. The American normative sample for the WAIS-IV included over 2,000 adults;

the Canadian normative sample was over 1,000 adults. Participants were selected to be generally representative of the population in terms of sex, education level, ethnicity, and region of the country. A French-language version of the Canadian edition is also available. Exhibit 7.1 provides details on the WAIS-IV subtests. Figure 7.2 illustrates sample items similar to those from subtests included in the WAIS-IV.

Exhibit 7.1 Wechsler Adult Intelligence Scale—Fourth Edition (WAIS-IV) Indexes and Subtests

Verbal Comprehension Scale

Similarities: After being presented with pairs of words (describing concepts or objects), the person is asked to provide an explanation of how the two concepts or objects are similar.

Vocabulary: The person is asked to define a series of orally and visually presented words.

Information: The person is asked a set of orally presented questions that address knowledge of events, objects, people, and places.

Comprehension: Questions about common concepts and problems are presented orally and the person is asked to provide the answers or solutions.

Perceptual Reasoning Scale

Block Design: The person is asked to use coloured blocks to create three-dimensional representations of two-dimensional geometric patterns.

Matrix Reasoning: The person is presented with incomplete patterns and, from a list of five choices, is asked to select the choice that completes each pattern.

Visual Puzzles: The person is presented with images, like pieces of a puzzle, and is asked to choose the images that go together to match the example given by the examiner.

Picture Completion: The person is presented with pictures of common objects and settings and is asked to identify the missing part.

Figure Weights: The person is asked to choose the "weight" depicted in a series of images that would be equivalent to the "weight" depicted in the example given by the examiner.

Working Memory Scale

Digit Span: The person is presented with a series of numbers and is asked to repeat them in the same sequence or in a reversed sequence.

Arithmetic: The person is asked to solve arithmetic problems and provide the answers orally.

Letter-Number Sequencing: Sequences of letters and numbers are presented orally and the person is asked to repeat them with the letters in alphabetical order and numbers in ascending order.

Processing Speed Scale

Symbol Search: The person is asked to indicate, by checking a box, whether target symbols occur in the group of symbols presented.

Coding: Using a key that matches numbers to symbols, the person is asked to rapidly provide the correct symbols to a list of numbers.

Cancellation: The person is presented with a series of shapes of different colours and is asked to cross out images that have a specific shape (e.g., circles) and a specific colour.

Adapted from Wechsler (2008).

Visual Puzzles

- Contributes to Perceptual Reasoning Composite
- More reliable measure than Object Assembly
- Requires no motor skills

Which three of these pieces go together to make this puzzle?

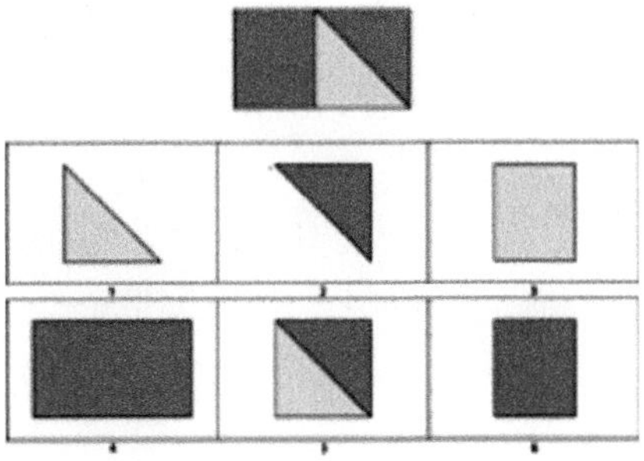

Figure Weights

- Contributes to Perceptual Reasoning Composite
- Measure of quantitative and analogical reasoning
- Requires no motor skills

Which one of these goes here to balance the scale?

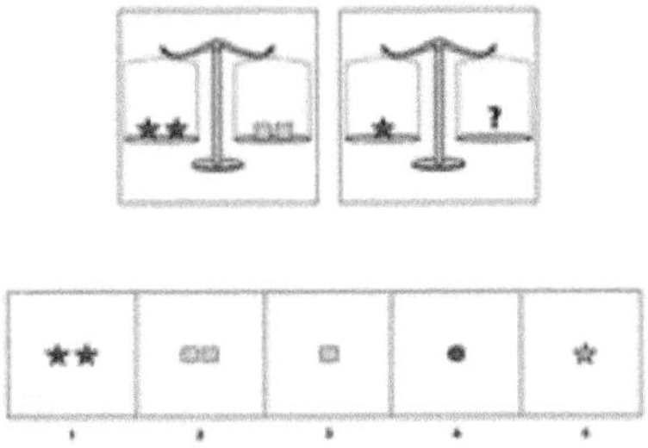

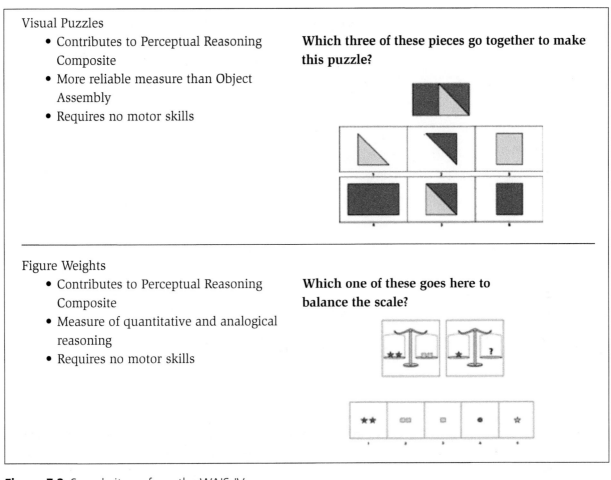

Figure 7.2 Sample items from the WAIS-IV

Previous versions of the WAIS were noted for their generally excellent reliability values. The WAIS-IV continues this trend, with the internal consistency coefficients derived from the normative sample for the FSIQ and the four index scores all equalling or exceeding .90. Greater variability is evident with the individual subtests, with reliability values ranging from .78 to .93 (only one subtest, Cancellation, is below a value of .80). As so many validity studies were conducted over the years for earlier versions of the WAIS, it is important to note that there are very high correlations among the IQ scores for the WAIS-IV and the WAIS-III. The pattern of subtest intercorrelations and factor analytic results reported in the test manual all support the continuing validity of the WAIS-IV. Despite all the encouraging validity data for the WAIS-IV, keep in mind that validity is not a property of a test, but rather a property that scores on a test have when used for a particular purpose with a specific group of people. The WAIS-IV (and the other Wechsler scales) must always be used and interpreted within the limits of the characteristics of the normative sample and the purposes for which it has established validity.

Early in this chapter, we encouraged you to adopt an attitude of caveat emptor when examining self-administered IQ tests. One of the most important ways that you can evaluate the quality of any psychological test is by considering the strength and extent of the reliability and validity evidence for the test. This is why we provide this kind of technical information about the Wechsler scales. If a family member was being assessed to determine whether he or she was eligible for admission to a giftedness program, you would probably want to be sure that he or she was assessed using the most valid measure possible.

Wechsler Intelligence Scale for Children—Fourth Edition (WISC-IV)

The fourth edition of the WISC was released in 2003 (Wechsler, 2003). A description of the subtests and the four indexes is presented in Exhibit 7.2. As you can see by comparing it with the information on the WAIS-IV subtests in Exhibit 7.1, there are many similarities in the type of tasks included on the two intelligence scales. The WISC-IV is designed to provide age appropriate assessment of children/adolescents between the ages of 6 and 17 years. To increase the developmental appropriateness of the scale, the developers simplified the instructions, including sample and/or practice items within each subtest, and made the test material more attractive and engaging for children. The WISC-IV was developed in the United States with a stratified sample of 2,200 children and adolescents. Subsequently, the Canadian normative study for the WISC-IV collected data from 1,100 Canadian children between the ages of 6 and 17 years. A French-language edition of the WISC-IV is also available for use in Canada.

Based on the normative data, the mean internal consistency reliability of the WISC-IV subtests is very good, with only two of the subtests having reliability values below .80. The reliability of the FSIQ is .97, a rather remarkable accomplishment for the scale. All of the four index scores have outstanding reliability values, ranging from .88 to .94. As with previous versions of the WISC, there is a great deal of

Exhibit 7.2 Wechsler Intelligence Scale for Children—Fourth Edition (WISC-IV) Indexes and Subtests

Verbal Comprehension Index

Similarities: After being presented with pairs of words (describing concepts or objects), the child is asked to provide an explanation about how the two concepts or objects are similar.

Vocabulary: The child is asked to name pictures that are presented and define words presented orally.

Comprehension: Questions about common concepts and social situations are presented orally and the child is asked to provide the answers or solutions.

Information: The child is asked to answer a set of orally presented questions that address knowledge of a wide range of general topics.

Word Reasoning: After being presented a series of clues, the child is asked to describe the underlying common concept.

Perceptual Reasoning Index

Block Design: The child is asked to use coloured blocks to create three-dimensional representations of three-dimensional models and two-dimensional geometric patterns.

Picture Concepts: The child is asked to choose pictures from rows of pictures in order to form a group that has a characteristic in common.

Matrix Reasoning: The child is presented with incomplete patterns and, from a list of five choices, is asked to select the choice that completes each pattern.

Picture Completion: The child is presented with pictures of common objects and is asked to point to or name the missing part.

Working Memory Index

Digit Span: The child is presented with a series of numbers and is asked to repeat them in the same sequence or in a reversed sequence.

Letter-Number Sequencing: Sequences of letters and numbers are presented orally and the child is asked to repeat them with the letters in alphabetical order and numbers in ascending order.

Arithmetic: The child is asked to solve arithmetic problems and provide the answer orally.

Processing Speed Index

Coding: Using a key that matches numbers or geometric shapes to symbols, the child is asked to rapidly provide the correct symbols to a list of shapes or numbers.

Symbol Search: The child is asked to indicate whether target symbols occur in the group of symbols presented.

Cancellation: The child is asked to mark target pictures in a series of pictures that includes both random arrangements and structured arrangements.

Adapted from Wechsler (2003).

validity information reported in the manual, including the intercorrelations among subtests and the factor structure of the scale. There are also numerous findings presented on the relation between the WISC-IV and other measures, including measures of similar and dissimilar constructs (i.e., convergent and discriminant validity). For example, the FSIQ correlates .89 with the FSIQ from the previous version of the WISC and with the FSIQ from the WAIS-III (based on data from 198 16-year-olds). In contrast, the correlations between a measure of emotional intelligence and the FSIQ and the four indexes ranged from .22 to .31, thus providing evidence of discriminant validity.

Wechsler Preschool and Primary Scale of Intelligence—Fourth Edition (WPPSI-IV)

The Canadian version of the WPPSI-IV was released shortly after the introduction of the American revision (Wechsler, 2012). There are 15 subtests, from which the psychologist uses a subset according to the age of the child. For children aged 2 years 6 months to 3 years 11 months, the psychologist administers five core subtests—Receptive Vocabulary, Information, Block Design, Object Assembly, and Picture Memory—and calculates the FSIQ based on all five. For children aged 4 years to 7 years 7 months, the psychologist administers six subtests to calculate the FSIQ: Information, Similarities, Block Design, Matrix Reasoning, Picture Memory, and Bug Search. The subtests are similar to those described in Exhibit 7.2 for the WISC-IV, but are age appropriate in content, with even less emphasis on both timed performance and reliance on verbal responses. These subtests provide the necessary information for the primary index scores (Verbal Comprehension, Visual Spatial, and Working Memory for the younger age group; Verbal Comprehension, Visual Spatial, Fluid Reasoning, Working Memory, and Processing Speed for the older age group). These index scores correspond to the main constructs of the Cattell-Horn-Carroll theory of intelligence. Additional subtests can be administered and scored as part of ancillary index scores. A French-language edition of the WPPSI-IV is available for use in Canada. As with the other Wechsler scales, the manual reports reliability data and validity data based on subtest intercorrelations and factor analytic results. Additional information is provided on correlations with measures of children's psychosocial functioning. Viewpoint Box 7.3 addresses the question of whether people are becoming more intelligent than those in previous generations.

Flynn effect: the observed trend that IQ scores in developed countries have increased over the past few decades.

VIEWPOINT BOX 7.3

THE FLYNN EFFECT

Are you more intelligent than your parents or your grandparents? According to research conducted by James Flynn (1987), the answer to this question is *yes*—at least at the population level. Flynn, a professor of political studies at a New Zealand university, analyzed changes in IQ scores in developed countries over the past few decades. He found that, on average, there was an annual increase of .33 IQ

CONTINUED . . .

score points in Western societies. In other words, an average undergraduate student today has an IQ that is approximately one standard deviation higher (i.e., 15 points) than that of the average undergraduate 40 years ago. Not all IQ measures or subtests are rising at the same rate. Flynn found that measures of visuospatial abilities—usually treated as measures of fluid intelligence (see the text section on Theories of Intelligence)—increased more than did measures of acquired knowledge (i.e., crystallized intelligence). Subsequent research demonstrated that the increase in IQ scores is greater in developing countries than in developed countries. Indeed, if the trend continues, by the end of this century there is likely to be few population-level differences in IQ across countries (Nisbett et al., 2012).

How can this be? Although it is always possible that part of these increases may be due to factors related to the tests themselves, this is rather unlikely. There is no evidence, for example, that people are generally aware of what the items are on IQ tests, or that they study for the tests prior to taking them, or that schools have altered their curricula to emphasize subjects related to *g*.

The span of a few decades seems too brief for such dramatic changes to be due to genetic factors. Changes stemming from genetic alterations within a population usually take centuries, not generations, to be evident. However, in the past century, we have witnessed unprecedented urbanization and mobility of human populations. As these factors have led to an increase in the human genetic variability due to the mating of individuals from genetically distinct subpopulations, Mingroni (2007) argued that such increased genetic variability is at least partially responsible for the observed changes in intelligence.

Can environmental influences be a significant driving force behind this rise in IQ? Flynn speculated that improvements in educational systems are an important contributory factor. These improvements include both increases in the number of people within a population who receive formal education and increases in the number of years of education completed. Flynn argued that other environmental influences must also be at work. These influences include improved nutrition, greater parental involvement with children, fewer severe childhood diseases, and rapid developments in technology such as television, video games, and computers that emphasize visuospatial skills (Neisser, 1998).

Yet, consider for a moment the fact that at least half of the variance in population IQ scores can be attributed to genetic factors. If these substantial rises in IQ are largely attributable to environmental factors, it might appear that alterations in these environmental factors over the past 50 years are absolutely enormous. In attempting to explain this "IQ paradox," Dickens and Flynn (2001) emphasized the importance of small but persistent alterations in the environment that, over generations, could influence IQ scores even though there is such a high genetic influence on IQ. For example, over the past century, the cognitive complexity of most jobs has increased, leisure time has increased, technologies in the home have increased, and average family size has decreased (allowing more time for parents to focus their attention on each child). The growing shift in the teaching of mathematics, from counting and simple arithmetic skills to more complex reasoning and logical analysis, has also been posited as playing a role in this change (Nisbett et al., 2012). Cumulatively, year after year, generation after generation, these changes may be responsible for rising IQ scores by providing stimulating environments that match the intellectual potential of more and more people in a population. By optimizing the gene–environment fit, Dickens and Flynn speculated that a multiplier effect is occurring in which small environmental forces can yield large IQ effects. However, as appealing as such a model may be, it is unlikely to be the last word on the pattern of rising IQ scores.

OTHER INTELLIGENCE SCALES

Although we have focused on the Wechsler intelligence scales because they are the most commonly used and have a strong evidence base, psychologists also use other scales to assess intellectual abilities. The Stanford-Binet Intelligence Scale, which is now in its fifth edition, is designed to assess intelligence in individuals from 2 to 85 years old (Roid, 2003). Like the Wechsler scales, the Stanford-Binet is standardized to have a mean of 100 and a standard deviation of 15. The subtests can be summed to provide an FSIQ and various composite factor scores. A normative American sample of 4,800 was selected based on 2000 census data. The reliability data for this sample were very strong, with all subtests having internal consistency values ≥ .84 and the composite and FSIQ scores ≥ .92. Validity data were obtained by correlating the scores with a host of intelligence and achievement tests included in the normative sample. Although the Stanford-Binet has a long historical tradition, its value outside of the United States is limited due to the lack of content adaptations and norms necessary for the validity of the instrument when used in other countries.

In developing tests of intellectual ability, Kaufman and Kaufman took a very different theoretical approach to that used in the Wechsler or Stanford-Binet scales. Rather than focusing on content areas that measure intellectual functioning, they constructed process-based measures (Lichtenberger, Broadbooks, & Kaufman, 2000). In other words, the Kaufman Assessment Battery for Children (Kaufman & Kaufman, 1983), now in a second edition, and the Kaufman Adolescent and Adult Intelligence Test (Kaufman & Kaufman, 1993) focus on how children and adults learn and assessed styles of learning rather than knowledge or skill areas. The subscales of the child version—Sequential Processing, Simultaneous Processing, Mental Processing Composite, and Achievement—are clearly different from those of the Wechsler scales. Comparing a person's scores on the processing scales with those obtained on the achievement scale identifies gaps between that person's potential to learn and what he or she has actually learned. As is typical with intelligence scales, normative data were collected on a large nationally representative (American) sample and extensive psychometric data were presented in the test manuals.

Although the Kaufman scales were designed to be culturally fair and relevant to educational contexts, they do not seem to be widely used by clinical psychologists. This may be due as much to the limited number of training programs that teach the use of these scales as it is to the need for traditional IQ scores in making a range of clinical diagnoses. Additionally, for those working outside of the United States, the lack of a country-specific standardized version of the scales is also a significant drawback.

How do the Kaufman intelligence tests differ from the Wechsler intelligence scales?

SELECTED COGNITIVE ASSESSMENT SCALES

To address some of the assessment questions described earlier in the chapter, clinical psychologists usually need to supplement the results from an intelligence test with information obtained on other tests that address cognitive functioning. In this section, we describe two of the tests most commonly used for this purpose. As with our presentation of intelligence tests, we will focus on Wechsler instruments in this section. Not only do these instruments have excellent norms and psychometric properties, they are also designed to address important clinical issues when used in combination with a Wechsler intelligence scale. The first test we consider is the Wechsler Memory Scale–Fourth Edition, a test that is typically used if there is a question of brain injury or brain dysfunction due to causes such as dementia, temporal lobe epilepsy, or Parkinson's disease. The second test we present is a standardized achievement test: the Wechsler Individual Achievement Test–Third Edition. An achievement test is used, along with a measure of intellectual functioning, in assessments focused on diagnosing learning disabilities and making recommendations for educational plans to address any observed learning problem.

Wechsler Memory Scale—Fourth Edition (WMS-IV)

The original WMS was published by Wechsler in 1945, revised in 1987, and revised again in 1997. The fourth edition of the WMS was released in 2009 and is substantially different from the previous versions in order to (a) reduce testing time for older adults, (b) improve the usefulness of the scale for forensic assessment purposes, (c) reduce the content overlap with the WAIS-IV, and (d) improve the assessment of working memory. To help you understand the constructs that the WMS-IV (Wechsler, 2009) assesses, consider what we know about memory processes. Lichtenberger, Kaufman, and Lai (2002) distinguished between *procedural memory*—involving skills and complex motor actions (such as riding a bike)—and *declarative memory*—involving symbolic representations (such as a phone number). Declarative memory can be further subdivided into **semantic memory** and **episodic memory**. Semantic memory involves general knowledge of words, concepts, and events, whereas episodic memory deals with the person's direct experiences. Although all of these forms of memory may be relevant in clinical contexts, the WMS-IV is designed to assess the episodic form of declarative memory.

semantic memory: memory of general knowledge of words, concepts, and events.

episodic memory: memory of a person's direct experiences.

The tasks involved in the WMS-IV require the examinee to respond to a number of stimuli, both auditory and visual. A brief cognitive status test is conducted at the beginning of the administration to identify significant cognitive impairment. The WMS–IV is designed to be flexible in terms of the subtests which are then used, in order to reduce the burden on the test-taker and to alter the test administration for test-takers who have motor difficulties. Combining the subtests leads to Immediate, Delayed, Visual, and Auditory Memory Index scores. Exhibit 7.3 provides details on the scale's primary subtests (the optional subtests are not presented) and index scores. For each subtest, as with the Wechsler intelligence scales, the mean is 10 and the standard deviation is 3. The index scores on the WMS-IV have a mean of 100 and a standard deviation of 15, just like an IQ score.

Exhibit 7.3 Wechsler Memory Scale—Fourth Edition (WMS-IV) Indexes and Subtests

Subtests

Designs I: The person is presented with designs placed on a grid. The card is withdrawn and a new card with designs is presented. The examinee is asked to place the correct designs in the correct location on a grid.

Designs II: The person is asked to recall the designs on the grid and then to place the correct designs in the correct location. At least 25 minutes after completing Designs I, a series of designs on grids is presented and the person is asked to choose those viewed in Designs I.

Logical Memory I: A story is read aloud and the person is asked to repeat back as much of the story as possible.

Logical Memory II: The person is asked to recall stories presented in Logical Memory I and is then asked a series of questions about the stories (at least 25 minutes must have passed from doing Logical Memory I).

Spatial Addition: Two pages with dots are presented and then removed. The person is asked to answer questions that require remembering the location of the dots in order to add or subtract dots from the remembered location.

Symbol Span: A set of designs is presented and then removed. The person is asked to select the correct designs, in the correct sequence from left to right, from a large set of designs.

Verbal Paired Associates I: A set of word pairs is read out. Following this, a single word is read out and the person is asked to provide the paired word.

Verbal Paired Associates II: At least 25 minutes after completing Verbal Paired Associates I, a set of word pairs is read out and the person is asked to indicate which word pairs were in the Verbal Paired Associates I.

Visual Reproduction I: The person is presented with a series of designs. After the designs are withdrawn, the person is asked to draw the designs.

Visual Reproduction II: At least 25 minutes after completing Visual Reproduction I, the person is asked to draw the designs from Visual Reproduction I and then is asked to identify the correct designs from a list of designs that is presented.

Index Scores

Auditory Memory: Logical Memory I & II, Verbal Paired Associates I & II

Visual Memory: Designs I & II, Visual Reproduction I & II

Visual Working Memory: Spatial Addition, Symbol Span

Immediate Memory: All four I subtests

Delayed Memory: All four II subtests

Adapted from Wechsler (2009).

The WMS-IV was normed with the WAIS-IV. This resulted in a representative normative sample of 1,400 adults (between the ages of 16 and 90 years) who completed both fourth-edition scales. A validation study with a Canadian sample confirmed the appropriateness of using American norms with Canadians. Based on the normative data, internal consistency values for the subtests ranged from .74 to .97, with short-term stability values ranging from .59 to .77. For the index scores, the internal consistency values ranged from .93 to .96 and the stability values from .81 to .83. Based on (a) correlations with other memory measures and a range of measures of psychosocial functioning and (b) comparisons among clinical samples included in the validation studies (including people with traumatic brain injuries, schizophrenia, major depression, learning disorders, intellectual disabilities, and Alzheimer's disease), there is considerable evidence that the WMS-IV can detect memory impairments and can differentiate between clinical groups. Evidence of validity for these tasks is especially important as the WMS-IV is the main measure used by clinical psychologists and neuropsychologists to assess memory impairment.

Wechsler Individual Achievement Test—Third Edition (WIAT-III)

The original WIAT was released in 1992. A revised test, the WIAT-II, was released in 2002, with a Canadian version released the following year. The Canadian version of the WIAT-III (Wechsler, 2010) was also made available a year after the American version was released. It is designed to evaluate a person's academic and problem-solving skills, from the age of 4 to 51 years. The manual provides linkage with scores from the Wechsler family of intelligence tests, allowing easy identification of discrepancies between intellectual functioning and academic achievement. As a result, the WIAT-III, when used in conjunction with any of the three Wechsler intelligence scales, can be used in the diagnosis of learning disabilities and can provide invaluable information for use in planning remedial educational efforts.

Exhibit 7.4 provides information on the main subtests of the WIAT-III. To give you a sense of the kinds of questions that are asked, a Sentence Composition question asks the person to write a response to a statement like *My favourite thing to do is . . .*, and a Reading Comprehension question involves the person reading a passage about kangaroos and then answering questions about how kangaroos move, where they live, and how they are born. The Canadian edition includes some items that differ from the American version. For example, pictures of coins used in some mathematics items were changed from American to Canadian currency, spelling changes were made to be consistent with

Canadian usage, and units of measurement were changed from imperial to metric. The subtests are organized into four composite scores: Reading, Mathematics, Written Expression, and Oral Language. The composite scores have substantial applied value, as they map onto the four areas that the Learning Disabilities Association of Canada have defined as critical in assessing the precise nature of a learning disability.

Exhibit 7.4 Wechsler Individual Achievement Test—Third Edition (WIAT-III) Composites and Subtests

Reading Composite

Word Reading: The person is asked to read aloud from a list of words.

Reading Comprehension: The person is asked to read sentences and short passages, answer questions about the text, and draw conclusions and inferences from the text.

Pseudoword Decoding: The person is asked to sound out unfamiliar or nonsense words.

Oral Reading Fluency: The person is asked to read sentences aloud and answer questions about the sentences.

Mathematics Composite

Numerical Operations: The person is asked to solve math problems of varying complexity.

Math Problem Solving: The person is asked to solve problems related to areas such as time, measurement, geometry, and probability.

Math Fluency—Addition: The person is asked to solve written addition questions within a 60-second time limit.

Math Fluency—Subtraction: The person is asked to solve written subtraction questions within a 60-second time limit.

Math Fluency—Multiplication: The person is asked to solve written multiplication questions within a 60-second time limit.

Written Expression Composite

Spelling: The person is asked to spell a word based on its meaning as used in a sentence.

Sentence Composition: The person is asked to write sentences using specific words and then write sentences that are equivalent in meaning to presented sentences.

Essay Composition: The person is asked to write a brief essay (10 minutes maximum) on a specified topic.

Oral Language Composite

Listening Comprehension: The person is asked to match spoken words/sentences to pictures.

Oral Expression: The person is asked to provide words that match a topic, repeat sentences, and tell a story based on presented pictures.

Adapted from Wechsler (2010).

What kind of information can psychologists obtain by comparing a person's results on an intelligence test with those on an achievement test?

As we described earlier in the chapter, research has found consistent American-Canadian differences in intelligence test scores. This fact, combined with different educational curricula in the two countries and national differences in the academic year (i.e., the Canadian school year is about 20 days longer than the American school year), led the developers of the WIAT-III to assume that there would be differences in achievement test scores in the two countries. Accordingly, extensive steps were taken to gather normative data for the Canadian version of the WIAT-III, including data from (a) students from prekindergarten to Grade 12 and (b) adults from the Canadian WAIS-IV normative sample.

As with the Wechsler intelligence scales, data from the normative sample demonstrate that the scores derived from the WIAT-III are likely to have excellent internal consistency values. For example, most of the average reliability values for the subtests were > .80 and the average reliability values for the composite scores ranged from .91 to .98. Short-term test-retest reliability values for the subtests and composites scores ranged from .73 to .97. The validity data presented in the test manual demonstrate expected patterns of association (a) among subtests and (b) among composite scores and other cognitive measures.

SUMMARY AND CONCLUSIONS

Our society prizes intelligence highly. It is not surprising, therefore, that the measurement of intelligence is a sensitive topic that arouses heated debate. Decisions about access to educational and rehabilitation services are frequently made based on the results of intellectual assessment. The assessment of intellectual and cognitive functioning has been an important professional activity for clinical psychologists for almost a century. Because significant decisions are made based on the results of intelligence tests, a great deal of effort has been made to ensure that tests are fair, that adequate normative data are gathered, and that assessments are both reliable and valid. The Wechsler scales are the most commonly used scales, allowing assessment of intelligence over different developmental periods, assessment of episodic memory, and assessment of academic achievement. In recent years, advances have been made in adapting the Wechsler scales for use in diverse contexts, including Canada.

KEY TERMS

crystallized intelligence: what we have learned in life, both from formal education and general life experiences.

episodic memory: memory of a person's direct experiences.

fluid intelligence: the ability to solve novel problems; innate intellectual potential.

Flynn effect: the observed trend that IQ scores in developed countries have increased over the past few decades.

Full Scale IQ: the total score for an intelligence scale obtained by summing scores on verbal and non-verbal scales; usually referred to simply as the IQ.

g: the general factor shared by all intellectual activities.

premorbid IQ: intellectual functioning prior to an accident or the onset of a neurological decline.

representativeness: extent to which a sample reflects the characteristics of the population from which it is drawn.

semantic memory: memory of general knowledge of words, concepts, and events.

KEY NAMES

Raymond Cattell   James Flynn   Charles Spearman   David Wechsler

ADDITIONAL RESOURCES

Books

Hunt, E. (2011). *Human intelligence.* Cambridge, UK: Cambridge University Press.

Sternberg, R. J., & Kaufman, S. B. (Eds.). (2011). *The Cambridge handbook of intelligence.* Cambridge, UK: Cambridge University Press.

Journals

Intelligence

Check It Out!

Information on Mensa can be found on the Mensa International and Mensa Canada pages:
www.mensa.org

www.mensacanada.org/home.htm

Take the Mensa workout (not an intelligence test!): www.mensa.org/workout.php

The Learning Disabilities Association of Canada website offers detailed information on learning disabilities: www.ldac-acta.ca

Pearson Canada Assessment is the publisher of the Wechsler scales. Visit their website for information on these scales and other measures of cognitive functioning: pearsonassess.ca/hai/ProductListing.aspx?Category=psychological-cognition-intelligence

The following website provides information on research on emotional intelligence. It also lets you see sample reports and learn about what a person might be encouraged to do based on the results of the Mayer-Salovey-Caruso Emotional Intelligence Test: www.unh.edu/emotional_intelligence/index.html

ASSESSMENT: SELF-REPORT AND PROJECTIVE MEASURES

8 CHAPTER

INTRODUCTION

Many people take psychology courses because they are interested in understanding better the differences among people in attitudes, beliefs, behaviours, and emotionality. Psychology examines the ways that we can identify differences among people and how we can use this knowledge to predict future behaviour. Having focused on differences in intelligence in Chapter 7, in this chapter we turn our attention to differences in personality and psychosocial functioning.

As social beings, people develop models for understanding and predicting other people's behaviour. If you were asked to describe the key psychological characteristics of your friends and family members, you probably wouldn't have difficulty coming up with a list. As you looked over your lists for the different people you know, you'd probably find that you used descriptors such as "friendly," "trustworthy," "sociable," "honest," "serious," "caring," and "fun-loving." These concepts refer to a person's tendency to consistently behave in a specific way—otherwise known as personality traits or dispositions. Moreover, we tend to use these concepts not just for those we know well, but also for ourselves, for people we barely know, characters in books and movies, and even for our pets. Over the course of a day, we seek patterns in the behaviours of others (*Seth is grumpy today*), generate hypotheses about why those patterns occur (*I wonder whether he's worried about the mid-term*), making inferences about other personal characteristics based on these patterns (*He can really be a perfectionist at times*), and predicting future behaviours from these patterns (*He'll probably be so hard on himself that he will be unbearable when he's doing his honours thesis next year*).

personality traits: the tendency to consistently behave in specific ways.

objective personality tests: tests that can be scored objectively, always using the same scoring system.

behaviour checklists: lists of behaviours that are rated for frequency, intensity, or duration.

projective personality tests: tests requiring drawings or a response to ambiguous stimuli, based on the assumption that responses reveal information about personality structure.

Over the past century, psychologists have constructed literally thousands of measures of individual differences. Many of these measures are designed to assess **personality traits**, which psychologists define as consistencies in behaviour, emotions, and attitudes that are evident across situations and across time. Personality theorists and researchers work to examine the influences of genetics and life experiences on the development of traits (Mischel, 2004) and how traits are expressed in everyday life (Hampson, 2012). Clinical psychologists are active in both researching personality traits and in assessing personality traits for clinical purposes. As you may know from taking a personality theory course, personality measures vary in the scope of the constructs they are designed to assess. Some are intended to measure very broad constructs such as extraversion or neuroticism; others focus on highly specific constructs such as perfectionism or motivation for academic tasks. Most personality measures are based on self-report data and are often called **objective personality tests** because they can be scored objectively (i.e., the same scoring system is always used). Other self-report measures are less complex than personality tests and are derived from descriptive characteristics of an experience or an event rather than from personality theories. These **behaviour checklists** or symptom checklists are designed to provide information about the nature of an individual's experience (e.g., psychological distress, mood states, and feared situations) and the frequency or severity of the experience. **Projective personality tests** represent a very different approach to assessing personality characteristics. Projective tests require the test-taker to respond either to ambiguous stimuli such as pictures or incomplete sentences or to generate drawings according to the assessor's instructions. Projective tests are based on the assumption that valuable information on aspects of the test-taker's personality structure can be gleaned from responses to these ambiguous stimuli.

In this chapter, we will review some of the major objective personality measures, behaviour and symptom checklists, as well as frequently used projective personality measures. To help you appreciate the strengths and weaknesses of these types of measures, we begin by discussing some of the considerations that influence their clinical usefulness and accuracy.

THE PERSON-SITUATION DEBATE

Since the late 1960s, researchers and clinicians have debated a fundamental question about personality. Although most people (and most personality theorists) believe that personality traits influence the way people behave and are, therefore, responsible for the apparent stability of behaviour across time and situations, others have raised the question: what if this stability is illusory? In other words, what would happen if measures of personality couldn't accurately predict individual differences among people or the behaviour of an individual? This was the challenge—often called the person-situation debate—that Walter Mischel launched in his 1968 book *Personality and Assessment*. Mischel reviewed decades of research into personality assessment and the relation between personality and actual behaviour. At that time, theorists and clinicians assumed a direct connection between personality traits or dispositions and actual behaviour. Therefore, it was believed that the more an individual possessed a certain trait, the more likely that person was to behave in a manner consistent with the trait in any environment or situation. For example, Amanda, who is an extraverted person, would be expected to always behave in an outgoing, confident way, at home, at school, and with friends. However, Mischel's literature review revealed that the link between trait scores and actual behaviour rarely exceeded a correlation of .30! Moreover, he also provided examples of research demonstrating that variations across situations seemed to be more important than personality measures in accounting for behavioural variability. To demonstrate this point, think about what is more likely to influence Amanda's behaviour at a party—her personality characteristics or contextual factors such as whether it was a student party, a reception given by a potential employer, or a party to celebrate her grandparents' wedding anniversary. Although she may score high on a measure of extroversion, is she likely to behave in a highly extroverted way regardless of the type of party?

Is there consistency between your behaviour and emotional reactions? In reviewing your own psychological reactions, how important do you think your personality is in determining your responses? How important are the demands of the situation you find yourself in, such as the expectations of others?

Mischel's work, combined with some other conundrums personality researchers were facing (such as the limits to self-knowledge; see Viewpoint Box 8.1), led many clinical psychologists to question the clinical value of personality measures. This scepticism coincided with the rising influence of behavioural approaches to treatment. Instead of relying on traditional personality measures, clinical psychologists using a behavioural approach to treatment preferred to use situation-specific

©iStock.com/MichaelDeLeon

People often behave differently in different contexts.

or disorder-specific checklists and rating scales. The current use of such checklists in clinical practice largely developed from the activities of these early behavioural and cognitive-behavioural clinicians and researchers. They viewed cross-situational variability in people's actions as a source of important information. For example, if Jacob, who is depressed, feels discouraged while on the job in an information technology company, but has great energy in his volunteer work at the animal shelter, it may be valuable to help him (a) learn about the conditions in which the symptoms are less severe and (b) use this knowledge to try to increase involvement in situations in which the symptoms are lower.

In the decades since the publication of Mischel's book, there have been substantial developments in the science of personality. It now appears that variability across situations co-exists with stability across time. Those emphasizing the power of situational influences and those emphasizing the power of personality were both correct (Fleeson, 2004; Fournier, Moskowitz, & Zuroff, 2008). Having information on both situational characteristics and personality characteristics can enhance the prediction of human behaviour. As you will see later in the chapter, the most commonly taught and used personality measures have been available for many decades. Unfortunately, advances in personality research have not been matched by changes in clinical assessment tools designed to assess personality.

VIEWPOINT BOX 8.1

HOW WELL DO WE (AND CAN WE) KNOW OURSELVES?

We usually take for granted that we can know ourselves fairly well. Most people feel confident in their ability to accurately describe themselves, their attitudes, and their personal preferences. The assumption that people can accurately describe themselves is implicit in all objective personality tests. Yet, for well over a century, psychological theorists and researchers have questioned the extent to which we can actually know our own mental states and the causes of our actions.

Based on early Freudian theories, many people view the non-conscious—or unconscious—aspect of our existence as something that can be accessed through a great deal of conscious effort. The metaphor often used is that of an archaeological dig that yields ever more fascinating material the deeper one digs into the past. In contrast, the contemporary view of the unconscious is rather less romantic than this. Most cognitive, social cognitive, and neuroscience researchers see the human mind as a collection of information processors that function largely out of our awareness and that probably developed long before consciousness emerged in our species (Wilson, 2002). According to this research-informed perspective, no amount of "digging" (i.e., introspection) is likely to result in a more accurate understanding of ourselves, our motives, or our past experiences.

Wilson and Dunn (2004) reviewed research relevant to the questions of (a) how well we can know and understand ourselves and (b) the obstacles that interfere with efforts to attain greater self-knowledge. Many of their conclusions may surprise you. First, despite decades

CONTINUED . . .

of theorizing and research, there is little compelling evidence for the existence of the Freudian concept of repression by which information is kept out of consciousness but is stored in memory. There is, however, substantial evidence for the existence of conscious suppression (i.e., trying not to think about or focus on something). Most research indicates that suppression often fails to accomplish the goal of rendering information unavailable to consciousness. Ironically, efforts to suppress thoughts, memories, or feelings can frequently result in people paying even more attention than usual to the information they are attempting to ignore (Wegner, 1994). See for yourself: for the next few minutes, actively try not to think about a sumo wrestler wearing a ballet tutu.

So, if the unconscious is not the repository of unwanted and undesirable urges and experiences, what is it then? Psychological research has firmly established that a great deal of non-conscious processing does occur but, according to Wilson and Dunn, this processing is largely related to matters of perception, attention, learning, and automatic judgments. Contrary to Freud's hypotheses, current research indicates there are no motivational or emotional impediments to people easily accessing this unconscious content. Instead, much of the unconscious is simply inaccessible to conscious inspection, either because it was never processed in consciousness to begin with (e.g., we are not consciously aware of what we do to perceive depth) or because a simple, repetitive task has become automatic and removed from conscious awareness (e.g., although when we learn to drive a car we are conscious of each action, as our skill develops, performing the various subtasks becomes automatic or unconscious).

If introspection cannot help us better understand ourselves, can we take other steps to increase the accuracy of our self-knowledge? Wilson and Dunn suggested that we could learn much about ourselves by attending to how others view us. However, research indicates that most people are unable to accurately learn about how others see them, especially if those views do not match their own views of themselves. Social cognitive research indicates that the best route to self-knowledge is to intentionally observe our own behaviours and decisions as they occur.

SELF-PRESENTATION BIASES

In many circumstances, people may be motivated to present themselves in a particular light. In some cases, such as those involving child custody evaluations or assessments to determine the suitability for police training, people may have a desire to downplay any personal problems and to appear as resilient and mentally healthy as possible. In other circumstances, such as when seeking compensation for work- or accident-related psychological problems, people may be inclined to overemphasize their distress and difficulties.

Can you think of times when you deliberately underemphasized or overemphasized physical problems or emotional difficulties that you were experiencing? Did this seem justified to you at the time? Did your presentation of your problems have the effect on other people that you hoped it would have? Are there times when you think other people are downplaying or highlighting their problems?

validity scales: scales designed to detect whether a person is faking good, faking bad, or responding randomly.

malingering: emphasizing negative characteristics and deliberately presenting a more problematic picture.

To address these possible biases, most personality inventories designed for clinical use, such as the Minnesota Multiphasic Personality Inventory (MMPI), the Millon Clinical Multiaxial Inventory (MCMI), and the Personality Assessment Inventory (PAI), include **validity scales**. Generally speaking, the validity scales focus on three possible tendencies that could distort the answers given by test-takers: emphasizing positive characteristics ("faking good"), **malingering** or emphasizing negative characteristics ("faking bad"), and inconsistent or random responding to test items (this can occur when the person does not take the test seriously or when the person is cognitively impaired). You will find more details on the validity of these validity scales when we present information on these inventories later in the chapter. In addition to malingering scales that are part of large-scale personality tests, there are also tests specifically designed to evaluate possible malingering. The Test of Memory Malingering (Tombaugh, 1997), for example, was designed to assess whether an individual with established or suspected neurological impairments is exaggerating his or her memory deficits. This test has been demonstrated to accurately detect almost half of individuals attempting to simulate memory problems (Mossman, Wygant, & Gervais, 2012)—a noteworthy outcome, given the relatively low base rate of this behaviour. Of course, psychologists often examine other data when they have concerns about the accuracy of information provided to them by those they are assessing. Information obtained from interviews with other people who know the person being assessed (e.g., partner, employer) and from a review of relevant records (e.g., medical records, police records, school records) can be invaluable in this regard.

To avoid the problem of intentional misrepresentation, many clinical psychologists have advocated the use of projective personality tests, reasoning that their ambiguous nature makes it difficult for clients to exaggerate or minimize psychological problems. The many studies on this issue have yielded inconclusive findings. In one study, Meisner (1988) instructed half of a sample of non-depressed undergraduate student participants to act as if they were depressed when responding to psychological tests. To assist them in this, he also provided them with a clinical description of depression and offered a cash incentive for convincingly displaying depression. Compared with the control group participants who completed the measures in an honest manner, those in the malingering condition had higher scores on the Beck Depression Inventory (a symptom checklist) as well as on several Rorschach indices of depression (a projective personality test). This suggests that the projective measure was just as susceptible to faking as the symptom checklist. In contrast, Bornstein, Rossner, Hill, and Stepanian (1994) found that, when instructed to deliberately present as dependent or independent, undergraduate student participants could do so effectively on a self-report measure of dependency but not on a Rorschach dependency scale. So, the research on whether projective tests are less easily faked is inconclusive.

DEVELOPING CULTURALLY APPROPRIATE MEASURES

How can we ensure that tests are culturally sensitive and appropriate?

Given the multicultural nature of most countries, personality measures must be relevant and unbiased across cultural and ethnic groups. Malgady (1996) proposed a radical change in the ways that clinical psychologists react when there is a paucity of research evidence. Rather than approaching these issues in the usual way that null hypotheses are generated—that no biases or differences exist—he argued that both practitioners and researchers should assume that measures *are* culturally biased unless there are data to suggest the opposite. This has provoked efforts to carefully examine the relevance of personality measures and the potential for bias across cultural and ethnic groups. Research has shown that a growing number of measures are suitable for use across cultural and ethnic groups; however, not all commonly used clinical instruments have such evidence supporting their use.

Tests can be biased or unfair in several ways. First, the test content may not be equally applicable or relevant to all cultural groups. Test items that accurately capture the essence of the underlying psychological construct for one cultural group may not be as appropriate for other cultural groups. In an early study on the influence of ethnicity on responses to the California Personality Inventory, for example, Cross and Burger (1982) found that African American and European American university students responded differently to more than a third of the test items. Jayawickreme, Jayawickreme, Atanasov, Goonasekera, and Foa (2012) found that although commonly used measures of depression and posttraumatic stress disorder (PTSD) were predictive of the functional impairment experienced by Sri Lankans directly affected by war, impairment was better predicted by scores on a measure of distress that used local idioms. Such evidence of incremental validity (see Chapters 4 and 5) demonstrates the possible value that culturally specific measures may have. Second, the pattern of validity coefficients may not be similar across groups. For example, an association between a negative attributional style and depressive symptoms may be much larger for one group than for another. Third, the use of a cut-off score on a scale to classify individuals may not be equally

Measures must be relevant and unbiased across cultural and ethnic groups.

accurate across groups. As described in Chapter 5, many personality inventories use *T*-scores (i.e., scores based on group means and standard deviations) of 65 or 70 to determine whether an individual's responses fall outside the normal range. Bias related to cut-off scores could mean that those in some cultural and ethnic groups could be over- or under-identified as having scores in the clinical range. Using the California Personality Inventory, Davis, Hoffman, and Nelson (1990) found that Native American women, compared with European American women, scored much higher on measures of passivity and assistance seeking. A clinical psychologist using this test with a Native American woman would, therefore, need to consider the impact of cultural influences when interpreting the meaning of the obtained test scores. A fourth form of bias could occur with respect to the test's underlying structure. Researchers frequently use a statistical procedure called factor analysis to explore exactly how components of a construct relate to each other. For example, a measure of anxiety may have a factor structure that has cognitive and physical components for one group but only a physical component for another. If this pattern of results occurred, it would mean that the test is tapping different constructs in the two groups.

So how should a clinical psychologist conduct an assessment with a client from an ethnic minority background? Haynes, Smith, and Hunsley (2011) suggested that psychologists should (a) use measures that have been shown to be psychometrically sound for people who come from the same ethnic group as the client; (b) consult published norms relevant to the client's ethnic group in interpreting the test results; and (c) adopt multiple assessment methods to minimize errors that might be associated with any one method or test. What if recommendations (a) and (b) cannot be followed? If the best measures available do not have such strong validation (including evidence of lack of test bias) and relevant norms, then caution must be exercised in interpreting the results obtained with the tests. At a minimum, the psychologist should indicate in the assessment report that the accuracy and validity of the results may be less than ideal. For example, the psychologist might report the test score and interpret it according to test norms, but qualify this by indicating that both the test items and the norms may not provide an optimal assessment of the client's psychological functioning. If the administration of the test was not standardized (e.g., if the psychologist translated some of the items to ensure that the client understood the questions) and/or if the psychologist has significant concerns about the accuracy of the test results, then the prudent course of action would be not to report test scores in a report and to use the test only to aid in generating hypotheses about client functioning (cf. Fernandez, Boccaccini, & Noland, 2007).

There is an increasing array of psychological tests that were developed in English and then translated and validated in another language. As guides to the translation and cross-cultural adaptation of tests become more commonly available (e.g., van Widenfelt, Treffers, de Beurs, Siebelink, & Koudijs, 2005), it is likely that the rate at which translated measures become available will also increase. According to the International Testing Commission (2001), translation and adaptation of a test requires five steps. First, items are translated into the second language, this version is translated back into the initial language by a second translator, and the two versions are compared. This procedure is known as back translation. Second, pilot testing should be conducted with the translated measure to ensure there are no problems with the comprehension of items. Third, evidence of good reliability should be obtained on the translated measure. Fourth, scores on the measure should be restandardized using norms specific to the translated measure. Fifth, construct validation efforts should be undertaken to determine whether the instrument measures the same psychological qualities in both languages. Of course, before a psychologist decides to use a translated test, it is critical to determine the extent to which the supporting research is relevant to the client being assessed. When assessing Spanish translations, Fernandez, Boccaccini, and Noland (2007) encouraged psychologists to consider the extent to which there is research support for a test in various Hispanic populations. This is critical, as a test adapted for use in Spain may not necessarily be appropriate for use with Hispanic Americans or residents of Latin America. Similarly, a test adapted for a French Canadian population would not necessarily be suitable for use with a European French or Haitian French population. Subtle linguistic differences among these populations might affect the way in which respondents interpret test items. Moreover, the reliability and validity data from one population may not necessarily generalize to other populations.

When using psychological tests with members of ethnic minority groups (including both translated tests and English-language tests validated for use with the minority group), psychologists must always ensure that they take into account the client's life circumstances when they interpret the test data and integrate these hypotheses with other clinical information. In particular, a large number of cultural factors must be considered. A fine example of how psychologists should approach the assessment of members of ethnic minority groups was provided by Acevdeo-Polakovich et al. (2007). Exhibit 8.1 presents these authors' recommendations regarding the types of issues that must be considered when addressing ethnicity or culture in psychological assessments.

Exhibit 8.1 Assessing Cultural and Linguistic Factors

Immigration History

- Length of time residing in the country.
- Circumstances surrounding migration from country of origin (e.g., immigration for economic reasons, refugee).
- Current legal status in the country.

Contact with Other Cultural Groups

- Ethnic composition of the area in which the client lives.
- Extent to which client stays within the area in which he or she lives.
- Frequency of changes in residence and impact on the client.

Acculturative Status

- Cultural norms, behaviours, and values.
- Exposure-adherence to traditional culture and exposure-adherence to the dominant culture.

Acculturative Stress

- Impact of acculturation on client (i.e., stress and distress).

Socioeconomic Status

- Financial resources (e.g., family income), interpersonal resources (e.g., educational level), and non-material resources (e.g., family structure).

Language

- Client language preference and ability/fluency in language(s) used in the assessment.
- Verbal and non-verbal communication skills.

Adapted from Acevedo-Polakovich et al. (2007).

THE CLINICAL UTILITY OF SELF-REPORT AND PROJECTIVE MEASURES

Given the challenges we described in the preceding sections, how useful are self-report and projective measures in practice? The volume of research on personality measures and behaviour/symptom checklists is staggering, involving many tens of thousands of published studies. There is replicated, cumulative research on scores of personality traits and behaviour/symptom profiles that has greatly advanced our knowledge of human functioning. For constructs such as anxiety, narcissism, self-esteem, attachment style, or optimism, psychologists have a wealth of empirical evidence to draw upon in understanding individual differences in human experience. In considering the impact of this research, it is essential to distinguish between basic and applied perspectives. Basic research has enriched our knowledge of personality enormously in the past few decades. We now know a great deal about the manner in which personality traits are expressed and the ways in which they are reciprocally influenced by the person's life circumstances (Mischel, 2004; Hampson, 2012).

Addressing the applied value of this research literature is a different matter. Simply because psychologists know a great deal about personality determinants, structure, and expression does not mean that all (or any) of this knowledge is useful in making changes in people's daily functioning. Instead, there must be firm evidence that the measures, and the research on the measures, have clinical utility. Hunsley and Bailey (1999) proposed distinct and increasingly stringent ways to define clinical utility by addressing three questions:

clinical utility: the extent to which a test and the resulting data improve upon typical clinical decision-making and treatment outcome.

1. Is the test considered useful by clinical practitioners?
2. Is there replicated evidence that the measurement data provide reliable and valid information about clients' psychological functioning?
3. Does the use of the test and the resulting data improve upon typical clinical decision-making and treatment outcome? In other words, does using the measure eventually make a difference in terms of the client's functioning?

With respect to the first definition of clinical utility, it is indisputable that self-report and projective tests are seen as useful for general clinical practice. Table 8.1 summarizes results from surveys of APA-accredited clinical training programs (Childs & Eyde, 2002), APA-accredited internships (Clemence & Handler, 2001), and clinical psychologist members of the APA (Camara, Nathan, & Puente, 2000) with respect to the most commonly taught or used psychological tests. In all three surveys, the Wechsler intelligence tests were consistently seen as the most important measures in clinical practice. As illustrated in Table 8.1, there is also remarkable consistency among endorsements of the self-report and projective measures. Among self-report personality measures, knowledge of the various versions of the MMPI and the MCMI was seen as

TABLE 8.1 ■ Rank Ordering of Self-Report and Projective Measures among All Clinical Tests

Test	Taught in Clinical Graduate Courses[1]	Recommended for Internship[2]	Used by Clinical Psychologists[3]
MMPI	3	2	2
MCMI	8	8	10 (tied)
BDI	--	4	10 (tied)
Rorschach	4	3	4
TAT	5	5	6

[1]Childs & Eyde (2002); [2]Clemence & Handler (2001); [3]Camara, Nathan, & Puente (2000).

essential. Two projective personality tests, the Rorschach Inkblot Test and the Thematic Apperception Test (TAT), were consistently ranked among the most important measures for students and practitioners. One self-report symptom checklist, the Beck Depression Inventory (BDI), was viewed as important for both internship training and general clinical practice.

Let's move now to the second definition—whether there is evidence that the test can provide reliable and valid information about clients. Again, voluminous data indicate that many self-report tests and some projective tests provide psychometrically sound information. Some examples from the comprehensive report on psychological testing by Meyer and colleagues (2001) illustrate this point. These researchers drew data from more than 125 meta-analyses to illustrate the validity of a number of psychological tests. As we mentioned in Chapter 4, effect sizes in meta-analysis can be expressed as either differences between groups or as correlation coefficients. Meyer et al. reported correlations including attributions for negative events and depression, $r = .27$; MCMI scale scores and ability to detect depressive or psychotic disorders, $r = .37$; Rorschach-derived dependency scores and dependent behaviour, $r = .37$; MMPI scale scores and conceptually relevant criterion measures, $r = .39$; and MMPI validity scales and detection of known or suspected malingering, $r = .45$.

So, what do these numbers mean? Is this good news or bad news? It may be useful to compare them with other validity findings in health care research. Meyer et al. (2001) reported that, for example, traditional electrocardiogram stress tests and a diagnosis of coronary artery disease are correlated at $r = .22$, screening mammogram results and detection of breast cancer within a year are correlated at $r = .32$, and conventional dental X-ray and diagnosis of between-tooth cavities are correlated at $r = .43$. So, compared with validity evidence from other health care assessments, the results for many psychological tests appear similar, suggesting that psychological tests may be as useful as assessments commonly used in health care systems. Nevertheless, these results should be interpreted cautiously. In contrast to the situation for many medical or dental tests, there is surprisingly little evidence that psychological test results provide information that makes a difference in treatment provision or treatment outcome (e.g., Garb, Klein, & Grove, 2002).

This leads us to the third definition of clinical utility. Unfortunately, even though the need for evaluations of clinical utility has been apparent for many years (e.g., Mash, 1979), there are limited data supporting the clinical utility of psychological tests (Nelson-Gray, 2003). The only tools with broad supporting evidence of their utility are (a) behaviourally oriented assessment strategies that rely on idiographic measurement and some behavioural/symptom checklists (Haynes, Leisen, & Blaine, 1997) and (b) treatment monitoring measures (Whipple & Lambert, 2011). Much of the research on the efficacy and effectiveness of psychological treatments has assessed patient variables with behaviour and symptom checklists. It would be reasonable to assume, therefore, that these checklists have substantial clinical utility. Yet there is little research that has examined the degree to which these measures are necessary for the success of these treatments. The same is true of the most commonly used personality tests. Despite decades of validity research and frequent clinical use, there is no scientific evidence that MMPI or Rorschach scores have a meaningful impact on the outcome of psychological services (Hunsley & Bailey, 2001).

Most of the instruments discussed in this chapter were designed to evaluate a person's psychosocial functioning. Many of them are very good at doing this. However, as you learned in Chapter 1, over the decades, clinical psychologists' principal activities have shifted from assessment to intervention. Consequently, these instruments have been increasingly used to inform treatment planning decisions—a purpose that they were never originally designed to serve. As you learned in Chapter 5, the validity of a test is very much conditional on the purpose for which it is being used and the population with which it is used. This means that an instrument that has scientific support for evaluating personality characteristics and psychosocial functioning is not necessarily valid for determining the optimal ways to enhance or improve problematic aspects of personality and psychosocial functioning. In other words, as you learned in Chapter 5, instruments that may be useful for assessment-focused evaluations may not be useful for intervention-focused evaluations.

What are criteria by which we can judge whether a test is useful?

The lack of evidence of intervention-related utility of self-report and projective tests is of great concern and makes it difficult to justify time-consuming and expensive personality assessments conducted for intervention-focused evaluative purposes. This gap in the literature could easily be addressed using straightforward research designs. For example, in an experimental design, all patients who are about to receive treatment could complete a self-report personality measure. Half of the therapists would be randomly selected to receive the results of this test and the others would receive nothing. This would allow the researcher to determine whether the test results influence (a) therapists to alter the nature of the treatment offered to clients and (b) the outcome of the treatment. Lima and colleagues (2005) used just such a design to examine the value of clinicians having access to patient MMPI-2 data at the beginning of treatment. They found that having these data available had no impact on the number of sessions patients attended, whether therapy ended prematurely, or overall patient improvement in functioning assessed at the end of treatment.

So, why has there been so little research on the utility of assessment instruments? You may recall learning in Chapter 1 the distinction between efficacy and effectiveness in the context of treatment research. There is a different emphasis on internal and external validity in these two types of studies, with efficacy trials constructed to be high on internal validity and effectiveness trials to be high on external validity. As we will describe later in the text, researchers have tended to ensure that a treatment works at the level of efficacy trials before moving on to examine effectiveness. It is likely that the same type of decision has occurred with psychological instruments. A great deal of research effort has been devoted to evaluating the reliability and validity of data provided by psychological instruments. In many ways, this is akin to the purpose of efficacy studies, inasmuch as the basic question addressed by the research is whether or not the test (or treatment) "works." The applied question of whether the test has utility in actual clinical services is similar to the question behind effectiveness trials (i.e., does this treatment work in real-world clinical settings?). Just as psychotherapy researchers are now beginning to attend more to effectiveness trials, some assessment researchers are now beginning to focus more of their efforts on the very important question of the clinical utility of our assessment instruments.

SELF-REPORT PERSONALITY MEASURES

In the following sections, we present the most commonly used personality inventories in clinical psychology (French-language versions are available for most). The original major personality inventory, the Minnesota Multiphasic Personality Inventory, is now available in forms appropriate for adults (MMPI-2) and adolescents (MMPI-A). These inventories provide broad coverage of many clinical syndromes and other characteristics relevant for typical assessment and intervention purposes. Based on a distinct theoretical approach to psychopathology and keyed to DSM conditions, the Millon Clinical Multiaxial Inventory-III (for adults) and the Millon Adolescent Clinical Inventory (for adolescents) are frequently used by clinicians because of their emphasis on personality styles and disorders. One of the newest multi-scale inventories, the Personality Assessment Inventory, is gaining support among clinical psychologists because its main scales are designed to address common DSM diagnoses. Table 8.2 provides summary information on the basic characteristics of the MMPI-2, MCMI-III, and PAI.

TABLE 8.2 ■ Comparing the MMPI-2, the MCMI-III, and the PAI

	MMPI-2	MCMI-III	PAI
# of items	567	175	344
Response format	True/False	True/False	4-point scale
Age range	18 and over	18 and over	18 and over
Reading level	Grade 6–8	Grade 8	Grade 4
Administration time	60–90 minutes	25–30 minutes	40–50 minutes

MMPI-2 and MMPI-A

Background Issues

The Minnesota Multiphasic Personality Inventory (MMPI) and the revised versions of the test, the MMPI-2 (for use with adults) and the MMPI-A (for use with adolescents), are the most commonly taught and used self-report (or objective) personality measures in clinical psychology. The original MMPI was published in 1943 by Starke Hathaway and J. Charnley McKinley based on their test development research at the University of Minnesota Hospitals. Their goal was to construct a self-report test that could provide accurate information on symptom severity and possible diagnoses for adult patients suspected of having mental disorders. Up until then, assessment data were collected via interviews by hospital staff, which entailed a great deal of time, effort, and expense. Also, as you may remember learning in Chapter 6, inter-rater reliability for unstructured interviews is generally poor. In developing the MMPI, the researchers relied on a test construction strategy known as an empirical criterion-keying approach, which involves the generation and analysis of a pool of items. Items are retained for inclusion in the test if they discriminate between two clearly defined groups (in this case, patients with mental disorders and a comparison group made up of patients' friends and family members, recent high school graduates, and patients with medical disorders). First, the researchers established a pool of 1,000 items from existing personality tests, clinical reports, and other sources of clinical information. Following data analyses of group differences in item responses, almost 500 items were eliminated. With the later inclusion of scales measuring masculinity-femininity and social introversion, the final version of the original MMPI consisted of 550 items. Within years, the MMPI became widely used and researched; the MMPI was also translated and validated for use in many countries outside the United States (Butcher & Beutler, 2003; Groth-Marnat, 2009).

empirical criterion-keying approach: a method of test construction that involves the generation and analysis of a pool of items; those items that discriminate between two clearly defined groups are retained in the scale.

Addressing concerns about the potential for test-takers to either intentionally or unconsciously influence the way in which they answered the items on the test, Hathaway and McKinley developed several scales to assess threats to the validity of responses to the MMPI (such as answering in an unrealistically positive manner). As time passed and the MMPI became the dominant self-report personality measure used by psychologists, concerns were raised about wording problems, the outdated content of some items, the non-representativeness of the original normative comparison group, and the test's technical shortcomings stemming from the use of empirical criterion-keying methods.

James Butcher headed a project to revise the MMPI that began in 1982. The researchers in this project faced a substantial challenge in attempting both to (a) improve upon the original test by using better test construction strategies and obtaining representative normative data and (b) ensure continuity with the original test by retaining the MMPI's main scales. After some items were updated and a number of provisional new items were added, data were collected from more than 2,500 American adults. Extensive data analysis led to the elimination of some old and some new items, which resulted in the 567-item MMPI-2 (Butcher, Dahlstrom, Graham, Tellegen, & Kaemmer, 1989). The first 370 items on the test contain all of the original validity and clinical scales, with the remaining items providing information for a range of additional scales designed to supplement the information available from the original MMPI scales. Many of these new scales were formed by means of a content approach to test construction, which involves developing items specifically designed to tap the construct being assessed. This approach to test construction is much more consistent with current views of optimal test development strategies.

content approach: a method of test construction that involves developing items specifically designed to tap the construct being assessed.

Many clinical psychologists who were familiar with the MMPI adopted the MMPI-2 slowly and cautiously. Changing from one version to the next required purchasing new test and scoring materials as well as learning how to interpret the new measure. Eventually, despite ongoing criticisms about weaknesses in the test construction procedures used by the restandardization committee (e.g., Helmes & Reddon, 1993), the revised test became even more popular than the original because of its improved content, coverage of psychological symptoms, and standardization sample. The MMPI-2 is now available in more than two dozen languages (Butcher & Beutler, 2003).

Over the years, problems specific to test use with adolescents became apparent: for example, the MMPI was too long for many youth to complete, the reading level was too high, and the norms were not suitable for use in interpreting the scores obtained by adolescents (Groth-Marnat, 2009). This led to the development of the MMPI-Adolescent (MMPI-A; Butcher et al., 1992). This test includes a normative sample of adolescents, fewer items (478) than the MMPI-2, as well as reworded and additional items of particular relevance to youth.

Exhibits 8.2, 8.3, and 8.4 provide information on the main scales found in both the MMPI-2 and the MMPI-A. As shown in Exhibit 8.2, the scales assess potential biased responding in several ways, by detecting overly negative, overly positive, and careless, random, or otherwise biased responses. The range of validity scales provide a thorough evaluation of biases in self-presentation, and even allow for the determination of whether the way in which a person responded to the test items changed as he or she took the test!

Exhibit 8.2 MMPI Validity Scales

Cannot Say (?): This scale is the total number of unanswered items. A large number of unanswered items indicates defensive responding.

Lie Scale (L): A measure of self-presentation that is unrealistically positive.

Infrequency Scale (F): A measure of self-presentation that is very unfavourable. This can indicate a desire to present oneself as having severe psychopathology *or* it can be an accurate report of substantial distress, disorganization, and confusion.

Defensiveness Scale (K): A measure of unwillingness to disclose personal information and problems. The scores on some of the clinical scales are adjusted based on the test-taker's *K* score.

Back F Scale (FB): Similar to the F scale, the items for this scale all occur in the final third of the inventory. The scale measures a possible change in self-presentation, which may be due to a change in test-taking strategy.

Variable Response Inconsistency Scale (VRIN): A number of the items for this scale have either similar or opposite content. The VRIN measures the tendency to answer these item pairs inconsistently and may reflect random or confused responding to the test.

True Response Inconsistency Scale (TRIN): The TRIN scale is based on answers to item pairs that are opposite in content. A very high score indicates a tendency to give "True" answers indiscriminately; a very low score indicates a tendency to give "False" answers indiscriminately.

Exhibit 8.3 provides details on the traditional clinical scales that were part of the MMPI and that were retained for the revised tests. Exhibit 8.4 provides information about the most clinically relevant scales. These so-called content scales were developed specifically to address some of the test users' needs (such as more thoroughly assessing anxiety and depressive symptoms and having information on factors related to family, work, and treatment contexts). Most psychologists examine the results obtained from both the basic clinical scales and the content scales.

Exhibit 8.3 MMPI Clinical Scales

Scale 1 (Hs: Hypochondriasis): Measures the tendency to be preoccupied with one's health and to be unlikely to connect psychological problems to the experience of some physical symptoms.

Scale 2 (D: Depression): Measures common cognitive, physical, and interpersonal symptoms of depression.

Scale 3 (Hy: Hysteria): Measures the tendency to develop physical symptoms when stressed and to minimize the extent of interpersonal problems.

Scale 4 (Pd: Psychopathic Deviate): Measures the tendency toward rebellious attitudes, conflict with authorities and family, and engagement in antisocial activities.

Scale 5 (Mf: Masculinity-Femininity): Measures gender-stereotyped interests, beliefs, and activities.

Scale 6 (Pa: Paranoia): Measures interpersonal sensitivity, feelings of being mistreated, and, at the extreme, delusions of persecution.

Scale 7 (Pt: Psychasthenia): Measures the tendency toward worry, apprehension, rumination, and fears of loss of control.

Scale 8 (Sc: Schizophrenia): Measures the tendency to withdraw and experience social alienation, feel inferior, and, at the extreme, experience delusions, hallucinations, and extreme disorganization.

Scale 9 (Ma: Hypomania): Measures the tendency toward hyperarousal, excessive energy, low frustration tolerance, and agitation.

Scale 0 (Si: Social Introversion): Measures introversion, lack of comfort in social contexts, and over-controlled style of coping.

Exhibit 8.4 MMPI Content Scales

Anxiety (ANX): A measure of general anxiety and worry.

Fears (FRS): A measure of the fear of specific objects, events, and situations.

Obsessiveness (OBS): A measure of indecisiveness and obsessiveness.

Depression (DEP): A measure of depressive symptoms.

Health Concerns (HEA): A measure of general health concerns.

Bizarre Mentation (BIZ): A measure of very peculiar or psychotic thought processes.

Anger (ANG): A measure of anger, aggression, and lack of control.

Cynicism (CYN): A measure of beliefs related to a general lack of trust in people and little faith in their intentions.

Antisocial Practices (ASP): A measure of antisocial attitudes and a history of engaging in antisocial acts such as stealing.

Type A Behavior (TPA): A measure of the Type A personality (i.e., characteristics of impatience, irritability, and being easily annoyed).

Low Self-Esteem (LSE): A measure of general self-esteem.

Social Discomfort (SOD): A measure of social introversion.

Family Problems (FAM): A measure of reported family conflict and the tendency to have characteristics that increase the likelihood of current interpersonal conflict.

Work Interference (WRK): A measure of work-related impairments.

Negative Treatment Indicators (TRT): A measure of negative attitudes toward health care professionals and mental health treatments.

Recent major developments with the MMPI involved the development of restructured clinical scales and the inclusion of the Symptom Validity Scale. One of the long-standing problems with the MMPI clinical scales was the high intercorrelations among scales—in some studies, the shared variance among pairs of scales has been 75% or higher (Nichols, 2006). Additionally, because small samples of patients were used in the original empirical criterion-keying approach to MMPI development, concerns about the validity and relevance of the clinical scales have often been raised. As a result, Tellegen et al. (2003) undertook a revision of the eight main clinical scales (i.e., not including scales 5 and 0). These researchers used a factor analytic strategy to develop scales that did not overlap and had items that were specific to the construct being assessed by the scale. To do this, they first identified a group of items from across the clinical scales that formed a general distress factor, which they labelled Demoralization. Then, by removing the variance due to this demoralization factor from each of the eight clinical scales, they were able to identify a set of unique items for each scale that best represented the underlying construct of the scale. So, for example, on the basis of such factor analyses, items were eliminated from scale 1 to yield the new restructured clinical scale they labelled Somatic Complaints. Although guidelines for scoring and interpreting the restructured clinical scales are available, there continues to be vigorous scientific debate on the validity and utility of these new scales (e.g., Butcher, 2010; Nichols, 2006; Rogers, Sewell, Harrison, & Jordan, 2006; Tellegen et al., 2006). The Symptom Validity Scale (known as FBS) is used to identify a test-taker who is reporting a very high number of psychological symptoms. Meta-analytic evidence, from over 80 studies, has demonstrated that this scale is correlated with other MMPI-2 validity scales and has some value in identifying individuals who may be making exaggerated claims of psychological impairment (Nelson, Hoelzle, Sweet, Arbisi, & Demakis, 2010).

Trainees learning to use the MMPI often complain about the number of scales to score and consider. Aside from the challenge of learning what all the different scales are meant to assess, can you see other difficulties stemming from this "embarrassment of riches"?

Norms, Reliability, and Validity

The normative sample for the MMPI-2 consisted of more than 1,400 American women and 1,100 American men. Participants were randomly selected within a sampling frame that was generally representative of the American population in terms of ethnicity, socioeconomic status, and geographical location. The only limitation is a slight under-representation of adults with lower education and lower income. Consequently, for these individuals, the cut-off scores for determining the presence of clinical problems may be too low. This means that the test is likely to yield a high number of false positives (i.e., inaccurately identifying substantial clinical problems) in the evaluation of patients of lower socioeconomic levels (Nichols, 2001). Clinicians therefore need to be aware of the possible tendency to overpathologize (i.e., exaggerate and overestimate the extent of psychopathology) such patients. As for the MMPI-A, the normative sample consists of more than 800 female adolescents and 800 male adolescents who were representative of the American population of adolescents in terms of ethnicity and geographic location. Although there have often been efforts to establish new regional norms when the tests have been translated, there is surprisingly little research on the degree to which the original MMPI-2 and MMPI-A norms are appropriate for English-speaking populations outside the United States.

overpathologize: the tendency to exaggerate and overestimate the extent of pathology.

How do some tests overpathologize test-takers and why is that a problem?

Research on the original clinical scales yielded a wide range of reliability values, with some values well below an alpha of .80. The median reliability values for the MMPI-2, based on the normative data analyses reported in the test manual, are .64 for the validity scales and .62 for the clinical scales. The higher median value for the reliability of the content scales, .86, is consistent with the improved approach to test construction used with the content scales. Nevertheless, based on data from the normative sample, it is evident that a number of MMPI scales are likely to have relatively weak internal consistency. As for test-retest reliability, the data are much more encouraging, with the median values for the validity, clinical, and content scales all exceeding .80. As we mentioned in Chapter 7, attention to these rather dry details is critically important in determining the strengths and weaknesses of the MMPI.

With respect to validity, it is extremely difficult to meaningfully summarize the voluminous research on the various MMPI scales. Meta-analyses of these scales typically find support for the validity of many scales for a range of purposes and populations (e.g., Parker, Hanson, & Hunsley, 1988; Hiller, Rosenthal, Bornstein, Berry, & Brunell-Neuleib, 1999). However, there are so many scales and so many studies that it is necessary to consider cumulative validity data on a scale-by-scale basis. For example, Gross, Keyes, and Greene (2000) reviewed the research on the validity of relevant clinical (Scale 2) and content (DEP) scales in predicting depression and found evidence of comparable validity for both scales. Further complicating the task of understanding MMPI validity is that, as we describe next, much of the interpretation of a test score involves a consideration of scale profiles (i.e., validity scale score, the highest two clinical scale scores, and the overall pattern of scores)

MMPI-2™ Basic Service Report
ID 10101010 Page 2

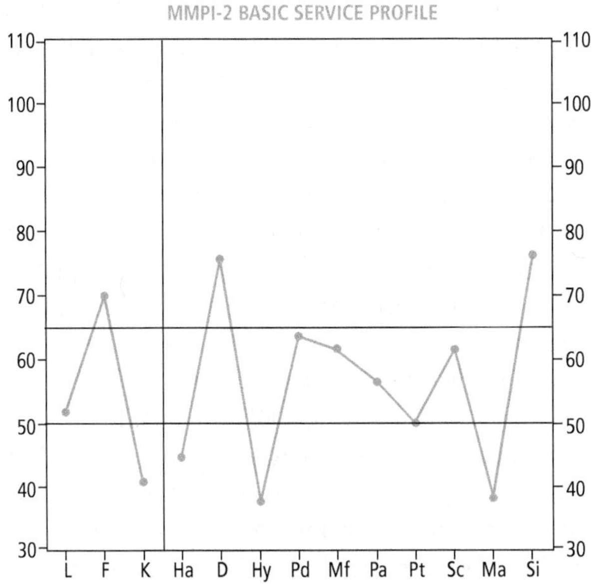

	L	F	K	Ha	D	Hy	Pd	Mf	Pa	Pt	Sc	Ma	Si
Raw Score:	4	11	11	5	31	15	25	32	12	16	22	13	49
T Score:	52	70	41	45	76	38	64	62	57	51	62	39	77

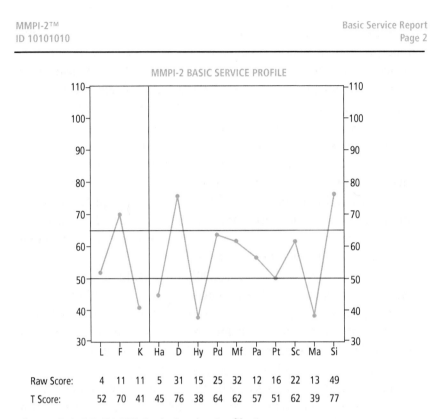

Figure 8.1 MMPI-2™ Basic Service Profile Report

rather than simply individual scales. Figure 8.1 is an example of a profile obtained with the main MMPI validity and clinical scales.

Administration, Scoring, and Interpretation Issues

Administering the MMPI-2 and MMPI-A is relatively straightforward. Nichols (2001) recommended that the assessor provide information on the overall purpose of the assessment and the nature of the MMPI. In providing test instructions, the assessor encourages the client to answer all the questions. Because the person must read the test, it is important to ensure that he or she has no visual impairment that interferes with test-taking (severely visually impaired patients typically use an audiotaped version of the test). The test requires reading comprehension at the Grade 8 or 9 level. Most people complete the test in one to two hours, although some psychiatric patients may require up to four hours.

Several standardized and objective scoring options are available. One option is to have the patient respond to the test using a computer scanning sheet that allows for direct entry and computerized scoring. Alternatively, the completed test response form may be sent to test scoring services that provide interpretive reports based on the patient's response. A third option is computerized administration and scoring (which has the additional advantage of reducing the time usually required to complete the test). The final and most cumbersome option is to hand score using templates available from the test publisher. Psychologists who use hand scoring must check carefully to ensure they make no scoring errors.

The MMPI-2 and MMPI-A provide a wealth of information on the patient's self-presentation, symptoms, severity of distress, personality style, and social functioning (Nichols, 2001). Several options are available to clinical psychologists for interpreting the test data, including interpretation by a test scoring service, the use of MMPI interpretation software, and reference to one of several professional books on the topic (e.g., Graham, 2011; Nichols, 2001). In most instances, psychologists use a combination of these sources of interpretive information.

code types: summary codes for the highest two clinical scale elevations on the MMPI scales.

Interpretation begins with examination of the validity scales to determine the degree to which responses to the clinical and content scales might be affected by response biases. The next stage involves categorizing the test profile into **code types**, which are summary codes for the highest two clinical scale elevations. Interpretive guidelines provide details on the possible meaning of code types, other high clinical scale scores, high content scale scores, and high restructured clinical scale scores. Regardless of the source of the interpretative information, it is imperative that factors related to age, ethnicity, and life context be taken into account when drawing conclusions from test data. Both individual circumstances and generational factors influence the nature of the patient's response. For example, Newsom, Archer, Trumbetta, and Gottesman (2003) found that the MMPI responses of typical adolescents have become more extreme over the past few decades, reflecting shifts in attitudes and experiences rather than increased distress and psychopathology. All guidelines for test interpretation, whether text-based or computer-based, are derived from expert summaries of the research literature, which vary in terms of completeness and accuracy (Butcher, Perry, & Atlis, 2000). Hence, for all these reasons, a computer-generated test report should never be used without careful review and analysis by a clinical psychologist who is knowledgeable about the test's strengths and limitations and about the current status of MMPI research.

Other Clinical Measures of Personality Functioning

The Million Measures: MCMI-III and MACI

Personality and psychopathology researcher **Theodore Millon** developed a set of personality inventories for use in a wide range of clinical settings. We will focus on two of these measures, the Millon Clinical

Multiaxial Inventory-III (MCMI-III; Millon, 1997) and the Millon Adolescent Clinical Inventory (MACI; Millon, 1993). Both measures were developed from Millon's theory of psychopathology, are oriented toward DSM diagnostic categories, and contain scales to assess validity, clinical personality patterns, and clinical syndromes.

The MCMI-III is a 175-item true-false self-report measure designed to assess personality styles and disorders (e.g., avoidant personality pattern, passive-aggressive personality pattern, borderline personality pathology) and major clinical syndromes (e.g., mood disorders, anxiety disorders, and substance dependency). It is intended for use with clients seeking mental health services and is not appropriate for use with adults with no psychological problems. Like the MMPI tests, the MCMI-III can be hand scored or computer scored. Computer interpretation software or text guidelines (e.g., Strack, 2008) can be used to interpret the test scores, including both the validity indices and the personality and syndrome scales. Normative data for the test are based on responses from almost 1,000 American and Canadian adults with psychiatric diagnoses. The normative sample under-represents ethnic minorities but is otherwise representative in terms of demographic characteristics. A set of norms based on data from more than 1,600 inmates in correctional facilities is available for use in correctional settings.

The internal consistency values based on the normative data are quite variable for the MCMI scales, with most values in the .70 to .90 range; one- to two-week test-retest values are typically higher than .80 (Millon, 1997). In developing and validating the third edition of the measure, Millon drew upon research on the previous two editions. This has led to substantial improvements, especially with respect to the psychometric properties of the personality disorder scales (Strack & Millon, 2007). Although research has generally supported the validity of the MCMI-III scales, two major concerns are often expressed about the test (e.g., Retzlaff & Dunn, 2003). First, there are concerns about the item overlap among scales (i.e., the same item may appear on more than one scale), which can artificially inflate correlations between scales. Second, due in part to item overlap, it is common for test-takers to have high scores on several scales and, thus, the MCMI-III has a tendency to overpathologize test-takers.

The MACI is a 175-item self-report inventory designed to assess personality styles and disorders (e.g., inhibited personality pattern, dramatizing personality pattern, oppositional personality pattern), expressed concerns (e.g., body disapproval, peer insecurity, family discord), and major clinical syndromes (e.g., eating dysfunctions, anxious feeling, suicidal tendency). It is intended for use with adolescent clients aged 13 to 19 years who are seeking mental health services. Scoring and interpretation options are similar to those described for the MCMI-III.

Data from more than 1,000 American and Canadian adolescents were used to develop the test norms and provide supporting psychometric data. Separate norms are available for young adolescent girls, young adolescent boys, older adolescent girls, and older adolescent boys. Although the psychometric data published with the inventory are encouraging, there has been only limited subsequent research on the inventory (Strack, 2008). Additional research, especially studies conducted by investigators other than the test developer, is crucial for establishing the validity of the inventory. The limited research on the MACI also restricts the extent to which new information can be added to the knowledge on which interpretation of the inventory is based.

Personality Assessment Inventory

Another broad-based personality inventory increasingly used by clinical psychologists is the Personality Assessment Inventory (PAI; Morey, 1991, 2007). The PAI is a 344-item self-report measure designed for use with adults. A version with fewer items has been developed and normed for use with adolescents (Personality Assessment Inventory—Adolescent). Although the PAI has many items, it requires only a Grade 4 reading level and can be completed in under an hour. The PAI contains 4 validity scales, 11 clinical scales (e.g., somatic complaints, antisocial features, borderline features), 2 interpersonal scales (dominance and warmth), and 5 treatment-oriented scales designed to provide information on respondent characteristics that might affect engagement in therapy or disrupt the process of therapy (e.g., aggression, stress, treatment rejection). It was developed using modern test construction principles, with extensive attention paid to both content validity and discriminant validity.

The PAI norms are based on data from 1,000 American adults who were representative of American census data in terms of age, gender, and ethnicity. The overall reliability of the scales is superior to the inventories described thus far. Based on data from the normative sample and samples of more than 1,000 patients and more than 1,000 university students, median internal consistency and test-retest values are above .80. There is an impressive body of research supporting the validity of many of the scales in this relatively new inventory. Research on use of the PAI in forensic, correctional, and rehabilitation services is growing dramatically. In 2007, a special issue of the *Journal of Personality Assessment* was devoted to PAI research developments (Blais & Kurtz, 2007). Like the other inventories we have presented, the PAI can be scored by hand or with computer software, and interpretations can be based on information in the manual test interpretation guides (Morey, 2003) or via computer software. As with the MMPI tests, the interpretation process involves an examination of validity indices, two-point code types, and then individual scales.

Self-Report Measures of Normal Personality Functioning

The self-report inventories we have discussed so far are intended for use with adolescents and adults who are likely to have some impairment in their psychosocial functioning. Some measures, such as the MMPI-A, are intended to provide information to help determine the presence and nature of the distress or disorder, whereas others, such as the MACI, are only appropriate for use with individuals who have already been determined to have clinically relevant problems.

A host of inventories focused on normal personality assessment are available for use in clinical practice and research. We present two of the most commonly used measures below. These types of measures may be especially appropriate in assessing clients in vocational or counselling contexts, in which the goal of the assessment is to obtain data to help improve or optimize the client's adjustment rather than to treat a mental disorder. For example, in dealing with a common event such as the ending of an intimate relationship, a person may seek psychological services as an aid to understanding what went wrong in the relationship and what could be done to enhance relationship functioning in the future. It may be advantageous in such a case for the psychologist to provide the client with research-based feedback on his or her personality as part of a discussion about personal preferences and styles that the client may wish to consider altering through treatment or through his or her own efforts. It is worth noting that, because of the focus on normal personality functioning, these types of inventories rarely include the types of validity scales that are common in the inventories we reviewed in the previous sections. It is assumed that respondents typically present an accurate picture of themselves, as there is little to be gained from presenting an overly positive or negative depiction of oneself in the situations in which these measures are commonly used.

The California Psychological Inventory (CPI; Gough & Bradley, 1996), now in its third edition, is a 434-item inventory with a similar structure to the MMPI. Roughly one-third of the CPI items also appear on the MMPI-2. Unlike the MMPI, though, the CPI largely focuses on normal interpersonal patterns and skills within the normal range of functioning and is composed of scales that measure constructs such as dominance, empathy, tolerance, and flexibility. The research base for the CPI is enormous, involving more than 2,000 studies (Groth-Marnat, 2009). The inventory's norms and psychometric values are all generally acceptable, and substantial information is available to assist clinicians in the use and interpretation of the CPI (e.g., Megargee, 2002).

The NEO Personality Inventory–3 (NEO PI-3; McCrae & Costa, 2010; McCrae, Costa, & Martin, 2005) is based on the five factor model of personality that is generally seen as the most scientifically supported personality theory (Wiggins & Trapnell, 1997). It is a 240-item test that measures the personality factors of neuroticism, extroversion, openness, agreeableness, and conscientiousness. The current version eliminated outdated and difficult items found in the previous edition, and completion of this instrument requires Grade 5 reading skills. The norms are based on data from 500 American youth and 635 American adults. Based on data from the normative samples, the internal consistency values for the factors are ≥ .89; no test-retest reliability values are reported. Validity data reported in the test manual provide extensive evidence for the factor scores. The research literature on the previous edition, the NEO PI-R, is voluminous, and the NEO PI-3 factors are very highly correlated with the parallel NEO PI-R factors (all values ≥ .98). Factors assessed by the inventory tap the basic structure of personality, so the evidence base for the inventory's validity continues to grow, with many studies on the NEO PI-R and NEO PI-3 appearing each year. Because of its growing use in clinical contexts, researchers have developed and evaluated validity scales for the instrument. Although empirical studies on these scales have provided mixed results, there is some indication that they could be a useful addition (e.g., Morasco, Gfeller, & Elder, 2007).

SELF-REPORT CHECKLISTS OF BEHAVIOURS AND SYMPTOMS

Many clinical psychologists have shifted from the use of broadband tests (such as personality inventories and projective tests) toward a greater use of self-report checklists of behaviours and symptoms (Groth-Marnat, 1999; Mash & Hunsley, 2004). These changes are fuelled by a number of factors, including changes in the reimbursement practices of insurance companies and health care organizations with respect to psychological assessments conducted as part of treatment provision (e.g., Stout & Cook, 1999) and clinicians' awareness of and demand for measures that aid in the formulation and evaluation of psychological services (Barkham et al., 2001; Bickman et al., 2000). Profile Box 8.1 introduces Dr. David A Clark who conducts research on cognitive assessment measures and has developed both self-report symptom measures and structured interviews.

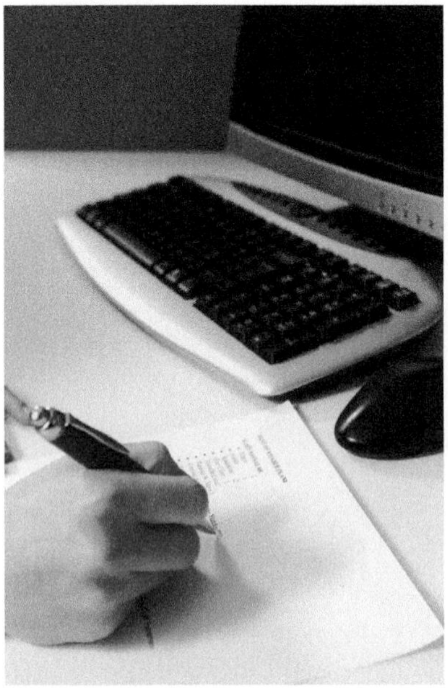

©iStock.com/savas keskiner

Current assessment practices often include self-report checklists.

As we discussed in the earlier section on clinical utility, there is currently little evidence that the use of personality inventories and projective tests improves clinical outcomes. In the absence of compelling evidence of clinical utility, psychologists must consider the value of the resulting test information in light of the expense of hours spent in administering, scoring, and interpreting self-report inventories and projective tests. It is also important to remember that, although often

PROFILE BOX 8.1

DR. DAVID A. CLARK

Courtesy of David Clark

I completed my B.Sc. in psychology at Houghton College, received an M.A. in social/experimental psychology from the New School for Social Research, and subsequently worked at a child guidance centre in Dartmouth, Nova Scotia. I then completed a master's of Philosophy in clinical psychology and a Ph.D. at the Institute of Psychiatry and Maudsley Hospital, University of London. I completed postdoctoral training in cognitive therapy at Aaron T. Beck's Center for Cognitive Therapy in Philadelphia. I am currently a full professor of psychology at the University of New Brunswick. My research focuses on cognitive behavioural assessment, theory, and treatment of adult depression and anxiety disorders. I have authored several books, including *Cognitive Therapy for Anxiety Disorders* and *The Anxiety and Worry Workbook*, and have developed several clinical questionnaires. I've given numerous workshops on cognitive behaviour therapy for depression, obsessive-compulsive disorder (OCD), and other anxiety disorders to mental health practitioners worldwide, I maintain a part-time private practice, and I'm licensed with the College of Psychologists of New Brunswick. I am a Founding Fellow of the Academy of Cognitive Therapy, and a Fellow of the Canadian Psychological Association.

HOW DID YOU CHOOSE TO BECOME A CLINICAL PSYCHOLOGIST?

Having been raised in a working class neighbourhood in the Maritimes, I witnessed poverty, injustice, and adversity in other people's daily lives. I wanted to do something to help and so I started by volunteering in a youth drop-in centre for street kids. For the first time I was confronted with significant emotional disturbance, substance abuse, abusive relationships, and truly dysfunctional families. I quickly realized that my ability to help was limited by my ignorance—I needed more knowledge and so decided to major in psychology. I became intrigued with the promises psychology could offer for improving our knowledge and treatment of mental illness.

WHAT IS THE GREATEST CHALLENGE YOU FACE AS A CLINICAL PSYCHOLOGIST?

An ever-expanding and demanding workload creates significant time pressures for clinical psychologists who also hold an academic position. Unlike teaching, which has a cyclical fluctuation, the pressures for research productivity are constant throughout the year. The second great challenge is the need to maintain razor-sharp clinical skills so I can offer students the most relevant, up-to-date training experience. This means maintaining some form of clinical practice and supervision. The need to balance research, teaching, clinical practice, and administrative duties requires strong commitment, efficiency, and a diligent work ethic.

TELL US ABOUT YOUR RESEARCH ON COGNITIVE ASSESSMENT STRATEGIES

My interest in cognitive assessment happened serendipitously. Starting with my doctoral research, I have maintained a primary research interest in unwanted intrusive thoughts and OCD. Often I would begin a research project on, for example, the control of unwanted intrusive thoughts and discover there were no good measures of the psychological phenomena of interest. This meant that I needed to develop my own measures in order to pursue my program of research. So, for my dissertation I wanted to know whether unwanted intrusive thoughts was a common experience in the general population, but since there were no accepted self-report measures of mental intrusions, I constructed the Distressing Thoughts Questionnaire. I discovered a number of problems with this measure and so, in subsequent studies, our research group

CONTINUED . . .

worked on a more accurate measure called the Revised Obsessional Intrusions Inventory. My two most important assessment projects have been the development of a published self-report symptom measure for OCD called the Clark-Beck Obsessive Compulsive Inventory. This has proven to be a useful instrument for screening individuals for obsessive and compulsive symptoms. The second assessment project is the recent development of a structured interview for unwanted intrusive thoughts called the International Intrusive Thoughts Interview Schedule, developed with Dr. Adam Radomsky from Concordia University and a team of psychologists from 13 countries. We have now collected the largest international dataset on unwanted intrusive thoughts and are in the process of analyzing these data for publication. I am also co-editing a book on cognitive assessment with Dr. Gary Brown of Royal Holloway University in London, England, that will be published next year.

HOW DO YOU INTEGRATE SCIENCE AND PRACTICE IN YOUR WORK?

There are several points of integration between my research and clinical practice. The first is that I maintain a private practice one day per week. Within this practice I strive to offer evidence-based assessment and treatment that is supported by my own research and that of other clinical researchers. Second, I am writing my second self-help book for the general public, which is an attempt to more widely disseminate research-based interventions to the general population. Third, I offer professional workshops and courses in our doctoral program in clinical psychology in which I emphasize diagnosis, assessment, and treatment strategies that have a strong research base. And finally, the research questions and objectives that guide our laboratory work are often derived from issues arising in the clinical setting.

WHAT DO YOU SEE AS THE MOST EXCITING CHANGES IN THE FIELD OF CLINICAL PSYCHOLOGY?

One of the most interesting developments has been the convergence between the neurosciences and cognitive-clinical psychology. Advances in neuroimaging technology have revealed a remarkable degree of agreement between cognitive research that has identified core cognitive processes involved in the regulation of emotion, and neuroimaging scans that show centres of the brain involved in the cognitive control of emotion. So, rather than representing a challenge to clinical theories of cognition and emotion, the neuroscience research is explicating the neurophysiological basis of emotion regulation. The advent of smartphones and other hand-held devices now makes it possible to collect real-time data on people's thoughts, feelings, and behaviour while interacting in the natural world. The availability of more sophisticated statistical analytic tools is enabling researchers to more accurately map the causal relationship between thoughts and feelings, thereby increasing the accuracy of our models of psychological disorders.

used for intervention-focused evaluation purposes, most of these instruments were not designed for this purpose. In contrast, behaviour and symptom checklists are very inexpensive and have direct and immediate relevance to treatment planning and monitoring. For example, it may be very useful for a clinical psychologist to track week-by-week changes in a patient's bingeing and purging. Based on checklist data, the psychologist is able to determine the success of treatment strategies and, if necessary, to discuss changes in treatment with the patient if there is no symptomatic improvement after several sessions of therapy.

There are numerous well-developed, psychometrically sound checklists. In the following pages, we provide only a small sample of the types of measures available to clinical psychologists for both research and clinical purposes. As you will see, some of these checklists cover a range of behaviours and symptoms, whereas others are problem-specific or disorder-specific. Just as the reading level required to complete personality inventories is an important consideration for their use, so too must developers of checklists be aware of how readability can affect test validity and utility. Although many self-report checklists are suitable for individuals with low levels of literacy, some require a reading level higher than the mean reading grade level of adults in the United States (McHugh & Behar, 2009).

Achenbach System of Empirically Based Assessment

As we described briefly in Chapter 3, the Achenbach System of Empirically Based Assessment (ASEBA; Achenbach & Rescorla, 2000, 2001, 2003; Achenbach, Newhouse, & Rescorla, 2004) is a family of questionnaires developed over many years by Thomas Achenbach. The original scale, the Child Behavior Checklist (CBCL), is a standardized questionnaire completed by a child's parents that includes competence items as well as diverse problems. For each item, the respondent is required to note whether it does not apply, applies occasionally, or applies frequently (Achenbach & Rescorla, 2001). The CBCL is one of the most widely used measures of child adjustment and has been demonstrated to be reliable and valid over hundreds of studies. Versions are available to be completed by parents of children aged 1.5 to 5 years and 6 to 18 years, as well as by caregivers and teachers. The Youth Self-Report (YSR) is a version of the CBCL that is completed by young people aged 11 to 18 years. Norms based on large national American samples are available for all the child and youth ASEBA measures, and a range of multicultural norms are available for the child measure. The ASEBA scales yield scores in the normal, clinical, or borderline (i.e., between normal and clinical) range. Scales yield a total problem score, as well as scores for two broad types of problems: internalizing problems and externalizing problems. Internalizing problems relate to distressed feelings, social withdrawal, worry, and sadness. Externalizing problems refer to acting-out and aggressive behaviours. In addition, scores are generated for a number of DSM-oriented scales. Most recently, the ASEBA has expanded to include measures and norms for adults 18 to 59 years (Achenbach & Rescorla, 2003) and older adults (60 to 90 years; Achenbach et al., 2004). These measures are the Adult Self-Report, Adult Behavior Checklist, Older Adult Self-Report, and Older Adult Behavior Checklist.

Computerized scoring of the ASEBA scales also provides an analysis of the degree of agreement between two raters (e.g., mother and youth), as well as a comparison of their degree of agreement about a problem with that of a normative group. This is a particularly useful feature of the ASEBA, as it is common to have parallel versions of the test completed by different informants. Using a wide range of measures, researchers have consistently found rather modest correlations among different raters rating the same individual. For example, pairs of parents rating their children have a mean correlation of .60, and correlations between youth self-ratings and parent ratings of the youth are typically not much more than .20 (e.g., Achenbach, McConaughy, & Howell, 1987). Likewise, correlations between adults' ratings of themselves and ratings of them by those who know them well are lower than you might think. For example, mean correlations for measures of substance use can be as high as .68, but mean correlation values for ratings of internalizing (.43) and externalizing problems (.44) are substantially lower (Achenbach, Krukowski, Dumenci, & Ivanova, 2005). With the ASEBA, data from different raters can be correlated and compared to normative data on what is a typical degree of concordance between raters. Thus, it is possible to determine if there is an average level of correspondence between the ratings, or whether the ratings are much more (or much less) similar than is usually found. This information aids the psychologist in interpreting and integrating the information provided by all informants.

VIEWPOINT BOX 8.2

TOP PROBLEMS: AN OPTION FOR TRACKING AND EVALUATING TREATMENT EFFECTS

As part of an initial session with clients seeking therapy, it is common for psychologists to ask questions such as *What led you to decide to seek treatment?* or *What are the main problems you hope to deal with in therapy?* A group of psychotherapy researchers looking to better understand how assessment might inform treatment planning and treatment implementation decided to see whether asking these types of questions, in a standardized manner, before and during treatment could provide useful assessment data. In a sample of 178 children referred for treatment, Weisz et al. (2011) asked children and their parents, separately, to identify the three *top problems* of greatest concern to them prior to treatment. Parents and children then provided, on a 0 to 10 scale, weekly ratings of the severity of these problems as treatment progressed. Children and parents also completed the CBCL and YSR (ASEBA measures described in this chapter) prior to treatment.

From week to week, the test-retest reliabilities of the identified top problems were high, ranging from .69 to .91. Using sophisticated mathematical growth models, the researchers found that the top problems approach provided reliable and valid estimates of change over time in treatment. However, almost all of the problems identified by the children and parents could be mapped onto ASEBA items that they

CONTINUED . . .

had endorsed. For example, a parent might endorse a CBCL item indicating that the child worries, but the top problem identified that the child worries about being socially rejected. This suggests that the top problems were likely to be serious ones, but it leaves open the question of whether it is useful to ask about these problems in addition to using a psychometrically strong symptom checklist.

To address this, the researchers then examined whether the ASEBA items that were comparable to the top problems appeared on CBCL or YSR scales in which the children scored in the clinical range of severity. They found that, for these items, approximately 40% of parents' top problems and 70% of children's top problems were *not* associated with scales that were in the clinical range. Additionally, for approximately 40% of parents and 80% of children, none of the identified top problems mapped onto ASEBA subscale scores that were in the clinical range. These findings are important because clinicians are most likely to attend to problems on scales in the clinical range, which would potentially cause them to overlook many serious additional problems. Accordingly, the researchers strongly recommended (a) that the top problems measurement approach be used as a complement to standardized self-report checklists and (b) that clinicians use top problem information when developing, providing, and evaluating the effects of treatment.

SCL-90-R

The Symptom Checklist-90-Revised (SCL-90-R; Derogatis, 1994) is a widely used general measure of distress. It is a 90-item measure with nine subscales that cover a range of symptom dimensions, including interpersonal sensitivity, phobic anxiety, and hostility. Respondents are asked to indicate the extent to which they have been distressed by various symptoms over the past two weeks. Norms—although not nationally representative—are available for various groups, including non-patient adults, non-patient adolescents, psychiatric inpatients, and psychiatric outpatients. The internal consistency and test-retest reliability values (over one week) based on data from these normative groups all exceed .75. The SCL-90-R has been used in hundreds of research studies. Although both the individual subscales and the global indices of distress available for the test have been demonstrated to be sensitive to treatment-related changes, there is considerable evidence that most subscales do not adequately measure the constructs they are designed to assess. Moreover, a commonly voiced concern among clinicians is that the scale tends to overpathologize. Finally, there is substantial intercorrelation among the subscales and little evidence for the divergent validity of the subscales (Groth-Marnat, 2009). As a result, the SCL-90-R is probably best conceptualized as a brief measure of general psychological distress.

Outcome Questionnaire 45

The 45-item Outcome Questionnaire (OQ-45; Lambert et al., 1996) is an increasingly popular measure for research and clinical purposes. The

OQ-45 is composed of three subscales: symptom distress, interpersonal relations, and social role functioning. These subscales provide a good overview of a client's psychosocial functioning that takes only five minutes or so to complete. Because of high inter-scale correlation, it is probably most appropriate that the total score be used as an indicator of client distress. Although the OQ-45 is a relatively new measure, there is growing evidence that it is psychometrically strong across a range of populations (e.g., Umphress, Lambert, Smart, Barlow, & Clouse, 1997; Vermeersch, Lambert, & Burlingame, 2000). There is also evidence that the OQ-45 is a useful tool for assessing change over the course of psychological services. Even more importantly, as we described in Chapter 5, meta-analytic results from more than 2,500 clients indicated that the use of the OQ-45 in monitoring treatment progress can both dramatically improve treatment success rates and reduce the rates of deterioration associated with treatment (Lambert et al., 2003). Figure 8.2 provides an example of an OQ-45 report. Data such as these have played a major role in the widespread adoption of the OQ-45 by clinical psychologists. A version of the measure is also available for use with children and adolescents (Burlingame et al., 2001). Taken together, these measures hold great promise for enhancing the impact of psychotherapeutic services offered to the public.

Beck Depression Inventory-II

The Beck Depression Inventory-II (BDI-II; Beck, Steer, & Brown, 1996) is a 21-item checklist with a multiple-choice format (i.e., several response options are available to describe each symptom). It is designed to evaluate the severity of depressive symptoms experienced in the past two weeks. Based on normative data, cut-offs are provided to classify the symptoms as minimal, mild, moderate, or severe. Although the BDI-II more closely maps onto DSM criteria than did the original BDI, it does not provide sufficient detail to determine whether a person meets diagnostic depression for a mood disorder. It is one of the most frequently used symptom checklists in clinical research, and there are studies of its reliability and validity in numerous populations, including psychiatric inpatients, patients with chronic pain, and university students. Although the precise factor structure and validity of the BDI-II vary somewhat across these groups, there is compelling evidence that the measure is a psychometrically strong tool for assessing depressive symptoms in adolescents and adults. It appears, though, that scores can drop appreciably simply due to repeated administration of the test (e.g., Longwell & Truax, 2005). Such findings are concerning, as they indicate that the BDI-II may yield imprecise results when used for treatment monitoring purposes.

©iStock.com/iPandastudio

The BDI-II has been identified as a psychometrically strong symptom checklist for use with university students.

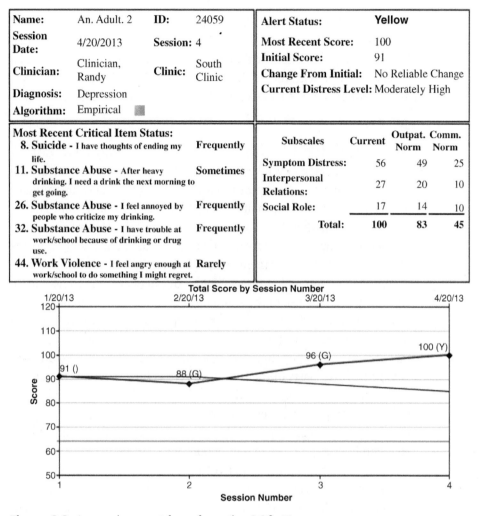

Name:	An. Adult. 2	**ID:**	24059
Session Date:	4/20/2013	**Session:**	4
Clinician:	Clinician, Randy	**Clinic:**	South Clinic
Diagnosis:	Depression		
Algorithm:	Empirical		

Alert Status:	**Yellow**
Most Recent Score:	100
Initial Score:	91
Change From Initial:	No Reliable Change
Current Distress Level:	Moderately High

Most Recent Critical Item Status:

8. Suicide - I have thoughts of ending my life.	**Frequently**
11. Substance Abuse - After heavy drinking. I need a drink the next morning to get going.	**Sometimes**
26. Substance Abuse - I feel annoyed by people who criticize my drinking.	**Frequently**
32. Substance Abuse - I have trouble at work/school because of drinking or drug use.	**Frequently**
44. Work Violence - I feel angry enough at work/school to do something I might regret.	**Rarely**

Subscales	**Current**	**Outpat. Norm**	**Comm. Norm**
Symptom Distress:	56	49	25
Interpersonal Relations:	27	20	10
Social Role:	17	14	10
Total:	**100**	**83**	**45**

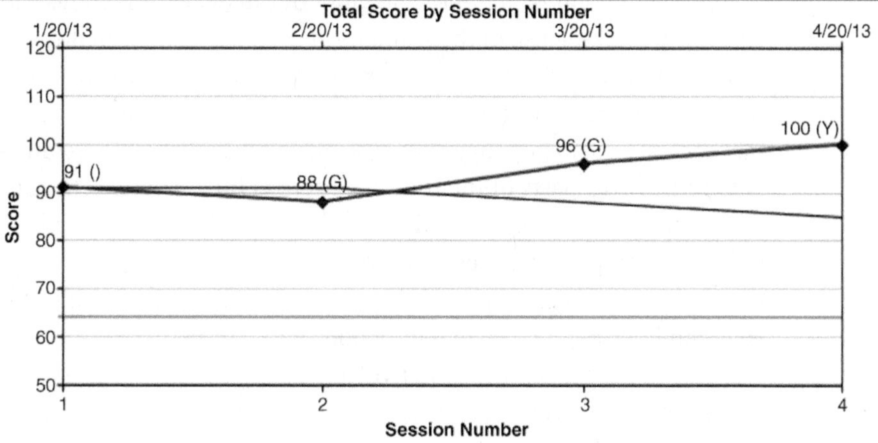

Figure 8.2 A sample report form from the OQ®-45

Reprinted with permission from OQ Measures.

Children's Depression Inventory 2

Similar in content and structure to the BDI-II, the Children's Depression Inventory 2 (CDI 2; Kovacs, 2010) is a self-report checklist designed to evaluate recent (in the past two weeks) symptoms of depression in children. The normative data, from 1,100 American chidren, were designed to be representative of U.S. census data. Although there are relatively few studies of the CDI 2, the original CDI yielded data that have been shown to have good reliability and validity, especially in community samples (Sitarenios & Kovacs, 1999). The research evidence suggests that it does not distinguish between heightened levels of depressive and anxious symptoms, but no depression checklist is particularly good at making this distinction. A meta-analysis of the original version revealed no socioeconomic status effects in CDI responses, although there may be effects due to ethnicity (Twenge & Nolen-Hoeksema, 2002). Unfortunately, consistent with data from the BDI, there is evidence that repeated testing with the original CDI can result in substantial decreases in reported symptoms (Twenge & Nolen-Hoeksema, 2002).

PROJECTIVE MEASURES OF PERSONALITY

A variety of personality instruments used by clinical psychologists fall under the general category of projective measures. These instruments have in common the presentation of ambiguous items or stimuli. That is, regardless of whether the measure relies on pictures, colours, incomplete sentences, drawings, or puppets, there is no inherent meaning to the stimulus material, just as there are no obvious right and wrong answers. A core assumption is that the ambiguity of the material requires the individual to make sense of the stimulus and, in the process of doing that, aspects of the individual's personality are revealed. The original concept of projection was developed by Freud and was seen as a type of defence mechanism in which people unconsciously attribute to others undesirable or negative parts of themselves. There is little evidence to support the existence of projection, and little doubt that the process involved in responding to projective tests doesn't rely on projection per se—rather, the process involves responses being influenced by a person's experiences and personality (Lilienfeld, Wood, & Garb, 2000).

What are the main differences between objective personality tests and symptom checklists?

There is some similarity between projective methods and some of the techniques developed for use in the cognitive sciences to examine unconscious mental processes (Westen, Feit, & Zittel, 1999). However, clinical use of projective measures is not characterized by the standardization and rigorous attention to scientific principles that are the hallmarks of cognitive science techniques. As we noted in Chapter 1, projective tests such as the Rorschach Inkblot Test, the Thematic Apperception Test, and projective drawings were not developed in a manner consistent with psychological test construction guidelines. Consequently, most projective tests used in clinical settings do not have standardized administration, scoring, or interpretation guidelines, and only the Rorschach has normative data (Hunsley, Lee, Wood, & Taylor, in press).

Projective measures can be subdivided into five broad but overlapping categories (Lilienfeld et al., 2000). In the following sections, we will present two examples from measures involving association techniques (i.e., those requiring people to report what a stimulus looks like) and construction techniques (i.e., those requiring the individual to produce a story or a drawing). Other categories of projective measures are completion techniques (e.g., sentence completion tasks), arrangement/ selection techniques (e.g., colour tests that require the rank ordering of preferred colours), and expression techniques (e.g., handwriting analysis). There is no denying the intuitive appeal of many of these techniques. However, after decades of research, many psychologists view them as invalid and unscientific measures.

Rorschach Inkblot Test

The Rorschach inkblots, developed by Swiss psychiatrist Hermann Rorschach, consist of 10 cards, each containing symmetrical inkblots, some coloured and some in black and white. Test-takers are asked to report what they see in these ambiguous stimuli. For much of the 20th century, there were several distinct approaches to the administration and scoring of the Rorschach, and clinicians tended to adopt elements of different systems and to "personalize" the scoring and interpretation of the Rorschach based on their own experiences. The Comprehensive System (CS) devised by John Exner (Exner, 1993) is now considered the principal scoring system for the Rorschach, although a new system, the Rorschach Performance Assessment System (R-PAS), was recently introduced (Meyer, Viglione, Mihura, Erard, & Erdberg, 2011). The CS offers clear information on administration and scoring, with extensive tables and computer software available to aid the interpretation of the test results. Directions specify the seating arrangements, the instructions to be given to examinees, the sequence of card administration, as well as permissible responses to examinee questions. Unfortunately, research indicates that (a) administration errors are easy to make even if the examiner is careful, has received training in the CS, and is well supervised, and (b) these errors are likely to have a substantial impact on the examinee's Rorschach responses and test scores (Lis, Parolin, Calvo, Zennaro, & Meyer, 2007).

What are the shortcomings of current practice in projective assessment?

After developing the CS, Exner published norms for different age groups that have become a cornerstone of the system's scientific basis (e.g., Exner, 1993). For the adult norms, convenience sampling strategies were used to obtain Rorschach protocols from approximately 1,300 volunteers over a 20-year period. From this pool, 700 protocols were selected in an attempt to match key demographic variables reported in the 1980 U.S. census. Although members of some minority groups were included in this selected sample, this is not sufficient to ensure that the norms are relevant for the clinical use of the Rorschach with members of minority groups (Gray-Little & Kaplan, 1998).

A major problem for the CS norms is the likelihood that nonpatient norms overpathologize normal individuals—a phenomenon found for both child and adult samples (Wood, Nezworski, Garb, &

Lilienfeld, 2001). The extent of this problem is vividly apparent in Hamel, Shaffer, and Erdberg's (2000) study involving data from 100 children who were selected for the absence of psychopathology and behaviour problems based on historical information and assessment of current functioning. When the Rorschach data from these children were scored and interpreted according to CS norms, a considerable number of children scored in the clinical range on Rorschach indices of psychopathology. As the authors wrote: "(T)hese children may be described as grossly misperceiving and misinterpreting their surroundings and having unconventional ideation and significant cognitive impairment. Their distortion of reality and faulty reasoning approach psychosis. These children would also be described as having significant problems establishing and maintaining interpersonal relationships and coping within a social context" (p. 291). According to the interpretation of their responses to the Rorschach inkblots, these children sound very troubled, but remember: none of these children had had psychological problems in the past, none was currently experiencing psychological distress, and all were doing very well in school and in social activities.

Because of the concerns about the quality of the CS norms, considerable efforts have been devoted to developing norms that meet the standards expected of psychological tests. To that end, a series of norms (called the International Reference Samples) has been published for the CS that draws on data from over 5,800 people from 16 countries (Shaffer, Erdberg, & Meyer, 2007). These norms are now recommended for scoring and interpreting adults' responses to the Rorschach (Meyer, Erdberg, & Shaffer, 2007), even though none of the normative samples were representative of the countries in which the data were collected. A major problem arose in trying to develop norms for data from youth, as substantial and erratic differences in CS scores occurred both within and across samples from the various countries. As a result, the primary researchers behind this international norming effort recommended against using available norms for Rorschach responses from children and adolescents (Meyer et al., 2007)—in other words, they indicated that the Rorschach should not be used with youth.

Scoring reliability of the Rorschach and CS has been much discussed. Acklin, McDowell, Verschell, and Chan (2000) reported inter-rater reliability values for most CS scores, for both normal and clinical samples. The median reliability value was slightly above .80, thus indicating (as with some of the self-report personality inventories described previously) that many, but not all, scores meet the level commonly seen as indicative of good reliability. Of concern, Guarnaccia, Dill, Sabatino, and Southwick (2001), however, found that both graduate students and practising psychologists made numerous errors in scoring Rorschach data. These errors were so extensive that the overall mean accuracy in scoring the major components of the CS was only 65%. As you will recall from Chapter 7, scoring errors on intelligence tests can also greatly affect the accuracy of the results obtained with these tests.

The literature on the validity of the Rorschach in general and the CS in particular is so large that it is impossible to review it within a few paragraphs. There have been very heated debates over the past 50 years about the quality of Rorschach research and its adequacy for supporting the widespread clinical use of the test. A number of clinical psychology journals, such as *Psychological Assessment* (Meyer, 1999, 2001), have published special sections on this topic. Some general conclusions can be drawn, however, about the scientific status of the Rorschach. For example, global meta-analyses of Rorschach validity (Parker et al., 1988; Hiller et al., 1999) have demonstrated that some Rorschach scales have reasonable validity, although typically lower than that found for MMPI scales. An extensive meta-analytic review of the research on CS variables found that the average correlation between the Rorschach variables and self-report measures of the same psychological constructs was only $r = .08$ (Mihura, Meyer, Dumitrascu, & Bombel, 2013). Although there is no question that this is a very weak association, the meaning of the association is rather controversial, with critics of the Rorschach seeing it as a major problem and Rorschach advocates seeing it as a reflection of the test's strengths! There is consensus, however, that the Rorschach should not be used to provide diagnostic information. Wood, Lilienfeld, Garb, and Nezworski (2000) reviewed more than 150 studies on the use of the Rorschach and diagnoses of mental disorders and found almost no evidence that the Rorschach could consistently detect major depressive disorder, posttraumatic stress disorder, antisocial personality disorder, or many other psychiatric diagnoses. On the other hand, even the harshest critics of the Rorschach agree that the test can provide valid information about intelligence and thought disorder, although evidence of validity does not suggest that the Rorschach is necessarily the best method to assess these constructs (Wood, Nezworski, & Garb, 2003).

The Rorschach is likely to have value in research examining personality structure and correlates. However, as we have emphasized throughout the text, clinical psychologists have a responsibility to evaluate their assessment and treatment services in light of professional standards and scientific evidence. As we discuss in the next chapter, even when used with other measures, the Rorschach is likely to overpathologize patients. The evidence of both

An inkblot pattern similar to those used in the Rorschach test.

substantial problems with scoring accuracy and the significant limitations of the youth norms suggest that the Rorschach simply has too many shortcomings to be clinically useful (Viewpoint Box 8.3 offers some thoughts on why psychologists continue to use this and other questionable tests). Only time will tell whether the new R-PAS approach to administering and scoring the test will provide sufficient research support to merit the clinical use of the Rorschach.

VIEWPOINT BOX 8.3

WHY DO QUESTIONABLE PSYCHOLOGICAL TESTS REMAIN POPULAR WITH SOME CLINICAL PSYCHOLOGISTS?

As we described in Chapter 5, for decades projective tests have been among the assessment tools most commonly used by clinical psychologists and most commonly taught in graduate programs. Clearly a large number of professionals believe that these tests are valuable in assessing patients' psychosocial functioning. Yet, as we have presented in this chapter, the research support for these tests is, at best, mixed and often non-existent. So the question that inevitably arises is why have these tests remained relatively popular among clinicians?

In addressing this question, Lilienfeld, Wood, and Garb (2006) have drawn upon a number of sources, including research on decision-making processes, in suggesting that five main factors are responsible for the continuing use of projective tests (and other tests with weak or non-existent research support).

The first factor is that of clinical tradition: many psychologists have been trained to use these measures and, not surprisingly, they continue to use them when they graduate from doctoral programs. Of course, if a program provides training in projective testing, it is highly likely that the scientific weaknesses of these tools are ignored, downplayed, or explained away as irrelevant to "real" clinical practice. Thus, many psychologists who use these instruments may not be fully aware of just how problematic these tests are.

Lilienfeld and colleagues suggested that two forms of decision-making errors, illusory correlation and the P. T. Barnum effect, also play a role in the continued use of projective tests. Illusory correlation is a phenomenon that involves the belief that there is a stronger statistical association between variables than there actually is. For example, patients whose projective drawings of human figures included overly large eyes have often been considered as being highly suspicious, even though there is almost no research evidence to support such an association. Of course, the proper way for a psychologist to consider the validity of a hypothesis of covariation between two variables is to search the research literature to evaluate the accuracy of the hypothesis.

The P. T. Barnum effect, named after the 19th-century circus entrepreneur, is a phenomenon in which an individual finds something of personal relevance in a generic statement that could apply to almost anyone. For example, the statement "There are times when you find it difficult to make certain decisions" probably applies to almost everyone. As Lilienfeld et al. reported, research has found that a person is much more likely to rate such statements as a more accurate reflection of his or her personality if the person was tested with the Rorschach rather than a self-report measure or an interview. In the context of clinical work, this suggests that patients may reinforce the clinician's belief that information of particularly high value is only available from projective tests.

The issue of whether a test leads to overestimating psychopathology has been discussed repeatedly in this

CONTINUED . . .

chapter and is the fourth factor viewed as contributing to the popularity of projectives. Most clinical psychologists work with people who have considerable problems. Therefore, in most assessment tasks, we go into the evaluation process expecting to find problems. If the Rorschach, for example, tends to classify too many people as having psychological problems, this may yield "evidence" consistent with clinicians' typical expectations. Rather than causing them to question the accuracy of the Rorschach, this is much more likely to reinforce the clinicians' belief in the value of the Rorschach.

The final factor that Lilienfeld et al. proposed as contributing to the popularity of projective tests is something they called the alchemist's fantasy. As you probably know, alchemy was based on the belief that, with the right processes and ingredients, base metals could be transmuted into gold. Well, according to Lilienfeld and colleagues, those who use projectives have a comparable belief, namely that, despite the lack of research evidence for the validity of the tests, there is something special that clinicians can do to take projective data and turn it into clinical "gold." Indeed one can find many examples in the literature on projective tests in which authors claim special clinical "powers" to discern patterns in projective data that sophisticated research designs and methods have been unable to detect.

Thematic Apperception Test

The Thematic Apperception Test (TAT; Murray, 1943) is a projective measure composed of 31 cards. The person being assessed is asked to tell stories about pictures printed on cards. The principle underlying the TAT is that, in creating these stories, the dominant needs, emotions, and conflicts of the person's personality are revealed. Moreover, it is assumed that at least some aspects of personality cannot be assessed by self-report, as they may not be consciously accessible to the person being assessed. Although the TAT was the first apperceptive measure developed, there are a number of other such measures, including some designed for use with children, older adults, and minority groups (Teglasi, 2010).

There is little survey information available on the extent to which practitioners follow or modify the original instructions developed by Murray for the TAT. What is clear, though, is that there is little consistency across clinicians and researchers in terms of how many cards are used in an assessment, which cards are used, the order in which the cards are presented, the instructions used in administering the test, and the scoring and interpretive principles used with the test (Groth-Marnat, 2009; Teglasi, 2010). Unlike the Rorschach, there is no single dominant scoring system and no norms are available for the measure. Even ardent proponents of the TAT admit that most clinicians using the TAT have abandoned a scientific approach to its use (Rossini & Moretti, 1997). Given this, any psychometric data on the measure available in the research literature are irrelevant to determining its actual reliability and validity as it is used by clinical psychologists. The current clinical status of the TAT is, therefore, best characterized as a measure that is taught and used in a manner that ignores scientific and professional standards (Hunsley et al., in press).

The neglect of science in the routine clinical use of the TAT is very unfortunate. Most importantly, for those assessed with the TAT, there is absolutely no evidence to support the validity of the conclusions drawn by the psychologist. Nevertheless, there is substantial research to suggest that standardized apperceptive methods have the potential to provide valid personality information. For example, using selected TAT cards and adding other specially developed picture stimuli, McClelland and colleagues conducted a programmatic series of studies on achievement, power, and affiliative needs (1989). This pioneering research has been continued by a number of researchers (e.g., Langan-Fox & Grant, 2006). The results of this research have provided compelling evidence that, when a standard set of cards and empirically supported scoring criteria are used, data from the modified TAT often outperform self-report measures in predicting subsequent behaviour (McClelland, Koestner, & Weinberger, 1989; Spangler, 1992).

SUMMARY AND CONCLUSIONS

The self-report and projective measures described in this chapter represent some of the key measures within the clinical psychologist's kit of assessment tools. In graduate training, psychologists learn how to administer, score, and interpret various instruments that are used in the objective assessment of personality and in projective assessment. Although the scoring of objective assessment measures is more standardized and straightforward than the scoring of projective measures, it is not immune from administrative errors that can distort scores. In the interpretation of both objective and projective personality assessment measures, clinical psychologists are faced with a complex array of interpretation methods that vary in their degree of empirical support. Unfortunately, important advances in research on personality have not been reflected in comparable advances in the clinical assessment of personality. There has been an important shift in measure validation in the recognition of the need to determine the suitability of measures developed in one population for use with another population. In addition to issues of standardization, reliability, validity, and norms, we must add the criterion that a test must be shown to be reliable and valid for the population in which it will be used. Without attention to these issues, there is a danger that psychological tests will overpathologize those who take the tests and, thus have iatrogenic effects. Another fundamental question about the value of psychological tests relates to the clinical utility of these assessment tools. Although limited utility data are available, there is growing recognition of the usefulness of cost-effective, brief measures that allow tracking of symptoms in treatment planning and monitoring.

KEY TERMS

behaviour checklists: lists of behaviours that are rated for frequency, intensity, or duration.

clinical utility: the extent to which a test and the resulting data improve upon typical clinical decision-making and treatment outcome.

code types: summary codes for the highest two clinical scale elevations on the MMPI scales.

content approach: a method of test construction that involves developing items specifically designed to tap the construct being assessed.

empirical criterion-keying approach: a method of test construction that involves the generation and analysis of a pool of items; those items that discriminate between two clearly defined groups are retained in the scale.

malingering: emphasizing negative characteristics and deliberately presenting a more problematic picture.

objective personality tests: tests that can be scored objectively, always using the same scoring system.

overpathologize: the tendency to exaggerate and overestimate the extent of pathology.

personality traits: the tendency to consistently behave in specific ways.

projective personality tests: tests requiring drawings or a response to ambiguous stimuli, based on the assumption that responses reveal information about personality structure.

validity scales: scales designed to detect whether a person is faking good, faking bad, or responding randomly.

KEY NAMES

Thomas Achenbach

James Butcher

John Exner

Starke Hathaway

J. Charnley McKinley

Theodore Millon

Walter Mischel

ADDITIONAL RESOURCES

Books

Antony, M. M. & Barlow, D. H. (Eds.). (2010). *Handbook of assessment and treatment planning for psychological disorders* (2nd ed.). New York: Guilford Press.

Butcher, J. N. (Ed). (2009). *Oxford handbook of personality assessment.* New York: Oxford University Press.

Wood, J. M., Nezworski, M. T., Lilienfeld, S. O., & Garb, H. N. (2003). *What's wrong with the Rorschach? Science confronts the controversial inkblot test.* San Francisco: Jossey-Bass.

Journals

Assessment

Journal of Personality Assessment

Journal of Psychopathology and Behavioral Assessment

Psychological Assessment

Check It Out!

MMPI-2, the publisher's site: psychcorp.pearsonassessments.com/HAIWEB/Cultures/en-us/Productdetail.htm?Pid=MMPI-2

MCMI-III, the publisher's site: psychcorp.pearsonassessments.com/HAIWEB/Cultures/en-us/Productdetail.htm?Pid=PAg505

PAI, the publisher's site: www4.parinc.com/Products/Product.aspx?ProductID=PAI

The International Personality Item Pool Representation of the NEO PI-R (including two versions of a five-factor personality test that can be taken online) can be found at: www.personal.psu.edu/~j5j/IPIP

ASEBA, the publisher's site: www.aseba.org

ASSESSMENT: INTEGRATION AND CLINICAL DECISION-MAKING

9 CHAPTER

case example **MELISSA**

We described in Chapter 3 some of the problems that Melissa was experiencing; in this chapter, we present the results of the evaluation of Melissa's problems. A new mother who had recently left her nursing career, Melissa reported a number of complaints related to worries about inadvertently injuring other people. These worries began in her work life after hearing media reports about errors in dispensing medication that had led to numerous deaths in hospitals in North America. She became increasingly preoccupied with the possibility of making such an error and spent excessive amounts of time checking and rechecking all of her work. Not surprisingly, this led to her becoming very inefficient at work and, consequently, receiving a poor annual evaluation from her supervisor. Melissa tried to follow through on the supervisor's recommendations to work faster, but this led to her becoming even more concerned about the likelihood of making critical errors. Her anxiety mounted, she became irritable with patients and colleagues and no longer looked forward to her workday. During her time away from work, Melissa grew increasingly agitated and anticipated a call from work telling her that one of the patients in her care had died because of a mistake she had made. When Melissa became pregnant, she and her husband, Erik, decided that the stress she was experiencing at work was simply not worth the effect it was having on her. So she quit the job that only two years previously she had cared so much about.

Both Melissa and Erik had noticed that her concerns about hurting other people through inattention had spread to her life outside of work. They had assumed that her worries about hitting someone while driving would disappear once the stress of work was removed from her life. Unfortunately, this did not occur. If anything, her fears seemed to worsen, for she was frequently worried about how minor alterations in her diet, activities, and emotional state might injure the developing foetus. Although Melissa would have preferred to stop driving altogether, she forced herself to continue because Erik sometimes had business trips away from home.

Preparations for the baby's room and the birth filled her with dread, for she imagined all the accidents that could occur during the birth and the baby's first weeks of life. Although the delivery was uneventful and Melissa and Erik had the help of family members in making the adjustment to their new roles as parents, Melissa became even more anxious and distressed. She worried about the baby's eating and sleeping patterns. She was concerned about her capacity to feed the baby and was anxious that her diet might cause the baby gastric problems. Melissa was also vigilant for risk of sudden infant death syndrome. If she had to leave the baby's room, she turned the baby monitor on and, if she heard the slightest sound, she rushed back to check the baby. Melissa laundered the baby's clothes and bed linens on noticing the slightest mark. Exhausted from giving birth and from looking after a newborn, she spent much of her time when the baby was asleep going over the house to ensure that it was "baby proof." Although the couple had already done this prior to the birth, Melissa was convinced that they had forgotten something. She started using baby gates to block off access to the stairs in the house. The couple argued repeatedly about this, with Erik pointing out that the baby was only a few weeks old and they were months away from needing to use the gates. Melissa also checked and rechecked all the cabinets in the kitchen, the bathrooms, the laundry room, and even the garage to make sure that all cleaning products, matches, and other hazardous materials were tightly sealed and stored at eye level.

Erik's concern about his wife's health mounted during the first months after the birth of their child. He saw Melissa's distress and exhaustion grow. Although he felt that she was a wonderful and caring mother, he was starting to worry that her fatigue and distractibility might actually lead her to make the kind of mistake that she dreaded. As her checking for possible problems consumed more and more of her time, her involvement in pleasurable activities diminished and the number of arguments between the couple increased. Following a tearful discussion, Erik and Melissa agreed she needed to talk to their family physician about her worries.

Melissa and Erik met with the physician the following week. Ten minutes into their appointment the physician was convinced that the situation they were describing went beyond the typical cautiousness of new parents. She then asked questions about whether Melissa's anxiety was evident in other areas of her life. When she heard the litany of concerns, she knew that Melissa needed to be assessed by a specialist. She asked Melissa if she would be willing to meet with a psychologist who would be better able to diagnose her difficulties and possibly help her overcome them. Melissa quickly agreed to this and the physician said that she would make a referral to a psychologist. The physician then suggested that Erik check about the extended health benefits he had through his work and, that afternoon, Erik contacted someone in his company's human resources department and learned that he did have coverage for services with a psychologist. The next day the receptionist in the physician's office phoned Melissa to tell her that a referral had been made for her to see a psychologist the following month.

You have probably heard of postpartum depression, a form of depression that can develop due to the many psychosocial and physical changes related to pregnancy, birth, and caring for a newborn.

Researchers and clinicians are now paying attention to anxiety disorders that develop or become more severe around the postpartum period (e.g., McGuinness, Blissett, & Jones, 2011). As illustrated by the case of Melissa, these anxiety problems can become very debilitating. Because much of the focus of this chapter is on integrating data and addressing factors that can affect the assessment's accuracy, we will use the case of Melissa to illustrate how clinical psychologists work to achieve an assessment that is comprehensive, accurate, and clinically useful.

All assessments are conducted to address a question. The psychologist refers to the question that prompted the assessment as a framework to guide the process of drawing together the various pieces of information available about the client(s). A question about a client's intellectual capabilities leads to the preparation of a report that highlights general intellectual functioning and more specific cognitive strengths and weaknesses. Emotional and interpersonal factors that affect the client's ability to achieve his or her potential are also considered in such an assessment, but they are secondary to a clear presentation of the client's intellectual skills. In contrast, an assessment report summarizing data relevant to the question of whether Jeff, a depressed teacher, is able to return to work would have a very different focus and structure. Jeff's symptoms, diagnostic information, and functional capabilities would have to be discussed first. After that, the psychologist would address the factors that led to Jeff's burnout, his motivation and readiness to return to work, and possible impediments (both psychological and interpersonal) that could affect the return to work. Cognitive sequelae of the depression, such as difficulty in decision-making and planning that would affect Jeff's teaching abilities, would be addressed as secondary to the emotional issues.

Psychological assessment may be conducted to determine if someone is suitable to return to work after an injury or disorder.

In Chapter 5, we described some of the general issues in psychological testing and assessment. Psychological assessment involves gathering and integrating multiple forms of information from multiple sources and perspectives. Based on the purposes of the assessment and the initial hypotheses to be explored, the clinical psychologist selects the most appropriate assessment methods and tools to conduct the assessment. As the psychologist gains a better understanding of the person (or couple or family) being assessed, additional assessment procedures may be used to narrow or expand the focus of the assessment.

In Chapters 6, 7, and 8, you learned about the most commonly used assessment methods and tools: interviews, observations, intellectual assessment measures, cognitive assessment measures, self-report measures, and projective measures. It is now time to consider the final phases of the assessment process, namely the integration of the diverse data collected about the client and the clinical use of the completed assessment. As you learned in Chapter 5, the clinical psychologist must examine all the assessment information, consider both consistencies and contradictions in the information, generate hypotheses about the client, and formulate conclusions or clinical recommendations about the client based on the overall picture emerging from the assessment. These tasks are necessary whether the psychologist is providing an assessment-focused service or an intervention-focused assessment service. In this chapter, we describe the process by which psychologists integrate assessment data and the product of this integration. To do this, we will present research on the process of case formulation, threats to the validity of psychological assessments, and use of assessment reports and feedback about the assessment findings. Our goals are to convey to you both the challenges in integrating assessment data and the potential value for clients of an integrated psychological assessment.

INTEGRATING ASSESSMENT DATA

What are the challenges involved for psychologists in synthesizing all of the information collected as part of a psychological assessment?

Think of what it is like for you to collect and use the information necessary to write a term paper. You need to get material from a number of sources, often including books, journal articles, and websites. Once you have all the necessary material, you have to sift through it to determine what is useful, what isn't, and what is redundant. Then, you have to find a way to put all of the various pieces of information together in a manner that makes sense. The challenges in integrating data gathered as part of a psychological assessment are similar to the challenges of putting all the material together in a coherent term paper.

The clinical psychologist has many tasks in integrating data obtained during an assessment. At the simplest level, this integration requires providing a descriptive account of the client's present psychological functioning. Even providing this "simple" account may be a very complex task. Depending on the nature of the assessment, a simple account might involve a consideration of the client's personality structure, level of emotional distress, coping resources, and/or intellectual capacity. In many instances, this description includes diagnosis using a classification system such as the DSM-5. As comorbidity is common in clinical diagnoses, with many clients receiving more than one diagnosis, the psychologist must indicate how these diagnoses are related to each other and to the person's overall psychosocial functioning. It is possible for someone to receive one or more diagnoses but to still function relatively well in many life domains. Psychological assessment requires an understanding of the person in his or her social and interpersonal environment. For example, the examination of the impact of diagnostic status on global psychosocial functioning is an important aspect of assessments conducted to determine a person's suitability to return to work or a parent's fitness to have primary physical custody of a child.

Unlike pieces of a jigsaw puzzle, data obtained in psychological assessments infrequently fit together smoothly and neatly—rarely does one piece of information perfectly conform to a related piece of information. As described in previous chapters, it is important for the psychologist to gather information using different methods and, often, from different informants. Yet each source of data has its own strengths, limitations, and potential biases that must be taken into account when integrating the data and drawing conclusions. Assessments of children and adolescents typically require that, in addition to the information gathered directly from the young client, information also be obtained from significant others such as parents and teachers. In assessing adults, it is less common to obtain data from multiple informants, although for some assessment purposes (such as treatment planning for couples therapy or evaluating the daily impact of dementia on a patient), obtaining information from others can also be critical.

The use of data from multiple informants can provide a fuller picture of a person's psychological functioning.

Some fascinating findings on apparent discrepancies among informants were reported by De Los Reyes, Henry, Tolan, and Wakschlag (2009) in their study assessing young children with high levels of disruptive behaviours. Measures of disruptive behaviour were available for each child, from both mothers and teachers. Additionally, using a structured observation procedure, each child's behaviours were observed in the research laboratory during interactions with the mother and with a research assistant. Children who were described as having significant disruptive behaviour problems by the mothers but not by the teachers displayed considerable disruptive behaviours (such as problems with anger modulation and behavioural regulation) during the lab interaction with the mothers—but not during the interaction with the research assistant. In contrast, children who were described as having significant disruptive behaviour problems by the teachers but not by the mothers displayed considerable disruptive behaviours during the lab interaction with the research assistant—but not during the interaction with the mothers. In other words, both mother and teacher reports were correct! By the way, children who were described as having significant disruptive behaviour problems by *both* mothers and teachers displayed considerable disruptive behaviours during both types of lab interactions. These kinds of complexities are similar to those described in Viewpoint Box 9.1, which illustrates some of the challenges in meaningfully integrating data obtained from different informants.

VIEWPOINT BOX 9.1

INTEGRATING DATA FROM MULTIPLE INFORMANTS

The psychological assessment of children and youth often involves collecting data from multiple informants. For example, in assessing 12-year-old Kaleb, who has been suspended from school for aggressive behaviour, data may be gathered from Kaleb, his parents, and his teachers. The computer-generated profile based on Kaleb's responses reveals that he does not consider himself to have any problems with aggression, although he acknowledges feeling sad and having difficulties paying attention. In contrast, his father's profile shows that he sees Kaleb as having externalizing problems in the borderline range; his mother's profile indicates that she sees her son as having clinically significant attentional problems and borderline problems with anxiety, depression, and externalizing behaviours; and his teacher's profile suggests that she perceives Kaleb as having clinically significant attentional problems and borderline problems with externalizing behaviours. It sounds as though we have four different descriptions of the same youth. How do we make sense of these apparently conflicting reports? Is Kaleb "faking bad" by exaggerating his worry and sadness to avoid punishment? Is his father's perspective realistic or is he minimizing the problem? Is the mother realistic or is she oversensitive to her son's distress? Did the teacher rate the correct child or did she perhaps mix Kaleb up with someone else in her class?

As we have described in previous chapters, it is common for there to be only limited correspondence between the ratings of different informants regarding a target individual. Likewise, informant ratings and the self-ratings of the individual are typically only moderately correlated. Given the low concordance between raters, how does a clinical psychologist proceed to make sense of the differing information provided by these reports? Should the psychologist ignore some of the reports or try, somehow, to integrate the various perspectives?

One way in which researchers have addressed this important clinical problem is to examine the value of different decision-making rules in using multiple sources of data. For example, if a psychologist uses the "*or* rule," the decision is based on the assumption that the variable targeted in the assessment is present if any informant reports it. On the other hand, the use of the "*and* rule" means that the psychologist requires evidence of the presence of the variable from two or more informants before assuming that the variable is actually present. Perhaps, not too surprisingly, which rule to follow appears to depend on the variable being assessed.

In their research on youth bipolar disorder, Youngstrom et al. (2004) compared the diagnostic accuracy of six different instruments designed to screen for bipolar disorder in children and adolescents. Three of these instruments involved parent reports, two involved youth self-reports, and one relied on teacher reports.

Across all measures, the parent-based measures consistently outperformed the other measures in identifying bipolar disorder among youth (as determined by a structured diagnostic interview of the youth and parent). In addition, the researchers found that the prediction of bipolar disorder was not improved by combining data from other informants with the parent-based reports.

However, a different picture emerges when considering attention-deficit/hyperactivity disorder (ADHD) in youth. Pelham, Fabiano, and Massetti (2005) synthesized the results of several years of research on the use of multi-informant data in diagnosing ADHD. Among their conclusions: (a) consistent with diagnostic criteria, confirmatory data from both teachers and parents are necessary for the accurate diagnosis of ADHD (i.e., the "*and* rule"); and (b) in ruling out an ADHD diagnosis, it is not necessary to use both parent and teacher data, because if either informant does not endorse ADHD items, the youth is

CONTINUED . . .

unlikely to have a diagnosis of ADHD (i.e., a variation of the "*or* rule). So, to return to Kaleb, this would suggest that, based on the nature of the information provided by the various informants, the psychologist should definitely assess for the presence of ADHD. Additionally, although there are no clear research findings to guide this decision, it would also be prudent for the psychologist to more fully explore the extent to which aggressive, depressive, and anxious symptoms are present.

Combining information from multiple psychological tests or even from multiple scales within a self-report personality test can be a daunting task. Common psychological practice is to begin by examining the client's test responses at the most global level. This would mean, for example, that on the MMPI-2 (Minnesota Multiphasic Personality Inventory-2) the psychologist would first consider scores on the various validity scales and then move to examine the MMPI-2 code type (i.e., the highest two scores on the clinical scales). The validity score data allow the psychologist to evaluate the extent to which the other scale scores are likely to accurately reflect the client's personality and psychosocial functioning. In this way, the code type information serves as the foundation for generating hypotheses about the client, with other MMPI-2 scales and other sources of assessment data added to this foundation (Levak, Hogan, Beutler, & Song, 2011).

Psychologists must be aware that data from other self-report tests and interviews are not independent sources of information that can be used to confirm initial hypotheses. Whether the client provides information about himself or herself during an interview, on one psychological test, or on many psychological tests, these data sources all represent client self-report. Additional assessment data from sources other than self-report (such as reports by significant others, clinical observation, or archival records such as hospitalization data) have the potential to independently corroborate or nuance hypotheses based on self-report data. However, if all the sources of assessment data are based on what is essentially the same source or form of information (such as different self-report measures completed by the same person), then the apparent convergence of data can lead to misplaced confidence regarding the validity or accuracy of the hypotheses or conclusions (Hunsley & Meyer, 2003).

Case Formulation

Many assessment questions require the psychologist to go beyond a descriptive account of the client. Often the purpose of the assessment is to provide directions for possible alleviation or remediation of problems. This includes assessments to address educational

In what ways is the process of developing a case formulation a scientific endeavour?

concerns (e.g., does the client require some form of special education services?), vocational questions (e.g., are the client's career aspirations realistic in light of his or her intellectual abilities, personality, and interests?), rehabilitation services (e.g., does the client need assistance in developing new strategies for daily living to cope with the effects of a severe closed head injury?), and possible referrals for psychotherapy (e.g., are the client's problems amenable to treatment and how motivated is the client to engage in therapy?). In such cases, the psychologist needs to formulate hypotheses about how the problems developed and the factors that maintain them. Typically, the clinical psychologist is also expected to develop a fuller perspective on how the client's current functioning fits with his or her life history and how well the client may be able to function in the future. Then, based on these hypotheses and conclusions, the psychologist provides recommendations of ways to improve the client's functioning. These recommendations frequently, but not necessarily, include suggestions for psychological services. Other suggestions may include obtaining further assessment data from other health care specialists (such as internists, neurologists, or audiologists) or involving health care specialists or other professionals (e.g., teachers, lawyers, or residential care staff) in service planning.

case formulation: a description of the patient that provides information on his or her life situation, current problems, and a set of hypotheses linking psychosocial factors with the patient's clinical condition.

As described in Chapter 5, the term **case formulation** refers to the task of both describing the patient in his or her life context and developing a set of hypotheses that pull together a comprehensive clinical picture in sufficient detail that the psychologist can make decisions about treatment options. Exhibit 9.1 summarizes the ways in which a good case formulation can aid in planning clinical services. A detailed case formulation is particularly useful when a patient has numerous or complex clinical problems, for it allows the psychologist to make informed decisions about the timing, sequence, duration, and specific focus of interventions (Haynes, O'Brien, & Kaholokula, 2011; Mumma, 1998). Even when assessment is followed by treatments that are evidence-based, case formulations are critical. They may provide, for example, information to assist the psychologist in choosing among evidence-based treatment options. Once the option has been chosen (in consultation with the client, of course), the case formulation will guide the psychologist in determining what issues should be emphasized in treatment and how the steps in a treatment manual can be individualized to match client needs.

Clinical psychologists of all theoretical orientations use assessment data to develop case formulations. Eells, Kendjelic, and Lucas (1998) found that, across orientations, case formulations tended to include four major components: symptoms and problems, events or

Exhibit 9.1 The Benefits of a Clinical Case Formulation

- Provides a way of understanding the connections between a patient's various problems
- Provides guidance on the type of treatment to consider (including whether the treatment should be conducted in an individual, couple, family, or group modality)
- Predicts the patient's future functioning if treatment is not sought and how this functioning will be different if treatment is successful
- Provides options to consider if difficulties are encountered in implementing and following through on treatment
- Indicates options, outside of psychological services, for the patient to consider
- Provides alternative treatment options to consider if the initial treatment is unsuccessful

Adapted from Persons (1989).

stressors that led to the symptoms and problems, predisposing life events or stressors (i.e., pre-existing vulnerabilities), and a hypothesized mechanism that linked the first four components together to offer an explanation for the development and maintenance of the problems and symptoms. Exhibit 9.2 summarizes the steps that Mariush (2002) suggested all psychologists should follow in developing a case formulation.

Exhibit 9.2 Developing a Case Formulation

Step 1. Develop a comprehensive problem list, including the patient's stated problems and other problems indicated by referral agents or identified by other informants during the assessment.

Step 2. Determine the nature of each problem, including its origin, current precipitants, and consequences.

Step 3. Identify patterns or commonalities among the problems; this may yield an indication of previously unidentified factors that serve to maintain, exacerbate, or lessen the problem.

Step 4. Develop working hypotheses to explain the problems.

Step 5. Evaluate and refine the hypotheses, using all information gathered during the assessment and the patient's feedback on the hypotheses.

Step 6. If the psychologist moves from conducting an assessment to providing treatment, the hypotheses should be reconsidered, re-evaluated, and revised (as necessary) based on data gathered during treatment.

Adapted from Mariush (2002).

A major challenge in case formulation is that the psychologist must accurately detect patterns in the wealth of data gathered during an assessment, including patterns that may be primarily attributable to

©iStock.com/SilviaJansen

The psychologist must integrate assessment findings, identifying patterns evident in the data.

cultural factors (Ridley & Kelly, 2006). Even if the assessment is limited to an interview with the client and some self-report measures completed by the client before the interview, it is not an easy task to detect patterns. Then, assuming that the psychologist has been able to recognize patterns in the data, he or she must then try to relate these patterns to specific causes and outcomes.

We address the challenges of this exercise more fully in the next section. At this point, we will illustrate the difficulty of these tasks with one example. O'Brien (1995) presented clinical psychology graduate students with a very limited but clear set of assessment data: daily self-monitoring data (for 14 days) from a client who presented with frequent and severe headaches. Each day of self-monitoring data included information on the client's overall stress level, hours of sleep, interpersonal conflicts, number of headaches, severity and duration of the headaches, and the number of analgesics taken to deal with the headaches. The students' task was to estimate the magnitude of the relation between precipitating factors (such as reduced sleep, high stress, and frequency of arguments) and headache symptoms (such as frequency, severity, and duration). Across the 14 days of self-monitoring data, the students were able to accurately detect the factors most highly correlated with symptoms only 50% of the time!

Thus far we have not directly addressed the influence of the clinical psychologist's theoretical orientation in the development of a case formulation. Theoretical orientation plays a central role in all aspects of the assessment process, from the nature of the initial hypotheses made about the client, to the selection of assessment tools, to the manner in which the assessment data are used to build a full clinical picture of the client. Berman (1997) described case formulation as having two key features. The first is a succinct analysis of the client's core strengths and weaknesses, which Berman called the premise. The second is the supporting material, which involves an in-depth analysis of these strengths and weaknesses. According to Berman, the premise of the case formulation is tied to the clinician's theoretical perspective. Indeed, the type of constructs to be included in both the premise and the supporting material is enormously influenced by orientation. Interpersonally oriented psychodynamic case formulations are likely to focus on dysfunctional relationship styles (called *cyclical maladaptive patterns*) as the premise for the formulations, whereas process-experiential formulations are likely to use information about the client's emotional processing and insight into emotional issues in developing the main premise (Berman, 1997; Eells, 2006).

Given exactly the same clinical information, clinicians of differing orientations are likely to develop very different formulations. Plous and

Zimbardo (1986) found, for example, that in formulating hypotheses about the development of psychological symptoms, psychoanalysts emphasized dispositional and personality factors, whereas behaviour therapists focused on either situational influences or the interaction of situational and dispositional influences. Of course, this raises the question of just who is right. Unfortunately, there is very limited research on the validity of case formulations (Beiling & Kuyken, 2003; Garb, 1997).

There is, however, growing research on the reliability of case formulations. This line of research provides evidence on the extent to which clinical psychologists within an orientation are likely to formulate the same case formulation for a given patient. Jacqueline Persons has devoted considerable effort to developing an approach to case formulation that clinical psychologists can easily learn and use. Her Cognitive-Behavioral Case Formulation approach emphasizes the importance of identifying the patient's overt problems (such as psychological symptoms, interpersonal conflicts, or legal problems) and long-standing beliefs (called *schemas*) that, when activated by life events, are believed to cause the overt problems (Persons, 1989, 2008). She found that clinicians, when presented with detailed case information, accurately identified about two-thirds of a client's main presenting problems, and that the mean inter-rater reliability of patient schemas was $r = 0.72$ (Persons & Bertagnolli, 1999). Similar reliability results have been reported for psychodynamic case formulations that focus on core relationship conflicts (Barber & Crits-Christoph, 1993). Such findings suggest that, within an orientation, there can be considerable similarity in the case formulations developed by clinicians. There is also growing evidence that, regardless of orientation, some basic training in developing case formulations can greatly enhance the quality of clinicians' formulations (Kendjelic & Eells, 2007).

case example **MELISSA**

The clinical psychologist to whom Melissa was referred specialized in providing cognitive-behavioural treatments for anxiety and related problems. Based on the referral from the physician, the psychologist assumed that a major part of the assessment would involve an evaluation of obsessive-compulsive symptoms. However, knowing from the research literature that patients who have an anxiety disorder often have a comorbid mood disorder or another anxiety disorder, the psychologist was prepared to assess a full range of potential anxiety and mood symptoms. As people with anxiety disorders often use alcohol or other drugs in an attempt to moderate their symptoms, the evaluation also addressed the possibility of a substance abuse problem. Finally, because individuals with obsessive-compulsive disorder (OCD) may not be fully aware of the extent or severity of their problems, the psychologist planned to briefly interview Erik as part of the assessment. (More details on these assessment issues can be found in Abramowitz [2008] and McLean and Woody [2001].) An interview with Erik provided an opportunity to determine (a) Erik's perspective on the extent to which the baby might be in any significant danger because of Melissa's symptoms leading her to neglect or forget about the baby, and (b) his willingness to assist in his wife's treatment (with his wife's agreement, of course). Accordingly, based on knowledge of both the psychopathology and treatment literatures, the psychologist planned to use the following assessment tools: an interview with Melissa, an interview with Erik, self-monitoring diaries with Melissa (and possibly with Erik), the MMPI-2, the Yale-Brown Obsessive Compulsive Scale-II (Y-BOCS-II; Storch et al., 2010), the Beck Depression Inventory-II (BDI-II), the Penn State Worry Questionnaire (Meyer, Miller, Metzger, & Borkovec, 1990), and the Fear Questionnaire (Marks & Mathews, 1979). Of course, tools might be dropped or added based on the psychologist's initial case formulation following the interviews.

Having reviewed criteria for OCD, major depressive disorder, and generalized anxiety disorder prior to the interview, the psychologist conducted an interview with Melissa that focused largely on her symptoms. Questions were also asked about her understanding of the development of her problems, her efforts to cope with her symptoms, and her concerns regarding the symptoms' effects on her baby and Erik. After approximately 45 minutes, the psychologist concluded this first interview with Melissa. The importance of using standardized symptom measures was then explained to Melissa and she was asked to complete the four symptom checklists (not including the MMPI-2) while Erik was interviewed. During his interview, Erik was asked about how Melissa was coping with her problems, his understanding of her problems, and how his life was affected by Melissa's distress. The psychologist also asked Erik how they were both dealing with the demands of being new parents and how Erik saw Melissa in her role as a mother. After 30 minutes or so, the psychologist concluded the interview with Erik, checked that Melissa had completed the measures, and invited her to join Erik in the psychologist's office.

At this point, the psychologist shared some initial impressions with the couple. After commenting on how well they were dealing with the challenges they both faced, the psychologist stated that it appeared Melissa was indeed suffering from OCD. Although the tests would need to be scored and further information would be required to determine if other clinical problems were evident, it was clear that Melissa should consider treatment for this disorder. The psychologist briefly described the main evidence-based psychological and pharmacological treatments for OCD, but emphasized that Melissa would not need to make any treatment-related decisions until the assessment was concluded. As a final step in this initial feedback session, the psychologist provided Melissa with a simple self-monitoring form to record some information (duration of anxiety, level of anxiety, and efforts to cope with the anxiety) each time she noticed that she was anxious about inadvertently harming someone and about the possibility of having left dangerous materials in the house. Melissa understood that recording these details would help the psychologist better understand the nature of her anxiety and readily agreed to do the self-monitoring each day until the next assessment appointment six days later.

Between the first and second appointments with Melissa, the psychologist scored the symptom measures and summarized diagnostic hypotheses from the interviews. Melissa clearly met criteria for OCD and both the obsessions and the compulsions subscales of the Y-BOCS-II were in the OCD range. There were a number of situations that Melissa indicated on the Fear Questionnaire that she tended to avoid but, other than trying to avoid thoughts of injury or illness, none of the items indicated evidence of a clinical problem. On the worry measure, she scored above the 70th percentile, but the interview data suggested that she did not meet criteria for generalized anxiety disorder as all of her worries were better accounted for by the OCD diagnosis. Melissa scored in the moderately depressed range on the BDI-II, but the interview data indicated that she did not currently meet criteria for a mood disorder—it did seem likely to the psychologist that such a disorder might develop if her OCD was not treated.

At the second appointment, the psychologist met with Melissa for 30 minutes to review the self-monitoring data and to ask Melissa about her symptoms over the past few days. The psychologist also checked whether she had any questions about the information discussed in their first meeting. After the interview, Melissa completed the MMPI-2. To allow sufficient time for the psychologist to review the assessment data, a full feedback session was scheduled for two weeks later. Melissa asked if Erik could attend the meeting; the psychologist immediately agreed to this.

In interpreting the MMPI-2, the psychologist was particularly interested in the code type of Melissa's responses (i.e., her highest scores on the Clinical scales) and the scores on some of the Content scales. All Validity scale scores were in the normal range, indicating that she had responded in a consistent and forthright manner to the MMPI-2 items. This was in line with observations of Melissa during the two interviews, for she clearly took all the interview questions seriously and tried to give full and accurate answers even when she became upset in describing some of her difficulties. With respect to code type, Melissa's highest two scores in the clinical range were 7 (Pt) and 8 (Sc), with 7 being much higher than 8. This code type is typically found among people who are having problems with ruminations, obsessions, anxiety, and depression, who have frequent health concerns, and who are feeling stressed out. On the Content scales, there were elevations with anxiety, obsessiveness, and health concerns, but the Depression scale did not quite reach the clinical level. Finally, the psychologist scored the test for the supplemental scores available to evaluate addiction and substance abuse. Consistent with interview data, there was no indication that Melissa was relying on alcohol or other substances to alleviate her anxiety.

PROFILE BOX 9.1

DR. HEATHER HADJISTAVROPOULOS

Courtesy of Trevor Hopkin, University of Regina

After receiving my Ph.D. in clinical psychology from the University of British Columbia in 1995, I became registered as a doctoral psychologist in Saskatchewan in 1996. I am currently a full professor of psychology and director of clinical training at the University of Regina (U of R). I teach an advanced undergraduate course in clinical psychology and graduate courses in psychological assessment and professional issues. I founded the Psychology Training Clinic at the U of R in 2002. In this clinic, clients from Regina and surrounding area are seen by doctoral students in clinical psychology under the supervision of faculty members. In 2010, I founded the Online Therapy Unit for Service Education and Research (onlinetherapyuser.ca). The unit oversees trained therapists (students and community providers) in the provision of online cognitive behaviour therapy (Online-CBT) to residents of Saskatchewan. Through the unit, research is conducted on the delivery of Online-CBT. I currently hold research funding from the Canadian Institutes of Health Research and the Saskatchewan Health Research Foundation to conduct research in this area. In 2012, I was president of the Canadian Association of Cognitive and Behavioural Therapies. I have a small part-time private practice that is focused on the assessment and treatment of clients with anxiety and mood disorders, or clients who are experiencing psychological problems related to comorbid medical conditions (e.g., chronic pain).

CONTINUED . . .

HOW DID YOU CHOOSE TO BECOME A CLINICAL PSYCHOLOGIST?

I first became interested in clinical psychology in high school. My interest in the area was solidified once I took courses in abnormal psychology and personality in university. I always knew that I would enjoy helping clients who had psychological problems. Something that I had not expected when I was in high school was how much I would also enjoy research. In my fourth year as an undergraduate student, I became particularly interested in clinical health psychology, or the application of knowledge from clinical psychology and health psychology into practices that promote health or treat illness or disability.

WHAT IS THE GREATEST CHALLENGE YOU FACE AS A CLINICAL PSYCHOLOGIST?

My position as a professor of psychology involves teaching, research, clinical practice, and administration. My greatest challenge is finding time to do a good job in all of these roles, while at the same time ensuring I have free time for my family and for myself. Many days I feel torn in many directions.

TELL US ABOUT HOW YOU TRAIN STUDENTS TO INTEGRATE ASSESSMENT DATA AND ENGAGE IN RESEARCH-INFORMED CLINICAL DECISION-MAKING.

Central to training students to integrate assessment data and make research-informed clinical decisions is first to ensure that students have foundational knowledge that they need before they work with clients. This means having knowledge of research on psychopathology and assessment, as well as on evidence-based interventions. Also key to this training is ensuring that students have the opportunity to assess many clients with many different problems and with varying complexity under supervision. This supervision helps students to appropriately integrate information from various sources (e.g., tests, interviews, observation) and to consider relevant research when making clinical decisions.

HOW DO YOU INTEGRATE SCIENCE AND PRACTICE IN YOUR WORK?

My clinical practice is informed by research evidence when assessing clients (e.g., selecting tests with strong psychometric properties, using structured interviews for diagnosis). My therapeutic orientation is cognitive behavioural, which is also evidence-based. Given my academic and research work, I spend considerable time reading the literature and subsequently work to incorporate evidence-based clinical findings into my clinical practice. My research is currently focused on examining the efficacy of Online-CBT and how to best train therapists and integrate this treatment into community settings. This research is directly informed by clinical practice, in that clients often have a difficult time accessing mental health care, and there is a need to examine new ways of delivering care in order to improve the under-treatment of mental health problems.

WHAT DO YOU SEE AS THE MOST EXCITING CHANGES IN THE FIELD OF CLINICAL PSYCHOLOGY?

Given advances in technology, I am very excited by the attention being given to finding novel ways to provide psychological services to individuals with mental health problems. Use of technology such as the Internet, telephone, smartphone applications, and virtual reality environments has enormous potential to improve both access to mental health care and the efficacy of clinical psychology services. Before technology is used in everyday clinical practice, however, more research is needed on the efficacy of interventions that incorporate technology, and attention needs to be given to the dissemination of findings to health care providers.

THREATS TO THE VALIDITY OF ASSESSMENTS AND CASE FORMULATIONS

Patient/Client Factors

As you know from Chapter 8, clinical psychologists are well aware that people may selectively choose how they depict themselves during a psychological evaluation. To achieve certain ends, people may consciously highlight either their strengths or their weaknesses. Some people who are required to undergo an evaluation for court-mandated reasons may attempt to render their results invalid by purposely responding to test items in a random manner. As we described previously, there are measures to detect such attempts at impression management. There are also more subtle biases that can affect the validity of patient-provided data. These biases are not necessarily consciously intended and, therefore, are much less likely to be detected by responses to validity scales or measures of malingering.

A basic assumption underlying the use of interviews and self-report measures is that people accurately recall and report events in their lives. The truth of this assumption seems so obvious that, in our daily lives, we rarely have any reason to question it. After all, we are usually certain about what we were doing when important events occurred in our lives, whether they be events of personal significance (such as learning of the death of a family member) or of more global significance (such as what we were doing when we learned that planes had struck the World Trade Center in New York City in 2001). However, when psychologists study the accuracy of these recalled memories, it appears that there is good reason to be sceptical about the general accuracy of memory. We will examine several lines of research bearing on the accuracy of self-report data that relies on **retrospective recall**.

retrospective recall: using data that rely on people to remember events that happened to them at some point in the past.

Gosling, John, Craik, and Robins (1998) videotaped research participants in a group discussion. Following the interaction, each participant was asked to recall how frequently he or she had engaged in specific acts such as "I persuaded others to accept my opinion on the issue." Using the videotapes, observers recorded each instance of the participant engaging in these acts. Across 12 different acts that were coded with high reliability (an alpha > .80), the average correlation between participants' recall and observers' records was only .40! For highly observable acts (e.g., "The participant reminded the group of their time limit"), there was much greater agreement than there was for acts that required some inference on the part of observers (e.g., "The participant took the opposite point of view just to be contrary"). The desirability of the acts also seemed to have an effect on the correlation between participant and observer data. Compared with observer act counts, participants tended to over-report the frequency with which they engaged in socially desirable acts (e.g., "Participant settled the dispute among other members of the group") and to under-report engaging in less desirable acts (e.g., "Participant yelled at someone"). Taken together, these results, which are consistent with prior research findings, suggest that there may be considerable variability in the accuracy of people's reports of how they acted in a particular situation, even when the reports are given shortly after the situation occurred. The clinical implications are clear: first, we should not assume complete accuracy when using checklists that ask clients to indicate the frequency of occurrence of behaviours, symptoms, or other experiences; and, second, we should expect that the desirability of the experience being reported may influence the accuracy of the information provided by the client.

A second line of research relevant to the issue of memory effects on self-report measures compares people's recording of events as they happen (or shortly after they happen) with their later recall of the events. For example, Shiffman and colleagues (1997) asked people who had recently quit smoking to record their smoking lapses and temptations to smoke. Twelve weeks later, participants were asked to provide retrospective accounts of these events. The overall pattern of results suggested that recalled information was highly inaccurate: only 57% of participants were able to accurately recall whether they had a lapse within a two-week period, and the recalled number of cigarettes smoked was three times greater than the number reported during the lapses. Perhaps most strikingly, people were highly confident in the accuracy of their recall but there was no statistically significant relation between confidence ratings and accuracy. Stone and colleagues (1998) also examined the relation between immediate reports of participants' attempts to cope with daily stressors and the recall of their coping efforts two days later. On average, approximately one-third of people failed to retrospectively report coping efforts they recorded using during the actual occurrence of their efforts; a similar number retrospectively reported using coping strategies that they did not report using during the events in question. As a final example, Halford, Keefer, and Osgarby (2002) asked 60 heterosexual couples to keep a daily diary of events in their relationship for one week. At the end of the week, all participants were asked to describe the week overall, and their descriptions were then coded in terms of positive and negative comments about the relationship. The researchers were particularly interested in whether participants' satisfaction with their relationship would colour their recall of events. Consistent with their hypotheses, when these summary comments were compared with the daily diaries, low relationship satisfaction was significantly related to a tendency to recall the relationship events in an overly negative manner.

Research indicates that it is not just minor daily events that are difficult to accurately recall. As part of an ongoing project based in New Zealand to track health and development, Henry, Moffitt, Caspi, Langley, and Silva (1994) used data from more than 1,000 young adults to compare retrospectively recalled events at age 18 with data on these events that were obtained throughout the participants' childhood and adolescence. The researchers found enormous variability in the accuracy of the recollections, with correlations between recalled events and actual details of the events ranging from -.02 to .77! Although correlations were relatively high for reports on the number of housing moves ($r = .76$) and height and weight just prior to puberty ($r \geq .59$), accuracy was very poor for recall of psychosocial variables such as the extent of conflict in the family prior to age 15 ($r \leq .25$), maternal depression prior to age 15 ($r \leq .20$), and the extent of depressive or hyperactive symptoms in participants prior to age 11 ($r \leq .12$). As these psychosocial variables are the ones that clinicians typically ask about during initial assessments, it appears that there are considerable grounds for doubting the veracity of these reports.

©iStock.com/Rubberball

Studies suggest recall memory is not always accurate.

As we described in previous chapters, clinical psychologists may be asked to assess individuals to determine their level of ability or functioning prior to an event such as a workplace injury or a motor vehicle accident. Many studies suggest that it is important to gather archival information, such as medical, school, or police records, as part of this assessment rather than relying on patient self-report. Greiffenstein, Baker, and Johnson-Greene (2002), for example, compared self-reported and actual academic performance among people with head injuries who were or were not involved in lawsuits based on the accident that led to the injuries. Compared with the non-litigating group, those who had filed lawsuits showed a much greater tendency to overestimate their scholastic performance.

Does it feel to you that your memories of recent and more distant events might be flawed? Can you think of examples of memories you have that seem very clear but you know are not entirely accurate?

Clinician Factors

Since the groundbreaking work of cognitive psychologists Tversky and Kahneman (1974), there has been dramatic growth in our knowledge of how subtle influences can affect judgment, reasoning, and decision-making processes. We now know a great deal about how experience, expectations, attributions, and stereotypes all shape the ways in which people make both relatively minor and major decisions. For example, hundreds of studies have examined the tendency for people to see themselves in a generally positive light, even when such positivity may not be warranted. A meta-analysis conducted by Mezulis, Abramson, Hyde, and Hankin (2004) included 266 studies of the **self-serving attributional bias**. This bias involves people making more internal, stable, and global attributions for positive events in their lives than they do for negative events (e.g., *I got an A on the paper because I worked hard for it. I am always a hard worker, in every area of my life, so it is no wonder that good things occur in my life.* versus *I really didn't deserve a C on the paper. It really wasn't my fault that my computer crashed. I usually get things done on time—I know that I left things late this time, but if my hard drive hadn't crashed I would have been fine.*). Health care professionals are not immune to this bias, which can lead to substantial overestimates about one's competence and the quality of the services one provides (Brosnan, Reynolds, & Moore, 2008; Davis et al., 2006).

self-serving attributional bias: a tendency to take more personal credit for successes than for failures, by attributing success but not failure to internal, stable, and global causes.

Generally speaking, **biases** involve judgments that are systematically different from what a person should conclude based on logic or probability. **Heuristics** are mental shortcuts that people often use to ease the burden of decision-making, but which also tend to result in errors in decision-making. Thus, heuristics are at the heart of cognitive biases. Since the 1980s, **Howard Garb** has contributed much to our understanding of how biases and heuristics influence routine clinical tasks (e.g., Garb, 1997, 2005), and his 1998 book provides an excellent summary of the large literature indicating that simply being trained to provide psychological services does not make a person immune to human information processing biases. Exhibit 9.3 provides a summary of common biases and heuristics that can affect clinical decision-making. Although we present this table in the section on clinician factors that affect the validity of assessment, these biases and heuristics apply equally to patient reports.

biases: judgments that are systematically different from what a person should conclude based on logic or probability.

heuristics: mental shortcuts that make decision-making easier and faster but often lead to less accurate decisions.

Biases and heuristics are likely to lead to errors in decision-making. However, not all errors are created equal: some are potentially more damaging than others and small errors may not really make much of a difference. For example, failing to administer one item on an intelligence test because the clinician didn't think that the person could get the correct answer will affect the overall total test score, but is unlikely to affect the global interpretation of the client's score as being average or above average. In other words, not all errors result in mistakes that have real-world consequences. With respect to psychological services,

Exhibit 9.3 Common Decision-Making Biases and Heuristics

Fundamental Attribution Error: In attempting to understand why a person acted in such a manner, there is a tendency to overestimate the influence of personality traits and to underestimate the influence of situational effects on the person's behaviour.

Inattention to Base Rates: A psychologist may believe that a certain pattern of responses on a test is indicative of a specific diagnosis, and support this belief with information on some relevant cases. However, without full knowledge of the base rate of (a) the pattern of test responses and (b) the diagnosis, it is not possible to determine the extent to which the test responses accurately predict the diagnosis.

Belief in the Law of Small Numbers: Results drawn from small samples are likely to be more extreme and less consistent than those obtained from large samples. Nevertheless, the clinical psychologist may be tempted to attend more to information gained from two or three patients with a specific disorder than to the results of research on the disorder. Direct experience with a small number of patients may feel more relevant and compelling, even though it is less likely to yield accurate information compared with data drawn from research samples.

Regression to the Mean: Because of the nature of measurement error, a person who obtains an extreme score on a test at one point in time is likely to obtain a less extreme score when next taking the test. This apparent change in test scores has nothing to do with real alterations in the person's life. (The standard error of measurement is available for many psychological tests so that psychologists can take this into account when comparing test scores from two time points.)

Inferring Causation from Correlation: A psychologist may note that there appears to be substantial co-occurrence of certain patient characteristics (such as a history of sexual abuse and the presence of borderline personality disorder) and infer that the earlier of the two characteristics causes the later characteristic (i.e., the abuse led to the development of the personality disorder). Before drawing causal inferences, though, other factors must be considered, including whether the later characteristic may influence the information provided about the earlier characteristic, and the possibility that both characteristics stemmed from a third variable (e.g., severely dysfunctional family environment).

Hindsight Bias: As the saying goes, "hindsight is 20/20." Most decisions (including clinical decisions) must be made without the benefit of all the pertinent information. After a decision has been made and, as a consequence, a certain course of action has been taken, new information may become available. It is tempting to validate or question the initial decision based on data gathered after the fact even though it was not possible to have these data inform the original decision.

Confirmatory Bias: Once a clinical hunch has been formed, it is tempting to gather information to support it. However, in testing a hypothesis, it is important to evaluate evidence both for and against the hypothesis. The clinical psychologist must avoid simply looking for evidence to support the hypothesis (such as a diagnosis or an emerging case formulation) and also actively look for evidence that would refute or temper the strength of the hypothesis.

Representativeness Heuristic: Relying on biases such as the belief in the law of small numbers to draw conclusions about the degree to which a symptom or behaviour is representative of an underlying disorder or condition.

Availability Heuristic: Making a decision based on easily recalled information, such as recent, extreme, or unusual examples that are relevant to the decision. Using only easily recalled examples (such as

CONTINUED . . .

the last person assessed with similar symptoms) will lead to an incomplete evaluation of the elements that must be considered in the decision. By definition, extreme examples are atypical and likely to bias a decision.

Affect Heuristic: When reaching a decision, the affective qualities (such as likeability, negativity, disgust, or pleasure) of cognitive representations of people or objects are rapidly considered. This usually occurs at an unconscious level and can lead to a judgment based solely on emotional considerations (such as the attractiveness of an individual), with only minimal attention paid to the full range of factors relevant to the decision.

Anchoring and Adjustment Heuristic: Initial conditions or characteristics determine a starting point for considering the nature of an individual or task (such as using the dealer's price when negotiating to buy a car). In clinical contexts, this means that, for example, first impressions may serve as the (possibly inaccurate) basis for considering and integrating all subsequent information gathered about a person.

What common heuristics are operating when we assume that a person who has been exposed to trauma is likely to be psychologically vulnerable?

and health care services more generally, it is almost certainly best for clinicians to try to minimize the effects of heuristics and biases, as we know that some clinician errors can have substantial consequences. Let's take the example of diagnosis. Inaccurate or unwarranted diagnoses can lead to unnecessary and costly treatment, considerable stigma, and a host of other negative social side effects. Kim and Ahn (2002) found that, when determining a diagnosis, clinical psychologists and graduate clinical psychology students are more likely to be influenced by their own causal theories than they are by the actual DSM criteria relevant to the diagnostic category. As another example, compared with actual occurrences of violence, clinicians typically over-predict the violence of male patients and under-predict the violence of female patients. Likewise, African American psychiatric inpatients and prison inmates are predicted by clinicians to be more violent than are White psychiatric inpatients and prison inmates (Garb, 1997, 2005). Other ethnic biases have also been found in clinical practice: for example, minority patients diagnosed with schizophrenia are almost twice as likely as White patients to receive excessive dosages of antipsychotic medication (Wood, Garb, Lilienfeld, & Nezworski, 2002).

If some clinical errors are so important, what gets in the way of clinicians—psychologists, physicians, psychiatrists, and others—identifying and correcting their mistakes? One of the main obstacles seems to be that people tend to be overconfident in the accuracy or correctness of their decisions (Griffin, Dunning, & Ross, 1990). Ryan and Schnakenburg-Ott (2003), for example, found that despite making substantial errors in scoring an intelligence test, both experienced psychologists and graduate students were very confident about the accuracy of their scoring efforts. In an attempt to understand the factors that lead to overconfidence in clinical decisions, Smith and Dumont (2002) asked 36 clinical psychologists to "think aloud" while they read case file material about a patient (including life history data and information about current events in the patient's life). The researchers coded several aspects of the thoughts reported by participants during the task, including the confidence expressed in the accuracy of their conclusions. Among the variables they investigated, the sole factor that predicted psychologists' confidence was the extent to which dispositional (as opposed to contextual) information was used. In other words, it appears that the fundamental attribution error (see Exhibit 9.3) may play a powerful role in leading clinicians to be overconfident in their interpretations, decisions, and conclusions.

Improving the Accuracy of Clinical Judgment

In light of the kinds of errors we have just described, it seems obvious that psychologists and other clinicians should be more cautious in their decision-making. Simply being aware of decision-making biases and the resultant errors is insufficient—clinical psychologists (and others who wish to reduce the role of biases in their decisions) must take concrete steps to tackle the potential for bias and error. In this regard, the evidence is overwhelming that the use of informal, unstructured strategies to integrate assessment data is inferior to strategies that rely on the structured application of empirical evidence (Ægisdóttir et al., 2006; Grove, Zald, Lebow, Snitz, & Nelson, 2000). This was the conclusion reached in the middle of the last century by Meehl (1954) who launched the so-called clinical versus actuarial debate. Meehl's conclusion has been repeatedly supported since then.

There is clear evidence that clinical experience per se has little impact on improving clinical judgment. Spengler et al. (2009) conducted a meta-analysis of 75 clinical judgment studies, involving over 4,600 clinicians, and found an overall correlation of .06 between clinical experience and accuracy in a range of judgment tasks. So, what *can* help to improve clinical judgment? Exhibit 9.4 describes a host of other simple, practical strategies that psychologists can follow in order to minimize the impact of bias and error in their work. Unfortunately, based on a review of courses offered in APA-accredited clinical psychology programs, very few graduate students in clinical psychology receive much classroom training in these strategies. Harding (2007) found that, in these programs, issues related to decision-making were most likely to be covered in non-required courses in cognitive psychology. Only 9% of these programs had required courses that included material on decision improvement strategies. That being said, psychologists who learn and routinely apply the strategies listed in Exhibit 9.4 will do a great deal to enhance the quality of their decision-making and reduce the likelihood of errors affecting the services they offer to the public.

Exhibit 9.4 Improving the Accuracy of Clinical Judgment

- Use psychological tests that are directly relevant to the assessment task and that have strong psychometric qualities.
- Check for scoring errors when using test data.
- Use computers as aids in the collection, scoring, and interpretation of clinical data whenever possible.
- Use normative data and base rate information whenever available.
- Use established diagnostic criteria when making diagnostic decisions.
- Use evidence-based decision aids, such as decision trees or clinical guidelines.
- In unstructured tasks, such as conducting interviews and reviewing assessment data, be as systematic, structured, and quantifiable as possible in order to obtain, consider, and use all relevant information.
- Be aware of relevant research in psychological assessment, psychopathology, and prevention/intervention.
- Be aware of personal biases and preconceptions.
- Be self-critical: search for alternative explanations for hypotheses and challenge evolving case formulations.
- Seek consultation from other professionals when unsure of the accuracy of conclusions.
- Don't rely on memory and don't rush any conclusion or decision.

A friend has just told you that someone she knows named Chris is interested in switching to psychology as a major. Without asking your friend any questions, do you assume that Chris is female or male? Obviously, the person's name can be either a man's or a woman's, so this doesn't give you any clues. However, you do know something about the base rate of men and women in psychology courses. For many years now, the majority of students majoring in psychology have been women. So, using this base rate information, your best guess about Chris's gender should be that Chris is a woman.

case example **MELISSA**

The psychologist assessing Melissa was concerned about a number of possible biases that might affect the validity of the assessment information. To deal with the possibility that Melissa might unwittingly underestimate the extent of her problems, symptom-related information was also collected from Erik. As Melissa might consciously downplay her difficulties, a measure with established validity scales was used (the MMPI-2). Because both Melissa and Erik's memories of her symptoms might be influenced by her most recent episodes of anxiety or by her most extreme episodes of anxiety, Melissa was asked to self-monitor her anxiety for a week. Finally, because both Melissa and Erik might have concerns about how Melissa's anxiety was influencing her ability as a parent, the psychologist asked each of them separately about this issue. This point was particularly important as the psychologist had a duty to contact child protection services if it appeared that the baby was in need of protection. After interviewing both parents, it was the psychologist's opinion that the baby was not in need of protection.

Several steps were taken to guard against biases that might affect the clinical psychologist's judgment; for example, DSM-5 criteria were used to make diagnostic decisions. Because the psychologist specialized in anxiety disorders, it was important to address the possibilities of overestimating the likelihood of an anxiety diagnosis and underestimating other diagnoses. To this end, several self-report measures were used to establish the nature of the anxiety and depressive symptoms. The MMPI-2 would also provide indications if other clinically significant disorders might be present. With respect to the possibility of errors in the assessment, standardized psychological tests were used that had relevant norms and solid psychometric properties. The psychologist checked all scoring of the measures and used software to generate interpretive statements for the MMPI-2. The psychologist obtained information from multiple informants and looked for independent confirmation of the main hypotheses generated early in the assessment with Melissa.

PSYCHOLOGICAL ASSESSMENT REPORTS AND TREATMENT PLANS

The assessment process culminates in writing a report and, usually, presenting the assessment findings to the individual or individuals who were the focus of the assessment. In addition to providing information to the agency or professional (or the client), the report serves as a record of the assessment that can be referred to subsequently and, in some instances, can also be a document used for legal purposes. In situations in which some form of treatment will follow the assessment, the report records the client's functioning prior to intervention. This baseline information is crucial in accurately determining the impact of any intervention.

What are the advantages of reviewing reports with clients?

Assessments may be requested by many people, including clients, the parents of young clients, physicians, insurance companies, employers, lawyers, or the courts. Accordingly, when conducting the assessment and writing the report, the psychologist must be cognizant of the potential uses of the report and the "audiences" for the report (Groth-Marnat & Horvath, 2008). This is especially true when the person being assessed is in a potentially adversarial position with the agency that requested the assessment. As described previously in the text, this can happen when an individual is making a claim for compensation based on injuries suffered and the agency responsible for adjudicating the claim seeks an independent evaluation of the individual's psychological state. Issues of informed consent and confidentiality are always important in the provision of psychological services. However, when there may be competing interests involved, it is especially important for the psychologist to emphasize and reiterate the rights and options available to the person who is being assessed.

In almost all jurisdictions, privacy legislation allows clients access to their psychological records, so the psychologist should write a report with this in mind. Although this should not change any conclusions or recommendations, it should affect how the report is written. Care must be taken to minimize or eliminate any stigmatizing or objectionable terms or descriptions in the report. Moreover, in integrating information from multiple sources, it is also crucial that the psychologist clearly attribute who said what. Reports are always potential legal documents that may have ramifications far beyond the original reasons for which the assessment was conducted. If based solely on client self-report, a statement such as "His father physically assaulted him on numerous occasions" should be written as "The client reported that his father had physically assaulted him on numerous occasions." Likewise, ambiguous terms should be avoided. In describing marital arguments, for example, the phrase "the couple often fights" could refer either to frequent arguments or physical violence. Exhibit 9.5 highlights some principles that clinical psychologists typically follow in order to maximize the validity and usefulness of their assessment reports.

Exhibit 9.5 Principles of Report Writing

- Clearly state the purpose of the report and explicitly address the referral questions.
- Identify common themes, integrating the findings across assessment procedures.
- Use all relevant sources of information about the client (including test results, behavioural observations, individual test responses, interview data, and case history) in generating hypotheses, formulating interpretations, and making recommendations.
- Be definitive when the findings are clear; be cautious when the findings are inconsistent; and be clear about your confidence in your conclusions.
- Use concrete examples to enhance the report's readability.
- Interpret the meaning and implications of a test score rather than simply citing test names and scores.
- Refrain from making diagnoses solely on the basis of test scores; consider all sources of information.
- Communicate clearly and eliminate unnecessary technical material in order to enhance the report's readability and ensure it can be understood by all who are likely to read it.

Adapted from Kvaal, Choca, Groth-Marnat, and Davis (2011) and Sattler (1992).

Earlier in the chapter, we described how computers could be used to improve the accuracy of some aspects of clinical decision-making. Despite the numerous benefits of using computers for various assessment-related tasks, clinical psychologists need to exercise considerable caution with computer-based interpretations (CBIs) when integrating the assessment data and writing the assessment report. Because CBIs are based on research using group level data, not all interpretative comments associated with, say, a specific MMPI-2 code type apply to the patient being assessed. The clinician needs to review the CBI and select only those narrative statements that accurately describe the patient in question. Next the psychologist must examine the relevance of any statement, given the reasons for the assessment (Kvaal, Choca, Groth-Marnat, & Davis, 2011). In most jurisdictions, the regulatory bodies for psychologists have clear guidelines on the use of CBIs in psychological assessment. Typically these include the need to ensure the relevance of the interpretations to the patients, and to clearly identify any statements that come directly from the computer report and that are the sole source of information for a specific point or conclusion. For these reasons, including an unedited computer report in an assessment report is not considered appropriate or responsible in routine practice.

computer-based interpretations: reports generated by computer programs that match a patient's general pattern of responses on a psychological test to summaries of research evidence about the typical characteristics of people with the same pattern of test responses.

Exhibit 9.6 presents the sections typically found in most psychological assessment reports focused on issues of psychological functioning. There are no standards dictating the necessary components of a report; the content and structure depend on the reasons for the assessment. Most reports are several single-spaced pages in length, although reports prepared for legal or forensic purposes tend to be substantially longer.

Exhibit 9.6 Sections of an Assessment Report Focused on Psychological Functioning Issues

- Identifying patient/client information
- Reason for referral
- Background information (including, as relevant, developmental history, educational history, employment history, family history, relationship history, medical history, history of symptoms and disorders)
- Assessment methods (including tests administered)
- Interview data and behavioural observations
- Test results (including interpretation of test scores)
- Diagnostic impressions and case formulation
- Summary
- Recommendations

Exhibit 9.7 presents the sections usually included in assessment reports prepared for treatment planning purposes. These treatment plans differ from the typical assessment report in that they focus primarily on using the assessment data to develop and structure a plan for intervening with the patient. This should also include some consideration of whether psychological treatment is warranted or appropriate at this time. Both types of reports serve to document the client's psychological functioning and to provide clinically informed formulations that draw on the assessment data. A treatment plan report involves problem identification, specification of the aims and goals of treatment, and a description of the strategies and tactics involved in the planned treatment (Mariush, 2002). Specific attention is also paid to the need for ongoing evaluation of the patient's functioning, because the monitoring of treatment impact is important in determining whether treatment should be discontinued or whether alternative treatment options should be considered. A growing number of agencies now require a treatment plan prior to the commencement of therapy, and sometimes require an updated plan if the clinical psychologist requests additional sessions for the patient's treatment. Viewpoint Box 9.2 deals with one of the challenges psychologists are likely to encounter in developing a treatment plan.

Exhibit 9.7 Elements of an Assessment Report Focused on Treatment Planning Issues

- Identifying patient/client information
- Reason for referral
- Evaluation of primary symptoms and problems
- Diagnosis
- Patient strengths
- Treatment-related goals and objectives
- Proposed treatment(s)
- Potential barriers to treatment
- Criteria for treatment termination or transfer to other service provider
- Service provider responsible for treatment implementation and evaluation of treatment

Adapted from Mariush (2002).

Assessment Feedback

For much of the history of psychological assessment, the results of the assessment process were delivered primarily to the medical or educational personnel who requested the assessment. In the assessment of child clients, parents often received some feedback on the results

VIEWPOINT BOX 9.2

MULTIPLE PERSPECTIVES ON TREATMENT GOALS

One of the first steps in offering intervention services is for the psychologist to help the client establish treatment goals (Nezu & Nezu, 1993). Psychological interventions for adult clients involve at least two perspectives: that of the client and that of the therapist. The psychologist asks questions to discover what the person hopes to get out of psychological services. Clients vary in the extent to which they have clear ideas about what needs to change to resolve the problem. The goals identified by the psychologist depend on the way the psychologist formulates the case, which in turn is influenced by the theoretical model that the psychologist uses in understanding problems. The core of an effective therapeutic alliance is the agreement on goals by client and therapist (Horvath & Luborsky, 1993). Agreement on goals is even more of a challenge in the delivery of psychological services to children and families. Children rarely refer themselves for services (Kazdin, 1988). Over years of clinical practice, we have yet to receive a call from a young person saying, *I realize that I am pretty tough to live with; my distractibility is getting in the way of meeting my academic goals and my impulsiveness leads to all kinds of trouble, so I think I need to see a psychologist.* Adults are usually the ones to request psychological services for children. As you saw in Viewpoint Box 9.1, there is often limited overlap in the ways that young people and their parents view their behaviour. So, if parents and children do not agree on what the problem is, how can they agree on treatment goals?

Hawley and Weisz (2003) asked 315 children and their parents attending community mental health centres about the problem for which they were seeking services. They also asked the children's therapists to identify the presenting problem. All three raters identified disobedience, temper tantrums, poor school work, and difficulties getting along with other children as the most common reasons for seeking services. However, beyond such generalities, the level of agreement among children, parents, and therapists was low. Only 23.2% of the triads (child-parent-therapist) agreed on the target problem for therapy; less than half of the triads agreed on the general area that needed to be addressed. Agreement was significantly higher for externalizing, or acting out, problems (41.3%) than it was for internalizing problems (6.7%). In general, there was higher agreement between therapists and parents than between children and either therapists or parents. Therapists offering services to children and families therefore face a dilemma. On the one hand, if they act according to the parents' identification of the problem, they are likely to set treatment goals that are not endorsed by the child. On the other hand, if they set goals according to what the child thinks is a problem, they risk alienating the parents, who may see the focus as misplaced. To engage both the child and the parents in psychological services, the psychologist must first find a way to formulate goals that are meaningful to both the child and parents. If the child does not see the point in services, he or she is unlikely to cooperate, and although parents may sometimes force the child's attendance, they cannot force meaningful involvement. As the parents are the ones who control access to services, it is essential that they be convinced that the services offered are relevant. Psychologists working with children and families must therefore be sensitive to the different perspectives of those seeking services and of those child clients who are referred to them.

of the assessment. Opportunities to present assessment feedback are invaluable in assisting other professionals in developing remedial or intervention strategies to use with the assessed client. However, with changes in ethical codes and legislation since the 1970s, it is now

sturti/Getty Images

Clinical psychologists typically provide detailed feedback to clients as the final stage in the assessment process.

commonplace for those who were assessed to also receive feedback from the clinical psychologist involved. Indeed, current ethical requirements underscore the importance of psychologists providing such feedback in most circumstances. As indicated in Exhibit 9.8, not only do clients have the right to receive feedback, but the provision of feedback also yields an opportunity for the psychologist to verify assessment findings and conclusions, correct any error or misunderstanding, and help clients begin to use the assessment findings in making modifications in their lives. For an assessment designed to address elements of a treatment plan, it is essential that the client and psychologist work collaboratively during the initial assessment phase and throughout the following treatment phases. Therefore, it is crucial that the psychologist explain the results of all assessments, including the initial assessment data and the data that are collected as part of the treatment monitoring and evaluation process.

Exhibit 9.8 The Purposes of Providing Assessment Feedback

- Verify the general accuracy of the assessment results
- Correct any errors or misunderstanding that occurred during the assessment process
- Refine the interpretation of the results to ensure an optimal fit with the individual's life circumstances
- Put the individual's symptoms, problems, and experiences in the context of his or her life history and current life circumstances
- Provide some psychological relief for the individual by presenting an integrated picture that helps make sense of the individual's difficulties
- Provide concrete information about steps the individual can take to address personal difficulties
- Help the individual identify potentially stressful situations that can exacerbate difficulties
- Collaborate with the individual in creating therapeutic goals that build on personal strengths

Adapted from Levak, Hogan, Beutler, and Song (2011).

In 2007, Smith, Wiggins, and Gorske published data from a survey of over 700 psychologists who frequently conducted either personality assessment or neuropsychological assessments for clinical purposes. Their survey included questions on a range of issues dealing with the psychologists' practices in providing assessment feedback and the value of providing assessment feedback. Despite differences in the focus of their assessment activities, there were relatively few statistically significant differences between the data on assessment feedback reported by the two groups of psychologists. Overall, the researchers found that most psychologists were likely to provide in-person feedback to the client who had been evaluated. Over 70% indicated that they usually or almost always provided this kind of direct verbal feedback; however, less than a quarter of the psychologists routinely provided clients with a copy of the actual assessment report. With respect to the benefits of providing assessment feedback to clients, most psychologists believed that receiving feedback allowed clients to (a) better understand their problems, (b) be more motivated to follow any recommendations that resulted from the assessment, and (c) actually feel better. Interestingly, the more strongly that psychologists believed in these positive effects of feedback, the more likely they were to spend an extended time (i.e., an hour or more) providing assessment feedback to their clients.

If you had been assessed by a clinical psychologist, would you want to receive a copy of the report? Are there any reasons why you wouldn't want a copy?

Building on a range of research evidence that suggested assessment feedback can influence client emotional functioning, **Stephen Finn** developed a **therapeutic model of assessment** (Finn, Fischer, & Handler, 2012; Finn & Tonsager, 1997). In this model, clients are active participants in all phases of the assessment. This includes discussing the reasons for assessment, reviewing the test results, and discussing the interpretation of the test scores. Particular efforts are made to (a) develop a strong working alliance with the client, (b) work collaboratively in defining the client's goals for the assessment, and (c) explore the assessment data with the client. Research evaluating aspects of this model has been encouraging: compared with assessment procedures focused solely on information gathering (i.e., little active collaboration with clients), clients receiving therapeutic assessment developed stronger working alliances with the psychologists and were less likely to prematurely terminate treatment (Hilsenroth & Cromer, 2007). Most of these studies were conducted in the context of providing short-term psychodynamic treatment to clients, but the results may also be relevant to other treatment forms. Therapist-client collaboration is a cornerstone of cognitive-behavioural treatments and findings such as these suggest that the collaborative approach to assessment and treatment may be instrumental in the well-documented success of the cognitive-behavioural therapies (see Chapter 14).

therapeutic model of assessment: an approach to psychological assessment in which clients are actively encouraged to participate in discussions about the reasons for the assessment, the results of the testing, and how the assessment data should be integrated and interpreted.

case example **MELISSA**

The psychologist drafted a report to be sent to Melissa and Erik's family physician and to the company that managed Erik's extended health care benefits. The psychologist summarized the reason for the assessment and Melissa's history of anxiety symptoms. The results of the testing, interviews, observations, and self-monitoring were described and a diagnosis of obsessive-compulsive disorder was indicated. Based on the nature of Melissa's symptoms and the treatment literature on OCD, the psychologist recommended that Melissa begin cognitive-behavioural treatment, emphasizing exposure and response prevention. It was also recommended that, if the couple were willing, Erik should participate in some sessions in order to assist Melissa with some of the exposure steps she would need to undertake.

The psychologist met with Melissa and Erik to provide feedback on the full assessment and to review details of the report. The couple were encouraged to ask questions about the results, but they had very few, as the findings were consistent with their own views. They were also encouraged to ask questions about the treatment options, including medication and partner-assisted exposure and response prevention. They had many questions on these matters and the psychologist took considerable time to explain the nature of the psychological treatment. They discussed, in particular, the symptoms that would be targeted in the treatment (e.g., thoughts about injuring people, checking for dangerous materials around the house, hitting someone while driving). The psychologist also emphasized that the treatment required substantial commitment from both Melissa and Erik to work on anxiety-related assignments between treatment sessions.

After noting two minor errors in the draft report (concerning the dates of work-related events), Melissa indicated that she felt comfortable with the report being sent to the physician and the health care company. Although the psychologist indicated that the couple could take their time to discuss treatment options between themselves, very little discussion was needed for Melissa and Erik to decide to go ahead with the psychological treatment. Accordingly, the psychologist booked an initial treatment appointment for both of them. Melissa was also asked to continue her self-monitoring activities, as these data would provide an important baseline for examining changes in anxiety symptoms during treatment.

SUMMARY AND CONCLUSIONS

In this chapter, we have described the final stage of the assessment process in which the psychologist integrates diverse material from different sources into a sound formulation. The task of drawing together information requires the same kind of scientific thinking needed to make sense of research results. The psychologist draws on a wealth of knowledge about psychological functioning, psychopathology, risk, and protective factors, as well as on a solid understanding of psychometric issues in reaching a meaningful conclusion about a particular client. Like other types of decision-making, clinical decision-making is prone to a host of biases and errors. The psychologist must be flexible in generating hypotheses and cautious in weighing the evidence in support of them or against them. Overconfidence in one's own wisdom and experience may lead to a premature conclusion that fails to take into account all relevant data. Even-handed consideration of confirming and disconfirming data is as essential in clinical practice as it is in the conduct of research.

Students of clinical psychology may initially feel discouraged to learn of all the potential pitfalls in clinical decision-making. However, it is important to remember that these decision-making errors apply to everyone; they apply in our personal lives and they occur in other types of decision-making. Clinical psychologists are not immune from the same kinds of errors in decision-making that affect other people. However, awareness of these pitfalls can lead to the use of strategies that minimize the likelihood of errors. As we discussed in earlier chapters, the different types of assessment information all have advantages and disadvantages. There is no single test that will yield a meaningful clinical formulation—the task of the clinical psychologist is much more complex. Research has established that clinical psychologists can effectively combine data from several imperfect methods to reach a clinically meaningful formulation that can guide services.

A psychological assessment report is the product of careful analysis of a specific client; it draws on research evidence developed from large groups of individuals, paying particular attention to the client's specific circumstances. In most situations, clients receive detailed feedback about the assessment and, in many instances, a copy of the assessment report. This move toward greater transparency and accountability in the delivery of health services fits well with the practice of providing feedback to clients following psychological assessment.

KEY TERMS

biases: judgments that are systematically different from what a person should conclude based on logic or probability.

case formulation: a description of the patient that provides information on his or her life situation, current problems, and a set of hypotheses linking psychosocial factors with the patient's clinical condition.

computer-based interpretations: reports generated by computer programs that match a patient's general pattern of responses on a psychological test to summaries of research evidence about the typical characteristics of people with the same pattern of test responses.

heuristics: mental shortcuts that make decision-making easier and faster but often lead to less accurate decisions.

retrospective recall: using data that rely on people to remember events that happened to them at some point in the past.

self-serving attributional bias: a tendency to take more personal credit for successes than for failures, by attributing success but not failure to internal, stable, and global causes.

therapeutic model of assessment: an approach to psychological assessment in which clients are actively encouraged to participate in discussions about the reasons for the assessment, the results of the testing, and how the assessment data should be integrated and interpreted.

KEY NAMES

Stephen Finn Howard Garb Jacqueline Persons

ADDITIONAL RESOURCES

Books

Antony, M. M., & Barlow, D. H. (2010). *Handbook of assessment and treatment planning for psychological disorders* (2nd ed.). New York: Guilford Press.

Eells, T. D. (Ed.). (2007). *Handbook of psychotherapy case formulation* (2nd ed.). New York: Guilford Press.

Garb, H. N. (1998). *Studying the clinician: Judgment research and psychological assessment.* Washington, DC: American Psychological Association.

McLeod, B. D., Jensen-Doss, A., & Ollendick, T. H. (Eds.). (2013). *Handbook of child and adolescent diagnostic and behavioral assessment.* New York: Guilford Press.

Check It Out!

If you would like more information on decision-making biases and heuristics, including some examples you can try that illustrate various biases and heuristics, look at the following websites:

www.nku.edu/~garns/165/pptj_h.html

www.prioritysystem.com/reasons1.html

In 2002, the cognitive psychologist Dr. Daniel Kahneman won the Nobel Prize for Economics for his research on how people make decisions under conditions of uncertainty. You can read his Nobel Prize lecture on his research here: nobelprize.org/nobel_prizes/economics/laureates/2002/kahnemann-lecture.pdf

Many websites provide examples of psychological assessment reports written for different purposes. Here are some, including sites that have computer-based interpretative reports for specific assessment instruments:

www.msresource.com/format.html

www.behaviordata.com

www.self-directed-search.com/sdsreprt.html

www4.parinc.com/WebUploads/samplerpts/PAI32.pdf

www.pearsonassessments.com/NR/rdonlyres/8C203588-0C96-4F0E-ACBA-59482E82B595/0/MCMIIII_Interp.pdf

www.pearsonassessments.com/NR/rdonlyres/A28D3A3E-BFA1-45F9-905E-984A19A01840/0/000000017MMPI2RFInterp20080301.pdf

10 CHAPTER

PREVENTION

INTRODUCTION

Harry sits in a comfortable chair watching the clock. Since the death of his wife five years ago, Harry has lived alone. An avid reader and expert horticulturalist, Harry spends many hours reading and tending his plants. His adult children maintain regular contact with weekly phone calls, but live too far away to allow frequent visits. Over the years Harry, now 83, has been troubled by osteoarthritis that causes him pain and debilitation. He has found it increasingly difficult to manipulate small objects as the joints in his hands are stiff and inflamed. Pain in his knees and hips makes walking difficult, although he attempts to be as active as possible. Harry adjusts his clothing, smoothing his tie and brushing lint off his jacket. He checks his watch, shaking it to make sure it has not stopped. On hearing a noise outside his door, Harry grasps his cane and pulls himself painfully to a standing position. As the door opens with a creak, Harry grumbles, "I'm hungry. I thought you were supposed to be here at 12:30." The cheery face at his door belongs to Anne, a sprightly 76-year-old who has been a volunteer since her retirement from teaching 11 years ago. Anne sets out Harry's lunch, asks how he's enjoying the book he's reading, admires the blooms on his azalea, commiserates with his disappointment that his daughter has had to postpone her next visit, gathers up the tray and dishes from yesterday's meal, and leaves to deliver other meals.

The Meals on Wheels organization operates in many countries to provide wholesome meals to older adults whose nutrition might otherwise be poor. The benefits to recipients of Meals on Wheels may extend beyond the physical advantages of having a good meal. For Harry, the regular, brief visits punctuate his day, reducing his isolation. For Harry's adult children who live far away, Meals on Wheels provides reassurance that he is having at least one good meal a day and that he is seen by an informed and caring person on days that meals are delivered. For volunteers such as Anne, there may be a sense of satisfaction in contributing to the well-being of others. The Meals on Wheels program is a non-profit, volunteer-based organization in many countries. It is a good example of a program designed to offer services to a vulnerable population and prevent the development of serious problems. Meals on Wheels is committed to offering a sustainable service that is accountable to government and sensitive to the needs of a diverse population. Meals on Wheels is a model program providing benefits for both physical and mental health.

Prevention programs were first established to prevent physical health problems. Programs to prevent the spread of infectious diseases involve simple practices such as hand-washing, more intrusive procedures such as quarantining and wearing masks, and challenging tasks such as the development and use of vaccines. According to the World Health Organization, the provision of clean drinking water and the development of vaccination programs have been effective in preventing illness and death for millions of people worldwide every year (World Health Organization, 2003). Although scientists have developed vaccinations that are cost-effective in preventing virulent diseases, tragically, these vaccines are under-used and 2 million children die each year from diseases that could be prevented at low cost (World Health Organization, 2003). Furthermore, although vaccines in general are effective, the utility of each vaccine must be evaluated and this process can take considerable time. For example, although an innovative program providing free influenza vaccinations to the entire population of Ontario (at an annual cost to the government of many million dollars) was introduced in 2000, the first data showing evidence that the program was associated with reduced flu-related mortality and reduced health care use were not published until 2008 (Kwong et al., 2008). Furthermore, a meta-analysis of studies assessing the efficacy and effectiveness of influenza vaccines (Osterholm, Kelley, Sommer, & Belongia, 2012) found that although there was evidence of moderate protection against viral influenza, there was no evidence of protection in adults aged 65 and older, a group that is often seen as especially vulnerable.

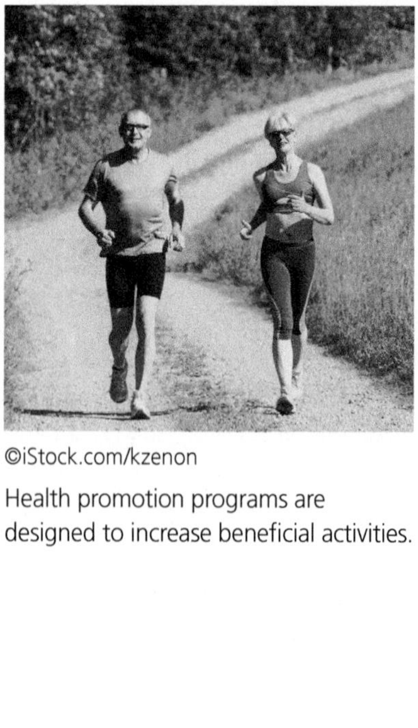

Health promotion programs are designed to increase beneficial activities.

Because lifestyle factors are associated with many health problems, many prevention efforts also focus on encouraging the development of healthy habits such as good nutrition, regular exercise, and adequate sleep. Efforts to introduce a healthy lifestyle are usually referred to as **health promotion**. Health promotion is usually designed to increase activities that are beneficial to many aspects of physical health.

health promotion: programs designed to increase activities that are beneficial to many aspects of physical health.

As we discussed in Chapter 1, clinical psychologists were not very involved in prevention activities until recently. Another branch of psychology, **community psychology**, focuses on the reciprocal relations between individuals and the community in which they live. Community psychologists have a long history of developing services that are offered to a vulnerable population (Viewpoint Box 10.1 examines vulnerability due to poverty). For many years, the training of clinical psychologists focused on understanding problems at the level of the individual, so it made sense that interventions would also be designed at that level. Clinical psychologists reasoned that if problems were related to the way a person thought, felt, or acted, then it made sense to help the person by finding ways to change the dysfunctional thoughts, feelings, or behaviours. Consequently, clinical psychologists developed interventions at the level of the individual, couple, or family. Efforts to evaluate the effectiveness of those psychological services showed that the services were definitely helpful for some people.

What are the similarities and differences between prevention programs for physical health problems and programs for mental health problems?

community psychology: a branch of psychology that focuses on research and practice on the reciprocal relations between individuals and the community in which they live.

VIEWPOINT BOX 10.1

POVERTY

In 2003, UNICEF released troubling results indicating that more than 1 billion children worldwide suffer the severe effects of poverty and are deprived of basic human rights such as adequate shelter, food, water, sanitation, and education. There is, however, no internationally agreed-on definition of poverty. As politicians and scholars point out, the definition of poverty varies according to a country's level of affluence. There are basically two ways to identify and track those who are vulnerable to the effects of poverty: in relative terms or in absolute terms. Relative definitions identify the proportion of the population whose income is significantly below the median income. This is a statistical definition. "Absolute" means identifying those people whose incomes are insufficient to purchase goods and services that are considered essential.

Critics argue that official poverty statistics drastically underestimate the number of children who live in poverty. The Luxembourg Income Study (2000), a landmark international initiative, adopted relative definitions to compare poverty rates across 25 countries by calculating the proportions of people whose income was 50% of the median income. Data for 1994 indicated that the highest proportion of children living in poverty among the 25 countries evaluated was Mexico (26.1%), followed by the United States (24.5%). Levels of child poverty were similar in Australia (15.8%), Canada (15.4%), Ireland (14.6%), and the United Kingdom (13.9%). The pattern with respect to older adults was somewhat different, with the bleakest statistics indicating that 31.0% of older Mexicans had incomes that were 50% of the median, followed by older adults in Australia (29.4%), the United States (20.6%), Ireland (17.3%), and the United Kingdom (15.1%). At 4.9%, the figures for older Canadians were dramatically lower than those for Canadian children living in poverty. Despite Canada's

CONTINUED . . .

sustained economic growth beginning in the 1990s and early 2000s and the implementation of a federal program of child benefits in 1998, the data for 2008 were only slightly better than in 1994, with 13.3% of all Canadian children living in poverty (Bradshaw et al., 2012). The comparable figure for the U.S. was 23.1% (Bradshaw et al., 2012).

For decades, social scientists have recognized the deleterious consequences of child poverty on children's mental and physical health status (Cybele, 2012). Scholars now see that children living in poverty are subject to multiple risk factors that have cumulative negative effects on their well-being. Poverty is harmful to the physical, socio-emotional, and cognitive well-being of children, youth, and their families (Evans, 2004). Compared with other children, children living in poverty are more likely to be exposed to family disruption and violence, and their parents are less responsive, read to them less frequently, and are less involved with their school activities. These children are more likely to be exposed to environmental pollutants, live in more crowded housing, and attend poorer quality daycare. So how is all of this relevant to clinical psychology? The most important message is that children living in poverty are being challenged on multiple fronts. They are compromised in all areas of their lives. Consequently, any efforts to prevent negative outcomes for these vulnerable children must take into account the effects not simply of one stressor or disadvantage, but of a pile-up of stressors. Although it may be conceptually easier to study the effects of children witnessing violence in one study and the children of alcoholic parents in another study, we now understand that there is tremendous overlap in the different populations—the child whom we identify as exposed to violence in one study may be the same child identified as the child of an alcoholic parent in another study, and as an aggressive child in a third study. The serious, cumulative, and chronic risks to which children in poverty are exposed require high dosage prevention programs to buffer children from the accumulation of challenges these children face. A meta-analysis of the effectiveness of preschool prevention programs (Nelson, Westhues, & MacLeod, 2003) provided encouraging data indicating that positive effects of intensive preschool interventions for children who are disadvantaged in multiple ways are sustained in the short, medium, and long term. Not surprisingly, the longer and more intense the intervention, the greater the gains.

According to UNICEF, 13.3% of Canadian children were living in poverty in 2008.

Services to help parents manage their children's behaviour are a good example. We know from studies of many species, from flatworms to humans, that (a) when a behaviour is followed by a positive outcome, that behaviour is likely to be repeated, and (b) when a behaviour is followed by a negative outcome, it is less likely to be repeated. Early parent education programs based on these simple reinforcement principles were helpful to many parents. Nevertheless, some people do not come for psychological services, some drop out after the first session, and others fail to do their between-session assignments designed to improve their parenting. Even though clinical psychologists know effective ways to help parents encourage appropriate behaviour, to help children manage their angry feelings and learn to share, etc., they are unable to reach some parents. Who are these people who are so difficult to reach? Parents who argued a lot tended to drop out of treatment, as did depressed mothers and women who felt isolated (Reyno & McGrath, 2006). The recognition that potentially effective strategies were not accessible to parents who needed them the most forced clinical psychologists to think outside the box and to develop innovative ways to prevent problems and to head off more serious problems. Increasingly, therefore, clinical psychologists have begun to develop programs that utilize the results of decades of community psychology research.

You may remember learning in Chapter 1 of the vast numbers of people who suffer from mental disorders, the severe psychological toll of these disorders on affected individuals and their families, and the escalating financial costs of mental health problems. Estimates suggest that the annual costs of mental disorders in Canada may be as high as $63 billion annually (Wilkerson, 2012). Mental disorders also increase the risk of physical illness. The World Economic Forum estimates that globally the cost of mental health conditions in 2010 was $2.5 trillion and will grow to $6 trillion by 2030 (Bloom et al., 2011). Experts agree, therefore, that the only sustainable way to reduce the burden of mental disorders is through prevention (World Health Organization, 2004a). Clinical psychologists working with people suffering from specific disorders are increasingly aware of the need to develop prevention programs (Dozois & Dobson, 2004). We admire the apparent simplicity of vaccination programs that allow the body to develop immunity to a virus before exposure to the actual virus. A trip to the clinic, tears of protest, and an afternoon with a slightly cranky child seem a small price to pay to protect a child from the dangers of polio! There is, however, no vaccine for child abuse, bullying, suicide, or eating disorders. Although we can all agree that prevention is a desirable goal, it is much more difficult to determine the most appropriate prevention program to develop, how it will be implemented, who will pay for it, and how we will measure its effectiveness.

Although intervention programs are much more common than are prevention programs, we have chosen to place the chapter on prevention before the chapters describing therapeutic intervention (like Benjamin Franklin's adage, "an ounce of prevention is worth a pound of cure"). It is clear that clinical psychology has the potential to help many people and to reduce the burden of care. It is also possible for clinical psychology to prevent the onset of mental disorders through the development and evaluation of programs for those at risk. You will notice that prevention programs are often delivered by trained health service providers, not clinical psychologists. In prevention programs the role of the clinical psychologist is more likely to be in program development, training, supervision, and/or evaluation than it is in front-line service provision.

©iStock.com/joecicak
An ounce of prevention is worth a pound of cure.

In this chapter, we outline different models that have guided the development of prevention programs. We present some key concepts in prevention science and illustrate them by briefly describing effective programs. Because prevention is based on the principle of early intervention, much of the work we highlight focuses on children and youth (Weissberg, Kumpfer, & Seligman, 2003). Although there are many innovative and promising prevention programs that target adults (Dozois & Dobson, 2004; Forsman, Schierenbeck, & Wahlbeck, 2011; Le, Muñoz, Ippen, & Stoddard, 2003; Townsend, Mathews, & Zembe, 2013), in this chapter, we highlight programs that target children and youth. We follow a developmental path, addressing programs to promote effective parenting, to prevent bullying and conduct disorder, to prevent internalizing disorders or problems, to prevent substance abuse, and to prevent problems in those exposed to trauma or loss. As prevention programs are not limited to the very young, later in the chapter Viewpoint Box 10.2 describes a program designed to promote physical activity in older adults. Two profile boxes describe the work of Canadian psychologists who are active in prevention science, Dr. Katreena Scott, who works to prevent child abuse, and Dr. Jonathan Weiss, who works to prevent mental health and behavioural problems in people with developmental disabilities.

Have you considered a professional role in which you would not necessarily be the direct service provider? How important is it to you that your work could affect a large number of people?

APPROACHES TO PREVENTION

How do primary and secondary prevention programs differ in their focus?

In the United States, the Commission on Chronic Illness (1957) identified three different types of intervention with respect to illness: primary, secondary, and tertiary. Primary intervention occurs before a disorder has developed and is designed to prevent the development of the disorder. Secondary intervention occurs when a disorder is evident; we usually refer to this type of intervention as treatment. Tertiary intervention occurs with respect to a chronic disorder and focuses on rehabilitation and long-term adaptation. The model of primary, secondary, and tertiary intervention that was originally designed to categorize services with respect to physical illness was then applied to mental disorders. Traditionally, the focus of psychological services has been at the level of secondary intervention, or treatment. As described in Chapter 1, clinical psychologists have extended their services both toward primary intervention in the prevention of problems and toward tertiary intervention in rehabilitation services.

It is also useful to think of distinctions among prevention programs. One distinction involves universal preventive interventions, selective preventive interventions, and indicated preventive interventions (Mrazek & Haggerty, 1994). As the name implies, **universal preventive interventions** are applied to an entire population. As a member of the general public, you will have been exposed to several universal preventive interventions. You may, for example, remember television advertising campaigns designed to reduce undesirable activities such as wife assault or smoking, or to promote healthy activities such as regular physical exercise. Your parents or grandparents probably remember the initial advertising campaigns to encourage the wearing of seat belts while driving. During the flu season, universal programs remind the public to reduce contagion by frequent and thorough hand-washing. **Selective preventive interventions** target people who are at elevated risk of developing a particular disorder or problem. So, during an outbreak of a contagious disorder, selective prevention programs might require people entering hospitals to wear masks. **Indicated preventive interventions** target people who do not meet criteria for a disorder, but who have elevated risk and may show detectable, but subclinical, signs of the disorder. Those who have come into contact with a confirmed case of an infectious disorder may be targets for indicated preventive interventions requiring a period of quarantine. We can probably all agree that the goal of preventing a debilitating, contagious, and potentially fatal disease is a good one. Nevertheless, there is controversy about the most effective prevention efforts. If you were a nurse in a hospital caring for patients with the disease, you would want compelling evidence that the prevention strategies were effective in protecting you from potentially fatal infection. Similarly, if your life was effectively put on hold for almost two weeks by imposed quarantine (missing school, recreation, and social life), you would probably want reassurance that this sacrifice was necessary to help contain the spread of the disease. This means that prevention programs should be evaluated to determine whether they are meeting their goals.

universal preventive intervention: a prevention program applied to an entire population, such as a media awareness campaign on the dangers of drinking and driving.

selective preventive intervention: a prevention program that targets people who are at elevated risk of developing a particular disorder or problem.

indicated preventive intervention: a prevention program that targets people who do not meet criteria for a disorder, but who have elevated risk and may show detectable, but subclinical, signs of the disorder.

Some prevention scientists consider that these categories of universal, selective, and indicated prevention rely too much on a disease model and have proposed that psychologists think instead in terms of promoting health (e.g., Kaplan, 2000). This of courses raises the question of what we mean by health. Health is not simply the opposite of illness. There is no universal definition of health—it all depends on the person's context. Younger people often consider health in terms of fitness, energy, and strength. Older people tend to see health in terms of their inner strength and their ability to meet life's challenges (World Health Organization, 2004a). There are similar challenges in defining mental health and promoting it. To this end, the World Health Organization defines mental health promotion activities as those designed to increase well-being and resilience.

primary prevention: the provision of conditions conducive to good health.

secondary prevention: prevention that targets groups of people who are identified as being at high risk (similar to selected and indicated prevention).

risk reduction model: an approach to prevention that reduces risks and promotes protective factors.

risk factors: characteristics of the individual or the environment that render a person more vulnerable to the development of a problem or disorder, or that are associated with more severe symptoms.

Different types of prevention programs are designed to reduce the symptoms and burden of mental disorders. **Primary prevention** is based on a behavioural model of functioning and does not rely on the concept of disease. It is focused on the provision of conditions conducive to good health and is similar to the concept of health promotion. **Secondary prevention** is more similar to selected and indicated prevention programs because it focuses on prevention in groups of people who are identified as being at high risk. The **risk reduction model** of prevention relies heavily on research to guide interventions (Mrazek & Haggerty, 1994). **Risk factors** are characteristics of the individual or the environment that render a person more vulnerable to the development of a problem or disorder, or that are associated with more severe symptoms. Once at-risk individuals are identified, they are the target of prevention programs designed to protect them from developing the problem or disorder. The other side of the coin is the identification of factors associated with resilience—those characteristics that protect high-risk individuals from developing the problem or disorder. If we understand the variables that are protective, then we can use such knowledge in developing effective prevention programs.

protective factors: characteristics of the individual or the environment that render a person less vulnerable to the development of a problem or disorder.

The science of prevention requires knowledge of a problem and its prevalence, variables that are causally involved in the problem's development, the mechanisms of risk transmission, and particular subgroups that are at high risk. Obviously not all risk factors are equally malleable, so it makes sense to target those risk factors that can be changed. Some risk and **protective factors** are specific to disorders, whereas others are generic. Potential risk and protective factors associated with the development of psychopathology in children and youth are listed in Exhibits 10.1 and 10.2.

If you were asked to design a program to prevent the development of behavioural problems using a risk reduction model, you would need to target risk and protective factors that are modifiable. Which of the factors listed in Exhibit 10.1 and Exhibit 10.2 are most likely to be modifiable?

Exhibit 10.1 Risk Factors for the Development of Psychopathology in Children and Youth

Individual Factors

- complications in pregnancy and/or birth
- physical health problems or disability
- difficult temperament
- poor nutrition
- intellectual deficit or learning disability
- attachment problems
- poor social skills
- low self-esteem
- impulsivity
- attention deficits

School Context

- bullying
- peer rejection
- deviant peer group
- inadequate behaviour management

Family/Social Factors

- parental isolation
- single parent
- antisocial role models in family
- exposure to family or community violence
- harsh or inconsistent discipline
- inadequate supervision and monitoring
- parental abuse or neglect
- long-term parental unemployment
- criminality in family
- parental psychopathology

Life Events and Situations

- abuse
- family disruption
- chronic illness or death of family member
- poverty
- unemployment
- homelessness
- parental imprisonment
- war or natural disasters
- witnessing trauma
- migration
- high-density living

CONTINUED . . .

- poor housing conditions
- isolation from support services, including transport, shopping, recreational facilities

Community and Cultural Factors

- socioeconomic disadvantage
- social or cultural discrimination
- isolation
- exposure to community violence or crime

Adapted from Barrett & Turner (2004).

Exhibit 10.2 Protective Factors against the Development of Psychopathology in Children and Youth

Individual Factors

- easy temperament
- adequate nutrition
- positive attachment
- above-average intelligence
- school achievement
- problem-solving skills
- social competence
- optimism
- positive self-esteem

Family/Social Factors

- supportive, caring parents
- authoritative parenting
- family harmony
- supportive relationship with another adult (aside from parents)
- strong family norms and prosocial values

School Context

- prosocial peer group
- required responsibility and helpfulness
- opportunities for some success and recognition of achievement
- school norms against violence
- positive school–home relations

Life Events and Situations

- adequate income
- adequate housing

Community and Cultural Factors

- attachment to networks within the community
- participation in church or other community groups

CONTINUED . . .

- strong cultural identity and ethnic pride
- access to support services
- community/cultural norms against violence

Adapted from Barrett & Turner (2004).

Once a program has been designed, the prevention scientist must carefully monitor its implementation to ensure that it is conducted as planned. This is especially important as the prevention program is likely to be implemented in numerous agencies that vary in their resources and staff skills. Both the program's short- and long-term outcomes must be monitored in order to fully evaluate its impact. Exhibit 10.3 describes the process that a researcher follows in developing a prevention program.

Exhibit 10.3 Designing and Evaluating Prevention Research

- Identify the target. What do you want to prevent?
- Determine how serious the problem is. How many people are affected? What are the costs of the problem, in human suffering, health care costs, etc.?
- Review the research evidence about the problem. What do you know about how the risk factors develop? What variables make it more likely that a problem will develop?
- Identify high-risk groups.
- What is known about protective factors? These are the factors that have been shown to moderate risk.
- Design the intervention. How will the target condition be prevented? Is there an evidence-based prevention program for this problem? If so, does it need to be modified for your community?
- Design the study. How will you know if the intervention is efficacious?

In assessing the effects of a treatment intervention, it is relatively easy to determine whether the treatment made a difference. We can assess whether those who received the service had a different outcome than those who did not receive the service: we can test whether there was a clinically significant reduction in symptoms, and determine whether or not they meet criteria for a diagnosis or whether they now score in the normal range on a particular measure. Determining the efficacy of a prevention program presents a much greater challenge. Researchers must assess whether the program resulted in fewer people developing a problem than would have been the case without the prevention program. **Incidence rates** are used to describe the number of new cases of a specific problem. So, some prevention researchers

incidence rates: the number of new cases of a specific problem.

Why is long-term systematic evaluation so important in prevention science?

measure the success of their program by examining the extent to which the incidence rate is reduced. Although more than 1,000 controlled studies have examined the effectiveness of programs designed to prevent mental health problems, relatively few have examined whether these programs are effective in reducing the incidence of new cases of a disorder (Cuijpers, 2003). One reason why this strategy is rarely used is that, in order to have the statistical power to detect a difference in the incidence of a disorder, it is necessary to have studies with very large samples. Alternative research strategies target high-risk samples, offer the program at high intensity, or rely on accumulating samples from different studies. Although used with increasing frequency, these strategies remain underutilized in evaluating the impact of prevention efforts. Yet another way to measure the success of a prevention program is by calculating the **number needed to treat**. This refers to the number of people who need to receive the intervention in order to prevent one person from developing the condition. Perhaps the best example of this is the well-known practice of regular use of Aspirin to lower the risk of heart attack for which the number needed to treat is 130. That means that for every 130 people who regularly take Aspirin, one person will be saved from having a heart attack. As you can see, this commonly used prevention strategy must be used by many people in order to have an effect on a single person.

number needed to treat: the number of people who need to receive the intervention in order to prevent one person from developing the condition.

Meta-analytic reviews of prevention programs are very useful in identifying the types of programs that have demonstrated effectiveness. In the following sections, we will describe the results of meta-analyses of programs designed to prevent a range of disorders. You may recall learning in Chapter 4 the distinction between efficacy and effectiveness. These concepts apply to the science of prevention just as they do to intervention research. Once a prevention program has been shown to be efficacious in controlled studies, it is likely to be adopted in other less strictly controlled settings. Effectiveness refers to the extent to which a prevention program achieves desired outcomes when used in an applied setting rather than in the original research conditions. Even if a program has been demonstrated to be effective in other settings and meta-analyses have yielded positive results, it is important that the program continue to be evaluated to determine its usefulness in each setting in which it is applied.

PROMOTING EVIDENCE-BASED PARENTING

Parents play a key role in their children's socialization. The task of parenting children is a demanding one that requires no licence, training, or supervision. As you saw in Exhibit 10.1, harsh or inconsistent discipline, poor supervision and monitoring of a child, parental abuse, and neglect are risk factors for the development of child and adolescent psychopathology. However, the availability of supportive, caring parents can protect children and youth from the development of psychopathology (Exhibit 10.2). Although the responsibilities of caring for children can be daunting at times to all parents, some parents are particularly vulnerable due to their age, isolation, distress, experience of ongoing conflict, or limited socioeconomic resources. There is strong evidence that children's functioning is challenged by poor parenting, conflict in the family, and parental psychopathology (Biglan, 2003; World Health Organization, 2004a). We describe below three evidence-based programs that have been developed to promote good parenting and therefore to decrease risk factors for diverse child problems.

Home Visiting Programs

A number of programs have demonstrated impressive results in targeting at-risk parents. In a seminal 27-year research program, Olds and colleagues developed, implemented, tested, and replicated a program offering services to low-income, teenage, single mothers expecting their first child (Olds, 2006). Home visits were conducted by trained nurses beginning during the pregnancy and continuing after the child's birth. During these visits, the nurses addressed the mother's concerns about the pregnancy, delivery, and care of the child. They taught skills in both self-care and child care and promoted use of the health care system. Figure 10.1 illustrates the model of program influences on maternal and child health and development.

In three large-scale randomized controlled trials in different communities, Olds and his colleagues found that the home visit program was effective in achieving the immediate goal of improving parental care. In the middle term, this had benefits for children in reducing child abuse and neglect, and in the long term in reducing the number of arrests, convictions, substance abuse problems, and sexual promiscuity in the children by the time they reached the age of 15. Furthermore, the program improved the life course of young mothers by increasing labour force participation and economic self-sufficiency. These positive effects are all the more remarkable as nurses completed only an average of 8 visits during the pregnancy and 25 visits during the child's first two years of life. Visits lasted up to an hour and a half, so these short- and long-term gains were accomplished in a very high-risk group with the investment of under 50 hours of direct contact between nurses and teenage mothers. In general, the most beneficial effects were found for the families who were at greatest risk. With hindsight, the investment of hours of nurses' time seems to have borne fruit, but at the time the

Home visiting programs are designed to help teenage mothers improve their ability to interact with and care for their babies.

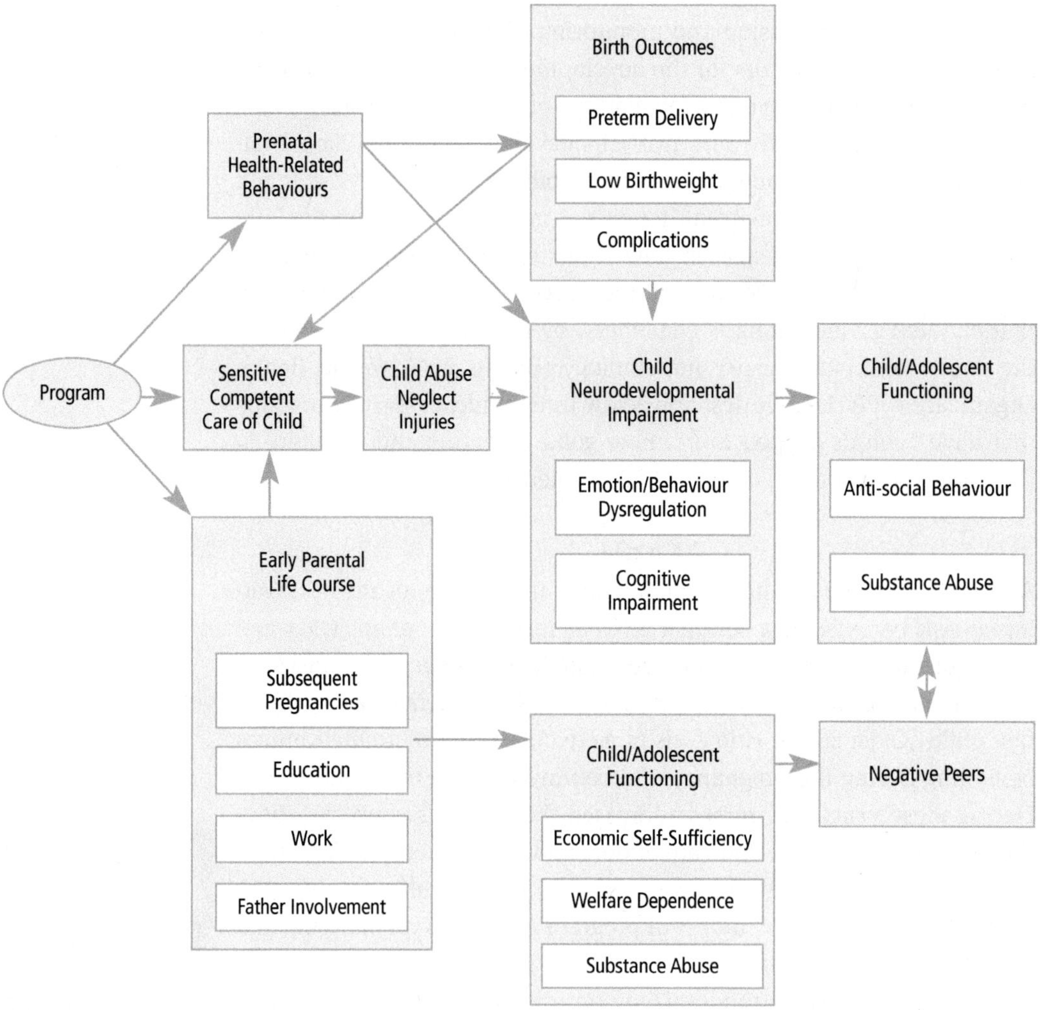

Figure 10.1 Model of influences of home visit program on maternal and child health and development

Reproduced from Olds (2002), with permission from Springer Science and Business Media.

program was developed, it must have been quite a challenge to get funding for these resources to be focused on teenage mothers.

Incredible Years

Developed and refined over 30 years of research by psychologist Carolyn Webster-Stratton, the Incredible Years training program was originally designed to help children aged three to eight who had been identified as having conduct problems (Webster-Stratton & Reid, 2010). As the program was found to be successful in treating conduct problems, it has been expanded to cover a wider age range and has been offered as a prevention program. The program uses group discussion, videotaped modelling, and behavioural rehearsal techniques to promote adult–child interactions that will facilitate children's development of social competence. The primary goal of the Incredible Years program is to train parents in skills so that they can effectively play with their child, provide praise for positive behaviours, and set limits on unacceptable behaviours using time-out, ignoring, appropriate consequences, and problem-solving. The basic program is available for different age ranges and includes a minimum of 12 sessions (although additional sessions may be required). An advanced 9- to 12-session program targets parents' interpersonal difficulties by teaching problem-solving, anger management, communication, emotional regulation skills, and support-seeking skills. A supplementary program, Supporting Your Child's Education, helps parents whose children are experiencing school difficulties. Complementary programs involve one for training teachers (Webster-Stratton, Reid, & Hammond, 2001) and a 22-week child training program (Webster-Stratton & Reid, 2010) that teaches emotional literacy, perspective-taking, friendship skills, anger management, and problem-solving. The effectiveness of this selective prevention program has been tested with more than 1,000 multi-ethnic, socioeconomically disadvantaged families. Results support the program's effectiveness in promoting good parenting, enhancing children's social competence, and preventing the development of conduct problems (Gross et al., 2003; Webster-Stratton & Reid, 2010).

Triple P

Developed by psychologist Matthew Sanders and his colleagues in Australia, the Triple P Positive Parenting Program is an evidence-based parenting program designed to (a) enhance the knowledge, skills, and confidence of parents; (b) promote safe environments for young people; and (c) promote children's competence through positive parenting practices (Sanders, 2012). Consistent with the idea of adapting programs to offer different "dosages" of intervention according to participants' needs, Triple P is a multi-level system that provides interventions of gradually increasing intensity, according to the level of need (Collins, Murphy, & Bierman, 2004).

Level 1, or Universal Triple P, is offered to all interested parents using a variety of media, including radio, television, and websites. The intention is to reduce stigma by acknowledging that parenting can be challenging, and to increase awareness of evidence-based information about general parenting strategies to deal with everyday issues and challenges. Universal Triple P may equip parents with all the information they need, or may facilitate help-seeking about parenting. Level 2 involves parenting seminars or brief (one- or two-session) services by phone or face to face to address parents' specific concerns. Level 3 is designed for parents of children with mild to moderate problems, who may benefit from a program delivered over three to four sessions by a primary health care provider. Parents of children with more severe behaviour problems may require Level 4, the Standard Triple P offered in either a group or individual format. Level 4 Triple P is also available online. The most intensive intervention is Level 5, Enhanced Triple P, which includes not only parenting skills but also additional sessions focused on parents' mood, coping, and partner support.

Program materials are designed for five developmental stages (infants, toddlers, preschoolers, children in elementary school, and teenagers). The program is designed to enhance protective factors and to decrease risk factors for children's problems. All Triple P services are designed around the principle that children benefit from a safe and engaging environment that offers opportunities for children to explore and discover. Assertive discipline practices are provided to manage misbehaviour. Parents are encouraged to adopt developmentally appropriate expectations about their child's behaviour. The importance of taking care of oneself as a parent is also stressed. A central tenet of the Triple P approach is that parents have a fundamental right to make choices about how they parent. Services are offered within a self-regulation framework that provides information about strategies that have been shown to be helpful, allowing parents to set their own goals and to select the strategies that they are interested in using. The Triple P approach involves intense training of practitioners, as well as continuing education for those who deliver the program.

There is a strong foundation of evidence in support of Triple P, based on randomized controlled trials that compare groups receiving Triple P interventions with wait-list control groups, as well as comparing different formats of Triple P (e.g., Sanders et al., 2004; Sanders, 2008). Meta-analyses (Nowak & Heinrichs, 2008; Thomas & Zimmer-Gembeck, 2007) have found that Triple P is efficacious in helping parents adopt positive parenting practices, which in turn is associated with fewer child problems, greater parental confidence, and enhanced parental well-being. The Triple P program has been adapted for use in diverse populations in several countries (Prinz & Sanders, 2007; Sanders, 2012).

PREVENTION OF VIOLENCE

Physical Abuse of Children

Physical abuse of children refers to the deliberate infliction of injury on a child. Experience of one type of child abuse is associated with multiple types of adversity (Sugaya et al., 2012). Furthermore, childhood abuse is associated with greater risk of a number of mental disorders

(Sugaya et al., 2012) and poorer response to treatment (Nanni, Uher, & Danese, 2012). Estimates of the incidence of physical abuse vary, as there are widely differing definitions of the boundary between acceptable discipline and abuse. A behaviour that constitutes reasonable punishment for one person may be considered abusive by another. Although a growing number of countries have banned the use of physical punishment, in Canada and the United States parents are permitted to punish their children physically, as long as they do not inflict physical harm. Data from the National Epidemiologic Survey on Alcohol and Related Conditions, collected in 2004–2005 on a sample of 43,093 adults in the U.S., revealed that 8% of respondents reported having been physically abused as children (Sugaya et al., 2012). The Ontario Child Health Study (MacMillan, Tanaka, Duku & Vaillancourt, 2013) found that almost a third of their sample of young adults reported having been physically abused. Although it is possible that such dramatic differences do exist between the two countries, it is also likely that there may be differences related to measurement and to the recency of the experience.

The risk of child abuse by poor, single, teenage mothers who participated in the home visiting programs described in the previous section (Olds, 2002) was half that of comparison mothers who did not participate. Both behavioural training and stress management training were effective in improving maternal reports of their own well-being and their child's welfare. These positive effects were evident both in the short term and at long-term follow-up. Unfortunately, improvements in parenting skills were evident in the short term only and were not maintained at follow-up. Multimodal programs appear to blend the benefits of both home visits and skills-based programs and have the advantage of minimizing participant attrition (O'Riordan & Carr, 2002). Profile Box 10.1 introduces Dr. Katreena Scott, whose work focuses on promoting positive parenting in men at risk for abusing their children.

PROFILE BOX 10.1

DR. KATREENA SCOTT

Courtesy of Katreena Scott

I completed my undergraduate studies at Queen's University, my graduate work in clinical psychology at the University of Western Ontario, an Internship at Sick Kids Hospital, and a postdoctoral placement at the University of New Hampshire. I am currently an associate professor in the Department of Applied Psychology and Human Development at the University of Toronto and I hold the Tier II Canada Research Chair in Family Violence Prevention and Treatment. My research program examines the development of violent relationships, the effect of abuse and trauma on children, and the impact of empirically

CONTINUED . . .

supported and ethically sound intervention and prevention programs for child abuse and domestic violence. One of the intervention programs I developed, Caring Dads: Helping Fathers Value Their Children, has been adopted for use in Canada as well as in the United Kingdom, Sweden, Germany, United States, Ireland, and Hong Kong.

HOW DID YOU CHOOSE TO BECOME A CLINICAL PSYCHOLOGIST?

My mother was a child protection worker, so it is perhaps not surprising that I have always been interested in understanding how we, as a society, can better support healthy child development. While completing my undergraduate degree in psychology, I discovered that training in clinical psychology offered the opportunity to do research and to develop skills to assess and provide treatment to children, youth, and families. This seemed like the perfect combination to me, as I was already beginning to appreciate the value of research for guiding practice and of clinical experience for helping to direct research. During my undergraduate studies, I refined my interest in child maltreatment and family violence and I applied to graduate programs that would support my continued learning in this area.

WHAT IS THE GREATEST CHALLENGE YOU FACE AS A CLINICAL PSYCHOLOGIST?

Ironically, the attraction of being able to develop skills in both research and practice is also clinical psychology's greatest challenge. Quite simply, it is very difficult as a student, and now as a professor, to develop expertise as a researcher while at the same time acquiring the skills, competencies, and experience necessary for exemplary clinical practice. Mostly, I worry that with so much to *do*, there is too little time to *think* critically about how our individual and collective work contributes to enhancing the safety and well-being of children and youth.

A second challenge I see for Canadian psychologists is articulating what our unique training offers to the health and social service systems. Among the diverse professional programs for preparing one to work in the mental health field, psychology offers rigorous training in research, program evaluation, consultation, and complex differential diagnosis. I think that the psychologists of the future will need to be able to better articulate how their training sets them apart from other mental health professionals and makes them ideal for leadership roles in mental health services.

TELL US ABOUT YOUR RESEARCH ON THE PREVENTION OF ABUSE IN INTIMATE RELATIONSHIPS AND FAMILIES

My research over the past 10 years has helped us understand how and why experiences of maltreatment in childhood lead to increased risk for dating violence in adolescence, and how schools and communities can effectively intervene to prevent the recurrence of relationship violence. I have explored the influence of motivation on the success of treatment for intimate partner violence and developed more efficacious ways to intervene with highly resistant male batterers. Over the next five years, my research will focus on three interrelated themes: recognizing and intervening with abusive fathers; integrating systems of intervention for perpetrators of domestic violence; and responding to maltreated children in the classroom. I use a range of research methods, including randomized control trials of intervention, longitudinal analyses of the predictors of abuse, qualitative examination of systems change, and secondary analysis of representative national data on family violence.

HOW DO YOU INTEGRATE SCIENCE AND PRACTICE IN YOUR WORK?

I am constantly straddling the gap between the science and practice, bringing research to inform clinical work, but also using experiences in practice to help guide research questions and interpret study results.

CONTINUED . . .

I continue to do some clinical work, mostly with men who have been violent in their families and children who have experienced abuse-related trauma. These experiences are invaluable in my consultation with policy-makers and my research in identifying best practices in intervention.

WHAT DO YOU SEE AS THE MOST EXCITING CHANGES IN THE FIELD OF CLINICAL PSYCHOLOGY?

Over the past 5 to 10 years, there has been increased recognition across the fields of psychology, medicine, sociology, criminology, and others that adverse experiences in childhood, such as abuse, neglect, and exposure to domestic violence, have profound, neurologically and environmentally mediated impacts on child and adult physical, mental, and social health. With this recognition has come an increased willingness of researchers and service providers to work together. An example from research is the University of Toronto's new Institute of Human Development that brings together researchers from across fields to support multidisciplinary research on questions relevant to healthy and unhealthy development of children, especially in their first five years of life. An example from clinical practice is the continued spread of multidisciplinary teams and group practices where many professionals work together in support of families. Integration of knowledge from across these fields promises to lead to some exciting insights and innovative new practices.

Risk of child physical abuse has also been assessed beyond the level of the individual parent, child, or family. In the U.S. Triple P population trial (Prinz, Sanders, Shapiro, Whitaker, & Lutzker, 2009), nine counties in which Triple P was implemented were compared with nine counties that received services as usual. Randomization in this study was at the level of the county rather than of the individual parent. Outcomes were also assessed at the level of the county. Positive program effects were found in terms of a reduced number of substantiated cases of child maltreatment, out-of-home placement, and child-maltreatment injuries requiring hospitalization.

©iStock.com/Mark Bowden

Parenting programs have been shown to reduce child maltreatment.

Youth Violence: Bullying and Conduct Disorder

One of the most common reasons children are referred to mental health clinics is for problems with aggressive and noncompliant behaviour (Miller & Prinz, 1990). A subgroup of children exhibits risk factors for the development of aggression from a very early age (Nagin & Tremblay, 1999). By the time these young people reach adolescence, their aggressive behaviour has brought them into conflict with the law and they are alienated from the school system (Fisher, 2003). Intervention at that stage has only limited success as these young people are very resistant to efforts to change their behaviour (Fisher, 2003). Therefore, if we have such limited success in treating conduct disorder once it has developed, it makes much more sense to try to prevent its development in the first place (Biglan, 2003; World Health Organization, 2004a).

In a previous section, we described programs for families with very young children such as home visits, Incredible Years, and Triple P that have been successful in promoting parenting, enhancing child competence, and reducing child aggression. School-based interventions have tended to focus on bullying, which is a phenomenon that overlaps with but is distinct from physical violence. Not all those who perpetrate violence engage in bullying and not all who bully engage in physical violence (Ttofi & Farrington, 2011).

The first successful comprehensive school-based program to reduce bullying in children aged 6–15 years was developed in Norway following the suicide of two youth who were the victims of bullying (Olweus, 1993). The program is designed to reduce both the opportunities and the rewards for bullying. This comprehensive program encourages changes in the school (an anti-bullying policy) and in the classroom (anti-bullying rules and discussion of alternatives to antisocial behaviour), and promotes links between family and schools. The program is effective not only in reducing bullying, but also in reducing antisocial behaviour in general and in enhancing student satisfaction with school. A study of 37 schools and 89 teachers who used the Olweus Bullying Prevention Program to varying degrees revealed that teachers are the key agent of change: their recognition of a problem with bullying and their commitment to the program are essential to its effective implementation (Kallestad & Olweus, 2003). The Olweus program has been applied in many countries. McCarthy and Carr (2002) reviewed four studies of its effectiveness, including data from 110 schools and almost 20,000 youths. They concluded that the program is effective in reducing reports of bullying as well as reducing reports of being bullied. These effects are evident in the short term and, importantly, are sustained over longer periods. Consistent with our previous comments about prevention program implementation, program effectiveness is determined by the extent to which program integrity is maintained. When the program is diluted, effects are reduced (McCarthy & Carr, 2002).

©iStock.com/CEFutcher

School-based anti-bullying programs can be effective in reducing bullying.

A large scale meta-analysis synthesizing results of 44 evaluations of a variety of school-based anti-bullying programs found evidence of average reductions in bullying of 20–23% and reductions in victimization of 17–20% (Ttofi & Farrington, 2011). Not surprisingly, the most effective programs included program components of parent meetings, firm disciplinary methods in response to bullying, and enhanced playground supervision. Ttofi and Farrington highlighted the innovative nature of the KiVa program implemented in Finland. KiVa is multi-component approach that includes a multimedia curriculum (including online questionnaires, films, computer games, discussion groups, and role plays) to change student attitudes, as well as enhanced monitoring and involvement with parents. The KiVa program has shown encouraging effects in reducing many forms of bullying (Salmivalli, Kärnä, & Poskiparta, 2011).

As we mentioned earlier, the problem of conduct disorder has also been a focus for prevention scientists. A multi-component prevention program, the Fast Track Program, was launched in 1990 by the Conduct Problems Prevention Research Group (CPPRG; 2002a). This trial project was based on available research on risk and protective factors in the development of conduct disorder. The CPPRG hypothesized that a toddler with biologically based difficulties in impulse control and regulation of behaviour is vulnerable to a cascade of challenges, as the parents may also have difficulties in behaviour regulation, making it more difficult for them to provide an optimal parenting environment. These effects would be magnified for a family living in an impoverished and disadvantaged environment. By the time of school entry, this child would have accumulated deficits that would make it difficult to learn and to establish friendships. Conflict with peers and teachers would reinforce a defensive and aggressive style that could reduce adult supervision and monitoring and promote association with delinquent peers.

The Fast Track Program expanded on a program developed to target high-risk children in kindergarten (Tremblay, Pagani-Kurtz, Mâsse, Vitaro, & Pihl, 1995). Screening of more than 9,000 kindergarten children identified a very high-risk sample of 891 children who were then randomly assigned to an intervention group or to a control group. A 10-year multi-component program was offered in the schools attended by the intervention-group children. The intervention included a child component designed to increase academic competence, emotion regulation, and social skills. Discipline, support of constructive behaviour, and monitoring of activities were targeted in the parent component. Group discussions were followed up by home visits. The classroom component involved a curriculum designed to promote self-control, emotional awareness, and social problem-solving. At the end of the first year, the program had been delivered successfully to most families, and the results were encouraging (CPPRG, 2002b). Compared with the control group, children in the intervention had more positive interactions with their peers and were less frequently rejected. Parents in the intervention group were more involved with their children, were more consistent in their discipline strategies, and were less reliant on harsh physical punishment. Teachers rated intervention parents as more involved with their children's education. School observations revealed that the intervention children had fewer behavioural problems than did the untreated control children.

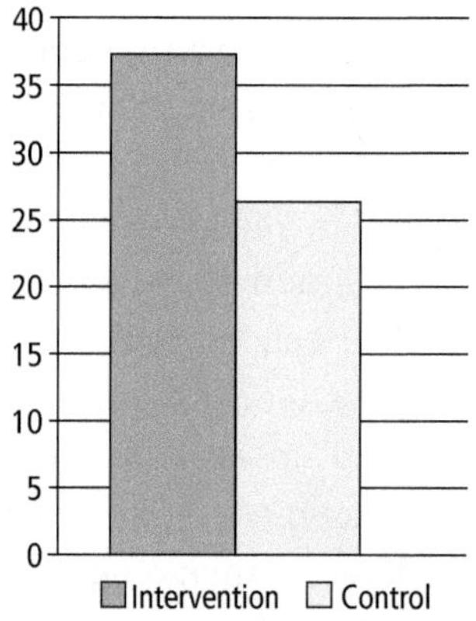

Figure 10.2 Proportion of intervention and control children classified as problem-free at the end of Grade 3

Conduct Problems Prevention Research Group (2002b). Reproduced with permission of Springer Science and Business Media.

As the goal of a prevention program is to reduce the incidence of problems in the future, longer-term assessment is essential. An assessment of the children at the end of Grade 3 revealed that although some gains had been maintained, several effects had disappeared. Children who received the intervention were less likely to show signs of serious conduct problems than were children in the control group. Figure 10.2 shows that more than a third of the children in the intervention group (37%) were classified as "problem-free" at the end of Grade 3, whereas just over a quarter of children in the control group were considered problem-free.

At first glance, these results may seem disappointing, as almost two-thirds of the children in the program were classified as having conduct problems. However, there is another way to look at these data. Although the total elimination of disorders or illnesses would be ideal, prevention programs usually have a more realistic goal of reducing the incidence of disorders. So, another way to think of the results is that the children who received the program were 37% less likely to have serious problems than were children in the control group. Follow-up at the end of Grades 4 and 5 indicated that high-risk children who participated in the program had better social competence, fewer problems in social cognition, less involvement with deviant peers, and fewer conduct problems than did high-risk children who did not participate (CPPRG, 2004). Although significant, these effects were small. By Grade 9, the effects of the program were evident only among the children at highest risk—and of those, the ones in the Fast Track Program showed a reduction in cases of conduct disorder and ADHD compared to the comparison group (CPPRG, 2007). Analyses conducted two years after the intervention ended confirmed that participation in this 10-year program reduced the risk of developing psychiatric disorders among those with the highest risk (CPPRG, 2011).

PREVENTION OF INTERNALIZING DISORDERS

You may recall learning in Chapter 3 that researchers have found it useful to consider problem behaviours along two dimensions: internalizing problems and externalizing problems. So far in this chapter, we have focused most of our discussion on the prevention of externalizing problems and on the promotion of good parenting. Externalizing problems are often dramatic and, when they result in injuries or damage to property, can yield sensational newspaper headlines. Internalizing problems, by definition, are more private. The person with internalizing problems may suffer quietly on his or her own without coming to anyone's attention. Internalizing problems are no less serious, however, and recent prevention efforts have also focused on ways to prevent the development of problems such as anxiety and depression.

The Canadian Community Health Survey, a national study of Canadians over the age of 15, revealed that similar numbers of Canadians suffer from anxiety disorders (4.7%) or depressive disorders (4.0%) as from chronic physical disorders such as heart disease, diabetes, or a thyroid condition (Statistics Canada, 2003). In addition to their psychological toll, these disorders result in the health care system and the economy incurring substantial costs. Internalizing problems are also evident in childhood. Some research suggests that anxiety problems in childhood may also be related to the development of depression in young people (Cole, Peeke, Martin, Truglio, & Seroczynski, 1998). Psychologists have therefore been at the forefront of efforts to prevent anxiety and depression in children.

Anxiety Disorders

Risk factors for the development of anxiety include individual factors such as inhibited temperament and an avoidant coping style, as well as overprotective parenting practices and parental anxiety (Barrett & Turner, 2004). A group of Australian researchers, led by Paula Barrett, developed a prevention program that was adapted from an effective treatment program for children with anxiety disorders (Barrett & Turner, 2001; Dadds et al., 1999; Lowry-Webster & Barrett, 2001). In a selected prevention program, schoolchildren were screened to identify those with mild to moderate anxiety problems (n = 128), and these children were then randomly assigned to an intervention group or to a monitoring group. The intervention was based on the Coping Koala program, with 10 sessions offered to children in a group format as well as three sessions offered to parents, followed by booster sessions. Children who received the intervention were found to have lower rates of anxiety disorder at the end of treatment. At the 12-month follow-up, differences between the intervention group and the comparison group had diminished. However, by the 24-month follow-up, 39% of children in the untreated group met criteria for an anxiety disorder, compared with only 20% of children in the intervention group (Dadds et al., 1999). This means that participation in the program was associated with an almost 50% reduction in the incidence of anxiety disorders at the 24-month follow-up.

Barrett and Turner (2001) adapted the Coping Koala program to a format that could be used in a universal prevention program delivered by teachers (Friends for Children and Friends for Youth). Within a sample of 489 children, assignment was made to one of three conditions: psychologist-led preventive intervention, teacher-led preventive intervention, or standard curriculum. The intervention included 10 weekly sessions and two booster sessions, as well as four parent sessions. Assessment at the end of the program revealed positive effects in both intervention conditions. These data suggest that the program can be effectively delivered by teachers. A meta-analysis of 65 outcome trials of anxiety prevention programs such as Coping Koala found small but significant effects in reduction of both symptoms and diagnoses of anxiety (Teubert & Pinquart, 2011). Greater effects were found for indicated/selected interventions than for universal programs.

Depression

Risk factors for the development of depression include individual variables such as interpersonal skills deficits and cognitive errors, family variables such as parental depression and marital conflict, as well as contextual factors such as negative life events (Lee & Asgary-Eden, 2009). Horowitz and Garber (2006) examined a wide range of programs designed to prevent depressive symptoms in children and adolescents. Horowitz and Garber found little meta-analytic evidence that universal programs are effective in preventing depression, but observed small yet significant effects for indicated and selective intervention. In a later meta-analysis, Stice, Shaw, Bohon, Marti, and Rohde (2009) reported similar findings, with small effects overall but larger effects for selective interventions. Both groups of researchers recommended that prevention efforts should focus on those most at risk for developing depression. In

©iStock.com/Matt_Brown

Indicated and selective prevention programs have been found to be helpful in reducing the incidence of depression.

light of this, it is very informative that a meta-analysis of 13 trials targeting children of parents with mental disorders found that prevention programs decreased the risk of the young people developing a mental disorder by 40% (Siegenthaler, Munder, & Egger, 2012).

Interestingly, a meta-analysis that examined prevention programs across the life span found that preventive interventions reduce the incidence of depressive disorders by 22% (Cuijpers, van Straten, Am Smit, Mihalopoulos, & Beekman, 2008). The researchers reported that, for depression prevention programs, the number needed to treat is 22—in comparison, as we described earlier in the chapter, the preventive effects of Aspirin on heart attacks has a number needed to treat of 130. Overall, these studies suggest that there is merit to developing programs to prevent the development of internalizing problems. Programs based on cognitive-behavioural and interpersonal principles are promising strategies to promote individual and interpersonal skills that will protect children and youth from developing internalizing disorders. School-based programs offer an appealing avenue to circumvent adolescents' avoidance of the stigma of mental health services. Researchers are working hard to identify the most cost-effective strategy to convey these skills to young people and to solicit the collaboration of their parents.

PREVENTION OF SUBSTANCE ABUSE

The societal costs of smoking, alcohol abuse, and drug abuse are enormous. Alcohol, tobacco, and drug use during pregnancy are associated with a host of deleterious consequences, such as premature delivery, low birth weight, perinatal mortality, and long-term neurological and cognitive-emotional problems (World Health Organization, 2004). It is estimated that tobacco is responsible for 4.1% of the total global economic costs due to disability, with alcohol accounting for another 4.0% (World Health Organization, 2004a). Substance abuse is a leading cause of adolescent morbidity and mortality because of its links with motor vehicle accidents and with sexual behaviour leading to unplanned pregnancies and HIV infection (Essau, 2004). Problems with smoking, alcohol, and drug abuse emerge during adolescence. There is evidence that the early onset of consumption is associated with higher risk of abuse (Essau, 2004).

©iStock.com/toxawww

Problems with smoking, alcohol, and drug abuse emerge during adolescence.

Alcohol use is common in society but, obviously, not all those young people who drink alcohol go on to abuse it. What factors are associated with greater risk? Risk can be considered at the level of the individual, the family, peer group, and community, and at a provincial or national level according to the laws governing access to cigarettes and alcohol. Individual-level risks include temperamental factors, coping skills, psychopathology, and exposure to negative life events. Unfortunately, some high-risk youth may also be at risk of school dropout and may therefore not receive a prevention or health promotion program if it is delivered in school (Zucker, 2003). Those at risk for one problem behaviour may also be at risk for others. For example, adolescent smoking is highly correlated with engagement in other problem behaviours, including alcohol abuse, antisocial behaviour, high-risk sexual behaviours, and academic failure (Biglan & Severson, 2003).

Problems of substance abuse are particularly acute in some indigenous populations. Although risk and protective factors for the development of substance abuse may be similar in American Indian populations and in the general population, there has been little systematic study of any culture-specific risk and protective factors, or of the effectiveness of prevention programs in these populations (Marlatt et al., 2003). As a step toward addressing this shortcoming in our knowledge, a group of researchers from the University of Washington collaborated with the Seattle Indian Health Board to develop a program grounded in the scientific knowledge about substance abuse that is also congruent with the culture of urban native youth (Hawkins et al., 2004).

Universal preventive interventions can focus on regulating young people's access to tobacco and alcohol as well as on education about their harmful effects. A series of meta-analyses by Tobler and colleagues (Tobler et al., 2000) distinguished between two types of programs: interactive and non-interactive. *Interactive programs* that foster the development of interpersonal skills yielded higher effect sizes than did lecture-based *non-interactive programs*. Efficacious programs begin by providing multiple sessions early in adolescence and following them with booster sessions in mid-adolescence (Coughlan, Doyle, & Carr, 2002). In addition to directly targeting youth, prevention programs can be designed to influence the behaviour of significant others and, indirectly, the behaviour of children and adolescents. A meta-analysis of 20 studies that examined parenting programs to reduce misuse of tobacco, alcohol, and drugs by youth found evidence that efficacy was associated with active parental involvement in developing social competence and self-regulation (Petrie, Bunn, & Byrne, 2007). Exhibit 10.4 summarizes the features of efficacious drug abuse prevention programs.

Although it makes sense to think that in choosing a prevention program, organizations would be guided by the results of the scientific

Exhibit 10.4 Key Elements of Efficacious Drug Abuse Prevention Programs

Skills Promoted In

- recognizing and resisting social pressure to use drugs
- assertiveness
- stress management
- social skills
- problem-solving
- decision-making

Multi-Systemic Involvement

- peer leaders
- peer group projects to explore alternatives to drug use
- home–school liaison about drug use prevention policy
- parent–child homework assignments about drug abuse prevention
- parent training in parent–adolescent communication, limit-setting, and supervision
- community involvement in a drug abuse prevention task force

General Design Features

- adequate training, support, and supervision of teachers, peer leaders, and program staff
- manualized program curricula
- accurate program implementation monitoring
- active training methods (modelling, rehearsal, corrective feedback, reinforcement, and extended practice)
- transition from primary to secondary school beginning when youngsters are aged 11 to 13
- extension over at least one school year and inclusion of booster sessions annually throughout high school
- incorporation into existing school curriculum
- sensitive to developmental stage
- social and cultural acceptability to the community, particularly where youngsters are from ethnic minorities
- rigorous evaluation and giving of evaluation feedback to implementation team and participants

Adapted from Coughlan, Doyle, & Carr (2002).

literature, unfortunately this is not always the case. For example, Ennett and colleagues (2003) surveyed a national sample of public and private schools in the United States about the programs they used to prevent substance abuse. Although Tobler's series of meta-analyses clearly identified that programs are most effective when they include interactive teaching strategies, only 17.4% of surveyed programs delivered material in an interactive style. Psychologists' ethical codes dictate that they should strive to deliver programs that work, and taxpayers expect

VIEWPOINT BOX 10.2

HEALTH PROMOTION AND PREVENTION PROGRAMS FOR OLDER ADULTS

Although most of the prevention and promotion programs we have presented target very young children, it would be a mistake to conclude that health promotion and the prevention of mental disorders focus exclusively on very young participants. With an aging population, there have been growing efforts to identify ways to promote resilience and decrease the risk of problems in older adults. These include programs to promote exercise and social support, early screening efforts, and programs to support caregivers (Depp, Vahia, & Jeste, 2010; World Health Organization, 2004a).

©iStock.com/monkeybusinessimages

Exercise has benefits for the physical and mental health of older adults

Studies have provided evidence of the multiple mental and physical benefits of regular exercise for older adults. Li, McAuley, Chaumeton, and Harmer (2001), for example, reported from a randomized controlled trial of the effects of Tai Chi that participants scored higher than did controls on measures of life satisfaction and positive affect, and had fewer depressive symptoms. Various factors contribute to the social isolation of older adults, including their lack of involvement in the labour force, decreased mobility due to disability, and bereavement due to the death of a spouse or friend. Although befriending programs are believed to have positive effects on the well-being of older women, there have been few systematic attempts to assess whether such programs are effective in enhancing social support (World Health Organization, 2004a). Early screening programs are designed to identify older adults requiring additional services. A small randomized controlled trial (Shapiro & Taylor, 2002) reported that provision of early in-home geriatric assessment to older adults at moderate risk for losing their ability to remain in their own homes was associated with higher subjective well-being and lower likelihood of institutionalization.

Family caregivers of older adults shoulder a significant financial, physical, and emotional burden in caring for their loved ones. Because the toll of such care giving is substantial, a number of programs have been designed to ease caregiver burden. Sörensen, Pinquart, and Duberstein (2002) conducted a meta-analysis of 78 caregiver intervention studies, and found that interventions yielded small to moderate effect sizes. Overall, programs were more effective in increasing knowledge than they were in reducing burden or depressed symptoms. The field of prevention of problems for older adults is an emerging one, with promising interventions. However, with the growing need for such programs to meet the demands of an aging population, it is essential that the evaluation of the usefulness of such programs be a priority.

that funds should be directed toward those programs that are most cost-effective. It is essential therefore that priority be given to developing scientifically based programs that are efficacious and effective in preventing problems and promoting health.

PREVENTION OF PROBLEMS IN THOSE EXPOSED TO TRAUMA OR LOSS

Within the mental health field, it is a commonly held belief that it is necessary to express and *work through* difficult experiences. This conviction has its origins in Freudian theories and has led to the widespread belief that mental health services are required by everyone who is the victim of or witness to an unpleasant event (Bonanno, 2004). News reports of tragedies such as high school shootings, train derailments, or murder–suicides inevitably end with the phrase "counsellors will be available on site to assist the survivors."

The strategy of critical incident stress debriefing was introduced as a preventive strategy to ensure that survivors and witnesses to tragedies had assistance in processing the details of the traumatic event at the time, in order to avoid the dangers of a delayed stress reaction. In critical incident stress debriefing, counsellors work with groups of up to 15 participants whom they instruct to recount details of the event they have witnessed. Participants are then asked to describe their thoughts, emotional reactions, and symptoms in response to the event. Finally, counsellors provide psychoeducation on coping skills before sharing a snack and returning participants to their regular environment (Enright & Carr, 2002).

The rationale for critical incident stress debriefing has an intuitive appeal. If indeed it were possible to protect people from developing posttraumatic stress disorder by devoting a couple of hours to hearing their stories, then it would certainly be time well invested. Unfortunately, outcome data do not support the effectiveness of critical incident stress debriefing and suggest that sometimes it can even be harmful as it may impede natural recovery processes (Bonanno, 2004; World Health Organization, 2004a). The basic problem with an approach such as critical incident stress debriefing is that it is based on the faulty assumption that there is only one path to recovery and that beneficial effects can be obtained by imposing the same solution on everyone. There is, however, ample evidence that there are multiple pathways to healthy functioning and that it is ineffective and sometimes harmful to insist that everyone be treated the same.

We see similarly faulty logic with respect to services for the bereaved. Although we assume that the death of a parent would be an appalling blow that would provoke serious mental health problems for children, research suggests that a substantial minority of bereaved children do not show any signs of adjustment problems (Lin, Sandler, Ayers, Wolchik, & Luecken, 2004). Nevertheless, it is common for bereaved children to be offered psychological services to prevent the development of problems. A meta-analysis of bereavement interventions with children found no evidence that they generated positive outcomes (Currier, Holland, & Neimeyer, 2007). As the majority of bereaved children are resilient in the face of their loss, showing either no symptoms or symptoms that are of a time-limited nature, services offered to bereaved children are likely to show little effect simply because many children do not need any intervention. In most cases, these children are helped by those who love and care for them.

The assumption that everyone resolves grief in a similar fashion led to the assumption that a person who does not show an overt grief reaction is an emotional time bomb who will inevitably one day experience a delayed grief reaction. There is no scientific evidence to support this assumption (Bonanno, 2004). It is clear that in our efforts to identify those who are suffering psychological pain, we have inadvertently overlooked the many people who are resilient in the face of adversity. By searching to better understand the qualities, behaviours, and resources of these individuals—who, despite enduring suffering, maintain their equilibrium and lead satisfying lives—we may be in a better position to mount effective prevention programs.

Prevention programs seem to be relatively effective for many psychological problems, so why aren't such programs more commonly used in our health care and educational systems?

There are certainly people who are adversely affected by life-threatening or traumatic events. Such individuals may well benefit from psychological services designed to minimize the effects of these events. A meta-analysis that examined the effects of different types of psychological services on children exposed to traumatic events found strong evidence for the helpfulness of individual and group cognitive-behaviour therapy (Wethington et al., 2008). Additionally, the researchers found that there was simply not sufficient evidence to conclude that the other interventions (play therapy, art therapy, medication, psychodynamic therapy, or psychological debriefing) were effective in reducing psychological harm in children exposed to trauma.

When you have had painful experiences, who did you turn to for support? What do you think it would be like to have a stranger tell you what you need to do to cope with a painful situation?

Profile Box 10.2 introduces Dr. Jonathan Weiss, who works with people with developmental disabilities to prevent the development of emotional and behavioural problems.

PROFILE BOX 10.2

DR. JONATHAN WEISS

Courtesy of Jonathan Weiss

I earned a Ph.D. in clinical developmental psychology from York University and completed an internship at Surrey Place Centre in Toronto. After that, I completed a postdoctoral fellowship in the Dual Diagnosis program at the Centre for Addiction and Mental Health, and was a research fellow in the Department of Psychiatry at the University of Toronto. I am an assistant professor in the Department of Psychology at York University, and a clinical psychologist registered with the College of Psychologists of Ontario. I hold the Canadian Institutes of Health Research Chair in Autism Spectrum Disorders Treatment and Care Research. My research focuses on the prevention and treatment of mental health and behaviour problems in people with developmental disabilities, including autism spectrum disorders or intellectual disabilities. My research involves individuals, their families, and larger systems of care.

HOW DID YOU CHOOSE TO BECOME A CLINICAL PSYCHOLOGIST?

I chose to become a clinical psychologist for a number of educational and clinical reasons that fit well within a scientist-practitioner framework. I had been pursuing an undergraduate degree in psychology, and found the scientific study of human behaviour and *why we do what we* do incredibly fascinating. I valued psychology's empirical approach, and could see myself working in a field where that was the accepted method of inquiry. I also knew that I enjoyed learning, and clinical psychology was a field where education was an ongoing part of the profession. As well, I had some important interpersonal experiences that directed me specifically to clinical psychology. I had been working for many years as a residential caregiver, providing support to adults with intellectual disabilities and autism in their homes. I found this work rewarding, and found myself wanting to work more to address my clients' mental health and well-being. Clinical psychology allowed me to do all of these things: I could continue to study and use science to answer questions about clinical issues, and take that knowledge to inform how I help people with clinical problems.

WHAT IS THE GREATEST CHALLENGE YOU FACE AS A CLINICAL PSYCHOLOGIST?

The greatest challenge is balancing the time it takes to do research with the time it takes for clinical practice. There is such a large need for both, but figuring out when to do each can be hard.

TELL US ABOUT YOUR RESEARCH ON THE PREVENTION OF MENTAL HEALTH PROBLEMS IN PEOPLE WITH DEVELOPMENTAL DISABILITIES.

I have studied how Special Olympics, a sport organization for children and adults with developmental disabilities, can enhance the mental health and well-being of participants. Athletes in Special Olympics show improvements in self-concept and in adaptive and maladaptive behaviours following participation, and different aspects of the program are related to the athletes' psychological well-being. Empirically identifying variables of import informs program developers about the aspects of the program that should be emphasized to promote mental health. My research extends beyond sport to examining a variety of contexts that can be protective in nature. These include studying how well-being in individuals with developmental disabilities is related to (a) their family's well-being and to (b) their ability to access health care and social services when they need them. Part of prevention means making sure we have the

CONTINUED . . .

capacity to provide service in a timely manner when someone says there is a need and before problems get worse. One of our research projects has been to study why there are so few clinical psychologists in Canada providing psychological services to individuals with developmental disabilities across the life span. Although graduate students clearly value training in developmental disabilities as part of their general clinical training, they also feel a need for additional training that will prepare them to provide effective services to this population. Building capacity in Canada to provide services in a timely and effective manner can help to address problems before they become severe.

HOW DO YOU INTEGRATE SCIENCE AND PRACTICE IN YOUR WORK?

My clinical practice and my research inform each other in an ongoing way, and the scientific method is important to both areas of my work. Most of my clinical practice involves providing psychological services to individuals with developmental disabilities or to their families, and this is the main focus of my research. So, what I learn through research and through others who study in this field translates into how I provide care. I regularly consult the literature when presented with clinical issues and use evidence-based interventions in my practice. As well, my interactions with clients inform the kinds of questions I ask or how I might interpret the results of the scientific studies that I am involved in.

WHAT DO YOU SEE AS THE MOST EXCITING CHANGES IN THE FIELD OF CLINICAL PSYCHOLOGY?

It is now recognized across health and allied health professions that there is a critical need to use research and evidence when making decisions about client care. This is very exciting to me because it means a method of providing responsible care for clients, where our choices of what we do are guided by sound science. Because of our training in science and in practice, clinical psychologists are ideally suited to be leaders in evidence-based practice. This includes being the ones to develop interventions, study them, and apply them in clinical situations.

VIEWPOINT BOX 10.3

UNSUNG HEROES

It is easy to get discouraged when we read the data from the World Health Organization that, despite the development of effective vaccines, millions of children die every year from infectious diseases, and that, despite the development of effective programs for the prevention of substance abuse, most programs are not delivered in an effective way. If you are contemplating a career in prevention science, you may be overwhelmed by the thought of having to master knowledge and skills not only in clinical psychology, but also in public health. You may doubt that you would have the charisma, vision, or persistence to become a member of a team that was successful in securing funding and getting cooperation from stakeholders in government, education, and the community. Does this mean you cannot contribute to the prevention of mental health problems? Let's consider Rachel's story.

Rachel's father, Daniel, was a Holocaust survivor, embittered by his suffering and haunted by guilt that he alone of all his family had survived the concentration camps of Nazi Germany. Daniel married, had two children, and built a life in Canada, working hard to provide safety for his son and daughter. His grief prevented him from ever experiencing much joy and he

CONTINUED . . .

was a hard taskmaster to his children. He punished his son harshly with a strap and was critical and demanding of Rachel. Rachel grew up with low self-esteem and poor coping skills. She married early and found herself in a relationship that mirrored the emotional abuse she suffered as a child. Nevertheless, she was a resourceful woman who was a devoted and loving mother to her own two children. Rachel sought psychological services for depression after leaving her abusive husband.

During the intake assessment, the psychologist asked her about other adults who might have been sources of support during her childhood and adolescence. Sadly, Rachel saw her mother as having failed to protect her from her father's rages. The person she remembered was the father of a friend of hers. On a rare free evening after school in Grade 9, Rachel had gone home with her friend Hillary. As the girls prepared a snack in the kitchen, they heard Hillary's father call up from the basement: "Is that you Hillary? Could you give me a hand please?" To Rachel's horror, Hillary yelled back, "Sure Dad, in a few minutes when we're done our snack." Rachel felt her heart pound and her hands get clammy as she braced for Hillary's dad to burst out of the basement in a rage because Hillary had not immediately complied with his request. She could not believe her ears when he replied, "OK honey, no rush." Rachel treasured the opportunities to visit Hillary—she found Hillary's relationship with her father amazing. Hillary's father may have shaken his head sadly at his daughter's shy friend and may have felt helpless to make a difference in the life of this young woman whose home life was overshadowed by the suffering of the Holocaust. Although he did not know it, Hillary's father provided a lifeline for Rachel. He gave her hope that young people could be treated respectfully by parents. Rachel nurtured that hope and acted on it with her own children, treating them as she had seen Hillary's father behave rather than as she had been treated.

Even if you do not choose a career in preventing mental health problems, you will have many opportunities to contribute to the prevention of emotional and behavioural difficulties. The principles for healthy development are relatively simple. You have already learned in other psychology courses about the importance of positive reinforcement, social support, modelling prosocial behaviour, and clear communication. As you put those principles into practice in your job, your family, your friendships, and your community, you will be making an important step in preventing problems. The protective factors listed in Exhibit 10.2 include many ways that you can contribute to mental health promotion.

SUMMARY AND CONCLUSIONS

We have summarized research on some of the many programs designed to prevent emotional and behavioural problems and to promote positive psychological functioning. The most successful programs have several features in common (Biglan, Mrazek, Carnine, & Flay, 2003). First, they are evidence-based. Each effective program was designed to target known risk and protective factors in the development of psychopathology. These prevention programs drew on psychological research that has identified those factors that make a person vulnerable to developing psychopathology, as well as those factors that act as a buffer against the development of problems. Second, many programs work to promote the same relatively simple principles, such as promoting positive adult–child relationships; allowing children ample opportunities to be rewarded for appropriate behaviour; providing adequate monitoring and supervision; providing mild corrective feedback for inappropriate behaviour; helping children manage emotions, treat one another with respect, and act assertively rather than aggressively; and facilitating the development of supportive networks (Biglan, 2003; Carr, 2002). Third, these programs are usually multifaceted, involving different components or modules that operate at the level of the individual, family, school, community, or legal system. This allows the same message to be conveyed by parents, teachers, peers, community leaders, and the government (Biglan, 2003; Weissberg et al., 2003). A fourth common feature among some of the most successful programs is that they were developed as an expansion of an efficacious treatment intervention that was modified and offered in a slightly diluted format to those with subclinical problems. Programmatic research is then carried out over many years to determine the program's effectiveness (Nation et al., 2003; Sanders, 2012). Fifth, successful programs are offered in convenient contexts. Services are offered in a milieu that minimizes obstacles to participation, by using schools, community centres, and home visits, as well as by offering childcare services so that parents can participate (Carr, 2002). Finally, the developers of effective prevention programs all stress the importance of program fidelity in adopting their interventions (e.g., Webster-Stratton, 2006). This means that it is necessary to use the same materials and protocols and to deliver the same number of sessions as the original program.

To ensure that people are receiving effective services, it is necessary to conduct outcome assessments of both competence and symptoms/risk factors. These programs are designed to reduce problems in the future, so it is essential that evaluations extend beyond the conclusion of a program in order to evaluate longer-term functioning. As those who receive preventive services are led to believe that these services will make a difference in their lives, we owe it to them to be certain that this is really the case.

KEY TERMS

community psychology: a branch of psychology that focuses on research and practice on the reciprocal relations between individuals and the community in which they live.

health promotion: programs designed to increase activities that are beneficial to many aspects of physical health.

incidence rates: the number of new cases of a specific problem.

indicated preventive intervention: a prevention program that targets people who do not meet criteria for a disorder, but who have elevated risk and may show detectable, but subclinical, signs of the disorder.

number needed to treat: the number of people who need to receive the intervention in order to prevent one person from developing the condition.

primary prevention: the provision of conditions conducive to good health.

protective factors: characteristics of the individual or the environment that render a person less vulnerable to the development of a problem or disorder.

risk factors: characteristics of the individual or the environment that render a person more vulnerable to the development of a problem or disorder, or that are associated with more severe symptoms.

risk reduction model: an approach to prevention that reduces risks and promotes protective factors.

secondary prevention: prevention that targets groups of people who are identified as being at high risk (similar to selected and indicated prevention).

selective preventive intervention: a prevention program that targets people who are at elevated risk of developing a particular disorder or problem.

universal preventive intervention: a prevention program applied to an entire population, such as a media awareness campaign on the dangers of drinking and driving.

KEY NAMES

Paula Barrett   Matthew Sanders   Carolyn Webster-Stratton

ADDITIONAL RESOURCES

Books

Dozois, D. A., & Dobson, K. S. (Eds). (2004). *The prevention of anxiety and depression: Theory, research, and practice.* Washington, DC: American Psychological Association Press.

Greenwood, C. R., Kratochwill, T. R., & Clements, M. (Eds). (2008). *Schoolwide prevention models: Lessons learned in elementary schools*. New York: Guilford.

Tolan, P., Szapocznik, J., & Sambrano, S. (Eds). (2006). *Preventing youth substance abuse: Science-based programs for children and adolescents*. Washington, DC: American Psychological Association Press.

Check It Out!

An American website providing information on the Incredible Years Program: www.incredibleyears.com

An Australian website providing information on Triple P: www.triplep.net

The website for the Blueprints for Violence Prevention programs that identifies efficacious prevention programs: www.colorado.edu/cspv/blueprints

11 CHAPTER

INTERVENTION: OVERVIEW

INTRODUCTION

When Rashad was diagnosed with ADHD, his parents felt relieved to know what was wrong with their son. Now they want to know how to help him.

Clayton has learned that his nightmares and the intrusive thoughts about the combat missions in which he participated are related to PTSD. He is eager to get on with his life but does not know what services would help.

Genevieve has been worried about her father's low mood, lack of motivation, and joyless life. She has been told her father, Alain, is suffering from a major depressive disorder. Now she is wondering whether anything can be done to help him.

In previous chapters, you have learned about the ways that psychologists conduct assessments (Chapters 5 to 9), as well as efforts to prevent the development of psychological disorders (Chapter 10). In this chapter and the following three, we discuss psychological interventions to help people like Rashad, Clayton, and Alain. As we described in Chapter 2, a major part of most psychologists' workload is devoted to providing psychological treatment; the vast majority of clinical psychologists report providing these services as part of their practice. Throughout the text we have drawn attention to the ethical principles that guide the delivery of psychological services. In this chapter, we will discuss ethical issues in the selection of treatments, in informed consent to services, and in the requirement for ongoing assessment of treatment usefulness. We will also highlight issues related to confidentiality. Then we will examine some major models that inform current evidence-based psychological interventions.

Instead of providing comprehensive coverage of theoretical approaches to psychotherapy, in this chapter we focus on major forms of therapy that have been shown to work. Although hundreds of different forms of psychotherapy are offered by mental health professionals, most of them have not been empirically evaluated, and so are not covered here. Instead, in keeping with both the scientific and ethical evolution of the field of clinical psychology, we focus on evidence-based approaches to psychotherapy. Accordingly, you will notice that we do not present any information on two large categories of therapy: those that have a long history but scant empirical support (e.g., psychoanalysis, Jungian analysis) and those more recently developed therapies that, likewise, are lacking empirical support and are largely discredited (e.g., primal scream therapy, neuro-linguistic programming, thought field therapy; for more examples of discredited treatments, see Norcross, Koocher, & Garofalo, 2006).

To provide you with a broad sense of the nature of psychotherapeutic services, we will consider the characteristics of people who seek and receive psychological interventions. Some psychologists refer to these individuals as *patients* and others use the term *clients*, so we will use the terms interchangeably in this and subsequent chapters. We will look at the paths by which people are referred (or self-refer) for psychotherapy. Although the majority of psychological interventions are delivered in one-to-one sessions in the psychologist's office, there is evidence that other modes of treatment delivery—such as couples therapy, family therapy, and group therapy—are also efficacious. There is also growing evidence of the efficacy of psychological treatments delivered without direct face-to-face contact. Accordingly, we will highlight recent innovations in the use of technology in the delivery of psychological interventions. Because of the diversity of those seeking therapy, as well as concerns to offer the most cost-effective services, psychologists have developed menus of treatments that can be calibrated according to the patient's level of need. We discuss the principles of this *stepped care* approach to treatment at the end of the chapter.

So, what is psychotherapy? Norcross (1990, pp. 218–220) defined psychotherapy as "the informed and intentional application of clinical methods and interpersonal stances derived from established psychological principles for the purpose of assisting people to modify their behaviors, cognitions, emotions, and/or other personal characteristics in directions that the participants deem desirable." This concise statement distinguishes psychotherapy from other helpful conversations that a person might have with friends, in online chats, or sitting on a bus. It emphasizes that psychotherapy is based on the body of knowledge in psychology, and that it can target changes in terms of how people act, think, and feel. Unfortunately, although most psychologists refer to the intervention services they provide as psychotherapy, the term is also commonly used to refer to many types of services that are *not* based on established psychological principles. Barlow (2004) suggested that the term *psychological treatments* be used to refer to evidence-based interventions to treat clinically significant problems (i.e., DSM-5 diagnoses).

Using Norcross' definition, the American Psychological Association (2013b) passed a resolution recognizing the effectiveness of psychotherapy. As you will learn in this and subsequent chapters, there is a great deal of evidence that many psychological interventions can be efficacious for a wide range of psychological problems experienced by people across the life span, and there is growing evidence that some of these interventions are also effective when applied in typical clinical settings.

The APA resolution was intended to promote the inclusion of psychotherapy in health care systems as a form of evidence-based practice. Although this is a laudable goal which most clinical psychologists support, it is possible the resolution would have been stronger if it had referred to specific psychological treatments rather than to psychotherapy. As psychotherapy includes not only services to address mental disorders but also counselling to address regular life challenges, the resolution covers a broad range of services. The resolution does not distinguish between therapies that have been empirically evaluated and those that have not. There is enormous variability in the extent of scientific evidence on the impact of psychotherapy for commonly experienced psychological problems. For example, compared with the voluminous evidence regarding the impact of treatments for depression in adults, the evidence base is not as well established for the treatment of depression in youth. There are debates about the appropriate scope of psychotherapy, with some treatment approaches focusing primarily on symptom reduction and improvement in psychosocial functioning and other approaches emphasizing self-actualization and broader changes in personality (e.g., Wampold, 2013). The current evidence base is not uniformly strong with respect to the usefulness of psychotherapy to address the full spectrum of treatment goals of the different approaches to psychotherapy.

THE ETHICS OF INTERVENTION

Psychotherapy is practised by professionals from many disciplines, including psychology, psychiatry, social work, medicine, and nursing. In most jurisdictions, the title *psychotherapist* is not licensed or restricted in any fashion. Accordingly, in most provinces, anyone can advertise his or her services as a psychotherapist. Those seeking psychotherapeutic services would be well advised, therefore, to obtain treatment from a registered or licensed health care professional. The following statement from the College of Psychologists of Ontario (2004) nicely captures the reasons for seeking services from a regulated professional.

> *As regulated health providers, psychologists and psychological associates are required by law to deliver competent, ethical and professional services and are accountable to the public, through the College, for their professional behaviour and activities. As members of the College, psychologists and psychological associates must meet rigorous professional entry requirements, adhere to prescribed standards, guidelines and ethical principles and participate in quality assurance activities to continually update and improve their knowledge and skill. In contrast, the College has no jurisdiction over unregulated service providers. There is no regulatory body to set minimum levels of education, training and competence or to establish and monitor professional and ethical standards of conduct. There is no regulatory body to protect the public interest and hold unregulated providers accountable for the services they provide.*

In Chapter 5, you learned about ethical issues in obtaining consent to psychological assessment and, in Chapter 6, we described confidentiality and the limits to confidentiality in psychological services. Given the central importance of these ethical principles in the delivery of all psychological services, it is critical to recognize their applicability in psychological interventions. A core ethical issue is that the psychologist cannot proceed with any psychological services without the client's agreement to receive the services. Furthermore, this agreement must be based on a reasonable understanding of what the services will entail and the likely outcomes of receiving or not receiving services. The process of obtaining informed consent recognizes the consumer's rights regarding psychological services. It is insufficient to simply obtain the client's signature at the bottom of a jargon-filled description of services; the psychologist must provide a comprehensible account so that the client can make an informed decision on whether to pursue services.

Each person who is involved in services must understand the nature of those services and must consent to receive them. In order to make a truly informed decision about treatment, patients should be informed of all evidence-based treatment options. This includes medication options, psychological interventions the psychologist can provide, *and* psychological interventions the psychologist does not have the training to provide (in which case a referral would be necessary). Ethical obligations to inform patients about treatment options must take precedence over the business consideration of whether the person will choose to receive therapy from the psychologist.

The next time you seek any type of health service, pay attention to informed consent issues. How does the service provider explain the options to you? Does it make a difference to you whether the service provider ensures you understand your choices?

In different jurisdictions, the issue of obtaining consent from children is treated in various ways, including setting chronological ages at which children are presumed competent to give consent, or requiring the psychologist to determine in each case whether a child is competent to give consent (Fisher, 2004). A child who is not competent to give consent still has a right to have procedures explained in a simple manner and is asked to give assent, which is the verbal form of consent. Obviously, the onus is on the psychologist to know and follow the legal requirements relevant to the jurisdiction in which he or she practises. Ability to provide consent can also be an issue in working with older clients who are experiencing significant cognitive impairment, such as can occur with the dementias. Careful evaluation of the client's capacity to understand options and make decisions is required in such situations.

Psychologists must explain their services to children in a language they can understand.

Once people have decided to begin therapy, what kinds of questions should they raise in their first appointment with a psychologist?

As you learned in Chapter 6, clients must be assured of the confidentiality of the services they receive, as well as the limits to confidentiality when a person's safety is in danger. They must also receive clear descriptions of the steps taken by the psychologist to protect their privacy. Many potential clients do not ask about confidentiality issues, financial arrangements, or treatment alternatives (e.g., Braaten, Otto, & Handelsman, 1993). They definitely should. Exhibit 11.1 provides some of the questions all clinical psychologists should be prepared to answer for potential clients.

Exhibit 11.1 Questions about Psychotherapy Services

- What kind of training and experience do you have in dealing with problems like the ones I have?
- What type of treatment is most effective for the kinds of problems I have, and do you provide this treatment?
- Is this treatment right for me? How likely is it that it will help me?
- Are there any disadvantages or side effects associated with the most effective treatment?
- Are there other effective treatment options that I should consider?
- What is the hourly rate for sessions?
- Do you offer a sliding fee based on individual or family income?
- Will my private health insurance cover all or part of the fees?
- How many sessions will treatment likely take? How often will we need to meet?

We have stressed that ethical issues are prominent at the beginning of psychological services. They do not end once consent has been obtained, confidentiality explained, and a course of services begun. As we have emphasized many times, the psychologist has an ethical responsibility to monitor the effectiveness of services. It would be unethical to persist in offering services to a client if those services did not prove helpful in addressing the problem. Although there is great merit in adopting an approach that has been shown to be effective in treating similar problems, the psychologist must be vigilant in monitoring its usefulness for each client. Ethical practice requires that the psychologist be attentive to the ongoing and potentially changing fit between the treatment plan, the client's needs, and the client's responses to treatment.

Think about a health service you have received recently. It might have been treatment for an infection, orthodontic services, or chiropractic services. How did the health care provider monitor the effectiveness of the services in helping you? Is it important to you to know that the services are making a difference in your life?

Many people ask what psychologists should do if there is no evidence-based treatment for the problem presented by a client. Fortunately, at this point in time, there is research evidence that is relevant to the treatment of almost all psychosocial problems. Although there may be no randomized controlled trials relevant to the problem, there are likely to be other types of pertinent research data, including uncontrolled treatment trials and case reports. As discussed in Chapter 1, evidence-based practice does not require that treatments be based solely on highly controlled, internally valid, replicated studies—it requires that the psychologist base treatment for a client on the *best available evidence*. In some cases the relevant evidence base may include many controlled treatment studies; in other cases it may be that there are only one or two case studies that provide evidence on how to treat the psychological problem. In other words, there is little justification for psychologists or other mental health professionals to offer treatments that are not informed by research evidence. In situations in which there is limited evidence about treatment efficacy, the client should be informed of this and asked to consent to treatment with full knowledge about the limited scientific basis for the treatment.

Another commonly encountered question is whether there are forms of intervention that should *not* be provided to clients. Although most psychological therapies do not have harmful side effects, there is a growing awareness, and research base, on psychological treatments that can cause harm. Two examples provided by Lilienfeld (2007) illustrate the general concern about some widely available treatments. "Scared straight" programs that try to frighten adolescents at risk for ongoing criminal behaviour actually increase the odds of subsequent criminal offending. Rebirthing therapy, in which children are wrapped in blankets and squeezed repeatedly to "simulate" the "trauma" of birth, has resulted in a number of deaths. These examples clearly demonstrate that some psychological treatments can cause harm, and underscore the need for psychologists to provide services that are strongly based in science.

How important is it that the research evidence be based on clients who are similar to the person seeking services? Does it matter whether the research was conducted with people of similar age, gender, ethnicity, or socioeconomic status? In general, it is highly unlikely that all aspects of human diversity—sexual orientation, religious beliefs, socioeconomic status—are adequately represented in the treatment research. A key question that the psychologist must ask is whether client characteristics affect the relevance of available research results that inform the type of treatment to offer to the client. Based on the extent to which the client is similar to the participants in research trials, the psychologist should adopt, adapt, or abandon an evidence-based treatment (cf. Morales & Norcross, 2010). If there is a reasonable fit between client characteristics and the research samples, the psychologist should *adopt* an evidence-based treatment and offer it to the client. If the fit is reasonable but it seems that some modification is required to respect important cultural characteristics or practices, then the psychologist should *adapt* the treatment to the client. Most evidence-based treatments offer considerable flexibility in how elements of the treatment are implemented, so this does not necessarily pose a problem, assuming that the psychologist is culturally sensitive and culturally competent. Guidance on when and how to adapt a treatment is available in the professional literature (e.g., Bernal, Jiménez-Chafey, & Rodríguez, 2009; Castro, Barrera, & Steiker, 2010), and there is considerable evidence of the efficacy of culturally adapted treatments (Smith, Rodríguez, & Bernal, 2011). The decision to *abandon* an evidence-based treatment option should never be undertaken lightly. However, in almost all instances it should be possible to offer other evidence-based treatment options, ones that offer a better fit to the client's characteristics and preferences. Profile Box 11.1 presents Dr. Christopher Mushquash and describes his efforts to develop culturally sensitive evidence-based mental health services for Aboriginal youth.

PROFILE BOX 11.1

DR. CHRISTOPHER MUSHQUASH

Courtesy of Christopher Mushquash

I obtained a B.Sc. (Hons.) in psychology and M.A. in experimental psychology at Lakehead University, and a Ph.D. in clinical psychology at Dalhousie University. I completed the northern pre-doctoral residency in the Department of Clinical Health Psychology at the University of Manitoba. I am an assistant professor in the Department of Psychology at Lakehead University, and have a cross-appointment in the Division of Human Sciences at the Northern Ontario School of Medicine. I am a member of Pays Plat First Nation, a small First Nation community on the north shore of Lake Superior. My identity is embedded in my Ojibway culture and my experiences growing up in a rural Northwestern Ontario community. In 2013, I was awarded the Canadian Psychological Association President's New Researcher Award. My work focuses on culturally appropriate assessment and intervention in the areas of addiction and mental health for First Nations people. I will soon begin the process of becoming a registered clinical psychologist.

HOW DID YOU CHOOSE TO WORK IN THE FIELD OF CLINICAL PSYCHOLOGY?

I am not sure I chose to become a clinical psychologist! When I began university, I knew I wanted to study science, in a way that would provide me with the skills needed to contribute to the health of Aboriginal people in Canada. To gain new skills, I worked as a research assistant at the Centre for Rural and Northern Health Research. In this position, I tried to learn as much as I could about issues facing rural and remote communities and Aboriginal peoples. I wanted to use the knowledge I gained and the skills I was developing to help my community and other First Nations communities in Canada. To do so, I pursued every opportunity presented to learn skills to help me toward this goal.

While completing my master's degree and still working at the Centre for Rural and Northern Health Research, I became fascinated by the potential to add a clinical perspective to continue to build my research skill set. I learned about research examining the delivery of distance-based treatments to rural communities and about the development of culturally relevant early interventions for alcohol misuse with Aboriginal youth in Nova Scotia. Joining Drs. McGrath, Stewart, and Comeau at Dalhousie University was the next step in pursuing my goal of working on improving health for First Nations communities. During my doctoral studies, we had the opportunity to collaborate with First Nations communities in Nova Scotia, Manitoba, and Saskatchewan. The

CONTINUED . . .

learning was immense! Through my research and clinical training at Dalhousie, I gained skills that have enabled me to work with others who are interested in improving the health and mental health of Canada's Aboriginal people.

WHAT IS THE GREATEST CHALLENGE YOU FACE AS A CLINICAL PSYCHOLOGIST?

With a research focus on Aboriginal addiction and mental health, an emphasis on evidence and critical appraisal, and a recognition that psychology is grounded in Western scientific understandings, I sometimes experience a disconnect between First Nations philosophies and mainstream psychology. Much of my work is in navigating these world views, examining where there is a discrepancy but also where there is overlap and potential for relationship building and collaboration.

TELL US ABOUT YOUR RESEARCH ON THE DEVELOPMENT OF MENTAL HEALTH SERVICES FOR ABORIGINAL YOUTH.

Related to the challenges above, my work has focused mostly on understanding how evidence-based psychological approaches can be integrated with traditional Aboriginal cultural healing practices to provide culturally appropriate services. I was very fortunate to work with excellent researchers during my time at Dalhousie University and owe a lot to a number of scholars who influenced my thinking and work.

HOW DO YOU INTEGRATE SCIENCE AND PRACTICE IN YOUR WORK?

My training had a strong scientist-practitioner focus with importance placed on determining assessment and interventions based on sound scientific evidence. My goal as a practitioner is to choose the best assessment and intervention techniques for the particular client I am working with. My approach tends to be holistic. I am interested in obtaining a wide picture of how a client is doing. I am very cognizant of cultural aspects as they relate to assessment and intervention, while understanding that the definition of culture is very broad. I am interested not only in how cultural affiliation impacts a client's access to services but also in how it impacts identity. To engage in culturally appropriate service provision, I try to choose well-validated, evidence-based measures to collect data, conduct semi-structured interviews to obtain broader information, and gather collateral information (where available) to create and test hypotheses. An important note is that my use of standardized measures occurs with careful attention to possible cultural effects and with regard to appropriate interpretation of scores.

WHAT DO YOU SEE AS THE MOST EXCITING CHANGES IN THE FIELD OF CLINICAL PSYCHOLOGY?

I am most excited about some recent developments in the integration of Western and traditional First Nations approaches to healing and well-being that I have been fortunate to be involved with. For example, Honouring Our Strengths (a collaboration between the National Native Addictions Partnership Foundation and the Assembly of First Nations, in partnership with Health Canada) engaged in a process of developing a renewed framework to address substance use issues among First Nations people in Canada. This process produced a culturally informed continuum of care that communities can use to guide their program development and administration.

THEORETICAL APPROACHES

Consistent with our commitment to evidence-based practice, we will present the forms of psychological therapies that have the strongest research support. These include short-term psychodynamic therapy, interpersonal psychotherapy, process-experiential therapy, and cognitive-behavioural therapy. As you will see, each approach is based on a distinct theory of psychological functioning and change processes. All of these approaches have at least a moderate amount of supporting data for use in the treatment of specific mental disorders. All have also been applied to the treatment of personality disorders, although the evidence of their impact is limited at this time. In Chapters 12 and 13, we will provide more details about specific evidence-based versions of each approach in working with adults, children, and youth. Because it is clear that treatments based on different theoretical approaches can be efficacious in dealing with the same problem, in Chapter 14 we provide information on ways in which efficacious treatments may have many elements in common.

As you read through the following sections on the different theoretical orientations, try to imagine what it would be like to receive the different forms of treatments and how you might respond to the different emphases across orientations.

Short-Term Psychodynamic Psychotherapies

short-term psychodynamic therapy: a treatment approach that emphasizes bringing to awareness unconscious processes, especially as they are expressed in interpersonal relationships, and helping the client to understand and alter these processes.

In response to concerns about the cost and effectiveness of extended psychoanalytic and psychodynamic interventions, a number of **short-term psychodynamic psychotherapies** (STPPs) were developed. STPPs are grounded in psychodynamic principles that originated in the work of Sigmund Freud (Messer, 2000). As you may recall from Chapter 1 and from other psychology courses, Freud's drive theory emphasized the importance of innate, biological drives that the individual must control in order to adapt to society. A number of psychodynamic models building on this theory were developed in the 20th century. Ego psychology, developed by Anna Freud, among others, focused on the process by which the very young child learns to construct a model of the world (Vakoch & Strupp, 2000). Themes from both drive and ego theories were blended in object relations theories that noted that infants tend to categorize their experiences into good and bad. As children mature, they learn that each person has both positive and negative qualities. If, however, they do not learn this, they are prone to chaotic relationships, because they act as though people are either all good or all bad (Vakoch & Strupp, 2000). As you can imagine, having such a dichotomous view of people is likely to lead to a great deal of disappointment, resentment, and interpersonal conflict.

Psychodynamic theories assume that individuals are prone to conflicts between id and ego. These conflicts are resolved when the ego learns to accept and tolerate the id impulses. However, there is a tendency for these impulses to be suppressed so that they are not within conscious awareness and tend to be re-enacted throughout the client's life. According to psychodynamic theorists, it is inevitable that the client's core interpersonal conflicts will be repeated in the relationship with the therapist through a process known as **transference** (Vakoch & Strupp, 2000). Most current forms of psychodynamic treatment use transference to assist clients in understanding their problems and making changes in their lives. Generally speaking, clients are helped to see how their core interpersonal conflicts are influencing the relationship with the therapist, how these conflicts developed, and how these conflicts have affected, and continue to affect, their lives. Psychodynamic theorists believe that by repeatedly attending to these issues, clients become aware of these conflicts, make choices about their interpersonal style, and behave in a manner that is less determined by their unconscious conflicts.

transference: the unconscious application of expectations and emotional experiences, based on important early relationships, to subsequent interpersonal relationships.

Brief psychodynamic therapies were championed in the 1960s and 1970s by psychiatrists Malan, Davanloo, and Sifneos, who proposed theoretical models in which change is proposed to occur by the therapist challenging the client's defences. The 1980s witnessed the development of another generation of brief therapies, including Lester Luborsky's supportive-expressive therapy (Luborsky, 1984) and Hans Strupp's time-limited dynamic therapy (e.g., Strupp & Binder, 1984). Although the various forms of psychodynamic therapy have different emphases and assign differing importance to various intervention strategies, these therapies have a great deal in common. Across the different types of STPPs, therapy is considered a process of understanding stages of psychological development, bringing to awareness unconscious processes, and re-enacting in the relationship with the therapist issues that have troubled the client in the past (Messer, 2001). Luborsky's research on core conflictual relationship themes has been studied with people suffering from a range of mental disorders, and has greatly influenced the manner in which contemporary STPP is conducted.

STPPs involve face-to-face sessions conducted once or twice a week for between 16 and 30 sessions (Leichsenring, Rabung, & Lebing, 2004). By limiting the number of sessions, the therapist encourages the client to anticipate that change will occur relatively quickly (Messer, 2001). Compared with traditional psychoanalytic therapists, STPP therapists are active, engaging in dialogue and challenging the client. The therapist's first task is to foster the development of a therapeutic alliance and positive transference by adopting an open-minded, non-judgmental stance and displaying interest in the client's experience (Cutler, Goldyne, Markowitz, Devlin, & Glick, 2004). Among the techniques used by the STPP therapist to alter maladaptive patterns are reflection (paraphrasing clients' statements or commenting on emotional states in order to enhance their awareness of current experiences), clarification (asking clients to attend more closely to some aspects of their experience in order to see connections or patterns), interpretation (commenting on a problem or experience and relating it to the use of defence mechanisms or underlying core conflictual themes), and confrontation (challenging clients to recognize that defence mechanisms are interfering with their optimal functioning or that core conflictual themes are responsible for aspects of their experience) (Messer, 2001).

Like most forms of psychodynamic therapy, examination of the transference relationship is a central theme of STPP. However, attention is paid to the present relationship, without necessarily connecting patterns to the client's past (Leichsenring et al., 2004). Examination of the transference relationship is considered an important tool in understanding how the client views the world; it is designed to bring to awareness unconscious fantasies and to reveal the ways that the client thinks about relationships (Blagys & Hilsenroth, 2000). Counter-transference refers to the therapist's emotional reaction to the client. Although Freud viewed counter-transference as a breach in therapeutic neutrality caused by the therapist's unconscious conflicts, STPP therapists take a more benign view, seeing counter-transference as providing useful information about the way the client's interpersonal behaviours affect others (Vakoch & Strupp, 2000). Exhibit 11.2 lists the therapeutic tasks of the different STPP stages.

Exhibit 11.2 Therapeutic Tasks in Short-Term Psychodynamic Psychotherapy

Phase 1: Developing a positive transference relationship
Identifying themes that are important for the patient
Phase 2: Analyzing the transference relationship
Exploring themes through clarification and confrontation
Phase 3: Terminating therapy
Dealing with loss
Dealing with expectable challenges in life

Adapted from Vakoch & Strupp (2000).

Early in therapy, the STPP therapist identifies specific themes or conflicts that will be the focus of attention. These themes reflect the therapist's formulation of the conflicts underlying the presenting problem

(Messer, 2001). Throughout therapy, the therapist maintains a focus on these themes, treatment goals, and termination issues. The therapist identifies defensive patterns that interfere with the client's life (Cutler et al., 2004). Consistent with their Freudian roots (Blagys & Hilsenroth, 2000), STPP theorists accord a central role to evoking emotions and to facilitating change through a process of catharsis (i.e., the release of previously suppressed emotional reactions). Goal-setting plays an important part in STPP, distinguishing it from long-term psychodynamic therapy and making it similar to other short-term treatment approaches (Messer, 2000).

As therapy moves toward termination, gains are consolidated. During this phase, the client faces issues of loss (of the therapist), separation (from the therapeutic relationship), and individuation (moving toward independence from the therapist). As STPP is, by definition, brief and time limited, issues of termination of services cannot be avoided. Theorists have proposed that the time-limited nature of therapy raises awareness of the time-limited nature of human life, making it particularly salient for clients who are dealing with mortality issues (Messer, 2000). There is strong evidence that STPP is efficacious in the treatment of depression, and initial evidence that psychodynamic therapy can be efficacious in the treatment of panic disorder, substance abuse, and borderline personality disorder (Gibbons, Crits-Christoph, & Hearon, 2008).

Interpersonal Psychotherapy for Depression

Departing from the intrapsychic focus of psychodynamic theories, Sullivan (1953) drew attention to interpersonal factors in psychopathology, suggesting that psychiatric problems were often related to difficulties in communication and to dysfunctional relationships. This theoretical framework laid the foundation for studies of the interpersonal context of a wide range of disorders. Compelling evidence regarding the interpersonal difficulties experienced by those suffering from depression fuelled interest in developing a therapy that addressed interpersonal factors associated with this disorder (Klerman, Weissman, Rounsaville, & Chevron, 1984). **Interpersonal psychotherapy** (IPT) for depression focuses on changing interpersonal problems that are related to the onset, maintenance, and relapse of depressive symptoms.

interpersonal psychotherapy: a treatment approach that emphasizes interpersonal elements in the development, maintenance, and alteration of psychological problems (especially grief, role disputes, role transitions, and interpersonal deficits).

IPT is a brief therapy that involves weekly meetings over three to four months. IPT is divided into distinct phases, as described in Exhibit 11.3. The first phase involves assessment of the symptoms of depression as well as an examination of the patient's relationships. The construction of an inventory of current and past relationships is essential in identifying the interpersonal themes that will be the focus of therapy. At the end of this assessment phase, the IPT therapist diagnoses the patient and provides an interpersonal formulation of the patient's difficulties. The patient is explicitly absolved of responsibility for symptoms, as these are attributed to the disorder of depression. The IPT therapist explains the ways that interpersonal issues maintain the depression and invites the patient to participate actively in changing current relationships.

Exhibit 11.3 Phases of Interpersonal Psychotherapy for Depression

Initial sessions (1–3):

Assess symptoms
Diagnose and explain depressive disorder
Assess interpersonal context (current and past)
Present IPT formulation of patient's problems

Intermediate sessions (4–12) addressing one or more of the following themes:

- **Grief**
  Help patient deal with a loss; promote healthy mourning
  Facilitate the development of new relationships
- **Role disputes**
  Identify dispute
  Formulate plan for dispute resolution
  Modify communication and/or change expectations to resolve dispute
- **Role transitions**
  Leave old role and mourn its loss if necessary
  Develop skills, coping strategies, and support for transition
- **Interpersonal deficits**
  Build social skills
  Increase social involvement

Termination phase (13–16):

Acknowledge worries and sadness related to ending therapy
Encourage awareness and practice of new skills
Anticipate future challenges in which new skills will be employed

Adapted from Weissman, Markowitz, & Klerman (2000).

The focus of subsequent IPT sessions is tailored to the client's specific needs and may include addressing one or all of the following themes: grief, role disputes, role transitions, and interpersonal deficits. In addressing grief issues, the therapist facilitates mourning of a lost relationship as well as the development of a new social network. If role disputes are identified as contributing to depressive symptoms, the patient and therapist collaborate on a plan for resolving the difficulty by renegotiating the problem, reaching an agreement that the dispute is insoluble, or dissolving the relationship. The patient is assisted in developing effective communication patterns and realistic expectations about relationships. Both IPT and STPPs address aspects of interpersonal functioning. An important difference is that IPT is designed to alter relational functioning, whereas STPPs use information about relationships to alter intrapsychic variables.

Imagine that you were seeking services to deal with conflicts that you are experiencing with one of your parents or someone in your family. How would the focus of services differ in STPP from IPT? Which one would focus more on altering the way you interact with that parent or that person? Which one would focus more on how you feel about that person and how being with him or her makes you feel?

Research has established that people are often vulnerable at times of role transition. Even though some transitions such as marriage, the birth of a child, or a new job are considered positive and may be welcomed, they create a challenge as the person adapts to new role demands. In IPT, the patient is first encouraged to leave the old role (e.g., moving from being a student to a professional, from being single to married, or from being employed to retired). Next the client is aided in developing skills that are required in the new role (e.g., adopting a more formal style, focusing on the challenges of living with another person, or finding ways to maintain an active social life). Some depressed patients may not be troubled by grief, role disputes, or role transitions, but may have an impoverished interpersonal network with few contacts and little opportunity for pleasant or supportive exchanges. In this case, the therapist focuses on the development of communication and relationship skills that are likely to promote the development of closer interpersonal ties. Within IPT, the termination phase of therapy offers an opportunity to consolidate gains made in previous phases. The therapist helps the client recognize and take credit for the changes that have occurred as well as prepare for future challenges. In therapy, the client communicates any misgivings and anxieties about ending the therapeutic relationship.

As interpersonal difficulties are found in all ages, the treatment protocol has been modified by Myrna Weissman and her colleagues to address the needs of people of various ages (Weissman, Markowitz, & Klerman, 2000). IPT-LL was developed to meet the needs of adults in late life (Sholomskas, Chevron, Prusoff, & Berry, 1983) by having brief sessions that

Medioimages/Photodisc

IPT examines the role of personal relationships in the maintenance of depression.

included help with practical matters, and that focused on ways to tolerate negative affect in relationships rather than withdrawing from them. Mufson and her colleagues (Mufson & Dorta, 2003; Mufson, Dorta, Moreau, & Weissman, 2004) developed IPT for adolescents (IPT-A) by including attention to developmental issues such as separation from parents, exploration of parental authority, the development of dyadic relationships, and peer pressure. In addition to strong evidence of efficacy in the treatment of depression (Cuijpers et al., 2011), there is also good evidence for a form of IPT (combined with behaviour therapy elements) in the treatment of bipolar disorder (Frank, 2005; Milkowitz et al., 2007). Finally, IPT has been adapted for use in different cultures (e.g., group treatment for depression in rural Uganda; Bolton et al., 2003) and has been modified for use with eating disorders, anxiety disorders, and substance use disorders (Weissman, Markowitz, & Klerman, 2000).

process-experiential therapy: a treatment approach that emphasizes the importance of becoming aware of emotions, understanding and expressing emotions, and transforming maladaptive to adaptive emotions.

Process-Experiential Therapies

With their origins as alternatives to psychodynamic and behavioural psychology, humanistic and experiential approaches to psychotherapy include client-centred therapy (Rogers, 1951), Gestalt therapy (Perls, Hefferline, & Goodman, 1951), and existential therapy (May, Angel, & Ellenberger, 1958). These approaches are based on the assumption that human nature is fundamentally growth-oriented, trustworthy, and guided by choice (Elliott, Greenberg, Watson, Timulak, & Freire, 2013).

You may recall learning in Chapter 1 that Rogers was committed to psychotherapy research. During the 1970s and the 1980s, however, research on humanistic and experiential approaches dwindled. Given the emphasis on the uniqueness of each individual's subjective experience, humanistic and experiential approaches have been the subject of less psychotherapy outcome research compared with other approaches. For many decades, humanistic and experiential theorists and therapists actively rejected attempts to evaluate their treatments with experimental designs. Consequently, by the early 1990s only one experiential therapy (emotion-focused therapy for moderately distressed couples; Johnson & Greenberg, 1985) had a strong evidence base (Elliott, 2001).

The efforts of Robert Elliott and Leslie Greenberg promoted a resurgence of well-designed research on the process-experiential (PE) approach that combines elements of client-centred and Gestalt approaches into an emotion-focused approach to treatment (Elliott et al., 2013). Combining these humanistic and experiential approaches with basic psychological research on emotions, Greenberg (2008) proposed that PE treatment should include the following elements: increasing the client's awareness of emotion, encouraging the client to express emotion, enhancing the client's emotion regulation abilities, aiding the client to reflect on emotions, and helping the client to transform maladaptive emotions into adaptive emotions. There is solid evidence of the efficacy of PE in treating depression and couple distress, and growing evidence of its value in treating adult survivors of childhood abuse (Greenberg, 2008).

A central characteristic of PE therapies is their emphasis on in-session experiencing of affect. It is assumed that changes occur when experiential processing is facilitated by guiding clients to focus their attention on their in-session experiences. In order to make these emotions more intense and vivid, PE emphasizes using the therapeutic relationship to help clients process their emotions and, subsequently, to create new meaning for their emotional experiences. The therapeutic relationship is considered to provide both support and guidance in the client's exploration of his or her experience. PE is a 12- to 20-session treatment in which the therapist facilitates the client's role as an active agent of self-change. This approach is clearly intrapsychic, placing emphasis on the client's self-exploration and understanding rather than on relationships with others. In contrast to early client-centred approaches, the PE therapist takes a more task-focused approach, largely emphasizing emotional content (Elliott, 2001). Exhibit 11.4 describes general features of process-experiential therapy.

Exhibit 11.4 Principles of Process-Experiential Therapy

Treatment Principles

- **Fostering a therapeutic relationship**
    - Enter and track client's experiences
    - Express empathy and genuine valuing of the client and the client's experience
    - Facilitate mutual involvement in setting the goals and tasks of therapy
- **Facilitating work on therapeutic tasks**
    - Facilitate optimal client experiential processing
    - Foster client growth and self-determination
    - Facilitate client completion of key therapeutic tasks
- **Experiential response modes**
    - Utilize simple empathy responses
    - Engage in empathic exploration of client experience in session
    - Guide the client in exploration of the experience
    - Encourage the client to stay "in the moment" to focus on the experience
- **Therapeutic tasks**
    - Aid the client in exploring the emotions and experiences
    - Use reflection and active expressions of client emotional states
    - Use the therapeutic relationship to support and facilitate client exploration

Adapted from Elliott (2001).

Cognitive-Behavioural Therapies

cognitive-behavioural therapy: a treatment approach that emphasizes the role of thoughts and behaviour in psychological problems and, therefore, focuses on altering beliefs, expectations, and behaviours in order to improve the client's functioning.

The many forms of behavioural, cognitive, and cognitive-behavioural therapies can be considered a single orientation. Behavioural approaches are based on the assumption that problem behaviours are learned and that faulty learning can be reversed through the application of learning principles. Cognitive approaches emphasize the role of thoughts and beliefs in the development and maintenance of psychological problems. A cognitive-behavioural approach combines both behavioural and cognitive elements in understanding and treating mental disorders.

The earliest application of behaviour therapy (BT) was the use of operant conditioning in treating patients who were considered untreatable: those with psychotic disorders and those with mental retardation. From its roots in the application of classical and operant conditioning, the field of BT has advanced to include procedures based on research findings from areas such as perception, cognition, and the biological bases of behaviour. Therapists focus on present functioning as opposed to childhood history. Accordingly, behavioural interventions focus on specific targets by reducing undesirable behaviours (e.g., intrusive thoughts about a traumatic event, self-harming behaviours, and avoidance), as well as increasing desirable behaviours (e.g., engaging in pleasant activities, calmly presenting a seminar, or assertively dealing with an angry customer). An essential feature is the application of scientifically derived principles in the treatment of problems. Throughout therapy, progress is assessed to determine whether the strategy should be modified. BT requires clear identification of goals and is oriented toward the future (Emmelkamp, 2013).

self-efficacy: a person's sense of competence to learn and perform new tasks.

Albert Bandura's seminal findings that learning could take place by observation and imitation have been applied in the treatment of both adults and children (Naugle & Maher, 2003). Self-efficacy, which refers to a person's sense of competence to learn and perform new tasks, is often found to be the best predictor of behaviour, such as approaching a phobic stimulus or attempting a new behaviour. Bandura's work laid the foundation for approaches that emphasize the importance of cognitions in mediating behavioural responses (Craighead, Hart, Craighead, & Ilardi, 2002). Using models developed to understand information processing, D'Zurilla and Goldfried (1971) introduced a problem-solving approach that was applied in the treatment of diverse problems such as weight control, clinical depression, and social skills deficits. The key elements of problem-solving in cognitive-behavioural treatments are defining and formulating the problem, generating

Time & Life Pictures/Getty Images

alternative solutions to deal with the problem, deciding on the best solution to implement, and implementing and evaluating the solution (D'Zurilla & Nezu, 1999).

Cognitive approaches, such as Ellis' Rational-Emotive Behavior Therapy and Aaron Beck's Cognitive Therapy, are based on the assumption that an individual's perception of events, rather than the events themselves, affect adjustment. Consequently, they focus on identifying automatic thoughts and changing maladaptive patterns of thinking that are associated with distress, anxiety, and depression (Hollon & Beck, 2013). Cognitive approaches foster a collaborative relationship in which the therapist and client work together to identify problems, test hypotheses, and re-evaluate beliefs. Like their behavioural relatives, cognitive and cognitive-behavioural approaches rely on the application of empirically derived strategies in the treatment of diverse disorders.

Cognitive-behavioural therapy (CBT) emphasizes the use of psychopathology research in understanding the problems experienced by clients. Although relevant research informs case conceptualization and treatment planning (e.g., referring to research on causes and concomitants of panic disorder), a cornerstone of all CBT approaches is the tailoring of assessment and treatment to the needs of the individual client. Another core element of CBT is the continuous monitoring of the client's responses to treatment in order to evaluate the effect of intervention and alter treatment plans if necessary. Perhaps because of the use of the psychopathology research evidence to develop treatments that are specific to a disorder, there is strong evidence that CBT is efficacious in treating a multitude of youth and adult disorders and conditions, including mood disorders, anxiety disorders, eating disorders, sleep disorders, somatoform disorders, substance abuse disorders, marital distress, and anger- and stress-related problems (Beck & Dozois, 2011; Nathan & Gorman, 2007). Exhibit 11.5 describes the typical phases of CBT, usually provided over 8 to 30 sessions.

CBT therapists assume a very active role in service provision. They probe the precise nature of the problem, seeking information on its intensity, frequency, and duration as well as contextual factors that are associated with variation in the problem. They collaborate with clients in establishing concrete treatment goals and in translating vague complaints into measurable outcomes toward which the client will work. CBT therapists provide information about the process of treatment, explaining the central role of homework assignments in gathering data, carrying out experiments, and practising new skills.

CBT therapists take responsibility for structuring each session, setting an agenda, and teaching new skills. Throughout treatment, the therapist uses a blend of didactic teaching methods (i.e., directions and

Exhibit 11.5 Phases of Cognitive-Behavioural Therapy

Assessment phase:

Integrate data from interview, direct observation, rating scales, and self-monitoring

Establish concrete, collaboratively agreed-upon treatment goals

Intervention phase:

1. Introduce skills in session:

   Behavioural skills could include assertiveness, relaxation, engaging in enjoyable activities, using self-reinforcement to develop and maintain behaviours, or exposing oneself to feared stimuli.

   Cognitive skills could include developing strategies to dispute automatic negative thoughts and using cognitive restructuring strategies to challenge and evaluate the accuracy of one's beliefs, assumptions, and expectations.

   Cognitive-behavioural skills could include developing problem-solving skills, stress management skills, and communication skills to improve interpersonal relationships.
2. Practise skills in session and then as homework assignments, reviewing them in the following session
3. Ensure that skills learned in session are generalized to the client's day-to-day life context
4. Review progress toward agreed-upon treatment goals session by session

Termination phase:

Review treatment goals and the extent to which they were achieved

Review skills learned in therapy and their application to daily life

Anticipate future challenges and how they could be handled

Booster sessions:

Review treatment goals and the extent to which they were achieved

Review skills learned in therapy and their application to daily life

Anticipate future challenges and how they could be handled

instructions) and Socratic questioning (i.e., asking questions that encourage the client to examine his or her beliefs and to be self-directed in skill acquisition) to help the client. To promote changes, the therapist engages in a process of collaborative empiricism with the client. This means that the client and therapist develop strategies to concretely test the client's dysfunctional beliefs. By encouraging self-examination and then working with the client to test the validity of his or her beliefs, the therapist actively encourages a process of guided discovery for the client. Thus, in contrast to many other forms of therapy, the most important changes are presumed to take place not *in* sessions but *between* sessions as the client completes and learns from homework assignments (Blagys & Hilsenroth, 2002).

The other theoretical orientations we have discussed consider termination in terms of the end of the therapeutic relationship. In CBT, the termination phase is seen as a time for consolidating skills, anticipating future challenges, and preparing the client to face inevitable slip-ups.

Termination is future-oriented. CBT also allows for the possibility of clients requiring one or two future "booster" sessions to help them get back on track. Viewpoint Box 11.1 presents ways that experts of three different theoretical orientations understood and proposed treatments for a young man experiencing depression.

Where would you place the four main evidence-based approaches to therapy presented in this chapter on a continuum with intrapsychic and interpersonal as endpoints?

VIEWPOINT BOX 11.1

THE CASE OF MICHAEL

Cutler et al. (2004) described a client, Michael, who was referred for treatment of depression. Experts of different theoretical orientations (long-term psychodynamic, interpersonal, and cognitive-behavioural) described how they would understand and treat Michael.

Although he had been a successful student as an undergraduate, in law school Michael developed a habit of procrastination and poor class attendance that led to him having to cram at exam time. He found this extremely stressful and started to feel increasingly depressed, began overeating and oversleeping, and had increasing trouble concentrating. Michael experienced prolonged feelings of sadness as well as decreased sexual desire and diminished pleasure in activities he used to enjoy.

After his parents divorced when he was an infant, Michael's father remarried and began a new family; his mother did not date or remarry. His father maintained contact twice a year, but did not engage in any meaningful parenting. As a pre-adolescent, Michael was cared for by his grandmother while his mother sought training in another city. The only times in which his father became engaged in Michael's life were when he was in trouble for skipping classes. As a student, Michael had a supportive mentoring relationship with a professor, but felt disappointed that the professor did not maintain the relationship when Michael moved to law school. During law school, Michael was troubled by phone calls from his mother expressing her distress and reproving him for not spending enough time with her. Another current stressor in his life was an unsatisfactory relationship with a student he had dated. Although the woman broke off the romantic relationship with Michael, she maintained regular contact with him.

Michael's style toward the therapist was deferential. He apologized for arriving late for some of the intake assessment interviews. After a couple of sessions, Michael reported that he had begun to feel better, had thrown away his prescription for antidepressant medication, and wished to engage in psychotherapy.

Dr. Glick, whose orientation is psychodynamic, assumes that Michael's depressive problems stem from conflicts of which he is not fully aware. The goal of therapy would be to promote Michael's exploration of the underlying meaning of his feelings. Dr. Glick would strive to respond to Michael in an open-minded manner to facilitate Michael's curiosity about himself and, eventually, his insight into the source of his problems. Dr. Glick assumes that in the context of a non-judgmental therapeutic relationship, Michael would learn to tolerate painful feelings. Exploration of the transference relationship is designed to facilitate greater awareness of defensive responding. The therapist would comment on aspects of Michael's behaviour toward him, offering possible interpretations of their significance. For example, "You missed a big part of each session. And today you seem to be staying on the surface of things. Might you be avoiding painful or troubling feelings about you?" (Cutler et al., 2004, p. 1571). Dr. Glick assumes that a core issue is Michael's unconscious feelings of unresolved anger toward his parents, whom he perceives as rejecting. His ambivalence toward his mother is then played out in his current

CONTINUED . . .

romantic relationship. Examination of the transference relationship would allow exploration of Michael's need for a nurturing father figure and his fears of being seen as needy and weak.

Dr. Markowitz, the interpersonal psychotherapist, is sensitive to Michael's various relational difficulties and their relation to his depression. He would probe Michael's emotions in reaction to perceived rejection or disappointment and ask whether Michael has communicated his reactions to the people in his life. The therapist would explicitly present an interpersonal formulation of Michael's problems in which his reactions are normalized. "Coming to terms with losses can be hard, especially when you've had as many dislocations as you've already had . . . . I suggest we work . . . on solving your law school role transition; as you gain greater comfort in your situation there, not only will that improve your life, but your mood symptoms should improve as well" (Cutler et al., 2004, p. 1570). Dr. Markowitz predicts that over the course of interpersonal psychotherapy, Michael would learn to respond more effectively to interpersonal challenges. Although no formal homework is given, Michael would be encouraged to increase his activity level. The final phase of services would allow Michael to consolidate his gains, taking credit for the new skills he has mastered. Termination would be a time to celebrate his gains as well as a time to be aware of the loss associated with the end of the therapeutic relationship.

Dr. Devlin, the cognitive-behavioural therapist, would establish goals and collaborate to help Michael better understand his depression and the links between his thoughts, feelings, and behaviours. Homework tasks would be assigned to help track links between different feelings and procrastination behaviours, as well as to identify exceptional occasions on which Michael experiences pleasure. Michael would be encouraged to conduct behavioural experiments to determine whether his thoughts are accurate. For example, the thought that *I don't enjoy anything anymore* could be tested by monitoring his mood as he engages in different activities. Michael would be encouraged to shift from making characterological statements about himself to recognizing the choices that he makes to behave in specific ways. As he becomes more active, Michael would be in a position to identify and challenge his core beliefs about his inadequacy.

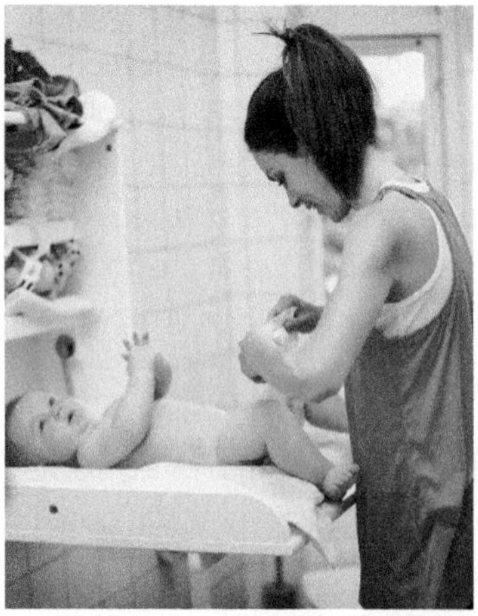

©iStock.com/Yuri_Arcurs

Life transitions may lead some people to seek psychological services.

SEEKING PSYCHOLOGICAL TREATMENT

People seek the services of a clinical psychologist for numerous reasons. Some people desire assistance and advice in managing the expectable challenges in life, such as problems in settling into university, dealing with a painful relationship breakup, or handling workplace difficulties. The transition from one phase of life to another, such as becoming a parent, brings new demands as well as new joys. Dealing with other expectable but painful life events—for example, the death of a parent or a spouse—may also lead some people to initiate therapy. In many cases, the person is seeking relief from emotional distress that interferes with daily functioning. Individuals often suffer from mental disorders for months or years before seeking professional services. Finally, some people who engage in therapy have only minimal levels of distress. These individuals are often seeking to address questions related to personal identity, values, or self-knowledge.

Evidence suggests that the overall use of mental health services has been increasing in recent decades. However, much of this increase is associated with the use of medication rather than psychological treatment. For example, in the United States, the use of psychotherapy provided by mental health professionals was found to have remained stable in the 10 years since 1998, but the use of psychotropic medication increased (Olfson & Marcus, 2010). During that period, the percentage of patient visits to psychiatrists involving psychotherapy declined from almost half of all visits to less than a third of visits (Mojtabai & Olfson, 2008). Similar data were obtained by Esposito et al. (2007) who conducted a telephone survey to determine the pattern of treatment for depression in Alberta. They found that, among those meeting diagnostic criteria for major depression, approximately 40% reported using antidepressant medication, whereas only 14% reported receiving some form of counselling or psychotherapy. Based on a population survey in Great Britain in 1993, 6.7% of women and 6.2% of men reported receiving psychotherapy for a mental disorder (Brugha et al., 2004). In 2000, there was no statistically significant change in this: 7.9% of women and 9.8% of men reported receiving psychotherapy. In stark contrast, the rates of psychotropic medication use during this period rose sharply for both women (9.6% to 20.1%) and men (9.7% to 19.1%).

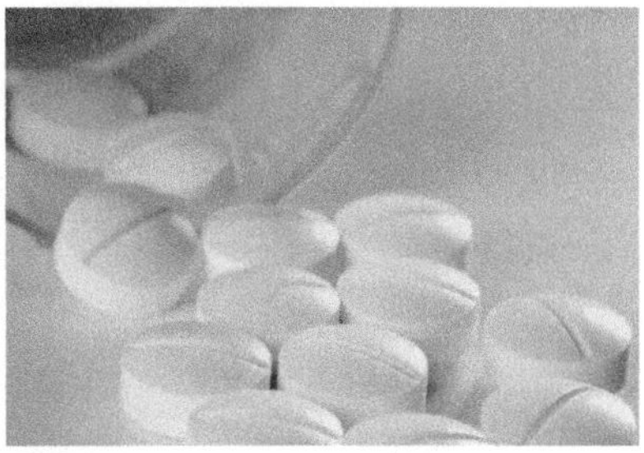

©iStock.com/VisualField

The use of psychoactive medication has increased dramatically in the last 20 years.

Who are the people who decide to seek therapy as either an alternative or an adjunct to medication? Over many decades there has been surprisingly little change in the sociodemographic characteristics related to the use of psychotherapy. Across all approaches to psychotherapy, two-thirds of psychotherapy clients are female, half have a college or university education, half are married, and the majority are young to middle-aged adults (Vessey & Howard, 1993). Unfortunately, consistent with the information we presented earlier in the book, Vessey and Howard's analysis also suggested that many of those most in need of such services (i.e., those with a diagnosable condition) never seek professional help of any kind.

Data from the 2002 Canadian Community Health Survey found that women were more likely than men to seek mental health services, as were those with post-secondary education compared to those with high school education (Vasiliadis, Tempier, Lesage, & Kates, 2009). These data also showed that low income was a significant barrier to accessing the services of a psychologist in Canada. The most detailed information on who seeks the services of a psychologist comes from the Canadian National Population Health Survey conducted in 1994–1995. Using this information, Hunsley, Lee, and Aubry (1999) found sociodemographic characteristics similar to those described by Vessey and Howard (1993) among those who reported consulting a psychologist for physical or

What may account for the difficulty many people experience in deciding to seek psychological services?

mental health reasons. Based on this survey, 2.2% of Canadians 12 years and older consulted a psychologist during the previous year. Not surprisingly, those who sought psychological services reported more stress and distress and lower life satisfaction than did the population at large. Consistent with the American data just described, many who might benefit from mental health services had not received it: for example, many Canadians suffering from depression had received neither therapy nor medication. Exhibit 11.6 provides further details about the findings from this survey.

Depending on the nature of the national health care system, there are many routes to receive treatment from clinical psychologists. In some countries, services provided by psychologists in hospitals or community clinics are covered by the national health care system. In other countries, such services may be covered by private insurance for most individuals, with only those in the lower-income brackets receiving government-supported services. Across most health care systems, it is possible to obtain services from clinical psychologists in private practice settings. Typically, this requires that clients directly pay for services. Some clients have extended health care benefits through their workplace that may cover part or all of the costs. A referral from a physician may be necessary for psychological services delivered in publicly funded settings (such as a hospital) and may be required by some insurance schemes; however, clients can usually self-refer when seeking the services of a private practitioner.

Exhibit 11.6 Characteristics of Canadians Receiving Psychological Services

- Women/girls are twice as likely as men/boys to consult a psychologist.
- People between the ages of 30 and 50 are most likely to see a psychologist.
- Canadians living in rural areas, compared with those in urban settings, are one-third as likely to consult a psychologist.
- A higher percentage of those consulting a psychologist have a university education than in the Canadian population.
- A higher percentage of those consulting a psychologist are parents and children in single-parent families than in the Canadian population.
- People experiencing significant pain that interferes with daily activities are twice as likely as other Canadians to consult a psychologist.
- People who receive psychological services also tend to be frequent users of other health care services.
- Adolescents and adults who feel so unhappy that they believe life is not worthwhile are five times as likely as other Canadians to seek psychological services.

Adapted from Hunsley, Lee, & Aubry (1999).

The financial costs of psychological services present a major obstacle for many potential clients. This economic burden comes on top of the multiple obstacles that many people face when making a decision to seek therapy. Saunders (1993) conceptualized the process of seeking psychotherapy as involving a series of four interrelated decisions: realizing that there is a problem, deciding that therapy might be of value, actually deciding to seek therapy, and then contacting a therapist or a clinic. In Saunders' research, the majority of those who eventually sought therapy reported that it took several months to move from recognizing that a significant problem existed to deciding that therapy might be useful. Even then, over half of the clients took at least several weeks to make the decision to seek treatment. The extent to which the potential client feels supported by significant others in this process can also influence decisions around seeking therapy (Saunders, 1996).

It is striking that Hunsley et al. (1999) found that Canadians living in rural areas were three times less likely to consult a psychologist compared with their counterparts in urban areas. Although the rates of psychological problems are no lower in rural settings, access to all health care professionals, including psychologists, is much lower. There are now a number of initiatives designed to address the challenges faced by those living in rural areas. To illustrate some of these initiatives, Profile Box 11.2 presents Dr. Karen Dyck, a rural clinical psychologist who is also the director of an innovative training program designed to address the needs of those in underserved rural areas.

PROFILE BOX 11.2

DR. KAREN DYCK

Courtesy of Karen Dyck

I received my Ph.D. in clinical psychology at the University of South Dakota (USD), a program known for its emphasis on cross-cultural and rural psychology. I have been a registered psychologist in Manitoba since 1997 and have had the opportunity to provide psychological services in rural/northern Manitoba for over 18 years. I am a faculty member in the Department of Clinical Health Psychology at the University of Manitoba and the director of the program in Rural and Northern Psychology. I was extremely honoured to receive the 2012 Canadian Psychological Association (CPA) Award for Distinguished Contributions to Psychology as a Profession for my work in rural psychology.

HOW DID YOU CHOOSE TO BECOME A RURAL CLINICAL PSYCHOLOGIST?

My interest in clinical psychology began in high school, fuelled by my interest in human behaviour and desire to help others. When I entered university, my long-term goal was to become a private practice child psychologist in a large urban centre. Although both my parents were raised on farms in rural Manitoba, they relocated to

CONTINUED . . .

Winnipeg before I was born and I never imagined living anywhere but a big city. That all changed, however, as I progressed through the Ph.D. program at USD and was exposed to models of community psychology applied in a rural setting. Aspects of rural and cross-cultural practice were intertwined throughout our coursework and clinical practica. I quickly came to appreciate the numerous benefits of rural practice (e.g., interdisciplinary work, opportunities to work across the age span, broad range of presenting problems, broad range of clinical responsibilities, opportunities for knowledge translation/transfer). Travelling to various small communities for my practica also helped me appreciate what my parents knew all along: the many joys of small town/rural life.

WHAT IS THE GREATEST CHALLENGE FACED BY RURAL CLINICAL PSYCHOLOGISTS?

Unfortunately, we really don't have good data to inform us about the challenges facing rural psychologists in Canada. Together with colleagues Dr. Judi Malone (Athabasca University) and Dr. Cindy Hardy (University of Northern British Columbia), I am in the process of developing and implementing a large-scale online survey for psychologists in Canada. One goal of this survey is to better understand the practice variables (including challenges) that impact recruitment and retention of rural, northern, and remote psychologists. So, we hope to have some data about this in the very near future. The conversations I've had with many rural psychologists in Canada, as well as my own personal experiences, suggest that limited resources (psychologists and other mental health professionals) continue to be a significant challenge for many rural clinical psychologists. As a result, many rural clinical psychologists face high workload demands, ethical issues (e.g., competency issues, multiple roles, boundary issues), and a sense of professional isolation. Fortunately, exciting new developments in the field and the inherent benefits of rural practice have the potential to offset these challenges.

TELL US ABOUT THE RURAL AND NORTHERN RESIDENCY PROGRAM.

The residency was established in 1996 with a grant from Manitoba Health. This is the only residency program in Canada offering a specialty residency in rural (two positions) and northern (one position) clinical psychology. Psychology residents complete six months of training in Winnipeg before beginning their second six-month rotation in a rural or northern Manitoba community. Working under the supervision of the staff psychologist in that community, psychology residents are exposed to generalist practice in which they provide a variety of psychological services (assessment, treatment, consultation) to a broad clientele that varies with respect to age, ethnicity, culture, and presenting problems. Rural and northern psychology residents also provide educational presentations to community and professional groups and work with other helpers (e.g., self-help organizations, school staff, psychiatrists, social workers, and psychiatric nurses). Psychology residents participate in weekly clinical and professional issues seminars, clinical case conferences, and monthly rural and northern journal club throughout the year. They attend these activities in person or via videoconference. I've been thrilled to see the changes in our applicant pool over the years (e.g., a tenfold increase in numbers, a greater proportion of applicants with rural/northern background).

HOW DO YOU INTEGRATE SCIENCE AND PRACTICE INTO YOUR WORK?

The direct provision of evidence-based services is an integral part of my practice. Additionally, psychologists in rural practices offer consultation to many peer support workers and health care providers from other disciplines. Within this general context, science and practice are integrated into my work through knowledge translation and transfer activities, capacity building, participation in program development and evaluation projects, needs assessments, and ongoing advocacy efforts aimed at increasing access to evidence-based treatments.

CONTINUED . . .

WHAT DO YOU SEE AS THE MOST EXCITING CHANGES IN THE FIELD OF RURAL CLINICAL PSYCHOLOGY?

Courtesy of Dr. Bob McIlwraith

I've been particularly excited by the increased interest in this area of practice as evidenced by membership rates to the Rural and Northern Psychology Section of the CPA, the increased number of high-calibre applicants to our rural and northern residency program, the inclusion of rural-specific psychology courses and practica at universities, and the growing number of publications in the area of Canadian rural/northern psychology. Although not a replacement for rural-based clinical psychologists, technological advances (e.g., telehealth/videoconferencing, computer-based treatment) have also been an exciting development with the potential to impact the field of rural psychology.

THE DURATION AND IMPACT OF PSYCHOTHERAPY

Mention the word psychotherapy to most people and their initial associations probably include a couch and a nodding therapist who says very little, but grunts enigmatically. As mentioned in Chapter 2, movies and television series frequently depict psychotherapy as a life-long form of treatment. Even if images such as these were accurate at one time, they do not correspond to current reality. The vast majority of people who receive psychotherapy attend fewer than 10 sessions, and evidence-based treatment, across orientations, requires a very active therapist. Across practice settings, countries, and client-presenting problems, the duration of psychotherapy has been remarkably consistent for decades (Garfield, 1994; Phillips, 1991): a substantial minority of clients attend only one or two sessions, and the median number of therapy sessions is typically in the range of 5 to 13. Over the years, several studies have examined clients' and therapists' expectations for a number of treatment-related factors, including the duration of treatment and reasons for the therapy termination (e.g., Hunsley, Aubry, Vestervelt, & Vito, 1999; Steenbarger, 1994). Ironically, compared with therapists' expectations, clients' expectations for treatment duration seem to be more in line with the actual duration of therapy. Likewise, clients generally report more benefits from treatment—even treatment of a brief duration—than do therapists. Viewpoint Box 11.2 presents strategies that have been employed to increase attendance at psychotherapy.

Findings reported by Hansen, Lambert, and Forman (2002) illustrate several aspects of what is known about the duration and impact of psychotherapy as it has been typically practised, based on data from more than 6,000 adult patients seen in a range of settings, including employee assistance programs, university counselling centres, community mental health clinics, and health maintenance organizations. One-third of patients attended only a single session of psychotherapy,

VIEWPOINT BOX 11.2

OPTIONS FOR INCREASING PSYCHOTHERAPY ATTENDANCE

There is both good and bad news in the fact that most clients attend only a small number of treatment sessions. The good news is that, for some people, a few sessions may be all that is necessary to achieve their treatment goals. Baldwin, Berkeljon, Atkins, Olsen, and Nielsen (2009), for example, reported that, in a sample of students receiving individual therapy at a large university counselling centre, approximately 35% of those who attended only three therapy sessions experienced clinically significant improvements. The bad news is that (a) up to 40% of people fail to follow up on a referral for psychotherapy (Hampton-Robb, Qualls, & Compton, 2003) and (b) approximately 20% of clients prematurely terminate treatment (Swift & Greenberg, 2012). Is there anything that can be done to reduce the number of people who refuse or fail to engage in treatment?

To address this question, Oldham, Kellett, Miles, and Sheeran (2012) searched the scientific literature and identified 31 published studies in which a randomized controlled trial design was used to evaluate the impact of various strategies designed to enhance therapy attendance. Researchers have been extremely creative in developing such strategies. To address treatment refusal, a range of interventions have been tested, including (a) education interventions for providing information about the nature and goals of therapy, outlining what it is like to be a therapy client, and detailing the responsibilities that come with starting psychotherapy, (b) using appointment letters that provide details about an initial appointment, and (c) allowing potential clients to see the therapist of their choice. With respect to efforts to reduce rates of premature termination, many strategies have been evaluated, including the use of telephone reminders about appointments, providing feedback to therapists on client progress, and assigning a case manager to clients with severe problems in order to assist those individuals with aspects of day-to-day life. Oldham and colleagues conducted a meta-analysis to examine the effects of these varied strategies on client therapy attendance. They found several strategies that were most effective across studies. These were allowing clients to choose a therapist and appointment times, using motivational interviewing techniques to explore clients' reasons for seeking treatment, preparing clients for what will be required of them in therapy, using appointment reminders, and implementing a case management service for severely distressed clients. The researchers also reported that the impact of attendance strategies was reduced for clients presenting with comorbid diagnoses.

So, on the basis of this research, what should clinical psychologists do? It appears that relatively small and inexpensive efforts on the part of the psychologist can have substantial effects for clients. Allowing some choice of therapist and appointment times and providing appointment reminders via telephone messages or texts are simple administrative tasks that should be feasible in most practice settings. Likewise, conducting a detailed review of clients' reasons for starting treatment and taking time to clarify the psychologist's expectations of the client are steps that all psychologists could take with new clients. Although providing case management services may not be possible in all settings, it should be possible to arrange for these services in settings that frequently provide treatment to individuals with chronic and severe mental disorders. This line of investigation nicely illustrates the potential benefits, for clients and psychologists, of putting research into practice.

with the median number of therapy sessions being three. Using data from the Outcome Questionnaire (OQ-45 that you learned about in Chapter 8), across settings, 8.2% of patients deteriorated during treatment, 56.8% experienced no change, and 35.0% improved or recovered. Similar findings were reported by Wampold and Brown (2005) based on analyses of data from over 6,100 American adults, all of whom were diagnosed with a mental disorder and who received therapy from a managed care company. In the Wampold and Brown sample, the median number of sessions attended was eight. Outcome data indicated that 29% of patients were seen as improved or recovered at the end of therapy.

These results for psychotherapy outcome may seem very discouraging and, in many ways, they are. At first glance, the data seem to suggest that psychotherapy, as routinely practised, benefits only about a third of those who enter treatment. On the other hand, if you take into account that the median number of therapy sessions reported in the American studies was in the single digits, it is not surprising that psychotherapy has such a limited impact. As you will see in Chapters 12 and 13 when we discuss specific evidence-based psychological treatments, most current treatments are designed to be short term, ranging from 10 to 30 sessions. It seems obvious that, just as with medication, if most people are not receiving the full treatment, the likelihood of experiencing therapeutic benefits is reduced. Moreover, it is likely that only some of this therapy is evidence-based, an issue to which we will return. In other words, the observed impact of routine psychotherapy in these studies may be weak for two separate reasons: most patients attended too few sessions and most therapists did not provide evidence-based treatments.

In contrast to these findings, it is informative to look at other data summarized by Hansen et al. (2002) based on data extracted from randomized controlled trials (RCTs) of evidence-based treatments. Across 28 studies and more than 2,100 patients, the average dose of therapy was 12.7 sessions, with 57.6% of patients meeting criteria for recovery (and 67.2% meeting criteria for improvement or recovery). Because of the use of untreated control groups in these studies, these positive results can be attributed directly to the effects of treatment. Hence, with more treatment, and treatment that is evidence-based, the success rate of psychotherapy improves substantially compared with treatment as usual. You might wonder whether the RCTs obtain better results because they are dealing with a less distressed sample of patients. In actual fact, the exact opposite is likely to be true: Stirman, DeRubeis, Crits-Christoph, and Brody (2003) reported that the average severity of symptoms reported in RCTs of evidence-based treatments is greater than that found in the patients seeking routine psychotherapy services. Evidence-based treatments did better than treatment as usual, even though the patients receiving the evidence-based treatments were more severely distressed.

There are indications that the impact of psychotherapy provided in routine clinical settings may be improving. Blais et al. (2012) reported on the treatment outcomes of over 800 patients receiving routine psychotherapy services in a multi-clinic academic psychiatry program located in a large urban American hospital. The patients presented with a range of disorders, most commonly anxiety disorders, mood disorders, or substance abuse disorders. Of those who received psychotherapy, 50% had improved or recovered following therapy; of those receiving psychotherapy and medication, 56% had improved or recovered. Although these results are not quite as strong as those reported by Hansen et al. (2002) for RCTs of evidence-based treatments, they are superior to the treatment-as-usual outcome rates reported by Hansen et al. and Wampold and Brown (2005). Do these results reflect an increased incorporation of evidence-based treatments in routine clinical practice, or do they simply indicate that these academic hospital clinics obtained better outcomes than are typically found across the entire gamut of clinical settings? The only way we will know is through replication attempts that use large sample of clients obtained from multiple clinical settings.

ALTERNATIVE MODES OF SERVICE DELIVERY

Although the vast majority of psychological interventions are delivered in individual sessions in the psychologist's office, psychological services are also delivered in other formats. For example, a variety of structured, brief couples therapies have been developed from different theoretical orientations, including behavioural marital therapy, cognitive-behavioural marital therapy, insight-oriented marital therapy, and emotion-focused couples therapy. Although some of these approaches were originally labelled *marital therapies*, the term *couples therapy* is now used as these approaches apply to intimate relationships in married and co-habiting heterosexual, gay, and lesbian couples. Based on the modest results of early efficacy trials of couples therapy, many approaches have been modified. So, for example, behavioural marital therapy was modified from a solely skill-based, behavioural exchange model designed to improve unsatisfactory relationships into an approach that also includes tasks designed to facilitate acceptance of an imperfect but adequate relationship (Jacobson, Christensen, Prince, Cordova, & Elridge, 2000).

Couples therapy is offered to treat distressed relationships and also to address psychological disorders such as depression that are associated with relationship dysfunction (Baucom, Epstein, & Gordon, 2000; Birchler & Fals-Stewart, 2002). Couples therapy is delivered primarily in conjoint sessions with both partners, but may also include individual sessions with each partner. Although there is a wealth of research on couples therapy (Sexton, Datchi, Evans, LaFollette, & Wright, 2013), there are no systematic data on the effectiveness of these approaches with ethnic minority couples (Gray-Little & Kaplan, 2000).

Like couples therapy, family interventions are practised by clinical psychologists of different orientations, as well as by other mental health professionals such as social workers and psychiatrists. A common aspect of family approaches is to identify interactions between family members that may inadvertently contribute to problems. However, whereas advocates of different theoretical approaches to couples therapy agree on a common goal of therapy, such as reduced conflict and increased satisfaction, there is no single type of family outcome that is sought across different approaches (Sexton, Alexander, & Mease, 2004). Family therapy may be sought to address difficulties associated with transitions, as well as to address mental disorders in one or more family members. Although early family approaches viewed the family as the source of a family member's problems, many current family approaches make no such assumption, instead considering the family an important part of the solution to problems.

David Young-Wolff/PhotoEdit Inc.

Family therapy can identify interactions between family members that may be inadvertently contributing to problems.

Given concerns over mounting health care costs, there are increasing pressures to find innovative ways to deliver services in as cost-efficient a manner as possible. One obvious solution is to offer group services to people who are facing the same types of difficulties. Like all other forms of psychotherapy, group approaches are based on a variety of theoretical models, including psychodynamic, interpersonal, experiential, and cognitive-behavioural. It is useful to distinguish between *process group* approaches, designed to capitalize on the dynamics of the group, and *structured group* approaches, which are extensions of treatments that are also offered in an individual format (Burlingame, MacKenzie, & Strauss, 2004). In addition to cost savings, group approaches offer unique opportunities to promote change through exchanges between participants (Yalom, 1995). Group therapy is offered both as a primary form of treatment for diverse types of problems and as an adjunct to individual therapy, as in the case of the treatment of substance abuse

(Burlingame et al., 2004). Group therapy is offered at different stages of the life span to children, adolescents, adults, and older adults (Brabender, Fallon, & Smolar, 2004).

Compared with individual treatment, do you think that there might be some disorders for which group treatment might be especially helpful?

Group therapy offers many promising mechanisms of change, including universality, support, and modelling. Universality refers to the experience of recognizing that one is not alone in facing a particular difficulty and that others share similar challenges and reactions. Support, both emotional and instrumental, may be provided in a group format, not only by the therapist but also by others in the group. Group contexts allow opportunities for modelling of behaviours, so that a client may learn new ways of coping by observing the efforts of another person. Unfortunately, groups allow the modelling of both positive and negative behaviours. Dishion, McCord, and Poulin (1999) reviewed evidence suggesting that when adolescents with significant problem behaviours received peer-group interventions, they learned aggressive behaviours from one another. Thus, group treatment had an iatrogenic effect, in that youth who received the group treatment did more poorly than did youth who did not receive the treatment. This finding underlines the essential requirement to continuously evaluate the effects of therapy, to determine whether therapy is helpful and to ensure that if therapy is harmful, it is terminated immediately.

Thus far we have discussed what might be termed *traditional* alternative modes of intervention. Since the 1980s, there has been dramatic growth in alternative intervention options. These include a range of **self-administered treatments** (also known as self-help) and a range of uses of technology to deliver or enhance services. It is abundantly clear that the extent of the need for mental health services in the population far exceeds the capacity of the health care system to provide individualized, face-to-face mental health services for all who need them. The only possible way to meet this need is to offer patients (and potential patients) a menu of these alternative modes of intervention services that have proven efficacy and effectiveness (Kazdin & Blasé, 2011).

self-administered treatment: treatment that the client engages in with no or minimal contact with a mental health professional.

It may seem strange to consider self-help as part of the clinical psychologist's menu of service options. After all, the shelves of any bookstore are replete with self-help books with advice from a host of health care professionals, famous and formerly famous celebrities, and self-promoting lifestyle gurus. Whereas the sales of some of these books may lead to improvements in the financial well-being of their authors, there is little evidence that they do much for improving the quality of the readers' lives. However, there are now self-help materials that have been demonstrated to have a meaningful clinical impact. What these have in common is that they are based on both well-established psychological principles and treatment protocols for psychotherapies that are evidence-based. Malouf and Rooke (2007) reviewed the research on the usefulness of self-help books readily available from bookstores. They found evidence of the usefulness of some books for several disorders, including depression, panic disorder, social anxiety, binge eating, and chronic fatigue. The book with the greatest empirical support, by far, was Burns' (1980) book on CBT techniques, *Feeling Good: The New Mood Therapy*.

Self-help materials can be used in different ways in treatment (Newman, Erickson, Przeworski, & Dzus, 2003). At one end of the continuum, treatment can be entirely self-administered, with the only therapist contact being an initial assessment of patient suitability. Alternatively, treatment can be predominantly self-administered with occasional therapist contact beyond an initial assessment to teach patients how to use the materials and check on their progress. The therapist contact may be via phone, email, or text. In turn, the client may submit homework assignments via email, text, or website. The degree of therapist involvement can be further increased—but still below the level found in traditional therapy—in minimal-contact therapy where the therapist actively aids the patient in using the self-help materials (which still remain the central focus of therapy). Finally, at the other end of the continuum, in traditional, predominantly therapist-administered treatments, self-help materials can be used as an adjunct to treatment. There is firm evidence that self-administered treatments, across this continuum, can be clinically effective in treating depression, anxiety disorders, and substance abuse disorders (Lewis, Pearce, & Bisson, 2012; Menchola, Arkowitz, & Burke, 2007).

For several decades, researchers have experimented with the possibility of delivering individual treatments via computers. Early programs were rather primitive and limited in scope but, with the rapid growth in computing power and memory, more recent programs are incredibly sophisticated and flexible. A number of experimental trials have found the efficacy of computer-based treatments to be comparable to that of traditional individual psychotherapy for some people and conditions (Marks, Shaw, & Parkin, 1998; Richards & Richardson, 2012). For example, Proudfoot et al. (2004) reported on a large randomized, controlled trial in England in which 274 primary care patients with anxiety and/or depression received, with or without medication, either a computerized CBT program, Beating

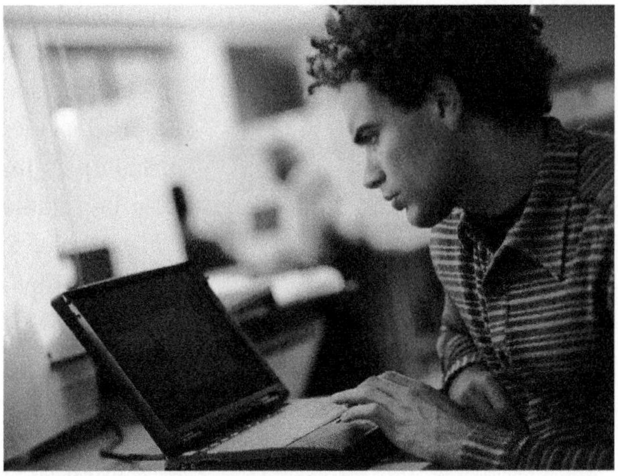

Ryan McVay/Photodisc/Getty Images

There has been an increase in the use of technology in psychological services, such as self-administered treatment, virtual reality treatments, and computer-based treatment delivery.

the Blues, or treatment as usual, as directed by the patient's primary care physician. The Beating the Blues program involves a brief video introduction followed by eight 50-minute computer sessions, with assigned homework to be completed between sessions. Compared with the treatment-as-usual condition, the patients who followed Beating the Blues showed significant improvements in depression, anxiety, work adjustment, and social adjustment. Interestingly, even though the cost of the computer-based treatment was £40 higher per patient than the usual treatments, lost employment costs were £407 less per patient (McCrone et al., 2004).

How do you feel about receiving psychological treatment based on a computer program provided under the supervision of a psychologist? Would your reaction change if you were able to start the computer-based treatment immediately, rather than having to wait weeks or months on a waiting list to receive therapy from a psychologist?

Other computer-based treatments are now available through the Internet, thus greatly expanding service delivery options for those who are far from a psychologist or who are too impaired by anxiety symptoms to travel for treatment (Kenwright & Marks, 2004). This use of information technology and telecommunications to provide health care services at a distance is known as **telehealth** (mentioned in Profile Box 11.2). Telehealth covers a range of delivery options, including telephone, videoconferencing, and computer-mediated communications (including email, chat rooms, and Internet-based services). The possibility of providing appropriate evidence-based services at a distance is extremely exciting and opens up countless opportunities for reaching people who might otherwise be unable or unwilling to seek necessary psychological services. For example, a growing literature on the efficacy of videoconferencing psychotherapy demonstrates that it can be successfully delivered to a wide range of clients and that the outcomes are comparable with those of face-to-face psychotherapy (Backhaus et al., 2012). To date, most of the research on telehealth treatments has involved adapting forms of CBT, and encouraging results have been obtained for the treatment of a number of disorders, especially depression and anxiety disorders (e.g., Carlbring et al., 2007; Mohr et al., 2005; Sloan, Gallagher, Feinstein, Lee, & Pruneau, 2011).

telehealth: the delivery of health care services via telephone, videoconferencing, or computer-mediated communications.

Survey data show that both psychologists and doctoral students in professional psychology programs are open to the idea of providing teleheath services, with those providing CBT services appearing to be the most comfortable with providing psychological services at a distance (Perle et al., 2013). The use of these technologies requires consideration of a host of ethical, legal, and training questions (Perle, Langsam, & Nierenberg, 2011). What additional training is required to prepare a psychologist who is competent at delivering evidence-based therapy to deliver the same types of treatment via videoconferencing? Is it legal for a psychologist to deliver Internet-based treatment to a patient who lives in a jurisdiction other than the one in which the psychologist is licensed? In 2011, to address such issues, the Association of Canadian Psychology Regulatory Organizations adopted standards for telepsychology service delivery. In addition to stressing that all such services must conform to the requirements of the Canadian Code of Ethics for Psychologists, the standards encourage psychologists to make plans for services in an emergency (including how to contact the psychologist and the availability of local services for the client) and to be prepared with alternatives if technological problems interfere with the delivery of services. The standards can be accessed at www.cpo.on.ca/assets/AA9EE26F-4A23-49F0-A947-21A6F25D6FB0.pdf.

For someone considering psychological treatment, what might the advantages be in considering self-administered treatments? What drawbacks might there be?

With this growing range of treatment options, models of **stepped care**, long available in medicine, are now being applied to psychological treatments. In an attempt to make the most of scarce health care resources, lower-cost interventions are offered first, with more intensive and more costly interventions provided only to those for whom the first-line intervention was insufficient (Haaga, 2000; Scogin, Hanson, & Welsh, 2003). Following a thorough assessment of the patient and the state of the research evidence for the available treatment options, self-help or computer-based treatments may be worth considering as initial treatments. If symptoms persist after the completion of such treatments, then individual or group therapy might be considered. In the treatment of bulimia nervosa, for example, Mitchell et al. (2011) reported that a stepped care approach involving therapist-assisted self-help, augmented by medication and individual therapy with CBT when necessary, resulted in substantial client improvement even one year after termination of treatment. If the likelihood is low that a patient will complete a treatment that does not involve ongoing contact with a health care professional, minimal contact treatments (i.e., three or four sessions) or group treatments might be the best initial options. With respect to providing services to children and families, less intense interventions may involve the use of therapeutic feedback, large group parenting training, or psychoeducational school-based programs (Stormshak & Dishion, 2002), as well as online services for parents (Sanders, Baker, & Turner 2012). Many details need to be worked out, and much research needs to

stepped care: an approach to health care service delivery in which lower-cost interventions are offered first, with more intensive and more costly interventions being provided only to those for whom the first-line intervention was insufficient.

be done, before stepped care models will be viable and widely accepted by patients and psychologists. What is clear, though, is that individual, face-to-face psychotherapy is no longer the only choice for many individuals seeking psychological services.

SUMMARY AND CONCLUSIONS

In this chapter, we have provided an introduction to psychological intervention. We described a number of psychological treatments that have empirical support. These therapies share some features, such as their short-term nature, the establishment of treatment goals, and the active role played by the therapist. Similarly, they share the view that the therapist must establish a positive relationship with the client. Most important, for all of these approaches, efforts have been made to evaluate their efficacy and effectiveness. They differ, however, in their assumptions about the nature of problems, the process by which change occurs, the importance of examining the past, and the relative benefits of insight, experimentation, and skills. These approaches differ in the role ascribed to the therapeutic relationship—whether it is seen as a mirror of the problems the client experiences, a support in exploration, or a resource to aid in experimenting and learning new skills.

Although the number of people seeking treatments for psychological problems has been increasing, this is largely accounted for by increased psychopharmacology rather than increased psychotherapy or other psychological services. It is clear that the majority of people who require psychological services do not have access to them, and Canadian data indicate that the need for psychological services among those living in rural areas is substantial. The popular stereotype of long-term psychotherapy does not match the data on the provision of psychotherapy, as important changes are made by many clients after weeks or months of psychological services. The short-term therapies we described are intended to create an expectancy of change as well as encouragement to think, behave, or feel in different ways. In addition to individual therapy, encouraging findings are reported from couples, family, and group therapy. Psychologists are also exploiting the enormous potential of computer and Internet technologies to extend services to sections of the population that have been underserved in the past. Rigorous evaluation of the effectiveness of psychological services allows the development of a range of interventions that can be offered according to clients' needs and preferences. Rather than imposing a one-size-fits-all approach to psychotherapy, it makes sense to tailor approaches to meet the needs of a diverse population.

KEY TERMS

cognitive-behavioural therapy: a treatment approach that emphasizes the role of thoughts and behaviour in psychological problems and, therefore, focuses on altering beliefs, expectations, and behaviours in order to improve the client's functioning.

interpersonal psychotherapy: a treatment approach that emphasizes interpersonal elements in the development, maintenance, and alteration of psychological problems (especially grief, role disputes, role transitions, and interpersonal deficits).

process-experiential therapy: a treatment approach that emphasizes the importance of becoming aware of emotions, understanding and expressing emotions, and transforming maladaptive into adaptive emotions.

self-administered treatment: treatment that the client administers without direct input from a mental health professional.

self-efficacy: a person's sense of competence to learn and perform new tasks.

short-term psychodynamic therapy: a treatment approach that emphasizes bringing to awareness unconscious processes, especially as they are expressed in interpersonal relationships, and helping the client to understand and alter these processes.

stepped care: an approach to health care service delivery in which lower-cost interventions are offered first, with more intensive and more costly interventions being provided only to those for whom the first-line intervention was insufficient.

telehealth: the delivery of health care services via telephone, videoconferencing, or computer-mediated communications.

transference: the unconscious application of expectations and emotional experiences, based on important early relationships, onto subsequent interpersonal relationships.

KEY NAMES

Albert Bandura | Aaron Beck | Robert Elliott
Leslie Greenberg | Lester Luborsky | Hans Strupp
Myrna Weissman

ADDITIONAL RESOURCES

Books

Lambert, M. L. (Ed.). (2013). *Bergin and Garfield's handbook of psychotherapy and behavior change* (6th ed.). Hoboken, NJ: John Wiley & Sons.

Norcross, J. C., Campbell, L. F., Grohol, J. M., Santrock, J. W., Selagea, F., & Sommer, R. (2013). *Self-help that works: Resources to improve emotional health and strengthen relationships.* New York: Oxford University Press.

Wood, J. C. (2007). *Getting help: The complete and authoritative guide to self-assessment and treatment of mental health problems.* Oakland, CA: New Harbinger Publications.

Journals

Annual Review of CyberTherapy and Telemedicine

CyberPsychology & Behavior

Journal of Telemedicine and Telecare

Psychotherapy

Psychotherapy Research

Check It Out!

Fact sheets on psychotherapy from the Society of Clinical Psychology: www.div12.org/member-login/toolkit/fact-sheets

Beating the Blues computer-based treatment of anxiety and depression: www.thewellnessshop.co.uk/products/beatingtheblues

The *FearFighter* Internet-based treatment of phobias and panic, and other Internet-based treatments: www.ccbt.co.uk

Some websites describing virtual reality treatments and treatment-related research (keep in mind the importance of empirical evidence in reviewing self-help books and websites offering treatment options):

www.virtuallybetter.com

www.vrphobia.com

INTERVENTION: ADULTS AND COUPLES

12

CHAPTER

INTRODUCTION

There has been a dramatic evolution in the nature of psychological treatment since the middle of the 20th century. Significant questions about whether or not psychotherapy works provoked a veritable explosion of research on the impact of psychological treatments which, in turn, led to the development of efficacious and (often) effective treatments for a wide range of disorders and presenting problems. In the first part of this chapter, we summarize these important events in the evolution of effective psychological treatments and describe strategies to accurately review treatment studies. We then outline recent initiatives to establish criteria for evidence-based treatments. In a growing number of countries, these efforts have culminated in the development of clinical practice guidelines that set out treatments of choice for both adult and child disorders.

In addition to presenting the big picture regarding the history and current state of research-based efforts to develop and promote psychological intervention, we will also provide several detailed examples of current evidence-based treatments for a number of disorders. This will give you a sense of what is involved in state-of-the-art treatments for common debilitating conditions such as depression, posttraumatic stress disorder (PTSD), and couple conflict. Because of the great volume of research and scholarly activity involved, it is not possible to do justice to all of this work in a single chapter. Accordingly, in this chapter we focus on treatments for adults and couples; the following chapter addresses treatments for children and adolescents.

DOES PSYCHOTHERAPY WORK? A CONTROVERSY AND ITS IMPACT

PsycINFO, the searchable database of psychological literature developed by the APA, covers the period from the second half of the 1800s to the present. If you search this database for empirical studies on psychotherapy for adults that were published in peer-reviewed journals prior to 1950, you will find zero entries. If you re-run the search for the years 1950 to 1980, you will find hundreds of entries, and if you search from 1980 to the present, you will find thousands of additional entries! Many scholars (e.g., Barlow, Bullis, Comer, & Ametaj, 2013) trace the beginning of this astonishing growth in empirical attention to the effects of psychotherapy to the publication of a single controversial paper. In 1952, Hans Eysenck published an article in which he argued that the rates of improvement among clients receiving psychodynamic or eclectic therapy were comparable to, or even worse than, rates of remission of symptoms among untreated clients. At that time, there were no randomized controlled trials (RCTs) of psychotherapy. Instead, proponents of various schools of psychotherapy authoritatively proclaimed the efficacy of their treatments on the basis of clinical experience and, occasionally, case histories of successfully treated patients. Eysenck, an early proponent of applying learning principles to alleviate psychological distress, reviewed data from 24 uncontrolled evaluations of psychoanalytic and eclectic therapies. He concluded that 44% of patients receiving psychoanalysis improved and 64% of those receiving eclectic treatments improved. He compared these results with two data sets in which *spontaneous recovery* occurred for 72% of *untreated* patients.

randomized controlled trial: an experiment in which research participants are randomly assigned to one of two or more treatment conditions.

As we discussed in Chapter 4, internal validity is an important aspect of any psychological research. If you look back at Exhibit 4.7, you can see that Eysenck's analysis of the data probably suffered from several threats to internal validity, including history, maturation, statistical regression, and selection biases. Without the use of appropriate control groups, in which participants are randomly assigned to treatment conditions, it is incorrect to compare the results from the different data sets. Without randomization, there is no way to determine whether the patients in the different samples were comparable in terms of disorder or severity of distress. It is also important to note that the so-called *untreated* groups were patients in residential treatment settings and patients making psychologically based disability claims who were treated by general medical practitioners. In other words, although they did not receive formal psychotherapy services, these *untreated* patients would have received some guidance and suggestions on their psychological difficulties as part of their treatment regimen. Critics of Eysenck's work, such as Luborsky (1954), also claimed that Eysenck's criteria for establishing clinical improvement were arbitrary and biased against finding positive therapeutic effects.

From the late 1950s to the early 1970s, a number of competing reviews of the impact of psychotherapy were published. Those who advocated the use of learning principles in developing psychological interventions, such as Eysenck (1966) and Rachman (1971), maintained that there was no compelling evidence supporting the efficacy of psychodynamic and other related forms of treatment. In stark contrast, proponents of these psychotherapies conducted reviews showing that not only did these therapies have positive effects, but their effects were also comparable to those reported for the newly developed behavioural therapies (Bergin, 1971; Luborsky, Singer, & Luborsky, 1975). Because each research group used different criteria to select studies for review, there was little overlap in the studies on which conclusions were based. Furthermore, different criteria were used to evaluate whether therapy worked. On top of that, interpretation of results was coloured by pre-existing biases for and against the value of traditional psychotherapies. For example, Bergin (1971) concluded that the research evidence demonstrated that psychodynamic and related psychotherapies worked and supported this claim by pointing out that significant results in 22 out of 60 studies showed these treatments to have a moderately positive effect. In contrast, critics of these therapies claimed the opposite, noting that 38 out of 60 studies failed to demonstrate clear evidence of positive treatment effects.

Half empty or half full? Do significant results in 22 out of 60 studies demonstrate or fail to demonstrate the effects of psychotherapy?

How important is it for you that psychological treatments be empirically evaluated? If you were considering seeking treatment (or were making recommendations to family members or friends about therapy), would it matter to you whether the support for the treatment was based on a clinician's experience or on the results of several large-scale RCTs?

META-ANALYSIS AND PSYCHOTHERAPY RESEARCH

Throughout the 1970s, as the debate about the impact of psychotherapy grew, so did the number of published treatment studies. The literature became so vast that anyone attempting to understand and integrate the research evidence on various forms of psychotherapy faced the daunting task of qualitatively reviewing hundreds of published studies. The publication of the first meta-analysis of the psychotherapy literature by Mary Smith and Gene Glass (1977) was a landmark in efforts to review scientific literature on treatment outcome.

meta-analysis: a set of statistical procedures for quantitatively summarizing the results of a research domain.

As you learned in Chapter 4, meta-analysis is a method for quantitatively reviewing research studies. We have mentioned results of meta-analytic studies in several preceding chapters. In this chapter and the remaining chapters of this book, we will be providing a bit more detail about the results of the meta-analytic studies we present. In order for you to be able to understand these results, you need a sense of the statistics used in meta-analyses. To allow for the meaningful integration of data across studies, researchers convert the results of studies into **effect sizes**. When based on group comparison statistics (such as t or F), effect sizes are typically expressed in standard deviation units: a between-groups effect size of $d = .5$ means that there is a difference of one-half standard deviation between treated and control groups. When correlational analyses are used (e.g., r or R), the effect size is expressed as an r statistic. It is also possible to convert d effect sizes into r effect sizes, and vice versa.

effect size: a standardized metric, typically expressed in standard deviation units or correlations, that allows the results of research studies to be combined and analyzed.

Effect sizes using the d statistic can also be represented in another way that is even more compelling. Let's consider a psychotherapy outcome research study in which there is a treated and an untreated group, and let's assume that the distribution of outcome scores for each group is normal in shape. If there were no group difference, then d would equal 0, and the two group distributions would overlap perfectly. However, if the treated group had better outcomes than the untreated group did (e.g., $d = .5$), then the distributions would overlap only partially as there is a half standard deviation difference between the means of the two groups. It is possible, therefore, to represent the d statistic as the percentage of participants in the untreated group whose scores are lower than that of the average participants in the treated group. Table 12.1 provides information on the equivalency among d, r, and the percentage of those in the untreated group falling below the mean of treated participants.

Arizona State University

Dr. Gene Glass co-authored the first meta-analysis of the psychotherapy literature in 1977.

By current research standards, the first attempt to employ meta-analytic techniques was rather crude. Nevertheless, based on data from more than 370 published and unpublished studies, Smith and Glass (1977) reported the average effect of psychotherapy to be $d = .68$. In percentage terms, this means that the average person receiving treatment was better off at the end of treatment than 74% of those who had not received treatment. Psychotherapy, in general, certainly seemed to have a substantial impact. In 1980, Smith, Glass, and Miller published a more extensive and more sophisticated meta-analysis of the psychotherapy literature. They reviewed 475 controlled studies of psychotherapy, including studies published in scientific journals and unpublished dissertations. Their overall finding was that psychotherapy had an average effect size of $d = .85$ (i.e., the average person receiving therapy was better off after therapy than 80% of people who did not receive therapy).

TABLE 12.1 ■ Equivalencies for Meta-Analytic Statistics

d	*r*	Percentage of untreated participants below the mean of treated participants
0.0	.00	50
0.2	.10	58
0.4	.20	66
0.6	.29	73
0.8	.37	79
1.0	.45	84
1.5	.60	93
2.0	.71	98

When Smith and colleagues calculated the efficacy of various types of treatment, they found the largest effect sizes (*d* values of 1.31 and 1.24, respectively) for cognitive and cognitive-behavioural treatments, followed by behavioural (.91), psychodynamic (.78), and humanistic treatments (.63). Generally speaking, all of these results are very encouraging with respect to the impact of various psychotherapies. These effect sizes cannot be directly compared, however, as clients treated within each type of treatment were not necessarily equivalent in the type and severity of problems. Smith et al. also examined the effects of psychotherapy across different disorders. Some of the largest effect sizes were for anxiety and mood problems and, again, some significant differences between treatments were evident. A subset of the studies they reviewed included direct comparisons of different forms of treatment (i.e., comparative treatment outcome studies in which participants were randomly assigned to different treatments). We will discuss these and other findings from this landmark meta-analysis in Chapter 14.

Criticisms of meta-analysis emerged rapidly (e.g., Eysenck, 1978; Wilson & Rachman, 1983). One criticism referred to the problem of *garbage-in, garbage-out;* in other words, if poor quality studies were included in a meta-analysis they could negatively influence the results. Similarly, the *apples and oranges* argument raised concern about the meaningfulness of including different treatments and different measures in a meta-analysis. For example, in considering the general effect of treatment, meta-analysts might give as much weight to a measure of patients' satisfaction with treatment as they do to data on whether a diagnosable condition was still present after treatment. In early meta-analyses, a number of mistakes were commonly made, such as not controlling for differences in sample sizes across studies, or using all results from each study rather than an average of all results (which meant that studies with a large number of analyses had more influence on the results of the meta-analysis). Fortunately, meta-analysts took these concerns seriously and current practices in meta-analysis address such shortcomings.

Throughout the 1980s and 1990s, the number of meta-analyses grew. Because Smith et al.'s (1980) general findings on the effectiveness of psychotherapy were replicated by other researchers (e.g., Landman & Dawes, 1982), meta-analyses became more focused. Instead of dealing with whether or not therapy had an effect, questions were transformed to: "How efficacious are the treatments for a specific disorder?" and "How efficacious is a specific treatment for a specific disorder?" Dobson (1989), for example, examined research on treatments for depression and found that cognitive therapy had a very large effect size compared with waiting-list controls ($d > 1.5$) but only a small relative advantage over other treatments such as behaviour therapy.

How has meta-analysis affected the field of psychotherapy?

The use of meta-analysis to review research is now the gold standard for evaluating treatment effects and most other areas of psychological research. Today, a PsycINFO search would reveal hundreds of meta-analyses published in the adult psychotherapy literature. Indeed, in examining the research on the efficacy of only cognitive-behavioural therapy (CBT) for a range of conditions, Hofmann, Asnaani, Vonk, Sawyer, and Fang (2012) identified 269 meta-analyses, published since 2000, that addressed this issue. Many meta-analytic reviews focus on the efficacy of treatments for specific disorders. A growing number, though, examine treatment effects in more detail. Olatunji, Cisler, and Tolin (2010), for example, examined the influence of comorbidity on the outcome of treatments for anxiety disorders. Overall, they found that comorbidity was unrelated to the effects of psychotherapies and drug treatments for these disorders. Interestingly, significant effects were found for specific diagnoses, with comordidity being *positively* related to treatment outcome for those with panic disorder, agoraphobia, or PTSD.

As you learned earlier, the quality of meta-analytic results is largely dependent on methodological decisions made by researchers who conduct the meta-analyses. These decisions in turn have the potential to impact the results of a meta-analysis. For example, as we described in Viewpoint Box 4.2, there is a tendency for journals to selectively publish research that has statistically significant results. This is known as publication bias, and there are concerns that conducting meta-analyses based on the results of published studies may, likewise, yield biased findings. Niemeyer, Musch, and Pietrowsky (2013) examined the data sets used in 19 meta-analyses on the efficacy of psychotherapy for the treatment of depression in adults. They detected the presence of publication bias in many of these meta-analytic studies; however, they also found that this bias had a negligible impact on evaluation of the effects of psychotherapies. We do not know, however, whether this conclusion might hold for the treatment of other conditions.

In an impressive series of multidimensional meta-analyses, Drew Westen and his colleagues examined how a number of methodological issues affected the results of treatment research for depression, bulimia nervosa, generalized anxiety disorder, panic disorder, PTSD, and obsessive-compulsive disorder (Bradley, Greene, Russ, Dutra, & Westen, 2005; Eddy, Dutra, Bradley, & Westen, 2004; Thompson-Brenner, Glass, & Westen, 2003; Westen & Morrison, 2001). These meta-analyses were designed to expand on previous meta-analyses by analyzing a number of other treatment-related variables in addition to treatment outcome. For example, in order to consider the external validity and the clinical utility of treatment studies, Westen and colleagues also examined variables such as the number of patients excluded from the RCTs for failure to meet inclusion criteria, recovery rates (not just symptom change), and the persistence of treatment benefits over time. By examining these types of variables, the researchers' intention was to determine (a) the clinical significance of obtained treatment results and (b) the applicability of the research results to the general population of patients receiving therapy.

To illustrate these points, we will consider their multidimensional meta-analysis on bulimia nervosa (Thompson-Brenner et al., 2003). These researchers found that, on average, more than 80% of patients who began the RCT completed the treatment—an important aspect to consider in understanding the potential impact of the treatments studied. When the usual effect sizes across treatments were calculated from 26 clinical trials, the average effect of therapy compared with no treatment was substantial, with d values in the range of .9 to 1.0. But how much of a difference did this make in the patients' lives? Approximately 40% of patients recovered completely, with the others continuing to experience some symptoms. Thirty-two percent of patients maintained their recovery a year after treatment. Although these findings indicated that treatments for this eating disorder can have a substantial impact on patients' functioning, it is clear that many patients continued to manifest some aspects of the disorder despite having received treatment.

Thompson-Brenner et al. were also concerned to find that, on average, 40% of patients were excluded from the RCTs they examined. Potential participants were excluded for a variety of reasons including the presence of psychotic disorders, substance abuse, or other major psychiatric problems. Such exclusion criteria may make good clinical sense, as it is probably important to address untreated substance abuse before beginning treatment for bulimia. However, this raises an important issue: is it possible that the RCTs routinely exclude from treatment too many patients who normally seek treatment, thereby greatly reducing the generalizability of findings?

Fortunately, this does not appear to be the case. As we mentioned in Chapter 11, Stirman and colleagues (2003) found that the average severity of symptoms reported in RCTs of evidence-based treatments is greater than that found in the patients seeking routine psychotherapy services. Moreover, it appears that even if a potential research participant might be excluded from an RCT because of the presence of a comorbid diagnosis, it is highly likely that the patient would meet commonly used inclusion criteria used in the RCTs for the comorbid diagnosis (Stirman, DeRubeis, Crits-Christoph, & Rothman, 2005). Thus, for example, someone excluded from an RCT for depression because of a comorbid panic disorder could be included in an RCT for panic disorder. The implications of this are that (a) there are likely to be efficacious treatment options (based on RCTs) for most patients, even those with comorbid diagnoses; and (b) in working with patients with comorbid diagnoses, psychologists must decide which diagnosis or condition should be addressed first and which problems should be addressed only after some initial changes in functioning have occurred. So, for example, in providing treatment to Olivia, a client experiencing both PTSD and bulimia nervosa, the psychologist might determine that the eating problem needs to be stabilized before initiating treatment for the trauma.

Should authors of treatment studies be required to report on the proportion of potential participants who were excluded from the studies and the proportion of participants who failed to complete treatment? What differences might these data make in interpreting the results of the study? Should this type of information influence a clinical psychologist when deciding on treatment options for a patient?

What are the advantages to the client of receiving evidence-based services?

EVIDENCE-BASED TREATMENTS: INITIATIVES AND CONTROVERSIES

Based on the efforts of psychotherapy researchers in numerous countries, there is now compelling evidence that psychotherapy has the potential to improve the psychosocial functioning of adult patients with a wide range of disorders. These include common psychological disorders—mood disorders, anxiety disorders, eating disorders, sleep disorders, sexual disorders, and substance-related disorders—and diseases and disorders that are routinely seen in primary care medical practices but are typically difficult to medically manage, including type 1 diabetes, chronic tension-type headaches, rheumatoid arthritis, chronic low-back pain, and chronic fatigue syndrome (First & Tasman, 2004; Hunsley, 2003a). Profile Box 12.1 presents Dr. Martin Provencher who conducts research on the treatment of bipolar disorder, a condition known to improve with the use of both mood stabilizing medication and specific forms of interpersonal psychotherapy and CBT.

PROFILE BOX 12.1

DR. MARTIN D. PROVENCHER

Courtesy of Magenta

I completed a Ph.D. in clinical psychology at l'Université Laval in Québec City and a clinical internship at the Calgary Regional Health Authority Consortium in Clinical Psychology. I then worked for five years as a clinical psychologist in Québec City. I am currently an associate professor at l'École de psychologie de l'Université Laval, a researcher at l'Institut universitaire en santé mentale de Québec, and the Director of the Cognitive Behavioral Therapy Unit at the university counselling centre. I am the current president of the Canadian Association of Cognitive and Behavioural Therapies (CACBT) and I am licensed as a clinical psychologist in Québec. My clinical and research interests include CBT for mood and anxiety disorders (in particular bipolar disorder, depression, and generalized anxiety disorder) and the dissemination of evidence-based treatments for these disorders. My current research program focuses on psychosocial interventions for bipolar disorder.

HOW DID YOU CHOOSE TO BECOME A CLINICAL PSYCHOLOGIST?

I was studying health sciences in college and was fascinated with understanding the body and mind connection. For these reasons, I took an elective course on introduction to general psychology. I was hooked from the start of the first class, and remember reading each chapter of the textbook with keen interest. I also took a course on the nature and management of stress in which I was introduced to one of the fundamental principles of cognitive-behavioural therapy (CBT), which is that it's not the events per se that affect how you feel or react to them, but rather how you perceive or interpret these events. This rather obvious principle rang true for me. I then went on to study anxiety and mood disorders during my doctoral training.

WHAT IS THE GREATEST CHALLENGE YOU FACE AS A CLINICAL PSYCHOLOGIST?

As a clinical psychologist, I'm interested in doing whatever I can to help patients deal with and overcome their mental health problems. This involves using evidenced-based treatments (EBTs), like CBT, for a wide range of disorders. Although the flexible use of treatment protocols and manuals, when based on an individualized case formulation, is very helpful for most patients, it doesn't always work as intended. This is the case for some severe and chronic patients with bipolar disorder I have treated. The dilemma then is to figure out how to best help these patients. I've found that closely monitoring treatment progress, constantly revising the case formulation using new data generated during and between sessions, and sticking to evidenced-based procedures have been the most helpful strategies. Consulting with colleagues about difficult cases and reviewing the existing literature and practice guidelines for such cases have also been useful.

TELL US ABOUT YOUR RESEARCH ON TREATMENT OF BIPOLAR DISORDER

Bipolar disorder (BD) is a severe mental illness characterized by phases of depression and mania that affects 2.2% of Canadians. Despite the best pharmacological treatment, relapse is common. Psychological interventions are

CONTINUED . . .

therefore recommended to help patients better manage their condition and improve the course of their disorder. For over 10 years, I have conducted clinical research on psychological interventions for BD. This has involved successfully implementing brief group psychoeducation in community mental health centres in Quebec and treating bipolar depression with CBT. I have also been interested in assessing factors that affect the course of the illness and treatment outcome. More recently, we've studied sleep problems, cognitive schemas, and comorbid anxiety in Canadians with BD. We found that patients with BD have significant daytime complaints like sleepiness, present a distinct cognitive profile, and fare worse when comorbid anxiety disorders are present. Currently, we are studying ways to better disseminate psychological interventions for BD and working on improving our existing treatments by including recent research findings on factors that affect treatment, such as sleep and comorbidity.

HOW DO YOU INTEGRATE SCIENCE AND PRACTICE IN YOUR WORK?

The scientist-practitioner model is at the core of my identity and work as a clinician and researcher. For example, while working as a clinical psychologist in the hospital, I routinely used EBTs for mood disorders. In working with severe cases of bipolar disorder and depression, there were times when treatment didn't work as well as I had planned. Understanding why this happens helps me formulate research questions that I can then study by designing research protocols to test out these ideas. The constant interaction between evidence-based clinical work and clinical research helps improve my understanding of these complex disorders and, ultimately, leads to improved treatments for severe mood disorders like BD.

WHAT DO YOU SEE AS THE MOST EXCITING CHANGES IN THE FIELD OF CLINICAL PSYCHOLOGY?

Without a doubt, widespread dissemination of EBTs in different countries is at the top of the list. For example, Improving Access to Psychological Therapies (IAPT) in the United Kingdom is at the forefront of these initiatives. The UK government invested over £300 million to train over 3,400 treatment providers to deliver CBT and other EBTs for anxiety disorders and depression. To date, over 1 million people have been successfully treated by these providers. In Canada, the Canadian Psychological Association (CPA) recently published a report from the CPA Task Force on Evidence-Based Practice of Psychological Treatments that strongly recommends the use of EBTs. The CACBT is committed to contributing to the effective dissemination of CBT in Canada by providing education, training, and credentialling for CBT providers (www.cacbt.ca). As it is now internationally recognized that EBTs significantly improve mental health disorders and are cost-effective, the next challenge will be to improve access to these psychological treatments in the health care system for all Canadians.

clinical practice guidelines: a summary of scientific research, dealing with the diagnosis, assessment, and/or treatment of a disorder, designed to provide guidance to clinicians providing services to patients with the disorder.

Clinical practice guidelines, based on the best available research, are a common way in which empirical evidence is used to assist clinicians in making assessment and treatment decisions. Many health professions, such as medicine, nursing, and psychiatry, have developed expert review panels to translate the knowledge gained from research into concrete guidelines intended to inform clinical practice. The American Psychiatric Association, for example, has practice guidelines listed on its website that address the treatment of dementias, mood disorders, several anxiety disorders, borderline personality disorder, eating disorders, substance use disorders, and schizophrenia.

Despite the extent and strength of psychotherapy research, organized clinical psychology has been very slow to develop clinical practice guidelines. The first initiative in this direction in clinical psychology began in the early 1990s when the APA Society of Clinical Psychology struck a task force on the promotion and dissemination of psychological procedures. The goal of the task force was to set a standard for defining treatment efficacy that was comparable to standards used in other areas of health care, such as approval criteria for pharmaceuticals. The impetus for this work came from increasing pressure in the United States for health care practices to be both clinically effective and cost-effective (Beutler, 1998). Legislation and state case law were being used to shape the nature of federal and state health care policy, and there appeared to be a very real danger that access to mental health and behavioural health care services might be curtailed because of perceptions that such services were both expensive and relatively ineffective.

Members of the original task force, chaired by **Dianne Chambless**, came from a range of employment settings and espoused a variety of theoretical orientations. The task force's strategy was to examine treatment research for specific disorders and conditions according to a number of criteria. For a treatment to be designated as an **empirically supported treatment** (EST), the task force required evidence of symptom reduction and/or improved functioning either from at least two independently conducted RCTs or from a large series of single-case studies. A report of the task force criteria and an initial list of ESTs were published in 1995 (Task Force on Promotion and Dissemination of Psychological Procedures, 1995). As the task force continued its work, the membership was expanded and additional issues were addressed in subsequent reports (Chambless et al., 1996; Weisz, Hawley, Pilkonis, Woody, & Follette, 2000). In a related effort, in 1998, a special section in the *Journal of Consulting and Clinical Psychology* was devoted to the topic of ESTs. To guide authors in reviewing the literature for the special section, Chambless and Hollon (1998) refined the criteria for designating ESTs. These criteria are presented in Exhibit 12.1.

empirically supported treatment: a psychotherapy that has been found, in a series of randomized controlled trials or single-participant designs, to be efficacious in the treatment of a specific condition.

What are the challenges in establishing a list of evidence-based treatments?

Critics of the EST initiative expressed concerns about issues ranging from the scientific soundness of the endeavour to the potential negative impacts on practising clinicians (e.g., Garfield, 1996; Henry, 1998; Silverman, 1996; Wampold, 1997). Moreover, as we described earlier in the chapter in discussing the meta-analyses of Westen and colleagues, even a large effect size (such as $d = 1.0$) does not guarantee that the majority of patients are symptom-free by the end of treatment or that they remain symptom-free for years after treatment. However, it is important to be aware that the standard used by most health care professions in defining preferred treatments is evidence of significant

©iStock.com/undergroundw

There are evidence-based psychological treatments for a wide range of problems, including substance abuse.

group differences from RCTs. We suggest, therefore, that at a minimum, clinical psychologists need to remain aware of both the strengths and limitations of psychotherapy research. This includes the important difference in all health care treatment research between *statistically significant differences* and *clinically significant differences* (as represented by such concepts as *improved quality of life, cure,* and *recovery*).

Furthermore, as you can see in Exhibit 12.1, one of Chambless and Hollon's criteria for ESTs is that the treatment be shown to be helpful on the basis of an RCT or equivalent design. As you learned earlier in the text, evidence-based treatments vary in the extent and nature of their supporting data—so a treatment could have an evidence base but, because no RCTs have been conducted on the treatment, it would not meet the criteria to be an EST. Therefore, the term evidence-based is broader and more inclusive than the term EST. Nevertheless, the EST initiative was an important step in the development and promotion of evidence-based practice in psychology.

Exhibit 12.1 Chambless and Hollon's (1998) Criteria for Empirically Supported Treatments

Methodological and Statistical Criteria for Treatment Studies

1. There must be a comparison of the treatment with a no-treatment control group, an alternative treatment group, or a placebo in an RCT, controlled single-case experiment, or an equivalent time-series research design.
2. The treatment must be statistically significantly superior to the comparison groups described above *or* the treatment must be equivalent to another treatment that is already of established efficacy.
3. The research must have sufficient statistical power to detect moderate differences.
4. The research must have been conducted with (a) a treatment manual or its equivalent; (b) a population treated for specified problems, for whom inclusion criteria have been delineated in a reliable and valid manner; (c) reliable and valid treatment outcome measures that, at a minimum, assess the problems addressed in the treatment; and (d) appropriate data analysis.

Designation Criteria for Treatments

Efficacious: The superiority of the EST must have been shown in at least two independent research settings (for single-case experiments, the sample size must have been at least three at each site). If the data from all studies of the treatment are conflicting, the preponderance of the well-controlled data must support the EST efficacy.

Possibly Efficacious: One study is sufficient for this designation, in the absence of conflicting evidence (for single-case experiments the study must have had a sample size of at least three).

Efficacious and Specific: The EST must have been shown to be statistically significantly superior to a pill, a psychological placebo, or an alternative bona fide treatment in at least two independent research settings. If there is conflicting evidence, the preponderance of the well-controlled data must support the EST's efficacy and specificity.

What do you think of Chambless and Hollon's criteria for ESTs? Do the criteria seem too demanding, or not demanding enough? Why do you think the requirements for efficacious treatments include the need for supporting evidence from at least two independent research groups?

Within an evidence-based approach to treatment, it is critical to distinguish between a treatment that is untested (which by definition could not be evidence-based) and a treatment that has been demonstrated to be ineffective or harmful. Treatments that have been shown to be harmful should not be used. It is highly likely that some existing but as yet untested treatments work for some patients. No doubt the next edition of this text will include new treatments that are currently being evaluated. According to the principles of evidence-based care, health care professionals and patients should consider a treatment with existing research support *before* they turn to untested treatments. This is true whether the clinical condition requiring treatment is depression, back pain, or diabetes, and whether the health care provider is a psychologist, a physician, or an occupational therapist.

In addition to the EST and evidence-based initiatives in North America, there have been evidence-based treatment initiatives in other countries. For example, in Germany, the federal government commissioned an expert report on psychotherapy that was used to guide the writing of laws to regulate psychotherapy. An important element of this expert report was the emphasis on ensuring access to psychotherapy services for which there is empirical evidence of efficacy (Schulte & Hahlweg, 2000). Another example comes from Australia and New Zealand, where the Quality Assurance Project has published several guidelines for the treatment of psychological disorders. These guidelines are based on the combined results of meta-analytic reviews of the empirical literature, surveys of practitioners, and the opinions of experts. Another approach was developed in the United Kingdom, when the National Health Service commissioned a report to guide the strategic policy review of psychotherapy services. The authors of this report used similar but less stringent criteria to those used by the Society of Clinical Psychology (Roth & Fonagy, 1996, 2005). Three criteria were used to determine whether there is evidence of treatment efficacy, each of which is less demanding than the EST criteria presented in Exhibit 12.1. First, there must be a minimum of a single, high-quality RCT showing treatment efficacy. Second, there must be a clear description of the treatment, preferably but not necessarily, in the form of a therapy manual. Third, there must be a clear description of the recipients of the therapy.

In a series of editions of a text examining the results of psychological and pharmacological treatment of mental disorders, Nathan and Gorman (1998, 2002, 2007) adopted an approach to reviewing and evaluating the therapy literature that was in line with the underpinnings of evidence-based practice. Expert contributors were asked to provide indications of the methodological adequacy of outcome studies that supported the various treatments for a specific disorder. This allowed experts to extend evidence-based guidance to the treatment of conditions for which the research was limited or was in an early stage of development. Three types of clinical trials were identified. In descending order of quality, Type 1 studies are high-quality RCTs, Type 2 studies are imperfect RCTs (e.g., very limited treatment duration, incomplete patient randomization), and Type 3 studies are **open trials** or pilot studies in which there are no control conditions. Additionally, experts could draw on the conclusions from quantitative literature reviews, such as meta-analyses (Type 4), qualitative literature reviews (Type 5), and case studies or professional consensus statements not based on research evidence (Type 6).

open trial: a type of initial, exploratory treatment study in which no control group is used and, typically, few participant exclusion criteria are applied.

Nathan and Gorman's consideration of all types of treatment studies is consistent with the approach to evidence-based practice you learned about in previous chapters. Indeed, most efforts to operationalize the concept of evidence-based practice rely heavily on a ranking system such as that used by Nathan and Gorman (2007) to establish a hierarchy of evidence. This is an important feature of evidence-based practice because, as you learned in Chapter 4, research designs vary in the extent to which they address threats to internal and external validity. Accordingly, basing treatment recommendations for a patient on the results of a single, non-replicated study is less desirable than basing the recommendations on the results from numerous studies of the same treatment. Similarly, though, making a treatment decision based on uncontrolled or correlational research is better than making it based solely on professional opinion. The establishment of a hierarchy of research evidence allows decisions to be made using the best available data with respect to a given disorder or condition. Defining precise requirements for research hierarchies can be very difficult, and it is not unusual for different groups of researchers or agencies to use slightly differently criteria for reviewing the research and making treatment recommendations. For example, there are several clinical guidelines with respect to the treatment of PTSD (Forbes et al., 2010). Because of the use of different criteria, there are some important differences in the recommendations made in these guidelines (e.g., the degree to which the use of antidepressants is recommended). As with any research report, understanding the research methodology is critical for truly understanding research-based conclusions and using these conclusions to guide clinical services.

Exhibit 12.2 provides a summary of Nathan and Gorman's review of psychological treatments for adult disorders, augmented with information from the Australian Psychological Society's (2010) review of evidence-based interventions. In order to provide a sense of the range of evidence-based treatment options available, we provide information on treatments that have the highest level of empirical support (primarily Type 1 and 2 studies, in Nathan and Gorman's terms). Psychopathology research about each disorder informed the development of almost all of the treatments listed and, subsequently, each treatment was evaluated for its efficacy. This means that these therapies were designed to treat a specific disorder. Thus, for example, although interpersonal therapies for bipolar disorder and bulimia share many elements in common (such as a focus on how others' reactions to the disorders affect those suffering from the disorders), each treatment has been uniquely tailored to address the key aspects of each of the disorders (such as symptoms, interpersonal problems, and cognitive distortions). In many ways, psychopathology research forms the foundation for all of these evidence-based treatments.

Exhibit 12.2 Evidence-Based Treatments for Common Adult Disorders

Mood Disorders

Major Depressive Disorder

- Behavioural Couples Therapy
- Cognitive-Behavioural Therapy
- Interpersonal Psychotherapy
- Process-Experiential Therapy
- Psychoeducation
- Short-Term Psychodynamic Psychotherapy
- Solution-Focused Brief Therapy

Bipolar Disorder

- Psychoeducation (including family members)
- Cognitive-Behavioural Therapy
- Interpersonal and Social Rhythm Therapy
- Some forms of Couples and Family Therapy

Anxiety and Related Disorders

Specific Phobias

- Cognitive-Behavioural Therapy

Anxiety Disorder

- Cognitive-Behavioural Therapy
- Short-Term Psychodynamic Psychotherapy

CONTINUED . . .

Panic Disorder with and without Agoraphobia
- Cognitive-Behavioural Therapy
- Psychoeducation

Generalized Anxiety Disorder
- Cognitive-Behavioural Therapy
- Short-Term Psychodynamic Psychotherapy

Obsessive-Compulsive Disorder
- Cognitive-Behavioural Therapy

Posttraumatic Stress Disorder
- Cognitive-Behavioural Therapy
- Eye Movement Desensitization and Reprocessing

Eating Disorders

Anorexia Nervosa
- Cognitive-Behavioural Therapy
- Short-Term Psychodynamic Psychotherapy
- Some forms of Couples and Family Therapy

Bulimia Nervosa
- Cognitive-Behavioural Therapy
- Interpersonal Psychotherapy

Binge-Eating Disorder
- Cognitive-Behavioural Therapy
- Interpersonal Psychotherapy

Substance-Related Disorders
- Cognitive-Behavioural Therapy
- Couples and Family Therapy
- Psychoeducation (including Motivational Interviewing)
- Solution-Focused Brief Therapy
- 12-Step Programs

Sleep Disorders
- Cognitive-Behavioural Therapy

Sexual Disorders
- Cognitive-Behavioural Therapy

Schizophrenia
- Cognitive-Behavioural Therapy
- Psychoeducation (including family members)

Personality Disorders

Avoidant Personality Disorder
- Cognitive-Behavioural Therapy

Borderline Personality Disorder
- Some forms of Cognitive-Behavioural Therapy (Dialectical Behaviour Therapy and Schema Therapy)
- Some forms of long-term Psychodynamic Therapy

Adapted from Nathan and Gorman (2007) and Australian Psychological Society (2010).

In examining this list, we encourage you to keep several points in mind. First, for some of the disorders listed, there are additional treatment options that have preliminary empirical support, although the support is not as strong as that for the treatments presented in the exhibit. For example, in the treatment of opiate dependence, there is some evidence that short-term psychodynamic treatment can be efficacious (Gibbons, Crits-Christoph, & Hearon, 2008). Second, there are many psychological disorders and problems not reviewed in the two sources we used for Exhibit 12.2. So, for example, we know that CBT, insight-oriented marital therapy, and emotionally focused couples therapy are all efficacious in treating couple conflict (Chambless & Ollendick, 2001). There are also efficacious psychological treatments for health problems and illnesses, such as irritable bowel syndrome, chronic fatigue syndrome, Raynaud's disease, tinnitus, and smoking, to name only a few (you will learn more about clinical health psychology in Chapter 15). Third, as you learned in Chapter 11, there is growing awareness of the need to examine the efficacy of treatments for a diverse population, but to date there is relatively limited research on efficacious psychotherapy options for ethnic minority clients. Although the evidence generally indicates that treatments found to be efficacious for patients with European ancestry can be efficacious for patients with other ethnic backgrounds, there may be a need to adapt these treatments in culturally appropriate ways (Miranda et al., 2005; Smith, Rodríguez, & Bernal, 2011). Finally, no matter how thoroughly the scientific literature was reviewed in developing a list of evidence-based treatments, the publication of new studies means that such a list must be frequently updated. Updating is especially important for treatments that have received little research attention, as data from one or two newly published studies may provide supporting evidence for a treatment that previously had none.

Three features in this exhibit are striking. The first is the range of conditions: there are evidence-based therapies for almost all commonly encountered mental disorders for adults, although personality disorders fare less well in this regard. This is partially due to the difficulties in treating personality disorders (which by definition are chronic and pervasive problems) and partially due to the difficulty in obtaining research funds and conducting clinical trials that are of a duration sufficient to address these disorders (i.e., typically longer than one year). A second striking feature is the strength of the evidence supporting the use of CBT treatments. In many instances, more than one form of CBT has been demonstrated to be efficacious in treating a disorder. As indicated in the Hofmann et al. (2012) review of meta-analyses of CBT, the sheer number of studies examining CBT for adult disorders is staggering.

The extent of the research indicates that, for most conditions, cognitive-behavioural interventions have been found to be efficacious in many independent replications, based on services provided by many hundreds of different clinicians to many thousands of different research participants.

The third feature is that, compared with the same exhibit in earlier editions of this text, this one shows the increasing number of process-experiential, interpersonal, and psychodynamic therapies that have been demonstrated to be efficacious in the treatment of some clinical conditions. Although the size of the research base is much smaller than for CBT, there is evidence for some conditions that the results achieved in efficacy studies with these approaches are comparable to those obtained with CBT. Treatment evaluation research has always been a central aspect of CBT, which explains, at least in part, why so many evidence-based treatments are cognitive-behavioural in nature. As this evaluation ethos is adopted by psychologists espousing other orientations, it is likely that there will be more non-CBT therapies added to the list of evidence-based treatments. Indeed, one could argue that one of the most important spin-offs from the movement toward evidence-based practice is that proponents of non-CBT approaches to psychotherapy are attending more to the need to empirically determine the impact of their treatments (cf. Elliott, Greenberg, Watson, Timulak, & Freire, 2013). Psychoanalysts, too, have been urged to conduct RCTs to establish an empirical basis for their treatment (Gabbard, Gunderson, & Fonagy, 2002).

As described in the first chapter of this book, based on a presidential task force report, the APA endorsed a set of policies and practices with respect to evidence-based practice (APA Presidential Task Force on Evidence-Based Practice, 2006). In the APA task force report, evidence-based practice in psychology was defined as the integration of the best available research and clinical expertise within the context of patient characteristics, culture, values, and treatment preferences. In contrast to most statements about evidence-based practice issued by health care professions, the statement was extremely cautious about the use of research evidence in planning psychological services and said little about how different forms of research evidence should be weighted in making treatment decisions. The task force's position that treatment should be *informed by* research evidence but *determined on* the basis of other clinical information, patient choice, and the likely costs and benefits of available treatment options suggested to some psychologists that research evidence might be the least important factor to consider in practising in an evidence-based manner (Stuart & Lilienfeld, 2007). With respect to patient values, the statement was silent on the need for psychologists to ensure that patient views were based on accurate information and not on mistaken assumptions about the nature of psychological disorders and psychological treatments. Regardless of these shortcomings, the fact that principles of evidence-based practice have been adopted as APA policy should increase the likelihood that greater numbers of psychotherapy clients will be receiving evidence-based treatments in the future.

The evidence-based practice model was endorsed by the Canadian Psychological Association (CPA Task Force on Evidence-Based Practice of Psychological Treatments, 2012). To avoid confusion around the value of research in evidence-based practice, the CPA policy explicitly stated that evidence-based practice relies, first and foremost, on published, peer-reviewed research. All research methodologies are recognized as having the potential to provide evidence that can guide practice, although preference is given to data collected via research designs that minimize threats to the validity of the research findings. To fully address all elements of evidence-based practice, psychologists are expected to collaborate with clients in providing services. This means that psychologists must apply their knowledge of the best available research, bearing in mind specific client characteristics, cultural backgrounds, and treatment preferences. Furthermore, psychologists are expected to monitor the effects of treatment on an ongoing basis and to be prepared to alter the treatment on the basis of such data. Viewpoint Box 12.1 describes ways that psychologists can search for the research evidence to inform their treatment planning.

VIEWPOINT BOX 12.1

SEARCHING FOR EVIDENCE

Evidence-based practice in psychology requires clinical psychologists to base service delivery on the best available evidence. This means psychologists must be able to access and evaluate relevant research. To what extent do psychologists do this? Are there resources to assist them in the lifelong process of education? Berke, Rozell, Hogan, Norcross, and Karpiak (2011) set out to address these questions in a survey of members of the APA Society of Clinical Psychology. A total of 549 clinical psychologists provided complete data to the survey of use and knowledge of evidence-based practice.

Approximately two-thirds of respondents indicated that most or all of their services were evidence-based (as defined by the APA policy), with only 10% reporting little or no provision of evidence-based services. The provision of evidence-based services was highest among respondents who endorsed a cognitive-behavioural orientation, followed by those who endorsed a humanistic/existential orientation, an integrative/eclectic orientation, and, finally, a psychoanalytic/psychodynamic orientation. Respondents were, on average, moderately knowledgeable about general research databases such as PsycINFO and

CONTINUED . . .

MEDLINE, but were much less knowledgeable about online databases designed specifically to provide integrated information on evidence-based health and mental health services. Slightly less than half of respondents reported feeling competent in using at least one of these evidence-based databases. As a result, Berke et al. stressed that training in accessing and utilizing the best available research evidence should be provided both to graduate students and practising clinicians.

What are the options available for locating the best available research evidence? Searching for the most relevant evidence in general research databases can be challenging. Let's say you wanted to find out the best treatment options for dealing with panic disorder. If you simply enter the search terms *panic disorder and treatment* in databases such as PsycINFO or MEDLINE, you need to be prepared to have to wade through hundreds of citations. So, let's go back to what it is that you wanted to find out. In searching for panic disorder treatment, perhaps you were mainly interested in learning what might be appropriate for treating panic disorder in older adults. By including information on age range in your search (and any other client or study characteristics that interest you), you will reduce the work involved in sorting through the citations because the database will have narrowed your search for you.

Alternatively, you could check out one of the evidence-based databases that have already done much of the work for you with respect to identifying relevant research and summarizing the findings. Bear in mind that, depending on when the summaries were written, they may not include the latest findings. Augmenting the information found in such summaries is relatively easily done by searching the general research databases, using multiple, specific search terms and limiting the search to the time period of interest (i.e., the years after the summary was published). Here are some evidence-based databases recommended for use by psychologists by Berke et al. (2011) and Falzon, Davidson, and Bruns (2010): Cochrane Database of Systematic Reviews, Database of Abstracts of Reviews of Effects, eMedicine Clinical Knowledge Database, National Guideline Clearinghouse, National Institute for Health and Care Excellence, Substance Abuse and Mental Health Services Administration, and Translating Research into Practice.

After locating and reviewing the research evidence, the next step is for psychologists to determine whether they are competent to provide to a client a service that has been identified as having the best research base. In some cases, a psychologist has the necessary training and experience, and can proceed to offer the service to the client. In other cases, a psychologist might have to seek training and/or supervision in order to be competent to provide the service. In the meantime, for psychologists in this situation, there is an ethical obligation to refer the client to a professional who is competent to provide an evidence-based service.

CLINICAL PRACTICE GUIDELINES

As you learned earlier in the chapter, clinical practice guidelines are used increasingly by many health care professions to promote evidence-based practice. For example, the Canadian Psychiatric Association has practice guidelines for the treatment of mood disorders, anxiety disorders, and schizophrenia. Health care professionals in the United Kingdom have been at the forefront of efforts to promote evidence-based health care. It is hardly surprising, therefore, that the UK National

Health Service (NHS) has been actively involved in efforts to translate research evidence into recommendations and priorities for health care services. Compared with the limited attention accorded mental health issues in most countries, the inclusion of mental health services in these efforts is especially noteworthy.

Because of a commitment to the translation of scientific findings into the provision of health care services, the NHS in England and Wales developed the National Institute for Health and Care Excellence (NICE) to guide health care professionals and patients in making decisions about health care treatment options. Independent from the NHS, NICE conducts extensive consultations with stakeholder organizations (both professional and consumer groups) in developing evidence-based clinical guidelines. Guidelines are reviewed and updated after several years to ensure their accuracy and completeness. There are clinical guidelines for assessment and treatment services for dozens of conditions. The Institut national d'excellence en santé et services sociaux in the province of Quebec provides guidelines and reviews for a range of health care services (although very little to date on mental health services) and the Institute of Medicine (2008) has called for the development of an American-based organization similar to NICE that would provide unbiased reviews of health care research.

Colin Young-Wolff/PhotoEdit Inc.

The National Institute for Health and Care Excellence (NICE) provides a guideline on the treatment of depression.

With respect to psychological/psychiatric conditions, there are currently guidelines for the treatment of anxiety disorders, mood disorders, eating disorders, substance abuse disorders, personality disorders, schizophrenia, self-harm, and violence, and several others are in development. To develop guidelines related to these conditions, NICE draws upon the expertise of the National Collaborating Centre for Mental Health, which is a joint venture between the British Psychological Society and the Royal College of Psychiatrists that also involves consumer groups and other professional organizations (e.g., those representing occupational therapists, nurses, pharmacists, and general medical practitioners). The involvement of a wide range of stakeholders is intended to ensure that the guidelines are comprehensive and professionally viable. NICE serves as an exemplary model that could be adopted by health care systems in other countries.

Because of the multidisciplinary and collaborative nature of the NICE guidelines development process and the prevalence of depression, we have selected the NICE guideline for the management of depression to illustrate the essence of an evidence-based clinical guideline (NICE, 2009). The 2009 guideline is an update of the initial guideline released in 2004; at the time this book was being written, consultation was underway to determine whether the 2009 version needed to be updated. Exhibit 12.3 provides details on the evidence-based steps recommended in the model. It is important to note the variability in the strength of evidence supporting each of these recommended steps, ranging from relatively strong (meta-analyses of RCTs) to relatively weak (expert committee reports or opinions of respected authorities). Moreover, there is currently no evidence to support the entire stepped care model. It is essential that as guidelines such as these are disseminated, researchers evaluate the validity and usefulness of recommended steps within the model and the service models themselves (cf. Bower & Gilbody, 2005).

What do you think of the NICE depression guideline, especially in terms of its emphasis on the provision of psychotherapy? What about the recommendations with respect to the use of antidepressants? If a friend of yours was looking for information about treatment of depression, would you find this kind of information helpful?

Exhibit 12.3 Stepped Care Model for the Management of Depression

Step 1. Identification and recognition

- Screening for depressive symptoms should be undertaken for patients with a past history of depression or chronic physical health problems with associated functional impairment.
- If there is an immediate risk of self-harm or risk to others, an urgent referral should be made for mental health services

Step 2. Treatment of persistent sub-threshold depressive symptoms or mild to moderate depression

- For these patients, there are a number of options to consider:
  - For those who do not want an intervention or who, in the opinion of the health care professional, may recover with no intervention, a further assessment should be arranged, normally within two weeks.
  - For those who prefer a low-intensity intervention, options include a guided self-help program based on CBT principles, computerized CBT, or structured group physical activity program.
  - For those who decline low-intensity interventions, group CBT should be considered.
- Antidepressants are not routinely recommended for the initial treatment of sub-threshold or mild depression.
- Although there is some evidence that St. John's wort may be of some benefit, it should not be prescribed because of uncertainty about the appropriate dosage to use, variations in the nature of the preparations, and the potential for harmful interactions with other commonly prescribed drugs.

CONTINUED . . .

Step 3. Treatment of (a) persistent sub-threshold depressive symptoms or mild to moderate depression with inadequate response to initial interventions and (b) moderate to severe depression

- For these patients, there are a number of options to consider:
  - Start with offering an antidepressant (normally a selective serotonin reuptake inhibitor SSRI).
  - Offer CBT, IPT, behavioural couples therapy (when appropriate), or behavioural activation (a form of behaviour therapy) to patients who prefer not to take antidepressant medication.
  - For those who decline these options, consider offering either short-term psychodynamic psychotherapy or general counselling.
- For patients with more severe depression, offer a combination of antidepressant medication and either CBT or IPT.

Step 4. Sequencing of treatments after initial inadequate response

- For patients whose depression does not change after initial treatment, the following options should be considered:
  - Offer treatments previously received only if they were inadequately delivered or adhered to.
  - Consider switching from one antidepressant to another antidepressant, but the evidence for the value of this is weak (either within or between classes of antidepressants).
  - Combine individual CBT and antidepressants.
  - Combine one antidepressant with another type of antidepressant medication.
- Augment an antidepressant with a mood stabilizer or an antipsychotic.

Step 5. Treatment of complex and severe depression

- For these patients, the treatment options typically involve multi-professional care:
  - Consider combining medication, psychosocial interventions, and crisis resolution/home treatment teams.
  - Consider inpatient treatment for patients at elevated risk of self-harm or suicide.
  - Consider electroconvulsive therapy for severe symptoms only after adequate trials of other treatments have been ineffective or the severe depression is considered to be potentially life threatening.
- There is insufficient evidence at this time to support the clinical use of transcranial magnetic stimulation, so this procedure should only be used in the context of research studies.

Adapted from NICE (2009).

EXAMPLES OF EVIDENCE-BASED TREATMENTS

CBT for Depression

In the previous chapter, we provided details on the use of IPT for the treatment of depression. We now briefly present another efficacious treatment for depression: cognitive-behavioural therapy. Many variants of CBT for depression have been extensively researched, ranging from those that are predominantly behavioural to those that are primarily cognitive (Emmelkamp, 2013; Hollon & Beck, 2013). We describe below the general form of CBT for depression described by Persons, Davidson, and Tompkins (2001).

The focus of CBT for depression is on altering the behaviours, negative automatic thoughts, and dysfunctional beliefs that are associated with the condition. In working with a depressed individual client using CBT, the psychologist conducts an initial assessment to determine the client's diagnostic status (including comorbid conditions) and to obtain a sense of the client's current life circumstances. Particular attention is paid to the client's relationships and social functioning, the client's psychological resources and strengths, recent events that may have precipitated the depressive episode, and the potential for suicidal behaviour. For example, Persons et al. (2001) described the case of Garrett, a musician who had lost a recording contract and a series of concert bookings. Based on initial assessment information, and in order to guide treatment, a case formulation was developed that related precipitating life events (e.g., loss of the contract and concert dates) to long-standing dysfunctional beliefs (e.g., *I'm a loser*). The case formulation also provided a framework for understanding Garrett's affective, cognitive, and behavioural symptoms. By spending time at home alone instead of his usual socializing, and by spending hours watching television instead of working on his music, Garrett felt increasingly depressed, discouraged, and listless.

Early in the treatment process the client is provided basic information about the nature of depression, the evolving case formulation, and the possible treatment options for addressing the depressive symptoms. As we described in Chapter 11, a CBT model emphasizes a collaboration in which the client participates actively in decision-making throughout treatment, which means that the therapist frequently provides information and lays out the options for addressing the agreed-upon targets for treatment. Throughout treatment, the client is asked to monitor symptoms and changes in functioning to determine the impact of therapy.

Initial sessions tend to focus primarily on behavioural activation tasks, such as getting the client to re-engage in some of the pleasurable activities that he or she used to do prior to the depressive episode. In order to do this, clients are first asked to self-monitor their activities during the day. In the typical case, this yields information that indicates that the client engages in very few pleasurable activities of any kind. To combat the lethargy and dysphoria common in depression, clients are encouraged to actively plan to increase their daily involvement in pleasant activities. This might involve activities such as exercise, going to a movie with a friend, reading a book, or making a special meal. Engaging in any of these pleasant activities is likely to reduce depressed feelings, whereas dwelling on past failures and ruminating about current problems are likely to increase depressed feelings.

As clients attempt to follow through on activity scheduling assignments, they typically express doubts about the point of the assignments and/or their abilities to carry them out. This provides an opportunity for the psychologist to point out the tendency to automatically focus on negative aspects of experiences and reasons for not attempting activities. Usually in the first few sessions this leads to the development of another form of homework assignment for clients that involves thought monitoring. This requires recording the types of thoughts that typically occur around upsetting or difficult situations. Persons et al. (2001) suggest the use of a thought record that includes a description of the situation (e.g., an event, a memory, or an attempt to do something), associated behaviours (e.g., getting into an argument and yelling at someone), associated emotions (e.g., frustration, sadness, and discouragement), and associated thoughts (e.g., *What's the point? I'm such a pushover, I'm such a total failure.)*. You can find some examples of self-monitoring records in Figures 6.2 and 6.3.

At the next stage in treatment, the therapist and client work together to examine how these thoughts influence decisions around behaviours (e.g., yelling rather than acting in a more assertive manner) and the resulting emotional states. The client is then coached to challenge the accuracy of these negative thoughts. Usually, it is easy for clients to acknowledge the link between thoughts such as *I'm a loser* and feelings of discouragement and disengagement from an activity. It takes a great deal of effort and repeated practice, however, for a client to counter this thought with a response such as *No, I'm not a loser; I'm just not very comfortable about handling conflict*. However, once the client is able to do this, it usually opens up a whole range of options for responding differently to a situation than was previously evident. At this point, depending on the client's needs, the psychologist may help the client develop skills in areas such as assertiveness, problem-solving, or time management.

In the next stage of treatment, the primary focus is on examining and challenging the long-standing beliefs or schemas held by the client that render the client vulnerable to depression when confronted by negative life events. This involves helping the client to see patterns in the assumptions the client makes about himself or herself and events in his or her life. These assumptions are often along the lines of beliefs such as *There is something basically wrong with me, good things never happen to me, I can never succeed at anything important,* and *I'm not a lovable person.* Building on the behavioural and cognitive skills honed earlier in treatment, the client is encouraged to challenge these beliefs both cognitively and by engaging in personal experiments to test the accuracy of the assumption.

The final stage of treatment focuses on relapse prevention. The gains achieved by the client are reviewed, as are the specific skills the client

Self-monitoring is an important element of CBT for depression.

learned or rediscovered. The clinician encourages the client to imagine events that might cause self-doubt and helps the client explore the most adaptive ways (both behavioural and cognitive) to respond to such events. Profile Box 12.2 introduces Dr. Peter Bieling who studies the use of CBT and related interventions in the treatment of adult depression.

PROFILE BOX 12.2

DR. PETER BIELING

Courtesy of Peter Bieling

I completed my B.Sc. (Hons.) at the University of Victoria, M.A. and Ph.D. at the University of British Columbia, an internship at the Centre for Addiction and Mental Health, University of Toronto, and a postdoctoral fellowship at the University of Pennsylvania Centre for Cognitive Therapy. I am now an associate professor in the Department of Psychiatry and Behavioural Neurosciences at McMaster University and a director in the Mental Health and Addiction Program at St. Joseph's Healthcare in Hamilton, Ontario. My research focuses on mood disorders, the effectiveness of cognitive therapy, emerging treatments and treatment models, and quality of mental health services delivery. I have been awarded research funding through provincial, national, and international agencies and have authored numerous articles and three books. I am a licensed psychologist in the province of Ontario.

HOW DID YOU CHOOSE TO BECOME A CLINICAL PSYCHOLOGIST?

During my adolescence, I loved two things that seemed to me to have nothing in common: people and science. I always found the details of people's lives interesting. I was fascinated not just by the fun, frivolous stuff, but also by why people struggled and endured, why they did what they did (even when it seemed to my teenage eye to be dysfunctional), and what they would do next. At that time, my other interest, science, seemed completely incompatible with my interest in people. I thought science was about beakers, Newton's laws, and equations. But that was fun, because science told you the truth in a way that human experience just couldn't.

It wasn't until I took an abnormal psychology course later in university that the light went on. I recognized that here was exactly the kind of mash-up I needed. Psychology involved working with people and their problems, to understand the people who had these problems and how we can help. Once I saw that, all other career options just went by the wayside. I became absolutely determined to become a psychologist and never really considered anything else. There are still days when I can't quite believe they pay me to be a psychologist, because it just feels like breathing to me.

WHAT IS THE GREATEST CHALLENGE YOU FACE AS A CLINICAL PSYCHOLOGIST?

There are just so many worthwhile things I feel I should spend my time on, and it's hard sometimes to prioritize when I'm pulled in lots of directions. Although I love that I don't just do the same thing every day, it can be a double- edged sword.

There's also been a real explosion in knowledge since I started seriously working in the field. The number of publications and the amount of data we generate are much harder to keep up with than when I started. It's a bit like surfing a wave of information: it requires a lot of work to stay on your board and you don't want to fall behind or feel swamped. It is never boring, that's for sure!

CONTINUED . . .

TELL US ABOUT YOUR RESEARCH ON TREATMENT OF DEPRESSION

Depression remains fascinating to me. It's a human emotion that we can all relate to, which makes it seem like the kind of problem that we ought to be able to grapple with quickly and completely. However, as a scientist and clinician, I realize that there is so much we do not know yet. Although decades of research have taught us a lot about depression, many fundamental issues are still murky. I find it totally satisfying to push at the boundaries of what we know. My curiosity has led me to ask questions about what kinds of treatments work best, whether different treatments work better at different points during the course of a person's depression, and whether it makes a difference what setting the treatment is delivered in. These questions we ask about depression need to be answered for almost every psychological and medical issue. Generally speaking, we don't spend enough time evaluating what we do, both with mental health and medical problems. In this sense, psychology has kind of a special place because we're the profession that cares the most deeply about science and practice, that believes strongly what we do makes a difference, and that can show many of our services work beyond any doubt.

HOW DO YOU INTEGRATE SCIENCE AND PRACTICE IN YOUR WORK?

The bottom line: by reading good sources and by practising with people what I learn from those sources. There's so much information generated through careful research that there are now all kinds of knowledge syntheses that summarize the research and tell you what you need to know. This effort to synthesize is relatively recent, and I think a boon to busy practitioners who want to do the best for their patients. It wasn't possible 20 years ago, and not even 10 years ago, to type a problem into a search engine and then generate a list of summaries of strategies that work for a problem (and, as importantly, that don't work).

WHAT DO YOU SEE AS THE MOST EXCITING CHANGES IN THE FIELD OF CLINICAL PSYCHOLOGY?

In my opinion, the world is coming to be increasingly focused on the evidence base for various health care services. Psychologists have always studied and evaluated what they do and tried to prove the difference they make. Medicine, economics, and politics have increasingly turned toward this same philosophy: that it isn't enough to do some kind of intervention and assume that things change for the better. You have to make sure that it works, to rule out other possible reasons for observed change, and to make sure that things you do don't also cause unintentional harm. There are so many fields now that begin with "evidence-based ...." It can be argued that we started all of that, and that we'll have a central place in those efforts.

Prolonged Exposure CBT for PTSD

You will notice similarities in the CBT approach to treating depression and PTSD, as there are features that are common to CBT treatment across disorders. These include the importance of a thorough initial assessment to develop a case formulation to guide treatment, the provision of information to the patient throughout treatment (about both the patient's condition and the rationale for specific treatment strategies), the development of a collaborative relationship between psychologist and patient, the use of between-session assignments, the ongoing monitoring of treatment impact, and attention to relapse prevention issues.

Media Bakery

Relaxation strategies are used in dealing with anxiety.

There are, however, several treatment components that are specific to the prolonged exposure treatment of PTSD (Cook, Schnurr, & Foa, 2004; Rothbaum & Schwartz, 2002).

Treatment begins with an assessment of the patient's condition and the provision of psychoeducational information about the nature of PTSD and the nature of the CBT approach. There are three broad components to CBT for PTSD: use of relaxation skills, imaginal exposure, and in vivo exposure. Because patients are asked to confront images and situations that cause them severe emotional upset, it is important that the psychologist help patients develop or enhance their relaxation skills. This can involve the use of progressive muscle relaxation, breathing retraining, and/or cognitive strategies for self-soothing. In many instances, patients are given reading materials or CDs to assist them in practising these relaxation skills at home. In most cases, treatment then moves to the use of imaginal exposure.

As part of the initial assessment process, patients will have already described the events, situations, and memories that are most disturbing to them. During treatment sessions patients are asked to close their eyes and to recount these traumatic experiences for an extended period (typically more than 30 minutes), using the present tense and providing as much contextual details as possible (e.g., smells, sounds, their own thoughts, and physical reactions). This imaginal exposure encourages the patient to begin to fully emotionally process the trauma that was experienced. This allows patients to (a) revisit details of the trauma and gain new perspective on what happened and what might have occurred; (b) distinguish between remembering the event (which is not inherently dangerous) and re-encountering the event (which could be dangerous); (c) develop a consistent, organized narrative of what occurred; (d) learn that remembering the events can lead to an overall reduction in anxiety and other symptoms; and (e) develop a new appreciation for what they did to survive the trauma (Cook et al., 2004). These imaginal exposure sessions are usually recorded, and the patient is asked to listen to the recording repeatedly between sessions in order to promote emotional processing.

In vivo exposure is used to assist patients in reducing distress associated with encountering stimuli that remind them of the trauma. This can include stimuli such as sounds (for a patient traumatized in a car accident, this could be hearing a car braking hard) and smells (for a patient who was raped, this could be the smell of the rapist's cologne), as well as common situations such as driving a car (for the car accident victim) or walking by a body of water (for someone who almost died in a flash flood). The psychologist develops a hierarchy of feared stimuli with the patient and encourages the patient to intentionally expose himself or herself to increasingly fearful stimuli. By having patients repeatedly expose themselves to these stimuli, anxiety is reduced, a sense of self-efficacy is developed, and the opportunity for engaging in a broader range of activities (instead of avoiding certain situations) is enhanced.

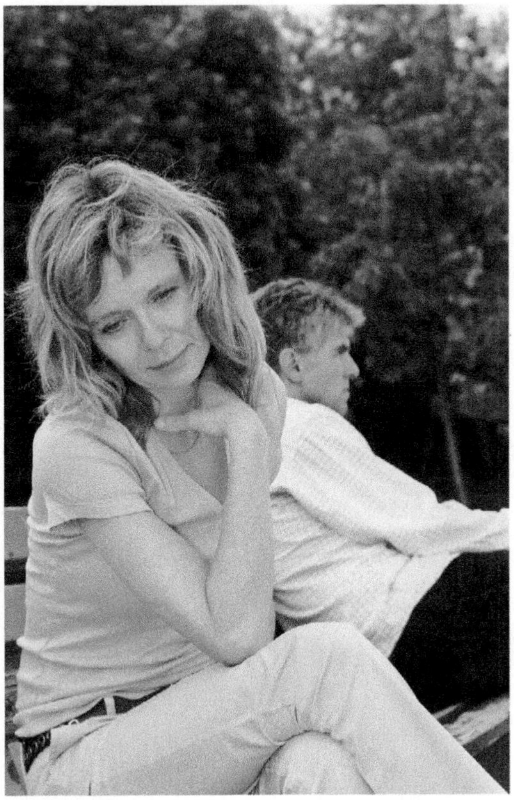

Media Bakery

EFT is designed to help couples re-establish an emotional bond.

EFT for Couple Distress

Emotionally focused couples therapy (EFT) is a process-experiential treatment combining an experiential approach to affect with a systemic focus on the way in which relationship behaviours can develop into cyclical, self-perpetuating interactional patterns. The key factors in relational distress are assumed to be the ongoing construction of absorbing states of negative affect and destructive interactional sequences that arise from, reflect, and then prime this distressing affect (Johnson, Hunsley, Greenberg, & Schindler, 1999). Accordingly, the main goals of EFT for couple distress are to (a) modify emotional responses and constricted, rigid interactional patterns and (b) foster the establishment or enhancement of a secure emotional bond in the couple (Johnson, 2004).

The psychologist providing EFT for couple distress must address each partner's affect and each partner's perspective on interactional problems. Partners are not seen as deficient in their ability to manage interpersonal issues, but rather as needing assistance in formulating and presenting their attachment-related needs and fears to each other. To bring about change in the couple, the psychologist must find ways to generate new emotional experiences and new interactional experiences for both partners. As with any form of couple treatment, this can be very challenging as partners in distressed relationships typically develop habitual strategies for protecting themselves and attributing the lion's share of responsibility for their problems to the other partner.

There are nine steps in EFT designed to bring about the necessary changes in the couple. In mildly distressed couples, it is common for both partners to work quickly through the nine steps at a similar pace. In couples with greater distress, the more withdrawn or passive partner is encouraged to go through the steps ahead of the other partner. It is assumed that as the more passive partner becomes engaged in the process, it will be easier for the more active or critical partner to trust that the passive partner is truly committed to the change process.

The first four steps involve assessment and de-escalation of problematic interpersonal cycles. Step 1 involves the formation of an alliance with each partner and the development and presentation of a case conceptualization of the couple's core conflicts from an attachment perspective. Step 2 is devoted to the identification of the problematic interpersonal cycle that maintains the insecure attachment and the affective distress. The third and fourth steps focus on accessing the emotions underlying each partner's position in the relationship and then presenting their core relationship conflicts as stemming from these underlying emotions and attachment needs.

The next three steps are designed to promote change in each partner's interactional position. In Step 5, each partner is encouraged to identify and accept psychological needs that he or she disowned or suppressed and to integrate these needs into the relationship. Step 6 requires each partner to learn to accept the other's new approach to the relationship. As partners adjust to these changes, Step 7 focuses on facilitating this adjustment by ensuring emotional engagement in the couple. The final two steps focus on developing new solutions to old relationship problems (Step 8) and consolidating these new solutions and the partners' new relationship positions (Step 9).

EFFECTIVENESS TRIALS

Throughout the text we have highlighted the distinction between efficacy and effectiveness several times. As we mentioned earlier in the book, it is important to know about the effectiveness of usual clinical treatments (Hansen, Lambert, & Forman, 2002). So far, we have presented a sample of the substantial literature on treatment efficacy. However, it is vital to consider evidence that efficacious treatments (developed in controlled research studies) are effective in clinical settings. As we discussed previously, reservations have been voiced about the representativeness of the patients included in typical efficacy trials (e.g., Westen & Morrison, 2001).

It is encouraging that accumulating data indicate that many treatments demonstrating positive results in efficacy trials also have a substantial impact in effectiveness trials. In other words, contrary to some initial concerns, it now appears that many efficacious treatments can be transported into routine clinical practice without much loss of treatment impact. Equally important, there is accumulating evidence that these treatments can be effective for patients from differing ethnic backgrounds (e.g., Miranda et al., 2005). There is, for example, evidence that CBT is effective for a range of anxiety disorders. Based on a meta-analysis of 56 effectiveness studies, Stewart and Chambless (2009) found that treatment outcomes were comparable to results obtained in high-quality RCTs of these treatments.

The strongest evidence for the transportability to clinical settings of a treatment for a specific adult disorder is for CBT for depression. Hans and Hiller (2013) conducted a meta-analysis on effectiveness studies of this treatment, drawing on 34 studies conducted in the United States, United Kingdom, and several continental European countries. These studies were conducted with patients who were seeking treatment for depression, and services were provided by clinicians who differed in (a) their background training (including both doctoral- and master-level clinicians) and (b) their experience in providing CBT for depression. The researchers found compelling evidence for the effectiveness of both individual and group formats of CBT, with within-group effect sizes of approximately $d = 1.0$. Although impressive, these effectiveness results were somewhat less than what has been obtained in the highest quality RCTs of these treatments. This may have been due, at least in part, to the greater heterogeneity found in effectiveness samples than in samples used in the RCTs.

How can the results of effectiveness studies add to our knowledge of the impact of psychological treatments?

In effectiveness studies, it is common to use what is known as a **benchmarking strategy** to evaluate the impact of a treatment. This involves using the results of efficacy trials to form a standard (or a benchmark) against which the services provided to *regular* patients by *regular* clinicians can be compared. In some cases, such as with the Stewart and Chambless (2009) and Hans and Hiller (2013) meta-analyses, the benchmark is based on results obtained from the best available RCTs of the treatments. Another option is to develop benchmarks based on meta-analyses of the treatment, which is what Hunsley and Lee (2007) did in their examination of treatment completion and treatment outcome in effectiveness studies. For example, in the treatment of adult depression and anxiety disorders, they found that more than 75% of patients in most effectiveness studies followed the course of services to completion. This was comparable to completion rates reported in relevant meta-analyses. In terms of the outcome of treatment, most of the effectiveness studies reported results that were comparable or superior to derived from meta-analytic estimates for each condition. Thus, based on the benchmarking strategy, there is evidence from various countries that evidence-based treatments can be very effective when used in routine practice settings. Viewpoint Box 12.2 presents some important examples of how evidence-based treatments are being disseminated in such settings.

benchmarking strategy: the use of data from empirical studies to provide a comparison against which the effectiveness of clinical services can be gauged.

Do you think that knowing that a treatment has supporting evidence in effectiveness studies is important? Are such data more important than data from efficacy studies? How do you think practising clinicians might view the relevance of effectiveness data?

VIEWPOINT BOX 12.2

DISSEMINATION OF EVIDENCE-BASED TREATMENTS

Demonstrating the efficacy of a treatment is a demanding and time-consuming task, requiring many years and the involvement of many, many people. Until recently, psychotherapy researchers paid relatively little attention to what happened after a treatment was shown to be efficacious. What needs to happen to ensure that clinicians adopt and use an efficacious treatment? In the past it was often assumed that (a) the onus was on the clinicians to somehow learn to use the treatment and (b) researchers had no role to play in facilitating the adoption of treatments, other than writing user-friendly treatment guides and providing one- or two-day training workshops. As you will see in the final sections of this chapter, this is no longer the case, and considerable efforts are made to understand how best to ensure that evidence-based treatments are available across a range of clinical settings.

Through the Veterans Health Administration, the U.S. Department of Veterans Affairs has been a leader in the dissemination and implementation of evidence-based psychological treatments, and in the subsequent evaluation of these services as they are delivered throughout the United States. These efforts have included treatments for PTSD (cognitive processing therapy, prolonged exposure therapy), depression (cognitive-behavioural therapy for depression), and insomnia (cognitive-behavioural therapy for insomnia), with full training and continuing supervision/consultation being provided to hundreds of clinicians working in Veterans Administration medical centres (Karlin et al. 2010; Karlin et al., 2012; Karlin, Trockel, Taylor, Gimeno, & Manber, 2013). Substantial decreases in symptoms and improvements in psychosocial functioning have been reported for patients receiving services in all of the dissemination projects. Importantly, across the dissemination projects, evaluations revealed that most of the clinicians continued to use the treatments in which they had trained.

In the most ambitious dissemination and implementation project to date, the Improving Access to Psychological Therapies (IAPT) initiative began in the National Health Service in England in 2006. The primary goal was to train, by 2014, 6,000 new therapists (including psychologists and many other mental health professionals) who could competently deliver evidence-based treatment for depression and anxiety disorders. As described by Clark (2013), by any standard this initiative has been an impressive success. Initial pilot projects were undertaken in two major sites, using the low-intensity therapies and stepped care model described in Exhibit 12.3. Many new therapists were recruited and trained. During the first year of the pilot work, more than 3,500 people received services, with over half of treated patients being evaluated as having recovered (i.e., having symptom scores below clinical cut-off levels).

Following the success of the pilot work, a phased national roll-out of the program commenced. Government funding was provided to train 3,600 new therapists (60% trained in CBT; 40% trained to provide low-intensity services) and to have these new therapists working in health care settings throughout England. Therapists are taught at least two evidence-based treatments for depression (cognitive behavioural therapy for depression, behavioural activation) and at least one evidence-based treatment for each anxiety disorder. Further funding will be used to train 2,400 therapists in the other psychological services recommended in the NICE (2009) guideline: interpersonal psychotherapy, behavioural couples therapy, brief psychodynamic psychotherapy, and counselling for depression. In 2013, across the country, approximately two-thirds of IAPT-treated patients showed reliable improvement, and almost half achieved clinical recovery. By 2014, IAPT services will be provided to approximately 900,000 per year, which is 15% of those in the community with clinically significant depression and anxiety condition, More details on the IAPT, along with relevant research reports, can be found at www.iapt.nhs.uk.

ADOPTION OF EVIDENCE-BASED TREATMENTS

Rarely a day goes by without a media announcement of a breakthrough in the treatment of some health condition or disease. Hearing such news reports, you probably realize that it will take time for the breakthrough to trickle down so that it is available in routine health services. It is unlikely, however, that the average person realizes all of the barriers that can impede the introduction of innovations into health care systems. In some cases, such as the introduction of a new vaccine, there are established laboratory and public health systems that can facilitate the relatively rapid development and distribution of the vaccine. Unfortunately, this is rarely the case for evidence-based innovations in psychological interventions.

There are a number of reasons for this state of affairs. One reason is that psychological interventions, unlike pharmaceutical interventions, cannot be patented. Pharmaceutical companies typically devote enormous sums of money to advertising and promoting their treatments. This includes targeting the health care professionals who prescribe the product and, in some countries, directly advertising to potential consumers. When a psychological treatment has been found to be efficacious (and even effective), there is no comparable process for disseminating the information and rapidly training psychologists to provide the treatment. Ethical codes and professional guidelines also prohibit most types of advertising of psychological services. A second reason is that there is often more to learning how to provide an efficacious psychological treatment than there is to learning how to appropriately prescribe a new medication. In this regard, the training necessary to appropriately provide the intervention is akin to what is required for surgeons to learn and use new surgical procedures. Reading the research reports and details on the indications and contraindications for a new drug may be sufficient for responsible prescribing, but such steps are unlikely to be sufficient for surgery or psychotherapy.

To effectively provide psychological services, the clinician requires background preparatory work, specialized training, and closely supervised experience in providing the intervention. Calhoun, Moras, Pilkonis, and Rehm (1998), for example, recommended that a clinical psychologist wishing to attain adequate skill in the delivery of a psychological treatment should be supervised in providing the treatment to at least three or four *typical* patients and a comparable number of *atypical* patients (i.e., those with more complex or chronic problems). At this time, even though many jurisdictions require clinical psychologists to engage in continuing education activities, there are few structured opportunities for practising psychologists to obtain this intensity of training (cf. Arnow, 1999). In a survey of 206 clinical psychologists and other mental health professionals, Nelson and Steele (2008) asked respondents about the treatment factors that influenced their selection of treatments to offer clients. As shown in Exhibit 12.4, psychologists were influenced by the availability of research supporting a treatment. Importantly, factors associated with learning a treatment were very influential in clinicians' decisions to use a treatment. This type of finding underscores the critical need for access to training opportunities in evidence-based treatments.

Exhibit 12.4 Treatment Factors Influencing Clinicians' Treatment Selection Decisions

1. Treatment flexibility
2. Research support in an effectiveness study
3. Recommended by trusted colleague(s)
4. Past success with the treatment in own practice
5. Easy to learn and implement
6. Easily accessible training and supervision in the treatment
7. Research support in an efficacy study
8. A focus on the therapeutic relationship
9. Reimbursement for treatment by insurance company
10. Short treatment duration

Adapted from Nelson and Steele (2008).

Beyond the issue of the availability of training, there are myriad potential barriers to the adoption of evidence-based treatments by psychologists and other health care professionals. These include systems-level factors such as the extent of organizational support for learning and providing cutting-edge interventions, and individual-level factors such as motivation, knowledge, and skill. Given the clear indication that there are evidence-based treatments for many (if not most) disorders, it is important to understand the barriers to their application. At the systems level, many institutions employing clinical psychologists are under great pressure to reduce waiting lists. There is, as a result, often a tension between the need to devote time to developing new skills and the need to devote this professional time to immediate patient care.

Even in doctoral training, where the expectation is that proportionally more time is devoted to skill development than to patient services, students may face significant challenges in learning about evidence-based treatments. Weissman et al. (2006) found that, in a survey of accredited doctoral programs in clinical psychology, 44% of Ph.D. programs and 67% of Psy.D. programs did not require any training in evidence-based treatments. Hays et al. (2002) reported that, in their survey of APA-accredited internships, 19% of internships reported little or no time spent on providing training and supervision in ESTs, with only 28% reporting that they spent more than 15 hours of training and supervision in ESTs during the internship year. Finally, and perhaps of greatest concern, in a survey of almost 1,200 graduate students in clinical psychology programs, Luebbe, Radcliffe, Callands, Green, and Thorn (2007) found that the nature of a treatment's empirical support was among the least important factors influencing students' treatment planning decisions. As guidance from supervisors was the most important factor in these decisions, this underscores the central roles that program requirements and faculty modelling of sound professional practices must play in the dissemination of evidence-based treatments.

Now that you know that clinical programs differ in the extent to which they provide training in evidence-based practice, if you were applying to graduate programs, how important would it be for you to find a program that has a strong commitment to training in evidence-based practice?

Addis, Wade, and Hatgis (1999) summarized many of the individual-level factors that obstruct the widespread adoption of evidence-based treatments by psychologists. These include concerns about the feasibility of implementing manual-based treatments, the possible lack of fit between client needs and available evidence-based treatments, the impact that manual-based treatments might have on the therapeutic relationship with clients, and the possibility for decreased job satisfaction among psychologists. In a survey of almost 900 psychologists, Addis and Krasnow (2000) found consistent associations between experience with offering manual-based treatments and attitudes toward such treatments: the psychologists with the strongest negative views on these treatments were those least likely to have familiarity with the nature of manual-based treatments.

If we know that a treatment is successful in research studies, what are the barriers to its routine implementation?

Despite individual- and systems-level challenges, many psychologists provide evidence-based treatments and are motivated to learn to use such treatments. For example, in a survey of clinical psychologists who provide treatments for eating disorders, Mussell et al. (2000) found that although 70% of respondents reported using evidence-based treatment techniques, approximately 75% of these psychologists reported having received no formal training in the provision of CBT or IPT for eating disorders. For many of these psychologists, this probably indicated a commitment on their part to learn these treatments on their own after graduation. Importantly though, more than 80% of respondents indicated a desire to obtain formal training in the approach. More recently, von Ransom, Wallace, and Stevenson (2013) interviewed 118 clinicians (including psychologists, psychiatrists, physicians, and social workers) who provided psychotherapy for eating disorders. As in the Mussell et al. survey, most respondents reported using components of evidence-based treatments. However, almost 20% reported never using CBT or IPT in the treatment of bulimia nervosa or binge-eating disorder (the only evidence-based treatments listed in Exhibit 12.2). Numerous reasons were given for not using these treatments (e.g., *incompatible with my clinical style; my clinical experience indicated the treatment was ineffective*), but the bottom line was that these clinicians appeared to be comfortable in routinely offering eating disorder treatments that did not have an evidence base.

Commitment to the use of evidence-based treatments may be influenced by the nature of the clients' presenting problems and the nature of the treatment. As discussed earlier in the chapter, exposure is a key component of efficacious treatments for PTSD. A survey of psychologists providing PTSD treatments found that only one in four had received training in the use of exposure and only 17% reported using any form of exposure in their treatments of clients with PTSD (Becker, Zayfert, & Anderson, 2004). Numerous reasons for not using exposure were reported, including lack of familiarity with the technique, concerns about the appropriateness of the technique (e.g., clients presenting with comorbid disorders), and concerns about complications that could arise from using exposure (e.g., increased symptoms, dissociation). Although concerns about client suitability and well-being strongly influenced psychologists' perceptions about the usefulness of exposure, few if any of their concerns are likely to be valid when exposure is used in a clinically sensitive manner (Cook et al., 2004). Indeed, exposure-based treatment for PTSD has been successfully adapted for use in other cultures, such as in the treatment of traumatized Ugandan refugees (Neuner, Schauer, Klaschik, Karunakara, & Elbert, 2004).

Clearly, much more must be done in the education and continuing education of clinical psychologists (and other mental health professionals) to promote the use of evidence-based practices. Accreditation requirements for training in these practices should continue to influence what is taught in both doctoral training programs and internships. Beyond that, many psychologists are working on developing models to develop, disseminate, and implement evidence-based treatments (e.g., Gotham, 2004; Rotheram-Borus, Swendeman, & Chorpita, 2012; Stirman, Crits-Christoph, & DeRubeis, 2004). A key element of such models is that psychologists who conduct treatment research and psychologists who provide real-world services must both be involved as active and equal participants in efforts to adapt and implement these treatments in clinical settings. Psychological science has much to offer patients suffering from diverse health conditions, but efforts to disseminate treatment breakthroughs must take into account the challenges facing the front-line clinicians who, ultimately, have the task of providing psychological services.

SUMMARY AND CONCLUSIONS

The second half of the 20th century was a period of rapid growth in the development and evaluation of psychological interventions for a variety of disorders. Passionate debates pitted proponents of one school of thinking against another. All of this occurred against a backdrop of shrinking health care budgets, increasing concerns about accountability, and growing reliance on practice guidelines. Psychologists used a range of strategies of varying methodological sophistication to examine whether or not their treatments worked. Meta-analysis became an important tool in integrating findings from the growing body of literature. Because meta-analysis requires an explicit statement about the decision rules for including a study and for weighting its findings, meta-analysis itself has been the subject of fierce debate, with many of the original criticisms of meta-analysis leading to important modifications in the procedure.

Many interdisciplinary efforts have focused on achieving consensus about (a) the criteria for determining when a treatment is evidence-based and (b) routes for disseminating information about efficacious treatments. Overall, the results with respect to psychological treatments are encouraging, as there appear to be effective treatments for many mental disorders and other health and mental health conditions. Cognitive-behavioural approaches are prominent in the lists of evidence-based treatments. This can be explained in part by CBT's emphasis on establishing clear treatment goals and requiring the ongoing monitoring of treatment efficacy. The armamentarium of effective treatments for some conditions also includes interpersonal, psychodynamic, and process-experiential interventions. With the encouraging data on treatment efficacy and growing evidence from effectiveness studies, there is a solid scientific basis for many treatments offered by clinical psychology. Nevertheless, there are barriers to the implementation of evidence-based services and they occur at many levels. They include limited graduate and postgraduate training opportunities and the limited interest of some clinicians to learn how to provide evidence-based treatments. Nevertheless, national dissemination efforts in the United States and England demonstrate that large numbers of psychologists and other mental health professionals can be trained to provide evidence-based treatments for common mental disorders in adults.

KEY TERMS

benchmarking strategy: the use of data from empirical studies to provide a comparison against which the effectiveness of clinical services can be gauged.

clinical practice guidelines: a summary of scientific research, dealing with the diagnosis, assessment, and/or treatment of a disorder, designed to provide guidance to clinicians providing services to patients with the disorder.

effect size: a standardized metric, typically expressed in standard deviation units or correlations, that allows the results of research studies to be combined and analyzed.

empirically supported treatment: a psychotherapy that has been found, in a series of randomized controlled trials or single-participant designs, to be efficacious in the treatment of a specific condition.

meta-analysis: a set of statistical procedures for quantitatively summarizing the results of a research domain.

open trial: a type of initial, exploratory treatment study in which no control group is used and, typically, few participant exclusion criteria are applied.

randomized controlled trial: an experiment in which research participants are randomly assigned to one of two or more treatment conditions.

KEY NAMES

Dianne Chambless

Hans Eysenck

Gene Glass

Mary Smith

Drew Westen

ADDITIONAL RESOURCES

Books

First, M. B., & Tasman, A. (2004). *DSM-IV-TR mental disorders: Diagnosis, etiology, and treatment.* New York: John Wiley & Sons, Inc.

Nathan, P., & Gorman, J. M. (Eds.). (2007). *A guide to treatments that work* (3rd ed.). New York: Oxford University Press.

Roth, A., & Fonagy, P. (2005). *What works for whom? A critical review of psychotherapy research* (2nd ed.). New York: Guilford Press.

Journals

American Journal of Psychiatry

Archives of General Psychiatry

Behavior Therapy

Clinical Psychology: Science and Practice

Journal of Consulting and Clinical Psychology

Check It Out!

There are many reputable sources of information on evidence-based psychotherapies. Here are some of the best websites available.

The Society of Clinical Psychology's site on Psychological Treatments: div12.org/PsychologicalTreatments

NICE Clinical Guidelines: www.nice.org.uk/page.aspx?o=guidelines.completed

Canadian Psychiatric Association Practice Guidelines: publications.cpa-apc.org/browse/documents/67

American Psychiatric Association Practice Guidelines: www.psychiatry.org/practice/clinical-practice-guidelines

Centre for Evidence-Based Mental Health: www.cebmh.com

Best Treatments (for mental health conditions, from the *British Medical Journal*): www.besttreatments.org/btus/health-topic/mental-health.jsp

Evidence-Based Behavioral Practice: www.ebbp.org

INTERVENTION: CHILDREN AND ADOLESCENTS

13 CHAPTER

INTRODUCTION

In Chapter 12, we described the debates over the efficacy and effectiveness of psychotherapy for adults, the development of psychotherapy research, issues and controversies over evidence-based practice, as well as the emergence of clinical practice guidelines. Many issues in the psychological treatment of childhood disorders mirror the themes that were presented with respect to adults. Because we assume that you are now familiar with the material in Chapter 12, we will first explore ways that child services are different from services for adults. We will then highlight landmarks in the evolution of evidence-based psychological treatments for childhood disorders. We will illustrate some evidence-based treatments for common childhood problems, and, finally, we will consider issues related to generalizing, from efficacy trials to regular clinical practice.

In this chapter, we return to the case of Noah, whom we introduced in Chapter 3. He is the adolescent boy who had been traumatized by the genocide in his country of origin. By describing the psychological treatment Noah received, we explain how evidence-based strategies can be applied in situations for which there is currently no comprehensive evidence-based treatment package.

WHO IS THE CLIENT IN PSYCHOLOGICAL SERVICES FOR CHILDREN AND ADOLESCENTS?

Adult psychotherapy usually involves an individual client working with a mental health professional to address an identified problem. In most cases, the adult seeks services after recognizing that there is a problem.

What are some of the major differences between services for children and adolescents and services for adults?

As you may remember learning in Chapter 11, psychological services cannot be imposed on a client: informed consent is required. Children and youth rarely refer themselves for psychological services. It is highly unlikely that 12-year-old Isaac would ask for psychological services because he realized that his inattentiveness, impulsiveness, and distractibility were interfering with his capacity to learn, that he was disrupting the class, and that the series of infractions at school seemed to be cascading toward expulsion. Similarly, it is unlikely that 7-year-old Sara, who has stayed home from school with a series of physical ailments that have no physiological basis and who is fearful of harm befalling her mother, would take the initiative to seek psychological help. Instead, young people are brought for psychological services by adults who are troubled or concerned by the young person's behaviour.

In Chapter 9, you learned that there is an imperfect match between the views of young people, their parents, and their teachers on the nature of the problem. Similarly, there is poor agreement between parents and youth about the goals for psychological services. The child or youth may not believe there is a problem: according to 9-year-old Raheem, for example, the only problem is that his mom is picky and his teacher is strict and, if only both those adults would get off his case and stop hassling him about the importance of tidying up his room and doing his homework, then there would be no problem. For his mother and teacher, though, Raheem's non-compliance has reached the point where both are frustrated in their search for ways to positively influence him. Fifteen-year-old Jia, who has been feeling very low and who cuts her arms when she is distressed, may know that there is a problem. Despite her parents' insistence that she see some doctor they found, she is far from confident that it would make any difference to talk to some old person of 35 who has a boring office with certificates on the wall and who couldn't possibly understand what she is feeling.

Children and youth do not have the resources to seek, attend, and pay for psychological services independently. Unless services are provided within the school context or parents facilitate attendance by seeking a referral, arranging transportation, and paying for services, it is unlikely that children and youth will receive outpatient psychological services. For example, data from the Great Smoky Mountain study of 1,420 adolescents revealed that only one in three adolescents requiring services for psychopathology received them (Costello, Copeland, Cowell, & Keeler, 2007).

©iStock.com/asiseeit

Adolescents and their parents often differ in their views on the need for treatment.

Parents generally serve as gatekeepers for psychological services for their children. This can have some important implications. Miller and Prinz (2003) found that when treatment of childhood conduct problems did not match parents' understanding of the child's problem, parents were less likely to engage in treatment. Furthermore, even though parent motivation seems to be a necessary condition for the young person to attend psychological services, it is not sufficient for positive change to be achieved. This was underscored in a study in which young people receiving outpatient mental health services and their parents rated the alliance with the therapist (Hawley & Weisz, 2005). The *parent*-therapist alliance was related to participation in therapy, with those parents who reported a stronger alliance participating more in services and cancelling fewer sessions. The *youth*-therapist alliance was related to reports of improvements in symptoms. The results of this study illustrate that unless parents are convinced that the therapy is useful, it will be difficult for the youth to participate; however, unless the young person is collaboratively engaged with the therapist, there will be limited change in his or her symptoms.

Legal issues around consent for psychological services for a child or adolescent are complex. Depending on the context in which services are offered (e.g., through schools, mental health clinics, hospitals, child protection agencies, or in the office of private psychologists), consent laws may be included in legislation that deals with education services, health services, or child protection. This means that the psychologist must be knowledgeable about the specific legislation that covers psychological services in the type of agency in which he or she works. In some jurisdictions, consent procedures are determined by the young person's chronological age. According to an age criterion, for example, children under 12 can receive psychological services only with the consent of a parent or legal guardian. In other jurisdictions, there is no age criterion and the psychologist must determine whether each young client can understand what is involved in treatment and therefore can legally consent to services. The psychologist must also be knowledgeable about consent laws concerning separated or divorced parents.

Jorge's situation illustrates how difficult these issues can be. Jorge is a 14-year-old who suffers from moderately severe symptoms of Tourette's disorder (frequent facial and vocal tics). He has developed severe social anxiety disorder because of his embarrassment about his tics. His parents, who are very concerned about his emotional and social functioning, brought him to see a clinical psychologist. Jorge's diagnostic status was clear to the psychologist based on interviews with the parents and an interview with Jorge. It was also clear to the psychologist, however, that Jorge generally understood the nature of his problems and was not willing to be involved in any treatment aimed at alleviating his distress. The psychologist explained both the likely benefits of therapy and the likely prognosis if his problems went untreated. Again, Jorge understood these things. According to the laws regarding competency to consent to health services in the jurisdiction, the psychologist had no choice but to explain to the distraught parents that their son was not willing to engage in treatment. The only option available for the family at that point was for the parents to consider involvement in a local family support group for Tourette's disorder or involvement in family-focused services (without Jorge) aimed at helping them encourage Jorge to increase his social activities.

It should not surprise you to learn that although legal consent to receive services is a necessary condition for treatment, it is not sufficient to ensure cooperation with the services. You can probably imagine the scene in which Jia's parents have insisted that she come to a mental health clinic. Not wanting to create a scene in front of a stranger, Jia has signed a consent to services, but she effectively communicates disinterest in the process by sitting hunched in the chair, her hoodie and hair concealing most of her face, rolling her eyes, and answering most questions with *I dunno*. Confidentiality issues are often complex in services with children and youth. The psychologist must clarify from the outset of services the circumstances under which confidentiality will be maintained and what information will be shared with parents. As we described in Chapter 6, laws require the psychologist to report situations in which a child is in need of protection. At the outset of services, the psychologist also explains who has access to material in the client's file. Profile Box 13.1 introduces Dr. Graham Reid, a clinical psychologist whose research focuses on access to and use of mental health services by children and their families.

Profile Box 13.1

DR. GRAHAM REID

Courtesy of Graham Reid

I completed my Ph.D. in child clinical psychology at Bowling Green State University in Ohio, my internship at the Children's Hospital of Eastern Ontario, and a postdoctoral fellowship in the area of pediatric pain at the IWK Children's Hospital (now part of the IWK Health Centre) in Halifax. After a short-term contract as a psychologist at the Nova Scotia Rehabilitation Centre and Victoria General Hospital in Halifax, I took a position at the Toronto General Hospital that combined clinical work and research focused on adult behavioural cardiology. My interest in child-clinical and health services research, and a desire to engage in research more intensively, led to my current joint appointment in Psychology and Family Medicine at Western University in Ontario. I have two lines of research: (a) access to and use of services for children and youth with mental health problems; and (b) common sleep problems among young children. In addition, I maintain a private practice in which I see individuals of all ages with a variety of psychological problems and disorders.

CONTINUED . . .

HOW DID YOU CHOOSE TO BECOME A CLINICAL PSYCHOLOGIST?

As an undergraduate student, I enjoyed the content of my psychology courses. I also always enjoyed working with children and youth. I was blessed with the opportunity to shadow a clinical psychologist who worked with adults with severe developmental disabilities. This led to a full-time summer placement in which I was involved in research and preparing my first conference presentation which examined the impact of having employees with a developmental handicap working in the city's recycling program. These experiences, along with working as a summer camp counsellor, helped me to secure another summer position in which I co-led a day treatment program for children with emotional and behavioural problems. Collectively, these experiences confirmed my desire to continue to pursue a career as a psychologist that would allow me to do both clinical and research work.

WHAT IS THE GREATEST CHALLENGE YOU FACE AS A CLINICAL PSYCHOLOGIST?

In research, my biggest challenge is narrowing down the range of options. I struggle to choose the right question that can be answered using the best methods, and which will be most likely to have a positive impact. In my clinical work, I would like every person that I work with to get better as quickly and efficiently as possible. I find it particularly difficult when, for any number of reasons, the things that I am doing to help people do not result in the outcomes that are hoped for.

TELL US ABOUT YOUR RESEARCH ON ACCESS TO AND USE OF MENTAL HEALTH SERVICES.

We began our study by trying to understand what happens to families who call for help but then, after months on the wait-list, do not respond when services are offered. This question prompted us to ask more about parents' contacts with children's mental health (CMH) services. We found that parents contacted an average of four agencies or professionals providing CMH services in the previous year and many had been involved with CMH for more than one year. It became clear that the ways in which families attempt to access mental health care for their children are considerably more complex than previously described in the literature. This led us to examine administrative visit data over extended periods of time from six CMH agencies across Ontario. We found five patterns of service use that were very stable across agencies. Among our key findings: (a) 20% of children will experience two or more episodes of care within a five-year period; and (b) 19% of children are involved with an agency for more than three and a half years from the date of their initial visit. These results suggest that one out of every five children receiving CMH care can be viewed as requiring ongoing care (i.e., care distributed over multiple years). Future studies will involve developing, and ultimately testing, new models of care for these children. We are also interested in examining what happens as these children with complex and ongoing mental health needs transition from CMH to adult mental health services.

HOW DO YOU INTEGRATE SCIENCE AND PRACTICE IN YOUR WORK?

My clinical practice helps to keep me grounded in the realities and struggles faced by children and youth with mental health problems and their families. When I have a clinical issue, I routinely look for current best practices. My research on pediatric sleep problems is also practice oriented. I developed the Parenting Matters program for parents of children 2–5 years old who have concerns about their children's sleep/bedtime and/or discipline. Treatment consists of self-help booklets and support from a telephone coach. The program was tested in a series of three randomized clinical trials involving 24 family medicine practices with over 550 parents. Currently I am part of a team of Canadian researchers that will develop and test Internet-based treatments for parents of children 1–10 years old with behavioural insomnia. When working with parents of preschoolers with

CONTINUED . . .

sleep or discipline issues, I often use my knowledge and experience from this research to inform my clinical work. Conversely, my clinical experience informed the development of the Parenting Matters treatment booklets.

WHAT DO YOU SEE AS THE MOST EXCITING CHANGES IN THE FIELD OF CLINICAL PSYCHOLOGY?

It is an ongoing challenge to provide best practices in both assessment and treatment to children, youth, and their families. Improving the capacity of our mental health system to care for more people also continues to be a challenge. New methods of treatment delivery, including Internet-based interventions and other distance treatment modalities, are needed. Easier and more rapid access to the best available treatments will hopefully result in improvements in what has, unfortunately, been a chronic problem for mental health service delivery—namely, that even when individuals finally do receive treatment, far too many drop out prematurely. I think an overarching principle is that we need to find ways to create a system that works for the people who need it, rather than trying to help people fit into a fragmented and confusing system.

In Chapter 10 (Exhibit 10.1), we presented risk factors for the development of psychopathology in children and youth. As you can see, many of the risk factors involve conditions over which the young person has very limited control, such as antisocial role models in the family, inadequate supervision and monitoring, parental psychopathology, bullying, or poverty. The protective factors (Exhibit 10.2) suggest some possible avenues for psychological services in the development of problem-solving skills, social competence, supportive family relationships, positive school–home relations, strong cultural identity, and ethnic pride. An examination of risk and protective factors influencing the development of psychopathology underlines that psychological services for children's psychological disorders must address the context in which the child's problem developed and is maintained. In Chapter 10, you learned about how knowledge of risk and protective factors informs the development of prevention programs. In this chapter, we focus on services for the treatment of diagnosable psychopathology in a child or adolescent. Early forms of child psychotherapy focused on intrapsychic factors but, as you will see later in the chapter, decades of research on developmental psychopathology have led to the development of treatments that attend to both intrapsychic and interpersonal factors.

LANDMARKS IN THE EVOLUTION OF EVIDENCE-BASED PSYCHOLOGICAL SERVICES FOR CHILDREN AND ADOLESCENTS

What are some of the reasons why there is less research on treatment of youth than on treatment of adults?

In general, the literature on psychological services for childhood disorders has followed a similar path to the one you learned about in Chapter 12 with respect to treatments for adults. Unfortunately, progress in the psychological treatment of children and adolescents has generally lagged behind the progress in psychological treatments for adults. There are simply fewer studies to examine in meta-analyses and, accordingly, compared with the adult literature, more limited and tentative conclusions must be drawn from the youth literature.

Do Psychological Treatments for Children and Adolescents Work?

Echoing Eysenck's 1952 report, Levitt (1957, 1963) concluded that there was no evidence for the efficacy of child psychotherapy. During the subsequent two decades, a variety of new approaches to the treatment of disorders of childhood were developed and numerous studies examined the efficacy of different types of child psychotherapy. In the 1980s and 1990s, four large-scale meta-analyses scrutinized the child psychotherapy outcome literature. Casey and Berman (1985) examined data from 75 studies covering services to treat diverse clinical problems using a large range of therapeutic approaches for young people under the age of 13. Across all techniques, they reported an effect size comparable to that reported by Smith and Glass (1977) in their review of the adult psychotherapy literature. A subsequent meta-analysis by Weisz, Weiss, Alicke, and Klotz (1987) examined 108 controlled studies (less than a third of which were also reviewed by Casey and Berman, 1985). Psychotherapy researcher John Weisz and his colleagues reasoned that if a treatment uses an artificial activity (like a computer task) to train a skill (like paying attention), then it is simply not fair to use a score on that same computer activity as a measure of treatment outcome. However, if the therapy is designed to treat fear of dogs, then a behavioural approach would focus on helping the child to approach dogs and an appropriate outcome measure would be the extent to which the child was able to comfortably interact with dogs. Using this reasoning, they excluded from analyses of outcomes any artificial or analogue activities that had been used in the treatment, but retained as outcome measures real-world activities that had been targeted in treatment. Based on their analyses, Weisz and his colleagues reported a mean effect size of .79, with larger effects found for behavioural approaches than for non-behavioural approaches.

A subsequent meta-analysis by Kazdin, Bass, Ayers, and Rodgers (1990) yielded a very similar effect size to those reported by Casey and Berman (1985) and Weisz et al. (1987). However, although the effect sizes looked encouraging, Alan Kazdin and his colleagues drew attention to a troubling discrepancy between the nature of psychotherapy research and the nature of clinical practice. They found that treatment studies often relied on volunteer samples recruited through schools and treated in a group format. In contrast, surveys indicated that clinical practice more commonly involved individual treatment in outpatient clinics of referred patients. Furthermore, Kazdin and his colleagues recommended that treatment researchers pay greater attention to characteristics of the child, parent, family, or therapist that might influence treatment outcome. As you will learn later in the chapter, these recommendations appear to have had a significant impact on the way that researchers have examined treatments for children, so that in the decades since their review, there is increasing attention to examining outcomes in samples of children who have been referred for treatment.

You learned in Chapters 4 and 12 that the use of meta-analysis has revolutionized the field of psychology by offering an explicit set of decision rules for synthesizing data from diverse studies and reporting findings using a common metric. Like other research tools, meta-analysis is not perfect. As problems in the procedure are identified, refinements are introduced. The fourth major meta-analysis of the effects of child psychotherapy (Weisz, Weiss, Han, Granger, & Morton, 1995) introduced a more conservative way of calculating effect sizes, using a statistical technique known as the *weighted least squares method.* As you know from your statistics courses, when sampling data from a population, there is always error (i.e., deviations from the true population values). Generally speaking, data from larger samples have less error variance and, therefore, are closer to population values. The weighted least squares method takes this into account by assigning less weight in the meta-analysis to studies with greater error variance and more heavily weighting those with less error variance. Based on a meta-analysis of 150 outcome studies that had not been previously reviewed, Weisz et al. (1995) reported a similar effect size to all the previous meta-analyses when they used unweighted least squares methods, but a lower effect size of .54 using the weighted strategy. Weisz et al. also examined data from follow-up studies and found encouraging evidence that treatment effects were evident not only at the end of services, but six months later as well.

All of the meta-analyses described thus far relied on published studies. Unfortunately, this may bias the results because journals are more likely to publish studies that report statistically significant findings than those that report non-significant results. McLeod and Weisz (2004) compared 134 published studies with 121 dissertations in terms of both their methodological adequacy and their findings. Overall, they found that the unpublished dissertations were stronger methodologically, but obtained lower effect sizes than did the published studies. This suggests that meta-analyses based on published studies may lead us to overestimate the effect sizes from child psychotherapy studies. McLeod and Weisz therefore recommended that future meta-analyses also include data from unpublished dissertations.

Although it is encouraging to know that psychological treatments can be efficacious in treating childhood disorders, the most important questions need much more precise answers. Researchers have focused, therefore, on examining the research on efficacious treatments for different types of childhood disorders. We now turn our attention to this research literature.

Which Treatments Work for Specific Disorders?

Psychotherapy researchers in various countries have developed psychosocial interventions and demonstrated that they can help children and adolescents who are dealing with diverse disorders and problems. These include disorders such as autism (Rogers & Vismara, 2008), anxiety (Silverman, Pina, & Viswesvaran, 2008; Silverman et al., 2008), depression (David-Ferdon & Kaslow, 2008; Watanabe, Hunot, Omori, Churchill, & Furukawa, 2007), ADHD (Pelham & Fabiano, 2008), disruptive behaviour (Eyberg, Nelson, & Boggs, 2008), and substance abuse (Waldron & Turner, 2008), as well as issues in primary care or medical practice such as adherence to treatment of chronic health conditions (Kahana, Drotar, & Frazier, 2008). Unfortunately, although there are numerous efficacious psychological treatments for various problems of childhood and adolescence, they are not routinely offered in standard care (Connor-Smith & Weisz, 2003). A meta-analysis of 32 studies comparing evidence-based treatments with usual clinical care found that evidence-based care consistently outperformed usual clinical care. Furthermore, the superiority of evidence-based treatment was also evident among minority youth and among youth with the most severe problems (Weisz, Jensen-Doss, & Hawley, 2006).

If evidence-based approaches seem to work better than care as usual, to be helpful to those with more serious problems and to be helpful to minority youth, why are they not used by all mental health professionals? One obstacle to the adoption of efficacious treatments is that clinicians may simply be unaware of them. The field of clinical psychology is constantly evolving, with exciting new research being published daily. The average clinician is unable to consult the literature and synthesize new findings into meaningful recommendations on a regular basis (Barwick et al., 2008). In addition, the average parent who is a potential consumer of psychological services can be faced with a bewildering array of contradictory messages about the most appropriate solution to the child's problem. If you browse through the parenting sections of bookstores or search the term *children's behaviour* on the Internet, you will see books advocating diverse ways to address children's problems. It is a challenge for parents to distinguish between experts whose message is based on solid research and those who are simply proposing something that makes sense to them but that lacks a solid empirical foundation.

To get a sense of the challenges faced by those seeking information about efficacious treatments for youth, check out the self-help sections of an online bookstore. Pick a childhood problem that interests you. How easy is it for you to tell whether the book is evidence-based?

Among the health disciplines, psychology is not alone in facing this dilemma of how to translate research findings into practice. Similar challenges are faced by clinicians trying to keep up-to-date with rapid advances in the knowledge base in professions such as nursing and medicine. As we explained in Chapter 12, a number of expert review panels have been set up to evaluate research findings and to develop clear evidence-based practice guidelines. Some of these review panels are organized within a particular discipline; others are multidisciplinary. Some are sponsored by a professional organization; others are the independent enterprise of a small number of researchers.

In the United States, an influential review of children's mental health services was initiated in response to a class action lawsuit on behalf of children with special needs. The settlement of the lawsuit involved an agreement by the state of Hawaii to develop a comprehensive system of care for those aged 0 to 20 years with mental health needs (Chorpita et al., 2002). As a first step, the Hawaii Department of Health established a task force to identify the empirical basis for services. This multidisciplinary group included health administrators, parents of children with special needs, clinical service providers, and academics in psychology (including anxiety and depression researcher Bruce Chorpita), psychiatry, nursing, and social work. The task force conducted a literature review of studies in psychology, psychiatry, and related mental health disciplines. The mandate of the Hawaii task force was to identify which treatments would work in the challenging context of isolated rural areas with multi-ethnic populations.

You learned in Chapter 12 of the APA division task forces that reviewed psychosocial treatments for adults. Similarly, the Society of Clinical Child and Adolescent Psychology (Division 53 of the American Psychological Association) commissioned a series of reviews on psychosocial treatments for disorders of childhood and adolescence that was published in the late 1990s. In the following decade, a large number of additional studies were published. The reviews were therefore updated and published in a special series of the *Journal of Clinical Child and Adolescent Psychology* (Silverman & Hinshaw, 2008). Authors examined the research using the criteria established by Nathan and Gorman (2002) as well as by Chambless and Hollon (1998) (see Chapter 12 for details on these criteria).

Why is it so important to have parents involved in many forms of treatment for children?

Over the last 20 years there have been concerted efforts in different countries and across different disciplines to identify the most helpful psychological treatments for childhood disorders. Exhibit 13.1 presents a list of the major evidence-based treatments for children and adolescents identified, in the reviews in the special series in the *Journal of Clinical Child and Adolescent Psychology,* as "well-established" or "probably efficacious" (Silverman & Hinshaw, 2008) or as having the highest levels of evidence in the Australian Psychological Society (2010) review of evidence-based interventions. You must remember that, like all such lists, this should be considered to reflect the state of knowledge in the area at the time of writing. The field is constantly evolving, so the list in the next edition of this book may look somewhat different. As evidence accumulates, some of the approaches that have promise and were labelled by the special series authors as "possibly efficacious" (or that had lower levels of evidence in the Australian Psychological Society review) may well have stronger support in the future.

You will notice that many of the evidence-based approaches are behavioural and cognitive-behavioural. In contrast to the treatments for adults that are offered to individuals, many of the efficacious treatments for children involve parents learning strategies to respond to their children's behaviour. As you can imagine, many parents who bring their children for psychological services are surprised to find that they are asked to participate by changing their behaviour toward the child or adolescent. Treatments for externalizing problems often include others who are trained to respond in a way that encourages desirable behaviour. Although treatments for internalizing problems usually focus directly on the child, many approaches also include parents in services (Barrett, Farrell, Pina, Peris, & Piacentini, 2008). In the treatment of adolescent depression, attention is also focused on interpersonal issues. Thus, most effective treatments of childhood disorders fall under the umbrella of behavioural, cognitive-behavioural, and interpersonal approaches. The involvement of parents is consistent with our earlier discussion of the importance of attending to protective factors in designing psychological interventions for youth. Due to developmental changes, it is also important when examining the usefulness of different treatment strategies (such as parental involvement) to take into account the child's age. However, as you may recall learning in Chapter 10, parental psychopathology may make it more difficult for parents to engage in and complete psychological services for their children.

Exhibit 13.1 Evidence-Based Treatments for Disorders in Children and Youth

Autistic Disorder
- Intensive behavioural treatment

Attention-Deficit/Hyperactivity Disorder
- Behavioural parent training
- Behaviour classroom management
- Intensive peer-focused behavioural interventions

Disruptive Behaviour Disorders
- Individual behavioural parent training
- Group behavioural parent training
- Individual CBT
- Group CBT
- Multisystemic therapy

Eating Disorders
- Family therapy

Exposure to Traumatic Events
- Individual trauma-focused CBT
- School-based group CBT

Depression
- Individual interpersonal psychotherapy
- Individual CBT
- Individual CBT with parental/family involvement
- Group CBT
- Group CBT with parental involvement

Obsessive-Compulsive Disorder
- Individual CBT

Phobic and Anxiety Disorders
- Individual CBT
- Group CBT
- Group CBT with parental component

Sleep Disorders
- Individual CBT

Substance Abuse
- Group CBT
- Individual CBT
- Multidimensional family therapy
- Functional family therapy
- Behavioural family therapy
- Multisystemic therapy

Imagine that you are a parent whose child is having psychological problems. How would you feel when the psychologist informs you that you will be expected to play an important role in the services your child will receive? What would you see as the advantages and disadvantages of being involved in the services?

The special series on evidence-based treatments also in the *Journal of Clinical Child and Adolescent Psychology* included a meta-analysis of studies that had examined efficacy in samples of ethnic minority youth (Huey & Polo, 2008). These authors found evidence that a number of treatments are probably efficacious in the treatment of minority youth, including combined medication and behavioural treatment for African American and Latino youth with ADHD, CBT for depressed Puerto Rican youth, Multisystemic Therapy (MST) for African American juvenile offenders, Lochman's CBT Coping Power program for aggressive African American youth, brief strategic family therapy for Latino youth with conduct problems, and multidimensional family therapy for diverse groups of ethnic minority youth. Additionally, in the treatment of traumatized minority youth, various CBT and peer-modelling approaches appear efficacious. Huey and Polo also examined the empirical question of whether treatments demonstrate *ethnic invariance* or *ethnic disparity*. A finding of ethnic invariance implies that an evidence-based treatment yields equivalent results for ethnic minority youth; ethnic disparity, on the other hand, implies that the treatment is not as powerful when applied to ethnic minority youth and, therefore, the treatment requires adaptation. Huey and Polo evaluated five studies that examined whether ethnicity moderated treatment effects. The results demonstrated ethnic disparity, but the disparity was not always in favour of the majority youth. In fact, for three studies, stronger effects were found for ethnic minority youth than for European American youth, whereas in two studies, better outcomes were obtained for European American youth than for ethnic minority youth. These findings underline the importance of the ongoing evaluation of the usefulness of treatment. A treatment should not be rejected simply because it has never been used in a particular population, but nor should the psychologist assume that because it worked with one sample it will definitely be helpful in another sample. The obligation to monitor treatment effectiveness is an ongoing requirement of evidence-based practice.

Clinical Practice Guidelines

In Chapter 12, you learned about the wealth of treatment guidelines that are available with respect to adult disorders. In contrast, the development of treatment guidelines for childhood disorders has lagged behind significantly. A number of professional organizations have sponsored reviews of the scientific literature to identify efficacious treatments that should be offered as routine care in the treatment of a specific problem. In 2010, the American Psychological Association established a framework for the development of clinical practice guidelines. The preparation of evidence-based guidelines for clinical practice in the treatment of depression, PTSD, and obesity are underway. Since 1997, the American Academy of Child and Adolescent Psychiatry has published many practice parameters and guidelines in the *Journal of the American Academy of Child and Adolescent Psychiatry,* addressing topics including the treatment of anxiety disorders, ADHD, autistic disorder, conduct disorder, obsessive-compulsive disorder, and PTSD. These practice parameters are based on the consensus of expert groups as well as the research evidence.

If you check practice guidelines you will notice that they, like many products in the grocery store, are identified with a *best before* date. This is an explicit acknowledgement that, although they represent the best recommendation based on available knowledge at the time they are released, research is ongoing, our understanding is constantly evolving, and guidelines must not be seen as the final word. Thus, ongoing updates of clinical practice guidelines based on new research are essential to the promotion of evidence-based practice.

It is inevitable that guidelines developed by one professional body may be seen to promote the approach favoured by that profession and may be seen to downplay the benefits of other approaches. There are, therefore, benefits to collaboration between different disciplines in identifying practices that are most helpful. One of the earliest multidisciplinary review panels on children's mental health was convened in the United States by the National Institutes of Health (NIH) to identify evidence-based treatment of ADHD (NIH, 1998). This resulted in the *NIH Consensus Statement on the Diagnosis and Treatment of Attention-Deficit/Hyperactivity Disorder,* which sets out standards for the evidence-based assessment and treatment of this condition.

In Chapter 12, we described the development in England and Wales of the National Institute for Health and Care Excellence (NICE), whose mandate is to guide health care professionals and patients in making decisions about health care treatment options. Although, to date, the bulk of the work in the mental health field has focused on adult disorders, NICE has published guidelines on the treatment of attention-deficit/hyperactivity disorder (NICE, 2008), conduct disorder (NICE, 2006, updated in 2013a), depression in children and adolescents (NICE, 2005), nocturnal enuresis (2010), and psychosis and schizophrenia (2013b). Although it is only in its infancy, the movement to develop interdisciplinary, evidence-based guidelines for the assessment and treatment of diverse childhood disorders is designed to inform policy-makers, consumers, and the mental health professionals who serve children with emotional and behavioural problems. The widespread application of research-based services has the potential to streamline services so that a greater proportion of the children in need can be helped.

Practice guidelines are designed to help practitioners deliver services that are based on current research findings. Parallel initiatives have been developed to provide consumers with plain language summaries of knowledge on a particular topic. The Canadian Psychological Association website includes a series of fact sheets, entitled *Psychology Works,* that synthesize research on a disorder or challenge and give a quick overview of treatment options. These can be found at www.cpa.ca/psychologyfactsheets.

EXAMPLES OF EVIDENCE-BASED TREATMENTS

It is clearly beyond the scope of this chapter to present all the evidence-based interventions that are listed in Exhibit 13.1. Instead we will examine some of the evidence-based treatments for different types of common problems of childhood. As disruptive behaviour disorders are the most frequent reason for referral to mental health services, we will examine some treatments that are helpful in the treatment of oppositional defiant disorder and conduct disorder. Next we will examine a treatment for adolescent depression.

Disruptive Behaviour Disorders

As we discussed earlier in the chapter, children do not refer themselves for treatment. It is perhaps not surprising that disruptive behaviour constitutes the most common reason for which adults refer children and youth for mental health services (Kazdin, 2004). Oppositional defiant disorder (ODD) reflects a pattern of persistent negativistic and hostile behaviour that is usually evident before the age of 8 years. Although all children sometimes fail to comply with parental requests, argue with adults, and are easily upset, children diagnosed with ODD behave like this consistently and their behaviour interferes with normal functioning. Children with ODD have problems in several contexts, such as home and school. ODD often precedes conduct disorder (CD), which involves a pattern of serious violation of the rights of others, including aggression, destructiveness, deceitfulness, and serious violation of rules. Young people diagnosed with ODD and CD are at risk for other mental health problems such as ADHD, learning problems, depression, and substance abuse. There is evidence that, left untreated, these problems persist into adolescence and adulthood.

The research on treatment for disruptive behaviour disorders has been the subject of many reviews. Eyberg, Nelson, and Boggs (2008) identified 16 evidence-based programs, many of which are behavioural parenting programs inspired by parent management training (PMT), developed and refined by Gerald Patterson and his colleagues at the Oregon Research Institute (Patterson, 1982). Although we recognize that the term *parent management training* may sound unappealing, it is important to understand Patterson's PMT, as it laid the foundation for most evidence-based parenting services. We will also describe Multisystemic Therapy (MST) for seriously disordered adolescents, developed by Scott Henggeler and his colleagues (Henggeler & Lee, 2003; Henggeler, Schoenwald, Borduin, Rowland, & Cunningham, 1998).

Parent Management Training

Parent management training (PMT) is grounded in social learning theory and the assumption that oppositional child behaviour can be changed by modifying the child's social environment rather than by working directly with the child. According to this theory, maladaptive patterns of parent–child interaction inadvertently encourage both parents and children to engage in inappropriate behaviours. During coercive exchanges the parent unintentionally rewards the child for whining or aggression (by withdrawing a demand or providing attention) and the child rewards the parent for giving in to his or her complaints (by ceasing the aversive behaviour). Patterson's team has conducted decades of systematic observations of families (Chamberlain & Smith, 2003; Patterson, 2005) and has found that, in all families, there are disagreements and conflicts that must be managed. In well-functioning families, children learn prosocial ways to resolve conflict (such as discussion and compromise), whereas in families with aggressive children, the child

coercive exchanges: parent–child interactions in which the parent unintentionally rewards the child for whining or aggression (by withdrawing a demand or providing attention) and the child rewards the parent for giving in to his or her complaints (by ceasing the aversive behaviour).

learns coercive ways to get what he or she wants. You have probably observed the classic example of a coercive exchange at the grocery store checkout. You first see a child grab a chocolate bar. The parent reminds the child that it is soon time for a meal, or that he or she has already had enough sugar. The child then launches into a routine that begins with wheedling, *Please, just one . . .*, then rapidly escalates in volume and aversiveness as the parent repeats quietly, *I said no*. The child may protest loudly that he or she is hungry, that the parent had promised, or that the parent allowed another sibling to have a chocolate bar the last time they were in the grocery store. The child may also demand an explanation for the parent's refusal (*Why are you always so mean to me?*). As the child's protests draw the attention of a growing number of onlookers, the parent's embarrassment mounts and he or she gives in to the child's demands. This sequence has rewarded the child for grabbing, whining, yelling, and persisting, as well as increased the likelihood that the child will do the same thing the next time. The parent's giving in is briefly rewarded by the short-term relief when the child's tantrum ends. Unfortunately, the coercive behaviours reinforced in the home are then applied in other contexts, so that the child behaves in a non-compliant and disruptive way with teachers, babysitters, coaches, and other children.

In their research, Patterson and his colleagues observed five parenting practices that are associated with the development of prosocial or deviant behaviour: skill encouragement, discipline, monitoring, problem-solving, and positive involvement (Patterson, 2005). The idea behind the treatment is simple: to train parents of children with behaviour problems to parent in the same way as parents whose children do not have problems. Patterson and his colleagues developed a program designed to help parents to encourage appropriate behaviour and to discourage unacceptable behaviours. Parents meet with a therapist who teaches them core skills (see Exhibit 13.2). An essential aspect of behavioural training is that complex skills are broken into small steps. First, parents establish a few simple rules on which they agree and which they are willing to impose consistently. Rules for child behaviour are basic guidelines about daily living, including the child's responsibilities and chores, daytime routines, and respectful ways of interacting. Lists of rules take into account the child's developmental level, circumstances, and any special needs.

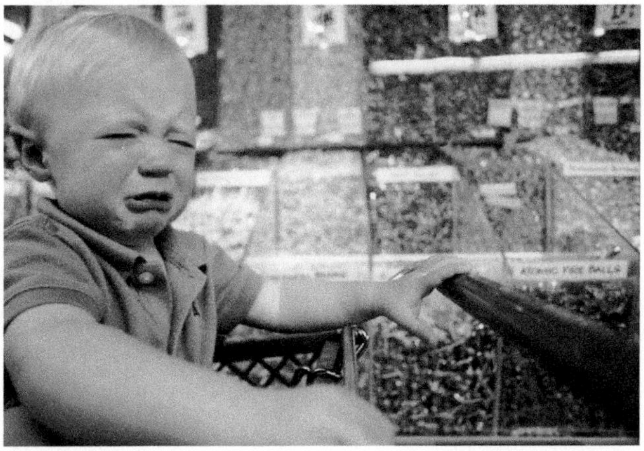

Media Bakery
Coercive exchanges set the stage for continued problems.

Exhibit 13.2 Core Parenting Skills

Positive Involvement

- Giving loving attention

Skill Encouragement

- Breaking behaviours into small steps. So, instead of telling the child *Get ready*, say:
  Put your coat on.
  Now do up the buttons.
  Slip on your boots.
  Close the tab.
- Prompting appropriate behaviour through clear rules and cues. So, instead of telling the child *Tidy up this mess*, say:
  Put your toys away.
  It's time to put everything away.
- Expressing contingent positive reinforcement (praise and incentives)
  Wow, you tidied up your toys—that's great!
  I like the way you played with Tyler and shared your toys. Would you like to pick a sticker?
  You've done your homework carefully, now you can have 30 minutes on the computer.

Discipline

- Setting limits
  Complete your homework after school.
  No hitting.
- Using mild sanctions (time out, removal of privileges)
  Because you did not complete your homework, you cannot have screen time.
  Because you hit your brother, you must take a time out for 10 minutes.

Monitoring

- Tracking the child's whereabouts and activities

Problem-Solving

- Establishing clear rules
- Establishing consequences
- Negotiating

The grocery store provides a great opportunity for naturalistic observation of parenting. The next time you are shopping, keep in mind the core skills and see if you can identify examples of parents using any of the five core skills of effective parenting.

Because research has consistently found that distressed families engage in fewer positive interactions than do non-distressed families, an important goal in treatment is to increase reinforcement for positive behaviour. As you have learned in other psychology courses, positive reinforcement is any consequence that increases the likelihood of a behaviour being repeated. Parents seeking mental health services for their children's oppositional behaviours often report that their interactions with their children are very negative. They feel at a loss in coming up with potential reinforcers. In fact, the list of potential reinforcers is very long. The benefits of social reinforcement through smiles, attention, verbal encouragement, and touch are often overlooked. In coming up with other potential reinforcers, the parents must put themselves in the child's position, so that they can appreciate the range of stickers, activities, and freedoms that can possibly serve as reinforcers of desirable behaviour. Parents may also worry about the long-term consequences of what they see as paying their children to behave well. By learning to use social reinforcers and by understanding the importance of fading out the use of material reinforcers, parents learn to intentionally use reinforcers without being haunted by the unrealistic fear of turning their child into a monster who will behave well only if bribed.

positive reinforcement: any consequence that increases the likelihood of a behaviour being repeated.

Think of times when you have been responsible for looking after children. What combination of social reinforcers, tangible reinforcers, and privileges did you find most helpful in encouraging the children to behave well?

Although establishing a system of positive reinforcement can go a long way toward resolving some behaviour problems, parents need to also develop skills in dealing with non-compliance. Patterson's approach offers mild punishment as an effective response to misbehaviour. Basically, punishment involves the withdrawal of reinforcers. This can include a range of losses according to the child's age and preferences. Punishment for a very young child may involve not being allowed to play with a favourite toy that he or she has just used to hurt another child, or turning off the TV or computer after the child has yelled and disturbed a sibling. For an older child, punishment may include an earlier curfew or loss of computer time or Internet access. Parents learn to use time out procedures in which the child does not have access to reinforcers for a brief period following misbehaviour.

time out: a parenting strategy in which the child does not have access to reinforcers for a brief period following misbehaviour.

Just as engaging in a restricted diet is not a permanent solution to weight problems (only a regular routine of healthy eating and exercise provides sustained effects), PMT is not offered as a quick fix for child

©iStock.com/digitalskillet

Parents learn to increase positive parent-child interactions.

behaviour problems. It is an approach to parenting in which the adult assumes an active role in monitoring and responding to the child's behaviours. Once the child's behaviour is more acceptable, parents cannot abandon this type of parenting or the problems will quickly return. With very young children, monitoring may include close physical supervision of the child's activities. As the child grows older, parental monitoring shifts so that parents learn to maintain a relationship with the young person, who informs parents about his or her whereabouts and activities. An essential component of parenting is recognizing that as children get older they should become more involved in decision-making. Therefore, parents learn negotiation and how to alter their expectations based on developmental changes.

PMT also highlights the importance of cognitive and affective variables that are related to treatment outcome. For example, if parents believe that the young person *intentionally* engages in misbehaviour, then they are less likely to adopt effective discipline strategies and are more likely to continue with strategies that actually increase the likelihood of misbehaviour. A parent who thinks that the child deliberately created a mess in order to get back at the parent is more likely to respond in a harsh and critical fashion than is a parent who understands the messiness is related to lack of coordination or attention. It is therefore necessary for PMT to focus not only on parents' behaviour toward the child, but also on the ways that parents understand the child's misbehaviour (Patterson, 2005). A core element of PMT is to increase the amount of positive interaction between parent and child. The importance of this affective dimension is underlined in studies showing that parent–child warmth is associated with **parental monitoring** and that adolescent–parent contempt is associated with inconsistent and disrupted parental monitoring, which in turn is associated with delinquency (Patterson, 2005).

parental monitoring: parents' awareness and tracking of the child's activities.

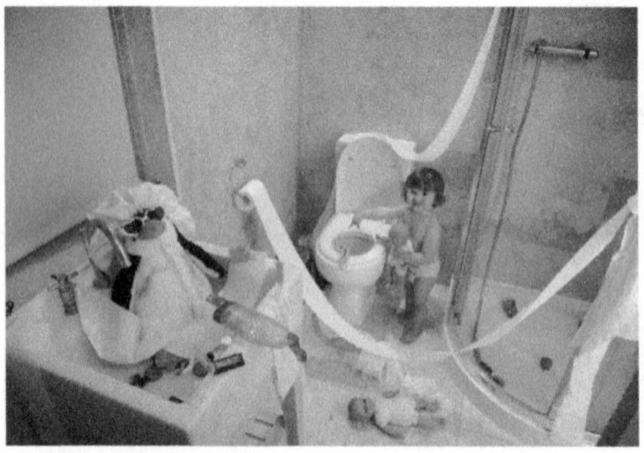

©iStock.com/sturti

Parents' attributions for the child's behaviour influence the way they respond.

A randomized controlled trial conducted in Norway demonstrated that this program was effective in improving parental discipline practices, improving teacher-rated social competence, and decreasing parent-rated externalizing problems in 112 children with conduct problems (Ogden & Hagen, 2008). Children in foster care are a vulnerable population that has a high rate of externalizing problems. A study of 700 foster families caring for children aged 5 to 12 compared outcomes in families randomly assigned to receive 16 weeks of parent management training and those assigned to usual care (Price et al., 2008). These investigators found that among an ethnically diverse, vulnerable population, the intervention increased the chances of a successful outcome of the foster placement; that is, children were more likely to be successfully reunited with their parents.

PMT is delivered in a structured format, using a treatment manual and repeated practice. The number of sessions varies according to the child's age and the severity of the disruptive behaviour: from 4 to 8 weeks with young mildly oppositional children to 12 to 25 weeks for clinically referred youth diagnosed with conduct disorder (Forgatch & Patterson, 2010; Kazdin, 2003). During sessions, parents practise skills through behaviour rehearsal and role-playing. Between sessions, they complete homework assignments related to the skills they have learned. Patterson's work has also inspired many variations of PMT that were described in Chapter 10, including the Incredible Years program and the Triple P program. A meta-analysis of 28 randomized controlled trials of the various forms of parent management training conducted in real-world settings (Michelson, Davenport, Dretzke, Barlow, & Day, 2013) found that they were effective in the treatment of children with disruptive behaviour disorders.

Multisystemic Therapy

How do services for children and services for adolescents differ?

Multisystemic Therapy (MST) is an approach designed to treat seriously disturbed delinquent adolescents by intervening in an integrated way in the multiple systems in which they are involved (Henggeler et al., 1998). These youth, who are at risk of being placed in out-of-home care, require costly services that consume a disproportionate amount of mental health resources (Henggeler & Lee, 2003). Grounded in an **ecological theory** of psychosocial functioning (Bronfenbrenner, 1979), MST works with these youth within the context of numerous systems, including the nuclear family, extended family, neighbourhood, school, peer, community, juvenile justice, child welfare, and mental health (Henggeler et al., 1998). This treatment approach is consistent with research findings that delinquent behaviour is not caused simply by one factor but, rather, is multiply determined. Within this model the caregiver (usually, but not always, a parent) plays a key role in the young person's short- and long-term adjustment. Exhibit 13.3 describes the nine principles that guide MST. The goals of the approach are positive and future-oriented. MST uses a behavioural approach that is designed to integrate services so that gains in one area will generalize to other contexts. A fundamental characteristic of this approach is that treatment effectiveness is evaluated continuously from the perspective of multiple stakeholders, including the youth, parents, and others in the educational, health, and justice systems.

ecological theory: a theory that examines a young person's functioning within the multiple contexts in which he or she lives—family, school, neighbourhood, etc.

Exhibit 13.3 MST Treatment Principles

Principle 1:	The primary purpose of assessment is to understand the fit between the identified problems and their broader systemic context.
Principle 2:	Therapeutic contacts emphasize the positive and use systemic strengths as levers for change.
Principle 3:	Interventions are designed to promote responsible behaviour and decrease irresponsible behaviour among family members.
Principle 4:	Interventions are present-focused and action-oriented, targeting specific and well-defined problems.
Principle 5:	Interventions target sequences of behaviour within and between multiple systems that maintain the identified problems.
Principle 6:	Interventions are developmentally appropriate and fit the developmental needs of the youth.
Principle 7:	Interventions are designed to require daily or weekly effort by family members.
Principle 8:	Intervention effectiveness is evaluated continuously from multiple perspectives, with providers assuming accountability for overcoming barriers to successful outcomes.
Principle 9:	Interventions are designed to promote treatment generalization and long-term maintenance of therapeutic change by empowering caregivers to address family members' needs across multiple systemic contexts.

Adapted from Henggeler, Schoenwald, Borduin, Rowland, & Cunningham (1998).

MST therapists work in teams of three to five people. Each therapist works with a very small caseload of four to five families. The therapist coordinates all the services that the youth and family receive. To reduce barriers to participation, services are offered in homes, schools, and neighbourhood centres rather than in hospitals or court clinics. Treatment is time limited, lasting only three to five months. It is, however, very intense, with therapists available 24 hours a day, seven days a week, to respond to crises.

The first phase of services involves an explanation of the MST model. The therapist works hard to develop a collaborative relationship with the caregiver. Assessment involves identification of the risk factors that contribute to the problem as well as strengths that can be drawn upon in every system in which the young person is involved. As you learned in Chapter 10, risk factors include low caregiver monitoring, low warmth, ineffective discipline, high conflict, caregiver psychopathology, and family criminal behaviour. Protective factors include secure attachment, a supportive family environment, and a harmonious couple relationship between the parents. At an early stage in services, the therapist works with the family to establish measurable long-term goals that can be broken down into measurable weekly goals. The therapist makes contact with any person or system that can affect the attainment of these goals in order to ensure cooperation. In collaboration with the caregiver and youth, the therapist then selects evidence-based treatments for each goal. As you can imagine, services to establish clear rules, to reward prosocial behaviour, and to encourage appropriate monitoring are very similar to PMT approaches. Caregivers are not always able to implement the recommendations, and their stress or psychopathology may pose a serious obstacle to successful treatment. Therefore the MST therapist also targets for intervention any caregiver characteristics that significantly limit the capacity to parent effectively.

Interventions that target the peer system depend on the nature of the problem. Peers can serve as a risk factor if they are anti-social or as a protective factor if they are socially competent. Youth lacking in social skills or assertiveness receive training in these areas. If the peer group is an antisocial one that encourages delinquent behaviour, the intervention focuses on limiting access to those peers, increasing parental monitoring, and developing more appropriate peer contacts through other activities.

Risk factors in the school system include learning problems, a chaotic school environment, and poor contact between family and school. Protective factors include strong intellectual functioning, a commitment to education, and good contact between family and school. MST therapists can play a key role in facilitating the development of a collaborative relationship between school and family to ensure a consistent approach between the two environments.

Individually oriented services target specific difficulties the youth may be experiencing using evidence-based approaches. For example, cognitive-behavioural strategies may be used to address problems with anxiety or depression. A referral may be made for a trial of medication in the treatment of ADHD in addition to parenting interventions and classroom interventions (Viewpoint Box 13.1 describes treatment for ADHD). As MST is a short-term intervention, considerable emphasis is placed on developing a supportive network so that the youth and family will be able to maintain the gains that they made when working directly with the therapist, after the therapist is no longer actively involved.

The developers of MST have established a quality assurance system to ensure that the approach is faithfully applied according to a manual by trained therapists who receive adequate supervision and consultation. Given the promising data on the efficacy of MST in reducing delinquent behaviour among seriously troubled youth, it is encouraging to learn that licensed MST programs operate in 30 American states, in Canada, and in several other countries (Henggeler & Lee, 2003). Ongoing research is examining the usefulness of this approach to treat other serious problems in adolescents (Henggeler & Sheidow, 2012).

VIEWPOINT BOX 13.1

TREATMENT OF CHILDHOOD ATTENTION-DEFICIT/HYPERACTIVITY DISORDER

ADHD is a neurological disorder. Reviews have consistently found evidence for the efficacy of stimulant medication in reducing symptoms of inattention, hyperactivity, and impulsivity (NICE, 2008; NIH, 1998; Schachar et al., 2002). You may wonder, therefore, why there is any need for psychosocial interventions to treat children with ADHD. There are many significant reasons why psychosocial treatment should be considered:

- Although problematic parent–child interaction does not cause ADHD, there is evidence that the presence of childhood ADHD is associated with disrupted parenting and this, in turn, affects the management of ADHD symptoms and the development of oppositional symptoms.
- Stimulants should not be prescribed to children under age 6 (NICE 2008; Paykina, Greenhill, & Gorman, 2007).
- A number of parents are unwilling to consider giving their children medication (Waschbusch & Hill, 2003).
- Although stimulant medication is effective in suppressing the symptoms of ADHD, the effect lasts only while the child is taking medication, with a return to regular functioning within 3 to 10 hours of ingesting a dose (NICE, 2008; Paykina et al. 2007).
- Thirty percent of children with ADHD do not respond to the medication (Paykina et al., 2007).
- Although stimulants are associated with reduction of core symptoms of ADHD, there is little evidence that medication is associated with improvement in academic or social skills (NIH, 1998).
- Although stimulants are not associated with serious side effects, there are minor unpleasant physiological symptoms, the most common of which is appetite suppression (NICE, 2008).
- Over time, there is a gradual decline in the numbers of children who adhere to their medication (Charach, Ickowicz, & Schachar, 2004). Unfortunately, it is impossible to predict which children will respond positively to medication (Paykina et al., 2007).

As medication is not suitable for all children and its positive effects are limited to the hours shortly after it has been administered, it is not surprising that behavioural approaches that have been used to treat other disruptive behaviour disorders have also been used to treat childhood ADHD. Similar to PMT for oppositional behaviour, behavioural treatments for children with ADHD are designed to help adults (parents and teachers) provide a structured, consistent environment in which the child is reinforced for appropriate behaviour and misbehaviour is ignored or mildly punished.

Pelham and Fabiano (2008) found evidence of positive treatment effects both at home and school regardless of whether the intervention was used by parents, teachers, or behavioural experts. However, echoing the findings for medication, although behavioural approaches have been demonstrated to be efficacious in the short term, sustaining treatment effects in the long run remains a challenge, and treatment effects generalize to other settings only if efforts are made to ensure that they are applied in different contexts (Hinshaw et al., 2002; Waschbusch & Hill, 2003). Furthermore, not all parents benefit from behavioural parent training (Chronis, Chacko, Fabiano, Wymbs, & Pelham, 2004). Similar to findings with respect to treatment of children with oppositional behaviour is the finding that parents facing environmental stressors (such as low family income, single parenthood, marital discord, and parental psychopathology) are least likely to benefit from standard behavioural parent training. For example, Sonuga-Barke, Daley, and

CONTINUED . . .

Thompson (2002) found that mothers who themselves had high levels of ADHD symptomatology demonstrated no improvement in parenting following training, whereas mothers with low or moderate ADHD symptoms demonstrated substantial improvement in parenting.

Given the promising but imperfect results from studies examining the separate effects of medication and of psychosocial treatment, a large group of researchers launched the Multimodal Treatment Study of Children with Attention-Deficit/Hyperactivity Disorder (MTA) (Richters et al., 1995). In this collaborative study, 579 children diagnosed with ADHD-combined type were recruited across six North American sites. Children were randomly assigned to 14 months of treatment in one of four treatment conditions: (a) medication management only (in which the dose of medication was adjusted in double-blind trials); (b) behavioural treatment with parents, child, and school; (c) a combination of medication management and behavioural treatment; and (d) a comparison of regular treatment in the community (which included medication for about two-thirds of the group).

The results from the MTA study varied according to the type of outcome measure as well as to characteristics of the child and family, suggesting that there is no one-size-fits-all treatment for all children with ADHD, but there is a menu of options from which to choose. Quite simply, because ADHD is a chronic disorder that causes serious debilitation in multiple contexts, as well as frequent comorbidity (oppositional behaviour, learning problems, and depression), it is unlikely that a single approach to treatment will be sufficient to address the problem for all children. A multidimensional approach is therefore recommended (NICE, 2008; Pelham & Fabiano, 2008). Researchers continue to develop enhancements to psychosocial interventions that will help a greater number of families benefit from this approach (Chronis et al., 2004; Hoza, Kaiser, & Hurt, 2007).

Adolescent Depression

Epidemiological studies indicate that major depressive disorder is almost as common in adolescence as it is in adulthood (e.g., Lewinsohn & Clarke, 1999). Data from the United States indicate that by the age of 18, one in five young people will have experienced an episode of major depressive disorder (Clarke et al., 2003). Depression is a chronic recurrent disorder that is associated with difficulties in peer relationships, poorer school functioning, and troubled family relationships (Seligman, Goza, & Ollendick, 2004). It is also associated with an increased rate of suicide (Clarke et al., 2003). Although adolescent depression is a serious problem, the literature on the topic is less extensive than the wealth of research on the treatment of adult depression. Reviews of this literature have concluded that there is support for CBT and for IPT (David-Ferdon & Kaslow, 2008; Watanabe et al., 2007; Weisz, McCarty, & Valeri, 2006).

Guidelines for the treatment of depression in children (NICE, 2005) recommend that the initial assessment address risk and protective factors in the child's social networks. If there is evidence that the young person is exposed to bullying, school and health professionals should develop strategies to deal with the bullying. Mental health professionals should consider whether it is necessary to treat parental psychopathology in parallel with the services offered to the young person. The young person should be advised of the benefits of lifestyle factors, including regular exercise, adequate sleep, and good nutrition. The NICE guidelines recommend that antidepressant medication *not* be prescribed to treat mild depression. Instead, monitoring, non-directive supportive therapy, or group CBT is recommended. The first line of treatment for youth with moderate or severe depression is individual CBT, IPT, or short-term family therapy. According to the guidelines, antidepressant medication should be offered only in combination with a psychological treatment.

In Chapter 11, we described the ways that IPT, which was originally developed to treat depression in adults, has been modified to meet the needs of adolescents (Mufson & Dorta, 2003; Mufson, Weissman, Moreau, & Garfinkel, 1999). In Chapter 12, we described CBT for adult depression. In order to give you a sense of how CBT can be provided to youth, we will describe a CBT approach developed for adults that has been modified specifically to treat adolescent depression.

Coping with Depression in Adolescence

Coping with Depression in Adolescence (CWDA) is a program developed by Peter Lewinsohn and his colleagues (Lewinsohn & Clarke, 1999; Clarke et al., 2003) as an adaptation of the Coping with Depression course (Lewinsohn, Antonuccio, Steinmetz, & Teri, 1984) that was found to be efficacious in the treatment of depressed adults. The two coping programs are based on a model of depression that applies to both adults and adolescents. It is assumed that there are genetic risk factors for depression that, when combined with maladaptive learned thoughts and behaviours, heighten the chances of experiencing clinically significant depressive symptoms (Clarke et al., 2003). In CWDA, treatment focuses on behaviours, cognitions, and management of affect. Behavioural interventions include increasing pleasant activities and developing problem-solving skills, assertiveness skills, communication skills, and conflict resolution skills (Clarke & DeBar, 2010). Cognitive techniques include promoting the use of positive self-talk, self-monitoring, coping, and cognitive restructuring. The affective component involves learning strategies for dealing with negative emotions, including relaxation and anger management. Parents may be involved to develop their parenting, conflict resolution, and communication skills. Just as with CBT for adult depression, mood monitoring is a central activity that is introduced at the beginning of the program and is continued throughout the course of services. The

mood monitoring: tracking mood on a regular basis, usually using a chart.

focus of initial sessions is on behavioural change, with an emphasis on the practice of social skills and an increase in pleasant activities. This flows logically into an examination of dysfunctional cognitions. The end of the program focuses on strategies to ensure the maintenance of gains, progress toward goals, and the prevention of relapse. Participants are told that not every skill will be equally useful to all participants, but they are required to attempt every activity. Booster sessions can be offered at four-month intervals for two years after completing the program.

The CWDA program is delivered according to a treatment manual in a group format. Between six and 10 depressed adolescents (aged 13 to 18) take part in each group. The **psychoeducational** approach presents material in a way similar to the way other subjects are taught in school. This style of conveying material is assumed to be less stigmatizing to young people who may feel very uncomfortable with the idea of receiving treatment of a mental disorder. Treatment includes 16 two-hour sessions that are scheduled over an eight-week period. The course uses a workbook with readings, quizzes, and forms for homework. Materials are designed to be engaging for young people, using popular newspaper cartoons to illustrate common dysfunctional thoughts. Therapists are active and engage participation by seeking examples and facilitating the exchange of ideas between group members. Skills are presented in the session and are practised using role play. Participants are then assigned homework tasks that involve the application of the skills in their everyday lives. As you can see, there are more similarities than dissimilarities between the treatment of adult and youth depression. The major difference is in adapting the psychoeducational material to make it more engaging to young people and in developing modules that include parents.

psychoeducation: teaching psychological concepts to clients in a manner that is accessible to them.

CALVIN AND HOBBES © Watterson. Dist. By UNIVERSAL PRESS SYNDICATE.

EFFICACY, EFFECTIVENESS, AND THE DISSEMINATION OF EVIDENCE-BASED TREATMENTS

In Chapter 12, we discussed the challenges of moving from efficacy in clinical trials to establishing effectiveness in clinical practice. The issues raised with respect to adults are equally important with respect to children and adolescents. In the previous sections of this chapter, we have described the progress that has been made in identifying efficacious psychological treatments for children and adolescents. There is growing evidence that standard community care for child and adolescent disorders is generally not effective (Ollendick & King, 2004). For example, Weersing and Weisz (2002) compared the outcomes of depressed youth receiving care in community mental health centres with those outcomes obtained in clinical trials. It is very troubling that the effects of community-based services were more similar to what is found for youth in no-treatment control conditions than what is found in the treatment condition of RCTs. The two crucial issues confronting the field are therefore (a) whether efficacious treatments established in methodologically sound studies are also effective when they are applied as part of regular clinical practice; and, assuming the first question is answered affirmatively, (b) how these evidence-based treatments can be disseminated so that they are more widely available.

In Chapter 12, you learned about the Hunsley and Lee (2007) review that compared data from effectiveness studies to benchmarks from meta-analyses. Hunsley and Lee reported on 21 studies of treatment for adult disorders and 14 for treatment of problems in childhood and adolescence. With the growth in the youth treatment literature, Lee, Horvath, and Hunsley (2013) conducted an updated review of the effectiveness literature that identified an additional 20 studies of treatments for disorders in children and adolescents conducted in regular clinical settings. All of the effectiveness studies for children and youth included in that review found that more than 75% of patients followed the course of services to completion. Improvement rates for treatment of internalizing problems were comparable to those reported in efficacy trials. There was greater variability in outcomes for parenting interventions to treat disruptive behaviour problems, with several studies yielding superior results compared with the benchmark, and a smaller number yielding results that were poorer. Thus, based on the benchmarking strategy, there is evidence from various countries that evidence-based treatments for children and youth can be very effective when used in routine practice settings.

Some people have raised concerns that the use of treatment manuals to guide services will interfere with the development of a therapeutic alliance. To test whether this was the case, Langer, McLeod, and Weisz (2011) randomly assigned youth with internalizing disorders seeking services in community clinics to receive either manualized services or non-manualized usual care. Observer ratings found that early in services, youth receiving manualized services had a stronger alliance with their therapists than did youth receiving usual care. By the end of services, there were no differences between groups. Although this single study requires replication in other samples, it is interesting that not only was there no evidence that manualized services impaired the therapeutic relationship, but these services were in fact associated with enhancing the early alliance.

A growing body of research indicates that evidence-based treatments for anxiety, depression, ADHD, and disruptive disorders appear to be as effective for African American and Latino youths as they are for European American youths (Miranda et al., 2005). Unfortunately, despite progress in the identification of efficacious treatments, dissemination of those treatments appears slower with respect to treatment of childhood disorders than for adult disorders (Herschell, McNeil, & McNeil, 2004). For example, Herschell et al. found twice as many journal articles devoted to treatment dissemination for adult disorders than for disorders of childhood and adolescence. Exhibit 13.4 lists some of the strategies proposed by Herschell and colleagues to improve dissemination of evidence-based treatments. As you can see, some of the strategies require action on the part of the developers of interventions (e.g., making treatment manuals widely available, providing opportunities for training and supervision). Other recommendations target graduate training programs and licensing bodies. It is clear that the process of learning does not end with the awarding of the doctorate, but is a career-long endeavour. Profile Box 13.2 introduces Dr. Melanie Barwick who works to support the implementation of evidence-based mental health services for children and adolescents in Ontario.

Exhibit 13.4 Strategies to Facilitate the Dissemination of Evidence-Based Treatment

- Development of manuals that allow flexible implementation
- Graduate education in evidence-based treatment
- Continuing education in evidence-based treatment
- Training protocols such as workshops, supervision, and consultation
- Increased research on effective dissemination strategies

Adapted from Herschell, McNeil, & McNeil (2004).

PROFILE BOX 13.2

DR. MELANIE BARWICK

Courtesy of Michelle Quance Photography, Toronto

I completed a bachelor's degree in psychology at McGill University, a master's degree at the Ontario Institute for Studies in Education at the University of Toronto in the Special Education program, and then a Ph.D. in educational psychology at McGill. After graduation, I was hired at the Hospital for Sick Children in Toronto as a scientist and to oversee implementation and data management for Ontario's outcome measurement initiative. I am now an associate scientist at the hospital, where I am the scientific director of knowledge translation within the Child Health Evaluative Sciences program of the Research Institute, and conduct a program of research in implementation science and knowledge translation. I hold appointments as associate professor in the Department of Psychiatry and the Dalai Lama School of Public Health at the University of Toronto. I also lead a technical support team for 107 service provider organizations, supporting Ontario's outcome measurement initiative for children's mental health. I provide training in knowledge translation internationally for researchers and practitioners. I consult to government and service providers in the child and youth mental health sector.

TELL US ABOUT HOW YOU BECAME AN IMPLEMENTATION SCIENTIST

Learning about research is about learning good procedures, documentation, method, and analysis. All of my early jobs as a research assistant helped to cultivate these skills while paving a network of established professionals that would provide guidance and references for my next step. My postdoctoral studies at the Hincks Institute focused on language and learning disorders in children and youth referred for mental health issues. As part of our research, we developed plain language summaries of our research findings to share with knowledge users. I came to realize that sharing research knowledge was necessary but insufficient, and that we had to concentrate on implementation—that is, how knowledge users adopt evidence-based practices and how they adapt their organizational and individual ways of working. The path to becoming an implementation scientist was really a natural progression of my interests in supporting the journey of research to evidence-based practice in the real world.

TELL US ABOUT YOUR WORK IN KNOWLEDGE TRANSLATION

My interest in knowledge translation (KT) began with my work as part of a team that selected an outcome measure that could be used in child and youth mental health service provider organizations across Ontario to determine whether services were making a difference in children's adjustment. To date, we have trained thousands of practitioners in Ontario to use the Child and Adolescent Functional Assessment Scale (CAFAS), developed by Dr. Kay Hodges. Through this work, we began to understand the challenges of facilitating change in an entire workforce of service providers and we began to seek out strategies to support practitioners' adoption of evidence-based practices at a time when little was written or understood about KT or implementation of evidence-based practices. Thus began my foray into knowledge translation, which we now recognize as activities designed to support the knowledge, use, and application of research evidence.

Over the last decade, my colleagues and I have developed a national community of KT researchers and practitioners (www.ktecop.ca), our CAFAS in Ontario team continues to support practitioners using the CAFAS measure (www.cafasinontario.ca), and I lead and participate in research in KT and implementation.

CONTINUED . . .

In particular, I study how best to support the implementation of research evidence in practice environments, including children's mental health, school systems, and hospital systems. In 2004, I began the development of what has become a nationally acclaimed course to support KT knowledge and practice among scientists, KT practitioners, and clinical educators (Scientist Knowledge Translation Training™). Later, my colleagues and I developed the Knowledge Translation Professional Certificate™, a course for professionals working in KT across many disciplines and sectors www.sickkids.ca/Learning/AbouttheInstitute/Programs/Knowledge-Translation/Knowledge-Translation-Professional-Certificate/Knowledge-Translation-Professional-Certificate.html.

WHAT DO YOU SEE AS THE MOST EXCITING CHANGE IN SERVICES FOR CHILDREN AND ADOLESCENTS?

We have made great strides in the development and empirical study of psychological interventions, and we now have a strong repertoire of interventions to address many psychological problems. Although it is important to conduct treatment outcome research, we also now recognize that currently much of what has already been discovered lies inactive. Unfortunately, much of our evidence does not make its way down the research pipeline to the real world, where it can be used to improve health and well-being. As such, the challenge ahead of us now is to develop an evidence base for knowledge translation and implementation. This challenge is not unique to psychology, as many health professions are wrestling with the same issues. At a time of limited economic resources and greater public need, we must become better at sharing and using what we already know works. Related challenges include building a workforce of practitioners with the skills and competencies to work in an evidence-based culture. Institutions of higher learning play a key role in ensuring that they are teaching the skills and values that equip future service providers to embrace evidence-based practice. It also means we must develop supports and tools to help provider organizations manage the implementation of evidence-based practices and interventions. As we work to develop and test KT and implementation strategies, we are focusing on uncovering the complexities of the change processes involved, including system, organizational, and individual considerations. We are also focusing on research to identify the factors that play important roles in implementation success and in developing measures that can help us both plan for implementation and measure its ultimate outcomes. Knowledge translation and implementation is a rich, nascent, and rapidly developing field, and I am so excited to be in the midst of it all, making my own contribution and learning, always learning.

Although there has been great progress in identifying helpful treatments for problems in children and adolescents, there is still considerable room for improvement. Weisz, Doss, and Hawley (2005) reviewed published, methodologically sound RCTs for anxiety (82 studies), depression (18 studies), ADHD (40 studies), and conduct problems (96 studies). These authors highlighted a number of threats to both internal validity and external validity that limited the extent to which results could be generalized. For example, in many studies there was no reliable determination of the diagnosis. Most studies were underpowered: they had too few participants in each condition to provide the statistical power to detect meaningful group differences. Few studies had participants from clinical settings: in the majority of studies, participants were recruited rather than drawn from contexts in which they were seeking treatment. Furthermore, the authors reported that two-thirds of the studies were conducted in the United States and that learning-based treatments were 8 to 10 times more likely to be studied than were insight-based treatments (i.e., psychodynamic treatments). Thus, although there has been progress in the study of psychological treatments for children and adolescents, it is essential that research be conducted to determine the extent to which promising treatments are useful for the populations who require services.

One of the most pressing questions is to identify the ingredients in treatment that are responsible for change (Kazdin, 2003). Clinical psychologists are faced with an overwhelming array of treatment protocols with varying degrees of support. In an attempt to address this, Chorpita and Daleiden (2009) undertook an innovative analysis of the practice elements that were used in 322 randomized clinical trials of treatments for children and adolescents. They were able to identify clusters of strategies that have consistently been found to be helpful in dealing with specific problems. For example, in the treatment of anxiety, treatments commonly included modules dealing with exposure, relaxation, cognitive interventions, modelling, and psychoeducation with the child. Based on this work, Chorpita and Daleiden recommended that clinicians consider individualizing treatments by selecting and integrating treatment modules that best correspond to a client's presenting problems.

You will have noticed that up until now, we have presented results of research examining treatments for specific disorders. Unfortunately, children and youth who meet diagnostic criteria for one disorder frequently have other problems too. To address this issue, Weisz and his colleagues (Weisz et al., 2012) tested the usefulness of offering modular treatment for depression, anxiety, and conduct problems in young people aged 7 to 13. Community clinicians were randomly assigned to one of three conditions: (a) treatment as usual; (b) an evidence-based treatment for anxiety, depression, or conduct problems; or (c) a modularized approach in which clinicians flexibly delivered modules that integrated the three evidence-based approaches as needed. Weisz et al. found that modular treatment outperformed both usual care and a single problem-focused evidence-based treatment. The modular treatment approach advocated by Chorpita and Daleiden (2009) and Weisz et al. (2012) appears to hold great promise in the dissemination of evidence-based psychological services for youth.

As we have indicated throughout this chapter, there are a number of challenges in providing psychological services for children and adolescents. To give you a sense of how some of these challenges play out in the actual treatment of an adolescent, Viewpoint Box 13.2 presents information on the treatment of Noah who was introduced in Chapter 3.

VIEWPOINT BOX 13.2

PSYCHOLOGICAL TREATMENT FOR NOAH

In Chapter 3, we introduced Noah, a 12-year-old boy exposed to the trauma of genocide. Noah suffered from diverse symptoms, including anxiety, persistent re-experiencing of the events, avoidance of stimuli associated with the trauma, somatic complaints, and sleep disturbance. Noah's symptoms were consistent with a diagnosis of PTSD. The initial assessment led to a formulation of Noah's problems in terms of his initial exposure to genocide when he was 3 years old as well as the re-emergence of threat when he was 9 years old. Counterbalancing these serious risk factors were the protective factors of his strong attachment to his mother and twin sister. Noah's mother did not connect her son's symptoms of anxiety to his horrific experiences. She was bewildered that, now the family was safe in Canada, her son was showing signs of "craziness." In understanding the mother's reaction, it is important to bear in mind that she, too, had been exposed to trauma, with the murder of her husband and threats to herself and her children. She, too, suffered from PTSD and experienced characteristic numbing and avoidance of stimuli that made it hard for her to acknowledge the source of Noah's difficulties.

In treatment planning, psychologists must first consider whether there are evidence-based treatments for the client's problem. Although there are efficacious treatments for adults with PTSD, the treatment of childhood and adolescent PTSD is not as well developed (Silverman et al., 2008). There is evidence of the usefulness of some approaches in treating childhood PTSD resulting from a single traumatic event such as a car accident (Scotti, Morris, Ruggiero, & Wolfgang, 2002). However, Noah was exposed to unremitting trauma over the course of months. There is also evidence of the usefulness of CBT approaches in treating children who suffer PTSD as a result of sexual abuse (Silverman et al., 2008), and case studies of exposure in the treatment of Lebanese children suffering war-related PTSD (Feeny, Foa, Treadwell, & March, 2004), but no studies on the treatment of children and adolescents exposed to genocide. As you learned in Chapter 12, efficacious treatments for adults with PTSD include relaxation, imaginal exposure, and in vivo exposure. Important prerequisites for treatment are that the person must be safe and there must be people available to support him or her during the painful period of habituation to the stimuli associated with symptoms. Although Noah was safe in Canada, his refugee claim was pending. In the event that his family's claim for refugee status was denied and they were forced to return to their home country, he would again be exposed to danger. Noah's mother was devoted to her children's well-being, but she also suffered from PTSD, so her capacity to support him emotionally was diminished.

In the absence of an evidence-based treatment package that matches the client's needs, the psychologist must consider whether there are elements of evidence-based approaches that are relevant (Connor-Smith & Weisz, 2003). Fortunately, the treatment of anxiety disorders in childhood includes many efficacious strategies (Cartwright-Hatton, Roberts, Chitsabesan, Fothergill, & Harrington, 2004; Kazdin, 2003; Roberts et al., 2003). Accordingly, the treatment goals for Noah included the development of relaxation and stress-management strategies, as well as the accurate identification of emotions and changes in his belief systems. A critically important goal was the reduction of avoidance of stimuli associated with the trauma. In a feedback session with Noah and his mother, the psychologist provided information about PTSD, linking

CONTINUED . . .

it to the events they had experienced. Noah and his mother agreed to parallel services in which each would work on PTSD symptoms and develop effective stress-management skills.

Noah attended 13 sessions. Initial sessions focused on the development of a collaborative relationship through non-threatening activities. For example, Noah learned to expand his vocabulary of emotions through Internet-based activities in which he had to match facial expressions to emotion labels (e.g., scared, disappointed, frustrated, grumpy, worried). Next, he worked to generate possible explanations for emotions (e.g., worried because a test is coming up, embarrassed because he does not want to look stupid). Noah agreed to keep a sleep log in which he recorded his nighttime routine and any awakening, as well as the thoughts he had when unable to sleep. Subsequently, he learned relaxation activities including both breathing exercises and progressive muscle relaxation. At the same time, his mother was also learning relaxation strategies. Noah then practised these relaxation activities when he went to bed and whenever he awoke in the night. Noah observed that the relaxation strategies were helpful in reducing the time spent awake.

In the next phase of services, Noah's cognitions were targeted. Following an episode in which he lay awake for hours having heard what he thought was an intruder in the house, Noah learned to distinguish between "real" emotional alarms and "false" emotional alarms. The therapist used the example of firefighters to illustrate this. Noah learned that when the bell sounds in the fire hall, the firefighters get ready to fight a fire; as they put on their gear and travel to the possible fire, they are ready for action. Once at the site, they check carefully to see whether there is a fire. In the event that there is a fire, they work to extinguish it. However, in the event that there is a false alarm, they return to the fire hall and resume their activities. Applying this analogy in his own life, Noah was able to remind himself that, like the firefighters, he should check to see whether there was a reason for the alarm by checking that the doors were locked and that no one had access to the house; once he had established that it was a false alarm, he could use the relaxation strategies to fall back to sleep.

As the anniversary of the genocide approached, Noah talked about his ambivalence in participating in memorial activities. Equipped with his expanded vocabulary of feelings, he communicated his desire to avoid the extreme sadness and anger of remembering the horror, balanced by his desire to connect to other people who had shared the experience. Noah recognized that participation did not have to be an all-or-nothing decision, and he chose to be involved in some activities, such as a candlelight vigil, but to limit others, such as watching hours of television footage of the carnage. With the psychologist, Noah practised communicating his preferences to his mother. Subsequently, Noah reported satisfaction that he was able to make choices and exhaustion at the emotional toll of the memorial, but also appreciation of a greater feeling of connectedness with others in his extended family and community. At the end of services, Noah reported that he no longer suffered from sleep disturbance or somatic complaints. The persistent re-experiencing of the trauma had diminished and he was less avoidant of stimuli associated with it.

In adapting treatment for this young client, it was necessary for the psychologist to deliver material in a developmentally appropriate fashion. Whereas a younger child might be engaged in cutting pictures from a magazine and pasting them into a collage that illustrates different emotions, Noah found it cool to point and click at images on a website. As a young man on the verge of adolescence, Noah was most comfortable with individual services in which he could enjoy privacy with the therapist. Nevertheless, from the provision of information about PTSD that reduced the mother's intolerance of her son's anxious behaviour, to the encouragement that both mother and son practise relaxation exercises, the coordination of services for the adult and youth was essential.

SUMMARY AND CONCLUSIONS

Compared with the evidence base for adult treatments, far less is known about the effects of psychotherapy for children and adolescents. Nevertheless, meta-analyses indicate that treatments for youth can have substantial effects on psychological symptoms, with some estimates indicating almost comparable treatment effects for adults and youth. Various organizations have worked to develop listings of evidence-based interventions for children and adolescents and, at present, there are scientifically supported psychosocial treatments for the most commonly occurring mental disorders. Clinical practice guidelines for addressing mood disorders, anxiety disorders, ADHD, and externalizing disorders are now available for both clinicians and patients and their families. Despite these advances, much more work needs to be done to encourage treatment research that is more clinically representative, to understand exactly what the ingredients of successful treatment are, and to promote the use of evidence-based treatments in real-world settings.

KEY TERMS

coercive exchanges: parent–child interactions in which the parent unintentionally rewards the child for whining or aggression (by withdrawing a demand or providing attention) and the child rewards the parent for giving in to his or her complaints (by ceasing the aversive behaviour).

ecological theory: a theory that examines a young person's functioning within the multiple contexts in which he or she lives—family, school, neighbourhood, etc.

mood monitoring: tracking mood on a regular basis, usually using a chart.

parental monitoring: parents' awareness and tracking of the child's activities.

positive reinforcement: any consequence that increases the likelihood of a behaviour being repeated.

psychoeducation: teaching psychological concepts to clients in a manner that is accessible to them.

time out: a parenting strategy in which the child does not have access to reinforcers for a brief period following misbehaviour.

KEY NAMES

Bruce Chorpita
Alan Kazdin
Peter Lewinsohn
Gerald Patterson
John Weisz

ADDITIONAL RESOURCES

Books

Kendall, P. C. (Ed.). (2012). *Child and adolescent therapy: Cognitive-behavioral procedures* (4th ed). New York: Guilford Press.

Weisz, J. R., & Kazdin, A. E. (Eds.). (2010). *Evidence-based psychotherapies for children and adolescents* (2nd ed). New York: Guilford Press.

Check It Out!

Information on evidence-based treatments, sponsored by the Society of Clinical Child and Adolescent Psychology: effectivechildtherapy.com/content/about-child-adolescent-symptoms

The *British Medical Journal* provides reviews of the literature on the treatment of physical and mental disorders: www.clinicalevidence.org

The American Academy of Child and Adolescent Psychiatry Practice Parameters: www.aacap.org/cs/root/member_information/practice_information/practice_parameters/practice_parameters

Multisystemic Therapy: www.mstservices.com

INTERVENTION: IDENTIFYING KEY ELEMENTS OF CHANGE

14 CHAPTER

INTRODUCTION

Consistent with our emphasis on clinical psychology as an evidence-based profession, Chapters 12 and 13 examined the research on interventions that work in the treatment of a variety of disorders and problems. However, it is important also to consider the large body of evidence that focuses on patient/client, therapist, and therapeutic process variables that influence treatment outcome. It is essential that this research inform the evidence-based practice of clinical psychology. As we described in the previous chapters, hundreds of studies have examined the outcome of treatments and the comparative outcome of different types of treatment. In addition, many hundreds of studies have examined elements of psychotherapy, such as the alliance between patient and therapist, and the way these process elements are related to the impact of treatment. These approaches to studying psychotherapy are known as, respectively, process research and process-outcome research. In the first part of this chapter, we illustrate what can be learned about psychotherapy from **process research** and **process-outcome research**.

As we mentioned in Chapter 2, many clinical psychologists describe their theoretical orientation as a combination of two or more of the major approaches to treatment, such as experiential and cognitive-behavioural. In considering the use of more than one approach, it is important to consider **common factors** in successful treatment that cut across specific approaches to therapy (e.g., Garfield, 1994; Norcross & Goldfried, 1992). In the latter part of the chapter, we examine both theories and research on these common (or non-specific) factors. As some theorists propose that common factors are responsible for most of the impact of any form of psychotherapy, we review evidence with

process research: research that examines patterns, using therapist and/or client data, that are evident within and across therapy sessions.

process-outcome research: research that examines the relation between variables related to the process of providing psychotherapy and the outcome of therapy.

common factors: therapeutic elements that occur in all or most treatments and are believed to be critical for successful client outcomes.

respect to the possibility that all forms of psychotherapy have equivalent effects.

As you learned in the previous two chapters, findings from treatment outcome research have been used to develop evidence-based recommendations for the treatment of specific disorders and conditions. The results of process research and process-outcome research have also been used to formulate clinical guidelines for psychologists. In the final part of this chapter, we examine these guidelines in detail. One set of initiatives focused on developing guidelines that explicitly emphasized client characteristics and therapy relationship factors found to be related to treatment outcome. A second initiative to develop guidelines involved combining research findings on client, therapist, client-therapist relationship, and treatment characteristics to develop evidence-based principles of therapeutic change that can be applied to all forms of treatment.

PSYCHOTHERAPY PROCESS AND PROCESS-OUTCOME RESEARCH

To understand the relation between treatment-outcome research and process-outcome research, it is useful to consider a sports analogy. A team's performance over a season can be analyzed in a number of ways. For example, you can simply count the number of wins during a season; or the number of wins under specific circumstances, such as when a team plays at home or away, or on natural or synthetic surfaces; or the team's record against specific opponents. Like treatment-outcome research, all of these examples focus on outcomes, outcomes under varying conditions, or how the team fared compared with other teams. None of this reveals much about *how* the team achieved its record. To do this, we need to examine *processes* within each game and then examine the consistency of these processes across all games the team played. For example, how well does the team do if they score first? What happens if the star offensive player has a poor game? Or what is the effect on the outcome if there are a greater than average number of penalties called against the team? All of these questions explore the issue of what is occurring during a game that is associated with the team being relatively successful or unsuccessful. Such questions are similar to those posed by process-outcome psychotherapy researchers.

©iStock.com/skynesher

Psychotherapy, like sports, can be analyzed in terms of how you win as well as whether you win.

These ways of examining the record of a sports team (or of psychotherapy) address different questions. Similarly, different types of psychotherapy research are designed to address different questions. Treatment-outcome research addresses the question of *which* intervention is more efficacious, whereas process research and process-outcome research ask about *how* an intervention works. Identifying the best team or comparing teams to one another requires different data and a different approach to data analysis than does determining the factors that contribute to a team's success or whether these same factors account for the performance of all the teams in the league.

In a review of the history of process-outcome research, David Orlinsky and colleagues (Orlinsky, Rønnestad, & Willutzki, 2004) traced the development of this line of psychotherapy research. In the 1950s and 1960s, psychologists interested in the process of psychotherapy began using two important sources of data: recordings of psychotherapy sessions, and standardized measures of clients' and therapists' experience of the treatment process. Since then, the number of strategies for studying what transpires in therapy (process research) and how it is related to client change (process-outcome research) has grown dramatically and grown more complex. Exhibit 14.1 provides an overview of the different levels at which psychotherapy researchers have addressed these important questions.

EXHIBIT 14.1 Levels of Analysis for Psychotherapeutic Process and Process-Outcome Studies

TIME FRAME	TIME SCALE	PROCESS FOCUS	OUTCOME FOCUS
Liminal	Split-seconds	Facial expressions, shifts in gaze	None
Momentary	Minutes	Specific statements, changes in direction of conversation	Emergence of specific experiences, such as insight or catharsis
Situational	Hours	Changes in dynamics across sessions, dealing with alliance problems	Immediate improvements in mood or motivation
Daily	Days	Homework assignments, between-session experiences	Change in functioning, improved handling of problems
Monthly	Weeks	Development of alliance, phases of treatment	Ongoing improvements in functioning and reduction of symptoms
Seasonal	Months	Addressing recurrent themes in treatment, entire course of treatment	Changes in adaptation and identity
Perennial	Years	Long-term treatment events	Personality change

Adapted from Orlinsky, Rønnestad, & Willutzki (2004).

As you will see throughout this chapter, by examining process questions, and by then relating this information to treatment outcome, psychotherapy researchers have learned a great deal about how therapy works. For example, many studies have examined the ways in which the therapist's behaviour during treatment sessions varies across different theoretical orientations. In general, even though there is considerable similarity across therapist behaviours, therapists tend to behave in ways that are consistent with the theoretical orientations they espouse (e.g., Blagys & Hilsenroth, 2000). In the following pages, we describe some of the intriguing results obtained in process-outcome research. By using this research to inform their therapeutic practices, clinical psychologists can improve the services they offer clients. Our description of the research on sudden client gains in treatment in Viewpoint Box 14.1 is an example of the important discoveries that have been made in process-outcome research.

VIEWPOINT BOX 14.1

SUDDEN GAINS IN THERAPY

After reading the chapters on psychological treatment, you may be wondering what the process of therapeutic change looks like. How can you tell if the client is improving? Is it a steady progression of small, barely perceptible but important changes that cumulatively result in altered psychosocial functioning? Or, does change occur the way it is often portrayed in movies, so that after weeks of non-productive sessions, a client experiences a dramatic breakthrough that results in a qualitatively different view of him- or herself?

This was the question that Tang and DeRubeis (1999) addressed when they undertook a session-by-session review of the treatment progress of depressed patients in two cognitive-behavioural therapy (CBT) efficacy trials. Although they found different patterns of progress across patients, they noticed that more than one-third of patients experienced large reductions in depressive symptoms early in treatment. Closer examination revealed that these patients made sudden large gains in functioning around session 4, 5, or 6. The sudden gains in functioning were very large—they involved at least a 25% reduction in pre-treatment symptom levels—and were made during a single period of time between two sessions. Those who experienced these sudden gains were less depressed than other patients at the end of treatment and they tended to maintain their gains up to 18 months after treatment. Using a different CBT efficacy trial data set, Tang, DeRubeis, Beberman, and Pham (2005) replicated their original findings. They found clear evidence of the same pattern of sudden gains and also found evidence that, prior to the sudden gains, substantial cognitive changes occurred among the patients who experienced sudden gains. Consistent with the cognitive theory of change proposed by cognitive therapists (described in Chapter 11), it appears that changes in the way in which patients thought about themselves and their life situations were causally related to the observed changes in symptoms.

Sudden gains have also been found in depressed patients receiving other forms of treatment. Tang, Luborsky, and Andrusyna (2002), for example, reported sudden gains in an efficacy trial of short-term psychodynamic treatment. These sudden gains were of similar magnitude to those reported by Tang and DeRubeis (1999), and occurred for a similar percentage of patients early in treatment. Although patients with sudden gains were, in comparison with those without sudden gains, significantly better at the end of treatment, the two groups had similar levels of depression six months after treatment ended. Using data from patients receiving

CONTINUED . . .

cognitive therapy for depression, Tang, DeRubeis, Hollon, Amsterdam, and Shelton (2007) reported that patients who experienced sudden gains were far less likely than other patients to experience relapse in the two years following treatment. Sudden gains have also been found in interpersonal psychotherapy for depression, but the experience of sudden gains did not affect the likelihood of patients achieving a remission of symptoms at the end of treatment (Kelly, Cyranowski, & Frank, 2007).

Evidence of sudden gains has also come from two British studies using data from routine treatment settings. Hardy et al. (2005) examined the progress of clients receiving cognitive therapy for depression in a National Health Service clinic: 40% of clients experienced changes almost identical to those reported by Tang and DeRubeis (1999). Stiles et al. (2003) examined data from 135 clients with a variety of disorders and problems who were treated with a variety of approaches (including cognitive therapy, psychodynamic therapy, and experiential therapies). Seventeen percent of those clients experienced the sudden gains, with half of the clients achieving them by the fifth treatment session. As in most other studies, by the end of treatment, these clients were significantly improved relative to the clients who did not experience sudden gains. Finally, Vittengl, Clark, and Jarrett (2005) found evidence of sudden treatment gains in two data sets that involved cognitive therapy for major depressive disorder. Sudden gain patterns similar to those reported by Tang and DeRubeis (1999) were found using both patient data and therapist data. What is particularly noteworthy, though, is that Vittengl and colleagues also found evidence of sudden gains in patients who received pill placebos as well as in those who received antidepressant medication.

The repeated independent replication of the sudden gains pattern lends credibility to the validity of the phenomenon. In a meta-analysis of 16 studies examining the phenomenon of sudden gains in the treatment of anxiety and depression, Aderka, Nickerson, Bøe, and Hofmann (2012) found consistent evidence of the occurrence of sudden gains and the substantial impact they usually have on treatment outcome. Interestingly, the impact of sudden gains on treatment outcome was significantly greater for CBT compared with other treatments. The fact that the effect of sudden gains on treatment outcome is evident in many, but not all, forms of intervention has raised the question of whether there might be different mechanisms of change operating in different types of treatment. It is likely that future research will investigate the important questions of what is responsible for the sudden gains and whether the outcome-related impact of sudden gains may occur for different reasons in different psychotherapies.

Think about an "intervention" you have begun recently. It could be yoga for relaxation, physiotherapy for knee pain, strips to whiten your teeth, or spinning to improve your cardiovascular fitness. If you were to experience sudden gains after a few sessions, how would that affect your likelihood of persisting with the intervention?

Examining Client Factors

As you learned in Chapters 12 and 13, the vast majority of randomized controlled trial (RCT) psychotherapy studies examine treatment outcomes for different groups of clients classified on the basis of diagnoses or presenting problems. However, it would be a mistake to think of people

How important is it that clients and therapists be similar in terms of key demographic variables? Can a male therapist possibly help a female client, or can a young therapist possibly help an older adult client?

Top row: Left, ©iStock.com/SPC-HQ; Middle, ©iStock.com/digitalskillet; Right, ©iStock.com/theboone

Bottom row: Left, ©iStock.com/jordanchez; Middle, ©iStock.com/DanielBendjy; Right, ©iStock.com/theboone

Client age is unrelated to treatment outcome.

only in terms of their psychological symptoms. No psychotherapy researcher believes that diagnosis is the primary factor that determines treatment outcome. Client characteristics other than diagnosis may be very important predictors of treatment success or failure. Consequently, a large literature has examined the influence of client variables on psychotherapy. Much of this research comes from studies of treatments provided in real-world clinic settings, but a growing number of studies are derived from RCTs in which investigators have sought to identify mediators and moderators (discussed in Chapter 4) of treatment efficacy (Kazdin, 2007).

The first challenge in examining client variables is determining which variables to evaluate. Which client characteristics should be taken into account? Among the myriad potential variables are personality characteristics, current life circumstances, life experiences, family of origin characteristics, ethnicity and cultural factors, beliefs about psychological problems, and expectations regarding treatment. If clinical psychologists know the potential impact of such characteristics on therapy, they can formulate a treatment to be optimally responsive to the needs of the client. Efforts to synthesize results of the voluminous research on client factors in therapy have been hampered by the non-systematic nature of the studies. In other words, different researchers have tended to examine a variable, such as clients' treatment expectations, in different ways across studies. It is extremely difficult to detect patterns across studies that used different types of measures (e.g., completion of a self-report measure versus coding of statements made during a therapy session) and different timing of the assessment (e.g., prior to commencing treatment or after one session of therapy). As succinctly summarized by Petry, Tennen, and Affleck (2000), the unfortunate consequence of this variability is that, despite thousands of empirical studies, we still have only a rudimentary appreciation of how client variables affect treatment responses. Exhibit 14.2 provides a summary of the most consistent findings in the empirical literature.

Exhibit 14.2 Client Variables That Influence Treatment

Sociodemographic Characteristics

Socioeconomic Status

- Higher socioeconomic status is associated with a greater likelihood of engaging in and staying in treatment.

Ethnicity

- Similarity in client and therapist ethnicity is associated with a somewhat greater likelihood of clients staying in treatment and of making therapeutic change.

CONTINUED . . .

Gender

- Women are more likely to seek therapy than are men, but there is no gender difference in premature termination of services.
- Matching of client and therapist gender has little influence on treatment outcome or treatment satisfaction.

Age

- Client age is positively related to staying in treatment, but unrelated to treatment outcome.

Psychological Functioning

Symptom Severity

- Greater severity of psychological symptoms is related to poorer treatment outcome.

Functional Impairment

- Greater overall impairment in functioning (i.e., in various social roles and health status) is related to poorer treatment outcome.

Personality Characteristics

Personality Disorders

- The presence of a personality disorder diagnosis is associated with premature termination, problems in the process of therapy, and less therapeutic change during treatment.

Ego Strength

- Ego strength (broadly defined as the capacity to use personality resources to manage negative emotional states and threats to personal identity) is related to positive treatment outcome.

Psychological Mindedness

- Psychological mindedness (broadly defined as the ability to understand people and problems in psychological terms) is usually related to positive treatment outcome.

Psychological Reactance

- Clients low in reactance (broadly defined as the tendency to react against attempts to influence or limit one's behaviours or options) tend to experience greater therapeutic gains in more directive treatments, whereas clients high in reactance tend to experience greater therapeutic gains in less directive treatments.

Treatment Expectations

- Positive expectations for treatment are associated with remaining in treatment and greater therapeutic gains.

Adapted from Bohart & Wade (2013); Clarkin & Levy (2004); Constantino, Glass, Arnkoff, Ametrano, & Smith (2011); Petry, Tennen, & Affleck (2000); and Swift and Greenberg (2012).

The information in Exhibit 14.2 provides clear guidance to help clinical psychologists tailor their treatment plans for the individual client. Let's take the example of socioeconomic status. Knowing that a client with a lower socioeconomic status is at heightened risk for premature termination, psychologists can take steps early in treatment to enhance the likelihood that the client will engage in treatment. So, in providing services to Shari, a single mother of two young children who has a part-time job with irregular working hours, the psychologist

©iStock.com/quavondo

Sensitivity to the client's life circumstances may reduce the likelihood of dropout from treatment.

could explicitly discuss options to help Shari fit therapy appointments into her schedule. Rather than a regular appointment during standard office hours, the psychologist could offer appointments that do not require Shari to take time off work or to make arrangements for extra child care. Furthermore, many psychologists in private practice have sliding fee scales that allow patients with lower incomes (and limited private insurance coverage) to pay reduced fees. Access to affordable services may make the difference between Shari engaging in therapy and prematurely ending services.

It is important to keep in mind that pre-existing client variables, such as current life context, life experiences, and personality, may have the greatest impact on client decisions about seeking and engaging in therapy. Once treatment starts, the relationship between client and psychologist is likely to generate a far more powerful influence on the course and outcome of treatment (cf. Clarkin & Levy, 2004). The ultimate outcome of treatment is affected by the way the client feels about the psychologist, the psychologist's responses to client questions and challenges, the degree of benefit the client experiences early in treatment, and the extent to which treatment influences the client's daily life. In a large-scale study of the treatment of depression, for example, patients who initially expected treatment to be effective remained in therapy and engaged actively and constructively in therapy sessions, which resulted in reductions in their symptoms (Elkin et al., 1999; Meyer et al., 2002).

Given what you learned in Chapter 9 about the possible effects of heuristics and biases in clinical decision-making, do you think that there are any dangers associated with using research on client factors to guide treatment planning for a specific client? What steps can a psychologist take to ensure that the research information is used in an appropriate manner?

Examining Therapist Factors

Just as researchers have explored the impact of *client* variables on treatment processes and outcome, so too have they addressed the ways in which *therapist* variables affect aspects of psychotherapy. This research has yielded subtle and nuanced findings about the impact of the psychotherapist on the patient's response to treatment. As mentioned previously with respect to client variables, this is partly because of

(a) the manner in which interactions between patient and therapist occur and evolve over the course of treatment and (b) the power such interactions exert on the process of therapeutic change. Exhibit 14.3 summarizes the main findings on the contribution of therapist factors to psychotherapy process and outcome.

Exhibit 14.3 Therapist Variables That Influence Treatment

Sociodemographic Characteristics

Ethnicity

- Very limited systematic research has examined the main effect of therapist ethnicity or cultural background on treatment outcome, with no consistent pattern of effects apparent.

Gender

- Therapist gender has no consistent effect on treatment outcome.

Age

- Therapist age is unrelated to treatment outcome.
- Similarity in age between client and therapist does not contribute significantly to treatment outcome.

Professional Background

Professional Discipline

- Therapists trained in a mental health discipline tend to have better treatment outcomes than those trained in a health discipline (i.e., general practitioners).
- Research is inconclusive regarding the relative effectiveness of therapists trained in different mental health disciplines (i.e., clinical psychologists, psychiatrists, social workers, marriage and family counsellors).

Professional Experience

- Although there is considerable variability in the evidence, overall, the research indicates that therapist experience (measured in years or number of clients treated) is small, but positively related to treatment outcome.

Personality Characteristics

Personality Traits

- Therapist personality traits have little association with treatment outcome.

Emotional Well-Being

- Therapist emotional well-being is consistently positively associated with treatment outcome.

Values, Attitudes, and Beliefs

- No consistent pattern of results has been found regarding the influence of therapists' values, attitudes, and beliefs on the process and outcome of therapy.

Use of Self-Disclosure

- Self-disclosure (broadly defined as the therapist's judicious sharing of personal experiences or views in the process of therapy) has been found to have a small but positive effect on treatment outcome.

Adapted from Beutler et al. (2004) and Teyber & McClure (2000).

©iStock.com/asiseeit

©iStock.com/nullplus

Therapist gender does not influence treatment outcome.

The research described in Exhibit 14.3, like that summarized for client variables in Exhibit 14.2, is based on an examination of the individual contribution of specific therapist variables on the therapeutic process. However, many therapist variables may interact in therapy. It seems intuitively obvious that the "sum" of the therapist's personal qualities should be an important ingredient in any recipe for good therapy. After all, a good psychotherapist must have considerable knowledge, technical skills, interpersonal sensitivity, and tolerance for distress. For example, Lafferty, Beutler, and Crago (1989) studied trainee therapists in clinical psychology, psychiatry, clinical social work, and psychiatric nursing working in an outpatient clinic. Based on the treatment results for two randomly selected clients for each trainee, they selected 30 therapists for whom both clients improved and 30 for whom neither client improved. Data from patients and therapists were used to examine differences in the therapists between these two groups. Although there were only small differences between the groups of therapists in terms of emotional adjustment or general life values, analyses revealed an important group difference in what transpired during treatment. Specifically, patients of the more effective therapists reported feeling more understood in treatment than did the patients of the less effective therapists.

But what do we know about overall differences in therapeutic effectiveness among fully qualified and practising therapists? The results of RCTs are likely to underestimate the true variability in effectiveness across therapists because of the standardization of treatment and treatment delivery essential to this type of experimental design. Nevertheless, variability in client outcomes due to therapist factors has been noted in RCTs (e.g., Kim, Wampold, & Bolt, 2006) and in clinical settings in which therapists had been trained to deliver a specific type of evidence-based treatment for posttraumatic stress disorder (PTSD) (e.g., Laska, Smith, Wislocki, Minami, & Wampold, 2013). Baldwin and Imel (2013) reviewed the research on therapist effects on treatment outcome and found that most studies reported significant variability in therapist effectiveness. On average, they found that therapist effects accounted for 3% of the treatment outcome in efficacy trials and 7% of the treatment outcome in effectiveness trials and naturalistic studies of psychotherapy provision. Although these may seem like relatively small effects, over the duration of therapists' careers, the cumulative difference between the least effective and the most effective therapists is likely to be substantial. Findings such as these demonstrate that variability in therapist effectiveness can exert a powerful influence on the delivery and impact of psychological interventions.

The nature of therapist effects is far from straightforward. For example, in their study of 119 therapists and 10,786 patients in the UK,

Saxon and Barkham (2012) found that differences in therapist effectiveness were most noticeable when treating patients with high levels of problem severity. The impact of therapist effects on treatment outcome was three times greater for patients with the most severe problems compared to those with the least severe problems. Kraus, Castonguay, Boswell, Nordberg, and Hayes (2011) collected data on the outcome of 6,690 patients treated by 696 therapists in the U.S. They explored patient improvement across a number of domains (e.g., anxiety, depression, mania, psychosis, sexual functioning, social functioning, and violence). Across domains, the percentage of patients who improved by the end of therapy ranged from 13% (with respect to symptoms of mania) to 55% (with respect to symptoms of depression). They also identified therapists who were harmful, which they defined as those whose average patient showed deterioration in functioning in a domain, and therapists who were effective, which they defined as those whose average patient showed improvement in functioning in a domain. To their surprise, they found a large number of therapists whose average patient ends treatment worse off than at the start of treatment in one or more domains (ranging from 3% harmful therapists with respect to treating symptoms of depression to 16% harmful therapists with respect to treating symptoms of substance abuse and violence). On the flip side of this, there were substantial numbers of effective therapists (ranging from 29% when dealing with symptoms of problems in sexual functioning to 67% when dealing with symptoms of depression). Indeed, the majority of therapists were effective in at least three domains of client functioning, with 30% of therapists being effective in seven or more domains of client functioning. Thus, based on this study, it would be inaccurate to label therapists as globally effective or harmful. Rather, therapists appear to have relative strengths and weaknesses in their competencies to address client problems across a wide range of conditions. As a result of the widespread evidence of differences in the effectiveness of therapists, suggestions have been made that there should be an emphasis on certifying *therapists*, rather than treatments, as effective in dealing with specific types of patient conditions (Krause, Lutz, & Saunders, 2007).

Examining Treatment Factors

In previous chapters, we described some of the characteristics of the current main approaches to psychotherapy and presented evidence for their efficacy and effectiveness in treating specific conditions. Researchers have examined, both within specific treatment orientations and across orientations, whether some aspects of therapy are especially important in achieving therapeutic change. Is it important for therapists to explicitly interpret clients' behaviour? Is it better to focus on symptom reduction or on achieving insight? Does the use of between-session assignments make any difference in treatment? Process-outcome researchers have investigated these questions and many others. In this section, we consider some of the main findings from this line of inquiry.

Interpretation

Interpretation of client behaviour often occurs in psychodynamic and experiential approaches to therapy. This can include explanations for the client's problems as well as the labelling of unconscious processes that are believed to influence thoughts, emotions, and behaviours. In their review of the research on interpretations, Beutler and colleagues (2004) found no consistent pattern of results across studies. Although the weighted average effect size was a nonsignificant $r = .07$, there were a number of studies in which interpretations were strongly correlated with positive outcome. In general, these studies suggested that therapist interpretations were most successful with clients who had good interpersonal skills. You can well imagine the mixed reactions people would have to frequent comments on the reasons for their behaviours and emotions. A high degree of interpersonal competence would probably be important in helping the client to openly discuss such affectively charged therapist comments.

Directiveness

How directive should the therapist be? Is it better to have an active, guiding therapist, or is a neutral, reflective stance more conducive to positive outcomes? Based on their review, Beutler et al. (2004) reported a weighted average effect size of $r = .06$, which was statistically nonsignificant. However, the range of effect sizes across studies varied enormously, from $-.17$ to $.79$. With such wide variation, it is obvious that calculating the mean across studies is likely to obscure some important information. In all likelihood, in this instance, there are moderating variables that influence the extent to which therapist directiveness is appropriate. When we consider the evidence summarized in Exhibit 14.1, it seems likely that the optimal degree of therapist directiveness is determined, at least in part, by the client's level of psychological reactance. Psychological **reactance** is the tendency to react against attempts to directly influence one's behaviour. Low-reactant clients are usually open to therapists being directive in therapy, whereas high-reactant clients tend to prefer therapists being less directive.

reactance: the tendency to react against attempts to directly influence one's behaviour.

Across all treatment approaches, it is possible for therapists to flexibly adjust their interactional style in order to differentially emphasize the provision of direct guidance versus client self-exploration and self-directedness. Indeed, there have been a number of RCTs in which the impact of therapist directiveness and client reactance were examined. Most relevant for clinical purposes, these studies examined what occurs when there is a match between client reactance and therapist directiveness (i.e., high-reactant client and low therapist directiveness, or low-reactant client and high therapist directiveness) or mismatch between client reactance and therapist directiveness (i.e., high-reactant client and high therapist directiveness, or low-reactant client and low therapist directiveness). In a meta-analysis examining the treatment outcomes of these studies, Beutler, Harwood, Michelson, Song, and Holman (2011) found a mean effect size of $d = 0.82$ favouring matched over mismatched conditions.

So what would this actually mean for psychologists in providing services? Let's consider the initial appointment for Florio, a middle-aged man referred because of recent panic attacks. When the clinic receptionist called to schedule the appointment, Florio insisted on talking to the psychologist directly. When the psychologist later phoned him back, Florio asked a series of questions about the psychologist's training, her experience with treating people with problems similar to his, and whether she could guarantee that the treatment would help. During the first session, the psychologist's attempts to structure the interview and to gather information about his anxiety and panic and his family history were met with frequent comments, such as *Just let me tell you my story in my own time*; *Not so fast, I don't think I want to answer that question;* and *So why do you want to know that*? Whenever the psychologist made an empathic statement about how Florio seemed to be feeling, he rebuffed her with statements such as *Not at all* and *You're off the mark there, doc*. Halfway through the session, the psychologist concluded that her usual approach to gathering information was simply not going to work with Florio. She told Florio that, in order to try to help him with his panic attacks, she needed precise information about what was going on in his life that seemed to be related to the panic. She said that, although she normally asked a series of questions to help gather this information, as he was a "take charge" kind of person, she was willing to be guided by Florio in how she gathered this information. She invited Florio to tell her what he thought was important and stated that she would ask only an occasional question if she needed something clarified. At this point, Florio laughed and said, *Well, you've got my number doc. I just don't like being bossed around and told what to do. But don't worry—I don't bite, just ask whatever you want when you want. Don't push too hard though*. The interview then proceeded more smoothly, with the psychologist gathering less information than was usual in a first session, but with Florio making a commitment to come to a second assessment session.

Insight versus Symptom Reduction

In a comparison of treatments focused on achieving patient insight or patient symptom reduction, Beutler, Harwood, Kimpara, Verdirame, and Blau (2011) reported that symptom-focused interventions had superior outcomes compared with insight-focused intervention, with an overall effect size of $d = 0.85$. However, patient coping style is an important moderator of the relation between the focus of treatment and treatment outcome. By and large, focusing on enhancing patient self-awareness and understanding of their problems works best for patients who are introspective or introverted or who have an internalizing style. In contrast, patients who are impulsive or under-controlled or who have an externalizing style respond best to a focus on symptom alleviation.

Examining the research in which treatment focus (i.e., insight or symptom reduction) was matched or mismatched to client coping style, Beutler et al. (2011) found a mean effect size of $d = 0.55$ favouring the matching of treatment focus to client coping style. That being said, most current treatments focus on helping the client to (a) better understand his or her experiences and problems *and* (b) make changes in his or her day-to-day life. As with the degree of therapist directiveness, regardless of orientation, it is possible for therapists to adjust the focus of treatment to take into account individual differences in client styles and preferences.

If you were seeking psychological services, how important would it be to gain an understanding of why you were having a particular problem? If you were able to get over the problem without fully understanding why it occurred, would that be sufficient for you?

Between-Session Assignments

Between-session assignments (also known as homework assignments) are used by many clinical psychologists and other psychotherapists of various theoretical orientations (Kazantzis, Busch, Ronan, & Merrick, 2007; Kazantzis, Lampropoulos, & Deane, 2005). But does it really matter whether a therapist assigns homework in order to consolidate something addressed in the session, and does it matter whether the clients actually do the homework? The answer to both these questions is yes. In a meta-analysis of 27 cognitive-behavioural therapy (CBT) studies, Kazantzis, Deane, and Ronan (2000) reported an effect size of $r = .36$ for the association between the use of homework assignments and positive treatment outcomes and an effect size of $r = .22$ for the association between the degree of patient completion of assignments and positive treatment outcomes. Research conducted by Westra, Dozois, and Marcus (2007) suggests that patient compliance in completing homework acts as a moderator of the relation between positive treatment expectations and initial improvement in functioning. In other words, getting involved in between-session assignments appears to be critical in turning hopes for improvement into actual improvement.

Were you aware that clients are often required to do homework between sessions? How can homework completion affect treatment outcome?

PROFILE BOX 14.1

DR. HENNY WESTRA

Courtesy of Henny Westra

I received my Ph.D. in clinical psychology from the University of Western Ontario. After seven years as a staff psychologist at the Queen Elizabeth II Health Sciences Centre in Halifax, Nova Scotia, I returned to Ontario as clinical leader of the Mood and Anxiety Disorders Service at the London Health Sciences Centre. I am currently an associate professor and the Director of the Anxiety Research Clinic in the Department of Psychology at York University in Toronto. I am also a licensed clinical psychologist and maintain a small private practice. My research centres on integrating methods for enhancing motivation for change, such as motivational interviewing (MI), with existing effective treatments, such as cognitive-behavioural therapy (CBT), for the treatment of anxiety disorders. I also study the effects of motivation and expectations for change on factors such as response to therapeutic rationales provided by clinicians, the quality and development of the therapeutic relationship, and adherence to recommended treatment procedures. I am also interested in psychotherapy process research using both quantitative and qualitative methods (such as client accounts of their treatment experiences). I am particularly interested in the investigation of observational measures of therapy engagement, such as client-demonstrated resistance within sessions.

HOW DID YOU CHOOSE TO BECOME A CLINICAL PSYCHOLOGIST?

Consciously, I have always been curious about what motivates people. I was also attracted to clinical psychology as a way of discovering more about myself. Practising clinical psychology is at once highly rewarding and challenging, in that it forces one to come face to face with unresolved issues in one's own life. Developing and honing such self-awareness is one of the keys to becoming a more effective therapist.

CONTINUED . . .

WHAT IS THE MOST REWARDING PART OF YOUR JOB AS A CLINICAL PSYCHOLOGIST?

It is the privilege of bearing witness as clients share stories about the most intimate and meaningful struggles in their lives. It is an honour to journey with clients as they courageously endeavour to cope with and make sense of painful events and feelings in their lives. It is also extremely rewarding to witness our enormous potential for change and to know that one has been a part of giving birth to such changes. As a researcher, I find it enormously gratifying to struggle with understanding the complexities of change and human encounter, and to play a small part in helping to unravel these mysteries.

WHAT IS THE GREATEST CHALLENGE YOU FACE AS A CLINICAL PSYCHOLOGIST?

I was trained as a cognitive-behavioural therapist, and learning to integrate more humanistic models of practice, such as those underlying MI, is highly rewarding but also very challenging. CBT and MI rest on fundamentally different assumptions of people, the role of the therapist, and how change comes about. Although both have enormous merit, wrestling with the discrepancies in these underlying models and learning how to integrate these divergent models is not an easy task.

TELL US ABOUT YOUR RESEARCH ON TREATMENT EXPECTANCIES AND MOTIVATION FOR CHANGE

All of us feel ambivalent or torn about change in our lives, particularly for major changes such as those routinely faced by our clients. I became very interested in finding ways of working more effectively and humanely with client ambivalence when I found myself frequently and unproductively attempting to convince my clients that they should change. This is an understandable position in our role as helpers but, unfortunately, turns out to be unhelpful in the face of significant ambivalence about change. I became aware of MI, which was receiving a lot of empirical support in the addictions domain, and realized that ambivalence was no less a problem for my clients with anxiety. MI is a client-centred approach that focuses on understanding and becoming curious about the client's mixed feelings about treatment and change. The therapist becomes a guide or consultant as the client explores his or her views and fears about change, rather than acting as an advocate for change. Our research on extending MI to the treatment of anxiety has already demonstrated much promise in increasing engagement and outcomes with CBT, and we look forward to other researchers beginning work in this important area.

HOW DO YOU INTEGRATE SCIENCE AND PRACTICE IN YOUR WORK?

I have always felt passionately that the essence of clinical psychology, regardless of whether one is primarily pursuing clinical work or research, is the synergy between science and practice. One cannot exist without the other as they inform one another. My clinical practice is guided by my knowledge of the research, such as what has been demonstrated to be helpful for particular problems. My practice also allows me to identify important, clinically meaningful, unanswered questions that fuel my research, such as what are the barriers to utilizing empirically supported treatments.

WHAT DO YOU SEE AS THE MOST EXCITING CHANGES IN THE FIELD OF CLINICAL PSYCHOLOGY?

I see clinical psychology evolving to incorporate new insights that challenge the way we understand how psychotherapy works. Recent findings suggesting that common factors underlying varied treatments can account for more variance in outcomes than do specific techniques force us to grapple with how to accommodate this knowledge in practice. I also see clinical psychology moving toward becoming curious about and incorporating more humanistic principles (such as those outlined by Carl Rogers decades ago) into the more technically focused intervention models that are currently prominent. Clinical psychologists are striving to creatively blend the wisdom of humanistic principles with the advancements in treating specific problems that have emerged more recently.

Some Methodological Cautions

Almost all of the research we have discussed thus far in the chapter has examined ways in which some characteristic of the client, therapist, or treatment is related to the outcome of therapy. In other words, the researchers are examining correlations between the variables of interest. As we discussed in Chapter 4, it is important to avoid assuming that a significant correlation means that one variable causes the other. Instead, one should always carefully examine the study to determine if there may be some aspects of the study's theoretical framework, methodology, or statistical analyses that hold information critical to understanding what a significant correlation might mean.

As pointed out by Stiles (1988) and Stiles and Shapiro (1989), it is inappropriate to assume that a significant correlation necessarily means that a specific therapy process component is crucial in achieving the desired outcome. Likewise, they argued that a nonsignificant correlation does not necessarily mean that the process component is irrelevant to successful outcome. Clinical skill involves adapting the frequency and strength of techniques to match the patient's individual needs. For example, Jones and Pulos (1993) found that explaining the rationale for an intervention was characteristic of therapists providing CBT. However, once the patient clearly understands the rationale, it does not make sense to provide frequent (and unnecessary) explanations. Repeated explanations would be necessary only if there were consistent indications that the patient had not fully grasped the nature of the treatment. Process-outcome researchers underline the importance of therapist responsiveness in which the therapist's behaviour is influenced by the context of treatment. Awareness of such responsiveness, from both therapists and clients, is critical when interpreting process-outcome correlations (Crits-Christoph, Gibbons, & Mukherjee, 2013).

It is always important to carefully read the methods and results sections of research articles, as they contain information crucial for a complete understanding of the study. Because the results of treatment research (whether process-outcome research or treatment-outcome research) can have a significant impact on the provision of clinical services, it is essential that consumers of the scientific literature exercise critical and informed judgments in evaluating the relevance and applicability of this research.

Have you developed the habit of carefully reviewing the method and results sections of scientific articles? How easy is it for you to generate hypotheses about the ways that the methods of the study may have influenced their results?

COMMON FACTORS IN PSYCHOTHERAPY

Although there are clear differences in guiding theory and preferred intervention techniques among the major approaches to psychotherapy, many clinical psychologists believe that the effectiveness of all approaches stems from a common set of therapeutic factors. Rosenzweig (1936) was the first to identify a common set of therapeutic factors. He made two broad propositions about psychotherapy: first, all therapies share common therapeutic elements that are responsible for client improvement (in particular, the therapeutic relationship and an explanation for the existence of the client's problems); and, second, because all therapies rely on these common factors to bring about change, all therapies should be equivalent in outcome. In considering Rosenzweig's assertion, it is important to note that treatments at that time were all variations on psychoanalytic treatment and that Rosenzweig provided no evidence supporting his claim. Nevertheless, both of these claims have greatly influenced subsequent psychotherapy researchers. We examine the common factors proposition first and consider the equivalency proposition in a later section.

For much of the middle of the last century, the common factors proposition lay dormant and, as described in Chapter 1, there was a proliferation of new theoretical approaches to treatment. In the 1970s, Jerome Frank revisited the common factors perspective. Drawing on such diverse sources of data as studies of psychiatric practices, the placebo effect, and anthropological reports of the practices of shamans, Frank developed an intriguing and compelling model to explain all treatment effects (Frank, 1973, 1982). His model begins with a demoralized individual who is distressed and unable to resolve his or her problems. The individual seeks help from a socially sanctioned healer, who provides healing services that, if successful, result in the restoration of the individual's morale. This occurs by virtue of the healer working in a recognized healing setting, providing a rationale for the person's difficulties, instilling hope that improvement is possible, and using a set of healing rituals to resolve the problems. Frank argued that this model applies to all health care treatments, irrespective of differences in healers (psychologists, mystics), settings (hospitals, religious shrines), or rituals (free association while reclining on a couch, doing between-session assignments, or sacrificing animals to appease angry spirits).

Inspired by Frank's model, some psychologists began to develop generic models of psychotherapy that cut across theoretical orientations, to propose lists of possible common factors shared by psychotherapies, and to search for evidence of the influence of these factors. By the 1990s, the common factors perspective had become so popular that Weinberger (1995) identified an interesting dilemma: few proponents of the common factors explanation for psychotherapeutic changes agreed on what actually constituted the set of hypothesized common factors. Or, as Weinberger wryly noted in the title of his literature review, "Common Factors Aren't So Common." In attempting to bring order to the common factors perspective, Weinberger emphasized the importance of the therapeutic relationship, client expectations, confrontation of problems in therapy, the client's development of a sense of mastery, and the client's attributions for the treatment outcome.

Taking a different approach, Lambert and Ogles (2004) used three main dimensions of common factors (support factors, learning factors, and action factors) to categorize the most commonly suggested common factors. Their framework is presented in Exhibit 14.4.

EXHIBIT 14.4 Common Factors in Psychotherapy

Support Factors	Learning Factors	Action Factors
Reducing isolation	Advice	Practice
Providing reassurance	Cognitive learning	Modelling
Therapeutic alliance	Emotional experiencing	Reality testing
Therapist expertise	Insight	Facing fears
Therapist respect, empathy	Feedback	Working through issues of acceptance, warmth
Exploration of assumptions, beliefs, expectations	Development of mastery	Catharsis
	Behavioural regulation	Releasing tension

Adapted from Lambert & Ogles (2004).

The intuitive appeal of the common factors approach and its potential to harness the power of psychotherapy led to the promotion of integrative treatment models. These models adopt theories and techniques from the major therapeutic approaches to optimize the influence of the common factors regardless of the nature of the patient's problems or characteristics (e.g., Duncan, Miller, Wampold, & Hubble, 2009; Lampropoulos, 2000). The proliferation of integrative models reflects the appeal of the common factors approach. Yet the increasing number of such models raises questions of what integrative models have in common and whether they are substantially different from other treatment models. To examine some of these issues, Hickman, Arnkoff, Glass, and Schottenbauer (2009) questioned 24 experts in psychotherapy integration. Not surprisingly, when asked to describe the orientation that best described their clinical approach, three-quarters identified an integrative/eclectic approach. However, when asked to indicate the extent to which they adhered to psychodynamic, cognitive-behavioral,

integrative treatment models: theoretical models that explicitly incorporate aspects of multiple theoretical approaches and, frequently, common factors.

humanistic, and family systems approaches, 71% reported that only one had a major influence on their clinical work. Assuming that this sample is representative of psychotherapists, these findings suggest that the majority of clinicians espousing an integrative approach draw upon a primary therapeutic approach. This suggests that therapists espousing an integrative approach rely on the conceptual framework of a primary orientation that they complement with therapy techniques from other theoretical frameworks. In a survey of 201 psychotherapists, Thoma and Cecero (2009) found that, across orientations, the most commonly used techniques were demonstrating empathy, providing unconditional positive regard, challenging maladaptive or distorted beliefs, being genuine, and reflecting client feelings.

There is little doubt that many of the common factors are found in a variety of therapeutic approaches, but how can we tell whether they are the *main* elements of treatment responsible for client improvement? The diversity in the list of common factors and the inconsistencies in operationalizing the factors have resulted in little cumulative research addressing the importance of these common factors in achieving treatment outcome. One notable exception to this state of affairs: a *common* common factor that has received extensive attention from researchers is the **therapeutic alliance**—and it is to this research that we now turn.

therapeutic alliance: a concept that encompasses the quality and strength of the collaborative relationship between client and therapist.

Research Perspectives on Common Factors: The Therapeutic Alliance

How should the therapeutic alliance evolve over the course of a successful psychological intervention?

The therapeutic alliance refers to the quality and strength of the collaborative relationship between client and therapist (Horvath & Bedi, 2002). It includes positive affective bonds (e.g., mutual trust, liking, respect, and caring), consensus about and commitment to the goals of therapy, and a shared sense of partnership in the therapeutic process. Although originally developed within psychodynamic approaches, the construct of therapeutic alliance applies to all approaches to psychotherapy. A series of meta-analyses on the relation between therapeutic alliance, typically measured in the first few sessions of treatment, and treatment outcome found the alliance to be a consistent predictor of the impact of treatment. This finding is robust across treatments for adults (Horvath, Del Re, Flückiger, & Symonds, 2011), children and adolescents (Shirk, Karver, & Brown 2011), and couples and families (Friedlander, Escudero, Heatherington, & Diamond, 2011). The alliance can be assessed from the perspective of the patient, the therapist, and an observer rating recorded sessions. Although there is little evidence that the numerous measures of the therapeutic alliance are highly intercorrelated, meta-analyses yield comparable effect sizes (weighted *r*'s of .28, .19, and .26 for, respectively, adult, youth, and couples/family therapy).

Echoing the caution we introduced earlier in the chapter about interpreting the research on the alliance-outcome link, it is important not to infer causation from correlation. Although it seems obvious that a good alliance is necessary for a good outcome, methodological factors may temper this conclusion. First, a poor alliance can lead to the premature termination of treatment by clients—this has been found, for example, with both cognitive and psychodynamic treatments for borderline personality disorder (Spinhoven, Giesen-Bloo, van Dyck, Kooiman, & Arntz, 2007). So, because clients with good alliances are more likely to complete therapy, researchers have a greater chance of obtaining data on treatment effects in clients reporting a strong alliance. As a result, most of what we know about the effect of the therapeutic alliance on treatment outcome is based on data from those who experienced relatively positive therapeutic alliances. Second, as alliance is typically assessed after initial treatment sessions, it is possible that early client improvement may confound the relation between alliance and treatment outcome. In general, studies that were designed specifically to test this possibility have found that early alliance significantly predicts outcome even after statistically controlling for the effects of early improvement (e.g., Barber, Connolly, Crits-Christoph, Gladis, & Siqueland, 2000).

Before leaving this section on the therapeutic alliance, there is a final point to consider. The research on the alliance-outcome link appears compelling, which lends credence to claims about the power of common factors in therapy. But think back to Chapter 11, in which we described alternatives to traditionally delivered psychotherapy such as telehealth, self-administered, and computer-administered treatments. As we indicated in that chapter, there is growing evidence that these forms of psychological intervention, when grounded in evidence-based therapist-administered treatments, can be very helpful treatments for many people. Is it possible to build an alliance without being physically present with the client? It seems likely that a therapeutic alliance can be established with a health service provider who is hundreds of kilometres away and who is known to the patient only by video link or a voice on the telephone line. But what about the user of a self-help manual or a program delivered online: can there be a form of therapeutic alliance with the materials or the "invisible" developer of the materials? If there is a sense of connection, does this come from the material being presented in an engaging and empathic manner in order to enhance the active involvement of the client, or does it come from feedback that is programmed to the client's responses? Is it meaningful to consider this type of connection to be a form of therapeutic alliance, or is it something else?

It is fairly easy to understand how a good alliance can positively influence the outcome of treatment. So, how is it possible that treatments delivered without any apparent therapeutic alliance can be successful? What does this mean, if anything, about the role of therapeutic alliance in promoting change in therapy?

Research Perspectives on Common Factors: Psychotherapy Equivalence

As mentioned previously in the chapter, Rosenzweig (1936) proposed that, because all psychotherapies are based on common curative factors, they must be equivalent in their effects. He referred to this hypothesized equivalence of psychotherapies as the Dodo bird verdict. This is an allusion to Lewis Carroll's *Alice in Wonderland* in which an argument about who had won a race was resolved by the Dodo bird, who announced, "*Everybody* has won, and all must have prizes." Lewis Carroll's Dodo bird verdict was a satirical jab at political committees, as it described the outcome of a caucus race in which competitors started at different points and ran in different directions for half an hour.

Dodo bird verdict: in the context of psychotherapy research, the view that all psychotherapies are equally effective.

Are good therapists born or trained?

Like the common factors perspective itself, the concept of psychotherapy equivalence received little attention during the decades in which many forms of psychotherapy were being developed. However, the Dodo bird verdict was revitalized by Luborsky, Singer, and Luborsky's (1975) review of treatment research in which they concluded there was no substantial evidence of differential treatment effects. In subsequent literature reviews, Lester Luborsky and colleagues (Luborsky et al., 1993; Luborsky et al., 1999; Luborsky et al., 2002) reiterated this position and concluded there was overwhelming evidence that all therapies were equal and that psychotherapies did not have distinct, specific effects. As efforts to establish empirically supported treatments began, some psychologists (e.g., Bohart, O'Hara, & Leitner, 1998; Elliott, 1998) argued that psychotherapy itself is empirically supported and that, for effective treatment, all that is needed is a therapeutic alliance and efforts to mobilize the client's capacity to resolve problems and distress.

Getty Images

Lewis Carroll's Dodo bird.

To properly consider the evidence on the impact of different psychotherapies, it is important to impose some rules. Otherwise, like Carroll's caucus race, it is comparable to having competitors in a race start at different points and run in different directions. The first rule in evaluating the accuracy of the Dodo bird verdict is that empirical evidence must be considered. Rosenzweig's claim of general therapy equivalence was based solely on the hypothesis that all curative effects in therapy are due to common factors. By applying this first rule to current forms of psychotherapy, it is easy to see that this broad claim of equivalence (i.e., that any treatment provided by a psychotherapist, regardless of the nature of the client's problem or life context, is likely to be as effective as any other possible treatment) is untenable because not all forms of psychotherapy have been empirically evaluated. The second rule deals with the type of evidence that can be considered in evaluating the impact of different psychotherapies. In this regard, both treatment outcome studies and comparative treatment studies are relevant. Treatment outcome studies are experiments in which the impact of a treatment is compared with a control condition in which no services are provided (typically a wait-list control group). In contrast, comparative treatment studies are experiments in which the differential impacts of at least two treatments are compared, and a no-treatment control group may or may not be included. Of course, if there was evidence for psychotherapy equivalence from these types of studies, it would mean that only the psychotherapies that were evaluated in the studies could be assumed to be equivalent, as the subset of therapies that have been evaluated is by no means a representative sample of those therapies offered by clinicians (Kazdin, 1995).

As you learned in earlier chapters, to accurately consider the huge amount of treatment research, we must use meta-analyses. In Chapter 12, we described the general findings from the seminal meta-analysis by Smith, Glass, and Miller (1980) on the efficacy of various types of treatment based on treatment outcome studies. Smith et al. reported that cognitive and cognitive-behavioural treatments had the largest effect sizes (d values of 1.31 and 1.24, respectively), followed by behavioural (.91), psychodynamic (.78), humanistic (.63), and, finally, developmental treatments (including vocational-personal development counselling and "undifferentiated counselling") (.42). This evidence indicates that treatments are not equivalent. However, as the effect sizes were largely derived from RCTs in which one treatment was compared to a wait-list (or similar) control condition, and there were no direct comparisons, it is not appropriate to draw conclusions about the superiority of one type of treatment over another.

Smith et al. also conducted analyses on data from 56 comparative outcome studies of the behavioural and verbal classes of treatment. Even though cognitive therapy and CBT results were not classified with the other behavioural treatments, there were significant differences between the two classes of therapy (d = .96 for behavioural treatments and d = .77 for verbal treatments). Thus, although frequently cited as providing evidence in support of the Dodo bird verdict, the influential meta-analyses published by Smith et al. yielded numerous results that do not support a verdict of psychotherapy equivalence.

How can we explain the apparent effectiveness of different types of treatments for some specific disorders (such as depression)?

The results of other meta-analyses are relevant to an examination of the possibility of psychotherapy equivalence. As we described in Chapter 13, meta-analyses examining treatment effects in the child and adolescent treatment literature have found clear differences between treatment orientations (e.g., Weiss & Weisz, 1995). In a meta-analysis focused specifically on ensuring the clinical representativeness of their results, Shadish, Matt, Navarro, and Phillips (2000) selected studies in which clients, treatments, and therapists were representative of typical clinical settings. In the 90 studies they examined, the cognitive-behavioural family of treatments was more efficacious than other treatment approaches. There have also been numerous focused meta-analyses dealing with the treatment of such specific conditions as depression, insomnia, smoking cessation, and pain, the majority of which have shown evidence of differential treatment effects (Westmacott & Hunsley, 2007).

Like Luborsky, Bruce Wampold has been a vocal proponent of the psychotherapy equivalency position. He has been highly critical of evidence-based treatment initiatives because, in his view, they have tended to overemphasize differences among treatments (e.g., Wampold, 2007; Wampold & Bhati, 2004). In a direct test of the Dodo bird verdict, Wampold et al. (1997) conducted a meta-analysis with data from adult treatment studies published between 1970 and 1995 that compared at least two treatments. Wampold et al. reported an average *d* of .19 which, despite attaining statistical significance, was described as a small and relatively unimportant difference. Accordingly, they interpreted their results as supporting the Dodo bird verdict. They explicitly cautioned, however, that their results should not be taken as evidence that all psychotherapies are equally efficacious or as efficacious as those included in their sample. To put Wampold et al.'s results into context, using the concept of number needed to treat (introduced in Chapter 10), a *d* of .19 means that nine patients would need to be treated with the more efficacious treatment to have one more treatment success than what would occur if the less efficacious treatment was used. It has been pointed out, though, that the majority of the studies included in their analyses were comparisons among different forms of CBT, not different orientations (Crits-Christoph, 1997). Additionally, as emphasized by Chambless (2002), a relatively small average difference among treatments does not necessarily indicate that the difference between treatment options for a specific disorder is also small. As Chambless pointed out, even if the average effect is relatively small, there could be considerable variability in the size of differential treatment effects for a specific disorder.

Subsequent meta-analyses conducted by Wampold and his colleagues focused on the treatment of specific disorders have yielded results indicating that the differences in outcome across psychotherapies are limited and rather small (e.g., Benish, Imel, & Wampold, 2008). In contrast, other researchers have found important differences between treatments for specific conditions. For example, a meta-analysis conducted by Siev and Chambless (2007) illustrates that some treatments are more efficacious than others. There is evidence that both CBT and a much simpler form of treatment, relaxation therapy, can help with a number of anxiety disorders. These researchers examined all published studies in which these two therapies were compared specifically for the treatment of (a) generalized anxiety disorder and (b) panic disorder. With respect to generalized anxiety disorder, both treatments were comparable in improving symptoms of anxiety and anxiety-related thoughts; they were also equivalent in their ability to help patients achieve clinically significant changes in functioning (about 45% of patients for each treatment). A very different picture emerged with the treatment of panic disorder. In these studies, patients receiving CBT achieved significantly greater reductions in panic symptoms and panic-related thoughts compared to patients receiving relaxation therapy. In terms of achieving clinically significant changes in functioning, CBT outperformed relaxation therapy: 72% of CBT patients versus 50% of relaxation therapy patients achieved clinically significant changes. These results suggest that, for certain disorders, some efficacious treatments can be more efficacious than others.

We now return to the rules we originally described to evaluate the Dodo bird verdict, as there is an important hidden issue about comparative treatment studies that warrants attention. In order to mount a comparative treatment study, researchers need adequate financial resources to cover the costs of training and/or paying therapists, paying for the work of research assistants over several years, and paying for equipment (e.g., computers, recording equipment) used in the study. In most instances, these costs amount to at least hundreds of thousands of dollars, which means that researchers need financial support from a granting agency. This is likely to exert a critical, but typically unrecognized, effect on the nature of the study. For a granting agency to approve the funds for a comparative treatment study, there must be convincing evidence that the proposed study is worthwhile—that is, it must address a relevant question with a set of methods that are appropriate. Accordingly, to build the strongest possible case for the study, plans for comparative treatment studies almost always involve the head-to-head comparison of treatments that have already been shown to be efficacious. After all, the research is intended to determine which treatment is the best one. Research comparing a treatment that has established efficacy with one that has no empirical support is unlikely to be funded: in addition to being unethical, comparing a strong treatment with one that has no existing empirical support would be seen as a waste of time and money. The net result of this is that the comparative treatment literature largely consists of comparisons among treatments that are known to be efficacious. If all the studied treatments are efficacious, it is hardly surprising that only small differences among the treatments emerge from comparative treatment studies.

Even though there is no consensus on the question of psychotherapy equivalence, there is an alternative to the diametrically opposed positions of absolute equivalency and absolute specificity (Chambless, 2002; Westmacott & Hunsley, 2007). The evidence indicates that, for many conditions, the outcomes of different treatments are not equivalent. However, in some cases, such as adult depression, several different treatments have sufficient evidence to be considered as first-line options for clients, including several forms of cognitive-behavioural treatment, interpersonal psychotherapy, short-term psychodynamic therapy, and process-experiential therapy. For the treatment of other disorders, even if there is strong evidence of some treatments being more efficacious than others, it would be inappropriate to dismiss the possible value of the relatively less efficacious treatments. Evidence-based practice emphasizes first using the intervention that has the greatest support, but if the intervention proves to be unsuccessful with a given patient, turning to treatments with less empirical support (i.e., second- and third-line treatments) is entirely appropriate. The strategy of turning to other treatment options when a first-line treatment has not worked is used routinely in medicine, and there is no reason that the full range of evidence-based psychotherapy options should not be considered with psychotherapy patients. In this context, the debate over psychotherapy equivalence or specificity fades in importance, as what matters is replicated evidence that one or more treatments may potentially work for a client.

EVIDENCE-BASED PSYCHOTHERAPY RELATIONSHIPS

As we described at the outset of the chapter, research on psychological interventions comprises both studies of treatment outcome and studies of the relation between process and outcome. If you glance back at the evidence-based treatment initiatives we presented in Chapters 12 and 13, you will see that all of these efforts have been based solely on the results of treatment outcome studies. To highlight the relevance of process-outcome research for evidence-based psychological practice, the APA Psychotherapy Division (Division 29) established a task force in 1999 to identify, operationalize, and disseminate information on empirically supported therapy relationships. The two aims of the task force were to (a) identify elements of effective therapy relationships and (b) determine methods of tailoring therapy to individual patient characteristics. The results of the task force, chaired by John Norcross, were subsequently published as a book (Norcross, 2002). This work was later updated by a task force co-sponsored by the APA Divisions of

Psychotherapy (Division 29) and Clinical Psychology (Division 12), and those results were also published (Norcross, 2011). Together these works provide clinical psychologists with a wealth of information on **evidence-based psychotherapy relationships**.

evidence-based psychotherapy relationships: aspects of the therapeutic relationship that research has found to be associated with successful treatment.

As with other evidence-based initiatives, some of the key decision points addressed by the task force involved determining what type of evidence (experimental studies, correlational studies, or both) and how much evidence were required to conclude that a treatment element was empirically supported. In the end, the decision was made to include both experimental and correlational studies, to have task force members conduct meta-analyses of their topic area, and to categorize treatment elements as *demonstrably effective, probably effective,* and *promising but insufficient research to judge*. Unfortunately, as with most process-outcome research, most of the data included in the meta-analyses were based on studies of treatments for adults. Exhibit 14.5 presents the listings developed by this task force for the demonstrably and probably effective elements and methods of adapting treatment to client characteristics. Given the evidence presented previously, both in

Exhibit 14.5 Evidence-Based Psychotherapy Relationship Task Force Listing of General Elements of the Therapy Relationship and Methods of Adapting Psychotherapy to Client Characteristics

Demonstrably Effective Elements

- Alliance in individual adult psychotherapy
- Alliance in youth psychotherapy
- Alliance in couples/family therapy
- Cohesion in group therapy
- Empathy
- Collecting client feedback
- Adapting to client reactance/resistance level
- Adapting to client treatment preferences
- Adapting to client culture
- Adapting to client religion/spirituality

Probably Effective Elements

- Goal consensus
- Collaboration
- Positive regard (treating clients in a warm and accepting manner)
- Adapting to client stage of change
- Adapting to client coping style

Adapted from Norcross (2011).

this chapter and others, many of the elements listed in these exhibits will already be familiar to you.

Task Force Recommendations

As a final step, the APA task force issued a number of practice, training, research, and policy recommendations based on its findings. The practice and training recommendations from the task force are listed in Exhibit 14.6.

Consistent with the strength of evidence in the literature, the task force recommended that mental health training programs, including those in clinical psychology, provide specific training on elements of evidence-based psychotherapy relationships. They also encouraged mental health practitioners, including clinical psychologists, to actively use this information in their clinical work. It is especially noteworthy that the task force encouraged clinicians to (a) routinely monitor their treatment services and (b) strive to integrate aspects of evidence-based psychotherapy relationships and evidence-based treatments adapted to clients in their clinical work in order to provide the best services possible to clients. This integrated approach to intervention brings together much of what research on clinical psychology has to offer patients seeking help for psychological problems. It also avoids the unnecessary tendency, sometimes evident in clinical psychology, to pit evidence for common or non-specific treatment factors against what we have learned from treatment outcome research.

Exhibit 14.6 Evidence-Based Psychotherapy Relationship Task Force Practice and Training Recommendations

For Practice

1. Create a therapy relationship characterized by the elements found to be demonstrably and probably effective.
2. Adapt the therapy relationship to specific patient characteristics shown to enhance therapeutic outcome.
3. Monitor patients' responses to the therapy relationship and ongoing treatment in order to improve the process and outcome of treatment.
4. Use both evidence-based therapy relationships and evidence-based treatments adapted to the patient to obtain the best outcomes for the patient.

For Training

1. Train students in the demonstrably and probably effective elements of the therapy relationship and the methods for adapting therapy.
2. Provide continuing education for professionals in the demonstrably and probably effective elements of the therapy relationship and the methods for adapting therapy.
3. Develop accreditation and certification criteria for assessing the adequacy of training in evidence-based psychotherapy relationships.

Adapted from Norcross (2011).

EMPIRICALLY BASED PRINCIPLES OF THERAPEUTIC CHANGE

In an effort to provide clear and unambiguous guidance to clinicians on how best to integrate the empirically supported treatment and the empirically supported therapy relationships perspectives, psychotherapy researchers Louis Castonguay and Larry Beutler developed an initiative to identify empirically based principles of therapeutic change (Castonguay & Beutler, 2006a). Their starting point was the assumption that psychotherapy research is sufficiently advanced to allow definition of the basic principles of therapeutic change in a manner that is not tied to any specific orientation or narrowly defined set of concepts. According to Beutler and Castonguay (2006), such principles should be general statements that identify participant characteristics (i.e., both therapist and patient), relational conditions, therapist behaviours, and types of intervention that are likely to lead to therapeutic change. Principles should be more general than a description of techniques and more specific than theoretical models.

empirically based principles of therapeutic change: client, therapist, therapeutic relationship, and treatment factors that research has found to be associated with successful treatment.

©iStock.com/killerb10

Treatment should be informed by research on all the factors known to influence outcome.

In forming their task force, Castonguay and Beutler went to great lengths to ensure representation of a variety of perspectives by selecting experts in the adult treatment of each of four problem areas (mood disorder, anxiety disorders, personality disorders, and substance abuse disorders) who were also strongly affiliated with either the empirically supported treatment or the empirically supported therapy relationships perspectives. To adequately cover the relevant literature, they planned a 3 × 4 matrix with the domains of participant factors, relationship factors, and treatment factors cutting across the four problem areas. The experts focusing on participant factors were asked to review what was known about the patient and therapist characteristics covered in the original empirically supported therapy relationship report (Norcross, 2002) and other relevant reviews of this literature. Task force members working on relationship factors were also asked to assess the status of research by reviewing these sources of information. Finally, those working on treatment factors were asked to review Nathan and Gorman (1998, 2002), the empirically supported treatments chapter by Chambless and Ollendick (2001), and other relevant sources.

On completion of these reviews, members discussed the principles of change that emerged from the work. By comparing these emergent sets of principles, members distinguished between principles that were similar across the problem areas and those that were relatively unique to a specific problem area. Once common principles were identified, task force members worked on identifying and refining the list of principles that were specific to each problem area. Beutler and Castonguay (2006) cautioned that none of these principles has been empirically tested, which is why the term *empirically based* rather than *empirically supported* was used to describe them. The main common principles that resulted from this process are presented in Exhibit 14.7.

Exhibit 14.7 Common Empirically Based Principles of Therapeutic Change

Client variables hypothesized to *reduce* the likelihood of benefiting from therapy

- Greater pre-treatment impairment
- Presence of a personality disorder
- Financial/occupational difficulties
- Significant interpersonal problems during early development
- Unfavourable expectations about problems and their treatment

Relational conditions hypothesized to *increase* the likelihood of benefiting from therapy

- A strong therapeutic alliance established and maintained during treatment
- Strong level of group cohesion developed and maintained during group therapy

Therapist behaviours hypothesized to *increase* the likelihood of benefiting from therapy

- A high degree of collaboration with clients
- Empathic response
- Attitude of authenticity, caring, warmth, and acceptance
- A limited number of accurate relational interpretations
- Sensitivity to alliance ruptures, and addressing of these ruptures in an empathic and flexible way
- Provision of a structured treatment, with a consistent but flexible focus on the application of his or her interventions
- Skillful use of non-directive techniques

Intervention targets hypothesized to *lead* to therapeutic change

- Intrapersonal issues
- Interpersonal issues related to client's clinical problems
- Problematic cognitions
- Maladaptive behavioural, emotional, or physiological responses
- Client self-exploration
- Acceptance, tolerance, and full experience of emotions
- Controlling extreme emotions

Adapted from Castonguay & Beutler (2006b).

The information presented in Exhibit 14.7 represents the first attempt in the history of clinical psychology to use empirical evidence in fully considering the roles of participant, relationship, and techniques in therapy. This will serve as an important starting point for future evidence-based initiatives and could also be applied to the research on treatments for children and adolescents. As Castonguay and Beutler (2006b) cautioned, the principles governing these factors do not operate in isolation, as the successful implementation of an effective technique is based on a collaborative process within a well-established relationship in which the therapist is empathic and genuine. Researchers have just begun to examine these complex interactions, and the future of psychotherapy research holds the promise of many exciting findings that will lead to improvements in the quality and impact of our treatments.

The principles listed in Exhibit 14.7 are designed for services with adults. In services with children, adolescents, and families, steps have been taken to examine the components of evidence-based treatments in order to develop a repertoire of evidence-based treatment strategies. As you learned in Chapter 13, rather than focus on the treatment of a disorder per se, the emphasis is on matching specific strategies (originally developed as part of an evidence-based treatment for a disorder) to specific problems that may occur across disorders or even when a diagnosis is not warranted (Chorpita & Daleiden, 2009; Chorpita, Daleiden, & Weisz, 2005). So, for example, in many evidence-based treatments for youth, there are a common set of strategies to help improve assertiveness or problem-solving skills. A psychologist trained in using these strategies should be able to apply them whenever they are appropriate for a client, not just as part of an established evidence-based treatment. Similarly, McCarty and Weisz (2007) advocated determining whether there are common components across evidence-based treatments, regardless of the treatment orientation. For example, a range of evidence-based treatments for depressed youth, including CBT, interpersonal therapy, and attachment-based family therapy, all address issues of social relationship and communication skills. Therefore, when treating a depressed adolescent, it may be critical to (a) include some focus on these skills in treatment and (b) use treatment strategies that match the client's characteristics and needs in addressing these skills. Indeed, there is initial research indicating that evidence-based treatments for youth can be enhanced by having psychologists incorporate components of evidence-based treatments into a treatment package that best addresses the youth's presenting problems (Weisz et al., 2012).

SUMMARY AND CONCLUSIONS

Having identified in Chapters 12 and 13 that there are evidence-based psychological interventions that are helpful in treating diverse disorders in adults and children, in this chapter we considered the elements of psychotherapy that facilitate change. The identification of common factors that cut across treatments holds an intuitive appeal. However, the task of examining these common factors in a systematic and consistent fashion has proved challenging. Over time, research has become more sophisticated in attending to the relative significance of different factors in influencing the change process at different stages. In general, clients with long-standing serious interpersonal difficulties and current acute stressors face greater challenges in benefiting from psychotherapy. Considerable progress has been made in identifying other client characteristics that moderate the effects of different therapeutic approaches. In matching interventions to best meet client needs, psychologists must be sensitive to psychological variables such as reactance. Among the many variables examined in process-outcome research, one robust finding stands out: across all types of psychotherapy, the nature of the therapeutic relationship is an important ingredient facilitating change. The establishment of a collaborative relationship in which the client feels understood and in which the therapist and client agree on goals sets the stage for facilitating change.

We have highlighted some of the debates over interpretation of meta-analytic findings concerning the equivalence or differential effectiveness of different types of therapy. As with all research, careful analysis of the research methods and statistical analyses used in these meta-analyses is necessary to fully and accurately understand the empirical findings. Even though these debates will continue, an evidence-based approach to treatment recognizes that all treatments with established efficacy may play a role in the services provided to clients. Based on exhaustive reviews of the process-outcome literature and the treatment-outcome literature, there are a number of treatment principles that reflect the combined wisdom and expertise of proponents of evidence-based psychotherapy relationships and evidence-based treatments. Efforts such as these enable us to better understand the ways that psychological interventions can assist a diverse clientele with diverse problems.

KEY TERMS

common factors: therapeutic elements that occur in all or most treatments and are believed to be critical for successful client outcomes.

Dodo bird verdict: in the context of psychotherapy research, the view that all psychotherapies are equally effective.

empirically based principles of therapeutic change: client, therapist, therapeutic relationship, and treatment factors that research has found to be associated with successful treatment.

evidence-based psychotherapy relationships: aspects of the therapeutic relationship that research has found to be associated with successful treatment.

integrative treatment models: theoretical models that explicitly incorporate into their framework aspects of multiple theoretical approaches and, frequently, common factors.

process-outcome research: research that examines the relation between variables related to the process of providing psychotherapy and the outcome of therapy.

process research: research that examines patterns, using therapist and/or client data, that are evident within and across therapy sessions.

reactance: the tendency to react against attempts to directly influence one's behaviour.

therapeutic alliance: a concept that encompasses the quality and strength of the collaborative relationship between client and therapist.

KEY NAMES

Larry Beutler
Louis Castonguay
Jerome Frank
Lester Luborsky
John Norcross
David Orlinsky
Bruce Wampold

ADDITIONAL RESOURCES

Books

Castonguay, L. G. & Beutler, L. E. (Eds.). (2006a). *Principles of therapeutic change that work.* New York: Oxford University Press.

Lambert. M. J. (Ed.). (2013). *Bergin and Garfield's handbook of psychotherapy and behavior change* (6th ed). Hoboken, NJ: John Wiley & Sons, Inc.

Norcross, J. C. (Ed.). (2011). *Psychotherapy relationships that work: Evidence-base responsiveness* (2nd ed.). New York: Oxford University Press.

Norcross, J. C., Beutler, L. E., & Levant, R. F. (Eds). (2006). *Evidence-based practices in mental health: Debate and dialogue on the fundamental questions.* Washington, DC: American Psychological Association.

Journals

Journal of Clinical Psychology

Journal of Consulting and Clinical Psychology

Psychotherapy

Psychotherapy Research

Check It Out!

Information on evidence-based therapy relationships: www.nrepp.samhsa.gov/Norcross.aspx

The Society for Psychotherapy Research (a multidisciplinary organization that encourages research on all forms of psychotherapy): www.psychotherapyresearch.org

The Society for the Exploration of Psychotherapy Integration (an organization for mental health professionals interested in exploring the interface between differing approaches to psychotherapy): www.sepiweb.com

CLINICAL HEALTH PSYCHOLOGY, CLINICAL NEUROPSYCHOLOGY, AND FORENSIC PSYCHOLOGY

15 CHAPTER

The practice of psychology is the observation, description, evaluation, interpretation, and or modification of human behavior by the application of psychological principles, methods, or procedures, for the purpose of preventing or eliminating symptomatic, maladaptive, or undesired behavior, and of enhancing interpersonal relationships, work and life adjustment, personal effectiveness, behavioral health, and mental health.

Association of State and Provincial Psychology Boards

INTRODUCTION

Throughout this book we have emphasized the diversity of issues addressed by clinical psychologists, the range of settings in which they are employed, and the growing number of populations with which they work. Across all these types of work, clinical psychologists rely on their knowledge of normal functioning, research methods, professional issues, assessment, diagnosis, case formulation, and intervention. As an example of the requirements in one jurisdiction, Exhibit 15.1 provides a list of the areas in which candidates must be knowledgeable for licensure as a clinical psychologist in the province of Ontario.

As you learned in earlier chapters, clinical psychology has expanded its boundaries from an early focus on mental health to address a broad array of issues, including physical health (Belar, 2008; Graff, Kaouakis, Vincent, Piotrowski, & Ediger, 2012; Leventhal, Weinman, Leventhal, & Phillips, 2008), brain-behaviour links (Boake, 2008; Wilson, 2008), and forensic work (Magaleta & Verdeyen, 2005; Packer, 2008). In this chapter, we will examine in greater depth three areas of clinical practice: clinical health psychology, clinical neuropsychology, and forensic psychology. There is great variability in the definitions and scope of these areas of practice. Some jurisdictions have specialty requirements to practise in these areas, whereas in other jurisdictions, practice in these areas is subsumed under the umbrella of clinical psychology. Psychologists with advanced training in these specialized areas can earn board certification from the American Board of Clinical Health Psychology, the American Board of Clinical Neuropsychology, and the American Board of Forensic Psychology.

Exhibit 15.1 Areas of Knowledge Required for Registration as a Clinical Psychologist in the Province of Ontario

Foundational Areas in Psychology
- Biological bases of behaviour
- Cognitive-affective bases of behaviour
- Social bases of behaviour
- Psychology of the individual
- Learning

Scientific Issues
- Research design and methodology
- Statistics
- Psychological measurement

Professional Issues
- Ethical, legal, and professional issues

Assessment and Case Formulation
- Psychopathology
- Psychological assessment
- Psychodiagnostics

Intervention
- Intervention procedures; psychotherapy
- Evaluation of change

Those working with children and adolescents are also required to have a background in developmental psychology, as well as assessment and intervention with this population.

In addition, there are specialized skills listed for practice in the area of health psychology (Exhibit 15.2), clinical neuropsychology (Exhibit 15.6), and forensic psychology (Exhibit 15.8).

We have touched on some of these areas of practice in earlier chapters. In the chapter on intellectual assessment (Chapter 7), we introduced cognitive assessment, a central component of many clinical neuropsychological services; and in the chapter on prevention (Chapter 10), we discussed health promotion activities. Across several chapters, you have learned about the interface between psychology and the legal system.

All clinical psychologists must be knowledgeable about the links between physical and mental health, be sensitive to the possibility of organic problems contributing to psychological impairment, and be aware that their work may be subpoenaed and they may be required to testify in court. In this chapter, we profile psychologists in clinical health psychology (Dr. Christine Chambers), clinical neuropsychology (Dr. Colette Smart), and forensic psychology (Dr. Martin Lalumière).

Practice in these three areas involves collaboration with other professionals, including physicians, occupational therapists, lawyers, and judges. Psychologists must work collaboratively with other professions while maintaining their professional autonomy. Depending on the setting in which the psychologist works, this collaboration may entail infrequent contact via phone or reports, or may involve regular team meetings and case conferences (Belar, 2008).

To highlight the core knowledge and skills of these three practice areas, we (a) address assessment and intervention issues in each area and (b) present the requirements for licensure in these areas in the province of Ontario. Our presentation of the three specialties in this chapter is most representative of practice in North America but, where possible, we underscore similarities and differences with practices in other countries.

©iStock.com/Yuri

Lifestyle factors have replaced germs as the major threat to health. Research has established links between psychosocial stress and health outcomes.

CLINICAL HEALTH PSYCHOLOGY

Twentieth-century advances in sanitation and in medicine dramatically reduced the effects of infectious diseases on morbidity and mortality, so that lifestyle factors replaced germs as the major threat to a person's health (Poole, Hunt Matheson, & Cox, 2005). Health is affected by individual behaviours and habits including diet, sleep, level of physical activity, and consumption of alcohol and tobacco. In addition, it is affected by moods such as anger, anxiety, and sadness. The links between exposure to psychosocial stress and health outcomes are also well established (Schneiderman, Ironson, & Siegel, 2005). Finally, advances in medical technology greatly increased the life expectancy of people living with serious illnesses such as cardiovascular disease, cancer, and HIV/AIDS. All of these developments within public health, medicine, and psychology have set the stage for psychologists to play a significant role in health promotion, treatment of disease, and rehabilitation (Leventhal et al., 2008).

Definitions of Health and Disability

In 1980, the World Health Organization (WHO) developed the *International Classification of Functioning, Disability and Health* (ICF) to provide a standard language to describe health (see Chapter 3). The most recent update of the ICF defines *functioning* in terms of body functions, activities, and participation. In parallel, the ICF defines **disability** as impairment, activity limitation, and participation restriction (WHO, 2002). Within a medical model, disability is considered a characteristic

disability: impairment, activity limitation, and participation restriction.

biopsychosocial model: a model that takes into account biological, individual, and social factors.

of a person, requiring treatment of that person to correct the problem. In contrast, within a social model, disability is viewed as a function of both the physical environment and the social environment. WHO has adopted an integrated or **biopsychosocial model** that takes into account biological, individual, and social factors associated with the individual's participation in various activities. According to this model, an individual's functioning or disability is determined by the interaction between health conditions (diseases, disorders, and injuries) and contextual factors. Contextual factors include individual characteristics such as gender, age, coping style, social background, education, occupation, temperament, and behaviour, as well as variables that are external to the individual, including climate, physical environment, societal attitudes, and, finally, legal and social structures. Impairment can, but does not necessarily, lead to restrictions in activity and in diminished participation. For example, Chantalle, who has type 1 diabetes, has a bodily impairment (pancreatic dysfunction) that is controlled by insulin injections, so she has no limitation in activities. However, because she is anxious about independently monitoring her blood sugar levels (individual contextual variable) and no teacher has offered to support her (environmental contextual variable), she is unable to participate in a school trip. Interventions to help Chantalle could focus on diminishing her anxiety as well as on devising strategies to mobilize environmental supports. Edward, who sustained a spinal injury in a motorcycle accident, has a serious impairment (paralysis) as well as an activity limitation in that he is unable to drive or use public transport. However, he is a determined person who uses a specially adapted transportation system as he participates in a wide range of activities.

To get an idea of the scope of health-related problems, it is useful to look at national data on the numbers of people whose lives are affected by health problems. As part of the census, Statistics Canada asks a screening question on the limitation of everyday activities due to a health-related condition or problem. This is followed by a detailed survey, the Participation and Activity Limitation Survey (PALS). PALS data from 2006 revealed a 14.3% disability rate, indicating that 4.4 million Canadians reported that their activities were limited by health-related problems (Statistics Canada, 2007). Not surprisingly, the disability rate increases with age. The disability rate was lowest among children (3.7%), for whom the most common disability was related to a chronic health condition such as asthma or to a learning disability. In those aged 15 to 64, the disability rate rose to 11.5%. Among working-age adults, the most common type of disability was related to pain, followed by mobility and agility limitations. In adults aged over 65, the disability rate rose sharply to 43.4%, with the most common disability in that age group being mobility problems. More than half of those over 75 (56.3%) reported some kind of disability.

Although it is important to recognize the extent of disability, it is also important to consider the positive aspects of functioning. The concept of quality of life has been used by many health professions to assess various aspects of well-being for those living with diverse disorders, as well as for their caregivers. Many quality-of-life assessment tools have been developed for use with people suffering from mental and physical problems, and for people of different ages. Although there is concern over the lack of standardization of these measures (Barbotte, Guillemin, Chau, & the Lorhandicap Group, 2001), quality-of-life measures appear to be sensitive to change (Selwood, Thorgrimsen, & Orrell, 2005) and to have predictive validity in some populations (Frisch et al., 2005).

Activities of Clinical Health Psychologists

How does the role of a clinical health psychologist differ from that of a physician?

Health psychology involves application of psychological research in efforts to promote healthy lifestyles as well as to help people adjust to health problems. To conduct health psychology research, it is not necessary to have clinical training, but within North America, practising health psychologists have generalist training in clinical psychology, as well as knowledge of psychological issues related to health. The American Psychological Association uses the term *health psychologist* to refer to psychologists whose careers focus on research and teaching related to health, and the term *clinical health psychologist* to refer to those who are also health service providers (Belar, 2008).

Some jurisdictions, such as Ontario, require a person to have specialized knowledge to practise health psychology. Exhibit 15.2 describes the additional knowledge, beyond that described in Exhibit 15.1, required to practise in the area of health psychology in the province of Ontario. You will notice that practice with children requires knowledge in developmental psychology as well as knowledge of issues related to the health of children.

The role of health psychologists in Great Britain, Ireland, and the United States can also include elements related to the improvements in health care systems. The American Psychological Association *Guidelines for Psychological Practice in Health Care Delivery Systems* (American Psychological Association, 2013a) underline the need for psychologists to understand the health care system and to seek roles in which they can promote optimal delivery of services. In Great Britain and Ireland, psychologists may receive training that focuses entirely on health psychology, rather than training in health psychology as a practice area within clinical psychology. Health promotion activities include efforts to reduce smoking, reduce obesity, and encourage regular exercise. Initiatives to promote a healthy lifestyle and to prevent the development of health problems are key activities for a growing number of health psychologists. As we have already discussed issues related to health promotion in Chapter 10, we focus our discussion here on the activities of psychologists in providing psychological services to individuals with health problems related to pain.

Exhibit 15.2 College of Psychologists of Ontario: Additional Knowledge Requirements to Practise Health Psychology

Health Psychology

- Normal lifespan development
- Behavioural medicine and psychological issues related to health

Pediatric Health Psychology

- Behavioural medicine and psychological issues related to the health of children
- Developmental psychology

What are the requirements to practise health psychology in the province or territory in which you live? If you do not know the name of the licensing body for psychologists where you live, you can look it up on the website of the Canadian Psychological Association: www.cpa.ca/public/whatisapsychologist/regulatorybodies

Clinical health psychologists can work with patients dealing with any type of health problem, including essential hypertension, coronary heart disease, cancer, diabetes, arthritis, recurrent headaches, asthma, end-stage renal disease, peptic ulcers, irritable bowel syndrome, women's reproductive health (menstruation, fertility, pregnancy, birth, and menopause), organ transplant, genetic testing, and somatoform disorders. As it would be impossible to address the research in all of these areas in a single chapter, we will focus on the general issue of pain that may apply across the spectrum of health problems.

Like clinical psychologists, some clinical health psychologists engage in assessment and intervention. Exhibit 15.3 describes variables that would be taken into account in assessment and intervention in the clinical application of the biopsychosocial model. Health psychologists must be knowledgeable about the physical disorders from which their patients suffer. They need to know about the characteristics of the disorder, risk factors, and prognosis, as well as diagnostic and treatment procedures. In addition to these biological variables, the health psychologist must also consider psychological issues, whether the patient meets diagnostic criteria for a mental disorder in addition to a physical disorder, the patient's understanding of the condition, and how it is likely to affect his or her life. As the social context determines the demands that will be placed on the patient and his or her resources, the health psychologist must consider the quality of the person's relationships, the extent to which others are available to provide instrumental and emotional support, the nature of the relationship with health care professionals, as well as cultural issues. Finally, the patient's concerns must be considered in the context of the health care system to which the patient has access.

Exhibit 15.3 Clinical Application of the Biopsychosocial Model

I. Illness variables
   A. Symptoms and course of the illness
   B. Factors that elevate the risk of the illness
   C. Diagnostic procedures
   D. Treatment procedures
II. The patient
   A. Mental health and disorder
   B. Personality traits and coping styles or mechanisms
   C. Educational and vocational issues
   D. Impact of illness on subjective distress, social functioning, activity level, self-care, and overall quality of life
III. Social, family, and cultural contexts
   A. Quality of couple and family relationships
   B. Social support
   C. Relationship with health care providers
   D. Patient's cultural background
IV. The health care system
   A. Medical organization
   B. Insurance coverage for diagnostic and treatment procedures
   C. Geographical, social, and psychological barriers to accessing health services
   D. Existence of disability benefits for medical condition

Adapted from Smith, Nealey, & Hamann (2000).

Clinical health psychologists are often employed within a hospital or a community health clinic. However, issues related to health problems don't just occur in those settings, and so some clinical health psychologists also work in private practice. For example, a family sought private services from a psychologist because of concerns about their 7-year-old daughter, Laila, who was becoming fearful of school and reluctant to attend. Laila's father, Ben, had had an unsuccessful kidney transplant and had recently been diagnosed with cancer. Physicians had informed him that he could expect to deteriorate steadily over the coming months and that there was virtually no hope of slowing the rate of his decline. Although Ben had come to terms with having a terminal illness, he felt guilty and anxious at the thought of leaving his daughter. Laila's mother, Anna, was a tower of strength for the entire family. Since her husband's diagnosis, she had supplemented the family income by putting in additional hours at work. A psychological assessment revealed that Ben was suffering from a dysthymic disorder, Laila met criteria for a diagnosis of separation anxiety disorder, and Anna, although fatigued and distressed, did not meet criteria for any mental disorder. The psychologist identified three foci for intervention: (a) addressing Ben's depressive symptoms, (b) addressing Laila's anxious symptoms and facilitating regular attendance at school, and (c) helping Anna to mobilize supports by reducing her work hours and taking care of her emotional needs.

Assessment and Intervention Related to Pain

It is common for clinical health psychologists to assist their patients in dealing with pain stemming from their medical conditions and/or the medical treatments they receive for these conditions. Pain serves a useful function in alerting us to potential harm. The sharp pain you feel when you twist an ankle is an important signal that you need to take weight off the ankle, a scorching sensation warns you to move away from a fire, chafing lets you know that clothing is too tight, and stinging reminds you to keep away from certain plants or insects. Although most of us consider pain an unpleasant experience that we would rather avoid, the very rare individual who is insensitive to pain is vulnerable to life-threatening injuries because he or she does not experience the warning signals of pain. Because pain is a subjective experience, we rely on individual reports to let us know how much pain a person is suffering: there is no objective way in which we can judge another person's pain. This poses an important challenge in understanding the pain experiences of those who are incapable of verbalizing pain. Until relatively recently, many health care professionals assumed that babies and very young children did not feel pain (Poole et al., 2005). Consequently, it was considered reasonable to conduct procedures such as circumcision on male infants without using local anaesthesia, whereas such procedures would not be applied to an older male without some intervention to block or dull the pain. Patrick McGrath and his colleagues have developed innovative strategies to measure pain in infants and children, as well as in adults who are incapable of expressing pain verbally (McGrath & Finley, 2003; McGrath & Unruh, 1999). These include research-based strategies for asking children about pain, observing their behaviour, and watching facial expressions (Breau, McGrath, Camfield, & Finley, 2002; Chambers, Finley, McGrath, & Walsh, 2003).

It is important to distinguish between acute pain and chronic pain. Acute pain is a short-term sensation that serves an unpleasant but useful function. It can usually be relieved in different ways, including the application of heat or cold, rest, distraction, or the administration of analgesics. In contrast, pain that persists for more than six months is considered chronic. All people experience acute pain due to injuries, illness, and medical procedures. For example, all children are exposed to procedures such as vaccination, many experience minor surgery, and a few must face pain associated with invasive procedures associated with the treatment of serious conditions such as cancer.

Pain management is multidimensional, including physical measures such as the administration of medication and psychological interventions such as training in distraction strategies. As children are discharged from hospital very rapidly following minor surgery, parents are often responsible for managing their child's pain. McGrath and his colleagues (McGrath, Finley, Ritchie, & Dowden, 2003) prepared a booklet to help parents help children. Exhibit 15.4 includes strategies that can be helpful in addressing children's acute pain, as well as some commonly used strategies they describe as not helpful. Profile Box 15.1 introduces Dr. Christine Chambers, a Canadian clinical psychologist whose clinical work and research focus primarily on pain in children.

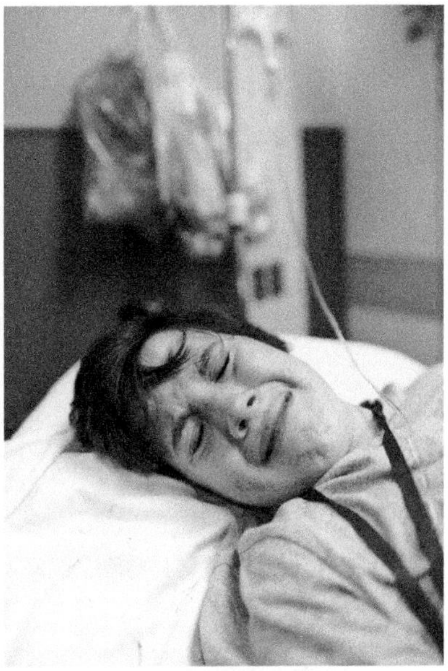

©iStock.com/Juanmonino

Psychological strategies can help children manage acute pain.

acute pain: a short-term sensation that serves an unpleasant but useful function; it can usually be relieved in different ways, including the application of heat or cold, rest, distraction, or the administration of analgesics.

chronic pain: pain that persists for more than six months.

Exhibit 15.4 Methods to Manage Children's Acute Pain

Psychological

- Presence of a parent or other special person
- Encouragement to ask questions and express feelings
- Provision of simple, accurate information about a medical procedure
- Provision of some control (e.g., sit on a lap or in a chair)
- Distraction: talking, video games, music, books
- Imagination: thinking of activities associated with being relaxed and calm
- Suggestion that the child let the pain slip away
- Play and silliness
- Encouragement that the child is doing well

CONTINUED . . .

Physical

- Deep breathing
- Comforting touch: stroking, swaddling, holding, rocking, cuddling
- Medication

Unhelpful strategies

- Denying the pain: *You won't feel a thing.*
- Ridiculing or shaming: *Only babies cry.*
- Giving false reassurance: *It only takes a second.*
- Focusing too much on pain: *I know you are worried it will hurt a lot.*

Adapted from McGrath, Finley, Ritchie, & Dowden (2003).

PROFILE BOX 15.1

DR. CHRISTINE CHAMBERS

Courtesy of Christine Chambers

I completed my Bachelor's (Hons.) degree in psychology at Dalhousie University and then completed my master's and Ph.D. in clinical psychology at the University of British Columbia. I am currently a full professor in the departments of Pediatrics and Psychology at Dalhousie University, where I hold a Canada Research Chair, an award sponsored by the federal government that allows me to spend most of my time conducting research on pain in children. Because of my research focus on children's health, my office and research lab are based at the IWK Health Centre, which is the major medical centre providing care to children and their families from across the Maritime provinces. I have also provided clinical services to patients through the Pediatric Health Psychology Service at the IWK, where I work with children with a variety of medical conditions and their families. My research and clinical interests lie in the area of pediatric psychology, which is a sub-type of clinical health psychology in which the principles of psychology are applied within the context of children's health.

HOW DID YOU CHOOSE TO BECOME A CLINICAL HEALTH PSYCHOLOGIST?

I was inspired to become a child psychologist after reading a book in elementary school about a psychologist who had made a difference in the lives of traumatized children. However, it wasn't until I completed my undergraduate degree in psychology that I became involved in psychological research and learned how the science and practice of psychology could be applied to help children with medical conditions and children undergoing medical procedures.

WHAT IS THE MOST REWARDING PART OF YOUR JOB AS A CLINICAL HEALTH PSYCHOLOGIST?

The most rewarding part of my job as a clinical health psychologist is the knowledge that the research in my field is making a difference in the lives of children and their families. It was not that long ago that many health professionals used to believe that children didn't feel pain, and they were often denied the benefits of appropriate pain management. Thanks to the considerable research that has been conducted on pain in children over the last 25 years, we know that this simply isn't true, and now, fortunately, more children are likely to benefit from both psychological and pharmacological pain management interventions.

CONTINUED . . .

WHAT IS THE GREATEST CHALLENGE YOU FACE AS A CLINICAL HEALTH PSYCHOLOGIST?

One of the greatest challenges I face as a clinical health psychologist is finding ways to have parents, children, and other health professionals "buy in" to the fact that psychological treatments can be very helpful. Fortunately, this is where the strong research base in support of the psychological treatments we use comes in handy. Related to this challenge is educating families and professionals that just because a psychological treatment works (e.g., in reducing pain) doesn't mean that the cause of the problem was psychological—many of the patients I work with (e.g., those who are referred for pain management) are worried that a referral to a psychologist means that people think that their problem is "all in their head."

TELL US ABOUT YOUR RESEARCH ON PEDIATRIC PAIN

My research examines the role of developmental, psychological, and social factors in children's pain. I'm interested in how we can better assess pain in children and the role that parents play in helping children learn how to cope with pain. Various groups of children of all ages help us out with our research, including children with medical conditions as well as healthy children. We observe children during medical procedures and we also conduct lab-based studies where we ask children to take part in experimental tasks like the cold pressor, an ethically acceptable task in which children are asked to lower an arm into cold water in order to induce pain. Trainees, including undergraduate and graduate students in psychology, are actively involved in our research.

HOW DO YOU INTEGRATE SCIENCE AND PRACTICE IN YOUR WORK?

Although I'm primarily a researcher, I've made it a priority to continue to see patients, and these patients have had a substantial impact on my research program. Patients often have a way of describing their difficulties and challenges that inspires research questions and reminds me why the work I'm doing is so important. Being involved in clinical work also provides an opportunity for me to determine whether my research questions are viable and whether they can be translated into practice.

Chronic pain is associated with a host of other problems, including sleep disturbances, depression, and anxiety (Ohayon, 2005). Among Canadians aged 12–44 years, approximately one in 10 live with chronic pain (Statistics Canada, 2010). Chronic pain is a fact of life for more than one in four Canadian older adults living in the community, and for those living in institutions, the number rises to almost four in 10 (Statistics Canada, 2008). Dennis Turk and his colleagues have highlighted the psychological aspects of chronic pain. The person's beliefs about pain influence the experience of pain: those who attribute their pain to a traumatic injury, who are fearful of causing further pain by engaging in activity, and who feel unable to control their pain report more intense pain symptoms (Turk & Okifuji, 2002). Psychological factors play an important role in determining whether the person will recover from the pain or will experience long-term disability (Keefe, Abernethy, & Campbell, 2005). Dysfunctional beliefs about pain, lack of social support, heightened emotional reactivity, low job satisfaction, and the possibility of compensation are associated with the experience of chronic problems (Turk & Okifuji, 2002). Psychologists may be consulted to conduct assessments in claims for disability due to pain-related injuries.

Psychological services to deal with pain may be offered within interdisciplinary services that include physicians and physiotherapists (Kerns, Sellinger, & Goodin, 2011). Psychological treatment may be directed at various goals, including the adoption of active coping strategies to manage pain, reduction of avoidance behaviours, improved sleep (see Viewpoint Box 15.1), adherence to a medication regimen, stress management, reduction of anxiety related to pain, resolution of interpersonal issues related to pain (e.g., communication difficulties and conflict with family members), and vocational issues (Hadjistavropoulos & Williams, 2004). Exhibit 15.5 lists psychological strategies frequently used in managing chronic pain. These interventions can be offered individually or in a group format. Treatment in interdisciplinary services for pain is as effective as pharmaceutical and surgical alternatives and is associated with a greater number of people being able to work (Turk & Burwinkle, 2005).

EXHIBIT 15.5 Psychological Approaches to the Management of Chronic Pain

Intervention	Strategy	Goal
Education about pain	Provide a rationale for the treatment	Patient motivation to take an active role in treatment
Goal-setting	Set short- and long-term goals, schedule activities, and pace activities	Realistic goals, recognition of gradual progress
Biofeedback	Gain awareness and control over bodily reactions	Reduction of muscle tension
Relaxation	Train and rehearse skills to achieve calm state	Capacity to reduce muscle tension
Hypnotherapy	Induce altered state of awareness	Focused relaxation
Mindfulness	In-the-moment experiencing	Separation of the sensation of pain from associated thoughts experience
Contingency management	Learn self-reinforcement of healthy behaviours	Reduction in use of analgesics, increase of appropriate exercise, increase of balanced response to pain
Exercise and fitness	Collaborate with physiotherapist/trainer	Address fears and avoidance of more active lifestyle
Cognitive restructuringa	Identify and challenge catastrophizing thoughts	Realistic appraisal of pain
Problem-solving	Address limitations and conflicts	Awareness of choices, capacity to activate support, clear communication
Acceptance and commitment	Observe thoughts and feelings to behave in a way consistent with values and goals	Reduction of attempts to control and avoid pain
Generalization and maintenance	Practise skills in relation to diverse issues, anticipate difficulties	Lifestyle changes so that skills are applied consistently

Adapted from Hadjistavropoulos & Williams (2004) and Kerns, Sellinger, & Goodin (2011).

VIEWPOINT BOX 15.1

INSOMNIA: NO NEED TO LOSE SLEEP OVER IT!

We all need sleep. As you may know from direct experience, without adequate sleep, infants, toddlers, children, and adults suffer cognitive and physical impairments (Bootzin & Epstein, 2011). Natural sleep-wake cycles are vulnerable to disruption by many variables including age, parental status, stress, and shift work (Williams, 2001), as well as by a host of physical variables, including chronic pain (Ohayon, 2005). Results of Statistics Canada's 2002 Canadian Community Health Survey revealed that 3.3 million Canadians aged 15 and over reported regular difficulty in either falling asleep or staying asleep (Statistics Canada, 2005).

Everyone occasionally suffers from insomnia triggered by life events, stressors, or an illness. Normal sleeping patterns usually return once the stressor or illness is over. However, an occasional bout of insomnia can develop into a chronic sleep disorder that takes on a life of its own, independent of the original trigger. Within DSM-5, insomnia disorder involves difficulties in initiating and/or maintaining sleep that are accompanied by fatigue-related impairment during the day (American Psychiatric Association, 2013). Chronic insomnia is often maintained by problematic behaviours and beliefs (Morin, 2004). Although the problem of insomnia is well recognized by the medical profession, the topic is not routinely covered in training in clinical psychology (Bootzin & Epstein, 2011) and sleep disorders are often overlooked by professional psychologists (De Koninck, 1997). Nevertheless, there is increasing evidence that psychological interventions may be very useful in the treatment of this common disorder, especially when the insomnia is chronic. As pharmacological interventions can lead to poor quality sleep, possible addiction, and rebound insomnia on withdrawal of the medication, there is a pressing need for effective psychological interventions.

Dr. Charles Morin of Laval University has been at the forefront of research in this area (Morin, Colecchi, Stone, Sood, & Brink, 1999; Morin, 2004). CBT interventions include three components: educational, behavioural, and cognitive (Morin, 2004). Educational strategies focus on knowledge of the physiology of sleep and on understanding the mechanics of how insomnia develops into a chronic problem. Education also focuses on the principles of **sleep hygiene** (i.e., good sleep practices): avoid caffeine and other stimulants in the evening; avoid smoking close to bedtime; avoid exercising too close to bedtime; and reduce noise, light, and excessive temperature (Morin, 2004). Behavioural strategies focus on stimulus control with five simple instructions: (a) go to bed only when sleepy; (b) use bed or bedroom only for sleeping; (c) get out of bed when unable to sleep and return only when sleepy; (d) get up at the same time every day no matter how little you have slept; and (e) do not take daytime naps. Two additional behavioural strategies include restricting sleep time and learning relaxation strategies. Cognitive interventions target and attempt to alter dysfunctional beliefs about sleep, including unrealistic expectations, feelings of lack of control, and catastrophic thinking about the consequences of being unable to sleep. Cognitive-behavioural interventions yield an average of 50–60% symptom reduction in those suffering from insomnia, a figure that is comparable with that obtained with pharmacotherapy (Morin, 2004). Furthermore, the effects of cognitive-behavioural interventions are better maintained over time.

Meta-analyses have shown that cognitive-behavioural interventions are efficacious in the treatment of insomnia (e.g., Morgenthaler et al., 2006; Morin et al., 2006). The effects of psychological and pharmacological treatments are comparable in the short term, but in the long term, psychological treatments produce better outcomes (Bootzin & Epstein, 2011). Despite evidence that psychological interventions are efficacious, they have been underused, as some people consider medication to be an easier alternative. Researchers have therefore focused their efforts on ways to deliver psychological interventions in brief and inexpensive ways. For example, a randomized controlled trial found that a brief (two-hour) cognitive-behavioural intervention for young and middle-aged

CONTINUED . . .

adults was more efficacious than either pharmacotherapy or combined cognitive-behavioural treatment and pharmacotherapy in the treatment of insomnia (Jacobs, Pace-Shott, Stickgold, & Otto, 2004). An evaluation of a national training program in Cognitive Behavior Therapy for Insomnia (CBT-I) in the U.S. Department of Veterans Affairs showed that clinicians were able to achieve competency in delivering this intervention and, in turn patients experienced significant reductions in symptoms of insomnia and depression, as well as an improved quality of life (Karlin, Trockel, Taylor, Gimeno, & Manber, 2013). This research suggests that CBT can be effectively delivered in inexpensive ways to address a common and troubling disorder.

In sum, the application of psychological knowledge to address issues related to health, including sleep and pain, is a growing area of practice. Over the relatively brief history of behavioural medicine and health psychology, psychologists have made an important contribution to the understanding of health, the promotion of healthy lifestyles, and the adjustment to health problems. Given the aging of our population and the increasing need for services to help people adjust to chronic health problems, it is highly likely that health psychology will become an even more important psychological service area in the coming years (Leventhal et al., 2008). Indeed, psychological services delivered in medical settings may dramatically enhance quality of life and reduce the financial burden on the health care system (Blount et al., 2007).

CLINICAL NEUROPSYCHOLOGY

Neuropsychology is the study of brain-behaviour relationships; *clinical neuropsychology* is the application of this knowledge in the assessment and remediation of neurological injury or illness (Boake, 2008). Clinical neuropsychology addresses the effects on functioning of neurological problems, including genetic problems such as Williams syndrome, birth-related injuries, head injuries resulting from sports accidents and car accidents, brain tumors, infections, demyelinating diseases such as multiple sclerosis, cerebrovascular diseases, epilepsy, neurodegenerative diseases such as Alzheimer's disease and Parkinson's disease, the effects of exposure to environmental toxins, and the effects of chemotherapy (Cairns, 2004).

Clinical neuropsychology developed after the Second World War, building on the work of Ward Halstead and Ralph Reitan in the United States, Donald Hebb in Canada, and Aleksandr Luria in the former Soviet Union (Groth-Marnat, 2000). Halstead, who was trained in physiological psychology, studied the behaviour of patients with neurological impairment. Dissatisfied with the academic focus of intelligence tests, he developed tests to assess specific adaptive deficits (Broshek & Barth, 2000). Over the course of his career, Reitan conducted numerous studies comparing performance on these tests between patients with brain damage and non-disordered individuals, and examining the usefulness of the battery in identifying the precise area of the brain that had been damaged (Broshek & Barth, 2000). The Halstead-Reitan battery is the most extensively investigated neuropsychological test and is widely considered a useful tool in evaluating cognitive functioning. However, the Halstead-Reitan is not without its flaws. Criticisms include the length of time required for administration; the failure to take into account differences according to age, education, and gender; and the lack of studies on diverse populations (Broshek & Barth, 2000). Luria's assessment approach was a qualitative one that yielded a profile of the patient's strengths and weaknesses, but that lent itself less readily to standardization in administration or scoring (Golden, Freshwater, & Vayalakkara, 2000). Current neuropsychological practices reflect an integration of the two traditions so that use of tests is complemented by careful analysis of functioning (Groth-Marnat, 2000).

Activities of Clinical Neuropsychologists

In addition to the knowledge base required for all clinical psychologists (see Exhibit 15.1), clinical neuropsychologists in the province of Ontario require additional specialized knowledge as listed in Exhibit 15.6. For example, to practise clinical neuropsychology, one must understand normal brain functioning (**neuroanatomy**); the ways that environmental toxins, chemotherapy, and recreational drugs affect brain functioning (pharmacology); and the ways that injuries and diseases affect the brain (**neuropathology**). In addition, clinical neuropsychologists must be knowledgeable about a wide array of assessment strategies to identify neuropsychological problems, as well as ways to adapt to these limitations.

neuroanatomy: normal brain functioning.

neuropathology: the ways that injuries and diseases affect the brain.

Training in clinical neuropsychology can be obtained in several ways: within generalist training in clinical psychology, in a small number of specialist clinical neuropsychology doctoral programs, or in postdoctoral training. The Division of Clinical Neuropsychology of the American Psychological Association identifies fulfillment of the requirements of the American Board of Clinical Neuropsychology as clear evidence of competence.

Exhibit 15.6 College of Psychologists of Ontario: Additional Knowledge Requirements to Practise Clinical Neuropsychology

- Neuroanatomy, physiology, pharmacology
- Human neuropsychology and neuropathology
- Neuropsychological assessment
- Clinical and neuropsychological intervention techniques
- Neuropsychology with children and adolescents: developmental psychology, as well as relevant assessment and intervention strategies

Clinical neuropsychologists work with clients across the lifespan and must be sensitive to issues in working with children (Middleton, 2004) and older adults (American Psychological Association Working Group on the Older Adult, 2004). Those working with children require knowledge of assessment and intervention that is suitable for children and must have a strong background in developmental psychology. In assessing older adults, the clinical neuropsychologist must take into account the physical and sensory changes that accompany aging, in addition to the cognitive changes that are the focus of the assessment (APA Working Group on the Older Adult, 2004; Lichtenberg, Murman, & Mellow, 2003). Profile Box 15.2 describes Dr. Colette Smart, a neuropsychologist who conducts research on self-regulation.

PROFILE BOX 15.2

DR. COLETTE SMART

Courtesy of Colette Smart

I obtained my first degree (M.A.) in psychology at the University of Glasgow in Scotland, followed by a master's and Ph.D. in clinical psychology at Loyola University Chicago. I then completed a two-year postdoctoral residency in clinical neuropsychology at the JFK-Johnson Rehabilitation Institute/New Jersey Neuroscience Institute in Edison, NJ, after which I stayed on for a further two years as an attending neuropsychologist. During that time I was fortunate to be part of a number of interdisciplinary teams, including those dealing with inpatient and outpatient brain injury, dementia, brain tumors, and movement disorders, as well as running mindfulness training groups in the cognitive rehabilitation program. Currently, I am an assistant professor in the Psychology Department at the University of Victoria (UVic). UVic is one of the few North American universities with a clinical psychology doctoral program that contains a dedicated neuropsychology track. As part of this program, I teach and supervise clinical neuropsychology graduate students, teaching classes on neuropsychological assessment and cognitive rehabilitation, as well as supervising clinical practice. I am currently licensed to practise in New York and am working toward registration in British Columbia.

HOW DID YOU CHOOSE TO BECOME A CLINICAL NEUROPSYCHOLOGIST?

I entered graduate training intending to specialize in clinical health psychology, with a particular focus on factors promoting adaptation to chronic and terminal illness. However, after my first practicum in neuropsychology, I fell in love with the field and decided to switch specializations. Being exposed to cognitive rehabilitation during my postdoctoral work, I finally found a way to weave together the various strands of my training—working with medical populations, understanding brain-behaviour relationships, conducting assessments, and delivering interventions to promote adaptation and resilience following life-changing illness and injury. Through my clinical experience, some very specific research questions arose, and it became clear to me that to pursue these to the depth that I wanted, I would be best served in an academic position, which prompted my move to UVic.

CONTINUED . . .

WHAT IS THE GREATEST CHALLENGE YOU FACE AS A CLINICAL NEUROPSYCHOLOGIST?

The thing that makes being a clinical neuropsychologist so fascinating and exciting is also one of its greatest challenges: trying to be an "expert" in so many different areas. To be fully competent in my work, I need to have an in-depth knowledge of functional neuroanatomy, of the medical illnesses that can impair cognitive and emotional functioning, of the appropriate tests to use to diagnose such impairments, and of evidence-based treatments, as well as of cognitive neuroscience and basic neuroscience. Being a clinical neuropsychologist means being a lifelong learner—which also means there is never room for boredom. Fortunately, I work with a very gifted and passionate group of collaborators, graduate and undergraduate students, who all bring their own experience and expertise to the work we do in our laboratory.

TELL US ABOUT YOUR RESEARCH ON SELF-REGULATION.

As a clinician I became fascinated by individuals with disorders of self-regulation—people who had problems being able to regulate cognitive function and emotion from one moment to the next. The unpredictable nature of their deficits was often more debilitating than the actual deficit itself. As a long-time meditator, it occurred to me that self-regulation was a big part of meditative practice. Lots of work had been done using techniques such as mindfulness with people with mood disorders and medical illnesses, but virtually nothing had been done with neurologic populations. While in clinical practice, I was the co-investigator in a study looking at the effects of mindfulness in people with traumatic brain injury. Since joining UVic, I have received funding for studies looking at mindfulness in older adults at risk for cognitive decline and children/adults with fetal alcohol spectrum disorders. I also conduct studies of expert Buddhist meditators, trying to understand basic mechanisms of self-regulation that could be used to inform the development of clinical interventions.

HOW DO YOU INTEGRATE SCIENCE AND PRACTICE IN YOUR WORK?

To remain current in clinical practice, I keep up with the scientific literature on new tests, procedures, and norms that are being developed, as well as with evidence-based treatments. I also read the cognitive neuroscience literature and collaborate with colleagues in that area in an effort to understand basic cognitive mechanisms and the way disruptions in these mechanisms can produce clinical symptoms. In turn, my clinical practice inspires new and exciting questions that fuel my research, questions that tend to have applied, practical value. As a clinical neuropsychologist, I believe that science and practice are not only inseparable, but mutually influential.

WHAT DO YOU SEE AS THE MOST EXCITING CHANGES IN THE FIELD OF CLINICAL NEUROPSYCHOLOGY?

In the early years of neuropsychology, it was believed that the brain had a limited ability to recover from illness or injury, and the primary function of the neuropsychologist was to diagnose and document the extent of the damage. However, an increasing body of basic science research (in both animals and humans) now shows the brain's potential for neuroplasticity and recovery across the lifespan. This research opens up exciting new opportunities in working with people with neurologic disorders. Clinical neuropsychologists, with their knowledge of brain-behaviour relationships, assessment, and treatment, as well as their understanding of the person in context, are uniquely positioned to develop meaningful interventions to help people with cognitive impairment not only survive but thrive after illness or injury.

Like other areas of clinical psychology, clinical neuropsychology has expanded and evolved over recent decades (Hayman-Abello, Hayman-Abello, & Rourke, 2003). As noted above, early clinical neuropsychology was primarily a diagnostic activity in which tests were developed to aid in the localization of lesions. Neuropsychological assessment was used to determine whether there was an organic basis for observed psychological and behavioural problems, and if so, to identify the precise area of the brain that was affected (Goldstein & McNeil, 2004). With the development of effective imaging techniques such as magnetic resonance imaging (MRI) and functional magnetic resonance imaging (fMRI), there are now alternative ways to identify the precise nature of brain dysfunction (Mellers, 2004). Clinical neuropsychology, in turn, has expanded its focus to also address cognitive, emotional, psychosocial, and behavioural difficulties that result from an insult to the brain (Laatsch et al., 2007; Livingston et al., 2005; Wilson, 2008).

Assessment

With the advent of advanced imaging techniques in neurology, what can clinical neuropsychologists contribute to the care of those patients with neurological impairments?

Neuropsychological assessment examines memory, abstract reasoning, problem-solving, spatial abilities, and the emotional consequences of brain dysfunction (Groth-Marnat, 2000). In Chapter 5, we noted that psychological assessment can be conducted for screening, diagnosis and case formulation, prognosis, treatment design and planning, treatment monitoring, and treatment evaluation. Similarly, neuropsychological assessment can address many different questions, as outlined in Exhibit 15.7.

Screening for organic problems may be conducted by a generalist clinical psychologist who then refers the patient for a full neuropsychological assessment if the screening indicates possible neuropathology. As you can see in Exhibit 15.7, the most common reasons for neuropsychological assessment are to address issues around diagnosis, prognosis, treatment planning, and legal issues. An increasing number of clinical neuropsychologists conduct assessments that are used in a forensic context (Boake, 2008). Diagnostic issues include determining whether the person's problem is primarily neurological or psychological. To conduct such an assessment, the clinical neuropsychologist must understand neuropathology and psychopathology.

Neuropsychologists are often requested to predict a patient's prognosis (Lemsky, 2000). For example, the neuropsychologist may be asked whether or not a person can return to work following a brain injury, and if so, to identify the types of tasks that may be difficult. Prediction of future functioning requires an understanding of the neuropathology and its course, as well as the person's developmental level. Some forms

Exhibit 15.7 Purposes of Neuropsychological Assessment

Diagnosis

- Does this child show signs of having been exposed to a toxic substance?
- Are this patient's memory complaints related to dementia or to depression?

Prognosis

- To what extent will this child's acquisition of language be affected by her head injury?
- How long is it reasonable to expect this person to live alone, given his declining memory and executive functioning?

Treatment Planning and Rehabilitation

- What kind of special learning aids will this child with a learning disability require?
- If this patient who has had a stroke returns to work, what kinds of adaptations will need to be made to compensate for deficits related to the stroke?
- What can be done to help this person with mild memory loss?

Legal Proceedings

- Is there evidence of brain dysfunction that could be related to the person committing a violent act?
- What is the extent of damage to this employee who sustained an electric shock?

of neuropathology are progressive; the person can expect a process of deterioration.

Other problems, such as those caused by a blow to the head, may lead to different problems at different ages. For example, following a mild concussion, a child may exhibit fewer symptoms than an adult would. However, there is some evidence that damage occurring at times of rapid development causes more harm than does damage occurring at times of slow development (Middleton, 2004). Counter-balancing this is the fact that the child's brain is in the process of development, so it may be possible for a child to recover from some types of injuries more easily than an adult could (Middleton, 2004). In assessing an adult who had difficulties with language following a head injury, the clinical neuropsychologist predicts the extent of recovery of functioning that can be expected. In assessing a three-year-old with a similar injury, the child clinical neuropsychologist predicts whether the child will acquire language at the same rate as non-injured peers or whether language delays can be expected (Middleton, 2004). In conducting neuropsychological assessment for the purposes of planning treatment and rehabilitation, the clinical neuropsychologist draws on knowledge of normal processes in memory, language, and executive functioning to make predictions that a person with a particular deficit could benefit from a particular intervention (Lemsky, 2000).

Neuropsychologists study driving in older adults.

In Chapter 5, we emphasized that psychological assessment and psychological testing are not synonymous. Similarly, neuropsychological assessment includes, but is not limited to, neuropsychological testing. The toolkit of the clinical neuropsychologist contains assessment strategies and instruments that we presented in earlier chapters, including interviews (Chapter 6) and psychometric tests such as the Wechsler Adult Intelligence Scale IV (WAIS IV), Wechsler Memory Scale IV, and Wechsler Individual Achievement Test III (Chapter 7). In choosing a neuropsychological test, the psychologist must consider the core psychometric elements that are required for all types of psychological tests: standardization (of stimuli, administration, and scoring), reliability, validity, and norms. There is no simple correspondence between performance on a neuropsychological test and performance of the activities of daily living (Goldstein & McNeil, 2004). The context of neuropsychological testing may actually mask some types of deficits (Lemsky, 2000). For example, an individual may perform better in the brief, structured one-to-one environment of a testing session than in the home setting with multiple distractions and simultaneous demands on attention. Therefore, it is essential that data be gathered from the individual and from others who are knowledgeable about that person's functioning, to determine his or her functional status in various domains.

In interpreting a score on a particular test, the clinical neuropsychologist refers to normative data. However, the usefulness of this comparison depends on the appropriateness of the normative group. Some widely used tests have norms for older adults. The WAIS IV (Wechsler, 2008), for example, provides normative data for the 70- to 90-year age range. Unfortunately, other commonly used neuropsychological tests were normed on small samples of convenience, so that an extreme score may represent a difference between the individual and the normative sample rather than a clinically meaningful difference (Crawford, 2004). Of particular concern, many norms for neuropsychological tests are based on samples that under-represent minority groups (Boake, 2008).

Media reports emphasize the need for society to adapt to an aging population. Normal aging is associated with declines in physical and cognitive functioning. In addition to these normal declines, the risk of Alzheimer's disease and other dementias increases with age. Most of us have experienced concerns about an older person we care about—a family member, neighbour, or friend—and the increasing difficulty he or she faces in driving, making financial decisions, or navigating the health care system. Our society values independence and the rights of the individual to determine where and how to live. However, the right to independence is balanced against the rights of others to be safe and the rights to be protected from exploitation.

Capacity assessment is designed to balance the need for autonomy with the need for protection. Capacity assessment requires an understanding of the ways in which functioning can be impaired by injury and degenerative processes. Capacity is not a unitary construct, as, for example, a person may be incapable of driving but still able to manage financial affairs. Psychologists have taken a leading role in the development of tools to assess a person's capacity to engage in various activities and to make various types of decisions (Moye, Marson, & Edelstein, 2013). The American Psychological Association in collaboration with the American Bar Association has produced three handbooks on the topic of capacity assessment, designed to inform psychologists, lawyers, and judges. This field of practice at the interface between psychology and the law is an excellent example of the way that practice is informed by research.

Intervention

Brain injuries affect approximately 1 million children a year in the United States (Laatsch et al., 2007). In addition, with an aging population, there are increasing numbers of people living with dementia (Turner, 2003). Furthermore, due to improvements in medical care, many people now survive strokes and serious head injuries. There is a clear need to offer effective services to help the growing numbers of people who are faced with the challenge of living with the effects of neurological problems (Wilson, 2004). Compared with the history of treatments for mental disorders, the history of interventions for individuals with neurocognitive impairment is relatively brief. Although these interventions include services to deal with the psychological consequences of the impairment, such as depression, a growing number of interventions are designed to remediate the problems that are identified in neuropsychological assessment. Viewpoint Box 15.2 provides a case example of neuropsychological assessment conducted to aid in treatment planning.

Despite the potential usefulness of neuropsychological assessment in treatment planning, it is not routinely available to all patients with neurological problems. A survey of rehabilitation programs within the American Hospital Association revealed that most patients were under 65 and had been hospitalized for a stroke or a brain injury (Stringer, 2003). The majority of these patients received individualized cognitive rehabilitation services over a period of one to six months, at a cost of $130 (U.S.) per session. These services were often delivered by speech therapists and occupational therapists. Few of these programs incorporated the results of neuropsychological assessment into the services offered.

VIEWPOINT BOX 15.2

NEUROPSYCHOLOGICAL ASSESSMENT TO AID IN DIFFERENTIAL DIAGNOSIS AND TREATMENT PLANNING

Peter (age 25) was referred for a neuropsychological assessment by a neurologist. He had difficulties with memory and concentration, slept poorly, suffered headaches, and felt anxious. Six months earlier, Peter had been a passenger in a car accident in which he sustained a mild head injury with loss of consciousness for 10 to 15 minutes. His close friend, who was the driver, was killed in the accident. A neuropsychological assessment was requested to determine whether Peter's symptoms were related to posttraumatic stress disorder (PTSD), a psychological disorder related to the effects of the severe accident in which a friend died, or to post-concussion syndrome (PCS), a physiological disorder resulting from a brain injury during the accident.

The neuropsychological assessment included an interview, as well as tests of intelligence, memory, perceptual and visual skills, and executive functioning. Results revealed that Peter experienced some symptoms of anxiety related to the accident, as well as grief over the death of his friend. However, he did not meet criteria for a diagnosis of PTSD, as he did not report re-experiencing the accident or intrusive thoughts about it. He did show evidence of significant cognitive difficulties in formal testing that were consistent with the problems he reported in daily living. These cognitive symptoms were more pronounced than those that would be seen after exposure to a traumatic event. The clinical neuropsychologist therefore concluded that Peter's symptoms reflected the residual effects of the brain injury (i.e., PCS), which were compounded by his emotional reaction to the accident and his friend's death. To address these issues, Peter was provided with information about head injuries and given strategies to address his memory and attention difficulties. He was advised to attempt a gradual return to work and was offered counselling to address the emotional sequelae of the accident.

Adapted from Goldstein & McNeil (2004).

Different theoretical models of cognitive rehabilitation lead to different strategies to help a person deal with the real-life problems caused by neurological problems (Lemsky, 2000). Rehabilitation is an interactive process between the patient and service providers designed to enable the person to function as adequately as possible. Using the terminology of the World Health Organization, some interventions are designed to overcome impairments by teaching the patient new strategies; other interventions are designed to compensate for impairments by modifying the environment or by using aids so that the patient is capable of carrying out an activity; and still other interventions address social, psychological, and physical barriers to the person's participation (Lemsky, 2000). Treatment planning involves collaborating with the client to identify desired outcomes. Wilson (2008) used the acronym SMART to underline the importance of establishing goals that are **s**pecific, **m**easurable, **a**chievable, **r**ealistic, and **t**imely.

The development of effective interventions relies on a solid understanding of cognitive processes such as memory and learning. In the treatment of memory deficits, efforts to retrain memory have been found to be ineffective, and external memory aids such as lists, calendars, electronic agendas, pagers, and personal digital assistants are widely used (Evans, 2004). It is clear that much more intervention research is needed to evaluate the impact of the wide range of available interventions.

The Committee on Empirically Supported Programs (COESP) of the Division of Clinical Neuropsychology of the American Psychological Association commissioned a review of literature on treatments for attentional problems (Riccio & French, 2004). Across all treatment programs and populations reviewed, they reported that there was insufficient methodologically adequate research to conclude that the treatments make a difference. Similarly, a review of cognitive rehabilitation for people with early stage Alzheimer's disease concluded that, although single case reports provided encouraging data, no randomized control trials have been conducted, so there is only limited evidence that individualized cognitive rehabilitation programs are efficacious for people with early-stage Alzheimer's disease (Clare & Woods, 2004). A meta-analysis of cognitive rehabilitation for individuals with acquired brain injury revealed that the majority of studies had methodological weaknesses and small sample sizes (Rohling, Faust, Beverly, & Demakis, 2009). Nevertheless, Rohling and colleagues found evidence of modest improvements in attention, visuo-spatial, and language deficits, but little evidence that treatment improved memory problems.

A systematic review of studies of cognitive and behavioural interventions for children with acquired brain injury (Laatsch et al., 2007) also found few high-quality randomized control trials and few studies with a large number of participants. However Laatsch et al. concluded that there was sufficient evidence to justify practice guidelines that children with acquired brain injury receive services to remediate memory and attention, and that comprehensive rehabilitation services should consider involving family members as active treatment providers. In addition, Laatsch et al. found preliminary evidence of the usefulness of providing an information booklet on traumatic brain injury to parents and caregivers of children seen in an emergency department for

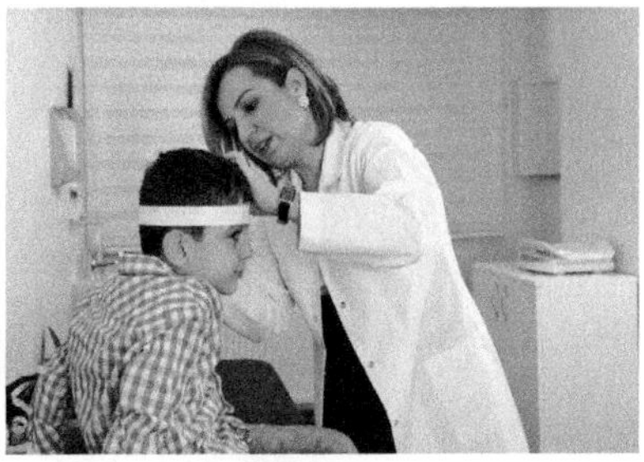

Brain injuries affect approximately 1 million children a year in the U.S.

such injuries. There is clearly an urgent need for increased research on neuropsychological rehabilitation so that we can identify the most efficacious programs for people dealing with impairment and disability related to neurological injury and disease.

FORENSIC PSYCHOLOGY

What are the roles for psychologists in dealing with those involved in the criminal justice system?

The American Psychological Association defines forensic psychology as "the professional practice by any psychologist working within any subdiscipline of psychology (e.g., clinical, developmental, social, cognitive) when applying the scientific, technical or specialized knowledge of psychology to the law to assist in addressing legal, contractual, and administrative matters" (APA, 2013b). Thus, forensic psychology, broadly defined, is the application of psychology in the legal and criminal justice systems. As in other types of clinical psychology, forensic psychologists engage in services related to prevention, assessment, treatment, and research. In earlier chapters, we raised issues that are important in forensic psychology, such as assessing whether a person making an insurance claim for injuries sustained in an accident is accurately reporting symptoms or is malingering (Chapter 8), developing programs to prevent the emergence of delinquent behaviour (Chapter 10), and treating victims of accidents or abuse (Chapters 12 and 13). We indicated that the work of psychologists may be subpoenaed and that, before beginning any services, psychologists must explain the limits of confidentiality to clients (Chapter 6). Forensic psychologists provide services to many stakeholders, including victims of crime, witnesses of crimes, offenders, parties in a legal dispute, police forces, and the courts. Other mental health professionals such as psychiatrists also offer forensic services based on interviews and examination of collateral data such as reports from schools, employers, or previous therapists. With their expertise in using data from psychological tests, psychologists are well positioned to offer expert opinion (Lally, 2003). The expert testimony of psychologists is presented in court on both civil and criminal matters (Packer, 2008).

Forensic psychologists are employed in myriad settings, including hospitals, private practice, court clinics, maximum security federal penitentiaries, provincial jails, provincial correctional centres, minimum security camps (both adult and youth), specialized treatment facilities, community probation and parole offices, and Aboriginal healing lodges. The vast majority of these psychologists are directly engaged in providing psychological services, but others are research psychologists or psychologists who work in the fields of policy and administration (Magaletta & Verdeyen, 2005). The nature of clinical psychologists' work in correctional facilities is greatly affected by high incarceration rates, overcrowding in prisons, and limited resources for psychological services. In their efforts to develop evidence-based clinical practice, psychologists in correctional settings must be acutely aware of the constraints associated with the environment in which they work (Clements et al., 2007).

©iStock.com/Rich Legg

Forensic psychologists conduct a variety of court-related assessments.

Activities of Forensic Psychologists

In Canada, most forensic psychologists have a doctorate in clinical psychology and field training in forensic psychology. Four universities—Carleton, Dalhousie, Québec à Trois Rivières, and Simon Fraser—offer structured programs in forensic psychology; another 20 universities offer some graduate work in forensic psychology (Helmus, Babchishin, Camilleri, & Olver, 2011). Exhibit 15.8 lists additional areas beyond those listed in Exhibit 15.1 in which a psychologist must be knowledgeable in order to practise forensic psychology in the province of Ontario. Given the nature of the problems with which they work, forensic psychologists must be knowledgeable about strategies for assessing and managing risk. In addition, those working with children must understand the criminal justice and legal systems with respect to children. Training in corrections is available through a few clinical psychology programs in Canada and in several clinical internship sites. Research forensic psychologists do not require training in clinical psychology. Profile Box 15.3 introduces Dr. Martin Lalumière, a forensic psychologist whose research is on sex offenders.

Exhibit 15.8 College of Psychologists of Ontario: Additional Knowledge Requirements to Practise Forensic Psychology

Forensic Psychology

- Criminal justice/legal systems
- Criminal behaviour
- Application of psychological principles within the federal and provincial legal systems
- Risk assessment
- Risk management

Child and Adolescent Forensic Psychology

- Criminal justice/legal systems with respect to children and adolescents
- Criminal behaviour
- Application of psychological principles within the federal and provincial legal systems
- Risk assessment
- Risk management

PROFILE BOX 15.3

DR. MARTIN LALUMIÈRE

Courtesy of Mélanie Provencher

I am a professor in the clinical program of the School of Psychology at the University of Ottawa. I obtained my Ph.D. from Queen's University at Kingston in 1995 and became a registered psychologist in Ontario in 1996. For a few years I was also a registered psychologist in Quebec, after receiving a master's degree from the University of Montreal in 1990. I currently conduct research in the areas of human sexuality and crime.

HOW DID YOU CHOOSE TO BECOME A FORENSIC PSYCHOLOGIST?

As an undergraduate, I signed up for a study on sexual conditioning. I was surprised to learn that my genital responses would be measured, but was impressed that the study involved such an objective measure of sexual arousal and interest. The professor running the laboratory impressed me with his insistence on scientific rigour in the study of abnormal psychology, and the importance of an empirical foundation for the assessment and treatment of psychological disorders.

As a doctoral student at Queen's University, my interest in forensic psychology blossomed. I learned about eyewitness testimony, the development of the paraphilias, the treatment of persistent antisocial behaviour, psychopathy, and so on. By the second year of my Ph.D., I was determined to become a professor of forensic psychology.

WHAT IS THE GREATEST CHALLENGE YOU FACE AS A FORENSIC PSYCHOLOGIST?

Forensic research often involves men and women who have been in trouble with the law, so there can be challenges with access to relevant populations. It is sometimes difficult to obtain funding to study offenders—an unpopular and stigmatized group. A few years ago, my colleagues and I obtained funding to study men with pedophilic interests who had never attempted to engage in sexual activities with children (other than using child pornography). The goal of the study was to identify protective factors among men at risk of sexually offending against children. In a media interview about the study, I mentioned that participation was voluntary and compensated by a small honorarium (to compensate for participants' time and to cover their travel expenses), as is often the case for any type of research involving human participants. Unfortunately, the reporter interpreted this as indicating that taxpayers' money would be used to reward pedophiles by having them watch pictures of children (we planned to use a standard assessment of pedophilic interest that involves exposing participants to pictures of children and adults in bathing suits). The article went nationwide, and we lost most of our recruitment sites.

TELL US ABOUT YOUR RESEARCH IN FORENSIC PSYCHOLOGY.

My doctoral research established that, in laboratory assessments, sexual offenders against women show greater relative genital arousal to descriptions of violent and non-consensual sexual activities than do other men. Recently we discovered that this pattern is distinct from sadism. Another line of research has

CONTINUED . . .

been on psychopathy, a constellation of such traits as impulsivity, manipulativeness, deception, promiscuity, parasitism, and glibness. I tested the hypothesis that psychopathy is a well-functioning, well-designed, and well-evolved strategy of social manipulation and dominance. So far, this hypothesis has been supported. For example, psychopaths do not show signs of neurodevelopmental perturbations characteristic of serious psychological disorders. Psychopaths are also nepotistic when it comes to their violent behaviour: that is, they tend to harm non-relatives to a greater extent (and relatives to a lesser extent) than do other violent offenders.

HOW DO YOU INTEGRATE SCIENCE AND PRACTICE IN YOUR WORK?

A lot of my research has direct practical implications. I have been involved in the training of clinicians who assess sex offenders, especially with regard to laboratory assessment of paraphilic interests. This training is very rewarding, because it allows for the application of research findings and also reveals gaps in knowledge. For example, when I gave a workshop for police detectives who deal with cases of sexual assaults, I presented an overview of what we know about sexually assaultive men. However, I learned from the feedback that most of what I talked about was irrelevant to their work, because the detectives were involved in cases in which the offenders are not known to the victims. These cases are extremely rare and, as researchers, we seldom study them. It is unclear whether men who assault strangers are different (or if their situation is different) from the more typical profile of men who offend against non-strangers.

WHAT DO YOU SEE AS THE MOST EXCITING CHANGES IN THE FIELD OF FORENSIC PSYCHOLOGY?

Like clinical psychology more generally, the field has significantly moved toward an evidence-based form of practice. For example, risk assessments to determine the relative likelihood of reoffending are now conducted using empirically based measures, and impressionistic clinical judgment has almost completely disappeared from this type of assessment. Treatment efforts have lagged, however, but there are promising signs, especially with juvenile offenders. Many recently graduated forensic psychologists have been trained in the scientist-practitioner model, which will likely lead to more research and evidence-based practice. Popular crime TV shows are sending hordes of students toward forensic psychology, leading to the selection and training of the best students—even though these same students are a bit disappointed to find out that what happens on these shows has little basis in reality.

Exhibit 15.9 lists some of the activities in which forensic psychologists engage. As you can see, the potential scope of activities is very broad. Few psychologists would be involved in offering all of these services, and it would be common for them to specialize in offering a small set of psychological services (e.g., assessment-focused work or offering treatment to offenders). As noted above, within the field of forensic psychology, a number of psychologists are employed within the correctional system.

Exhibit 15.9 The Scope of Forensic Psychology Services

Prevention Programs

To reduce violence and bullying

Court-Related Assessment

Assessment of Witnesses

- Credibility issues

Assessment of Victims

- Impact of an assault or injury
- Credibility versus malingering

Assessment of the Accused

- Evaluation of mental status at the time of an offence
- Competence to stand trial

Assessment of Disputing Parties

- Child custody evaluation

Assessment of Offenders

Risk of violence

Risk of sexual violence

Treatment Services for Offenders

To address mental health issues such as depression and anxiety

To address criminal behaviour

Research

To identify the best strategies to predict criminal behaviour

To identify the most effective treatments

Assessment

Lally (2003) surveyed expert forensic psychologists to identify the psychological assessment measures considered appropriate for different types of assessments. Exhibit 15.10 lists the measures that were deemed *recommended, acceptable,* or *unacceptable* in evaluating risk of violence and in evaluating competency to stand trial. Many of the assessment tools should be familiar to you from previous chapters. You will also notice that an instrument designed specifically for an offender population, the Psychopathy Checklist-Revised (Hare, 1991), is the most highly recommended tool for assessing risk of violence. This is rather surprising, as the checklist, which uses information gathered from a semi-structured interview and a review of the person's history and police/prison files, was not designed to be a tool for predicting future violence. A meta-analytic review of nine commonly used violence prediction tools found that the Psychopathology Checklist-Revised was the least powerful tool, among those evaluated, in predicting future violence among men

(Yang, Wong, & Coid, 2010). With the widespread attention given to this finding in the professional literature, it is likely that some of these other violence prediction tools will become more frequently used by forensic psychologists.

The majority of expert forensic psychologists who responded to the Lally (2003) survey did not consider projective tests acceptable in assessing the risk of violent behaviour or in determining competence to stand trial. A similar survey about instruments used in assessing young offenders' competence to stand trial indicated that (a) intelligence tests such as the Wechsler scales were used by the majority of experts in juvenile forensic assessment (82%); (b) around half of the survey respondents (56%) reported using the MMPI-A; and (c) only a small minority reported using projective tests such as the Rorschach (16%), TAT (12%), or sentence completion tests (10%) (Ryba, Cooper, & Zapf, 2003).

Exhibit 15.10 Expert Opinion on Tests for Forensic Evaluations

	Risk for Violence	Competency to Stand Trial
Recommended	Psychopathy Checklist-Revised	WAIS-III
		MacArthur Competence Assessment Tool
Acceptable	MMPI-2	MMPI-2
	Psychopathy Checklist-Screening version	Halstead-Reitan
		Stanford-Binet
	Violence Risk Appraisal Guide	Luria-Nebraska
	WAIS-III	Interdisciplinary fitness interview
	Personality Assessment Inventory	Personality Assessment Inventory
Unacceptable	Projective drawings	Projective drawings
	TAT	TAT
	Sentence completion	Sentence completion
	Rorschach	Rorschach
	16 PF	16 PF
		MCMI-II

Adapted from Lally (2003).

There are important similarities and differences between regular clinical practice and clinical practice within the corrections system. For example, correctional psychologists, like other clinical psychologists, should use evidence-based strategies in their assessment, treatment, and prevention activities. Any psychological assessment can have serious consequences for the well-being of the individual and society. However, one of the differences in a correctional context is that assessments usually involve public safety issues. This is especially evident in the context of risk assessments that focus on the likelihood of an individual re-engaging in violent criminal behaviour. Viewpoint Box 15.3 highlights issues in conducting these assessments.

risk assessment: predictions of the likelihood of an individual re-engaging in violent criminal behaviour.

VIEWPOINT BOX 15.3

RISK ASSESSMENT

One of the primary reasons for requesting a psychological assessment is to obtain a scientifically informed prediction about a person's behaviour. Psychological assessments may be used in predicting diverse outcomes such as suicidal risk, the ability to benefit from a social skills group, or the likelihood that the person will adhere to a medical regimen. When making predictions, the psychologist draws on research knowledge of risk and protective factors. The risks associated with making errors are carefully weighed. Although most psychological predictions are important, they are rarely the focus of public scrutiny. However, in the case of predictions of violent behaviour, the repercussions of errors are very serious. You may recall the media outcry that occurs when news breaks of a violent offence perpetrated by someone recently released from prison or on parole. There are often recriminations that mental health professionals had failed to predict and prevent the violent behaviour. The failure to predict that a person with a violent history will reoffend can have deadly consequences. However, overly conservative predictions based on single episodes of violence that are unlikely to be repeated can lead to the prolonged and unjust incarceration of an offender beyond the time when a sentence has been served.

A few decades ago, mental health professionals were ill-equipped to predict dangerousness (Monahan, 1981). Since that time, a number of evidence-based approaches have been developed to aid psychologists in making predictions (Hanson, 2005; Webster & Bailes, 2004). Armed with research-based assessment tools that allow more accurate prediction of violent and/or criminal behaviour, numerous correctional policies have been introduced in North America to protect the public from dangerous offenders. Canadian researchers such as Robert Hare have been at the vanguard of these research efforts. Hare's groundbreaking work on the construct of psychopathy has described the capacity of charming psychopaths to manipulate others without remorse. Hare's Psychopathy Checklist-Revised (PCL-R) is considered an excellent instrument for predicting recidivism among convicted criminals (Craig, Dixon, & Gannon, 2013), and has been demonstrated to be useful in diverse cultural contexts (Hare, Clark, Grann, & Thornton, 2000). Another commonly used measure, the Violence Risk Appraisal Guide (VRAG; Harris, Rice, & Quinsey, 1993), uses empirically derived combinations of common clinical variables to predict long-term recidivism. Specialized measures have also been developed for sub-populations such as young offenders or men who assault their wives (Hanson, 2005). There is a high degree of correlation between the different measures and many are moderately accurate in predicting future violence and recidivism in violent offenders (Hanson, 2005; Yang et al., 2010).

There are numerous challenges in ensuring that instruments such as these are used appropriately in professional work and that clinicians have an informed perspective on both their strengths and limitations. Adequate training and supervision in their use is essential, but even then difficulties can arise. For example, Miller, Kimonis, Otto, Kline, and Wasserman (2012) examined the inter-rater reliability of instruments commonly used to assess sex offenders' risk for reoffending,

CONTINUED . . .

and compared these values to those reported in the test manuals. They found much lower levels of inter-rater reliability when the instruments were used in forensic evaluations. Such variability in the scoring of the instruments could lead to differences in conclusions drawn about the likelihood of reoffending. Of course, as with any assessment procedure, risk assessment tools are not immune to the influence of heuristics and biases. For example, evidence has been found for an adversarial allegiance effect—that is, the scoring of some commonly used risk assessment measures has been found to be influenced by whether the assessment was intended to be used for defence or prosecution purposes (Murrie, Boccaccini, Guarnera, & Rufino, in press). Clearly there remains more work to be done in helping clinicians to more accurately predict the likelihood of criminal activity.

Intervention

Correctional psychology is not simply clinical practice with people who happen to live in a prison (Magaletta & Verdeyen, 2005). For example, for a correctional psychologist, treatment outcome is more likely to be measured in terms of **recidivism** (committing crimes after release from incarceration) rather than reduction in symptoms. This means that programs have traditionally been more likely to target factors associated with risk of criminal behaviour (e.g., association with delinquent peers, antisocial attitudes, anger and impulse control) than to target variables that are distressing to the offender but unrelated to criminal behaviour (e.g., low self-esteem) (Dowden & Andrews, 2004). For example, Don has a history of violent behaviour and has been incarcerated for physical assaults. Helping him learn to better control his anger may be an important goal for him, but it is also a critical aspect of reducing the likelihood that he will pose a threat to others when he has served his sentence.

recidivism: reoffending.

In the 1970s and 1980s, it was assumed that offender treatment had little chance of facilitating change. However, with the introduction of cognitive-behavioural programs that target risk factors, the portrait has changed considerably. A series of meta-analyses have supported the utility of CBT interventions for offenders (Dowden & Andrews, 2004). A meta-analysis, by Wilson, Bouffard, and MacKenzie (2005) examining studies on a range of cognitive behavioural interventions, including problem-solving, social skills training, cognitive restructuring, and impulse control, found that the methodologically strongest studies yielded a moderate effect size (d = .51). Translating this effect size into recidivism rates, treated offenders had a recidivism rate of 46%, whereas for untreated offenders the rate was 54% (Wilson et al., 2005). But, there are few randomized control trials and inconsistent use of strategies to address the substantial problem of high drop-out rates (Wormith et al., 2007). As in all therapy outcome research, it is important to move beyond examining the efficacy of research treatment programs to determining the effectiveness of these programs when they are widely applied.

Do you think it could be possible for a clinical psychologist to be a generalist who covers the areas of health psychology, neuropsychology, and forensic psychology? What would be the challenges involved for such a professional?

There are a number of challenges facing forensic psychologists who offer treatment services. These can stem from the context in which services are delivered, as well as from the clients themselves. Dowden and Andrews (2004) emphasized the importance of considering correctional staff practices in the delivery of effective treatment. It is clear that the considerable impact of environmental constraints and influences (e.g., restrictiveness of the setting, staff practices, what constitutes normative behaviour in a correctional setting) sets clinical practice in corrections apart from other types of mental health services provided by clinical psychologists. With respect to client issues, a prominent concern has to do with treatment drop-out. Wormith (2002), for example, underlined the importance of developing effective programs for offenders of Aboriginal ancestry who are particularly likely to drop out of treatment programs. Having debunked the notion that "nothing works" in the treatment of offenders, emerging approaches are moving beyond a simple risk reduction model to also address offender motivation for positive change in their lives (Day, Gerace, Wilson, & Howells, 2008; Wormith et al., 2007).

Across the different applied areas of practice described in this chapter, what knowledge and skill elements are common to all?

SUMMARY AND CONCLUSIONS

In addition to offering traditional mental health services, a growing number of clinical psychologists work in clinical health psychology, clinical neuropsychology, and forensic psychology. Practice in these areas is based on the core skill set found in clinical psychology, with additional specific knowledge and skills taught in graduate training, in internships, and on the job. Health psychologists, with their focus on health maintenance, illness prevention, assessment, and intervention, have a broad scope of practice potentially applicable to all age groups in all health care settings. Clinical neuropsychologists, with their knowledge of brain-behaviour connections, have been and continue to be key contributors to the health care of people with a wide range of neurological impairments. Forensic psychologists, working within and outside correctional facilities, have developed an increasingly efficacious set of assessment and intervention procedures. Across these areas of practice, psychologists strive to apply the science of psychology to the improvement of the lives of young and old alike. In these roles, psychologists are at the interface between psychology and the health care and legal systems. In addition to direct service provision, they have an important role to play in informing other professions about the contribution that psychology can make.

KEY TERMS

acute pain: a short-term sensation that serves an unpleasant but useful function; it can usually be relieved in different ways, including the application of heat or cold, rest, distraction, or the administration of analgesics.

biopsychosocial model: a model that takes into account biological, individual, and social factors.

chronic pain: pain that persists for more than six months.

disability: impairment, activity limitation, and participation restriction.

neuroanatomy: normal brain functioning.

neuropathology: the ways that injuries and diseases affect the brain.

recidivism: reoffending.

risk assessment: predictions of the likelihood of an individual re-engaging in violent criminal behaviour.

sleep hygiene: engaging in good sleep habits, such as avoiding stimulants before bedtime, developing pre-sleep routines, etc.

KEY NAMES

Ward Halstead

Robert Hare

Donald Hebb

Aleksandr Luria

Patrick McGrath

Charles Morin

Ralph Reitan

Dennis Turk

ADDITIONAL RESOURCES

Books

Belar, C. D., & Deardorff, W. W. (2008). *Clinical health psychology in medical settings: A practitioner's guidebook* (2nd ed.). Washington, DC: American Psychological Association.

Boyer, B. A., & Paharia, M. I. (Eds). (2008). *Comprehensive handbook of clinical health psychology.* New York: John Wiley & Sons.

Craig, L. A., Dixon, L., & Gannon, T. A. (Eds.). (2013). *What works in offender rehabilitation: An evidence-based approach to assessment and treatment.* Hoboken, NJ: Wiley-Blackwell.

Goldstein, L. H., & McNeil, J. E. (Eds.). (2004). *Clinical neuropsychology: A practical guide to assessment and management for clinicians.* Chichester, UK: John Wiley & Sons.

Lezak, M. D., Howieson, D. B., Bigler, E. D., & Tranel, D. (2012). *Neuropsychological assessment* (5th ed.). New York: Oxford University Press.

McConroy, M. A., & Murrie, D. C. (2007). *Forensic assessment of violence risk: A guide for risk assessment and risk management.* New York: John Wiley and Sons.

Check It Out!

Information on the IWK Health Centre and the Pediatric Pain Laboratory of the Psychology Department of Dalhousie University: www.pediatric-pain.ca

American Board of Clinical Health Psychology: www.abpp.org/i4a/pages/index.cfm?pageid=3308

The American Board of Clinical Neuropsychology: www.theabcn.org

American Board of Forensic Psychology: www.abpp.org/i4a/pages/index.cfm?pageid=3356

The Oliver Zangwill Centre for Neuropsychological Rehabilitation website provides resources on assessment and rehabilitation: www.ozc.nhs.uk

Details on the Canadian National Crime Prevention Strategy: www.ccsd.ca/cpsd/ccsd

MAJOR JOURNALS RELEVANT TO CLINICAL PSYCHOLOGY

1 APPENDIX

American Journal of Psychiatry

This journal is the official publication of the American Psychiatric Association. It includes articles on developments in biological psychiatry as well as on treatment innovations and forensic, ethical, economic, and social topics.

American Psychologist

This is the official journal of the American Psychological Association. Articles address current issues in psychology, the science and practice of psychology, and psychology's contribution to public policy.

Annual Review of Clinical Psychology

This journal provides reviews of major developments in clinical psychology, including theory, research, and application of psychological principles to the assessment and treatment of psychological disorders. Additionally, it includes a review of broader issues in the field, such as public policy and diversity issues.

Annual Review of Psychology

This journal presents authoritative, analytic reviews by eminent psychologists, covering the entire range of psychological research.

Archives of Clinical Neuropsychology

This journal includes articles on psychological aspects of the etiology, diagnosis, and treatment of disorders arising out of dysfunction of the central nervous system.

Assessment

This journal covers studies on the use of assessment measures within the domains of clinical and applied psychology, including practical applications of measurement methods, test development and interpretation strategies, and advances in the description and prediction of human behaviour.

Behavior Therapy

This journal is one of the two official publications of the Association for Behavioral and Cognitive Therapies. It includes reports and reviews of studies on the application of behavioural and cognitive sciences to clinical problems.

Behavioral Sciences and the Law

This journal covers topics at the interface of the law and the behavioural sciences, with theoretical, legal, and research articles on psycholegal topics, including mental health.

Behaviour Research and Therapy

This journal contains articles on cognitive-behavioural therapy applied to clinical disorders, behavioural medicine, and medical psychology.

British Journal of Clinical Psychology

Published by the British Psychological Society, this journal includes original contributions to scientific knowledge in clinical psychology. Articles include descriptive studies as well as studies of the etiology, assessment, and amelioration of disorders of all kinds, in all settings, and among all age groups.

British Journal of Psychiatry

Published by the Royal College of Psychiatrists, this journal includes editorials, review articles, and commentaries on contentious articles. The target readership is psychiatrists, clinical psychologists, and other mental health professionals.

Canadian Psychology

The official journal of the Canadian Psychological Association, this journal has articles in areas of theory, research, and practice that are potentially of interest to a broad cross-section of psychologists.

Clinical Case Studies

This journal is devoted entirely to the presentation of case studies, including cases involving individuals, couples, and families. All articles use a standard case presentation format that presents assessment, conceptualization, and treatment.

Clinical Child and Family Psychology Review

This journal includes research reviews and conceptual and theoretical papers related to infants, children, adolescents, and families. Topics covered include etiology, assessment, description, treatment and intervention, prevention, methodology, and public policy.

Clinical Psychological Science

This journal is published by the Association for Psychological Science. It focuses on advances in clinical psychology research on, for example, psychopathology diagnosis, assessment, treatment, and service delivery, the promotion of well-being, and the prevention of mental illness.

Clinical Psychology & Psychotherapy

This journal presents articles that focus on the integration of theory, research, and practice across different theoretical orientations.

Clinical Psychology Review

This journal presents reviews of research on topics such as psychopathology, psychotherapy, behavioural medicine, community mental health, assessment, and child development.

Clinical Psychology: Science and Practice

This is the official publication of the Society of Clinical Psychology (Division 12) of the American Psychological Association. It includes reviews of research related to assessment, intervention, service delivery, and professional issues.

Cognitive and Behavioral Practice

This journal is one of the two official publications of the Association for Behavioral and Cognitive Therapies. It contains clinically rich accounts of assessment and intervention procedures that are clearly grounded in empirical research.

Cognitive Therapy and Research

This is an interdisciplinary journal on the role of cognitive processes in human adaptation and adjustment. The journal includes experimental studies; theoretical, review, technical, and methodological articles; case studies; and brief reports.

Criminal Justice and Behavior

This is the official publication of the American Association for Correctional and Forensic Psychology. It includes scholarly evaluations of assessment, classification, prevention, intervention, and treatment programs.

Evidence-Based Mental Health

This multidisciplinary journal provides a digest of the most important clinical research relevant to clinicians in mental health.

Health Psychology

This journal is designed to further an understanding of the links between behavioural principles and physical health and illness.

JAMA: Psychiatry

This journal (formerly *Archives of General Psychiatry*) contains studies and commentaries of general interest to clinicians, scholars, and research scientists in psychiatry, mental health, behavioural science, and allied fields.

Journal of Abnormal Child Psychology

This is the journal of the International Society for Research in Child and Adolescent Psychopathology. It includes research on psychopathology in childhood and adolescence, with an emphasis on empirical studies of the major childhood disorders (the disruptive behaviour disorders, depression, anxiety, and pervasive developmental disorders).

Journal of Abnormal Psychology

This journal includes articles on basic research and theory in psychopathology, normal processes in abnormal individuals, pathological or atypical features of the behaviour of normal persons, experimental studies relating to disordered emotional behaviour or pathology, the influence of gender and ethnicity on pathological processes, and tests of hypotheses from psychological theories that relate to abnormal behaviour.

Journal of Behavioral Medicine

This interdisciplinary journal is devoted to furthering our understanding of physical health and illness through the knowledge and techniques of behavioural science.

Journal of Clinical Child and Adolescent Psychology

This is the official journal of the Society of Clinical Child and Adolescent Psychology (Division 53) of the American Psychological Association. It includes research on development and evaluation of assessment and intervention techniques, studies on the development and maintenance of problems, cross-cultural and sociodemographic variables that influence clinical child and adolescent psychology, training and professional practice issues, and child advocacy.

Journal of Clinical Psychology

This journal includes research studies, articles on contemporary professional issues, single case research, dissertations in brief, notes from the field, and news and notes. Topics include psychopathology, psychodiagnostics, and the psychotherapeutic process, as well as articles focusing on psychotherapy effectiveness research, psychological assessment and treatment matching, and clinical outcomes.

Journal of Consulting and Clinical Psychology

This journal includes articles on the development, validity, and use of techniques of diagnosis and treatment of disordered behaviour; studies of populations of clinical interest, such as hospital, prison, rehabilitation, geriatric, and similar samples; cross-cultural and demographic studies of interest for behaviour disorders; studies of personality and of its assessment and development that have a clear bearing on problems of clinical dysfunction; studies of gender, ethnicity, or sexual orientation that have a clear bearing on diagnosis, assessment, and treatment; and methodologically sound case studies pertinent to the preceding topics.

Journal of Family Psychology

This is the official publication of the Division of Family Psychology of the American Psychological Association (Division 43). It is devoted to the study of the family system from multiple perspectives and to the application of psychological methods to advance knowledge related to family research, intervention, and policy.

Journal of Marital and Family Therapy

This is the official journal of the American Association of Marital and Family Therapy. It has articles on research and clinical innovations in the areas of marital and family services.

Journal of Personality Assessment

This is the official publication of the Society for Personality Assessment. It contains articles dealing with the development, evaluation, refinement, and application of personality assessment methods. Articles address empirical, theoretical, instructional, and professional aspects of using psychological tests, interview data, and the applied clinical assessment process.

Journal of Psychopathology and Behavioral Assessment

This journal includes research investigations and clinical case summaries on psychopathology and mental disorders applicable to all ages, deviant or abnormal behaviours (including those related to medical conditions and trauma), and personality constructs.

Journal of Social and Clinical Psychology

This journal publishes research that applies theory and research from social psychology to the understanding of human functioning, including the alleviation of psychological problems and the improvement of psychological well-being.

Neuropsychology

This journal focuses on basic research, the integration of basic and applied research, and improved practice in the field of neuropsychology.

Professional Psychology: Research and Practice

This journal has articles on the application of psychology, including data-based and theoretical articles on techniques and practices.

Psychological Assessment

This journal presents empirical research on measurement and evaluation relevant to the broad field of clinical psychology. Topics include clinical judgment and the application of decision-making models; paradigms derived from basic psychological research in cognition, personality-social psychology, and biological psychology; and development, validation, and application of assessment instruments, observational methods, and interviews.

Psychological Bulletin

This journal includes evaluative and integrative research reviews and interpretations of issues in scientific psychology.

Psychotherapy

This is the official publication of the Division of Psychotherapy of the American Psychological Association (Division 29). The journal includes theoretical contributions, research studies, novel ideas, controversies, and examples of practice-relevant issues. The journal is designed to be of interest to theorists, researchers, and/or practitioners.

Psychotherapy Research

This journal is the official publication of the Society for Psychotherapy Research. It includes research findings relevant to practice, education, and policy formulation. The journal presents reports of original research on all aspects of psychotherapy, as well as methodological, theoretical, and review articles of direct relevance to psychotherapy research.

Training and Education in Professional Psychology

A joint publication of the American Psychological Association and the Association of Psychology Postdoctoral and Internship Centers, this journal publishes articles that contribute to the advancement of professional psychology education and training.

APPLICATIONS TO GRADUATE SCHOOL

2 APPENDIX

DO YOU WANT TO BE A CLINICAL PSYCHOLOGIST?

We hope that the descriptions we have provided of the diverse activities in which clinical psychologists engage help you imagine what it would be like to be a clinical psychologist. As you have learned, the term *clinical psychologist* covers many different types of professional activities, so that, for example, Dr. Randy Paterson's week is very different from a week in the life of Dr. Sheila Woody, whose work is different again from that of Dr. Clarissa Bush. Nevertheless, the work lives of these three psychologists have many features in common: (a) their work is based on a foundation of knowledge about human psychological functioning; (b) their work activities are diverse—they spend their work days in a variety of professional activities; (c) their work is demanding and they rarely feel they have enough hours in the day to do everything they wish to do; and, most importantly, (d) their work is rewarding—they feel a passionate commitment to what they do. These three psychologists are characterized by dynamism, energy, and a commitment to lifelong learning.

Throughout this book we have profiled clinical psychologists at different stages of their careers. When we asked them to tell us how they chose clinical psychology as a career, many described having discovered a passion for this field when they were undergraduate students. They were drawn to clinical psychology by the promise it offered to understand and treat health and mental health problems using research-based tools. All the clinical psychologists profiled in this book have varied jobs that require balancing the various activities in learning about new research developments, delivering services, training others, and contributing to the administration of the agency in which they work, as well as serving the broader community. If this appeals to you, then you may be interested in a career in clinical psychology. If your career goal is to spend a much larger proportion of your professional time delivering direct services to clients, you may wish to consider other professions, such as social work, counselling, or psychiatric nursing.

Many undergraduate students taking a course in clinical psychology are attracted to career possibilities in other areas of psychology. If you find that you have a passion for social psychology or for cognitive psychology, you should follow the steps we suggest in this appendix, but adapt them for the area of psychology that most interests you. In the past, it was possible for those with doctorates in non-applied areas of psychology to be registered as clinical psychologists. Due to the growing number of accredited clinical psychology training programs, the increasingly specialized nature of clinical training, and changes in registration requirements, this route for obtaining registration is closing. If you are interested in a career in clinical psychology but decide to pursue training in a different area of psychology, you should be fully aware that your chances of switching to work as a clinical psychologist are extremely limited. The best option for becoming a clinical psychologist is to complete a doctorate in an accredited clinical program.

DO YOU WANT TO GO TO GRADUATE SCHOOL?

Some students apply to graduate school without really taking the time to think about whether it is something that they want to do. As training in clinical psychology in Canada and the United States usually requires around six to seven years of further training after the completion of an honours baccalaureate, it is not something to be taken lightly. If you have high grades, you may have been encouraged by professors to apply to graduate school. However, you need to carefully consider whether this is something that you wish to do. Ideally, you should start thinking about applying to graduate school before the final year of your undergraduate program. This will allow you the time to consider different career options and to begin the process of gathering information about applying to graduate programs in clinical psychology.

You must consider your short- and long-term goals for both career and personal life. Are you willing to move? Are you willing to delay earning a good salary? Although clinical psychologists are typically well paid, there will be many years during graduate school when you will probably be earning much less than your peers who decided to enter the workforce. What kind of job do you hope to have 10 years from now? Graduate training does not occur in a vacuum. At the same time you are considering whether or not you wish to go to graduate school, you may also be reflecting on other decisions, for example, about relationships and when (or whether) you wish to become a parent. Although you may be fairly confident that parenthood is not in your plans in the next year or so, you may be less sure about your plans in three or four years' time. The decision to go to graduate school does not rule out having a family for the next six years. However, it does introduce challenges. Some programs have explicit policies with respect to parental leaves so that, for example, students are allowed one year longer to complete the program for each parental leave taken. Some scholarships now allow students to take a maternity leave. If you are a mature student who already has a family, you will no doubt be considering the ways that you can meet the financial and time demands of your multiple roles.

ARE YOU ELIGIBLE FOR ADMISSION TO A PROGRAM IN CLINICAL PSYCHOLOGY?

Competition for places in clinical psychology programs is fierce. As many programs accept only around 15% of the people who apply, all programs have demanding academic standards. Because research is such a strong component of the training, programs ensure that candidates they admit have the intellectual capacity to conduct original research. The selection system can be an unforgiving one: a bad grade in a single course may not sink your application, but a bad year just might. Most programs prefer to accept students who are likely to receive major scholarship funding, which means that places are offered to those candidates who have earned high grades in the baccalaureate degree. As we mentioned early in the book, programs in counselling psychology are often slightly less demanding in terms of the academic grades required.

Canadian Psychological Association (CPA) criteria for accredited programs in clinical psychology require students to have completed an honours baccalaureate degree in psychology or its equivalent (CPA, 2011). The honours thesis provides an excellent opportunity to learn about the various steps in conducting research. If you enjoy the process of reviewing the literature to formulate meaningful hypotheses, the intellectual challenge of designing a feasible study that will test those hypotheses, the careful consideration of ethical issues involved in the study, painstaking data collection, rigorous data analysis, and the satisfaction of writing it all up in a coherent report, then chances are good that you will savour the opportunity to conduct a doctoral dissertation. If, however, you find completing the honours thesis a tedious process, then you should think very carefully about whether you are attracted to a graduate program in clinical psychology in which one of the key requirements is the completion of a doctoral dissertation. Good grades and an honours thesis are necessary, but do not guarantee acceptance into graduate programs. Students with good grades can improve their chances of success if they also have varied research experience beyond their honours thesis.

FINDING OUT ABOUT PROGRAMS IN CLINICAL PSYCHOLOGY

What do you need to know about clinical training programs? The CPA requires accredited programs to make available information that will be useful to you in selecting the programs to which you wish to apply. Specifically, the CPA requires accredited programs to provide information on the program's philosophy and mission; the theoretical orientation and research interests of faculty members; the goals set by the program (as well as outcome data on the extent to which those goals have been met); the requirements and expectations of students in the program; the activities and practice functions for which the program prepares students; the training resources at the program's disposal; the usual size of the applicant pool; acceptance and attrition rates; gender, age, and self-reported diversity of students; availability of financial and other support; the percentage of graduates licensed; and evidence of accreditation. All of this information should be helpful to you in choosing the programs to which you will apply.

The website of the CPA provides lists of accredited clinical programs. At the time of writing, Canada has 24 accredited clinical psychology programs, five accredited counselling psychology programs, one accredited clinical neuropsychology program, and one accredited school psychology program. Reviewing a program website is probably the best strategy to get a general sense of what the program is like. Although all programs include training in the basics of clinical psychology, programs differ in their areas of strength. For example, some programs offer separate training in adult or child clinical psychology, whereas other programs offer combined training in both adult and child clinical psychology. Some programs have faculty members with a strong profile in clinical health psychology, others have special expertise in issues related to older adults, and some provide opportunities to learn about forensic psychology.

Accredited clinical psychology programs differ in the process by which students are selected. In some universities, students are accepted into the program and, during the first year of study, are matched to work with a particular thesis supervisor. In other programs, there must be a match with a thesis supervisor at the time of admission. You should become aware of the process for each program and tailor your application to each one you are considering. You should also be aware that there are differences among training programs in the sequence of degrees granted. Some universities accept students into a master's program that is then followed by a doctoral program; other universities accept students directly into a doctoral program. Both sequences require comparable coursework, research training, practica, and internship. The main difference is that students in the former programs must complete a master's thesis, which is required for the awarding of a master's degree.

THE APPLICATION PROCESS

The process of applying to graduate school consumes both time and money. The process consists of several phases, including gathering information and deciding whether you wish to apply to graduate school, choosing the programs to which you will apply, studying for and completing the Graduate Record Examination, preparing the application materials, obtaining letters of reference and submitting a full application, and, finally, making a decision about offers (one hopes) you have received. It is probably fair to say that the application process will take the same amount of your time as completing a one-term course.

Gathering Information

The information-gathering stage begins in your second or third year of undergraduate study. You can probably obtain enough information from websites to generate a list of programs that you wish to consider. You can increase your chances of obtaining a place by applying to several different programs. However, it is probably a waste of your time to apply to any programs that you know you do not wish to attend. In addition to the information from websites, you can ask professors for their opinion about different programs.

The Graduate Record Examination

Once you have decided to apply to graduate school and have selected a number of programs that interest you, you will have a better idea of the application requirements for each program. Most programs require candidates to submit scores on the Graduate Record Examination (GRE). As the GRE is available in English only, it is not usually required by programs providing instruction in French. The GRE includes both a general test that can be completed at any time of the year and a subject test that can be completed only in October, November, or April. The tests are completed at a licensed test centre either via computer or in a paper-and-pencil format. The general test takes up to three and three-quarter hours and assesses verbal reasoning, quantitative reasoning, and analytical writing skills. Practice material is available to applicants for the general test. The subject test lasts up to four hours and includes about 205 multiple choice questions of which 40% are oriented to natural science aspects of psychology, 43% are oriented to social science aspects of psychology, and 17% are on general psychology. In preparation for taking the GRE, you should visit the GRE website, review materials from psychology courses, and download a practice test from the GRE website.

Curriculum Vitae

Your curriculum vitae (CV) should provide contact information and detail educational accomplishments, honours and awards, scholarly conference presentations, publications, manuscripts submitted for publication, as well as work and volunteer experience. Volunteer experience in the mental health field can provide important opportunities to learn about different populations, the challenges they face, and the resources available to them. Paid or volunteer research experience provides the opportunity to learn research methods, to work more closely with a professor, and, in some cases, to gain valuable experience in conference presentations and the submission of manuscripts to scholarly journals.

Application Forms and Transcripts

Although many universities may use a provincial online application system, universities and programs all have different application forms. An increasing number of universities offer online applications. Ensure that your form is completed accurately. Printed or typed application forms are preferable to handwritten forms. There is also variability in the deadline by which all materials should be submitted, ranging from early December to the end of January, so check each date carefully. Most programs require you to arrange for official transcripts to be forwarded to the admission office. Allow plenty of time for the materials to arrive prior to the application deadline. Universities with online applications often have automated systems that will inform you about the status of your application. If you have not received a confirmation of receipt of all the necessary documents, it is prudent to contact the admissions office a couple of weeks before the final deadline to request confirmation that all the application materials have arrived safely and that your file is complete. As this is a busy time of year for all admissions offices, it is probably easier to do this via email rather than by phone.

Statements of Interest and Research Plans

Many programs ask candidates to submit a written statement about the areas in which they are interested, as well as their research plans. Programs do not expect candidates to have mapped out the study they will conduct for their doctoral dissertation. These written statements should describe your general areas of interest. If your statements are too specific, then you reduce the likelihood of finding a good match with a professor. It probably makes more sense to think in terms of whether you can imagine yourself joining in a professor's research group, than whether you can find someone whose ideas match yours perfectly. It is useful to tailor your statement of interest to match each program to which you are applying.

Letters of Reference

All applications for graduate school require reference letters. In general, these letters should be from psychology professors. Although you may obtain a glowing letter from a person in a community agency in which you have volunteered, the opinions of psychology professors are usually given greater weight in the selection process. Whereas professors in small universities may know undergraduate students by name, in larger universities, this occurs less frequently. So in your second or third year, you need to plan to make contact with professors who will be potential referees. You may wish to consider volunteering your services in a research project. Inform the professor that your goal is to apply to graduate programs in clinical psychology and that you are eager to obtain relevant experience.

Exhibit A2.1 highlights issues in obtaining a letter of reference. It is to your advantage to ask the professor whether he or she is willing to write a reference letter well ahead of the deadline. As you are aware, professors have numerous responsibilities, so if you make a request for a letter that is due in a week's time, you risk getting a brief letter, a late letter, or none at all. Once the professor has agreed to write the letter, it is most helpful if you prepare a complete package that contains all the material the professor will need in order to prepare letters to be sent to the various programs to which you are applying. It is beneficial for you to make the professor's task as straightforward as possible. Avoid asking for a series of letters as you decide to apply to different programs—make sure that you give the professor a complete list of programs you are applying to, rather than giving "updated" lists as you go through the process of deciding which programs to apply to. As online references cannot be submitted until your application is received, make sure that your application has been submitted prior to the time that professors submit their references. A week or so before the earliest application deadline, contact the professor to inquire politely whether the letters are ready or have been submitted electronically. Most professors who have gone to the trouble of preparing letters of reference for you will appreciate receiving a message of thanks and a message reporting the final outcome of the application process.

Exhibit A2.1 Letters of Reference

Who to ask

- Psychology professors who are familiar with your work
- Supervisor of your honours thesis
- Instructor in a small class
- Supervisor of your research assistantship or volunteer research

When to ask

- Once the professor is familiar with your work
- At least two months in advance

What to provide

- A full list of programs to which you are applying with addresses and deadlines
- Your CV
- A copy of your transcript
- A copy of the form(s) to be completed or a link to download the materials

Before the deadline

- Make a polite inquiry about whether the letter has been prepared

After you receive results

- Inform the professors who have written letters of the results and thank them

Universities have different policies concerning letters of reference. Some require the referee to send a letter directly to the university; others require the letters of reference to be given to the candidate in signed, sealed envelopes and included in the application package. Check the required procedure for each university.

Contacting Potential Supervisors

Email is a very easy way to contact potential supervisors. However, prior to contacting the potential supervisor, do your homework: find out all you can about the program in general and the work of that professor in particular. Exhibit A2.2 describes the process for contacting potential supervisors. During the fall term professors often receive many emails a week from potential students, so it is helpful to keep an initial email relatively brief. It is wise to verify whether the supervisor is planning to accept a new student that year; sometime this information is posted on the departmental website. It is important to know, for example, whether the professor is on parental leave, sabbatical leave, or close to retirement and not accepting a student.

Exhibit A2.2 Contacting Potential Supervisors

Prior to application

- Find out information from the university website
- Search for materials on PsycINFO
- Express interest via email
- Confirm that the professor is eligible to take a new student
- Offer to send materials (CV, transcript)
- Ask for copies of articles that are in press
- Inquire about future research planned by the professor
- Inquire about interviews
- Ask specific questions if the information is not available elsewhere

If you are contacted by a potential supervisor

- Ask questions that would give information to help you choose between two offers
- Ask about supervision style
- Ask to speak to current or recent graduate students

Once you have made a decision

- Inform the professor that you intend to accept his or her offer
- Inform the professor if you have accepted a place elsewhere

As published material is easily available electronically, it does not make sense to request copies of the professor's publications. You should do a bit of homework and read several of the professor's recent publications. If you are truly interested in working with this person, you may wish to ask to see a copy of work that is in press. Avoid clogging a professor's inbox with documents such as a transcript, your CV, and a copy of your honours thesis. However, it may be helpful to offer to send any of these materials if the professor would like to read them.

If you live within easy travelling of the university to which you are applying, you may wish to express your willingness to come for an interview. Many professors do not conduct interviews until after the deadline for admission (they simply do not have time to interview all potential candidates, so focus their energies on a few candidates who have met all the eligibility criteria and who are interested in research in their area). You may wish to ask a professor whether it is possible to meet or contact other graduate students.

FINANCING YOUR TRAINING

Unless you are independently wealthy, your planning should include consideration of how you will finance the years you will be in graduate school. On average, students take over six years after the bachelor's degree to complete a Ph.D. in clinical psychology. Expenses include tuition fees, as well as living expenses. Accredited programs in clinical psychology require full-time registration as a student for at least four years. That means that you are not allowed to work more than a small number of hours a week on work unrelated to your thesis (e.g., 10 hours a week in many universities). Part of your planning and decision-making should include finding out about all your potential sources of income.

In considering offers from different universities, it is often a challenge to know which university is offering the best financial support. For example, some universities offer generous funding in the first and second year, with lower amounts as the student progresses through the program. Other universities may offer a lower amount, but guarantee to provide it over the entire course of the program. It is useful to distinguish between money that is given to the student (i.e., a scholarship) and money that the student must earn (i.e., working as a teaching assistant).

Scholarships and Bursaries

You may be eligible to receive scholarships and bursaries from diverse sources, including the university in which you will be enrolled, and from provincial or federal funding agencies. Most scholarships are awarded on the basis of merit, which means that they are given to the students who have high grade point averages. If you have made a presentation at a scholarly conference, or have submitted a manuscript for publication, that will also strengthen your candidacy. Applications for federal and provincial funding are made a year in advance, so it is important to gather information and submit your application in plenty of time.

In addition to major funding, there may be many small scholarships for which you may be eligible. Some of these may be offered to students whose work is in a certain area, or to those in serious financial need. Some students are proficient at finding out about potential sources of funding and become competent at preparing application packages. Although a $500 scholarship will not solve all your financial concerns, it will help, and will of course be an important item to add to your CV.

Research Assistantships

You may be eligible to work part-time as a research assistant. The rates for research assistants vary from university to university. In addition to earning money, you will also be gaining experience in various research tasks. As well, the professor who supervises your research assistantship will be in a good position to observe your research skills and may be a good person to ask to prepare letters of reference for you in the future.

Teaching Assistantships and Teaching Courses

Many graduate students work part-time as teaching assistants with responsibilities in conducting laboratories, marking assignments, and even teaching a class or two. In some universities, graduate students also have the opportunity to teach a full course. If you are considering an academic job, this will be a great opportunity to develop your teaching skills.

Practica and Internships

In Canada, it is rare for students to be paid for completing practica. However, accredited clinical programs include a full one-year accredited paid internship. The salaries for internships vary tremendously from site to site. You will not be able to retire on your year's salary, but it will probably pay your living expenses for the internship year.

DECISION-MAKING

Unsuccessful Applications

The number of qualified applicants to programs in clinical psychology far exceeds the number of spaces available in accredited clinical psychology programs. That means that each year a number of candidates with high grade point averages, excellent letters of reference, and a passionate commitment to become a clinical psychologist fail to receive an offer of admission to an accredited clinical program. This is often a very disheartening experience—it may be the first sense of academic failure that you have experienced.

If your application is unsuccessful, it is important that you carefully examine the base rates. Across clinical programs there may be as many as 10 applicants for every position. In deciding what to do next, you must consider your chances for future years. If, for example, your grade point average is above the official cut-off but much lower than that of students admitted to clinical programs, then you may wish to consider alternative programs of study that are less stringent in terms of academic criteria. If you have highly specialized research interests in an area in which there are few supervisors, you may wish to broaden your interests. If you have applied to only one program, then you have seriously limited the odds of acceptance. If you decide to reapply next year, it makes sense to investigate strategies to enhance the chance of success. You may wish to consider ways to boost your GPA, or to study harder and retake the GRE. You may wish to consider a position in a research laboratory, and may wish to inquire about opportunities to become involved in a conference presentation or a manuscript submission.

Successful Applications

Although receiving a rejection letter is stressful, so too is receiving more than one offer of admission. Fortunately, all Canadian graduate programs in clinical psychology allow candidates until mid-April to accept offers of admission. Unfortunately, that can lead to chains of people waiting: candidate A has an offer from university 1, but really wants to go to university 2; candidate B has an offer from university 2, but really wants to go to university 3, and candidate C has an offer from university 3, but is not sure whether she or he wants to go into psychology or to law school. Although there is no foolproof way to avoid this kind of situation, it can be minimized if candidates gather all the information they need to make informed choices and develop a list of preferences.

ADDITIONAL RESOURCES

Books

American Psychological Association. (2013). *Graduate study in psychology: 2013 edition.* Washington DC: Author.

Sayette, M. A., Mayne, T. J., & Norcross, J. C. (2012). *Insider's guide to graduate programs in clinical and counseling psychology: 2012/2013 edition.* New York: Guilford.

Check It Out!

A listing of all Canadian graduate programs in psychology: www.cpa.ca/students/cpagraduateguide

A listing of all graduate programs accredited by the Canadian Psychological Association: www.cpa.ca/psychologyincanada/canadianuniversities/cpaaccreditedprograms

The Graduate Record Examination: www.gre.org

REFERENCES

Ablow, J. C., Measelle, J. R., Kraemer, H. C., Harrington, R., Luby, J., Smider, N., et al. (1999). The MacArthur three-city outcome study: Evaluating multi-informant measures of young children's symptomatology. *Journal of the American Academy of Child and Adolescent Psychiatry, 38,* 1580–1590.

Abramowitz, J. S. (2008). Obsessive-compulsive disorder. In J. Hunsley & E. J. Mash (Eds.), *A guide to assessments that work* (pp. 275–292). New York: Oxford University Press.

Acevedo-Polakovich, I. D., Reynaga-Abiko, G., Garriott, P. O., Derefinko, K. J., Wimsatt, M. K., Gudonis, L. C., & Brown, T. L. (2007). Beyond instrument selection: Cultural considerations in the psychological assessment of U.S. Latinas/os. *Professional Psychology: Research and Practice, 38,* 375–384.

Achenbach, T. M. (2002). *Manual for the Assessment Data Management Program (ADM) CBCL, YSR, TRF, YASR, YCBCL, SCICA, CBCL/2-3, CBCL/1.5-5 and C-TRF.* Vermont: University Medical Associates.

Achenbach, T. M. (2010). Multicultural evidence-based assessment of psychopathology at ages 1½–18 years. *Transcultural Psychiatry,* 2010, *47,* 707–726.

Achenbach, T. M., Krukowski, R. A., Dumenci, L., & Ivanova, M. Y. (2005). Assessment of adult psychopathology: Meta-analyses and implications of cross-informant correlations. *Psychological Bulletin, 131,* 361–382.

Achenbach, T. M., McConaughy, S. H., & Howell, C. T. (1987). Child/adolescent behavioral and emotional problems: Implications of cross-informant correlations for situational specificity. *Psychological Bulletin, 101,* 213–232.

Achenbach, T. M., Newhouse, P. A., & Rescorla, L. A. (2004). *Manual for ASEBA Older Adult Forms & Profiles.* Burlington, VT: University of Vermont, Research Center for Children, Youth, & Families.

Achenbach, T. M., & Rescorla, L. A. (2000). *Manual for ASEBA Preschool Forms & Profiles.* Burlington, VT: University of Vermont, Research Center for Children, Youth, & Families.

Achenbach, T. M., & Rescorla, L. A. (2001). *Manual for ASEBA School-Age Forms & Profiles.* Burlington, VT: University of Vermont, Research Center for Children, Youth, & Families.

Achenbach, T. M., & Rescorla, L. A. (2003). *Manual for ASEBA Adult Forms & Profiles.* Burlington, VT: University of Vermont, Research Center for Children, Youth, & Families.

Ackerman, M. J., & Ackerman, M. C. (1997). Custody evaluation practices: A survey of experienced professionals (revisited). *Professional Psychology: Research and Practice, 28,* 137–145.

Acklin, M. W., McDowell, C. J., Verschell, M. S., & Chan, D. (2000). Interobserver agreement, intraobserver reliability, and the Rorschach Comprehensive System. *Journal of Personality Assessment, 74,* 15–47.

Addis, M. E., & Krasnow, A. D. (2000). A national survey of practicing psychologists' attitudes towards psychotherapy treatment manuals. *Journal of Consulting and Clinical Psychology, 68,* 331–339.

Addis, M. E., Wade, W. A., & Hatgis, C. (1999). Addressing practitioners' concerns about manual-based psychotherapies. *Clinical Psychology: Science and Practice, 6,* 430–441.

Aderka, I. M., Nickerson, A., Bøe, H. J., & Hofmann, S. G. (2012). Sudden gains during psychological treatments of anxiety and depression: A meta-analysis. *Journal of Consulting and Clinical Psychology, 80,* 93–101.

Ægisdóttir, S., White, M. J., Spengler, P. M., Maugherman, A. S., Anderson, L. A., Cook, R. S., et al. (2006). The meta-analysis of clinical judgment project: Fifty-six years of accumulated research on clinical versus statistical prediction. *The Counseling Psychologist, 34,* 341–382.

Aiken, L. R. (2003). *Psychological testing and assessment* (11th ed.). Toronto: Pearson.

Albano, A. M., & Silverman, W. K. (1996). *Anxiety Disorders Interview Schedule for Children for DSM-IV (ADIS IV): Clinician manual for parent and child versions.* San Antonio, TX: Psychological Corporation.

American Educational Research Association, American Psychological Association, & National Council on Measurement in Education. (1999). *Standards for educational and psychological testing.* Washington, DC: American Educational Research Association.

American Psychiatric Association. (1994). *Diagnostic and statistical manual of mental disorders* (4th ed.). Washington, DC: Author.

American Psychiatric Association. (2000). *Diagnostic and statistical manual of mental disorders* (4th ed., text revision). Washington, DC: Author.

American Psychiatric Association. (2013). *Diagnostic and statistical manual of mental disorders* (5th ed.). Washington, DC: American Psychiatric Publishing.

American Psychological Association. (2003a). Guidelines on multicultural education, training, research, practice, and organizational change for psychologists. *American Psychologist, 58,* 377–402.

American Psychological Association. (2003b). PracticeNet survey: Clinical practice patterns. Retrieved April 8, 2005, from http://www.apapracticenet.net/results/Summer 2003/1.asp

American Psychological Association. (2004). Guidelines for psychological practice with older adults. *American Psychologist, 59,* 236–260.

American Psychological Association. (2010a). Ethical principles of psychologists and code of conduct. *American Psychologist, 57,* 1060–1073.

American Psychological Association. (2010b). Guidelines for child custody evaluations in family law proceedings. *American Psychologist, 65,* 863–867.

American Psychological Association. (2013a). Guidelines for psychological practice in health care delivery systems. *American Psychologist, 68,* 1–6.

American Psychological Association. (2013b). Recognition of psychotherapy effectiveness. *Psychotherapy, 50,* 102–109.

American Psychological Association Presidential Task Force on Evidence-Based Practice. (2006). Evidence-based practice in psychology. *American Psychologist, 61,* 271–285.

American Psychological Association Working Group on the Older Adult. (2004). What practitioners should know about working with older adults. *Professional Psychology: Research and Practice, 29,* 413–427.

American Psychological Association. (2002). *Guidelines on multicultural education, training, research, practice, and organizational change for psychologists.* Washington, DC: Author.

Anastasi, A., & Urbina, S. (1997). *Psychological testing* (7th ed.). Upper Saddle River, NJ: Prentice-Hall.

Anker, M. G., Duncan, B. L., & Sparks, J. A. (2009). Using client feedback to improve couple therapy outcomes: A randomized clinical trial in a naturalistic setting. *Journal of Consulting and Clinical Psychology, 77,* 693–704.

Antony, M. M. & Barlow, D. H. (Eds.). (2010). *Handbook of assessment and treatment planning for psychological disorders* (2nd ed.). New York: Guilford Press.

APA Publications and Communications Board Working Group on Journal Article Reporting Standards. (2008). Reporting standards for research in psychology: Why do we need them? What might they be? *American Psychologist, 63,* 839–851.

Arnow, B. A. (1999). Why are empirically supported treatments for Bulimia Nervosa underutilized and what can we do about it? *Journal of Clinical Psychology, 55,* 769–779.

Association of Family and Conciliation Courts. (2006). Model standards of practice for child custody evaluations. Retrieved February 5, 2008, from http://www.afccnet.org/pdfs

Association of State and Provincial Psychology Boards. (2005). *ASPPB code of conduct.* Montgomery, AL: Author.

Australian Psychological Society. (2010). *Evidence-based psychological interventions: A literature review* (3rd ed.). Melbourne, Australia: Author.

Backhaus, A., Agha, Z., Maglione, M. L., Repp, A., Ross, B., Zuest, D., et al. (2012). Videoconferencing psychotherapy: A systematic review. *Psychological Services, 9,* 111–131.

Baldwin, S. A., Berkeljon, A., Atkins, D. C., Olsen, J. A., & Nielsen, S. L. (2009). Rates of change in naturalistic psychotherapy: Contrasting dose-effect and good-enough level models of change. *Journal of Consulting and Clinical Psychology, 77,* 203–211.

Baldwin, S. A., & Imel, Z. E. (2013). Therapist effects: Findings and methods. In M. J. Lambert (Ed.), *Bergin and Garfield's handbook of psychotherapy and behavior change* (6th ed., pp. 258–297). Hoboken, NJ: John Wiley & Sons.

Barber, J. P., Connolly, M. B., Crits-Christoph, P., Gladis, L., & Siqueland, L. (2000). Alliance predicts patients' outcome beyond in-treatment change in symptoms. *Journal of Consulting and Clinical Psychology, 68,* 1027–1032.

Barber, J. P., & Crits-Christoph, P. (1993). Advances in measures of psychodynamic formulations. *Journal of Consulting and Clinical Psychology, 61,* 574–585.

Barbopoulos, A., & Clark, J. M. (2003). Practising psychology in rural settings: Issues and guidelines. *Canadian Psychology, 44,* 410–424.

Barbotte, E., Guillemin, F., Chau, N., & the Lorhandicap Group. (2001). Prevalence of impairments, disabilities, handicaps and quality of life in the general population: A review of the literature. *Bulletin of the World Health Organization, 79,* 1047–1055.

Barkley, R. et al. (2002). International Consensus Statement on ADHD. *Clinical Child and Family Psychology Review, 5,* 89–111.

Barlow, D. H. (2004). Psychological treatments. *American Psychologist, 59,* 869–878.

Barlow, D. H., Bullis, J. R., Comer, J. S., & Ametaj, A. A. (2013). Evidence-based psychological treatments: An update and the way forward. *Annual Review of Clinical Psychology, 9,* 1–27.

Bar-On, R. (2002). *BarOn Emotional Quotient Short Form (EQ-i: Short). Technical manual.* Toronto: Multi-Health Systems.

Barrett, P. M., Farrell, L., Pina, A. A., Peris, T. S., & Piacentini, J. (2008). Evidence-based psychosocial treatments for child and adolescent obsessive-compulsive disorder. *Journal of Clinical Child and Adolescent Psychology, 37,* 131–155.

Barrett, P., & Turner, C. (2001). Prevention of anxiety symptoms in primary school children: Preliminary results from a universal school-based trial. *British Journal of Clinical Psychology, 40,* 399–410.

Barrett, P., & Turner, C. (2004). Prevention of childhood anxiety and depression. In P. M. Barrett & T. H. Ollendick (Eds.), *Interventions that work with children and adolescents: Prevention and treatment* (pp. 429–474). Chichester, UK: John Wiley & Sons.

Barwick, M. A., Boydell, K. M., Stasiulis, E., Ferguson, H. B., Blase, K., & Fixsen, D. (2008). Research utilization among children's mental health providers. *Implementation Science, 3, 19.* Retrieved February 16, 2009, from www.implementationscience.com

Baucom, D. H., Epstein, N., & Gordon, K. C. (2000). Marital therapy: Theory, practice and empirical status. In C. R. Snyder & R. E. Ingram (Eds.), *Handbook of psychological changes: Psychotherapy processes and practices for the 21st century* (pp. 280–308). New York: John Wiley & Sons.

Bauer, S., Lambert, M. J., & Nielsen, S. L. (2004). Clinical significance methods: A comparison of statistical techniques. *Journal of Personality Assessment, 82,* 60–70.

Beach, S. R. H., & Amir, N. (2006). Self-reported depression is taxonic. *Journal of Psychopathology and Behavioral Assessment, 28,* 171–178.

Beck, A. T., & Dozois, D. J. A. (2011). Cognitive therapy: Current status and future directions. *Annual Review of Medicine, 62,* 397–409.

Beck, A. T., Steer, R. A., & Brown, G. K. (1996). *Beck Depression Inventory manual* (2nd ed.). San Antonio, TX: Psychological Corporation.

Becker, C. B., Zayfert, C., & Anderson, E. (2004). A survey of psychologists' attitudes towards and utilization of exposure therapy for PTSD. *Behaviour Research and Therapy, 42,* 277–292.

Bedi, R. P., Haverkamp, B. E., Beatch, R., Cave, D. G., Domene, J. F., Harris, G. E., et al. (2011). Counselling psychology in a Canadian context: Definition and description. *Canadian Psychology, 52,* 128–138.

Beiling, P. J., & Kuyken, W. (2003). Is cognitive case formulation science or science fiction? *Clinical Psychology: Science and Practice, 10,* 52–69.

Bekhit, N. S., Thomas, G. V., Lalonde, S., & Jolley, R. (2002). Psychological assessment in clinical practice in Britain. *Clinical Psychology and Psychotherapy, 9,* 285–291.

Belar, C. D. (2008). Clinical health psychology: A health care specialty in professional psychology. *Professional Psychology: Research and Practice, 39,* 229–233.

Benish, S. G., Imel, Z. E., & Wampold, B. E. (2008). The relative efficacy of bona fide psychotherapies for treating post-traumatic stress disorder: A meta-analysis of direct comparisons. *Clinical Psychology Review, 28,* 746–758.

Benton, S. A., Robertson, J. M., Tseng, W. C., Newton, F. B., & Benton, S. L. (2003). Changes in counseling center client problems across 13 years. *Professional Psychology: Research and Practice, 34,* 66–72.

Bergin, A. E. (1971). The evaluation of therapeutic outcomes. In A. E. Bergin & S. L. Garfield (Eds.), *Handbook of psychotherapy and behaviour change* (pp. 217–270). New York: John Wiley & Sons.

Berke, D. M., Rozell, C. A., Hogan, T. P., Norcross, J. C., & Karpiak, C. P. (2011). What clinical psychologists know about evidence-based practice: Familiarity with online resources and research methods. *Journal of Clinical Psychology, 67,* 329–339.

Berman, P. S. (1997). *Case conceptualization and treatment planning.* Thousand Oaks, CA: Sage Publications.

Bernal, G., Jiménez-Chafey, M. I., & Rodríguez, M. M. D. (2009). Cultural adaptation of treatments: A resource for considering culture in evidence-based practice. *Professional Psychology: Research and Practice, 40,* 361–368.

Beutler, L. E. (1998). Identifying empirically supported treatments: What if we didn't? *Journal of Consulting and Clinical Psychology, 66,* 113–120.

Beutler, L. E., & Castonguay, L. G. (2006). The task force on empirically based principles of therapeutic change. In L. G. Castonguay & L. E. Beutler (Eds.), *Principles of therapeutic change that work* (pp. 1–10). New York: Oxford University Press.

Beutler, L. E., Harwood, T. M., Kimpara, S., Verdirame, D., & Blau, K. (2011). Coping style. In J. C. Norcross (Ed.), *Psychotherapy relationships that work: Evidence-based responsiveness* (2nd ed., pp. 336–353). New York: Oxford University Press.

Beutler, L. E., Harwood, T. M., Michelson, A., Song, X., & Holman, J. (2011). Reactance/resistance level. In J. C. Norcross (Ed.), *Psychotherapy relationships that work: Evidence-based responsiveness* (2nd ed., pp. 261–278). New York: Oxford University Press.

Beutler, L. E., Malik, M., Alimohamed, S., Harwood, T. M., Talebi, H., Noble, S., et al. (2004). Therapist variables. In M. J. Lambert (Ed.), *Bergin and Garfield's handbook of psychotherapy and behavior change* (5th ed., pp. 227–306). New York: John Wiley & Sons.

Bickman, L. (1996). A continuum of care: More is not always better. *American Psychologist, 51,* 689–701.

Bickman, L., Rosof-Williams, J., Salzerm M. S., Summerfelt, W. T., Noser, K., Wilson, S. J., et al. (2000). What information do clinicians value for monitoring adolescent client progress and outcomes? *Professional Psychology: Research and Practice, 31,* 70–74.

Biglan, A. (2003). The generic features of effective childrearing. In A. Biglan, M. Wang, & H. J. Walberg (Eds.), *Preventing youth problems* (pp. 145–162). New York: Kluwer Academic.

Biglan, A., Mrazek, P. K., Carnine, D., & Flay, B. R. (2003). The integration of research and practice in the prevention of youth behavior problems. *American Psychologist, 58,* 433–440.

Biglan, A., & Severson, H. H. (2003). The prevention of tobacco use. In A. Biglan, M. Wang, & H. J. Walberg (Eds.), *Preventing youth problems* (pp. 63–85). New York: Kluwer Academic.

Birchler, G. R., & Fals-Stewart, W. S. (2002). Marital dysfunction. In M. Hersen (Ed.), *Clinical behavior therapy with adults and children* (pp. 216–235). New York: John Wiley & Sons.

Blagys, M. D., & Hilsenroth, M. J. (2000). Distinctive features of short-term psychodynamic interpersonal psychotherapy: A review of the comparative psychotherapy process literature. *Clinical Psychology: Science and Practice, 7,* 167–188.

Blagys, M. D., & Hilsenroth, M. J. (2002). Distinctive activities of cognitive-behavioral therapy: A review of the comparative psychotherapy process literature. *Clinical Psychology Review, 22,* 671–706.

Blais, M. A., & Kurtz, J. E. (2007). Personality Assessment Inventory [Special issue]. *Journal of Personality Assessment, 88(1).*

Blais, M. A., Sinclair, S. J., Baity, M. R., Worth, J., Weiss, A. P., Ball, L. A., & Herman, J. (2012). Measuring outcomes in adult outpatient psychiatry. *Clinical Psychology & Psychotherapy, 19,* 203–213.

Blanton, H., & Jaccard, J. (2006). Arbitrary metrics in psychology. *American Psychologist, 61,* 27–41.

Blashfield, R. K. (1991). Models of psychiatric classification. In M. Hersen, & S. M. Turner (Eds.), *Adult psychopathology and diagnosis* (2nd ed., pp. 3–22). New York: John Wiley & Sons.

Bloom, D. E., Cafiero, E. T., Jané-Llopis E., Abrahams-Gessel, S., Bloom., L. R., Fathima, S., et al. (2011). *The global economic burden of noncommunicable diseases.* Geneva: World Economic Forum. Retrieved from: www.weforum.org.EconomicsOfNCD

Blount, A., Schoenbaum, M., Kathol, R., Rollman, B. L., Thomas, M., O'Donohue, W., & Peek, C. J. (2007). The economics of behavioral health services in medical settings: A review of the evidence. *Professional Psychology; Research and Practice, 38,* 290–297.

Boake, C. D., (2008). Clinical neuropsychology *Professional Psychology: Research and Practice, 39,* 234–239.

Bohart, A. C., O'Hara, M., & Leitner, L. M. (1998). Empirically violated treatments: Disenfranchisement of humanistic and other psychotherapies. *Psychotherapy Research, 8,* 141–157.

Bohart, A. C., & Wade, A. G. (2013). The client in psychotherapy. In M. J. Lambert (Ed.), *Bergin and Garfield's handbook of psychotherapy and behavior change* (6th ed., pp. 219–257). Hoboken, NJ: John Wiley & Sons.

Bolton, P., Bass, J., Neugebauer, R., Verdeli, H., Clougherty, K. P., Wickramaratne, P., et al. (2003). Group interpersonal psychotherapy for depression in rural Uganda. *Journal of the American Medical Association, 289,* 3117–3124.

Bonanno, G. A. (2004). Loss, trauma, and human resilience. *American Psychologist, 59,* 20–28.

Bonanno, G. A. (2005). Resilience in the face of potential trauma. *Current Directions in Psychological Science, 14,* 135–138.

Bonanno, G. A., Westphal, M., & Mancini, A. D. (2011). Resilience to loss and potential trauma. *Annual Review of Clinical Psychology, 7,* 511–535.

Bongers, I. L., Koot, H. M., van der Ende, J., & Verhulst, F. C. (2003). The normative development of child and adolescent problem behavior. *Journal of Abnormal Psychology, 112,* 179–192.

Bootzin, R. R., & Epstein, D. R. (2011). Understanding and treating insomnia. *Annual Review of Clinical Psychology, 7,* 435–458.

Bornstein, R. F., Rossner, S. C., Hill, E. L., & Stepanian, M. L. (1994). Face validity and fakability of objective and projective measures of dependency. *Journal of Personality Assessment, 63,* 363–386.

Bowden, S. C., Lissner, D., McCarthy, K. A. L., Weiss, L. G., & Holdnack, J. A. (2007). Metric and structural equivalence of core cognitive abilities measured with the Wechsler Adult Intelligence Scale-III in the United States and Australia. *Journal of Clinical and Experimental Neuropsychology, 29,* 768–780.

Bowden, S. C., Saklofske, D. H., & Weiss, L. G. (2011). Augmenting the core battery with supplementary subtests: Wechsler Adult Intelligence Scale-IV measurement invariances across the United States and Canada. *Assessment, 18,* 133–140.

Bower, P., & Gilbody, S. (2005). Stepped care in psychological therapies: Access, effectiveness, and efficiency. *British Journal of Psychiatry, 186,* 11–17.

Bowman, M. L. (2000). The diversity of diversity: Canadian-American differences and their implications for clinical training and APA accreditation. *Canadian Psychology, 41,* 230–243.

Braaten, E. B., Otto, S., & Handelsman, M. M. (1993). What do people want to know about psychotherapy? *Psychotherapy, 30,* 565–570.

Brabender, V. A., Fallon, A. E., & Smolar, A. I. (2004). *Essentials of group therapy.* New York: John Wiley & Sons.

Bradley, R., Greene, J., Russ, E., Dutra, L., & Westen, D. (2005). A multi-dimensional meta-analysis of psychotherapy for PTSD. *American Journal of Psychiatry, 162,* 214–227.

Bradshaw, J., Chzhen, Y., Main, G., Martorano, B., Menchini, L., & de Neubourg, C. (2012). Relative income poverty among children in rich countries. *Innocenti Working Paper* No. 2012-01, UNICEF Innocenti Research Centre, Florence.

Breau, L. M., McGrath, P. J., Camfield, C. S., & Finley, G. A. (2002). Psychometric properties of the non-communicating children's pain checklist-revised. *Pain, 99,* 349–357.

British Psychological Society. (2003). *Professional Practice Guidelines: Division of Neuropsychology.* Retrieved January 15, 2005, from http://www.bps.org.uk

Brockington, I., & Mumford, D. (2002). Recruitment into psychiatry. *British Journal of Psychiatry, 180,* 307–312.

Bronfenbrenner, U. (1979). *The ecology of human development: Experiments by design and by nature.* Cambridge, MA: Harvard University Press.

Broshek, D. K., & Barth, J. T. (2000). The Halstead-Reitan Neuropsychological Test Battery. In G. Groth-Marnat (Ed.), *Neuropsychological assessment in clinical practice* (pp. 223–263). New York: John Wiley & Sons.

Brosnan, L., Reynolds, S., & Moore, R. G. (2008). Self-evaluation of cognitive therapy performance: Do therapists know how competent they are? *Behavioural and Cognitive Psychotherapy, 36,* 581–587.

Brown, T. A., Campbell, L. A., Lehman, C. L., Grisham, J. R., & Mancill, R. B. (2001). Current and lifetime comorbidity of the DSM-IV anxiety and mood disorders in a large clinical sample. *Journal of Abnormal Psychology, 110,* 585–589.

Brown, T. A., Di Nardo, P. A., & Barlow, D. H. (1994). *Anxiety Disorders Interview Schedule for DSM-IV (ADIS IV).* San Antonio, TX: Psychological Corporation.

Bruck, M., & Ceci, S. J. (2004). Forensic developmental psychology: Unveiling four scientific misconceptions. *Current Directions in Psychology.13,* 229–232.

Brugha, T. S., Bebbington, P. E., Singleton, N., Melzer, D., Jenkins, R., Lewis, G., et al. (2004). Trends in service use and treatment for mental disorders in adults throughout Great Britain. *British Journal of Psychiatry, 185,* 378–384.

Buchanan, T. (2002). Online assessment: Desirable or dangerous? *Professional Psychology: Research and Practice, 33,* 148–154.

Burlingame, G. M., MacKenzie, K. R., & Strauss, B. (2004). Small-group treatment: Evidence for effectiveness and mechanisms of change. In M. L. Lambert (Ed.), *Bergin and Garfield's handbook of psychotherapy and behavior change* (5th ed., pp. 647–696). New York: John Wiley & Sons.

Burlingame, G. M., Mosier, J. I., Wells, M. G., Atkin, Q. G., Lamber, M. J., Whooery, M., et al. (2001). Tracking the influence of mental health treatment: The development of the Youth Outcome Questionnaire. *Clinical Psychology and Psychotherapy, 8,* 361–379.

Burns, D. D. (1980). *Feeling good: The new mood therapy.* New York: Signet Books.

Butcher, J. N. (Ed). (2009). *Oxford handbook of personality assessment.* New York: Oxford University Press.

Butcher, J. N. (2010). Personality assessment from the nineteenth to the early twenty-first century: Past achievements and contemporary challenges. *Annual Review of Clinical Psychology, 6,* 1–20.

Butcher, J. N., & Beutler, L. E. (2003). The MMPI-2. In L. E. Beutler & G. Groth-Marnat (Eds.), *Integrative assessment of adult personality* (2nd ed., pp. 157–191). New York: Guilford Press.

Butcher, J. N., Dahlstrom, W. G., Graham, J. R., Tellegen, A., & Kaemmer, B. (1989). *Manual for administration and scoring: MMPI-2.* Minneapolis, MN: University of Minnesota Press.

Butcher, J. N., Perry, J. N., & Atlis, M. M. (2000). Validity and utility of computer-based test interpretations. *Psychological Assessment, 12,* 6–18.

Butcher, J. N., Williams, C. L., Graham, J. R., Archer, R., Tellegen, A., Ben-Porath, Y. S., et al. (1992). MMPI-A: *Manual for administration, scoring, and interpretation.* Minneapolis: University of Minnesota Press.

Cairns, N. J. (2004). Neuroanatomy and neuropathology. In L. H. Goldstein & J. E. McNeil (Eds.), *Clinical neuropsychology: A practical guide to assessment and management for clinicians* (pp. 23–55). Chichester, UK: John Wiley & Sons.

Calhoun, K. S., Moras, K., Pilkonis, P. A., & Rehm, L. P. (1998). Empirically supported treatments: Implications for training. *Journal of Consulting and Clinical Psychology, 66,* 151–162.

Camara, W. J., Nathan, J. S., & Puente, A. E. (2000). Psychological test usage: Implications in professional psychology. *Professional Psychology: Science and Practice, 31,* 141–154.

Canadian Association of University Teachers. (2012). *CAUT 2012-2013 Almanac of post-secondary education in Canada.* Ottawa, ON. Author.

Canadian Institute for Health Information (2011). *Canada's health care providers, 2000 to 2009: A reference guide.* Ottawa, ON: Canadian Institute for Health Information. Retrieved from http://secure.cihi.ca/cihiweb/products/CanadasHealthCareProviders2000to2009AReferenceGuide_EN.pdf

Canadian Psychiatric Association. (2013). *How many psychiatrists are there in Canada?* Retrieved from www.cpa-apc.org

Canadian Psychological Association. (1999). *Geographic locations survey of clinical psychologists in Canada.* Ottawa, ON: Author.

Canadian Psychological Association. (2000). *Canadian code of ethics for psychologists* (3rd ed.). Ottawa, ON: Author.

Canadian Psychological Association. (2001). *Guidelines for non-discriminatory practice.* Ottawa, ON: Author.

Canadian Psychological Association. (2011). *Accreditation standards and procedures for doctoral programmes and internships in professional psychology* (5th revision). Ottawa, ON: Author.

Cardeña, E., & Carlson, E. (2011). Acute stress disorder revisited. *Annual Review of Clinical Psychology, 7,* 245–267.

Carlbring, P., Gunnarsdottir, M., Hedensjo, L., Andersson, G., Ekselius, L., & Furmark, T. (2007). Treatment of social phobia: Randomised trial of internet-delivered cognitive-behavioural therapy with telephone support. *British Journal of Psychiatry, 190,* 123–128.

Carleton, R. N., Parkerson, H. A., & Horswill, S. C. (2012). Assessing the publication productivity of clinical psychology professors in Canadian Psychological Association-accredited Canadian psychology departments. *Canadian Psychology, 53,* 226–237.

Carr, A. (2002). Conclusions. In A. Carr (Ed.), *Prevention: what works with children and adolescents? A critical review of psychological prevention programmes for children, adolescents and their families* (pp. 359–372). Hove, UK: Brunner-Routledge.

Carroll, J. B. (1993). *Human cognitive abilities: A survey of factor analytic studies.* New York: Cambridge University Press.

Cartwright-Hatton, S., Roberts, C., Chitsabesan, P., Fothergill, C., & Harrington, R. (2004). Systematic review of the efficacy of cognitive behaviour therapies for childhood and adolescent anxiety disorders. *British Journal of Clinical Psychology, 43,* 421–436.

Caruso, J. C., & Cliff, N. (1999). The properties of equally and differentially weighted WAISIII factor scores. *Psychological Assessment, 11,* 198–206.

Casey, R. J., & Berman, J. S. (1985). The outcome of psychotherapy with children. *Psychological Bulletin, 98,* 388–400.

Cashel, M. L. (2002). Child and adolescent psychological assessment: Current clinical practices and the impact of managed care. *Professional Psychology: Research and Practice, 33,* 446–453.

Cassin, S. E., Singer, A. R., Dobson, K. S., & Altmaier, E. M. (2007). Professional interests and career aspirations of graduate students in professional psychology: An exploratory study. *Training and Education in Professional Psychology, 1,* 26–37.

Castonguay, L. G., & Beutler, L. E. (Eds.). (2006a). *Principles of therapeutic change that work.* New York: Oxford University Press.

Castonguay, L. G., & Beutler, L. E. (2006b). Common and unique principles of therapeutic change: What do we know and what do we need to know? In L. G. Castonguay & L. E. Beutler (Eds.), *Principles of therapeutic change that work* (pp. 353–369). New York: Oxford University Press.

Castro, F. G., Barrera, M., & Steiker, L. K. H. (2010). Issues and challenges in the design of culturally adapted evidence-based interventions. *Annual Review of Clinical Psychology, 6,* 213–239.

Cattell, R. B. (1963). Theory of fluid and crystallized intelligence: A critical experiment. *Journal of Educational Psychology, 54,* 1–22.

Chaimowitz, G. (2004). *Psychotherapy in psychiatry.* Ottawa, ON: Canadian Psychiatric Association.

Chamberlain, P., & Smith, D. K. (2003). Antisocial behaviour in children and adolescents: The Oregon multidimensional foster care model. In A. E. Kazdin & J. R. Weisz (Eds.), *Evidence-based psychotherapies for children and adolescents* (pp. 282–300). New York: Guilford Press.

Chambers, C. T., Finley, G. A., McGrath, P. J., & Walsh, T. M. (2003). The parents' postoperative pain measure: replication and extension to 2–6-year-old children. *Pain, 105,* 437–443.

Chambless, D. L. (2002). Beware the dodo bird: The dangers of overgeneralization. *Clinical Psychology: Science and Practice, 9,* 13–16.

Chambless, D. L., Caputo, G., Jasin, S. E., Gracely, E. J., & Williams, C. (1985). The Mobility Inventory for Agoraphobia. *Behaviour Research and Therapy, 23,* 35–44.

Chambless, D. L., & Hollon, S. D. (1998). Defining empirically supported therapies. *Journal of Consulting and Clinical Psychology, 66,* 7–18.

Chambless, D. L., & Ollendick, T. H. (2001). Empirically supported psychological interventions: Controversies and evidence. *Annual Review of Psychology, 52,* 685–716.

Chambless, D. L., Sanderson, W. C., Shoham, V., Bennett Johnson, S., Pope, K. S., Crits-Christoph, P., et al. (1996). An update on empirically validated therapies. *The Clinical Psychologist, 49(2),* 5–18.

Chambless, D. L., Sanderson, W. C., Shoham, V., Johnson, S. B., Pope, K. S., Crits-Christoph, P., et al. (1998). Update on empirically validated therapies, II. *The Clinical Psychologist, 51,* 3–16.

Charach, A., Ickowicz, A., & Schachar, R. (2004). Stimulant treatments over five years: Adherence, effectiveness, and adverse effects. *Journal of the American Academy of Child and Adolescent Psychiatry, 43,* 559–567.

Cherry, D. K., Messenger, L. C., & Jacoby, A. M. (2000). An examination of training model outcomes in clinical psychology programs. *Professional Psychology: Research & Practice, 31,* 562–568.

Childs, R. A., & Eyde, L. D. (2002). Assessment training in clinical psychology doctoral programs: What should we teach? What do we teach? *Journal of Personality Assessment, 78,* 130–144.

Chorpita, B. F., & Daleiden, E. L. (2009). Mapping evidence-based treatments for children and adolescents: Application of the distillation and matching model to 615 treatments from 322 randomized trials. *Journal of Consulting and Clinical Psychology, 77,* 566–579.

Chorpita, B. F., Daleiden, E. L., & Weisz, J. R. (2005). Identifying and selecting the common elements of evidence based interventions: A distillation and matching model. *Mental Health Services Research, 7,* 5–20.

Chorpita, B. F., Yim, L. M., Donkervoet, J. C., Arensdorf, A., Amundsen, M. J., McGee, C., et al. (2002). Towards large-scale implementation of empirically supported treatments for children: A review and observations by the Hawaii Empirical Basis to Services Task Force. *Clinical Psychology: Science and Practice, 9,* 165–190.

Chronis, A. M., Chacko, A., Fabiano, G. A., Wymbs, B. T., & Pelham, W. E. (2004). Enhancements to the behavioural parent training paradigm for families of children with ADHD: Review and future directions. *Clinical Child and Family Psychology, Review, 7,* 1–27.

Clare, L., & Woods, R. T. (2004). Cognitive training and cognitive rehabilitation for people with early-stage Alzheimer's disease: A review. *Neuropsychological Rehabilitation, 14,* 385–401.

Clark, D. M. (2013). Developing and disseminating effective psychological treatments: Science, practice, and economics. *Canadian Psychology, 54,* 12–21.

Clark, L. A., Watson, D., & Reynolds, S. (1995). Diagnosis and classification of psychopathology: Challenges to the current system and future directions. *Annual Review of Psychology, 46,* 121–153.

Clarke, G. N., & DeBar, L. L. (2010) Group cognitive-behavioral treatment for adolescent depression. In J. R. Weisz & A. E. Kazdin (Eds.), *Evidence-based psychotherapies for children and adolescents* (2nd ed., pp. 110–125). New York: Guilford Press.

Clarke, G. N., DeBar, L. L., & Lewinsohn, P. M. (2003). Cognitive-behavioral group treatment for adolescent depression. In A. E. Kazdin & J. R. Weisz (Eds.), *Evidence-based psychotherapies for children and adolescents* (pp. 120–134). New York: Guilford Press.

Clarkin, J. F., & Levy, K. N. (2004). The influence of client variables on psychotherapy. In M. J. Lambert (Ed.), *Bergin and Garfield's handbook of psychotherapy and behavior change* (5th ed., pp. 194–226). New York: John Wiley & Sons.

Clemence, A. J., & Handler, L. (2001). Psychological assessment on internship: A survey of training directors and their expectations for students. *Journal of Personality Assessment, 76,* 18–47.

Clements, C. B., Althouse, R., Ax, R. K., Magaletta, P. R., Fagan, T.J., & Wormith, J. S. (2007). Systemic issues and correctional outcomes: Expanding the scope of correctional psychology. *Criminal Justice and Behavior, 34,* 919–932.

Cohen, J. (1992). A power primer. *Psychological Bulletin, 112,* 115–159.

Cole, D. A., Peeke, L. G., Martin, J. M., Truglio, R., & Seroczynski, A. D. (1998). A longitudinal look at the relation between depression and anxiety in children and adolescents. *Journal of Consulting and Clinical Psychology, 66,* 451–460.

Cole, D. A., Tram, J. M., Martin, J. M., Hoffman, K. B., Ruiz, M. D., Jacquez, F. M., et al. (2002). Individual differences in the emergence of depressive symptoms in children and adolescents: A longitudinal investigation of parent and child reports. *Journal of Abnormal Psychology, 111,* 156–165.

College of Psychologists of Alberta. (2002). *Professional guidelines for psychologists: Child custody assessment.* Retrieved February 5, 2008, from http://www.cap.ab.ca/pdfs/HPAPGFP-ChildCustodyAssessment.pdf

College of Psychologists of Ontario. (2004). *Why choose a regulated service provider?* Retrieved December 21, 2004, from http://www.cpo.on.ca/AboutCollege/College.htm

Collier, R. (2010). DSM revision surrounded by controversy. *Canadian Medical Association Journal, 182,* 16–17.

Collins, L. M., Murphy, S. A., & Bierman, K. L. (2004). A conceptual framework for adaptive preventive interventions. *Prevention Science, 5,* 185–196.

Commission on Chronic Illness. (1957). *Chronic illness in the United States.* (Vol. 1). Cambridge, MA: Harvard University Press.

Conduct Problems Prevention Research Group. (2002a). The implementation of the Fast Track Program: An example of a large-scale prevention science efficacy trial. *Journal of Abnormal Child Psychology, 30,* 1–17.

Conduct Problems Prevention Research Group. (2002b). Evaluation of the first 3 years of the Fast Track prevention trial with children with high risk for adolescent conduct problems. *Journal of Abnormal Child Psychology, 30,* 19–35.

Conduct Problems Prevention Research Group. (2004). The effects of the Fast Track program on serious problem outcomes at the end of elementary school. *Journal of Clinical Child and Adolescent Psychology, 33,* 650–661.

Conduct Problems Prevention Research Group. (2007). The Fast Track randomized controlled trial to prevent externalizing psychiatric disorders: Findings from Grades 3 to 9. *Journal of the American Academy of Child and Adolescent Psychiatry, 46,* 1250–1262.

Conduct Problems Prevention Research Group. (2011). The effects of the Fast Track preventive intervention on the development of Conduct Disorder across childhood. *Child Development, 82,* 331–345.

Connor-Smith, J. K., & Weisz, J. R. (2003). Applying treatment outcome research in clinical practice: Techniques for adapting interventions to the real world. *Child and Adolescent Mental Health, 8,* 3–10.

Constantine, M. G. (2007). Racial microaggressions against African American clients in cross-racial counseling relationships. *Journal of Counseling Psychology, 54,* 1–16.

Constantino, M. J., Glass, C. R., Arnkoff, D. B., Ametrano, R. M., & Smith, J. Z. (2011). Expectations. In J. C. Norcross (Ed.), *Psychotherapy relationships that work: Evidence-based responsiveness* (2nd ed., pp. 354–376). New York: Oxford University Press.

Cook, J. M., Schnurr, P. P., & Foa, E. B. (2004). Bridging the gap between Posttraumatic Stress Disorder research and clinical practice: The example of exposure therapy. *Psychotherapy, 41,* 374–381.

Cook, T. D., & Campbell, D. T. (Eds.). (1979). *Quasi-experimentation: Design and analysis issues for field settings.* Chicago, IL: Rand McNally.

Copeland, W. E., Keeler, G., Angold, A., & Costello, E. J. (2007). Traumatic events and posttraumatic stress in childhood. *Archives of General Psychiatry, 64,* 577–584.

Costello, E. J., Copeland, W., Cowell, A., & Keeler, G. (2007). Service costs of caring for adolescents with mental illness in a rural community, 1993–2000. *American Journal of Psychiatry, 164,* 36–42.

Coughlan, B. J., Doyle, M., & Carr, A. (2002). Prevention of teenage smoking, alcohol use and drug abuse. In A. Carr (Ed.), *Prevention: what works with children and adolescents? A critical review of psychological prevention programmes for children, adolescents and their families* (pp. 267–286). Hove, UK: BrunnerRoutledge.

CPA Task Force on Evidence-Based Practice of Psychological Treatments. (2012). *Evidence based practice of psychological treatments: A Canadian perspective.* Ottawa, ON: Author.

CPA Task Force on Evidence-Based Practice of Psychological Treatments. (2012). *Evidence-based practice of psychological treatments: A Canadian perspective.* Retrieved from http://www.cpa.ca/docs/file/Practice/Report_of_the_EBP_Task_Force_FINAL_Board_Approved_2012.pdf

Craig, L. A., Dixon, L., & Gannon, T. A. (Eds.). (2013). *What works in offender rehabilitation: An evidence based approach to assessment and treatment.* Chichester, UK: Wiley-Blackwell.

Craighead, W. E., Hart, A. B., Craighead, L. W., & Ilardi, S. (2002). Psychosocial treatments for major depressive disorder. In P. E. Nathan & J. M. Gorman (Eds.), *A guide to treatments that work* (2nd ed., pp. 245–261). New York: Oxford University Press.

Crawford, J. R. (2004). Psychometric foundations of neuropsychological assessment. In L. H. Goldstein & J. E. McNeil (Eds.), *Clinical neuropsychology: A practical guide to assessment and management for clinicians* (pp. 121–140). Chichester, UK: John Wiley & Sons.

Creamer, M., O'Donnell, M. L., & Pattison, P. (2004). The relationship between acute stress disorder and posttraumatic stress disorder in severely injured trauma survivors. *Behaviour Research and Therapy, 42,* 315–328.

Creswell, J. W. (2012). *Qualitative inquiry and research design.* Thousand Oaks, CA: Sage Publications.

Crits-Christoph, P. (1997). Limitations of the dodo bird verdict and the role of clinical trials in psychotherapy research: Comment on Wampold et al. (1997). *Psychological Bulletin, 122,* 216–220.

Crits-Christoph, P., Gibbons, M. B. C., & Mukherjee, D. (2013). Psychotherapy process-outcome research. In M. J. Lambert (Ed.), *Bergin and Garfield's handbook of psychotherapy and behavior change* (6th ed., pp. 298–340). Hoboken, NJ: John Wiley & Sons.

Cross, D. T., & Burger, G. K. (1982). Ethnicity as a variable in responses to California Psychological Inventory items. *Journal of Personality Assessment, 46,* 153–158.

Cuijpers, P. (2003). Examining the effects of prevention programs on the incidence of new cases of mental disorders: The lack of statistical power. *American Journal of Psychiatry, 160,* 1385–1391.

Cuijpers, P., Geraedts, A. S., van Oppen, P., Andersson, G., Markowitz, J. C., & van Straten, A. (2011). Interpersonal psychotherapy for depression: A meta-analysis. *American Journal of Psychiatry, 168,* 581–592.

Cuijpers, P., van Straten, A., Smit, F., Mihalopoulos, C., & Beekman, A. (2008). Preventing the onset of depressive disorders: A meta-analytic review of psychological interventions. *American Journal of Psychiatry, 165,* 1272–1280.

Cukrowicz, K. C., Wingate, L. R. W., Driscoll, K. A., & Joiner, T. E. (2004). A standard of care for the assessment of suicide risk and associated treat. *Journal of Contemporary Psychotherapy, 34,* 87–100.

Currier, J. M., Holland, J. M., & Neimeyer, R. A. (2007). The effectiveness of bereavement interventions with children: A meta-analytic review of controlled outcome research. *Journal of Clinical Child and Adolescent Psychology, 36,* 253–259.

Cutler, J. L., Goldyne, A., Markowitz, J. C., Devlin, M. J., & Glick, R. A. (2004). Comparing cognitive behaviour therapy, interpersonal psychotherapy, and psychodynamic psychotherapy. *American Journal of Psychiatry, 161,* 1567–1573.

Cybele, R. C. (2012). Low income children's self-regulation in the classroom: Scientific inquiry for social change. *American Psychologist, 67,* 681–689.

Dadds, M. R., Holland, D. E., Barrett, P. M., Laurens, S. K., & Spence, S. (1999). Early intervention and prevention of anxiety disorders in children: Results at 2-year follow-up. *Journal of Consulting and Clinical Psychology, 67,* 145–150.

d'Ardenne, P., Ruaro, L., Cestari, L., Fakhoury, W., & Priebe, S. (2007). Does interpreter-mediated CBT with traumatized refugee people work? A comparison of patient outcomes in East London. *Behavioural and Cognitive Psychotherapy, 35,* 293–301.

David-Ferdon, C., & Kaslow, N. J. (2008). Evidence-based psychosocial treatments for child and adolescent depression. *Journal of Clinical Child and Adolescent Psychology, 37,* 62–104.

Davis, D. A., Mazmanian, P. E., Fordis, M., Van Harrison, R., Thorpe, K. E., & Perrier, L. (2006). Accuracy of physician self-assessment compared with observed measures of competence: A systematic review. *Journal of the American Medical Association, 296,* 1094–1102.

Davis, G. L., Hoffman, R. G., & Nelson, K. S. (1990). Differences between Native Americans and Whites on the California Personality Inventory. *Psychological Assessment, 2,* 238–242.

Day, A., Gerace, A., Wilson, C., & Howells, K. (2008). Promoting forgiveness in violent offenders: A more positive approach to offender rehabilitation? *Aggression and Violent Behavior, 13,* 195–200.

De Koninck, J. (1997). Sleep, the common denominator for psychological adaptation. *Canadian Psychology, 38,* 191–195.

De Los Reyes, A., Henry, D. B., Tolan, P. H., & Wakschlag, L.S. (2009). Linking informant discrepancies to observed variations in young children's disruptive behavior. *Journal of Abnormal Child Psychology, 37,* 637–652.

De Los Reyes, A., Thomas, S. A., Goodman, K. L., & Kundey, S. M. A. (2013). Principles underlying the use of multiple informants' reports. *Annual Review of Clinical Psychology, 9,* 123–149.

Depp, C., Vahia, I. V., & Jeste, D. (2010). Successful aging: Focus on cognitive and emotional health. *Annual Review of Clinical Psychology, 6,* 527–550.

Derogatis, L. R. (1994). *SCL-90-R: Administration, scoring, and procedures manual.* Minneapolis, MN: National Computer Systems.

Dickens, W., & Flynn, J. R. (2001). Hereditability estimates versus large environmental effects: The IQ paradox resolved. *Psychological Review, 108,* 346–369.

Dishion, T. J., McCord, J., & Poulin, F. (1999). When interventions harm: Peer groups and problem behavior. *American Psychologist, 54,* 755–764.

Dobson, K. S. (1989). A meta-analysis of the efficacy of cognitive therapy for depression. *Journal of Consulting and Clinical Psychology, 57,* 414–419.

Dobson, K. S., & Dozois, D. J. A. (2001). Professional psychology and the prescription debate: Still not ready to go to the altar. *Canadian Psychology, 42,* 131–135.

Dowden, C., & Andrews, D. A. (2004). The importance of staff practice in delivering effective correctional treatment: A meta-analytic review of core correctional practice. *International Journal of Offender Therapy and Comparative Criminology, 48,* 203–214.

Doyle, A. B., Edwards, H., & Robinson, R. W. (1993). Accreditation of doctoral training programmes and internships in professional psychology. In K. S. Dobson, & D. G. Dobson (Eds.), *Professional psychology in Canada* (pp. 77–105). Toronto, ON: Hogrefe & Huber.

Dozois, D. J. A., & Dobson, K. S. (Eds.). (2004). *The prevention of anxiety and depression: Theory, research, and practice.* Washington, DC: American Psychological Association.

Duncan, B. L., Miller, S. D., Wampold, B. E., & Hubble, M. A. (2009). *The heart and soul of change: Delivering what works in therapy* (2nd ed.). Washington, DC: American Psychological Association.

Duncan, L. E., & Keller, M. C. (2011). A critical review of the first 10 years of candidate gene-by-environment interaction research in psychiatry. *American Journal of Psychiatry, 168,* 1041–1049.

D'Zurilla, T. J., & Goldfried, M. R. (1971). Problem solving and behaviour modification. *Journal of Abnormal Psychology, 78,* 101–126.

D'Zurilla, T. J., & Nezu, A. M. (1999). *Problem-solving therapy: A social competence approach to clinical intervention* (2nd ed.). New York: Springer.

Eaton, W. W., Shao, H., Nestadt, G., Lee, B. H., Bienvenu, J., & Zandi, P. (2008). Population-based study of first onset and chronicity of major depressive disorder. *Archives of General Psychiatry, 65,* 513–520.

Eddy, K. T., Dutra, L., Bradley, R., & Westen, D. (2004). A multidimensional meta-analysis of psychotherapy and pharmacotherapy for obsessive-compulsive disorder. *Clinical Psychology Review, 24,* 1011–1030.

Eells, T. D. (Ed.). (2006). *Handbook of psychotherapy case formulation* (2nd ed.). New York: Guilford Press.

Eells, T. D., Kendjelic, E. M., & Lucas, C. P. (1998). What's in a case formulation? Development and use of a content coding manual. *Journal of Psychotherapy Practice and Research, 7,* 144–153.

Ekos. (2011). *Survey of Canadian attitudes toward psychologists and accessing psychological services.* Retrieved from: http://www.cpa.ca/docs/file/poll/National%20Findings%20(English).pdf

Elkin, I., Yamaguchi, J. L., Arnkoff, D. B., Class, C. R., Sotsky, S. M., & Krupnick, J. L. (1999). "Patient-treatment fit" and early engagement in therapy. *Psychotherapy Research, 9,* 437–451.

Ellenberger, H. F. (1970). *The discovery of the unconscious: The history and evolution of dynamic psychiatry.* New York: Basic Books.

Elliott, R. (1998). Editor's introduction: A guide to the empirically supported treatments controversy. *Psychotherapy Research, 8,* 115–125.

Elliott, R. (2001). Contemporary brief experiential psychotherapy. *Clinical Psychology: Science and Practice, 8,* 38–50.

Elliott, R., Greenberg, L. S., Watson, J., Timulak, L., & Freire, E. (2013). Research on humanistic-experiential psychotherapies. In M. L. Lambert (Ed.), *Bergin and Garfield's handbook of psychotherapy and behavior change* (6th ed., 495–540). Hoboken, NJ: John Wiley & Sons.

Elwood, L. S., Mott, J., Lohr, J. M. & Galovski, T. E. (2011). Secondary trauma symptoms in clinicians: A critical review of the construct, specificity, and implications for trauma-focused treatment. *Clinical Psychology Review, 31,* 25–36.

Emmelkamp, P. M. G. (2013). Behavior therapy with adults. In M. L. Lambert (Ed.), *Bergin and Garfield's handbook of psychotherapy and behavior change* (6th ed., 343–392). Hoboken, NJ: John Wiley & Sons.

Ennett, S. T., Ringwalt, C. L., Thirne, J., Rohrbach, L. A., Vincus, A., Simons-Rudolph, A., et al. (2003). A comparison of current practice in school-based substance use prevention programs with meta-analysis findings. *Prevention Science, 4,* 1–14.

Enright, S., & Carr, A. (2002). Prevention of post-traumatic adjustment problems. In A. Carr (Ed.), *Prevention: What works with children and adolescents? A critical review of psychological prevention programmes for children, adolescents and their families* (pp. 314–335). Hove, UK: Brunner-Routledge.

Esposito, E., Wang, J. L., Adair, C. E., Williams, J. V., Dobson, K., Schopflocher, D., et al. (2007). Frequency and adequacy of depression treatment in a Canadian population sample. *Canadian Journal of Psychiatry, 52,* 780–789.

Essau, C. A. (2004). Prevention of substance abuse in children and adolescents. In P. M. Barrett & T. H. Ollendick (Eds.), *Interventions that work with children and adolescents: Prevention and treatment* (pp. 517–539). Chichester, UK: John Wiley & Sons.

Evans, G. W. (2004). The environment of child poverty. *American Psychologist, 59,* 77–92.

Evans, J. J. R. (2004). Disorders of memory. In L. H. Goldstein & J. E. McNeil (Eds.), *Clinical neuropsychology: A practical guide to assessment and management for clinicians* (pp. 143–163). Chichester, UK: John Wiley & Sons.

Exner, J. E. (1993). *The Rorschach: A comprehensive system. Vol. 1. Basic foundations* (3rd ed.). New York: John Wiley & Sons.

Eyberg, S. M., Nelson, M. M., & Boggs, S. R. (2008). Evidence-based psychosocial treatments for children and adolescents with disruptive behaviour. *Journal of Clinical Child and Adolescent Psychology, 37,* 215–237.

Eyding, D., Lelgemann, M., Grouven, U., Härter, M., Kromp, M., Kaiser, T., et al. (2010). Reboxetine for acute treatment of major depression: Systematic review and meta-analysis of published and unpublished placebo and selective serotonin reuptake inhibitor controlled trials. *British Medical Journal, 341,* doi: http://dx.doi.org/10.1136/bmj.c4737

Eysenck, H. J. (1952). The effects of psychotherapy: An evaluation. *Journal of Consulting Psychology, 16,* 319–324.

Eysenck, H. J. (1966). *The effects of psychotherapy.* New York: International Science Press.

Eysenck, H. J. (1978). An exercise in meta-silliness. *American Psychologist, 33,* 517.

Eytan, A., Durieux-Paillard, S., Whitaker-Clinch, B., Loutan, L., & Bovier, P. A. (2007). Transcultural validity of a structured diagnostic interview to screen for major depression and posttraumatic stress disorder among refugees. *Journal of Nervous and Mental Disease, 195,* 723–728.

Falzon, L., Davidson, K. W., & Bruns, D. (2010). Evidence searching for evidence-based psychology practice. *Professional Psychology: Research and Practice, 41,* 550–557.

Feeny, N. C., Foa, E. B., Treadwell, K. R. H., & March, J. (2004). Posttraumatic stress disorder in youth: A critical review of the cognitive and behavioural outcome literature. *Professional Psychology: Research and Practice,* 35, 466–476.

Feifel, D., Moutier, C. Y., & Swerdlow, N. R. (1999). Attitudes toward psychiatry as a prospective career among students entering medical school. *American Journal of Psychiatry, 156,* 1397–1402.

Fernandez, K., Boccaccini, M. T., & Noland, R. M. (2007). Professionally responsible test selection for Spanish-speaking clients: A four-step approach for identifying and selecting translated tests. *Professional Psychology: Research and Practice, 38,* 363–374.

Feske, U., & Goldstein, A. (1997). Eye movement desensitization and reprocessing treatment for panic disorders: A controlled outcome and partial dismantling study. *Journal of Consulting and Clinical Psychology, 65,* 1026–1035.

Finn, S. E., Fischer, C. T., & Handler, L. (Eds). (2012). *Collaborative/therapeutic assessment: A casebook and guide.* Hoboken, NJ: John Wiley & Sons.

Finn, S. E., & Tonsager, M. E. (1997). Information-gathering and therapeutic models of assessment: Complementary paradigms. *Psychological Assessment, 9,* 374–385.

First, M. B., Spitzer, R. L., Gibbon, M., & Williams, J. B. W. (1997). *Structured Clinical Interview for DSM-IV Axis I Disorders (SCID-I CV)—Clinician Version.* Washington, DC: American Psychiatric Press.

First, M. B., & Tasman, A. (2004). *DSM-IV-TR mental disorders: Diagnosis, etiology, and treatment.* New York: John Wiley & Sons.

Fisher, C. B. (2004). Informed consent and clinical research involving children and adolescents: Implications of the Revised APA Ethics Code and HIPAA. *Journal of Clinical Child and Adolescent Psychology, 33,* 832–839.

Fisher, P. A. (2003). The prevention of antisocial behaviour: Beyond efficacy and effectiveness. In A. Biglan, M. Wang, & H. J. Walberg (Eds.), *Preventing youth problems* (pp. 5–31). New York: Kluwer Academic.

Flanagan, D. P., & Kaufman, A. S. (2009). *Essentials of WISC-IV assessment.* (2nd ed.). New York: John Wiley & Sons.

Fleeson, W. (2004). Moving personality beyond the person-situation debate: The challenge and opportunity of within-person variability. *Current Directions in Psychological Science, 13,* 83–87.

Flynn, J. R. (1987). Massive IQ gains in 14 nations: What IQ tests really measure. *Psychological Bulletin, 101,* 171–191.

Forbes, D., Creamer, M., Bisson, J. I., Cohen, J. A., Crow, B. E., Foa, E. B., et al. (2010). A guide to guidelines for the treatment of PTSD and related conditions. *Journal of Traumatic Stress, 23,* 537–552.

Forgatch, M. S., & Patterson, G. R. (2010). Parent management training. In J. R. Weisz & A. E. Kazdin (Eds.), *Evidence-based psychotherapies for children and adolescents* (2nd ed., pp. 159–178). New York: Guilford Press.

Forsman, A. K., Schierenbeck, I., & Wahlbeck, K. (2011). Psychosocial interventions for the prevention of depression in older adults: Systematic review and meta-analysis. *Journal of Aging and Health, 23,* 387–416.

Fournier, M. A., Moskowitz, D. S., & Zuroff, D. C. (2008). Integrating dispositions, signatures, and the interpersonal domain. *Journal of Personality and Social Psychology, 94,* 531–545.

Frances, A. (2013a). *Essentials of psychiatric diagnosis: Responding to the challenge of DSM-5.* New York: Guilford Press.

Frances, A. (2013b). *Saving normal.* New York: William Morrow.

Frank, E. (2005). *Treating bipolar disorder: A clinician's guide to interpersonal and social rhythm therapy.* New York: Guilford Press.

Frank, J. D. (1973). *Persuasion and healing.* Baltimore: Johns Hopkins University Press.

Frank, J. D. (1982). Therapeutic components shared by all psychotherapies. In J. H. Harvey & M. M. Parks (Eds.), *The Master Lecture Series: Vol. 1. Psychotherapy research and behavior change* (pp. 5–38). Washington, DC: American Psychological Association.

Friedlander, M. L., Escudero, V., Heatherington, L., & Diamond, G. M. (2011). Alliance in couple and family therapy. *Psychotherapy, 48,* 25–33.

Frisch, M. B., Clark, M. P., Rouse, S. V., Rudd, M. D., Paweleck, J. K., Greenstone, A., et al. (2005). Predictive and treatment validity of life satisfaction and the Quality of Life Inventory. *Assessment, 12,* 66–78.

Gabbard, G. O., Gunderson, J. G., & Fonagy, P. (2002). The place of psychoanalytic treatments within psychiatry. *Archives of General Psychiatry, 59,* 505–510.

Galea, S., Brewin, C. R., Gruber, M., Jones, R. T., King, D. W., King, L. A., et al. (2007). Exposure to hurricane-related stressors and mental illness after Hurricane Katrina. *Archives of General Psychiatry, 64,* 1427–1434.

Garb, H. N. (1997). Race bias, social class bias, and gender bias in clinical judgment. *Clinical Psychology: Science and Practice, 4,* 99–120.

Garb, H. N. (1998). *Studying the clinician: Judgment research and psychological assessment.* Washington, DC: American Psychological Association.

Garb, H. N. (2005). Clinical judgment and decision making. *Annual Review of Clinical Psychology, 1,* 67–89.

Garb, H. N. (2007). Computer-administered interviews and rating scales. *Psychological Assessment, 19,* 4–13.

Garb, H. N., & Boyle, P. A. (2003). Understanding why some clinicians use pseudoscientific methods: Findings from research on clinical judgment. In S. O. Lilienfeld, S. J. Lynn, & J. M. Lohr (Eds.), *Science and pseudoscience in clinical psychology* (pp. 17–38). New York: Guilford Press.

Garb, H. N., Klein, D. F., & Grove, W. M. (2002). Comparison of medical and psychological tests. *American Psychologist, 57,* 137–138.

Gardner, H. (1983). *Frames of mind: The theory of multiple intelligences.* New York: Basic Books.

Gardner, H. (1999). *Intelligence reframed: Multiple intelligences for the 21st century.* New York: Basic Books.

Garfield, S. L. (1994). Research on client variables in psychotherapy. In A. E. Bergin & S. L. Garfield (Eds.), *Handbook of psychotherapy and behavior change* (4th ed., pp. 190–228). New York: John Wiley & Sons.

Garfield, S. L. (1996). Some problems associated with "validated" forms of psychotherapy. *Clinical Psychology: Research and Practice, 3,* 218–229.

Gibbons, M. B. C., Crits-Christoph, P., & Hearon, B. (2008). The empirical status of psychodynamic therapies. *Annual Review of Clinical Psychology, 4,* 93–108.

Golden, C. J., Freshwater, S. M., & Vayalakkara, J. (2000). The Luria-Nebraska Neuropsychological Battery. In G. Groth-Marnat (Ed.), *Neuropsychological assessment in clinical practice* (pp. 263–289). New York: John Wiley & Sons.

Goldner, E. M., Abass, A., Leverette, J. S., & Haslam, D. R. (2001). *Evidence-based psychiatric practice: Implications for education and continuing professional development.* Retrieved June 6, 2008, from http://publications.cpa-apc.org/media.php?mid = 128&xwm = true

Goldstein, L. H., & McNeil, J. E. (2004). General introduction: What is the relevance of neuropsychology for clinical psychology practice? In L. H. Goldstein & J. E. McNeil (Eds.), *Clinical neuropsychology: A practical guide to assessment and management for clinicians* (pp. 3–20). Chichester, UK: John Wiley & Sons.

Goleman, D. (1995). *Emotional intelligence: Why it can matter more than IQ.* New York: Bantam.

Gonon F., Konsman J-P., Cohen, D., & Boraud, T. (2012). Why most biomedical findings echoed by newspapers turn out to be false: The case of attention deficit hyperactivity disorder. *PLoS ONE 7(9)*: e44275. doi:10.1371/journal.pone.0044275

Gornall, J. (2013). DSM-5: A fatal diagnosis. *British Medical Journal,* 346. doi: http://dx.doi.org/10.1136/bmj.f3256

Gosling, S. D., John, O. P., Craik, K. H., & Robins, R. W. (1998). Do people know how they behave? Self-reported act frequencies compared with online codings by observers. *Journal of Personality and Social Psychology, 74,* 1337–1349.

Gosling, S. D., Vazire, S., Srivastava, S., & John, O. P. (2004). Should we trust web-based studies? *American Psychologist, 59,* 93–104.

Gotham, H. J. (2004). Diffusion of mental health and substance abuse treatments: Development, dissemination, and implementation. *Clinical Psychology: Science and Practice, 11,* 160–176.

Gottfredson, L. S. (1997). Mainstream science on intelligence: An editorial with 52 signatories, history, and bibliography. *Intelligence, 24,* 13–23.

Gøtzsche, P. C., Hróbjartsson, A., Marić, K., & Tendal, B. (2007). Data extraction errors in meta-analyses that use standardized mean differences. *Journal of the American Medical Association, 298,* 430–437.

Gough, H. G., & Bradley, P. (1996). *California Psychological Inventory manual* (3rd ed.). Palo Alto, CA: Consulting Psychologists Press.

Graff, L. A., Kaoukis, G., Vincent, N., Piotrowski, A., & Ediger, J. (2012). New models of care for psychology in Canada's health services. *Canadian Psychology, 53,* 165–177.

Graham, J. R. (2011). *MMPI-2: Assessing personality and psychopathology.* New York: Oxford University Press.

Gray-Little, B., & Kaplan, D. A. (1998). Interpretation of psychological tests in clinical and forensic evaluations. In J. Sandoval, C. L. Frisby, K. F. Geisinger, J. D. Scheuneman, & J. R. Grenier (Eds.), *Test interpretation and diversity: Achieving equity in assessment* (pp. 141–178). Washington, DC: American Psychological Association.

Gray-Little, B., & Kaplan, D. (2000). Race and ethnicity in psychotherapy research. In C. R. Snyder & R. E. Ingram (Eds.), *Handbook of psychological changes: Psychotherapy processes and practices for the 21st century* (pp. 591–613). New York: John Wiley & Sons.

Greenberg, L. (2008). Emotion and cognition in psychotherapy: The transforming power of affect. *Canadian Psychology, 49,* 49–59.

Greiffenstein, M. F., Baker, W. J., & Johnson-Greene, D. (2002). Actual versus self-reported scholastic achievement of litigating postconcussion and severe closed head injury claimants. *Psychological Assessment, 14,* 202–208.

Griffin, D. W., Dunning, D., & Ross, L. (1990). The role of construal processes in overconfident predictions about the self and others. *Journal of Personality and Social Psychology, 59,* 1128–1139.

Gross, D., Fogg, L., Webster-Stratton, C., Garvey, C., Julion, W., & Grady, J. (2003). Parent training with multi-ethnic families of toddlers in day care in low-income urban communities. *Journal of Consulting and Clinical Psychology, 71,* 261–278.

Gross, K., Keyes, M. D., & Greene, R. L. (2000). Assessing depression with the MMPI and MMPI-2. *Journal of Personality Assessment, 75,* 464–477.

Groth-Marnat, G. (1999). Financial efficacy of clinical assessment: Rational guidelines and issues for future research. *Journal of Clinical Psychology, 55,* 813–824.

Groth-Marnat, G. (2000). Introduction to neuropsychological assessment. In G. Groth-Marnat (Ed.), *Neuropsychological assessment in clinical practice* (pp. 3–25). New York: John Wiley & Sons.

Groth-Marnat, G. (2009). *Handbook of psychological assessment* (5th ed.). Hoboken, NJ: John Wiley & Sons.

Groth-Marnat, G., & Horvath, L. S. (2008). The psychological report: A review of current controversies. *Journal of Clinical Psychology, 62,* 73–81.

Grove, W. M., Zald, D. H., Lebow, B. S., Snitz, B. E., & Nelson, C. (2000). Clinical versus mechanical prediction: A meta-analysis. *Psychological Assessment, 12,* 19–30.

Grubb, W. L., & McDaniel, M. A. (2007). The fakability of Bar-On's Emotional Quotient Inventory Short Form: Catch me if you can. *Human Performance, 20,* 43–59.

Guarnaccia, V., Dill, C. A., Sabatino, S., & Southwick, S. (2001). Scoring accuracy using the Comprehensive System for the Rorschach. *Journal of Personality Assessment, 77,* 464–474.

Guilford, J. P. (1956). The structure of intellect. *Psychological Bulletin, 53,* 267–293.

Haaga, D. A. F. (2000). Introduction to the special section on stepped care models in psychotherapy. *Journal of Consulting and Clinical Psychology, 68,* 547–548.

Hadjistavropoulos, T. (2011). Empirical and theory-driven investigations of the Canadian Code of Ethics for Psychologists *Canadian Psychology, 52,* 176–179.

Hadjistavropoulos, H., & Williams, A. C. (2004). Psychological interventions and chronic pain. In T. Hadjistavropoulos & K. D. Craig (Eds.), *Pain: Psychological treatment perspectives* (pp. 271–301). New Jersey: Lawrence Erlbaum.

Halford, W. K., Keefer, E., & Osgarby, S. M. (2002). "How has the week been for you two?" Relationship satisfaction and hindsight memory biases in couples' reports of relationship events. *Cognitive Therapy and Research, 26,* 759–773.

Hamel, M., Shaffer, T. W., & Erdberg, P. (2000). A study of nonpatient preadolescent Rorschach protocols. *Journal of Personality Assessment, 75,* 280–294.

Hammen, C., Shih, J. H., & Brennan, P. A. (2004). Intergenerational transmission of depression: Test of an interpersonal stress model in a community sample. *Journal of Consulting and Clinical Psychology, 72,* 511–522.

Hampson, S. E. (2012). Personality processes: Mechanisms by which personality traits "get outside the skin." *Annual Review of Psychology, 63,* 315–339.

Hampton-Robb, S., Qualls, R. C., & Compton, W. C. (2003). Predicting first-session attendance: The influence of referral source and client income. *Psychotherapy Research, 13,* 223–233.

Hankin, B. L., Fraley, R. C., Lahey, B. B., & Waldman, I. D. (2005). Is depression best viewed as a continuum or discrete category? A taxometric analysis of childhood and adolescent depression in a population-based sample. *Journal of Abnormal Psychology, 114,* 96–110.

Hans, E., & Hiller, W. (2013). Effectiveness of and dropout from cognitive behavioral therapy for adult unipolar depression: A meta-analysis of nonrandomized effectiveness studies. *Journal of Consulting and Clinical Psychology, 81,* 75–88.

Hansen, N. B., Lambert, M. J., & Forman, E. M. (2002). The psychotherapy dose-response effect and its implications for treatment delivery services. *Clinical Psychology: Science and Practice, 9,* 329–343.

Hanson, R. K. (2005). Twenty years of progress in violence risk assessment. *Journal of Interpersonal Violence, 20,* 212–217.

Harding, T. P. (2007). Clinical decision-making: How prepared are we? *Training and Education in Professional Psychology, 1,* 95–104.

Hardy, G. E., Cahill, J., Stiles, W. B., Ispan, C., Macaskill, N., & Barkham, M. (2005). Sudden gains in cognitive therapy for depression: A replication and extension. *Journal of Consulting and Clinical Psychology, 73,* 59–67.

Hare, R. D. (1991). The Hare Psychopathy Checklist-Revised. Toronto, ON: Multihealth Systems.

Hare, R. D., Clark, D., Grann, M., & Thornton, D. (2000). Psychopathy and the predictive validity of the PCL-R: An international perspective. *Behavioral Sciences and the Law, 18,* 623–645.

Harris, C. (2003). Editorial. *Psychological Bulletin, 129,* 3–9.

Harris, G. T., Rice, M. E., & Quinsey V. L. (1993). Violent recidivism of mentally disordered offenders: The development of a statistical prediction instrument. *Criminal Justice and Behavior, 20,* 315–335.

Harvey, A. G., & Bryant, R. G. (2002). Acute stress disorder: A synthesis and critique. *Psychological Bulletin, 128,* 886–902.

Hawkins, E. H., Cummins, L. H., & Marlatt, G. A. (2004). Preventing substance abuse in American Indian and Alaska native youth: Promising strategies for healthier communities. *Psychological Bulletin, 130,* 304–323.

Hawley, K. M., & Weisz, J. R. (2003). Child, parent, and therapist (dis)agreement on target problems in outpatient therapy: The therapist's dilemma and its implications. *Journal of Consulting and Clinical Psychology, 71,* 62–70.

Hawley, K. M., & Weisz, J. R. (2005). Youth versus parent working alliance in usual clinical care: Distinctive associations with retention, satisfaction, and treatment outcome. *Journal of Clinical Child and Adolescent Psychology, 34,* 117–128.

Hayes, S. C., Barlow, D. H., & Nelson-Gray, R. O. (1999). *The scientist practitioner: Research and accountability in the age of managed care* (2nd ed.). Needham Heights, MA: Allyn & Bacon.

Hayman-Abello, B. A., Hayman-Abello, S. E., & Rourke, B. P. (2003). Human neuropsychology in Canada: The 1990s (a review of research by Canadian neuropsychologists). *Canadian Psychology, 44,* 100–138.

Haynes, S. N., Leisen, M. B., & Blaine, D. D. (1997). Design of individualized behavioral treatment programs using functional analytic clinical case methods. *Psychological Assessment, 9,* 334–348.

Haynes, S. N., O'Brien, W. H., & Kaholokula, J. K. (2011). *Behavioral assessment and case formulation.* Hoboken, NJ: John Wiley & Sons.
Haynes, S. N., Smith, G., & Hunsley, J. (2011). *Scientific foundations of clinical assessment.* New York: Taylor & Francis.
Haynes, S. N., & Yoshioka, D. T. (2007). Clinical assessment applications of ambulatory biosensors. *Psychological Assessment, 19,* 44–57.
Hays, K. A., Rardin, D. K., Jarvis, P. A., Taylor, N. M., Moorman, A. S., & Armstead, C. D. (2002). An exploratory survey on empirically supported treatments: Implications for internship training. *Professional Psychology: Research and Practice, 33,* 207–211.
Hearn, M. T., & Evans, D. R. (1993). Applications of psychology to health care. In K. S. Dobson & D. G. Dobson (Eds.), *Professional psychology in Canada* (pp. 248–284). Toronto, ON: Hogrefe & Huber.
Helbok, C. M., Marinelli, R. P., & Walls, R. T. (2006). National survey of ethical practices across rural and urban communities. *Professional Psychology: Research and Practice, 37,* 36–44.
Helmes, E., & Reddon, J. R. (1993). A perspective on developments in assessing psychopathology: A critical review of the MMPI and the MMPI2. *Psychological Bulletin, 113,* 453–471.
Helmus, L., Babchishin, K. M., Camilleri, J., & Olver, M. (2011). Forensic psychology opportunities in Canadian graduate programs: An update of Simourd and Wormith's (1995) survey. *Canadian Psychology, 52,* 122–127.
Henggeler, S. W., & Lee, T. (2003). Multisystemic treatment of serious clinical problems. In A. E. Kazdin & J. R. Weisz (Eds.), *Evidence-based psychotherapies for children and adolescents* (pp. 301–324). New York: Guilford Press.
Henggeler, S. W., Schoenwald, S. K., Borduin, C. M., Rowland, M. D., & Cunningham, P. B. (1998). Multisystemic treatment of antisocial behaviour in children and adolescents. New York: Guilford Press.
Henggeler, S. W., & Sheidow, A. J. (2012). Empirically supported family-based treatments for conduct disorder and delinquency in adolescents. *Journal of Marital and Family Therapy, 38,* 30–58.
Henry, B., Moffitt, T. E., Caspi, A., Langley, J., & Silva, P. A. (1994). On the "Remembrance of Things Past": A longitudinal evaluation of the retrospective method. *Psychological Assessment, 6,* 92–101.
Henry, G. T. (1990). *Practical sampling.* Newbury Park, CA: Sage Publications.
Henry, W. P. (1998). Science, politics, and the politics of science: The use and misuse of empirically validated treatment research. *Psychotherapy Research, 8,* 126–140.
Herrnstein, R. J., & Murray, C. A. (1994). *The bell curve: Intelligence and class structure in American life.* New York: Free Press.
Herschell, A. D., McNeil, C. B., & McNeill, D. (2004). Clinical child psychology's progress in disseminating empirically supported treatments. *Clinical Psychology: Science and Practice, 11,* 267–288.
Hertzsprung, E. A. M., & Dobson, K. S. (2000). Diversity training: Conceptual issues and practices for Canadian clinical psychology programs. *Canadian Psychology, 41,* 184–191.
Hickman, E. E., Arnkoff, D. B., Glass, C. R., & Schottenbauer, M. A. (2009). Psychotherapy integration as practiced by experts. *Psychotherapy, 46,* 486–491.
Hiller, J. B., Rosenthal, R., Bornstein, R. F., Berry, D. T. R., & Brunell-Neuleib, S. (1999). A comparative meta-analysis of Rorschach and MMPI validity. *Psychological Assessment, 11,* 278–296.
Hilsenroth, M. J., & Cromer, T. D. (2007). Clinician interventions related to alliance during the initial interview and psychological assessment. *Psychotherapy, 44,* 205–218.
Himelein, M. J., & Putnam, E. A. (2001). Work activities of academic clinical psychologists: Do they practice what they teach? *Professional Psychology: Research and Practice, 32,* 537–542.
Hinshaw, S. P., Klein, R. G., & Abikoff, H. B. (2002). Childhood Attention-Deficit Hyperactivity Disorder: Nonpharmacological treatments and their combination with medication. In P. E. Nathan & J. M. Gorman (Eds.), *A guide to treatments that work* (2nd ed., pp. 3–55). New York: Oxford University Press.
Hofmann, S. G., Asnaani, A., Vonk, I. J. J., Sawyer, A. T., & Fang, A. (2012). The efficacy of cognitive behavioral therapy: A review of meta-analyses. *Cognitive Therapy & Research, 36,* 427–440.
Hogan, T. P. (2007). *Psychological testing: A practical introduction.* Hoboken, NJ: John Wiley & Sons.
Hoge, M. A., Tondora, J., & Stuart, G. W. (2003). Training in evidence-based practice. *Psychiatric Clinics of North America, 26,* 851–865.
Hollifeld, M., Hewage, C., Gunawardena, C. N., Kodituwakku, P., Bopagoda, K., Weerarathnege, K., et al. (2008). Symptoms and coping in Sri Lanka 20–21 months after the 2001 tsunami. *British Journal of Psychiatry, 192,* 39–44.
Hollon, S. D., & Beck, A. T. (2013). Cognitive and cognitive-behavioral therapies. In M. L. Lambert (Ed.), *Bergin and Garfield's handbook of psychotherapy and behavior change* (6th ed., 393–442). Hoboken, NJ: John Wiley & Sons.
Holmbeck, G. N. (1997). Toward terminological, conceptual, and statistical clarity in the study of mediators and moderators: Examples from the child-clinical and pediatric literatures. *Journal of Consulting and Clinical Psychology, 65,* 599–610.
Hopwood, C. J., & Richard, D. C. S. (2005). Graduate student WAIS-III scoring accuracy is a function of Full Scale IQ and complexity of examiner tasks. *Assessment, 12,* 445–454.
Horn, J. L., & Cattell, R. B. (1966). Refinement and test of theory of fluid and crystallized intelligence. *Journal of Educational Psychology, 57,* 253–270.
Horowitz, J. L., & Garber, J. (2006). The prevention of depressive symptoms in children and adolescents: A meta-analytic review. *Journal of Consulting and Clinical Psychology, 74,* 401–415.
Horrell, S. C. V., Holohan, D. R., Didion, L. M., & Vance G. T. (2011). Treating traumatized OEF/OIF veterans: How does trauma treatment affect the clinician? *Professional Research and Practice, 42,* 79–86.
Horvath, A. O., & Bedi, R. P. (2002). The alliance. In J. C. Norcross (Ed.), *Psychotherapy relationships that work: Therapist contributions and responsiveness to patients* (pp. 37–69). London: Oxford University Press.
Horvath, A., Del Re, A. C., Flückiger, C., & Symonds, D. (2011). The alliance in adult psychotherapy. *Psychotherapy, 48,* 9–16.
Horvath, A. O., & Luborsky, L. (1993). The role of the therapeutic alliance in psychotherapy. *Journal of Consulting and Clinical Psychology, 61,* 561–573.
Horvath, L. S., Logan, T. K., & Walker, R. (2002). Child custody cases: A content analysis of evaluations in practice. *Professional Psychology: Research and Practice, 33,* 557–565.
Hoza, B., Kaiser, N.M., & Hurt, E. (2007). Multimodal treatments for childhood attention-deficit/hyperactivity disorder: Interpreting outcomes in the context of study designs. *Clinical Child and Family Psychology Review, 10,* 318–334.
Huey, S. J., & Polo, A, J. (2008). Evidence-based psychosocial treatments for ethnic minority youth. *Journal of Clinical Child and Adolescent Psychology, 37,* 262–301.
Humbke, K. L., Brown, D. L., Welder, A. N., Fillion, D. T., Dobson, K. S., & Arnett, J. L. (2004). A survey of hospital psychology in Canada. *Canadian Psychology, 45,* 31–41.
Hunsley, J. (2003a). Cost-effectiveness and cost offset considerations in psychological service provision. *Canadian Psychology, 44,* 61–73.
Hunsley, J. (2003b). Introduction to the special section on incremental validity and utility in clinical assessment. *Psychological Assessment, 15,* 443–445.
Hunsley, J., Aubry, T. D., Vestervelt, C. M., & Vito, D. (1999). Clients' and therapists' perspectives on reasons for psychotherapy termination. *Psychotherapy, 36,* 380–388.
Hunsley, J., & Bailey, J. M. (1999). The clinical utility of the Rorschach: Unfulfilled promises and an uncertain future. *Psychological Assessment, 11,* 266–277.
Hunsley, J., & Bailey, J. M. (2001). Whither the Rorschach? An analysis of the evidence. *Psychological Assessment, 13,* 472–485.
Hunsley, J., Crabb, R., & Mash, E. J. (2004). Evidence-based clinical assessment. *The Clinical Psychologist, 57(3),* 25–32.
Hunsley, J., & Lee, C. M. (2007). Research-informed benchmarks for psychological treatments: Efficacy studies, effectiveness studies, and beyond. *Professional Psychology: Research and Practice, 38,* 21–33.
Hunsley, J., Lee, C. M., & Aubry, T. (1999). Who uses psychological services in Canada? *Canadian Psychology, 40,* 232–240.
Hunsley, J., Lee, C. M., Wood, J., & Taylor, W. (in press). Controversial and questionable assessment techniques. In S. O. Lilienfeld, S. J. Lynn, & J. Lohr (Eds.), *Science and pseudoscience in clinical psychology* (2nd ed.). New York: Guilford Press.
Hunsley, J., & Mash, E. J. (2007). Evidence-based assessment. *Annual Review of Clinical Psychology, 3,* 29–51.
Hunsley, J., & Mash, E. J. (Eds.). (2008). *A guide to assessments that work.* New York: Oxford University Press.

Hunsley, J., & Meyer, G. J. (2003). The incremental validity of psychological testing and assessment: Conceptual, methodological, and statistical issues. *Psychological Assessment, 15,* 446–455.

Hunsley, J., Ronson, A., & Cohen, K. R. (2013). Professional psychology in Canada: A survey of demographic and practice characteristics. *Professional Psychology: Research and Practice, 44,* 118–126.

Hunt, E. (2011). *Human intelligence.* Cambridge, UK: Cambridge University Press.

Hussein, A. H., & Sa'Adoon, A. A. (2006). Prevalence of anxiety and depressive disorders among primary health care attendees in Al-Nasiriyah, Iraq. *Journal of Muslim Mental Health, 1,* 171–176.

Hyman, S. F. (2010). The diagnosis of mental disorders: The problem of reification. *Annual Review of Clinical Psychology, 6,* 155–179.

Institute of Medicine. (2001). *Crossing the quality chasm: A new health system for the 21st century.* Washington, DC: National Academy Press.

Institute of Medicine. (2002). *Medical innovation in the changing healthcare marketplace: Conference summary.* Washington, DC: National Academy Press.

Institute of Medicine. (2008). *Knowing what works in health care: A road map for the nation.* Retrieved October 9, 2008, from http://www.iom.edu/Object.File/Master/50/721/Knowing%20What%20Works%20report%20brief%20FINAL%20for%20web.pdf

International Testing Commission. (2001). International guidelines for test use. *International Journal of Testing, 1,* 93–114.

Ioannidis, J. P. A. (2011). Excess significance bias in the literature on brain volume abnormalities. *Archives of General Psychiatry, 68,* 773–778.

Ivanova, M. Y., Achenbach, T. M., Rescorla, L. A., Dumenci, L., Almqvist, F., Bilenberg, N., et al. (2007). The generalizability of the Youth Self-Report syndrome structure in 23 societies. *Journal of Consulting and Clinical Psychology, 75,* 729–738.

Iverson, G. L., Lange, R. T., & Viljoen, H. (2006). Comparing the Canadian and American WAIS-III normative systems in inpatient neuropsychiatry and forensic psychiatry. *Canadian Journal of Behavioural Science, 38,* 348–353.

Jackson, J. L., Passamonti, M., & Kroenke, K. (2007). Outcome and impact of mental disorders in primary care at 5 years. *Psychosomatic Medicine, 69,* 270–276.

Jacobs, G. D., Pace-Shott, E. F., Stickgold, R., & Otto, M. W. (2004). Cognitive behavior therapy and pharmacotherapy for insomnia. *Archives of Internal Medicine, 164,* 1888–1896.

Jacobson, N. S., Christensen, A., Prince, S. E., Cordova, J., & Elridge, K. (2000). Integrative behavioral couple therapy: An acceptance-based, promising new treatment for couple discord. *Journal of Consulting and Clinical Psychology, 68,* 351–355.

Jacobson, N. S., & Truax, P. (1991). Clinical significance: A statistical approach to defining meaningful change in psychotherapy research. *Journal of Clinical and Consulting Psychology, 59,* 12–19.

James, R. L., & Roberts, M. C. (2009). Future directions in clinical child and adolescent psychology: A Delphi survey. *Journal of Clinical Psychology, 65,* 1009–1020.

Jayawickreme, N., Jayawickreme, E., Atanasov, P., Goonasekera, M. A., & Foa, E. B. (2012). Are culturally specific measures of trauma-related anxiety and depression needed? The case of Sri Lanka. *Psychological Assessment, 24,* 791–800.

Johnson, S. M. (2004). *The practice of emotionally focused marital therapy: Creating connection.* New York: Bruner/Routledge.

Johnson, S. M., & Greenberg, L. (1985). Emotionally focused couples therapy: An outcome study. *Journal of Marriage and the Family, 11,* 313–317.

Johnson, S. M., Hunsley, J., Greenberg, L., & Schindler, D. (1999). Emotionally focused couples therapy: Status and challenges. *Clinical Psychology: Science & Practice, 6,* 67–79.

Johnston, E. A., & Stewart, D. W. (2000). Clinical supervision in Canadian academic and services settings: The importance of education, training, and workplace support for supervisor development. *Canadian Psychology, 41,* 124–130.

Jones, E. E., & Pulos, S. M. (1993). Comparing the process in psychodynamic and cognitive-behavioral therapies. *Journal of Consulting and Clinical Psychology, 61,* 306–316.

Kahana, S., Drotar, D., & Frazier, T. (2008). Meta-analysis of psychological interventions to promote adherence to treatment in pediatric chronic health conditions. *Journal of Pediatric Psychology, 33,* 590–611.

Kallestad, J. H., & Olweus, D. (2003). Predicting teachers' and schools' implementation of the Olweus Bullying Prevention Program: A multilevel study. *Prevention and Treatment, 6, Article 21.* Retrieved October 21, 2004, from http://journals.apa.org/prevention/volume6/pre0060021a.html

Kamieniecki, G. W., & Lynd-Stevenson, R. M. (2002). Is it appropriate to use United States norms to assess the "intelligence" of Australian children? *Australian Journal of Psychology, 54,* 67–78.

Kangas, M., Henry, J. L., & Bryant, R. A. (2005). The relationship between acute stress disorder and posttraumatic stress disorder following cancer. *Journal of Consulting and Clinical Psychology, 73,* 360–364.

Kaplan, R. M. (2000). Two pathways to prevention. *American Psychologist, 55,* 382–396.

Kaplan, R. M., & Saccuzzo, D. P. (2001). *Psychological testing: Principles, applications, and issues* (5th ed.). Belmont, CA: Wadsworth/Thomson Learning.

Karlin, B. E., Brown, G. K., Trockel, M., Cunning, D., Zeiss, A. M., & Taylor, C. B. (2012). National dissemination of cognitive behavioral therapy for depression in the Department of Veterans Affairs Health Care System: Therapist and patient-level outcomes. *Journal of Consulting and Clinical Psychology, 80,* 707–718.

Karlin, B. E., Ruzek, J. I., Chard, K. M., Eftekhari, A., Monson, C. A., Hembree, E. A., et al. (2010). Dissemination of evidence-based psychological treatments for posttraumatic stress disorder in the Veterans Health Administration. *Journal of Traumatic Stress, 23,* 663–673.

Karlin, B. E., Trockel, M., Taylor, C. B., Gimeno, J., & Manber, R. (2013). National dissemination of cognitive behavioral therapy for insomnia in veterans: Therapist and patient-level outcomes. *Journal of Consulting and Clinical Psychology.* doi: 10.1037/a0032554.

Karney, B. R., Davila, J., Cohan, C. L., Sullivan, K. T., Johnson, M. D., & Bradbury, T. N. (1995). An empirical investigation of sampling strategies in marital research. *Journal of Marriage and the Family, 57,* 909–920.

Kaufman, A. S., & Kaufman, N. L. (1983). *Manuals for the Kaufman Assessment Battery for Children.* Circle Pines, MN: American Guidance Service.

Kaufman, A. S., & Kaufman, N. L. (1993). *Manual for the Kaufman Adolescent and Adult Intelligence Test.* Circle Pines, MN: American Guidance Service.

Kaufman, A. S., & Lichtenberger, E. O. (1999). *Essentials of WAIS-III assessment.* New York: John Wiley & Sons.

Kazantzis, N., Busch, R., Ronan, K. R., & Merrick, P. L. (2007). Using homework assignments in psychotherapy: Differences by theoretical orientation and professional training? *Behavioural and Cognitive Psychotherapy, 35,* 121–128.

Kazantzis, N., Deane, F. P., & Ronan, K. R. (2000). Homework assignments in cognitive and behavioral therapy: A meta-analysis. *Clinical Psychology: Science and Practice, 7,* 189–202.

Kazantzis, N., Lampropoulos, G. K., & Deane, F. P. (2005). A national survey of practicing psychologists' use and attitudes toward homework in psychotherapy. *Journal of Consulting and Clinical Psychology, 73,* 742–748.

Kazdin, A. E. (1981). Drawing valid inferences from case studies. *Journal of Clinical and Consulting Psychology, 49,* 183–192.

Kazdin, A. E. (1988). *Child psychotherapy: Developing and identifying effective treatments.* New York: Pergamon.

Kazdin, A. E. (1993). Evaluation in clinical practice: Clinically sensitive and systematic methods of treatment delivery. *Behavior Therapy, 24,* 11–45.

Kazdin, A. E. (1995). Scope of child and adolescent psychotherapy research: Limited sampling of dysfunctions, treatments, and client characteristics. *Journal of Clinical Child Psychology, 24,* 125–140.

Kazdin, A. E. (1999). Overview of research design issues in clinical psychology. In P. C. Kendall, J. N. Butcher, & G. N. Holmbeck (Eds.), *Handbook of research methods in clinical psychology* (2nd ed., pp. 3–30). New York: John Wiley & Sons.

Kazdin, A. E. (2003). Psychotherapy for children and adolescents. *Annual Review of Psychology, 54,* 253–276.

Kazdin, A. E. (2004). Psychotherapy for children and adolescents. In M. L. Lambert (Ed.), *Bergin and Garfield's handbook of psychotherapy and behavior change* (5th ed., pp. 543–589). New York: John Wiley & Sons.

Kazdin, A. E. (2006). Arbitrary metrics: Implications for identifying evidence-based treatments. *American Psychologist, 61,* 42–49.

Kazdin, A. E. (2007). Mediators and moderators of change in psychotherapy research. *Annual Review of Clinical Psychology, 3,* 1–27.

Kazdin, A. E., & Bass, D. (1989). Power to detect differences between alternative treatments in comparative psychotherapy outcome research. *Journal of Consulting and Clinical Psychology, 57,* 138–147.

Kazdin, A. E., Bass, D., Ayers, W. A., & Rodgers, A. (1990). Empirical and clinical focus of child and adolescent psychotherapy research. *Journal of Consulting and Clinical Psychology, 58,* 729–740.

Kazdin, A. E., & Blasé, S. L. (2011). Rebooting psychotherapy research and practice to reduce the burden of mental illness. *Perspectives in Psychological Science, 6,* 21–37.

Keefe, F. J., Abernethy, A. P., & Campbell, L. C. (2005). Psychological approaches to understanding and treating disease-related pain. *Annual Review of Psychology, 56,* 601–630.

Keller, M. L., & Craske, M. G. (2008). Panic disorder and agoraphobia. In J. Hunsley & E. J. Mash (Eds.), *A guide to assessments that work* (pp. 229–253). New York: Oxford University Press.

Kelly, M. A. R., Cyranowski, J. M., & Frank, E. (2007). Sudden gains in interpersonal psychotherapy for depression. *Behaviour Research and Therapy, 45,* 2563–2572.

Kendell, R., & Jablensky, A. (2003). Distinguishing between the validity and utility of psychiatric diagnoses. *American Journal of Psychiatry, 160,* 4–12.

Kendjelic, E. M., & Eells, T. D. (2007). Generic psychotherapy case formulation training improves formulation quality. *Psychotherapy, 44,* 66–77.

Kendler, K. S. (2008). Explanatory models for psychiatric illness. *American Journal of Psychiatry, 165,* 695–702.

Kendler, K. S., Gardner, C.O., Annas, P., Neale, M. C., Eaves, L. J., & Lichtenstein, P. (2008). A longitudinal twin study of fears from middle childhood to early adulthood: Evidence for a developmentally dynamic genome. *Archives of General Psychiatry, 65,* 421–429.

Kenwright, M., & Marks, I. M. (2004). Computer-aided self-help for phobia/panic via internet at home: A pilot study. *British Journal of Psychiatry, 184,* 448–449.

Kerns, R. D., Sellinger, J., & Goodin, B. R. (2011). Psychological treatment of chronic pain. *Annual Review of Clinical Psychology, 7,* 411–434.

Kessler, R. C., Merikangas, K. R., Berglund, P., Eaton, W. W., Koretz, D. S., & Walters, E. E. (2003). Mild disorders should not be eliminated from the DSM-V. *Archives of General Psychiatry, 60,* 1117–1122.

Kettman, J. D. J., Schoen, E. G., Moel, J. E., Cochran, S. V., Greenberg, S. T., & Corkery, J. M. (2007). Increasing severity of psycopathology at counseling centers: A new look. *Professional Psychology: Research and Practice, 38,* 523–529.

Kim, D. M., Wampold, B. E., & Bolt, D. M. (2006). Therapist effects in psychotherapy: A random effects modeling of the NIMH TDCRP data. *Psychotherapy Research, 16,* 161–172.

Kim, N. S., & Ahn, W. (2002). Clinical psychologists' theory-based representations of mental disorders predict their diagnostic reasoning and memory. *Journal of Experimental Psychology: General, 131,* 451–476.

Kirk, S. A. (2004). Are children's DSM diagnoses accurate? *Brief Treatment and Crisis Intervention, 4,* 255–270.

Klerman, G. L., Weissman, M. M., Rounsaville, B. J., & Chevron, E. S. (1984). *Interpersonal psychotherapy for depression.* New York: Basic Books.

Korotitsch, W. J., & Nelson-Gray, R. O. (1999). An overview of self-monitoring research in assessment and treatment. *Psychological Assessment, 11,* 415–425.

Kovacs, M. (2010). *Children's Depression Inventory (CDI 2).* San Antonio, TX: Pearson.

Kozey, M., & Siegel, L. S. (2008). Definitions of learning disabilities in Canadian provinces and territories. *Canadian Psychology, 49,* 162–171.

Kraemer, H. C., Kupfer, D. J., Clarke, D. E., Narrow, W. E., & Regier, D. A. (2012). DSM-5: How reliable is reliable enough? *American Journal of Psychiatry, 169,* 13–15.

Kraemer, H. C., Morgan, G. A., Leech, N. L., Gliner, J. A., Vaske, J. J., & Harmon, R. J. (2003). Measures of clinical significance. *Journal of the American Academy of Child & Adolescent Psychiatry, 42,* 1524–1529.

Kraemer, H. C., Wilson, G. T., Fairburn, C. G., & Agras, W. S. (2002). Mediators and moderators of treatment effects in randomized clinical trials. *Archives of General Psychiatry, 59,* 877–883.

Kratochwill, T. R. (2007). Preparing school psychologists for evidence-based school practice: Lessons learned and challenges ahead. *American Psychologist, 62,* 829–843.

Kraus, D. R., Castonguay, L., Boswell, J. F., Nordberg, S. S., & Hayes, J. A. (2011). Therapist effectiveness: Implications for accountability and patient care. *Psychotherapy Research, 21,* 267–276.

Krause, M. S., Lutz, W., & Saunders, S. M. (2007). Empirically certified treatments or therapists: The issue of separability. *Psychotherapy, 44,* 347–353.

Krishnamurthy, R., VandeCreek, L., Kaslow, N. J., Tazeau, Y. N., Miville, M. L., Kerns, R., et al. (2004). Achieving competency in psychological assessment: Directions for education and training. *Journal of Clinical Psychology, 60,* 725–739.

Krueger, R. F., Chentsova-Dutton, Y. E., Markon, K. E., Goldberg, D., & Ormel, J. (2003). A cross-cultural study of the structure of comorbidity among common psychopathological syndromes in the general health care setting. *Journal of Abnormal Psychology, 112,* 437–447.

Krueger, R. F., & Markon, K. E. (2006). Reinterpreting comorbidity: A model-based approach to understanding and classifying psychopathology. *Annual Review of Clinical Psychology, 2,* 111–133.

Krueger, R. F., Watson, D., & Barlow, D. H. (2005). Introduction to the special section: Toward a dimensionally based taxonomy of psychopathology. *Journal of Abnormal Psychology, 114,* 491–493.

Kvaal, S., Choca, J., Groth-Marnat, G., & Davis, A. (2011). The integrated psychological report. In T. M. Harwood, L. E. Beutler, & G. Groth-Marnat, *Integrative assessment of adult personality* (3rd ed., pp. 413–445). New York: Guilford Press.

Kwong, J. C., Stukel, T. A., Lim, K., McGeer, A. J., Upshur, R. E. G., Johansen, H. et al. (2008). The effect of universal influenza immunization on mortality and health care use. Retrieved February 16, 2009, from www.plos .medicine.org

La Rue, A., & Watson, J. (1998). Psychological assessment of older adults. *Professional Psychology: Research and Practice, 29,* 5–14.

Laatsch, L., Harrington, D., Hotz, G., Marcantuono, J., Mozzoni, M. P., Walsh V., et al. (2007). An evidence-based review of cognitive and behavioral treatment studies in children with acquired brain injury. *Journal of Head Trauma Rehabilitation, 22,* 248–256.

Lafferty, P., Beutler, L. E., & Crago, M. (1989). Differences between more and less effective psychotherapists: A study of select therapist variables. *Journal of Consulting and Clinical Psychology, 57,* 76–70.

Lally, S. J. (2003). What tests are acceptable for use in forensic evaluations? *Professional Psychology: Research and Practice, 34,* 491–498.

Lambert, M. J., Hansen, N. B., Umphress, V., Lunnen, K., Okiishi, J., Burlingame, G., et al. (1996). *Administration and scoring manual for the Outcome Questionnaire (OQ 45.2).* Wilmington, DE: American Professional Credentialing Services.

Lambert, M. J., & Ogles, B. M. (2004). The efficacy and effectiveness of psychotherapy. In M. J. Lambert (Ed.), *Bergin and Garfield's handbook of psychotherapy and behavior change* (5th ed., pp. 139–193). New York: John Wiley & Sons.

Lambert, M. J., Whipple, J. L., Hawkins, E. J., Vermeersch, D. A., Nielsen, S. L., & Smart, D. W. (2003). Is it time for clinicians to routinely track patient outcome? A meta-analysis. *Clinical Psychology: Science and Practice, 10,* 288–301.

Lampropoulos, G. K. (2000). Evolving psychotherapy integration: Eclectic selection and prescriptive applications of common factors in therapy. *Psychotherapy, 37,* 285–297.

Landman, J. T., & Dawes, R. M. (1982). Psychotherapy outcome: Smith and Glass' conclusions stand up under scrutiny. *American Psychologist, 37,* 504–516.

Langan-Fox, J., & Grant, S. (2006). The Thematic Apperception Test: Toward a standard measure of the big three motives. *Journal of Personality Assessment, 87,* 277–291.

Langer, D. A., McLeod, B. D., & Weisz, J. R. (2011). Do treatment manuals undermine youth-therapist alliance in community clinical practice? *Journal of Consulting and Clinical Psychology, 79,* 427–432.doi: 10.1037/a0023821

Laska, K. M., Smith, T. L., Wislocki, A. P., Minami, T., & Wampold, B. E. (2013). Uniformity of evidence-based treatments in practice? Therapist effects in the delivery of cognitive processing therapy for PTSD. *Journal of Counseling Psychology, 60,* 31–41.

Le, H., Muñoz, R. F., Ippen, C. G., & Stoddard, J. L. (2003). Treatment is not enough: We must prevent major depression in women. *Prevention and Treatment, 6, Article 10.*

Lee, C. M., & Asgary-Eden, V. (2009). Family-based approaches to the prevention of depression in at risk children and youth. In C. Essau (Ed.). *Treatment of adolescent depression* (pp. 177–214). Oxford: Oxford University Press.

Lee, C. M., Horvath, C., & Hunsley, J. (2013). Does it work in the real world? The effectiveness of treatments for psychological problems in children and adolescents. *Professional Psychology: Research and Practice,* 81–88.

Lee, J., Lim, N., Yang, E., & Lee, S. M. (2011). Antecedents and consequences of three dimensions of burnout in psychotherapists: A meta-analysis. *Professional Psychology: Research and Practice, 42,* 252–258.

Lee, W., Bindman, J., Ford, T., Glozier, N., Moran, P., Stewart, R., & Hotopf, M. (2007). Bias in psychiatric case-control studies. *British Journal of Psychiatry, 190,* 204–209.

Leichsenring, F., Rabung, S., & Lebing, E. (2004). The efficacy of short-term psychodynamic psychotherapy for specific psychiatric disorders. *Archives of General Psychiatry, 61,* 1208–1216.

Lemsky, C. M. (2000). Neuropsychological assessment and treatment planning. In G. Groth-Marnat (Ed.), *Neuropsychological assessment in clinical practice* (pp. 535–574). New York: John Wiley & Sons.

Levak, R. W., Hogan, R. S., Beutler, L. E., & Song, X. (2011). Applying assessment information: Decision making, patient feedback, and consultation. In T. M. Harwood, L. E. Beutler, & G. Groth-Marnat, *Integrative assessment of adult personality* (3rd ed., pp. 373–412). New York: Guilford Press.

Leventhal, H., Weinman, J., Leventhal, E. A., & Phillips, L. A. (2008). Health Psychology: The search for pathways between behaviour and health. *Annual Review of Clinical Psychology, 4,* 477–505.

Levitt, E. E. (1957). The effects of psychotherapy with children: An evaluation. *Journal of Consulting Psychology, 21,* 189–196.

Levitt, E. E. (1963). The results of psychotherapy with children: A further evaluation. *Behaviour Research and Therapy, 60,* 326–329.

Levitt, J. M., Saka, N., Romanelli, L. H., & Hoagwood, K. (2007). Early identification of mental health problems in schools: The status of instrumentation. *Journal of School Psychology, 45,* 163–191.

Lewinsohn, P. M., Antonuccio, D. O., Steinmetz, J. L., & Teri, L. (1984). *The coping with depression course: A psychoeducational intervention for unipolar depression.* Eugene, OR: Castilia.

Lewinsohn, P. M., & Clarke, G. N. (1999). Psychosocial treatments for adolescent depression. *Clinical Psychology Review, 19,* 329–342.

Lewis, C., Pearce, J., & Bisson, J. I. (2012). Efficacy, cost-effectiveness and acceptability of self-help interventions for anxiety disorders: Systematic review. *British Journal of Psychiatry, 200,* 15–21.

Li, F., McAuley, E., Chaumeton, N. R., & Harmer, P. (2001). Enhancing the psychological well-being of elderly individuals through Tai Chi exercise: A latent growth curve analysis. *Structural Equation Modeling, 8,* 53–83.

Lichtenberg, P. A., Murman, D. L., & Mellow, A. M. (2003). Integrated case studies. In P. A. Lichtenberg, D. L. Murman, & A. M. Mellow (Eds.), *Handbook of dementia* (pp. 403–412). New York: John Wiley & Sons.

Lichtenberger, E. O., Broadbooks, D. Y., & Kaufman, A. S. (2000). *Essentials of cognitive assessment with KAIT and other Kaufman measures.* New York: John Wiley & Sons.

Lichtenberger, E. O., Kaufman, A. S., & Lai, Z. C. (2002). *Essentials of WMS-III assessment.* New York: John Wiley & Sons.

Lilienfeld, S. O. (2007). Psychological treatments that cause harm. *Perspectives on Psychological Science, 2,* 53–70.

Lilienfeld, S. O., Lynn, S. J., & Lohr, J. M. (2003). Science and pseudoscience in clinical psychology: Initial thoughts, reflections, and considerations. In S. O. Lilienfeld, S. J. Lynn, & J. M. Lohr (Eds.), *Science and pseudo-science in clinical psychology* (pp. 1–14). New York: Guilford Press.

Lilienfeld, S. O., Wood, J. M., & Garb, H. N. (2000). The scientific status of projective techniques. *Psychological Science in the Public Interest, 1,* 27–66.

Lilienfeld, S. O., Wood, J. M., & Garb, H. N. (2006). Why questionable psychological tests remain popular. *The Scientific Review of Alternative Medicine, 10,* 6–15.

Lima, E. N., Stanley, S., Kaboski, B., Reitzel, L. R., Richey, J. A., Castro, Y., et al. (2005). The incremental validity of the MMPI-2: When does therapist access not enhance treatment outcome? *Psychological Assessment, 17,* 462–468.

Lin, E., Goering, P., Offord, D. R., Campbell, D., & Boyle, M. H. (1996). The use of mental health services in Ontario: Epidemiologic findings. *Canadian Journal of Psychiatry, 41,* 572–577.

Lin, K. K., Sandler, I. N., Ayers, T. S., Wolchik, S. A., & Luecken, L. J. (2004). Resilience in parentally bereaved children and adolescents seeking preventive services. *Journal of Clinical Child and Adolescent Psychology, 33,* 673–683.

Lis, A., Parolin, L., Calvo, V., Zennaro, A., & Meyer, G. (2007). The impact of administration and inquiry on Rorschach Comprehensive System protocols in a national reference sample. *Journal of Personality Assessment,* 89, S193–S200.

Livingston, G., Johnston, K., Katona, C., Paton, J., Lyketsos, C.G., & Old Age Task of the World Federation of Biological Psychiatry. (2005). *American Journal of Psychiatry, 162,* 1996–2021.

Loe, S. A., Kadlubek, R. M., & Marks, W. J. (2007). Administration and scoring errors on the WISC-IV among graduate student examiners. *Journal of Psychoeducational Assessment, 25,* 237–247.

London School of Economics Centre for Economic Performance Mental Health Policy Group. (2006). *The depression report: A new deal for depression and anxiety disorders.* Retrieved June 3, 2008, from www.lse.ac.uk

Longwell, B. T., & Truax, P. (2005). The differential effects of weekly, monthly, and bimonthly administration of the Beck Depression Inventory-II: Psychometric properties and clinical implications. *Behavior Therapy, 36,* 265–275.

Love, S. M., Koob, J. J., & Hill, L. E. (2007). Meeting the challenges of evidence-based practice: Can mental health therapists evaluate their practice? *Brief Treatment and Crisis Intervention, 7,* 184–193.

Lowry-Webster, H. M., & Barrett, P. M. (2001). A universal prevention trial of anxiety and depressive disorders in childhood: Preliminary data from an Australian study. *Behaviour Change, 18,* 36–50.

Luborsky, L. (1954). A note on Eysenck's article "The effects of psychotherapy: An evaluation." *British Journal of Psychology, 45,* 129–131.

Luborksy, L. (1984). *Principles of psychoanalytic psychotherapy: A manual for supportive expressive (SE) treatment.* New York: Basic Books.

Luborsky, L., Diguer, L., Luborsky, E., Singer, B., Dickter, D., & Schmidt, K. A. (1993). The efficacy of dynamic psychotherapies: Is it true that "Everyone has won and all must have prizes"? In M. E. Miller, L. Luborsky, J. P. Barber, & J. P. Docherty (Eds.), *Psychodynamic treatment research: A handbook for clinical practice* (pp. 497–516). New York: Basic Books.

Luborsky, L., Diguer, L., Seligman, D. A., Rosenthal, R., Krause, E. D., Johnson, S., et al. (1999). The researcher's own therapy allegiance: A "wild card" in comparisons of treatment efficacy. *Clinical Psychology: Science and Practice, 6,* 95–106.

Luborsky, L., Singer, B., & Luborsky, E. (1975). Comparative studies of psychotherapies: Is it true that "Everybody has won and all must have prizes"? *Archives of General Psychiatry, 32,* 995–1008.

Luby, J. L., Belden, A., Sullivan, J., & Spitznagel, E. (2007). Preschoolers' contribution to their diagnosis of depression and anxiety: Uses and limitations of young child self-report of symptoms. *Child Psychiatry and Human Development, 38,* 312–338.

Luebbe, A. M., Radcliffe, A. M., Callands, T. A., Green, D., & Thorn, B. E. (2007). Evidence-based practice in psychology: Perceptions of graduate students in scientist-practitioner programs. *Journal of Clinical Psychology, 63,* 643–655.

Luxembourg Income Study (2000). *Relative poverty rates for the total population, children and the elderly.* Retrieved October 22, 2004, from http://www.lisproject.org/keyfigures/povertytable.htm

MacCallum, R. C., & Austin, J. T. (2000). Applications of structural equation modeling in psychological research. *Annual Review of Psychology, 51,* 201–226.

MacCallum, R. C., Zhang, S., Preacher, K. J., & Rucker, D. D. (2002). On the practice of dichotomization of quantitative variables. *Psychological Methods, 7,* 19–40.

MacMillan, H. L., Tanaka, M., Duku, E., & Vaillancourt, T. (2013). Child physical and sexual abuse in a community sample of young adults. *Child Abuse and Neglect, 37,* 14–21.

MacMillan, H. L., Wathen, C. N., Jamieson, E., Boyle, M., McNutt, L.-A., Worster, A., et al. (2006). Approaches to screening for intimate partner violence in health care settings. *Journal of the American Medical Association, 296,* 530–536.

Magaletta, P. R., & Verdeyen, V. (2005). Clinical practice in corrections: A conceptual framework. *Professional Psychology Research and Practice, 36,* 37–43.

Maheu, M. M., Pulier, M. L., McMenamin, J. P., & Posen, L. (2012). Future of telepsychology, telehealth, and various technologies in psychological research and practice. *Professional Psycholgy: Research and Practice,* 613–621.

Malgady, R. G. (1996). The question of cultural bias in assessment and diagnosis of ethnic minority clients: Let's reject the null hypothesis. *Professional Psychology: Research and Practice, 27,* 73–77.

Malloy, D. C., Hadjistavropoulos, T., Douaud, P., & Smythe, W. E. (2002). The codes of ethics of the Canadian Psychological Association and the Canadian Medical Association: Ethical orientation and functional grammar analysis. *Canadian Psychology, 43,* 244–253.

Malouf, J. M., & Rooke, S. E. (2007). Empirically supported self-help books. *The Behavior Therapist, 30,* 129–131.

Mancini, A. D., & Bonanno, G. A. (2006). Resilience in the face of potential trauma: Clinical practices and illustrations. *Journal of Clinical Psychology, 62,* 971–985.

Mariush, M. E. (2002). *Essentials of treatment planning.* New York: John Wiley & Sons.

Marks, I. M., & Mathews, A. M. (1979). Brief standard self-rating for phobic patients. *Behaviour Research and Therapy, 17,* 263–267.

Marks, I., Shaw, S., & Parkin, R. (1998). Computer-aided treatments of mental health problems. *Clinical Psychology: Science and Practice, 5,* 151–170.

Marlatt, G.A., Larimer, M. E., Mail, P. D., Hawkins, E.H. Cummins, L.H., Blume, A. W., et al. (2003). Journeys of the Circle: A culturally congruent life skills intervention for adolescent drinking. *Alcoholism: Clinical and Experimental Research, 27,* 1327–1329.

Martin, L., Saperson, K., & Maddigan, B. (2003). Residency training: challenges and opportunities in preparing trainees for the 21st century. *Canadian Journal of Psychiatry, 48,* 225–231.

Mash, E. J. (1979). What is behavioral assessment? *Behavioral Assessment, 1,* 23–29.

Mash, E. J., & Foster, S. L. (2001). Exporting analogue behavioral observation from research to clinical practice: Useful or cost-defective? *Psychological Assessment, 13,* 86–98.

Mash, E. J., & Hunsley, J. (1993). Assessment considerations in the assessment of failing psychotherapy: Bringing the negatives out of the darkroom. *Psychological Assessment: A Journal of Consulting and Clinical Psychology, 5,* 292–301.

Mash, E. J., & Hunsley, J. (2004). Behavioral assessment: Sometimes you get what you need. In S. N. Haynes & E. M. Heiby (Eds.), *The comprehensive handbook of psychological assessment, Volume 3: Behavioral assessment* (pp. 489–501). New York: John Wiley & Sons.

Mash, E. J., & Hunsley, J. (2007). Assessment of child and family disturbance: A developmental-systems approach. In E. J. Mash & R. A. Barkley (Eds.), *Assessment of childhood disorders* (4th ed., pp. 3–50). New York: Guilford Press.

Mash, E. J, & Sattler, J. M. (1998). Introduction to clinical assessment interviewing. In J. M. Sattler, *Clinical and forensic interviewing of children and families* (pp. 2–44). San Diego, CA: Jerome Sattler.

May, R., Angel, E., & Ellenberger, H. (Eds). (1958). *Existence: A new dimension in psychiatry and psychology.* New York: Basic Books.

Mayer, J. D., Roberts, R. D., & Barsade, S. G. (2008). Human abilities: Emotional intelligence. *Annual Review of Psychology, 59,* 507–536.

Mayer, J. D., Salovey, P., & Caruso, D. R. (2008). Emotional intelligence: New ability or eclectic traits? *American Psychologist, 63,* 503–517.

Mayer, J.D., Salovey, P., Caruso, D. R., & Sitarenios, G. (2003). Measuring emotional intelligence with the MSCEIT V2.0. *Emotion, 3,* 97–105.

McCarthy, O., & Carr, A. (2002). Prevention of bullying. In A. Carr (Ed.), *Prevention: What works with children and adolescents? A critical review of psychological prevention programmes for children, adolescents and their families* (pp. 205–221). Hove, UK: Brunner-Routledge.

McCarty, C. A., & Weisz, J. R. (2007). Effects of psychotherapy for depression in children and adolescents: What we can (and can't) learn from meta-analysis and component profiling. *Journal of the American Academy of Child and Adolescent Psychiatry, 46,* 879–886.

McClelland, D. C., Koestner, R., & Weinberger, J. (1989). How do self-attributed and implicit motives differ? *Psychological Bulletin, 96,* 690–702.

McCrae, R. R., & Costa, P. T., Jr., (2010). *NEO Inventories: Professional manual.* Lutz, FL: Psychological Assessment Resources, Inc.

McCrae R. R., Costa P. T., & Martin T. A. (2005). The NEO-PI-3: A more readable revised NEO personality inventory. *Journal of Personality Assessment, 84,* 261–270.

McCrone, P., Knapp, M., Proudfoot, J., Ryden, C., Cavanagh, K., Shapiro, D. A., et al. (2004). Cost-effectiveness of computerised cognitive-behavioural therapy for anxiety and depression in primary care: Randomised controlled trial. *British Journal of Psychiatry, 185,* 55–62.

McFall, R. M. (1991). Manifesto for a science of clinical psychology. *The Clinical Psychologist, 44,* 75–88.

McFall, R. M. (2006). Doctoral training in clinical psychology. *Annual Review of Clinical Psychology, 2,* 21–49.

McGrath, P. J., & Finley, G. A. (Eds.). (2003). *Pediatric pain: Biological and social context.* Seattle, WA: IASP Press.

McGrath, P. J., & Unruh, A. (1999). The measurement and assessment of paediatric pain. In P. D. Wall & R. Melzack (Eds.), *Textbook of pain* (4th ed., pp. 371–384). London: Churchill Livingstone.

McGrath, P. J., Finley, G. A., Ritchie, J., & Dowden, S. J. (2003). *Pain, pain, go away: Helping children with pain.* Halifax, NS: Dalhousie University.

McGuinness, M., Blissett, J., & Jones, C. (2011). OCD in the perinatal period: Is postpartum OCD (ppOCD) a distinct subtype? A review of the literature. *Behavioural and Cognitive Psychotherapy, 39,* 285–310.

McHugh, R. K., & Barlow, D. H. (2010). The dissemination and implementation of evidence-based psychological treatments: A review of current efforts. *American Psychologist, 65,* 73–84.

McHugh, R. K., & Behar, E. (2009). Readability of self-report measures of depression and anxiety. *Journal of Consulting and Clinical Psychology, 77,* 1100–1112.

McIlwraith, R.D., Dyck, K. G., Holms, V. L., Carlson, T. E., & Prober, N. G. (2005). Manitoba's rural and northern community-based training program for psychology interns and residents. *Professional Psychology: Research and Practice, 36,* 164–172.

McLean, P. D., & Woody, S. R. (2001). *Anxiety disorders in adults: An evidence-based approach to psychological treatment.* New York: Oxford University Press.

McLellan, F. (2003). Research by US psychiatrists in danger of extinction. Expert committee recommends steps to strengthen research training in psychiatry residency. *Lancet, 362,* 1732.

McLeod, B. D., Jensen-Doss, A., & Ollendick, T. H. (Eds.). (2013). *Handbook of child and adolescent diagnostic and behavioral assessment.* New York: Guilford Press.

McLeod, B. D., & Weisz, J. R. (2004). Using dissertations to examine potential bias in child and adolescent clinical trials. *Journal of Consulting and Clinical Psychology, 72,* 235–251.

Measelle, J. R., Ablow, J. C., Cowan, P. A. & Cowan, C. P. (1998). Assessing young children's views of their academic, social and emotional lives: An evaluation of the self-perception scales of the Berkeley Puppet Interview. *Child Development, 69,* 1556–1576.

Measelle, J. R., John, O. P., Ablow, J. C., Cowan, P. A., & Cowan, C. P. (2005). Can children provide coherent, stable, and valid self-reports on the Big Five dimensions? A longitudinal study from ages 5 to 7. *Journal of Personality and Social Psychology, 89,* 90–106.

Meehl, P. E. (1954). *Clinical versus statistical prediction: A theoretical analysis and a review of the evidence.* Minneapolis, MN: University of Minnesota Press.

Megargee, E. I. (2002). *The California Psychological Inventory handbook* (2nd ed.). San Francisco: Jossey-Bass.

Meisner, S. (1988). Susceptibility of Rorschach distress correlates to malingering. *Journal of Personality Assessment, 52,* 564–571.

Mellers, J. D. C. (2004). Neurological investigations. In L. H. Goldstein & J. E. McNeil (Eds.), *Clinical neuropsychology: A practical guide to assessment and management for clinicians* (pp. 57–77). Chichester, UK: John Wiley & Sons.

Menchola, M., Arkowitz, H. S., & Burke, B. L. (2007). Efficacy of self-administered treatments for depression and anxiety. *Professional Psychology: Research and Practice, 38,* 421–429.

Merikangas, K. R., He, J-P., Burstein, M., Swanson, S.A., Avenevoli, S., Cui, L., et al. (2010). Lifetime prevalence of mental disorders in US adolescents: Results from the National Comorbidity Study-Adolescent Supplement (NCS-A). *Journal of the American Academy of Child and Adolescent Psychiatry,* 49, 980–989.

Messer, S. B. (2000). What makes brief psychodynamic therapy time efficient? *Clinical Psychology: Science and Practice, 8,* 5–22.

Meyer, G. (Ed.). (1999). The utility of the Rorschach in clinical assessment [Special section: I]. *Psychological Assessment 11,* 235–302.

Meyer, G. (Ed.). (2001). The utility of the Rorschach in clinical assessment [Special section: II]. *Psychological Assessment 13,* 419–502.

Meyer, G. J., Erdberg, P., & Shaffer, T. W. (2007). Toward international normative reference data for the Comprehensive System. *Journal of Personality Assessment, 89,* S201–S216.

Meyer, G. J., Viglione, D. J., Mihura, J. L., Erard, R. E., & Erdberg, P. (2011). *Rorschach Performance Assessment System: Administration, coding, interpretation, and technical manual.* Toledo, Ohio: Rorschach Performance Assessment System, LLC.

Meyer, T. J., Miller, M. L., Metzger, R. L., & Borkovec, T. D. (1990). Developmental validation of the Penn State Worry Questionnaire. *Behaviour Research and Therapy, 28,* 487–496.

Meyer, B., Pilkonis, P. A., Krupnick, J. L., Egan, M. K., Simmens, S. J., & Sotsky, S. M. (2002). Treatment expectancies, patient alliance, and outcome: Further analyses from the National Institute of Mental Health Treatment of Depression Collaborative Research Program. *Journal of Consulting and Clinical Psychology, 70,* 1051–1055.

Meyer, G. J., Finn, S. E., Eyde, L., Kay, G. G., Moreland, K. L., Dies, R. R., et al. (2001). Psychological testing and psychological assessment: A review of evidence and issues. American Psychologist, 56, 128–165.

Mezulis, A. H., Abramson, L. Y., Hyde, J. S., & Hankin, B. L. (2004). Is there a universal positivity bias in attributions? A meta-analytic review of individual, developmental, and cultural differences in the self-serving attributional bias. *Psychological Bulletin, 130,* 711–747.

Michelson, D., Davenport, C., Dretzke, J., Barlow, J., & Day, C. (2013). Do evidence-based interventions work when tested in the "real world"? A systematic review and meta-analysis of parent management training for the treatment of child disruptive behavior. *Clinical Child and Family Psychology Review, 16,* 18–34.

Middleton, J. A. (2004). Clinical neuropsychological assessment of children. In L. H. Goldstein & J. E. McNeil (Eds.), *Clinical neuropsychology: A practical guide to assessment and management for clinicians* (pp. 275–300). Chichester, UK: John Wiley & Sons.

Mihura, J. L., Meyer, G. J., Dumitrascu, N., & Bombel, G. (2013). The validity of individual Rorschach variables: Systematic reviews and meta-analyses of the Comprehensive System. *Psychological Bulletin.* Advance online publication. doi: 10.1037/a0029406.

Miklowitz, D. J., Otto, M. W., Frank, E., Reilly-Harrington, N. A., Wisniewski, S. R., Kogan, J. N., et al. (2007). Psychosocial treatments for bipolar depression: A 1-year randomized trial from the Systematic Treatment Enhancement Program. *Archives of General Psychiatry*, 64, 419–427.

Miller, C. S., Kimonis, E. R., Otto, R. K., Kline, S. M., & Wasserman, A. L. (2012). Reliability of risk assessment measures used in sexually violent predator proceedings. *Psychological Assessment, 24,* 944–953.

Miller, G. E., & Prinz, R. J. (1990). Enhancement of social learning family interventions for childhood conduct disorder. *Psychological Bulletin, 108,* 291–307.

Miller, G. E., & Prinz, R. J. (2003). Engagement of families in treatment for childhood conduct problems. *Behavior Therapy, 34,* 517–534.

Millon, T. (1997). *Millon Clinical Multiaxial Inventory-III manual.* Minneapolis, MN: National Computer Systems.

Mingroni, M. A. (2007). Resolving the IQ paradox: Heterosis as a cause of the Flynn effect and other trends. *Psychological Review, 114,* 806–829.

Miranda, J., Bernal, G., Lau, A., Kohn, L., Hwang, W.-C., & LaFromboise, T. (2005). State of the science on psychosocial interventions for ethnic minorities. *Annual Review of Clinical Psychology, 1,* 113–142.

Mischel, W. (2004). Toward an integrative science of the person. *Annual Review of Psychology, 55,* 1–22.

Mitchell, J. E., Agras, S., Crow, S., Halmi, K., Fairburn, C. G., Bryson, S., & Kraemer, H. (2011). Stepped care and cognitive-behavioural therapy for bulimia nervosa: Randomised trial. *British Journal of Psychiatry, 198,* 391–397.

Mohr, D. C., Hart, S. L., Julian, L., Catledge, C., Honos-Webb, L., Vella, L., et al. (2005). Telephone-administered psychotherapy for depression. *Archives of General Psychiatry, 62,* 1007–1014.

Mojtabai, R., & Olfson, M. (2008). National trends in psychotherapy by office-based psychiatrists. *Archives of General Psychiatry, 65,* 962–970.

Mokdad, A. H., Marks, J. S., Stroup, D. F., & Gerberding, J. L. (2004). Actual causes of death in the United States, 2000. *Journal of the American Medical Association, 291,* 1238–1245.

Monahan, J. (1981). *Predicting violent behaviour: An assessment of clinical techniques.* Beverly Hills, CA: Sage Publications.

Morales, E., & Norcross, J. C. (2010). Evidence-based practices with ethnic minorities: Strange bedfellows no more. *Journal of Clinical Psychology, 66,* 821–829.

Morasco, B. J., Gfeller, J. D., & Elder, K. A. (2007). The utility of the NEO-PI-R validity scales to detect response distortion: A comparison with the MMPI-2. *Journal of Personality Assessment, 88,* 276–283.

Morey, L. C. (1991). *The Personality Assessment Inventory professional manual.* Odessa, FL: Psychological Assessment Resources.

Morey, L. C. (2003). *Essentials of PAI assessment.* New York: John Wiley & Sons.

Morey, L. C. (2007). *Personality Assessment Inventory professional manual* (2nd ed.). Lutz, FL: Psychological Assessment Resources.

Morgan, D. L., & Morgan, R. K. (2001). Single participant research design: Bringing science to managed care. *American Psychologist, 56,* 119–217.

Morgenthaler, T., Kramer, M., Alessi, C., Friedman, L., Boehlecke, B., et al. (2006). Practice parameters for the psychological and behavioral treatment of insomnia: An update. An American Academy of Sleep Medicine Report. *Sleep, 29,* 1415–1419.

Morin, C. M. (2004). Cognitive-behavioral approaches to the treatment of insomnia. *Journal of Clinical Psychiatry, 65 (suppl 16),* 33–40.

Morin, C. M., Bootzin, R. R., Buysse, D. J., Edinger, J. D., Espie, C. A., et al. (2006). Psychological and behavioral treatment of insomnia: Update of the recent evidence (1998–2004). *Sleep, 29,* 1398–1414.

Morin, C. M., Colecchi, C., Stone, J., Sood, R., & Brink, D. (1999). Behavioral and pharmacological therapies for late-life insomnia: A randomized controlled trial. *Journal of the American Medical Association, 281,* 991–999.

Morley, S., & Adams, M. (1989). Some simple statistical tests for exploring single-case time-series data. *British Journal of Clinical Psychology, 28,* 1–18.

Mossman, D., Wygant, D. B., & Gervais, R. O. (2012). Estimating the accuracy of neurocognitive effort measures in the absence of a "gold standard." *Psychological Assessment, 24,* 815–822.

Moye, J., Marson, D. C., & Edelstein, B. (2013). Assessment of capacity in an aging society. *American Psychologist, 68,* 158–171.

Mrazek, P. J., & Haggerty, R. J. (1994). *Reducing risks for mental disorders: Frontiers for preventive research.* Washington, DC: National Academy Press.

Mueller, M., & Pekarik, G. (2000). Treatment duration prediction: Client accuracy and its relationship to dropout, outcome, and satisfaction. *Psychotherapy, 37,* 117–123.

Mufson, L., & Dorta, K. P. (2003). Interpersonal psychotherapy for depressed adolescents. In A. E. Kazdin & J. R. Weisz (Eds.), *Evidence-based psychotherapies for children and adolescents* (pp. 148–164). New York: Guilford Press.

Mufson, L., Dorta, K. P., Moreau, D., & Weissman, M. M. (2004). *Interpersonal psychotherapy for depressed adolescents* (2nd ed.). New York: Guilford Press.

Mufson, L., Weissman, M. M., Moreau, D., & Garfinkel, R. (1999). Efficacy of interpersonal psychotherapy for depressed adolescents. *Archives of General Psychiatry, 56,* 573–579.

Mullen, E. J., & Streiner, D. L. (2004). The evidence for and against evidence-based practice. *Brief Treatment and Crisis Intervention, 4,* 111–121.

Mumma, G. H. (1998). Improving cognitive case formulation and treatment planning in clinical practice and research. *Journal of Cognitive Psychotherapy, 12,* 251–274.

Munafò, M. R., & Flint, J. (2010). How reliable are scientific studies? *British Journal of Psychiatry, 197,* 257–258.

Murray, H. A. (1943). *Thematic Apperception Test manual.* Cambridge, MA: Harvard University Press.

Murrie, D. C., Boccaccini, M. T., Guarnera, L. A., & Rufino, K. A. (in press). Are forensic experts biased by the side that retained them? *Psychological Science.*

Mussell, M. P., Crosby, R. D., Crow, S. J., Knopke, A. J., Peterson, C. B., Wonderlich, S. A., et al. (2000). Utilization of empirically supported psychotherapy treatments for individuals with eating disorders: A survey of psychologists.

International Journal of Eating Disorders, 27, 230–237.

Myers, L. L., & Thyer, B. A. (1997). Should social work clients have the right to effective treatment? *Social Work, 42,* 288–297.

Nagin, D., & Tremblay, R. E. (1999). Trajectories of boys' physical aggression, opposition, and hyperactivity on the path to physically violent and nonviolent juvenile delinquency. *Child Development, 70,* 1181–1196.

Naglieri, J. A., Drasgow, F., Schmit, M., Handler, L., Prifitera, A., Margolis, A.M., et al. (2004). Psychological testing on the Internet, *American Psychologist, 59,* 150–162.

Nanni, V., Uher, R., & Danese, A. (2012). Childhood maltreatment predicts unfavorable course of illness and treatment outcomes in depression: A meta-analysis. *American Journal of Psychiatry, 169,* 141–151.

Nathan, P. E. (2004). When science only takes us so far. *Clinical Psychology: Science and Practice, 11,* 216–218.

Nathan, P., & Gorman, J. M. (Eds.). (1998). *A guide to treatments that work.* New York: Oxford University Press.

Nathan, P., & Gorman, J. M. (Eds.). (2002). *A guide to treatments that work* (2nd ed.). New York: Oxford University Press.

Nathan, P. E., & Gorman, J. M. (Eds.). (2007). *A guide to treatments that work* (3rd ed.). New York: Oxford University Press.

Nation, M., Crusto, C., Wandersman, A., Kumpfer, K. L., Seybolt, D., Morrissey-Kane, E., et al. (2003). What works in prevention: Principles of effective prevention programs. *American Psychologist, 58,* 449–456.

National Institute for Clinical Excellence. (2005). *Depression in children: Identification and management of depression in children and young people in primary, community and secondary care.* Retrieved February 15, 2005, from http://www.nice.org.uk

National Institute for Health and Clinical Excellence. (2006). *Conduct disorder in children: Parent training/education programmes: Guidance.* Retrieved June 5, 2009, from http://guidance.nice.org.uk/TA102/Guidance/pdf/English

National Institute for Health and Clinical Excellence. (2008, September). *Attention deficit hyperactivity disorder: Diagnosis and management of ADHD in children, young people, and adults.* Retrieved October 31, 2008, from www.nice.org.uk

National Institute for Health and Clinical Excellence. (2009). *Depression in adults: The treatment and management of depression in adults.* Retrieved from http://www.nice.org.uk/nicemedia/live/12329/45888/45888.pdf

National Institute for Health and Clinical Excellence. (2010). *Nocturnal enuresis: The management of bedwetting in children and young people. National Clinical Guideline Number 111.* Retrieved from http://guidance.nice.org.uk

National Institute for Health and Clinical Excellence. (2013a). *Antisocial behavior and conduct disorders in children and young people. National Clinical Guideline Number 158.* Retrieved from http://guidance.nice.org.uk

National Institute for Health and Clinical Excellence. (2013b). *Psychosis and schizophrenia in children and young people: Recognition and management. National Clinical Guideline CG155.* Retrieved from http://guidance.nice.org.uk

National Institutes of Health. (1998). *Diagnosis and treatment of attention deficit hyper-activity Disorder (ADHD), NIH Consensus Statement, 16,* 1–37. Kensington, MD: Author.

National Opinion Research Center. (2012). *Doctorate recipients, by subfield of study: 2001–11.* Retrieved from http://www.nsf.gov/statistics/sed/2011/pdf/tab15.pdf

Naugle, A. E., & Maher, S. (2003). Modeling and behavioral rehearsal, In W. O'Donohue, J. E. Fisher, & S. C. Hayes (Eds.), *Cognitive behavior therapy: Applying empirically supported techniques in your practice* (pp. 238–246). New York: John Wiley & Sons.

Neisser, U. (Ed.). (1998). *The rising curve: Longterm gains in IQ and related measures.* Washington, DC: American Psychological Association.

Nelson, G., Westhues, A., & MacLeod, J. (2003 December 18). A meta-analysis of longitudinal research on preschool prevention programs for children. *Prevention and Treatment, 6, Article 31.* Retrieved October 21, 2004, from http://journals.apa.org/prevention/volume6/pr e0060031a.html

Nelson, N. W., Hoelzle, J. B., Sweet, J. J., Arbisi, P. A., & Demakis, G. J. (2010). Updated meta-analysis of the MMPI-2 symptom validity scale (FBS): Utility in forensic practice. *Clinical Neuropsychology, 24,* 701–724.

Nelson, T. D., & Steele, R. G. (2008). Influences on practitioner treatment selection: Best research evidence and other considerations. *Journal of Behavioral Health Services & Research, 35,* 170–178.

Nelson-Gray, R. O. (2003). Treatment utility of psychological assessment. *Psychological Assessment, 15,* 521–531.

Neuner, F., Schauer, M., Klaschik, C., Karunakara, U., & Elbert, T. (2004). A comparison of narrative exposure therapy, supportive counseling, and psychoeducation for treating posttraumatic stress disorder in an African refugee settlement. *Journal of Consulting and Clinical Psychology, 72,* 579–587.

Newman, D. L., Moffitt, T. E., Caspi, A., & Silva, P. A. (1998). Comorbid mental disorders: Implications for treatment and sample selection. *Journal of Abnormal Psychology, 107,* 305–311.

Newman, M. G., Erickson, T., Przeworski, A., & Dzus, E. (2003). Self-help and minimal-contact therapies for anxiety disorders: Is human contact necessary for therapeutic efficacy? *Journal of Clinical Psychology, 59,* 251–274.

Newsom, C. R., Archer, R. P., Trumbetta, S., & Gottesman, I. I. (2003). Changes in adolescent response patterns on the MMPI/MMPI-A across four decades. *Journal of Personality Assessment, 81,* 74–84.

Nezu, A. M., & Nezu, C. M. (1993). Identifying and selecting target problems for clinical interventions: A problem-solving model. *Psychological Assessment, 5,* 254–263.

Nichols, D. S. (2001). *Essentials of MMPI-2 assessment.* New York: John Wiley & Sons.

Nichols, D. S. (2006). The trials of separating bath water from baby: A review and critique of the MMPI-2 restructured clinical scales. *Journal of Personality Assessment, 87,* 121–138.

Niemeyer, H., Musch, J., & Pietrowsky, R. (2013). Publication bias of meta-analyses of efficacy of psychotherapeutic interventions for depression. *Journal of Consulting and Clinical Psychology, 81,* 58–74.

Nisbett, R. E., Aronson, J., Blair, C., Dickens, W., Flynn, J., Halpern, D. F., & Turkheimer, E. (2012). Intelligence: New findings and theoretical developments. *American Psychologist, 67,* 130–159.

Norcross, J. C. (1990). An eclectic definition of psychotherapy. In J. K. Zeig & W. M. Munion (Eds.), *What is psychotherapy? Contemporary perspectives* (pp. 218–220). San Francisco, CA: Jossey-Bass.

Norcross, J. C. (Ed). (2002). *Psychotherapy relationships that work: Therapist contributions and responsiveness to patients.* London: Oxford University Press.

Norcross, J. C. (Ed.). (2011). *Psychotherapy relationships that work: Evidence-based responsiveness* (2nd ed.). New York: Oxford University Press.

Norcross, J. C., Campbell, L. F., Grohol, J. M., Santrock, J. W., Selagea, F., & Sommer, R. (2013). *Self-help that works: Resources to improve emotional health and strengthen relationships.* New York: Oxford University Press.

Norcross, J. C., Ellis, J. L., & Sayette, M. A. (2010). Getting in and getting money: A comparative analysis of admission standards, acceptance rates, and financial assistance across the research–practice continuum in clinical psychology programs. *Training and Education in Professional Psychology, 4,* 99–104.

Norcross, J. C., & Goldfried, M. R. (1992). *Handbook of psychotherapy integration.* New York: Basic Books.

Norcross, J. C., & Karpiak, C. P. (2012). Clinical psychologists in the 2010s: 50 years of the APA Division of Clinical Psychology. *Clinical Psychology: Science and Practice, 19,* 1–12.

Norcross, J. C., Kohout, J. L., & Wicherski, M. (2005). Graduate study in psychology: 1971–2004. *American Psychologist, 60,* 959–975.

Norcross, J. C., Koocher, G. P, & Garofalo, A. (2006). Discredited psychological treatments and tests: A Delphi poll. *Professional Psychology: Research and Practice, 37,* 515–522.

Norcross, J. C., Sayette, M. A., Mayne, T. J., Karg, R. S., & Turkson, M. A. (1998). Selecting a doctoral program in professional psychology: Some comparisons among Ph.D. counseling, Ph.D. clinical, and Psy.D. clinical psychology programs. *Professional Psychology: Research and Practice, 29,* 609–614.

Norton, J., De Roquefeuil, G., Boulenger, J.-P., Ritchie, K., Mann, A., & Tylee, A. (2007). Use of the PRIME-MD patient health questionnaire for estimating the prevalence of psychiatric disorders in French primary care: Comparison of family practitioner estimates and relationship to psychotropic medication use. *General Hospital Psychiatry, 29,* 285–293.

Nowak, C., & Heinrichs, N. (2008). A comprehensive meta-analysis of Triple P-Positive Parenting program using hierarchal linear modeling: Effectiveness and moderating variables. *Clinical Child and Family Psychology Review, 11*, 114–144.

Nunnally, J. C., & Bernstein, I. H. (1994). *Psychometric theory* (3rd ed.). New York: McGraw-Hill.

O'Brien, W. H. (1995). Inaccuracies in the estimation of functional relationships using self-monitoring data. *Journal of Behavior Therapy and Experimental Psychiatry, 26*, 351–357.

Ogden, T., & Hagen, K. A. (2008). Treatment effectiveness of parent management training in Norway: A randomized controlled trial of children with conduct problems. *Journal of Consulting and Clinical Psychology, 76*, 607–621.

Ohayon, M. M. (2005). Relationship between chronic painful physical conditions and insomnia. *Journal of Psychiatric Research, 39*, 151–159.

Olatunji, B. O., Cisler, J. M., & Tolin, D. F. (2010). A meta-analysis of the influence of comorbidity on treatment outcome in the anxiety disorders. *Clinical Psychology Review, 30*, 642–654.

Oldham, M., Kellett, S., Miles, E., & Sheeran, P. (2012). Interventions to increase attendance at psychotherapy: A meta-analysis of randomized controlled trials. *Journal of Consulting and Clinical Psychology, 80*, 928–939.

Olds, D. L. (2002). Prenatal and infancy home visiting by nurses: From randomized trials to community replication. *Prevention Science, 3*, 153–172.

Olds, D. L. (2006). The nurse-family partnership: An evidence-based preventive intervention. *Infant Mental Health Journal, 27*, 5–25.

Olfson, M., & Marcus, S. C. (2010) National trends in outpatient psychotherapy. *American Journal of Psychiatry, 167*, 1456–1463.

Ollendick, T. H., & King, N. J. (2004). Empirically supported treatments for children and adolescents: Advances toward evidence-based practice. In P. M., Barrett & T. H. Ollendick (Eds.), *Interventions that work with children and adolescents: Prevention and treatment* (pp. 3–25). New York: John Wiley & Sons.

Olweus, D. (1993). *Bullying at school: What we know and what we can do.* Oxford: Blackwell.

O'Riordan, B., & Carr, A. (2002). Prevention of physical abuse. In A. Carr (Ed.), *Prevention: What works with children and adolescents? A critical review of psychological prevention programmes for children, adolescents and their families* (pp. 154–180). Hove, UK: BrunnerRoutledge.

Orlinsky, D. E., Rønnestad, M. H., & Willutzki, U. (2004). Fifty years of psychotherapy process-outcome research: Continuity and change. In M. J. Lambert (Ed.), *Bergin and Garfield's handbook of psychotherapy and behavior change* (5th ed., pp. 307–389). New York: John Wiley & Sons.

Ormel, J., Petukhova, M., Chatterji, S., AguilarGaxiola, S., Alonso, J., Angermeyer, M. C., et al. (2008). Disability and treatment of specific mental and physical disorders across the world. *British Journal of Psychiatry, 192*, 368–375.

Osterholm, M. T., Kelley, N. S., Sommer, A., & Belongia, E. A. (2012). Efficacy and effectiveness of influenza vaccines: A systematic review and meta-analysis. *Lancet: Infectious Diseases, 12*, 36–44.

Pachana, N. A., Helmes, E., & Koder, D. (2006). Guidelines for the provision of psychological services for older adults. *Australian Psychologist, 41*, 15–22.

Packer, I. K. (2008). Specialized practice in forensic psychology: Opportunities and obstacles. *Professional Psychology: Research and Practice, 39*, 245–249.

Palmiter, D. J. (2004). A survey of the assessment practices of child and adolescent clinicians. *American Journal of Orthopsychiatry, 74*, 122–128.

Parker, J. D. A., Saklofske, D. H., Wood, L. M., Eastabrook, J. M., & Taylor, R. N. (2005). Stability and change in emotional intelligence: Exploring the transition to young adulthood. *Journal of Individual Differences, 26*, 100–106.

Parker, K. C. H., Hanson, R. K., & Hunsley, J. (1988). MMPI, Rorschach, and WAIS: A meta-analytic comparison of reliability, stability, and validity. *Psychological Bulletin, 103*, 367–373.

Patsopoulos, N. A., Analatos, A. A., & Ioannidis, J. P. A. (2005). Relative citation impact of various study designs in the health sciences. *Journal of the American Medical Association, 293*, 2362–2366.

Patterson, G. R. (1982). *Coercive family process.* Eugene, OR: Castilia.

Patterson, G. R. (2005). The next generation of PMTO models. *The Behavior Therapist, 28*, 27–33.

Paykina, N.L., Greenhill, L., & Gorman, J. M. (2007). Pharmacological treatments for attention-deficit/hyperactivity disorder. In P. E. Nathan, & J. M. Gorman (Eds.). *A guide to treatments that work* (3rd ed., pp. 29–70). New York: Oxford University Press.

Pelham, W. E., & Fabiano, G. A. (2008). Evidence-based psychosocial treatments for attention-deficit/hyperactivity disorder. *Journal of Clinical Child and Adolescent Psychology, 37*, 184–214.

Pelham, W. E., Fabiano, G. A., & Massetti, G.M. (2005). Evidence-based assessment of attention deficit hyperactivity disorder in children and adolescents. *Journal of Clinical Child and Adolescent Psychology, 34*, 449–476.

Perle, J. G., Langsam, L. C., & Nierenberg, B. (2011). Controversy clarified: An updated review of clinical psychology and tele-health. *Clinical Psychology Review, 31*, 1247–1258.

Perle, J. G., Langsam, L. C., Randel, A., Lutchman, S., Levine, A. B., Odland, A. P., et al. (2013). Attitudes toward psychological telehealth: Current and future psychologists' opinions of Internet-based interventions. *Journal of Clinical Psychology, 69*, 100–113.

Perls, F. S., Hefferline, R. F., & Goodman, P. (1951). *Gestalt therapy.* New York: Julian Press.

Persons, J. B. (1989). *Cognitive therapy in practice: A case formulation approach.* New York: Norton.

Persons, J. B. (2008). *The case formulation approach to cognitive-behavior therapy.* Washington, DC: APA Publications.

Persons, J. B., & Bertagnolli, A. (1999). Inter-rater reliability of cognitive-behavioral case formulations of depression: A replication. *Cognitive Therapy & Research, 23*, 271–283.

Persons, J. B., Davidson, J., & Tompkins, M. A. (2001). *Essential components of cognitive-behavior therapy for depression.* Washington, DC: American Psychological Association.

Peterson, D. R. (2004). Science, scientism, and professional responsibility. *Clinical Psychology: Science and Practice, 11*, 196–210.

Peterson, R., McHolland, J., Bent, R., David-Russell, E., Edwall, G., Polite, K., Singer, D., & Stricker, G. (1991). *The core curriculum in professional psychology.* Washington, DC: American Psychological Association.

Petrie, J., Bunn, F., & Byrne, G. (2007). Parenting programmes for preventing tobacco, alcohol, or drugs misuse in children under 18: A systematic review. *Health Education Research, 22*, 177–191.

Petry, N. M., Tennen, H., & Affleck, G. (2000). Stalking the elusive client variable in psychotherapy research. In C. R. Snyder & R.E. Ingram (Eds.), *Handbook of psychological change: Psychotherapy processes & practices for the 21st century* (pp. 88–108). New York: John Wiley & Sons.

Pew Internet. (2013). *Health online 2013.* Retrieved from http://www.pewinternet.org/Reports/2013/Health-online/Summary-of-Findings.aspx

Phillips, E. L. (1991). George Washington University's international data on psychotherapy delivery systems: Modeling new approaches to the study of therapy. In L. E. Beutler & M. Crago (Eds.), *Psychotherapy research: an international review of programmatic studies* (pp. 263–273). Washington, DC: American Psychological Association.

Piotrowski, C., Belter, R. W., & Keller, J. W. (1998). The impact of "managed care" on the practice of psychological testing: Preliminary findings. *Journal of Personality Assessment, 70*, 441–447.

Plous, S., & Zimbardo, P. G. (1986). Attributional biases among clinicians: A comparison of psychoanalysts and behavior therapists. *Journal of Consulting and Clinical Psychology, 54*, 568–570.

Poole, G., Hunt Matheson, D., & Cox, D. N. (2005). *The psychology of health and health care: A Canadian perspective* (2nd ed). Toronto, ON: Pearson, Prentice Hall.

Pope, K. S. (2003). Logical fallacies in psychology: 18 types. Retrieved July 8, 2004, from http://www.kspope.com/fallacies/fallacies.php

Price, J. M., Chamberlain, P., Landsverk, J., Reid, J. B., Leve, L. D., & Laurent, H. (2008). Effects of foster parent training intervention on placement changes of children in foster care. *Child Maltreatment, 13*, 64–75.

Prinz, R. J., & Sanders, M. R. (2007). Adopting a population-level approach to parenting and family support interventions. *Clinical Psychology Review, 27*, 739–749.

Prinz, R., Sanders, M., Shapiro, C., Whitaker, D., & Lutzker, J. (2009). Population-based prevention of child maltreatment: The US Triple P system population trial. *Prevention Science, 10*, 1–12.

Proudfoot, J., Ryden, C., Everitt, B., Shapiro, D. A., Goldberg, D., Mann, A., et al. (2004). Clinical efficacy of computerised cognitive-behavioural therapy for anxiety and depression in primary care: Randomised controlled trial. *British Journal of Psychiatry, 185,* 46–54.

Rachman, S. (1971). *The effects of psychotherapy.* Oxford: Pergamon Press.

Rae, W. A., Jensen-Doss, A., Bowden, R., Mendoza, M., & Banda, T. (2008). Prescription privileges for psychologists: Opinions of pediatric psychologists and pediatricians. *Journal of Pediatric Psychology, 33,* 176–184.

Rae, W. A., & Sullivan, J. R. (2003). Ethical considerations in clinical psychology research. In M. C. Roberts & S. S. Ilardi (Eds.), *Handbook of research methods in clinical psychology* (pp. 52–70). Oxford: Blackwell Publishing Ltd.

Rai, D., Skapinakis, P., Wiles, N., Lewis, G., & Araya, R. (2010). Common mental disorders, subthreshold symptoms and disability: Longitudinal study. *British Journal of Psychiatry, 197,* 411–412.

Raimy, V. C. (Ed.). (1950). *Training in clinical psychology.* New York: Prentice-Hall.

Rapaport, C., Gill, M., & Schafer, J. (1968). *Diagnostic psychological testing* (rev. ed.). Chicago: Year Book.

Reese, R. J., Toland, M. D., Slone, N. C., & Norsworthy, L. A. (2010). Effect of client feedback on couple psychotherapy outcomes. *Psychotherapy, 47,* 616–630.

Regier, D. A., Kaelber, C. T., Rae, D. S., Farmer, M. E., Knauper, B., Kessler, R. C., et al. (1998). Limitations of diagnostic criteria and assessment instruments for mental disorders: Implications for research and policy. *Archives of General Psychiatry, 55,* 109–115.

Regier, D. A., Narrow, W. E., Clarke, D. E., Kraemer, H. C., Kuramoto, S. J., Kuhl, E. A., & Kupfer, D. J. (2013). DSM-5 field trials in the United States and Canada. Part II: Test-retest reliability of selected categorical diagnoses. *American Journal of Psychiatry, 170,* 59–70.

Retzlaff, P. D., & Dunn, T. (2003). The Millon Clinical Multiaxial Inventory-III. In L. E. Beutler & G. Groth-Marnat (Eds.), *Integrative assessment of adult personality* (2nd ed., pp. 192–226). New York: Guilford Press.

Reyno, S. M., & McGrath, P. J. (2006). Predictors of parent training efficacy for child externalizing behaviour problems—a meta-analytic review. *Journal of Child Psychology and Psychiatry, 47,* 99–111.

Riccio, C. A., & French, C. L. (2004). The status of empirical support for treatments of attention deficits. *The Clinical Neuropsychologist,* 18, 528–558.

Richards, D., & Richardson, T. (2012). Computer-based psychological treatments for depression: A systematic review and meta-analysis. *Clinical Psychology Review, 32,* 329–342.

Richters, J. E., Arnold, L. E., Jensen, P. S., Abikoff, H., Conners, C. K., Greenhill, L. L., et al. (1995). The National Institute of Mental Health Collaborative Multisite Multimodal Treatment Study of Children with Attention-Deficit Hyperactivity Disorder (MTA) I: background and rationale. *Journal of the American Academy of Child and Adolescent Psychiatry, 34,* 987–1000.

Ridley, C. R., & Kelly, S. M. (2006). Multicultural considerations in case formulation. In T. D. Eells (Ed.), *Handbook of psychotherapy case formulation* (2nd ed., pp. 33–64). New York: Guilford Press.

Roberts, C., Kane, R., Thomson, H., Hart, B., & Bishop, B. (2003). The prevention of depressive symptoms in rural school children: A randomized controlled trial. *Journal of Consulting and Clinical Psychology, 71,* 622–628.

Roberts, M. C., Lazicki-Puddy, T. A., Puddy, R. W., & Johnson, R. J. (2003). The outcomes of psychotherapy with adolescents: A practitioner-friendly research review. *Journal of Clinical Psychology/In session, 59,* 1177–1191.

Robiner, W. N. (2006). The mental health professions: Workforce supply and demand issues, and challenges. *Clinical Psychology Review, 26,* 600–625.

Rogers, C. R. (1951). *Client centered therapy.* Boston: Houghton Mifflin.

Rogers, R., Sewell, K. W., Harrison, K. S., & Jordan, M. J. (2006). The MMPI-2 restructured clinical scales: A paradigmatic shift in scale development. *Journal of Personality Assessment, 87,* 139–147.

Rogers, S. J., & Vismara, L. A. (2008). Evidence-based comprehensive treatments for early autism. *Journal of Clinical Child and Adolescent Psychology, 37,* 8–38.

Rohling, M. L., Faust, M. E., Beverly, B., & Demakis, G. (2009). Effectiveness of cognitive rehabilitation following acquired brain injury: A meta-analytic re-examination of Cicerone et al.'s (2000, 2005) systematic reviews. *Neuropsychology, 23,* 20–39.

Roid, G. (2003). *Stanford-Binet Intelligence Scales* (5th ed.). Itasca, IL: Riverside Publishing.

Romanow, R. J., & Marchildon, G. P. (2003). Psychological services and the future of health care in Canada. *Canadian Psychology, 44,* 283–295.

Rosa-Alcázar, A. I., Sánchez-Meca, J., Gómez-Conesa, A., & Marín-Martínez, F. (2008). Psychological treatment of obsessive–compulsive disorder: A meta-analysis. *Clinical Psychology Review, 28,* 1311–1325.

Rosenthal, R., & DiMatteo, M. R. (2001). Meta-analysis: Recent developments in quantitative methods for literature reviews. *Annual Review of Psychology, 52,* 59–82.

Rosenzweig, S. (1936). Some implicit common factors in diverse methods of psychotherapy. *American Journal of Orthopsychiatry, 6,* 412–415.

Rossini, E. D., & Moretti, R. J. (1997). Thematic Apperception Test (TAT) interpretation: Practice recommendations from a survey of clinical psychology doctoral programs accredited by the American Psychological Association. *Professional Psychology: Research and Practice, 28,* 393–398.

Roth, A., & Fonagy, P. (1996). *What works for whom? A critical review of psychotherapy research.* New York: Guilford Press.

Roth, A., & Fonagy, P. (2005). *What works for whom? A critical review of psychotherapy research* (2nd ed.). New York: Guilford Press.

Rothbaum, B. O., & Schwartz, A. C. (2002). Exposure therapy for posttraumatic stress disorder. *American Journal of Psychotherapy, 56,* 59–75.

Rotheram-Borus, M. J., Swendeman, D., & Chorpita, B. F. (2012). Disruptive innovations for designing and diffusing evidence-based interventions. *American Psychologist, 67,* 463–476

Rumstein-McKean, O., & Hunsley, J. (2001). Interpersonal and family functioning of female survivors of childhood sexual abuse. *Clinical Psychology Review, 21,* 471–490.

Rupert, P. A., & Kent J. S. (2007). Gender and work setting differences in career-sustaining behaviors and burnout among professional psychologists. *Professional Psychology: Research and Practice, 38,* 88–96.

Ruscio, J., & Ruscio, A. M. (2000). Informing the continuity controversy: A taxometric analysis of depression. *Journal of Abnormal Psychology, 109,* 473–487.

Ryan, J. J., Glass, L. A., & Brown, C. N. (2007). Administration time estimates for Wechsler Intelligence Scale for Children-IV subtests, composites, and short forms. *Journal of Clinical Psychology, 63,* 309–318.

Ryan, J. J., & Schnakenberg-Ott, S. D. (2003). Scoring reliability on the Wechsler Adult Intelligence Scale-Third Edition (WAIS-III). *Assessment, 10,* 151–159.

Ryba, N. L., Cooper, V. G., & Zapf, P. A. (2003). Juvenile competence to stand trial evaluations: A survey of current practices and test usage among psychologists. *Professional Psychology: Research and Practice, 34,* 499–507.

Sabin-Farrell, R., & Turpin, G. (2003). Vicarious traumatization: implications for the mental health of health workers. *Clinical Psychology Review, 23,* 449–480.

Sackett, D. L., Rosenberg, W. M., Gray, J. A., Haynes, R. B., & Richardson, W. S. (1996). Evidence-based medicine: What it is and what it isn't. *British Medical Journal, 312,* 71–72.

Salmivalli, C., Kärnä, A, & Poskiparta, E. (2011). Counteracting bullying in Finland: The KiVa program and its effect on different forms of being bullied. *International Journal of Behavioral Development, 35,* 405–411.

Salmon, K. (2001). Remembering and reporting by children: The influence of cues and props. *Clinical Psychology Review, 21,* 267–300.

Salovey, P., & Mayer, J. D., (1990). Emotional intelligence. *Imagination, Cognition and Personality, 9,* 185–211.

Sanders, M. R. (2008). The Triple P-Positive Parenting Program as a public health approach to strengthening parenting. *Journal of Family Psychology, 22* (4), 506–517.

Sanders, M. R. (2012). Development, evaluation, and multinational dissemination of the Triple P-Positive Parenting Program. *Annual Review of Clinical Psychology, 8,* 345–379.

Sanders, M. R., Baker, S., & Turner, K. M. T. (2012). A randomized controlled trial evaluating the efficacy of Triple P Online with parents of children with early-onset conduct problems. *Behaviour Research and Therapy, 50,* 675–684.

Sanders, M. R., Markie-Dadds, C., Turner, K., & Ralph, A. (2004). Using the Triple P system of intervention to prevent behavioural problems in children and adolescents. In P. M. Barrett & T. H. Ollendick (Eds.), *Interventions that work with children and adolescents: Prevention and*

Treatment (pp. 489–516). Chichester, UK: John Wiley & Sons.

Santor, D. A., & Coyne, J. C. (2001). Evaluating the continuity of symptomatology between depressed and nondepressed individuals. *Journal of Abnormal Psychology, 110,* 216–225.

Sareen, J., Cox, B. J., Afifi, T. O., Stein, M. B., Belik, S-L., Meadows, G., & Asmundson, G. J. G. (2007). Combat and peacekeeping operations in relation to prevalence of mental disorders and perceived need for care: Findings for a large representative sample of military personnel. *Archives of General Psychiatry, 64,* 843–852.

Sattler, J. M. (1992). *Assessment of children* (3rd ed.). San Diego, CA: Jerome Sattler.

Sattler, J. M. (2001). *Assessment of children: Cognitive applications* (4th ed.). San Diego, CA: Author.

Saunders, S. M. (1993). Applicants' experience of the process of seeking therapy. *Psychotherapy, 30,* 554–564.

Saunders, S. M. (1996). Applicants' experience of social support in the process of seeking psychotherapy. *Psychotherapy, 33,* 617–627.

Saxon, D., & Barkham, M. (2012). Patterns of therapist variability: Therapist effects and the contribution of patient severity and risk. *Journal of Consulting and Clinical Psychology, 80,* 535–546.

Sayette, M. A., Norcross, J. C., & Dimoff, J. D. (2011). The heterogeneity of clinical psychology Ph.D. programs and the distinctiveness of APCS programs. *Clinical Psychology: Science & Practice, 18,* 4–11.

Schachar, R., Jadad, A. R., Gauld, M., Boyle, M., Booker, L., Snider, A., et al. (2002). Attention-deficit hyperactivity disorder: Critical appraisal of extended treatment studies. *Canadian Journal of Psychiatry, 47,* 337–348.

Schneiderman, N., Ironson, G., & Siegel, S. D. (2005). Stress and health: Psychological, behavioral and biological determinants. *Annual Review of Clinical Psychology, 1,* 607–628.

Schoenberg, M. R., Lange, R. T., & Saklofske, D. H. (2007). A proposed method to estimate premorbid Full Scale Intelligence Quotient (FSIA) for the Canadian Wechsler Intelligence Scale for Children-Fourth Edition (WISC-IV) using demographic and combined estimation procedures. *Journal of Clinical and Experimental Neuropsychology, 29,* 867–878.

Schulte, D., & Hahlweg, K. (2000). A new law for governing psychotherapy for psychologists in Germany: Impact on training and mental health policy. *Clinical Psychology: Science and Practice, 7,* 259–263.

Scogin, F. R., Hanson, A., & Welsh, D. (2003). Self-administered treatment in stepped-care models of depression treatment. *Journal of Clinical Psychology, 59,* 341–349.

Scotti, J. R., Morris, T. L., Ruggiero, K. J., & Wolfgang, J. (2002). *Post-traumatic stress disorder.* In M. Hersen (Ed.), *Clinical behaviour therapy: Adults and children* (pp. 361–382). New York: John Wiley & Sons.

Sechrest, L. (1963). Incremental validity: A recommendation. *Educational and Psychological Measurement, 23,* 153–158.

Seitz, J., & O'Neill, P. (1996). Ethical decision-making and the code of ethics of the Canadian Psychological Association. *Canadian Psychology, 37,* 23–30.

Seligman, L. D., Goza, A. B., & Ollendick, T. H. (2004). Treatment of depression in children and adolescents. In P. M. Barrett & T. H. Ollendick (Eds.), *Interventions that work with children and adolescents: Prevention and treatment* (pp. 301–328). New York: John Wiley & Sons.

Selwood, A., Thorgrimsen, L., & Orrell, M. (2005). Quality of life in dementia—a one year follow-up study. *International Journal of Geriatric Psychiatry, 20,* 232–237.

Sexton, T. L., Alexander, J. F., & Mease, A. L. (2004). Levels of evidence for the models and mechanisms of therapeutic change in family and couple therapy. In M. L. Lambert (Ed.), *Bergin and Garfield's handbook of psychotherapy and behavior change* (5th ed., pp. 590–646). New York: John Wiley & Sons.

Sexton, T. L., Datchi, C., Evans, L., LaFollette, J., & Wright, L. (2013). The effectiveness of couple and family-based clinical interventions. In M. L. Lambert (Ed.), *Bergin and Garfield's handbook of psychotherapy and behavior change* (6th ed., 587–639). Hoboken, NJ: John Wiley & Sons.

Shadish, W. R., Matt, G. E., Navarro, A. M., & Phillips, G. (2000). The effects of psychological therapies under clinically representative conditions: A meta-analysis. *Psychological Bulletin, 126,* 512–529.

Shaffer, T. W., Erdberg, P., & Meyer, G. J. (2007). Introduction to the *JPA* special supplement on the international reference samples for the Rorschach Comprehensive System. *Journal of Personality Assessment, 89,* S2–S6.

Shapiro, A., & Taylor, M. (2002). Effects of a community-based early intervention program on the subjective well-being, institutionalization, and mortality of low-income elders. *The Gerontologist, 42,* 334–341.

Shapiro, E. S., & Cole, C. L. (1999). Self-monitoring in assessing children's problems. *Psychological Assessment, 11,* 448–457.

Shea, S. (1991). Practical use of DSM-III-R. In M. Hersen & S. M. Turner (Eds.), *Adult psychopathology and diagnosis* (2nd ed., pp. 23–43). New York: John Wiley & Sons.

Sherman, M. D., & Thelen, M. H. (1998). Distress and professional impairment among psychologists in clinical practice. *Professional Psychology: Research & Practice, 29,* 79–85.

Shiffman, S., Hufford, M., Hickcox, M., Paty, J. A., Gnys, M., & Kassel, J. D. (1997). Remember that? A comparison of real-time versus retrospective recall of smoking lapses. *Journal of Consulting and Clinical Psychology, 65,* 292–300.

Shiffman, S., Stone, A. A., & Hufford, M. R. (2008). Ecological momentary assessment. *Annual Review of Clinical Psychology, 4,* 1–32.

Shimokawa, K., Lambert, M. J., & Smart, D. W. (2010). Enhancing treatment outcome of patients at risk for treatment failure: Meta-analytic and mega-analytic review of a psychotherapy quality assurance system. *Journal of Consulting and Clinical Psychology, 78,* 298–311.

Shirk, S., Karver, M., & Brown, R. (2011). The alliance in child and adolescent psychotherapy: A meta-analysis. *Psychotherapy, 48,* 17–24.

Shojaei, T., Wazana, A., Pitrou, I., Gilbert, F., Bergeron, L., Valla, J. P., & Kovess-Masfety, V. (2009). Psychometric properties of the Dominic Interactive in a large French sample. *Canadian Journal of Psychiatry, 54,* 767–776.

Shojaei, T., Wazana, A., Pitrou, I., Gilbert, F., Bergeron, L., Valla, J. P., & Kovess-Masfety, V. (2009). Psychometric properties of the Dominic Interactive in a large French sample. *Canadian Journal of Psychiatry, 54,* 767–776.

Sholomskas, A. J., Chevron, E. S., Prusoff, B. A., & Berry, C. (1983). Short-term interpersonal therapy (IPT) with the depressed elderly: Case reports and discussion. *American Journal of Psychotherapy, 37,* 552–566.

Shore, J. H., Savin, D., Orton, H., Beals, J., & Manson, S. M. (2007). Diagnostic reliability of telepsychiatry in American Indian veterans. *American Journal of Psychiatry, 164,* 115–118.

Siegenthaler, E., Munder, T., & Egger, M. (2012). Effect of preventive interventions in mentally ill parents on the mental health of the offspring: Systematic review and meta-analysis. *Journal of the American Academy of Child and Adolescent Psychiatry, 51,* 8–26.

Siev, J., & Chambless, D. L. (2007). Specificity of treatment effects: Cognitive therapy and relaxation for generalized anxiety and panic disorders. *Journal of Consulting and Clinical Psychology, 75,* 513–522.

Silverman, D. (2011). *Interpreting qualitative data* (4th ed.). Thousand Oaks, CA: Sage Publications.

Silverman, W. H. (1996). Cookbooks, manuals, and paint-by-numbers: Psychotherapy in the 90s. *Psychotherapy, 33,* 207–215.

Silverman, W. K., & Hinshaw, S. P. (2008). The second special issue on evidence-based psychosocial treatments for children and adolescents: A 10-year update. *Journal of Clinical Child and Adolescent Psychology, 37,* 1–7.

Silverman, W. K., & Ollendick, T. H. (2008). Child and adolescent anxiety disorders. In J. Hunsley & E. J. Mash (Eds.), *A guide to assessments that work* (pp. 181–206). New York: Oxford University Press.

Silverman, W. K., Ortiz, C. D., Viswesvaran, C., Burns, B. J., Kolko, D. J., Putnam, F. W., & Amaya-Jackson, L. (2008). Evidence-based psychosocial treatments for children and adolescents exposed to traumatic events. *Journal of Clinical Child and Adolescent Psychology, 37,* 156–183.

Silverman, W. K., Pina, A. A., & Viswesvaran, C. (2008). Evidence-based psychosocial treatments for phobic and anxiety disorders in children and adolescents. *Journal of Clinical Child and Adolescent Psychology, 37,* 105–130.

Sinclair, C. (1993). Codes of ethics and standards of practice. In K. S. Dobson & D. G. Dobson (Eds.), *Professional psychology in Canada* (pp. 167–224). Toronto, ON: Hogrefe & Huber.

Sinclair, C. (1998). Nine unique features of the Canadian code of ethics for psychologists. *Canadian Psychology, 39,* 167–176.

Singer, A. R., Cassin, S. E., & Dobson, K. S. (2005). The role of gender in the career aspirations of professional psychology graduates: Are there more similarities than differences? *Canadian Psychology, 46,* 215–222.

Sitarenios, G., & Kovacs, M. (1999). Use of the Children's Depression Inventory. In M. E.

Maruish (Ed.), *The use of psychological testing for treatment planning and outcomes assessment* (2nd ed., pp. 267–298). Mahwah, NJ: Erlbaum.

Sloan, D. M., Gallagher, M. W., Feinstein, B. A., Lee, D. J., & Pruneau, G. M. (2011). Efficacy of telehealth treatments for posttraumatic stress-related symptoms: A meta-analysis. *Cognitive Behaviour Therapy, 40,* 111–125.

Smith, J. D., & Dumont, F. (2002). Confidence in psychodiagnosis: What makes us so sure? *Clinical Psychology and Psychotherapy, 9,* 292–298.

Smith, M. L., & Glass, G. V. (1977). Meta-analysis of psychotherapy outcome studies. *American Psychologist, 32,* 752–760.

Smith, M. L., Glass, G. V., & Miller, T. I. (1980). *The benefits of psychotherapy.* Baltimore: Johns Hopkins University Press.

Smith, R. E., Fagan, C., Wilson, N. L., Chen, J., Corona, M., Nguyen, H., et al. (2011). Internet-based approaches to collaborative therapeutic assessment: New opportunities for professional psychologists. *Professional Psychology: Research and Practice, 42,* 494–504.

Smith, S. R., Wiggins, C. M., & Gorske, T. T. (2007). A survey of psychological assessment feedback practices. *Assessment, 14,* 310–319.

Smith, T. B., Rodríguez, M. M. D., & Bernal, G. (2011). Culture. In J. C. Norcross (Ed.), *Psychotherapy relationships that work* (2nd ed., pp. 316–335). New York: Oxford University Press.

Smith, T. C., Ryan, M. A. K., Wingard, D. L., Slymen, D. J., Sallis, J. F., & Kritz-Silverstein, D. (2008). New onset and persistent symptoms of post-traumatic stress disorder self-reported after deployment and combat exposures: Prospective population-based US military cohort study. *British Medical Journal.* Retrieved February 29, 2008, from www.bmj.com

Smith, T. W., Nealey, J. B., & Hamann, H. A. (2000). Health psychology. In C. R. Snyder & R. E. Ingram (Eds.), *Handbook of psychological change: Psychotherapy processes and practices for the 21st century* (pp. 562–590). New York: John Wiley & Sons.

Snyder, D. K., Heyman, R. E., & Haynes, S. N. (2008). Couple distress. In J. Hunsley & E. J. Mash (Eds.), *A guide to assessments that work* (pp. 437–463). New York: Oxford University Press.

Sommers-Flanagan, J., & Sommers-Flanagan, R. (2012). *Clinical interviewing* (4th ed). New York: John Wiley & Sons.

Sonuga-Barke, E. J. S., Daley, D., & Thompson, M. (2002). Does maternal ADHD reduce the effectiveness of parent training for preschool children's ADHD? *Journal of the American Academy of Child and Adolescent Psychiatry, 41,* 696–702.

Sörensen, S., Pinquart, M., & Duberstein, P. (2002). How effective are interventions with caregivers? *The Gerontologist, 42,* 356–372.

Spangler, W. D. (1992). Validity of questionnaire and TAT measures of need for achievement: Two meta-analyses. *Psychological Bulletin, 112,* 140–154.

Spearman, C. (1927). *The abilities of man.* New York: Macmillan.

Spengler, P. M., White, M. J., Ægisdóttir, S., Maugherman, A. S., Anderson, L. A., Cook, R. S., et al. (2009). The meta-analysis of clinical judgment project: Effects of experience on judgment accuracy. *The Counseling Psychologist, 37,* 350–399.

Spinhoven, P., Giesen-Bloo, J., van Dyck, R., Kooiman, K., & Arntz, A. (2007). The therapeutic alliance in schema-focused therapy and transference-focused psychotherapy for borderline personality disorder. *Journal of Consulting and Clinical Psychology, 75,* 104–115.

Spitzer, R. L., Kroenke, K., Linzer, M., Hahn, S. R., Williams, J. B., deGruy, F. V., et al. (1995). Health-related quality of life in primary care patients with mental disorders: Results from the PRIME-MD 1000 study. *Journal of the American Medical Association, 282,* 1511–1517.

Spitzer, R. L., Williams, J. B. W., & Endicott, J. (2012). Standards for DSM-5 reliability. *American Journal of Psychiatry, 169,* 537.

Statistics Canada. (2003, September 3). Canadian Community Mental Health Survey: Mental health and well-being. *The Daily.* Retrieved November 11, 2004, from www.statcan.ca/Daily/English/030903/d0309 03a.htm

Statistics Canada. (2005). Insomnia. *The Daily, November 16, 2005.* Retrieved October 1, 2008, from www.statcan.ca

Statistics Canada. (September 2007). Factors associated with Internet use: Does rurality matter? *Rural and Small Town Canada Analysis Bulletin, Catalogue No. 21—6-XIE.*

Statistics Canada (2008). Chronic pain in seniors. *The Daily, February 21, 2008.* Retrieved October 1, 2008, from www.statcan.ca

Statistics Canada (2008a). 2006 Census: Ethnic origin, visible minorities, place of work and mode of transportation. *The Daily, April 2, 2008.* Retrieved May 1, 2008, from www.statcan.ca

Statistics Canada (2008b). Aboriginal Peoples in Canada in 2006: Inuit, Métis and First Nations, 2006 Census. *The Daily, January 15 2008.* Retrieved January 15, 2008, from www.statcan.ca

Statistics Canada. (2010). Chronic pain at ages 12–44. *Health Matters.* Catalogue no. 82-003-XPE. Retrieved from www.statcan.ca

Statistics Canada. (2011). *Canadian Internet use survey.* Retrieved from http://www.statcan.gc.ca/daily-quotidien/110525/dq110525b-eng.htm

Steenbarger, B. N. (1994). Duration and outcome in psychotherapy: An integrative review. *Professional Psychology: Research and Practice, 25,* 111–119.

Steering Committee of the Empirically Supported Therapy Relationship Task Force. (2001). Empirically supported therapy relationships: Conclusions and recommendations of the Division 29 Task Force. *Psychotherapy, 38,* 495–497.

Sternberg, R. (1985). *Beyond IQ: A triarchic theory of human intelligence.* New York: Cambridge University Press.

Sternberg, R. J., Nokes, K., Geissler, P. W., Prince, R., Okatcha, F., Bundy, D. A., et al. (2001). The relationship between academic and practical intelligence: A case study in Kenya. *Intelligence, 29,* 401–418.

Stewart, R. E., & Chambless, D. L. (2009). Cognitive-behavioral therapy for adult anxiety disorders in clinical practice: A meta-analysis of effectiveness studies. *Journal of Consulting and Clinical Psychology, 77,* 595–606.

Stice, E., Shaw, H., Bohon, C., Marti, C. N. & Rohde, P. (2009). A meta-analytic review of depression prevention programs for children and adolescents: Factors that predict the magnitude of intervention effects. *Journal of Consulting and Clinical Psychology, 77,* 486–503.

Stiles, W. B. (1988). Psychotherapy process-outcome correlations may be misleading. *Psychotherapy, 25,* 27–35.

Stiles, W. B., Leach, C., Barkham, M., Lucock, M., Iveson, S., Shapiro, D. A., et al. (2003). Early sudden gains in psychotherapy under routine clinic conditions: Practice-based evidence. *Journal of Consulting and Clinical Psychology, 71,* 14–21.

Stiles, W. B., & Shapiro, D. A. (1989). Abuse of the drug metaphor in psychotherapy process-outcome research. *Clinical Psychology Review, 9,* 521–543.

Stirman, S. W., Crits-Christoph, P., & DeRubeis, R. J. (2004). Achieving successful dissemination of empirically supported psychotherapies: A synthesis of dissemination theory. *Clinical Psychology: Science and Practice, 11,* 343–359.

Stirman, S. W., DeRubeis, R. J., Crits-Christoph, P., & Brody, P. E. (2003). Are samples in randomized controlled trials of psychotherapy representative of community outpatients? A new methodology and initial findings. *Journal of Consulting and Clinical Psychology, 71,* 963–972.

Stirman, S. W., DeRubeis, R. J., Crits-Christoph, P., & Rothman, A. (2005). Can the randomized controlled trial literature generalize to nonrandomized patients? *Journal of Consulting and Clinical Psychology, 73,* 127–135.

Stone, A. A., Schwartz, J. E., Neale, J. M., Shiffman, S., Marco, C. A., Hickcox, M., et al. (1998). A comparison of coping assessed by ecological momentary assessment and retrospective recall. *Journal of Personality and Social Psychology, 74,* 1670–1680.

Storch, E. A., Larson, M. J., Goodman, W. K., Rasmussen, S. A., Price, L. H., & Murphy, T. K. (2010). Development and psychometric evaluation of the Yale-Brown Obsessive-Compulsive Scale—Second Edition. *Psychological Assessment, 22,* 223–232.

Stormshak, E. A., & Dishion, T. J. (2002). An ecological approach to child and family clinical and counseling psychology. *Clinical Child and Family Psychology Review, 5,* 197–215.

Stout, C. E., & Cook, L. P. (1999). New areas for psychological assessment in general health care settings: What to do today to prepare for tomorrow. *Journal of Clinical Psychology, 55,* 797–812.

Strack, S. (2008). *Essentials of Millon inventories assessment* (3rd ed.). Hoboken, NJ: John Wiley & Sons.

Strack, S., & Millon, T. (2007). Contributions to the dimensional assessment of personality disorders using Millon's model and the Millon Clinical Multiaxial Inventory (MCMIIII). *Journal of Personality Assessment, 89,* 56–69.

Streiner, D. L. (2002). Breaking up is hard to do: The heartbreak of dichotomizing continuous data. *Canadian Journal of Psychiatry, 47,* 262–266.

Streiner, D. L. (2003). Being inconsistent about consistency: When coefficient alpha does and doesn't matter. *Journal of Personality Assessment, 80,* 217–222.

Streisand, R., & Efron, L. A. (2003). Pediatric sleep disorders. In R. M. Roberts (Ed.), *Handbook of pediatric psychology* (3rd ed., pp. 578–598). New York: Guilford Press.

Stringer, A. Y. (2003). Cognitive rehabilitation practice patterns: A survey of American Hospital Association rehabilitation programs. *The Clinical Neuropsychologist, 17,* 34–44.

Strupp, H. H., & Binder, J. (1984). *Psychotherapy in a new key.* New York: Basic Books.

Stuart, R. B., & Heiby, E. M. (2007). To prescribe or not prescribe: Eleven exploratory questions. *Scientific Review of Mental Health Practice, 5,* 4–32.

Stuart, R. B., & Lilienfeld, D. O. (2007). The evidence missing from evidence-based practice. *American Psychologist, 62,* 613–614.

Sue, D. W., & Sue, D. (2008). *Counseling the culturally different: Theory and practice* (5th ed.). New York: John Wiley & Sons.

Sugaya, L., Hasin, D. L., Olfson, M., Lin., K-H., Grant, B. F., & Blanco, C. (2012). Child physical abuse and mental health: A national study. *Journal of Traumatic Stress, 25,* 384–392.

Sullivan, G., Vasterling, J. J., Han, X., Tharp, A. T., Davis, T., Deitch, E. A., & Constans, J. I. (2013). Preexisting mental illness and risk for developing a new disorder after Hurricane Katrina. *Journal of Nervous and Mental Disease, 201,* 161–166.

Sullivan, H. S. (1953). *The interpersonal theory of psychiatry.* New York: Norton.

Summerfeldt, L. J., & Antony, M. M. (2002). Structured and semistructured diagnostic interviews. In M. M. Antony, & D. H. Barlow (Eds). *Handbook of assessment and treatment planning for psychological disorders* (pp. 3–37). New York: Guilford Press.

Sutin, A. R., Terracciano, A., Milaneschi, Y., An, Y., Ferrucci, L., & Zonderman, A. B. (in press). The trajectory of depressive symptoms across the adult lifespan. *JAMA Psychiatry.*

Swift, J. K., & Greenberg, R. P. (2012). Premature discontinuation in adult psychotherapy: A meta-analysis. *Journal of Consulting and Clinical Psychology, 80,* 547–559.

Takushi, R., & Uomoto, J. M. (2001). The clinical interview from a multicultural perspective. In L. A. Suzuki, J. G. Ponterotto, & P. J. Meller (Eds.). *Handbook of multicultural assessment: Clinical, psychological, and educational applications* (2nd ed. pp. 47–66) San Francisco: Jossey-Bass.

Tamaskar, P., & McGinnis, R. A. (2002). Declining student interest in psychiatry. *Journal of the American Medical Association, 287,* 1859.

Tang, T. Z., & DeRubeis, R. J. (1999). Sudden gains and critical sessions in cognitive-behavioral therapy for depression. *Journal of Consulting and Clinical Psychology, 67,* 894–904.

Tang, T. Z., DeRubeis, R. J., Beberman, R., & Pham, T. (2005). Cognitive changes, critical sessions, and sudden gains in cognitive-behavioral therapy for depression. *Journal of Consulting and Clinical Psychology, 73,* 168–172.

Tang, T. Z., DeRubeis, R. J., Hollon, S. D., Amsterdam, J., & Shelton, R. (2007). Sudden gains in cognitive therapy of depression and depression relapse/recurrence. *Journal of Consulting and Clinical Psychology, 75,* 404–408.

Tang, T. Z., Luborsky, L., & Andrusyna, T. (2002). Sudden gains in recovering from depression: Are they also found in psychotherapies other than cognitive-behavioural therapy? *Journal of Consulting and Clinical Psychology, 70,* 444–447.

Task Force on Promotion and Dissemination of Psychological Procedures. (1995). Training in and dissemination of empirically-validated psychological treatments: Report and recommendations. *The Clinical Psychologist, 48,* 3–23.

Taylor, S. E., & Brown, J. D. (1988). Illusion and well being: A social-psychological perspective on mental health. *Psychological Bulletin, 103,* 193–210.

Teglasi, H. (2010). *Essentials of TAT and other storytelling assessments* (2nd ed.). Hoboken, NJ: John Wiley & Sons.

Tellegen, A., Ben-Porath, Y. S., McNulty, J. L., Arbisi, P. A., Graham, J. R., & Kaemmer, B. (2003). *The MMPI-2 restructured clinical scales: Development, validation, and interpretation.* Minneapolis: University of Minnesota Press.

Tellegen, A., Ben-Porath, Y. S., Sellbom, M., Arbisi, P. A., McNulty, J. L., & Graham, J. R. (2006). Further evidence on the validity of the MMPI-2 restructured clinical scales: Addressing questions raised by Rogers, Sewell, Harrison, and Jordan and Nichols. *Journal of Personality Assessment, 87,* 148–171.

Teubert, D., & Pinquart, M. (2011). A meta-analytic review on the prevention of symptoms of anxiety in children and adolescents. *Journal of Anxiety Disorders, 25,* 1046–1059.

Teyber, E., & McClure, F. (2000). Therapist variables. In C. R. Snyder & R. E. Ingram (Eds.), *Handbook of psychological change: Psychotherapy processes & practices for the 21st century* (pp. 62–87). New York: John Wiley & Sons.

Tharyan, P., John, T., Tharyan, A., & Braganza, D. (2001). Attitudes of "tomorrow's doctors" towards psychiatry and mental illness. *National Medical Journal of India, 14,* 355–359.

Thoma, N. C., & Cecero, J. J. (2009). Is integrative use of techniques in psychotherapy the exception or the rule? Results of a national survey of doctoral-level practitioners. *Psychotherapy, 46,* 405–417.

Thomas, J. C., & Rosqvist, J. (2011). Introduction: Science in the service of practice. In J. C. Thomas & M. Hersen (Eds.), *Understanding research in clinical and counseling psychology,* (2nd ed., pp. 3–28). Mahwah, NJ: Lawrence Erlbaum Associates.

Thomas, R., & Zimmer-Gembeck, M. J. (2007). Behavioral outcomes of parent-child interaction therapy and TripleP—positive parenting program: A review and meta-analysis. *Journal of Abnormal Child Psychology, 35,* 475–495.

Thompson-Brenner, H., Glass, S., & Westen, D. (2003). A multidimensional meta-analysis of psychotherapy for bulimia nervosa. *Clinical Psychology: Science and Practice, 10,* 269–287.

Thurstone, L. L. (1938). *Primary mental abilities.* Chicago: University of Chicago Press.

Tobler, N. S., Roona, M. R., Ochsborn, P., Marshall, D. G., Streke, A. V., & Stackpole, K. M. (2000). School-based adolescent drug prevention programs: 1998 Meta-analysis. *Journal of Primary Prevention, 20,* 275–336.

Tombaugh, T. N. (1997). The Test of Memory Malingering (TOMM): Normative data from cognitively intact and cognitively impaired individuals. *Psychological Assessment, 9,* 260–268.

Townsend, L., Mathews, C., & Zembe, Y. (2013). A systematic review of behavioral interventions to prevent HIV infection and transmission among heterosexual, adult men in low and middle income countries. *Prevention Science, 14,* 88–105.

Tremblay, R. E., Pagani-Kurtz, L., Mâsse, L. C., Vitaro, F., & Pihl, R. O. (1995). A bimodal preventive intervention for disruptive kindergarten boys: Its impact through mid-adolescence. *Journal of Consulting and Clinical Psychology, 63,* 560–568.

Truax, C. B. (1966). Reinforcement and nonreinforcement in Rogerian psychotherapy. *Journal of Abnormal Psychology, 71,* 1–9.

Tryon, G. S. (2000). Doctoral training issues in school and clinical child psychology. *Professional Psychology: Research and Practice, 31,* 85–87.

Ttofi, M. M., & Farrington, D. P. (2011). Effectiveness of school-based programs to reduce bullying: A systematic and meta-analytic review. *Journal of Experimental Criminology, 7,* 27–56.

Turk, D. C., & Burwinkle, T. M. (2005). Clinical outcomes, cost-effectiveness, and the role of psychology in treatment of chronic pain sufferers. *Professional Psychology: Research and Practice: 36,* 602–610.

Turk, D. C., & Okifuji, A. (2002). Psychological factors in chronic pain: Evolution and revolution. *Journal of Consulting and Clinical Psychology, 70,* 678–690.

Turner, R. J., & Lloyd, D. A. (2004). Stress burden and the lifetime incidence of psychiatric disorders in young adults. *Archives of General Psychiatry, 61,* 481–488.

Turner, R. S. (2003). Neurologic aspects of Alzheimer's disease. In P. A. Lichtenberg, D. K. Murman, & A. M. Mellow (Eds.), *Handbook of dementia* (pp. 1–24). New York: John Wiley & Sons.

Tversky, A., & Kahneman, D. (1974). Judgments under uncertainty: Heuristics and biases. *Science, 185,* 1124–1131.

Twenge, J. M., & Nolen-Hoeksema, S. (2002). Age, gender, race, socioeconomic status, and birth cohort differences on the Children's Depression Inventory: A meta-analysis. *Journal of Abnormal Psychology, 111,* 578–588.

Ullman, J. B. (2006). Structural equation modelling: Reviewing the basics and moving forward. *Journal of Personality Assessment, 87,* 35–50.

Umphress, V. J., Lambert, M. J., Smart, D. W., Barlow, S. H., & Clouse, G. (1997). Concurrent and construct validity of the Outcome Questionnaire. *Journal of Psychoeducational Assessment, 15,* 40–55.

U.S. Department of Health and Human Services. (1999). *Mental health: A report of the Surgeon General.* Rockville, MD: Author.

Vakoch, D. A., & Strupp, H. H. (2000). Psychodynamic approaches to psychotherapy: Philosophical and theoretical foundations of effective practice. In C. R. Snyder & R. E. Ingram (Eds.), *Handbook of psychological changes: Psychotherapy processes and practices for the 21st century* (pp. 200–216). New York: John Wiley & Sons.

Valla, J-P., Bergeron, L., & Smolla, N. (2000). The Dominic-R: A pictorial interview for 6–11-year-old children. *Journal of the American Academy of Child and Adolescent Psychiatry, 39,* 85–93.

Vallis, T. M., & Howes, J. L. (1996). The field of clinical psychology: Arriving at a definition. *Canadian Psychology, 37,* 120–127.

van Widenfelt, B. M., Treffers, P. D. A., de Beurs, E., Siebelink, B. M., & Koudijs, E. (2005). Translation and cross-cultural adaptation of assessment instruments used in psychological research with children and families. *Clinical Child and Family Psychology Review, 8,* 135–147.

Vasiliadis, H. M., Tempier, R., Lesage, A., & Kates, N. (2009). General practice and mental health care: Determinants of outpatient service use. *Canadian Journal of Psychiatry, 54,* 468–476.

Verkuil, B., Brosschot, J. F., & Thayer, J. F. (2007). Capturing worry in daily life: Are trait questionnaires sufficient? *Behaviour Research and Therapy, 45,* 1835–1844.

Vermeersch, D. A., Lambert, M. J., & Burlingame, G. M. (2000). Outcome Questionnaire 45: Item sensitivity to change. *Journal of Personality Assessment, 74,* 242–261.

Vessey, J. T., & Howard, K. I. (1993). Who seeks psychotherapy? *Psychotherapy, 30,* 546–553.

Vittengl, J. R., Clark, L. A., & Jarrett, R. B. (2005). Validity of sudden gains in acute phase treatment of depression. *Journal of Consulting and Clinical Psychology, 73,* 173–182.

von Ransom, K. M., Wallace, L. M., & Stevenson, A. (2013). Psychotherapies provided for eating disorders by community clinicians: Infrequent use of evidence-based treatment. *Psychotherapy Research, 23,* 333–343.

Voros, V., Osvath, P., Kovacs, L., Varga, J., Fekete, S., & Kovacs, A. (2006). Screening for suicidal behaviour and mental disorders with Prime-MD questionnaire in general practice. *Primary Care & Community Psychiatry, 11,* 193–196.

Waehler, C. A., Kalodner, C. R., Wampold, B.E., & Lichtenberg, J. W. (2000). Empirically supported treatments (ESTs) in perspective: Implications for counseling psychology training. *The Counseling Psychologist, 28,* 657–671.

Wakefield, J. C. (1992). The concept of mental disorder: On the boundary between biological facts and social values. *American Psychologist, 47,* 373–388.

Wakefield, J. C. (1997). Diagnosing DSMIV—Part 1: DSM-IV and the concept of disorder. *Behaviour Research and Therapy, 35,* 633–649.

Waldron, H. B., & Turner, C. W. (2008). Evidence-based psychosocial treatments for adolescent substance abuse. *Journal of Clinical Child and Adolescent Psychology, 37,* 238–261.

Wampold, B. E. (1997). Methodological problems in identifying efficacious psychotherapies. *Psychotherapy Research, 7,* 21–43.

Wampold, B. E. (2007). Psychotherapy: The humanistic (and effective) treatment. *American Psychologist, 62,* 858–873.

Wampold, B. E. (2013). The good, the bad, and the ugly: A 50-year perspective on the outcome problem. *Psychotherapy, 50,* 16–24.

Wampold, B. E., & Bhati, K. S. (2004). Attending to the omissions: A historical examination of evidence-based practice movements. *Professional Psychology: Research and Practice, 35,* 563–570.

Wampold, B. E., & Brown, G. S. (2005). Estimating variability in outcomes attributable to therapists: A naturalistic study of outcomes in managed care. *Journal of Consulting and Clinical Psychology, 73,* 914–923.

Wampold, B. E., Mondin, G. W., Moody, M., Stich, F., Benson, K., & Ahn, H. (1997). A meta-analysis of outcome studies comparing bona fide psychotherapies: Empirically, "All must have prizes." *Psychological Bulletin, 122,* 203–215.

Wang, P. S., Gruber, M. J., Powers, R. E., Schoenbaum, M., Speier, A. H., Wells, K. B., et al. (2008). Disruption of existing mental health treatments and failure to initiate new treatment after Hurricane Katrina. *American Journal of Psychiatry, 165,* 34–41.

Waschbusch, D. A., & Hill, G. P. (2003). Empirically supported, promising, and unsupported treatments for children with attention-deficit/hyperactivity disorder. In S. O. Lilienfeld, S. J. Lynn, & J. M. Lohr (Eds.), *Science and Pseudoscience in Clinical Psychology* (pp. 333–362). New York: Guilford Press.

Watanabe, N., Hunot, V., Omori, I. M., Churchill, R., & Furukawa, T. (2007). Psychotherapy for depression among children and adolescents: A systematic review. *Acta psychiatricia Scandanavica, 116,* 84–95.

Watkins, M. W. (2003). IQ subtest analysis: Clinical acumen or clinical illusion? *The Scientific Review of Mental Health Practice, 2,* 118–141.

Webster, C. D., & Bailes, G. (2004). Assessing violence risk in mentally and personality disordered individuals. In C. R. Hollin (Ed.), *The essential handbook of offender assessment and treatment* (pp. 17–30). Chichester, UK: John Wiley & Sons.

Webster-Stratton, C. (2006). Quality training, supervision, ongoing monitoring, and agency support: Key ingredients to implementing The Incredible Years programs with fidelity. In T. K. Neill (Ed.), *Helping others help children: Clinical supervision of psychotherapy.* Washington, DC: American Psychological Association.

Webster-Stratton, C., & Reid, M. J. (2010). The Incredible Years parents, teachers, and children training series: A multifaceted treatment approach for young children with conduct problems. In J. Weisz & A. E. Kazdin (Eds.). *Evidence-based psychotherapies for children and adolescents* (2nd ed., pp. 194–210). New York: Guilford Press.

Webster-Stratton, C., Reid, M. J., & Hammond, M. (2001). Preventing conduct problems, promoting social competence: A parent and teacher training partnership in Head Start. *Journal of Clinical Child Psychology, 30,* 283–302.

Wechsler, D. (1939). *The measurement of adult intelligence.* Baltimore, MD: Williams and Wilkins.

Wechsler, D. (1996). *Wechsler Intelligence Scale for Children* (3rd ed.): *Canadian manual supplement.* Toronto: The Psychological Corporation.

Wechsler, D. (2003). *Wechsler Intelligence Scale for Children* (4th ed.). San Antonio, TX: The Psychological Corporation.

Wechsler, D. (2008). *Wechsler Adult Intelligence Scale* (4th ed.). San Antonio, TX: Pearson Education, Inc.

Wechsler, D. (2009). *Wechsler Memory Scale* (4th ed.). San Antonio, TX: Pearson Education, Inc.

Wechsler, D. (2010). *Wechsler Individual Achievement Test* (3rd ed.): *Canadian manual.* Toronto: Pearson Canada.

Wechsler, D. (2012). *Wechsler Preschool and Primary Scale of Intelligence* (4th ed.): *Canadian manual.* Toronto: Pearson Canada.

Weersing, V. R., & Weisz, J. R. (2002). Community clinical treatment of depressed youth: Benchmarking usual care against CBT clinical trials. *Journal of Consulting and Clinical Psychology, 70,* 299–310.

Wegner, D. M. (1994). Ironic process of mental control. *Psychological Review, 101,* 34–52.

Weigold, A., Weigold, I. K., & Russell, E. J. (2013). Examination of the equivalence of self-report surevy-based paper-and-pencil and Internet data collection methods. *Psychological Methods, 18,* 53–70.

Weinberger, J. (1995). Common factors aren't so common: The common factors dilemma. *Clinical Psychology: Science and Practice, 2,* 45–69.

Weiss, B., & Weisz, J. R. (1995). Relative effectiveness of behavioral versus nonbehavioral child psychotherapy. *Journal of Clinical and Consulting Psychology, 63,* 317–320.

Weissberg, R. P., Kumpfer, K. L., & Seligman, M. E. P. (2003). Prevention that works for children and youth. *American Psychologist, 58,* 425–432.

Weissman, M. M., Markowitz, J. C., & Klerman, G. L. (2000). *Comprehensive guide to interpersonal psychotherapy.* New York: Basic Books.

Weissman, M. M., Verdeli, H., Gameroff, M. J., Bledsoe, S. E., Betts, K., Mufson, L., et al. (2006). National survey of psychotherapy training in psychiatry, psychology, and social work. *Archives of General Psychiatry, 63,* 925–934.

Weisz, J. R., Chorpita, B. F., Frye, A., Ng, M. Y., Lau, N., Bearman, S. K., et al. (2011). Youth Top Problems: Using idiographic, consumer-guided assessment to identify treatment needs and track change during psychotherapy. *Journal of Consulting and Clinical Psychology, 79,* 369–380.

Weisz, J. R., Chorpita, B. F., Palinkas, L. A, Schoenwald, S. K., Miranda, J., Bearman, S. K., & Research Network on Youth Mental Health. (2012). Testing standard and modular designs for psychotherapy treating depression, anxiety, and conduct problems in youth. *Archives of General Psychiatry, 69,* 274–282. doi: 10.10001/archgenpsychiatry.2011.147.

Weisz, J. R., Doss, A. J., & Hawley, K. M. (2005). Youth psychotherapy outcome research: A review and critique of the evidence base. *Annual Review of Psychology, 56,* 337–363.

Weisz, J. R., Hawley, K. M., Pilkonis, P. A., Woody, S. R., & Follette, W. C. (2000). Stressing the (other) three Rs in the search for empirically supported treatments: Review procedures, research quality, relevance to practice and the public interest. *Clinical Psychology: Science and Practice, 7,* 243–258.

Weisz, J. R., Jensen-Doss, A., &. Hawley, K. M. (2006). Evidence-based youth psychotherapies versus usual clinical care. *American Psychologist, 61,* 671–689.

Weisz, J. R., McCarty, C. A., & Valeri, S. M. (2006). Effects of psychotherapy for depression in children and adolescents: A meta-analysis. *Psychological Bulletin, 132,* 132–149.

Weisz, J. R., Weiss, B., Alicke, M. D., & Klotz, M. L. (1987). Effectiveness of psychotherapy with children and adolescents: A meta-analysis for clinicians. *Journal of Consulting and Clinical Psychology, 55,* 542–549.

Weisz, J. R., Weiss, B., Han, S. S., Granger, D. A., & Morton, T. (1995). Effects of psychotherapy with children and adolescents revisited: A meta-analysis of treatment outcome studies. *Psychological Bulletin, 117,* 450–468.

Westen, D., Feit, A., & Zittel, C. (1999). Methodological issues in research using projective methods. In P.C. Kendall, J. N. Butcher, & G. N. Holmbeck (Eds.), *Handbook of research methods in clinical psychology* (2nd ed., pp. 224–240). New York: John Wiley & Sons.

Westen, D., & Morrison, K. (2001). A multidimensional meta-analysis of treatments for depression, panic, and Generalized Anxiety Disorder: An empirical examination of the status of empirically supported treatments. *Journal of Consulting and Clinical Psychology, 69,* 875–899.

Westmacott, R., & Hunsley, J. (2007). Weighing the evidence for psychotherapy equivalence: Implications for research and practice. *Behavior Analyst Today, 8,* 210–225.

Westra, H. A., Dozois, D. J. A., & Marcus, M. (2007). Expectancy, homework compliance, and initial change in cognitive-behavioral therapy for anxiety. *Journal of Consulting and Clinical Psychology, 75,* 363–373.

Westra, H. A., Eastwood, J. D., Bouffard, B. B., & Gerritsen, C. J. (2006). Psychology's pursuit if prescriptive authority: Would it meet the goals of Canadian Health Care Reform? *Canadian Psychology, 47,* 77–95.

Wethington, H. R., Hahn, R. A., Fuqua-Whitely, D.S., Sipe, T. A., Crosby, A. E., Johnson, R. et al. (2008). The effectiveness of interventions to reduce psychological harm from traumatic events among children and adolescents: A systematic review. *American Journal of Preventive Medicine, 35,* 287–313.

Whaley, A. L., & Davis, K. E. (2007). Cultural competence and evidence-based practice in mental health services: A complementary perspective. *American Psychologist, 62,* 563–574.

Whipple, J. L., & Lambert, M. J. (2011). Outcome measures for practice. *Annual Review of Clinical Psychology, 7,* 87–111.

Wicherts, J. M., Borsboom, D., Kats, J., & Molenaar, D. (2006). The poor availability of psychological research data for reanalysis. *American Psychologist, 61,* 726–728.

Wickrama, K. A., & Kaspar, V. (2007). Family context of mental health risk in Tsunami-exposed adolescents: Findings from a pilot study in Sri Lanka. *Social Science and Medicine, 64,* 713–723.

Widiger, T. A. (2004). Looking ahead to DSM-V. *The Clinical Psychologist, 57(1/2),* 18–24.

Widiger, T. A., & Sankis, L. M. (2000). Adult psychopathology: Issues and controversies. *Annual Review of Psychology, 51,* 377–404.

Widiger, T. A., & Trull, T. J. (2007). Plate tectonics in the classification of personality disorders: Shifting to a dimensional model. *American Psychologist, 62,* 71–83.

Wiggins, J. S., & Trapnell, P. D. (1997). Personality structure: The return of the big five. In R. Hogan, J. Johnson, & S. Briggs (Eds.), *Handbook of personality psychology* (pp. 737–766). San Diego, CA: Academic Press.

Wilkerson, B. (2012, August). *Mental health in the workplace.* Paper presented at the Annual Conference of the International Society of Certified Employee Benefit Specialists, San Francisco, CA. Retrieved from Global Business and Economic Roundtable on Addiction and Mental Health website: http://www.mentalhealthroundtable.ca/oct_12/San%20Francisco%20speech%20to%20International%20Conference.pdf

Wilkinson, L., & the Task Force on Statistical Inference. (1999). Statistical methods in psychology journals: Guidelines and explanations. *American Psychologist, 54,* 594–604.

Williams, C. (2001). You snooze, you lose? Sleep patterns in Canada. *Canadian Social Trends,* 10–14. Catalogue No. 11-008. Ottawa, ON: Minister of Industry.

Wilson, B. A. (2004). Theoretical approaches to cognitive rehabilitation. In L. H. Goldstein & J. E. McNeil (Eds.), *Clinical neuropsychology: A practical guide to assessment and management for clinicians* (pp. 345–366). Chichester, UK: John Wiley & Sons.

Wilson, B. (2008). Neuropsychological rehabilitation. *Annual Review of Clinical Psychology, 4,* 141–162.

Wilson, T. D. (2002). *Strangers to ourselves: Discover the adaptive unconscious.* Cambridge, MA: Harvard University Press.

Wilson, D. B., Bouffard, L. A., & MacKenzie, D. L. (2005). A quantitative review of structured, group-oriented, cognitive-behavioral programs for offenders. *Criminal Justice and Behavior, 32,* 172–204.

Wilson, G. T., & Rachman, S. J. (1983). Meta-analysis and the evaluation of psychotherapy outcomes: Limitations and liabilities. *Journal of Consulting and Clinical Psychology, 56,* 54–64.

Wilson, T. D., & Dunn, E. W. (2004). Self-knowledge: Its limits, value, and potential for improvement. *Annual Review of Psychology, 55,* 493–518.

Wittchen, H. U., Jacobi, F., Rehm, J., Gustavsson, A., Svensson, M., Jönsson, B., et al. (2011). The size and burden of mental disorders and other disorders of the brain in Europe 2010. *European Neuropsychopharmacology, 21,* 655–679.

Wise, E. A. (2004). Methods for analyzing psychotherapy outcomes: A review of clinical significance, reliable change, and recommendations for future directions. *Journal of Personality Assessment, 82,* 50–59.

Wood, J. M., Garb, H. N., Lilienfeld, S. O., & Nezworski, M. T. (2002). Clinical assessment. *Annual Review of Psychology, 53,* 519–543.

Wood, J. M., Lilienfeld, S. O., Garb, H. N., & Nezworski, M. T. (2000). The Rorschach test in clinical diagnosis: A critical review, with a backward look at Garfield (1947). *Journal of Clinical Psychology, 56,* 395–430.

Wood, J. M., Nezworski, M. T., & Garb, H. N. (2003). What's right with the Rorschach? *The Scientific Review of Mental Health Practice, 2,* 142–146.

Wood, J. M., Nezworski, M. T., Garb, H. N., & Lilienfeld, S. O. (2001). The misperception of psychopathology: Problems with the norms of the comprehensive system for the Rorschach. *Clinical Psychology: Science and Practice, 8,* 350–373.

World Health Organization. (1992a). *International Statistical Classification of Diseases and Related Health Problems* (10th ed.). Geneva: Author.

World Health Organization. (1992b). *The ICD-10 classification of mental and behavioural disorders: Clinical applications and diagnostic guidelines.* Geneva: Author.

World Health Organization. (2002). *Towards a common language for functioning, disability, and health.* Retrieved February 4, 2005, from http://www.who.int/classification/icf

World Health Organization. (2003). *The history of vaccination.* Retrieved October 22, 2004, from http://www.who.int

World Health Organization. (2004a). *Prevention of mental disorders: Effective interventions and policy options.* Retrieved October 28, 2004, from www.who.int

World Health Organization. (2004b). *Mental health: The bare facts.* Retrieved January 5, 2013, from http://www.who.int/mental_health/en

World Health Organization. (2005). *Project Atlas: Resources for mental health and neurological disorders.* Retrieved from http://apps.who.int/globalatlas/default.asp

World Health Organization. (2007). Mental health: Strengthening mental health promotion. Fact sheet No. 220. Retrieved March 4, 2009 from www.who.int/mediacentre/factsheets/

World Health Organization World Mental Health Survey Consortium. (2004). Prevalence, severity, and unmet need for treatment of mental disorders in the World Health Organization World Mental Health Surveys. *Journal of the American Medical Association, 291,* 2581–2590.

Wormith, J. S. (2002). Offender treatment attrition and its relationship with risk, responsivity, and recidivism. *Criminal Justice and Behavior, 29,* 447–471.

Wormith, J. S., Althouse, R., Simpson, M., Reitzel, L. R., Fagan, T. J., & Morgan, R. D. (2007). The rehabilitation and reintegration of offenders. *Criminal Justice and Behavior, 34,* 879–892.

Wright, A. G. C., Krueger, R. F., Hobbs, M. J., Markon, K. E., Eaton, N. R., & Slade, T. (2013). The structure of psychopathology: Toward an expanded quantitative model. *Journal of Abnormal Psychology, 122,* 281–294.

Yalom, I. D. (1995). *The theory and practice of group psychotherapy.* New York: Basic Books.

Yang, M., Wong, S. C. P., & Coid, J. (2010). The efficacy of violence prediction: A meta-analytic comparison of nine risk assessment tools. *Psychological Bulletin, 136,* 740–767.

Yavchitz A., Boutron I., Bafeta A., Marroun I., Charles, P., et al. (2012). Misrepresentation of randomized controlled trials in press releases and news coverage: A cohort study. *PLoS Med 9(9)*: e1001308. doi:10.1371/journal.pmed.1001308

Youngstrom, E. A. (2013). Future directions in psychological assessment: Combining evidence-based medicine innovations with psychology's historical strengths to enhance utility. *Journal of Clinical Child & Adolescent Psychology, 42,* 139–159.

Youngstrom, E. A., Findling R. L., Calabrese, J. R., Gracious, B. L., Demeter, C., et al. (2004). Comparing the diagnostic accuracy of six potential screening instruments for bipolar disorder in youths aged 5 to 17 years. *Journal of the American Academy of Child and Adolescent Psychiatry, 43,* 847–858.

Zucker, R. A. (2003). Causal structure of alcohol use and problems in early life. In A. Biglan, M. Wang, & H. J. Walberg (Eds.), *Preventing youth problems* (pp. 33–61). New York: Kluwer Academic.

NAME INDEX

C

SUBJECT INDEX

J

K